D1484142

SCOTTISH HISTORY SOCIETY

FIFTH SERIES

VOLUME 19

Scottish Schools and Schoolmasters
1560–1633

Scottish Schools and Schoolmasters
1560–1633

† John Durkan

Edited and revised by
Jamie Reid-Baxter

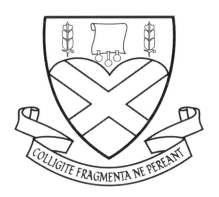

COLLIGITE FRAGMENTA NE PEREANT

SCOTTISH HISTORY SOCIETY
2006

THE BOYDELL PRESS

First published 2013

A Scottish History Society publication
in association with The Boydell Press
an imprint of Boydell & Brewer Ltd
PO Box 9, Woodbridge, Suffolk IP12 3DF, UK
and of Boydell & Brewer Inc.
668 Mt Hope Avenue, Rochester, NY 14620–2731, USA
website: www.boydellandbrewer.com

ISBN 978–0–906245–28–6

A CIP catalogue record for this book is available
from the British Library

The publisher has no responsibility for the continued existence or accuracy
of URLs for external or third-party internet websites referred to in this
book, and does not guarantee that any content on such websites is,
or will remain, accurate or appropriate.

Papers used by Boydell & Brewer Ltd are natural, recyclable products
made from wood grown in sustainable forests

Printed and bound in Great Britain by
TJ International Ltd, Padstow, Cornwall UK

CONTENTS

ACKNOWLEDGEMENTS

This book has been a long time in the preparation. It began with my discovery that the Registers of Deeds in the Scottish Record Office were worth exploring for the signatures of schoolmasters (and occasionally for their contracts of employment), and for indications of schools. Examination of the Registers took well over a year of daily visits to the Register House. During that time I was fortunate to have aroused the interest in my project of many colleagues and co-workers on early records; these anonymous helpers I would like to thank. Especially helpful was Mr John Ballantyne who not only directed my attention to sources I might have ignored, but made a point of collecting names of schools and schoolmasters in registers post-dating 1633 where my own explorations ended. Another diligent helper was Professor Robert Adam of the History Department of St Andrews University, collecting material regarding the north-east.

All this information I assembled on cards, where the schools were listed in alphabetical order and map-references supplied for less immediately identifiable school sites. In this I owe a particular debt of gratitude to Miss Patricia Martin of Glasgow University Library. The transfer of this material by word-processor into an alphabetically arranged sequence for publication, the compilation of the alphabetical list of schoolmasters, a list of abbreviations and a bibliography were all the work of Helen Cummings, without whom these researches would never have seen the light. She was also responsible for typing part of the introduction. The rest was typed by Jamie Reid-Baxter, Honorary Research Fellow in Scottish History at Glasgow, who gave up some twelve months of paid work in Luxembourg, over several years, to work on the whole text. His work was held up for several years when the almost finished product was lost in a computer disaster in the Baillie Room of Glasgow University's Scottish History Department, and so I must finally thank the Scottish History Society for their patience in awaiting delivery.

John Durkan
Lenzie, February 2006

PREFACE

A word of explanation is required with regard to the unpardonably long delay in getting this monument of John Durkan's scholarship into print. The original commissioners of this book, albeit not in anything like its present form, were the Scottish Record Society, the idea being to make available all the results of John's years-long search through all surviving records for the names of schoolmasters throughout Scotland between 1560 and 1633, in the shape of the Lists which form the second part of the present volume.

The preparation of the Lists of Schoolmasters had already been dealt with and typed up by Mrs Helen Cumming, working as a paid assistant on a short-term contract; in July 1995, it was my immense privilege to begin what turned out to be several summers of work as a volunteer assistant, by means of taking large blocks of unpaid leave from my job in Luxembourg with the European Parliament. My task was, on the one hand, to check references, and on the other, to type up the Introduction Dr Durkan was writing to put the Lists of Schoolmasters into context. That Introduction grew and grew – and grew. Once that task of transcription was complete, I did much reordering and reshaping of the material, all with Dr Durkan's approval: he read each version of the Introduction as I supplied it. At the end of summer 1999, the work was wellnigh complete when I left University Gardens late at night on the eve of yet another return to Luxembourg – and failed to make a back-up diskette copy of that final version.

I was never informed of the identity of the person who shortly thereafter crashed the Baillie Room computer, wiping its hard disk, and thus eliminating the final electronic version of the Introduction and of the List of Schoolmasters. It was this setback that caused the initial delay to the publication. Mercifully, there were hard copies of recent versions of the Introduction, and these were duly scanned in 2000. But scans are never perfect, and the work of proofreading them stretched out, as my own life and its demands increasingly intervened. Being based in Luxembourg (as I would be until May 2012) hardly made matters easier. It then transpired that the ancient computer on which Helen Cumming had painstakingly typeset the all-important Lists had 'died'. The Lists were salvaged from the hard disk, but the typesetting had gone haywire, and though a hard copy existed, it could not be found. When Roger Mason of the University of St Andrews asked me why nothing was happening with *Schools and Schoolmasters*, I explained the impasse and asked Dr Mason (as he then was) if he could perhaps supply a team of postgraduate students who could help me 'blitz' what remained to be done and get the book out. One of the students who was put forward at that time was John McCallum, though it would in fact be some years before he was able to turn his attention to the tasks outstanding. In the meantime, it turned out that John Durkan had never checked with the Scottish Record Society as to whether they could afford to print so vast a piece of prose as the fullscale book that he had written to introduce the 'Lists', and it turned out that they could not. Dr Mason then suggested that the Scottish History Society take over the publication, and the Record Society most courteously agreed. The single existing hard copy of the 'Lists' having been rediscovered, Dr Durkan was duly informed that publication was now not so very far off. Alas, he was to die in 2007 without seeing his work in print. For that, I must take full responsibility. *Scottish Schools and Schoolmasters* has come before the public thanks to the commitment shown by Dr John McCallum in recent years. Without his labours on re-typesetting the Lists of Schoolmasters, in particular, but also on double-checking the entire text, the present work would never have reached publication yet. We are all in his debt.

A very small number of uncertainties in the text have not been resolved. These concern missing references for entries in the List of Schoolmasters, which (mainly due to the lack of indices for the relevant parts of the Register of Deeds) have not been identified. The decision has been taken to include the entries in the List as in the surviving text, but to italicise the dates in either the entry or the portion of the entry which depends upon the missing or unclear reference, and to include an explanatory footnote. This was felt to be preferable to excluding the information altogether, since it may provide leads which future researchers can follow. Readers will also notice one or two footnoted references that postdate Dr Durkan's death. However, the actual text of the book is as Dr Durkan last saw and approved it. Despite all the years that have elapsed since then, it still represents an enormous contribution to the study of the history of education in Scotland, and a more than worthy memorial to the palaeographical, prosopographical, bibliographical and historical skills of the great-hearted Scottish schoolmaster and scholar who so selflessly dedicated so many years to assembling this vast databank. *Lux aeterna luceat ei.*

Jamie Reid-Baxter
Feast of St Herman of Alaska, December 2012

ABBREVIATIONS

Printed Volumes

Aberdeen Burgess Reg.	'Register of Burgesses of Guild and Trade of the Burgh of Aberdeen', ed. A.M. Munro, *New Spalding Misc.*, i (1890)
Aberdeen Burgh Accts.	'Extracts from the Accounts of the Burgh of Aberdeen', ed. J. Stuart, *Spalding Misc.*, v (Aberdeen, 1852)
Aberdeen Council Register	*Extracts from the Council Register of the Burgh of Aberdeen*, ed. J. Stuart (Spalding Club, 1844–1848)
Aberdeen Court Bk	*Records of the Sheriff Court of Aberdeenshire*, ed. D. Littlejohn (New Spalding Club, 1904–7)
Aberdeen Fasti	*Fasti Aberdonenses: Selections from the Records of the University and King's College of Aberdeen*, ed. C. Innes (Spalding Club, 1854)
Aberdeen Reg.	*Registrum Episcopatus Aberdonensis* (Spalding and Maitland Clubs, 1845)
Aberdeen Univ. Graduates	*Officers and Graduates of the University and King's College Aberdeen*, ed. P.J. Anderson (New Spalding Club, 1893)
Acta Facultatis	*Acta Facultatis Artium Universitatis Sanctiandree*, ed. A.I. Dunlop (SHS, 1964)
APS	*The Acts of the Parliaments of Scotland*, ed. T. Thomson & C. Innes (Edinburgh, 1814–75)
Arbroath Liber	*Liber Sancte Thome de Aberbrothoc 1178–1329*, ed. C. Innes (Bannatyne Club, 1848–56)
Autobiography and Diary	*The Autobiography and Diary of Mr James Melvill*, ed. R. Pitcairn (Wodrow Society, 1842)
Ayr Burgh Accts.	*Ayr Burgh Accounts 1534–1624*, ed. G.S. Pryde (SHS, 1937)
Ayr-Galloway Coll.	*Archaeological and Historical Collections relating to Ayrshire and Galloway* (Edinburgh, 1878–1899)
Banff Annals	*The Annals of Banff*, ed. W. Cramond (New Spalding Club, 1891–93)

Bannatyne Misc.	*The Bannatyne Miscellany* (Bannatyne Club, 1827–1855)
Bon Record	*Records and Reminiscences of Aberdeen Grammar School*, ed. H.F.M. Simpson (Aberdeen, 1906)
Brechin Reg.	*Registrum Episcopatus Brechinensis* (Bannatyne Club, 1856)
BUK	*The Booke of the Universall Kirk of Scotland*, ed. T. Thomson (Maitland Club, 1839–1845)
Cal. Scot. Supp.	E.R. Lindsay et al. (eds.), *Calendar of Scottish Supplications to Rome* (SHS, 1934)
Cal. State Papers Eliz.	J. Stevenson (ed.), *Calendar of State Papers, Foreign Series of the Reign of Elizabeth 1561–62* (London, 1866)
Cal. State Papers Scotland	J. Bain et al. (eds.), *Calendar of State Papers relating to Scotland and Mary, Queen of Scots, 1547–1603* (Edinburgh, 1898–1969)
Canongate Bk	*Book of Records of the Ancient Privileges of the Canongate*, ed. M. Wood (SRS, 1955)
Clan Campbell	H. Paton (ed.), *The Clan Campbell* (Edinburgh, 1913–1922)
Common Good	'Extracts from the Accounts of the Common Good of Various Burghs in Scotland, relative to Payments for Schools and Schoolmasters, between the years 1557 and 1634', *Maitland Misc.* (Edinburgh, 1840)
Coupar Angus Chrs.	D.E. Easson (ed.), *Charters of the Abbey of Coupar Angus* (SHS, 1947)
Coupar Angus Rental	*Rental Book of the Cistercian Abbey of Cupar Angus*, ed. C. Rogers (Grampian Club, 1879–1880)
Dempster, *Historia*	*Thomae Dempsteri Historia Ecclesiastica Gentis Scotorum: sive De Scriptoribus Scotis*, ed. D. Irving (Bannatyne Club, 1829)
Diary	*The Diary of Mr James Melvill*, ed. G.R. Kinloch (Bannatyne Club, 1829)
Dryburgh Liber	*Liber Sancte Marie de Dryburgh*, ed. W. Fraser (Bannatyne Club, 1847)
Dumfriesshire Trans.	*Transactions of the Dumfriesshire and Galloway Natural History and Antiquarian Society*
Dunfermline Burgh Recs.	E. Beveridge (ed.), *The Burgh Records of Dunfermline* (Edinburgh, 1917)
Dunfermline Recs.	*Extracts from Burgh Records of Dunfermline*, ed. A. Shearer (Edinburgh, 1951)
Dunfermline Reg.	*Registrum de Dunfermelyn* (Bannatyne Club, 1842)

Dunkeld Rentale	*Rentale Dunkeldense*, ed. R.K. Hannay (SHS, 1915)
East Lothian Trans.	*Transactions of the East Lothian Antiquarian and Field Naturalists' Society*
Edinburgh Apprentices	*Register of Apprentices of the City of Edinburgh, 1583–1666*, ed. F.J. Grant (Edinburgh, 1906)
Edinburgh Burgh Recs.	M. Wood (ed.), *Extracts from the Records of the Burgh of Edinburgh, 1589–1603* (Edinburgh, 1927)
Edinburgh Marriages	*Register of Marriages of the City of Edinburgh 1595–1700*, ed. H. Paton (Edinburgh, 1905)
Edinburgh Testaments	F.J. Grant (ed.), *The Commissariot Record of Edinburgh: Register of Testaments* (SRS, 1897–9)
Elgin Kirk Recs.	W. Cramond (ed.), *Extracts from the Records of the Kirk Session of Elgin* (Elgin, 1897)
Elgin Recs.	W. Cramond (ed.), *The Records of Elgin*, ii (New Spalding Club, 1908)
Exchequer Rolls	G.P. McNeill (ed.), *The Exchequer Rolls of Scotland, 1557–1567* (Edinburgh, 1898)
Fasti	H. Scott, *Fasti Ecclesiae Scoticanae* (Edinburgh, 1915–1981)
Fraser Papers	*Papers from the Collection of Sir William Fraser* (SHS, 1924)
Glasgow Burgesses	J.R. Anderson (ed.), *The Burgesses and Guild Brethren of Glasgow* (SRS, 1925)
Glasgow City Chrs.	J.D. Marwick, *Charters and Other Documents relating to the City of Glasgow* (SBRS, 1894–1906)
Glasgow Prot. Bk	R. Renwick (ed.), *Abstracts of Protocols of the Town Clerks of Glasgow* (Glasgow, 1894–1900)
Glasgow Recs.	*Extracts from the Records of the Burgh of Glasgow 1573–1642*, ed. J.D. Marwick (SBRS, 1876–1916)
Glasgow Reg.	*Registrum Episcopatus Glasguensis* (Bannatyne and Maitland Clubs, 1843)
Hist. MSS Comm.	*Reports of the Royal Commission on Historical Manuscripts* (London, 1870–)
Holyrood Liber	*Liber Cartarum Sancte Crucis* (Bannatyne Club, 1840)
Inverness Recs.	W. Mackay et al., *Records of Inverness* (New Spalding Club, 1911)
IR	*Innes Review*
Irvine Muniments	*Muniments of the Royal Burgh of Irvine*, Ayr-Galloway Coll. (Edinburgh, 1878–1899)
Kelso Liber	*Liber Sancte Marie de Calchou 1113–1567*, ed. C. Innes (Bannatyne Club, 1846)
Kinloss Recs.	J. Stuart (ed.), *Records of the Monastery of Kinloss* (Edinburgh, 1872)

Kirkcaldy Recs.	L. Macbean (ed.), *The Kirkcaldy Burgh Records* (Kirkcaldy, 1908)
Kirkcudbright Recs.	John, Marquis of Bute & C.M. Armet (eds.), *Kirkcudbright Town Council Records 1606–1658* (Edinburgh, 1958)
Kirkwall Chrs.	J. Mooney (ed.), *Charters and Other Records of the City and Royal Burgh of Kirkwall* (Third Spalding Club, 1952)
Lag Chrs.	A.L. Murray (ed.), *The Lag Charters 1400–1720* (SRS, 1958)
Laing Chrs.	J. Anderson (ed.), *Calendar of the Laing Charters 854–1837* (Edinburgh, 1899)
Lamont Papers	N. Lamont (ed.), *An Inventory of Lamont Papers* (SRS, 1914)
Lanark Recs.	R. Renwick (ed.), *Extracts from the Records of the Royal Burgh of Lanark* (Glasgow, 1893)
Lanark Testaments	F.J. Grant (ed.), *The Commissariot Record of Lanark: Register of Testaments 1595–1800* (SRS, 1903)
Lindores Chartulary	J. Dowden (ed.), *Chartulary of Lindores Abbey* (SHS, 1903)
Lindores Liber	*Liber Sancte Marie de Lundoris*, ed. W.B.D. Turnbull (Abbotsford Club, 1841)
Maitland Misc.	*Miscellany of the Maitland Club* (Maitland Club, 1833–53)
MAUG	C. Innes (ed.), *Munimenta Alme Universitatis Glasguensis* (Maitland Club, 1854)
Melrose Recs.	C.S. Romanes (ed.), *Selections from the Records of the Regality of Melrose* (SHS, 1914–1917)
Midlothian Chrs.	*Registrum Domus de Soltre … Charters of the Hospital of Soltre, of Trinity College, Edinburgh, and Other Collegiate Churches in Midlothian*, ed. D. Laing (Bannatyne Club, 1861)
Moray Reg.	*Registrum Episcopatus Moraviensis* (Bannatyne Club, 1837)
Munro Writs	C.T. McInnes (ed.), *Calendar of Writs of Munro of Foulis* (SRS, 1940)
Newbattle Reg.	*Registrum Sancte Marie de Neubotle* (Bannatyne Club, 1849)
New Spalding Misc.	*Miscellany of the New Spalding Club* (New Spalding Club, 1890–1908)
Nichols, *Progresses*	J. Nichols, *The Progresses and Public Processions of Queen Elizabeth* (London, 1788–1821)

Paisley Burgh Chrs.	W.M. Metcalfe (ed.), *Charters and Documents relating to the Burgh of Paisley* (Paisley, 1902)
Paisley Reg.	*Registrum Monasterii de Passelet*, ed. C. Innes (Maitland Club, 1832)
Peebles Chrs.	W. Chambers (ed.), *Charters and Documents relating to the Burgh of Peebles* (SBRS, 1872)
Peebles Recs.	W. Renwick (ed.), *Extracts from the Records of the Burgh of Peebles* (SBRS, 1910)
Pitcairn, *Trials*	R. Pitcairn (ed.), *Ancient Criminal Trials* (3 vols., Edinburgh, 1833)
Register of Ministers	A. Macdonald (ed.), *Register of Ministers, Exhorters and Readers and of their Stipends* (Maitland Club, 1830)
Reports	'Reports on the State of Certain Parishes in Scotland', ed. A. Macdonald, *Maitland Misc.* (Maitland Club, 1835)
Retours	*Inquisitionum ad Capellam Domini Regis Retornatarum … Abbrevatio*, ed. T. Thomson (Edinburgh, 1811–1816)
RKSSA	Records of the Kirk Session of St Andrews: *Register of the Minister, Elders and Deacons of the Christian Congregation of St Andrews*, ed. D.H. Fleming (SHS, 1898–90)
RMS	*Registrum Magni Sigilii Regum Scotorum*, ed. J.M. Thomson et al. (Edinburgh, 1882–1914)
RPC	*The Register of the Privy Council of Scotland*, ed. J.H. Burton et al. (Edinburgh, 1877–1908)
RPSA	*Registrum Prioratus Sancti Andree* (Bannatyne Club, 1841)
RSCHS	*Records of the Scottish Church History Society*
RSS	*Registrum Secreti Sigilli Regum Scotorum*, ed. M Livingstone et al. (Edinburgh, 1908–)
St Andrews Testaments	F.J. Grant, *The Commissariot Record of St Andrews: Register of Testaments, 1549–1800* (SRS, 1902)
St Giles Reg.	*Registrum Cartarum Ecclesie Sancti Egidii de Edinburgh*, ed. D. Laing (Edinburgh, 1859)
Scot. Antiq.	*Scottish Antiquary*, 1886–1903
SHR	*Scottish Historical Review*
South Leith Recs.	D. Robertson (ed.), *South Leith Records* (Edinburgh, 1911)
Spalding Misc.	*Miscellany of the Spalding Club* (Spalding Club, 1841–1852)

Spottiswoode Misc.	*The Spottiswoode Miscellany* (Spottiswoode Society, 1844–1845)
Stirling Recs.	R. Renwick (ed.), *Extracts from the Records of the Royal Burgh of Stirling* (Glasgow, 1887–1889)
Thirds of Benefices	G. Donaldson (ed.), *Accounts of the Collectors of Thirds of Benefices* (SHS, 1949)
Treasurer's Accounts	T. Dickson et al. (eds.), *Accounts of the Lord High Treasurer of Scotland* (Edinburgh, 1877–1970)
Wodrow Misc.	*Miscellany of the Wodrow Society* (Wodrow Society, 1844)
Yester Writs	C.C.H. Harvey & J. Macleod (eds.), *Calendar of Writs preserved at Yester House* (SRS, 1930)

General Abbreviations

AbK	Aberdeen, King's College
AbM	Aberdeen, Marischal College
Ed	Edinburgh University
EUL	Edinburgh University Library
Gl	Glasgow University
GRO	General Register Office for Scotland, Edinburgh
GUA	Glasgow University Archives
GUL	Glasgow University Library
MRf	Map Reference
NAS	National Archives of Scotland
NLS	National Library of Scotland
SA	St Andrews University
SAL	St Andrews, St Leonard's College
SAM	St Andrews, St Mary's College
SAS	St Andrews, St Salvator's College
SBRS	Scottish Burgh Records Society
SGTS	Scottish Gaelic Texts Society
SHS	Scottish History Society
SRS	Scottish Record Society
STS	Scottish Text Society

n.d.   no date

b	burgess	par	parish
c	chaplain	pr	precentor
ch	chorister	r	reader
cl	(session) clerk	reg	regent
d	doctor, didascalus	s	servitor
exh	exhorter	sc	scribe
i	instructor	t	teacher
min	minister	u	usher
n	notary	v	'vulgar', vernacular
p	preceptor		

Other designations are given in full.

INTRODUCTION

The present work falls into two parts. The first, in eight sections, surveys the history of Scottish schooling down to 1633, and examines a wide range of aspects of education in Scotland. The second part consists of a List which sets out the documentary evidence for the existence of individual schools and schoolmasters between 1560 and 1633. A Supplementary List provides far less exhaustive evidence for the period 1634 to 1660. The information assembled in the present work has resulted from tackling manuscript sources insufficiently researched hitherto, as earlier investigators have blenched before the vastness of the undertaking. Our Lists embody, above all, the recorded presence of schoolmasters, so designated, as witnesses signatory to legal documents. The major source of such documents is the General Register of Deeds. For our period, to December 1633, the relevant volumes (i.e. to RD1/458) are uncatalogued and unindexed from RD1/51 (July 1595). Even for the earlier volumes, the existing catalogue, indexed only to RD1/32, is of very little use in identifying the names, let alone the professions, of witnesses signatory. Other major collections featuring lists of names, such as burgh registers of deeds and court registers, are entirely uncatalogued, and no town council minutes and other proceedings have been published in their entirety.

1560 and 1633 were chosen as terminal dates because of their importance in the history of Scottish education in the Reformation and Renaissance period. 1560 saw the *First Book of Discipline* set out its ambitious educational project, and it was in 1633 that the Scottish Parliament, as distinct from other agencies, began to twist the arms of heritors and others to bring the book's proposals into greater effect at national level. The *Book of Reformation or of Discipline*, compiled by the 'Six Johns', Knox, Spottiswood, Row, Winram, Douglas and Willock, pointed out to the Protestant lords the need for an ambitious programme of great care for the virtuous education and godly upbringing of the younger generation. In every notable town, especially one where a superintendent was assigned, there was to be a college with provision at least for logic and rhetoric as well as Latin grammar, along with the sacred tongues, Greek and Hebrew: in these colleges poor students unable to maintain themselves, especially country boys 'from landward', were to be assisted to do so. In this way scholars could be kept at their books in a school near home, under the eye of family and friends. These schools were to be staffed by professional schoolmasters, qualified for the purpose and properly paid. This college, 'of full exercise' (i.e. with a complete pre-university course), was based on a French model found at Bordeaux and Nîmes, on which the Swiss colleges, particularly that of Geneva, were established. It was the top tier of the grammar school type.

The second tier schools were to teach grammar and Latin as the foundation of all current learning of the period. Less prestigious than those of the top tier, they were likewise to be based in urban centres, and to have at least one schoolmaster. The third tier were highland ('upaland') schools, at which daily attendance, unlike weekly 'convening to doctrine', was not envisaged; the job of the reader or minister was to have charge of the 'children and youth' to instruct them in basic grammar, 'the first rudiments', and especially the catechism as translated from the French of Calvin. Later, in 1565, the General Assembly made this compulsory, under the threat of removal from office. In other words the need, 'of necessitie', was to have a schoolmaster in 'every severall kirk', but there was no immediate prospect of that, and emergency arrangements had to be made.

The ideal of a school for 'every severall kirk' was not new. Martin Bucer had cherished the same ideal, reminding his contemporaries that the 'holy fathers of old wished for a school at every church' and that there was a present need to restore that ideal state of affairs.[1] In 1549 the Scottish Catholic provincial council had adopted the reforms of the fifth session of the Council of Trent as its programme: not only the restoration of theology lectures where not at present active, but also school provision in notable or populous towns, in cathedrals and the urban collegiate churches. In churches whose yearly income was slight and there were few clerics or laymen, there also ought to be a schoolmaster, chosen by the bishop and chapter and supported while in office by church funds: in other words a school and a grammar master in every parish. The Reformed Kirk had to match and, where possible, surpass this programme. The *Book of Discipline* was well-suited to achieving this, in that its requirements were more explicit, accounting for specifically national difficulties such as school provision in highland terrain.[2] The 1560 proposals, though never ratified by parliament, established a model for the future. What, however, was the school provision that the men of 1560 inherited from the past?

---

[1] *The First Book of Discipline,* ed. J. K. Cameron (Edinburgh, 1960), 54–7, 129–36.
[2] D. Patrick (ed.), *Statutes of the Scottish Church* (SHS, 1907), 99.

I. Schools before the Reformation

The main sources of information about pre-Reformation education, especially with regard to numbers and types of school, are episcopal and monastic registers. These are by no means still extant for all episcopal sees or monastic houses. Burgh records, too, are likewise scarcely available for these centuries, apart from those of Aberdeen, Peebles and Edinburgh, selections from which have been published, while a few others, like those of Ayr and Wigtown, exist mostly in manuscript. Before the twelfth century, records are almost non-existent. A further problem is that the records seldom refer to education as such, while chaplains and others engaged in teaching prefer, when they do appear in public documents, to style themselves as ecclesiastics rather than as schoolmasters. The extensive protocols of the Ayr chaplain and notary Gavin Ros, for instance, nowhere hint that for a time he had charge of the town's grammar school.[1]

I.1 Celtic schools

The first mention of schooling in Scotland is in the first half of the eleventh century, when Sulien, subsequently bishop of St David's (1011–1091), decided to make the sea journey to Ireland to sample the learning in the schools there. However, gusts of wind blew him off course and he landed in that country 'which they call by the well-known name of Albania' (Alba, that is, Scotland), where he remained for five years imbibing cupfuls 'fragrant with mellifluous aroma' from the 'sevenfold fountain' of the seven liberal arts, which included not only grammar school subjects but also others that in revised form would soon be reserved to the universities. Ten more years of scripture study in Ireland completed Sulien's course.[2] From the same century we have a very fulsome letter to Queen Margaret from Theobald of Etampes, then teacher in Caen, presumably looking for a post in her household, in which he praises her fame as a person of honour, munificence and liberality, a fame not confined to Margaret's neighbours, but known the world over. Theobald wrote that he would visit her, were not sea-travel so unsafe. (The queen's reply has not survived; possibly Theobald's strong anti-monastic views held little appeal.) He did eventually cross those unsafe waters, and became the earliest known master to teach in the little English

---

[1] See J. Durkan, 'Education in the century of the Reformation', in D. McRoberts (ed.), *Essays on the Scottish Reformation* (Glasgow, 1962), 167.

[2] M. Lapidge, 'The Welsh-Latin poetry of Sulien's family', *Studia Celtica*, viii–ix (1973/4), 68–106. I owe this reference to Dr Nerys Ann Jones.

village of Oxford.[3] At the beginning of the next century, in 1124, the new bishop of St Andrews, the Englishman Eadmer, was met on his arrival by the scholars and people, scholars of a school which, as we shall see, had a Celtic inheritance.[4]

With the twelfth century, our records multiply somewhat, at a time when the old Celtic schools were beginning to yield to Norman incomers. This change can hardly have been painless, though the pain is more evident in Ireland.[5] Early schooling there is much illuminated by Irish records, which our own cannot match. Scotland and Ireland have in common, however, the Gaelic term, *fer léiginn or ferleyn*, Latinised as *ferlanus*, referring to a principal teacher or rector. The first one noted at Kells died in 993, yet Iona, known as a literary centre, provides no such early mention. We also hear of a *taiseach na scoloc* or *toisech na mac legind*, overseer of students, terms recalling the *macleins et scolloci* at Dunkeld (c.1214), Macbeth, *rex scolarum* at Dunblane (c.1214), and Mael-domnaig, *rex scolarum* at Muthill. This 'chief of the schools' had a lower place in the hierarchy of Celtic educators than the *ferleyn* proper.[6] The latter name was preserved as Macnerlin, 'son of the ferleyn', a surname found in fifteenth-century Islay at Kilchoman.[7]

Already in the twelfth century we have mention of scholars and schools at St Andrews, Turriff (1132), Arbuthnott (1163), Kirkcudbright (1164), Iona (1164) and Abernethy (1193).[8] Later in the thirteenth century, we have records of schools at Fetteresso (the name Dufscolock at least indicates a school's former existence, even if by that date, 1204, it is derived from the tenancy of scoloc lands rather than from the scholar himself), Muthill, Dunkeld, Dunblane and Ellon (1265).[9] 'Felanus', or possibly Ferlanus, was by 1316 rector of the schools of Inverness.[10] The ferleyn was not only qualified in

3   *Patrologia Latina*, ed. J.P. Migne (Paris, 1893), clxlii, col. 765; A.F. Leach (ed.), *Educational Charters and Documents 1598–1909* (Cambridge, 1911), 105.

4   A.U. Anderson (ed.), *Scottish Annals from English Chroniclers* (London, 1908), 142.

5   M. Sheehy, *When the Normans Came to Ireland* (Dublin, 1975).

6   M. Herbert, *Iona, Kells and Derry* (Oxford, 1988), 98, 100; F. McGrath, *Education in Ancient and Medieval Ireland* (Dublin, 1979), 89–90; G.W.S. Barrow, 'The lost Gaedhealtachd', in G.W.S. Barrow (ed.), *Scotland and its Neighbours in the Middle Ages* (London, 1992), 123; D.S. Thomson, 'Gaelic learned orders and literati in medieval Scotland', *Scottish Studies*, xii (1968), pp. 57–78. For the *ard fer legind* of Armagh who was St Malachy's father, but does not, although 'chief ferleyn', seem to be of higher status, see A. Gwynn, *The Irish Church in the Eleventh and Twelfth Centuries* (Dublin, 1992), 193; *Lindores Chartulary*, 35, 49, 50 (Dunkeld, Dunblane, Muthill).

7   G.F. Black, *The Surnames of Scotland* (New York, 1962), 551.

8   *The Book of Deer*, ed. J. Stuart (Spalding Club, 1869), 93; J. Robertson, 'On scholastic offices in the Scottish Church', *Spalding Misc.*, v, 62, 69; ibid., 210; Reginald of Durham, *Libellus de administratione beati Cuthberti virtutibus* (Surtees Society, 1835), 179; A.O. Anderson (ed.), *Early Sources of Scottish History* (Edinburgh, 1922), ii, 253; *RPSA*, 116.

9   *Arbroath Liber*, i, 60; Robertson, 'Scholastic offices', 58.

10   W. Fraser, *Chiefs of Grant* (Edinburgh, 1883), iii, 258.

the seven arts, but might be master in theology, and even have done his higher studies in Ireland. It is worth noting that future Scottish Gaelic-speaking schoolmasters may be among the students from Scotland expected to repair for their training to Armagh in 1169 under a grant made by the king of Ireland, on behalf of himself and his successors, to the *fer léiginn* of Armagh to instruct the youth of Ireland and Alba (Scotland) in literature.[11] Among the textbooks there might be the *Ars Maior* of Aelius Donatus as commented on and theorised about by Murethach *Scotus* in the early ninth century.[12]

Non-Gaelic speakers inherited previous scholastic traditions and even, in one instance, their nomenclature. After 1200 there was a disagreement between the Augustinian canons and Laurence, archdeacon and ferleyn of St Andrews, resident 'in the ferleyn's house', in company with the master of the schools and the poor scholars, fighting the claims of the canons to school property, possibly in favour of their own almonry at St Leonard's. In this deed there is a clear distinction between ferleyn and master of schools. St Andrews had no chancellor, and hence the archdeacon had (and continued to have) equivalent powers over schooling in that town and diocese. The compromise reached, we are told, was to be infringed neither by ferleyn, nor by master of schools, nor by poor scholars.[13] Further north, it is evident that Domangart, ferleyn of Turriff, is a Gael, although his St Andrews counterpart Laurence is not. After Robert Bruce's harrying of Buchan, Gaelic speech, even in the north east, retreated into more highland areas, where it becomes harder to follow the development of schooling.[14] But as Gaelic education receded, it did leave mementoes of itself: church tenants of Kilmany and Strathmiglo are called 'scolocs', as also in Monymusk; while the 'clerics' of Deer and Methven could well represent actual schools at those places.[15]

I.2 Post-Celtic schools

The Augustinian canons of St Andrews were only one of the new foreign-based orders whose introduction proved momentous for cultural change. The lead was given, notably, by that thoroughgoing innovator David I. It

11 Anderson (ed.), *Early Sources*, ii, 267, cites the Ulster Annals in English; *Annals of Ulster*, ed. B. MacCarthy (Dublin, 1893), ii, 160 (in Gaelic); 163 (English).
12 L. Holtz, *Donat et la tradition de l'enseignement grammatical* (Paris, 1981), 294; *Corpus Christianorum Continuatio Mediaevalis*, ed. L. Holtz (Turnhout, 1979), p. xl.
13 *RPSA*, 316–18. The *Domus ferlani* may have been the hospital of St Nicholas associated with poor scholars in 1293, I. Macphail (ed.), *Highland Papers* (SHS, 1916), ii, 127.
14 Discussion in D.E.R. Watt, 'Education in the Highlands in the Middle Ages', in L. Maclean (ed.), *The Middle Ages in the Highlands* (Inverness Field Club, 1981), 79–90.
15 Barrow, 'The lost Gaedhealtachd', 123–5; W.D. Simpson, 'The Augustinian priory and parish church, Monymusk', *Proceedings of the Society of Antiquaries of Scotland*, lix (1924), 43.

is worth highlighting the fact that the schools now mentioned for the first time are located in what were, or were about to be, the seats of sheriff-doms, and not in ecclesiastical or noble sites. We have Roxburgh, Perth, Stirling, Lanark, Linlithgow in the twelfth century, and Berwick-on-Tweed, Ayr, Aberdeen in the thirteenth, followed by mentions of Dumfries, Cupar, Edinburgh and Haddington in the next. Dundee, mentioned in c.1219, is an exception. These were all town schools as well as church schools. Though the appointments were made by monastic or other church patrons (as in 1378 with Adam de Camis, master of the schools of 'the church' of Edinburgh, who ventured as far as Montpellier), the day-to-day supervision was effected by the town.[16] Clearly some of these schools pre-date their first occurrence in extant record: it is hard to credit that Edinburgh had no schoolmaster till 1378!

This is not the place to discuss the development of studies in these centuries. But one thing is obvious, namely that the 'master of the schools' had more status in the earlier period than later. This may be due to the gradual emergence of schoolmasters who were not qualified in anything beyond the seven liberal arts (the *trivium* of grammar, rhetoric, logic, and the *quadrivium* of mathematics, arithmetic, astronomy, music), or who could simply go no further than the rudiments of grammar. Another factor will have been the increasing hold exercised over contemporary minds by the newly rediscovered Greek philosophers; the birth of universities meant increased professionalism and specialism at one end of the spectrum, with higher prestige accruing to teachers within universities, at the expense of those outside. There is some visible unease at this progress into the technicalities of philosophy. Adam of Dryburgh accepted the traditional seven arts as the basis for sacred studies, and gave passing recognition to ethics, logic and physics.[17] His more conservative and eloquent correspondent, John, abbot of Kelso, flayed philosophy as 'inane and sterile', attacking some moderns for their 'profane novelties', quite in the spirit of Bernard of Clairvaux attacking Abelard.[18] Adam of Dryburgh had some knowledge of Greek and at least knew the Hebrew alphabet. Pagan authors read by him include Plautus and Juvenal.[19] In this monastic context, we might also mention a more famous Scot, Richard of St Victor, 'a Scot by nation … whom the Scottish land

---

[16] *Kelso Liber*, 5 (Roxburgh); *Dunfermline Reg.* 56 (Perth and Stirling); *RPSA*, 63 (Linlithgow); *Paisley Reg.*, 164 (Ayr); *Dryburgh Liber*, 196 (Lanark); *Glasgow Reg.*, i, 137 (Berwick); *Arbroath Liber*, i, 193 (Aberdeen); *Exchequer Rolls*, i, 303 (Dummies, 'schools of the church'); *APS*, i, 507–8 (Cupar); *Calendar of Entries in the Papal Registers: Petitions*, ed. W.H. Bliss (London, 1896), i, 549 (Edinburgh); *Exchequer Rolls*, ii, 603 (Haddington); *Lindores Liber*, 17 (Dundee).

[17] *Patrologia Latina*, ed. Migne, clxxxviii, col. 770.

[18] Ibid., cols. 623–5. Another correspondent was Walter, prior of St Andrews, ibid., col. 843.

[19] Ibid., cols. 446, 727; F. Petit (ed.), *Ad Viros Religiosos: Quatorze Sermones d'Adam Scot* (Antwerp, 1934), 24–5.

bore in a happy birth', as his tombstone had it.[20] Although monasteries were primarily meant to be schools of virtue rather than to become secular academies, their contribution is easily undervalued.

There were considerable educational developments in the secular cathedrals in the twelfth century, although much of this remains hidden due to lack of documentation. Around 1259 the chancellor's function at Glasgow is given as governing the schools, while the subchanter's is to govern the song school through his 'official'.[21] This is on the model of Salisbury cathedral, but the records now available are silent as to how anybody was educated in Glasgow before that date and as to whether the chancellor's powers at Glasgow extended to the diocese, or whether he too could deputise to other local masters of schools in the shires, in the same way as the archdeacon could deputise to his deans of Christianity. It seems not, as the almost contemporary Aberdeen statutes declared that the chancellor was to provide a fit master to have the governance of the schools of Aberdeen, able to educate boys in grammar and logic.[22] Elgin cathedral, however, was modelled on Lincoln and, presuming the statutes were adhered to, nobody could lecture in the city without the chancellor's leave; he was able to appoint as he wished to all the schools in the shire, except those in prebendal churches.[23] (That this procedure was followed in Lincoln itself is evident.)[24] What happened in other Scottish shires? In 1442, in the shire town of Ayr we still find a schoolmaster claiming to hold the rectorship not only of all schools in Ayr burgh whatever 'the faculty', but also to have power throughout the shire to close schools which were 'partial schools' with incomplete Latin courses, such as reading and song schools, and to prosecute their rectors (this would not have affected Irvine, as it presumably had a full curriculum of Latin grammar to match that at Ayr).[25]

The names of some of these early 'masters of schools' survive because of the status accorded to them by contemporaries. In St Andrews we find Master Patrick (c.1212), Master John (c.1231) and John Scot de Moneydie near Strathmiglo (1285); at Perth, Adam (1210); at Roxburgh, Thomas (1241); at Cupar, Nicholas (1357); at Aberdeen, Thomas de Bennum or Benholm (1263).[26] At Ayr in 1234 the master of the schools, Allan, was not a graduate,

20 *Patrologia Latina*, ed. Migne, clxxxxii, pp. x–xi. For his significance see A. Broadie, *A History of Scottish Philosophy* (Edinburgh, 2009), 4.
21 There was as yet no subchanter, *Glasgow Reg.*, i, 170.
22 *Aberdeen Reg.*, ii, 44–5.
23 *Moray Reg.*, 58.
24 Leach (ed.), *Educational Charters and Documents*, 280.
25 J. Durkan & J. Kirk, *The University of Glasgow 1451–1577* (Glasgow, 1977), 6.
26 D.E.R. Watt, *Biographical Dictionary of Scottish Graduates* (Oxford, 1977), 40 (Aberdeen), 426 (Cupar), 446, 476, 488 (St Andrews), 530 (Roxburgh).

but he was a papal judge-delegate nevertheless.[27] Mr William de Travement occurs at Haddington (1375).[28] After 1412, when Scotland had acquired a university of its own, and obscure chaplains took up rural schooling – thus breaking the urban monopoly – names are less easily identifiable, since an ecclesiastical title carried more kudos than that of schoolmaster. (We should also allow for the fact that poor children in rural areas, who could not afford the expense of education in town, would have received informal teaching, e.g. as altar servers or choirboys, from whatever cleric had charge in country parishes or in lairds' households.) Grammar was fundamental, the rest of the seven liberal arts less so. Yet, though there was continuity in terms of the textbooks used, the traditional terminology of teaching masks a changing pattern of instruction.

The hopes and fears of the twelfth century, as revealed in the contrasting attitudes of men like John of Kelso and Richard of St Victor, were borne out in subsequent developments. The Franciscan, John Duns Scotus, won international fame at Oxford, Paris and Cologne, where he died; on the other hand, two decades later we have a report of a certain Thomas Scotus, found in the Iberian peninsula. He is recorded by Alvaro Pelayo, who in 1333 became a bishop in Portugal and reported Thomas's radical views, very different from those of John Duns. Although some commentators feel that Thomas's presence in Spain and imprisonment in Lisbon rule out a Scottish origin, the phrase 'this selfsame Scots heretic' (*iste Scotus hereticus*) sounds decisive. According to this Franciscan apostate, Moses, Christ and Mohammed were all deceivers and impostors; his other heresies included the claim that as Aristotle said, the world was eternal, and that Augustine and Bernard were traitors to the truth.[29]

An extremist of a very different kind was Robert Gardiner at St Andrews in 1435, who exalted canon law above the seven liberal arts. His opinions were not so much heretical as 'offensive to pious ears' – he poured scorn on grammar and the rudiments of Priscian; on logic and the sophisms and arguments of logicians; on rhetoric and the smooth words of Cicero; on the natural philosophy of the time for the proportions of the four elements, the impressions made by vapours and exhalations, the complexions of animals and whatever human nature can investigate by reason; on arithmetic and the battles of numbers; on music and the modulations of sounds; on geometry and the measurements of quantity; on astrology (so-called) and the heavenly influences. The university should avoid the barbarism and solecisms of gram-marians, the deceptive fallacies and sophisms of Aristotle, and above all else,

---

[27] *Paisley Reg.*, 168.
[28] Watt, *Biographical Dictionary*, 536.
[29] M. Esposito, 'Les hérésies de Thomas Scotus d'après le "Collirium Fidei" d'Alvare Pelage', *Revue d'Histoire Ecclésiastique*, xxxiii (1937), 56–69; 'iste Scotus hereticus' appears on p. 62.

it should speak of the supreme truth. All copies of Gardiner's harangue were ordered to be destroyed.[30] For Laurence of Lindores, Gardiner had launched nothing less than an all-out attack on the value of a general education. It was enough of a problem to persuade parents to send their sons for education, without letting a university insider play into their hands: many parents believed their children could be more usefully employed at home on the farm, and some nobles preferred their sons to cultivate the arts of chivalry rather than memorise the contents of the Latin grammars of Donatus or Priscian.

Attention was drawn in 1988 to two Scottish followers, it would seem, of the Englishman, William of Ockham, whose views were condemned by the University of Paris in 1340 for their radical tendencies: John Rait, later bishop of Aberdeen, and Walter Wardlaw, later cardinal of Glasgow. Rait was criticised by Gregory of Rimini; Wardlaw is guilty by association, his manuscripts at Oxford and Seville awaiting investigation still.[31] At the other end of the spectrum, the realist, pro-Albertist manuscripts of John Athilmer, formerly in the medieval library of Glasgow, have disappeared with the rest of that library.[32] Other Scottish manuscript material which has not survived must, of course, include manuscript grammars, possibly edited by Scottish schoolmasters.

I.3 Monastery schools

I.3.1 Benedictines, including Tironensians and Cluniacs

The new monasteries of the twelfth century and thereabouts were made responsible for appointing the schoolmasters in the new, up and coming trading towns, but did they have schools themselves? Kelso Abbey patronised the schools of Roxburgh, yet it had its own almonry school, as we gather from a grant by the lady of Mow (Moue) to get the abbey to 'exhibit' in favour of her son William, in 1260.[33] He was to take his meals not in 'the house of the poor', but at table along with the better (and better off) scholars, i.e. including some noblemen's sons, eating in the almonry. About 1165, Dunfermline Abbey received a grant from the bishop of St Andrews not only of the school at Perth and that of Stirling, but of all the schools belonging to the abbey, by reason of churches appropriated to Dunfermline:

---

[30] *Acta Facultatis*, i, 39–41.

[31] K. Tachau & W. Courtenay, 'Ockham, Ockhamists and the English-German nation at Paris, 1339–1341', *History of Universities*, ii (1982), 53; K. Tachau, *Vision and Certitude in the Age of Ockham* (Leiden, 1988), 358–9, 368–70.

[32] Durkan & Kirk, *University of Glasgow*, 77–8; cf. works of Albertus Magnus in J. Durkan, 'Richard Guthrie: books left at Arbroath Abbey in 1473', *Bibliotheck*, iii (1962), 146.

[33] *Kelso Liber*, i, 142.

Musselburgh might have been one such school.[34] Dunfermline's own town grammar school, however, may have originated in an almonry school, for the abbot continued to appoint its master into the sixteenth century, when John Moffat was still describing himself as 'priest, master of the schools and of the grammar school of Dunfermline'. Thus, in abbey and town, all schooling was under Moffat's charge.[35] His predecessor, the poet Robert Henryson, must have inherited similar powers.

It looks as though the Dunfermline grammar school was in the monastery before moving into town. In 1433, the witnesses to a deed included 'the scholars of the whole town',[36] and in 1468 Abbot Richard Bothwell reminded the authorities in Rome that he had assigned a house for the dwelling place of the town schoolmaster and had made provision for the upkeep of poor scholars to be taught free of charge by the said master.[37] Such scholars, some of them kinsfolk nominated by the monks, could be boarded in the almonry house of St Catherine at the abbey gate, close to the town's west port.[38] This house existed from at least 1328. Leftovers from the novices' meal and the final dish of the monks themselves were to be distributed by the almoner or his servant to the abbey's associates and to the poor in the almonry and thus the monk almoner was excused from the liturgy of the afternoon hour and from evening compline in order to facilitate the distribution.[39] The almoner also had the St Catherine chapel beside the almonry for his and their use.[40] About 1420 the almoner of the time, clearly also keeper of the abbey rental book, reported to Rome how he had already in part rebuilt this chapel, which had become so ruinous that it had proved necessary to demolish it.[41]

Other properties within and outwith Dunfermline supported this St Catherine almonry, and we find two almoners of later date, Denes Patrick Fawside and Edward Skaithmure, pursuing the almshouse rights in the burgh court; a burgh court deed of 1492 makes it clear that it is St Catherine's which was here in question.[42] An almoner of 1541, John Boswell, was also styled keeper of the rental books like his predecessor of 1420.[43] John Angus, a monk of Dunfermline from at least 1539, was named principal almoner

34 *Dunfermline Reg.*, 58.
35 *Dunfermline Burgh Recs.*, no. 168.
36 NLS, Adv MS 29.4.2, vi, 106.
37 *Calendar of Papal Registers: Petitions*, viii, 297.
38 *Dunfermline Burgh Recs.*, pp. xxvii–xxix; I.B. Cowan & D.E. Easson, *Medieval Religious Houses, Scotland* (New York, 1976), 174–5.
39 *Dunfermline Reg.*, 253.
40 Ibid., 253.
41 E.R. Lindsay & A.I. Cameron (eds.), *Calendar of Scottish Supplications to Rome* (SHS, 1934), i, 238.
42 *Dunfermline Burgh Recs.*, nos. 32, 297; also introduction, p. xxviii.
43 *Laing Chrs.*, no. 453.

in post-Reformation deeds.[44] As almoner, he had charge of the singing boys and of the grammar boys lodged in the almonry; but we may well ask whether Angus, as a skilled composer, did not teach them music prior to becoming almoner.[45] However, 'the master of the boys', to whom payment is recorded in 1557 and 1580 (latterly at a reduced rate), would more often have been a secular cleric.[46] The boys under him, few in number, were trained to sing the more complex polyphonic music that existed alongside Gregorian plainsong, especially for services in the Lady chapel.[47] As many as fifteen non-monastic chaplains could be available at Dunfermline as well; it has to be remembered that altars in the nave were served by such secular chaplains, while monks served as 'tutors' to the choir altars.[48]

With regard to Paisley Abbey's almonry, an entry in the Book of Assumptions might lead us to assume that it existed merely for the daily doles to the poor, and did not necessarily indicate the existence of a school – especially in view of the hitherto accepted opinion that Paisley school was a post-Reformation foundation. However, it has now been shown that the scholars of Paisley were witnesses to several early sixteenth-century deeds, in which the schoolmaster notaries were secular chaplains in the nave of the abbey church.[49] The choir singers also performed in the chapter-house Lady chapel. The rental in question, a careless copy of one dated 1561, states that £700 were spent every year in the alms distributed week by week (*hepdomadatim*) by the Paisley almoner.[50] The monastery gatehouse, which may have included the almonry, was observed by Richard Augustine Hay in the seventeenth century. The large pend 'of huge elevation', open at both ends, supported a strong tower, an arrangement reminiscent of the ancient 'transe' (passageway) in St Leonard's College (former almonry) in St Andrews. The magnificent Paisley gatehouse may have been destroyed when the massive abbey wall came down a century or so after Hay's visit.[51] Here almonry-boys could have been accommodated or fed. No specific song schoolmaster is ever named, but it is clear that the 'bairns of the choir' of 1545 were trained boy choristers.[52] By Hay's time the chapel of the almonry had gone, but it is reasonable to deduce its existence: after all, our sole surviving reference

[44] *Laing Chrs.*, no. 431; *RMS*, v, 2969.
[45] S. Sadie (ed.), *New Grove Dictionary of Music and Musicians* (London, 1981), i, 435. For details of recordings, see p. 153n.
[46] *Yester Writs*, nos. 678, 838.
[47] N. Orme, *English Schools in the Middle Ages* (London, 1973), 246–7.
[48] *Dunfermline Burgh Recs.*, no. 265.
[49] EUL, Dc.4.32, 27; J. Durkan, 'Paisley Abbey in the sixteenth century', *IR*, xxvii (1976), 110–26; the earliest mention of grammar is in 1519.
[50] J. Lees, *The Abbey of Paisley* (Paisley, 1878), p. cl.
[51] J. Durkan, 'Paisley Abbey and Glasgow archives', *IR*, xiv (1963), 50. The Gatehouse at Arbroath Abbey is another example.
[52] Durkan, 'Paisley Abbey in the sixteenth century'.

to the almoner himself is as late as 1560. There was thus both a grammar and song school at Paisley, and conceivably provision for schoolboy boarders.

To the almonry at the wealthy Tironensian abbey of Arbroath there are, by contrast, abundant but sadly uninformative references. The first mention of an almoner occurs in a deed of 1325 concerning the hospital of St John Baptist, about whose chapel the country's almoner general would enquire in 1464.[53] References to the almonry croft and the monk-almoner are plentiful,[54] yet only one is named, Brother William Ardross (1467).[55] The chapel of St John was consecrated by the Greek bishop of Dromore, formerly of Athens, in 1481;[56] presumably this chapel was identical with the 'infirmary' chapel of 1490 which had undergone repairs after being 'utterly destroyed'.[57] These repairs appear to have followed the 1464 visit by Richard Guthrie, almoner general, representing the king, and the Dominican prior of St Andrews representing the church authorities. In this visitation we learn of the almonry adjoining St Michael's chapel immediately outside the abbey, surrounded by a high garden wall.[58] (A century later, the destruction of the religious wars led to a sale of the monastery timber in 1563, including the infirmary and its chapel with the 'tofallis' and thirty rib beams in the infirmary 'tofall'.[59]) In 1486, a graduate, Archibald Lamb, cleric, was appointed, for 'the instruction of novices and our young brethren'. This seems to point to the establishment of an internal school, and could be interpreted as circumventing the need for monastic personnel to attend an external grammar school; such a supposition is confirmed by Lamb's reappearance as a monk himself in the records twelve years later. He was paid twice yearly in cash, plus receiving a daily 'portion' such as the monks got.[60] Arbroath's was an educated community, with a monk specifically in charge of its library.[61] At the Reformation, a Mr Robert Cumming was schoolmaster; he was accused in the 1562 General Assembly of infecting the youth of Arbroath

53 *Arbroath Liber*, i, 309; ii, 141–3.
54 Ibid., i, 94, 163, 503, 523, 528; ii, 142, 188.
55 Ibid., i, 155.
56 Ibid., ii, 226.
57 Ibid., ii, 263.
58 Ibid., ii, 141–3; 'the great garden wall', ibid., ii, 56.
59 Durkan, 'Paisley Abbey and Glasgow archives', 50–1; G. Hay, *History of Arbroath* (Arbroath, 1876), 91, records the order to demolish the dormitory in 1580. A 'tofall' is an annexe. The almonry area was later referred to as 'almerie close' and the school was nearby.
60 *Arbroath Liber*, ii, 245, 316; cf. A. Ross, 'Notes on the religious orders', in D. McRoberts (ed.), *Essays on the Scottish Reformation, 1513–1625* (Glasgow, 1962), 125–6, offers a different explanation.
61 *Arbroath Liber*, ii, 329 (in 1500), 473 (in 1527). There are many entries in *Retours*, Forfar, 421, 501, 505, to the almonry croft. The chapel of St Michael is nowhere mentioned in these Retours.

with idolatry.[62] In 1564 he was succeeded by David Black, a former monk of the abbey, but it is likely that the funds to support poor boarders were no longer available, for Black was dependent on the town's grant from the revenue of the Lady chapel (at the bridge) and fee-paying pupils. Black had probably taught in the abbey earlier, since he had owned *The Discipline of Scholars* by Boethius when he was a monk.[63]

The 'Almerylandis' of Kelso, where there was an early almonry, continue to be mentioned in post-Reformation deeds.[64] At Lindores, the 'almerie cruik' existed in 1560, and one monk there, Thomas Wode (i.e. Wood), was a fine penman and a passionate lover of fine church music. This suggests no more than a song school at Lindores, but its nearby burgh of Newburgh had a school, fleetingly referred to, which probably taught Latin.[65] Coldingham priory also had an almonry.[66]

I.3.2 Augustinians and Premonstratensians

The houses of Augustinian canons are other places to look for almonries, without which we cannot postulate almonry schools. It may be that in the twelfth century houses dependent on reformed Augustinian monasteries like Arrouaise frowned on lay students disturbing the monastic peace. However, Scots like Richard of St Victor were attracted to the famous schools in Paris, for which Hugh of St Victor wrote his *Didascalicon* to promote a new approach to the reading of texts.[67] No school is known to have existed in Dryburgh in 1184, when a papal letter confirmed that the abbot was to protect not only the school of Lanark, a parish appropriated to Dryburgh, but also the schools in others of their parishes, and that this should not be a pretext for imposing harsh financial demands.[68]

The almonry of St Leonard's at St Andrews was attached to the town's cathedral priory, and originally seems to have been a hospice for pilgrims. Its history needs closer attention than we can give it here; it might be assumed that it harboured only old men and women, were it not for a reference in 1544 to a gate between St Leonard's church and 'the old school', that was

62   *BUK*, i, 25.
63   Hay, *Arbroath*, 259; J. Durkan & A. Ross, *Early Scottish Libraries* (Glasgow, 1961), 76.
64   *RMS*, vii, 1342; *Retours*, Roxburgh, 52, 156, 267, 282, 318, 341.
65   A. Laing, *Lindores Abbey and its Burgh of Newburgh* (Edinburgh, 1876), 423; Sadie, *New Grove Dictionary*, and D.J. Ross, *Musick Fyne* (Edinburgh, 1993), 65–7, 87–8; in 1540 a new *infirmatorium* was under construction, NAS, NP1/96, 97.
66   J. Raine, *History and Antiquities of North Durham* (London, 1852), appendix, 233.
67   I. Illich, *In the Vineyard of the Text* (Chicago, 1993); and for the wider context, R.W. Southern, *Scholastic Humanism and the Unification of Europe* (Oxford, 1995), i, passim; J. Chatillon, *Le mouvement canoniale au moyen âge* (Paris/Turnhout, 1992), 403–18.
68   *Dryburgh Liber*, 196.

to be kept shut unless the church door was closed.[69] The medieval survivals in the college library include standard grammar books like the grammar of Alexandre de Villedieu, the *Catholicon* of G. Balbi, the *Margarita poetica*, and newer, Renaissance-influenced texts like the *Elegantiae* of Lorenzo Valla, the *Precepts* of Agostino Dati, and the grammar and *Cornucopia* of Perotti. New arrivals in the college, we learn, were to be 'sufficiently instructed' in plainsong. They were not to rush through the chant on feastdays, and to sing with devotion and without syncopation at vespers (evensong). Polyphony too was evidently no stranger to these college students, for difficult masses were to be gone over in advance especially by those unused to singing. The priory novices were at least initially educated here behind the college's closed walls.[70] From an earlier age, the musical heights achieved in the thirteenth century are testified to by the monumental St Andrews Choirbook, abstracted to Germany by Marcus Wagner in 1553 (thus escaping the wholesale destruction of liturgical material at the Reformation), and long held in the Ducal Library at Wolfenbüttel. It contains extremely virtuosic music for the mass and office, not only by the great masters of the Notre Dame school, but also by native Scots.[71] But almost nothing survives of the music made in later centuries, such as the nine part mass in honour of the angelic orders composed by the future reformer Patrick Hamilton.[72] Thomas Wode of Lindores, however, succeeded in preserving two fine polyphonic pieces from the pen of David Peebles, canon of St Andrews (d.1578).[73]

Some light on Cambuskenneth is thrown by Robert Richardson, a student at St Victor in Paris and a former student of John Mair. He envisages religious life in a house with no almonry, thinking perhaps of Cambuskenneth rather than Scone (which even after total destruction still had its 'Almerland'),[74]

[69] Cowan & Easson, *Medieval Religious Houses*, 190; J. Herkless & R.K. Hannay, *The College of St Leonard* (Edinburgh, 1905), 198.
[70] 'Inventories of Buikis in the Colleges of Sanctandrois, 1588–1690', *Maitland Misc.*, i (1833), p. 319; Herkless & Hannay, *St Leonard*, 23, 46–7, 200.
[71] Many French pieces from the St Andrews Music Book have been recorded, but always sourced to MS 'W1', whose Scottish provenance is generally passed over in silence. See Edward Roesner, 'The origins of W1', *Journal of the Plainsong & Mediaeval Music Society*, xxix (1976), 337–80; J. Brown et al., 'Further observations on W1', *Journal of the Plainsong & Mediaeval Music Society*, iv (1981), 4 (1981), 53–80; Mark Everist, 'From Paris to St. Andrews: the origins of W1', *Journal of the Plainsong & Mediaeval Music Society*, xliii (1990), 1–42. Cappella Nova plan a series of recordings of the Scottish compositions recorded in the Music Book.
[72] D. McRoberts, 'The glorious house of Andrew', *IR*, xxv (1974), 127–9.
[73] *Si quis diligit me* (c.1530) and *Quam multi domine* (1576), recorded by Music Fyne (cassette CMF 004) and Edinburgh University Renaissance Singers (CD EURS 3); the former also by Cappella Nova (CD ASV Gaudeamus). See Ross, *Musick Fyne*, 65–74. Both works printed in K. Elliott & H.M. Shire (eds.), *Music of Scotland 1500–1700* (3rd edn, London, 1975).
[74] *RMS*, vi, 1820; *Retours*, Perth, 106 etc.

although he was addressing the junior brethren at both places. The inadequate instruction of novices and boys (schoolboys) is listed among causes of the decay of religious life. Stirling, of course, had a grammar school quite independent of Cambuskenneth. But there is clearly schooling in polyphonic music within the abbey; Richardson forcefully states his preference for the simplicity of the plainsong practised at Stirling's Chapel Royal. Even at Scone, where the presence of the composer-monk Robert Carver indicates the esteem in which lavish polyphony was held, it may be the case that musical settings of the mass were scaled down in response to criticism made by reform-minded Augustinians like Richardson[75] (who, despite his far from Ciceronian Latin, incidentally seems to have acquired some Greek, but whether at Cambuskenneth or Paris we can only surmise).[76]

Holyrood's ancient church school was probably at the gatehouse opposite St Thomas's chapel and almhouse on the other side of the Watergate. There are persistent references to St Anne's yards to the south east or east of the palace, and yet we find no altar of that dedication in Holyrood abbey church. However, there are early unprinted mentions of the walls of St Anne's which are identically sited in an area said to be divided off from King's Park by the Almerie Walls mentioned in a second document: this is clearly the location of a former almonry with its former chapel of St Anne. Some centuries later, St Anne's yards became Holyrood Gardens.[77] The earliest Edinburgh (later Canongate) scholars would have been boarded here. We have no documentary proof of provision for teaching music at Holyrood, as at other Augustinian houses, but one of the conventual brethren there before the Reformation was the composer Andro Blackhall,[78] who later opened a music school at Inveresk.[79] Post-Reformation Inchaffray still had its 'Almerieyaird', pointing to an almonry there at least, if not to an external school. In Inchmahome the poet-musician Alexander Scott, was appointed

---

[75] *Commentary on the Rule of St Augustine by Robertus Richardinus*, ed. C.G. Coulton (SHS, 1935), 81, 82. See Ross, *Musick Fyne*, 43–4.

[76] *Richardinus*, 56, 68, 132; these are among references overlooked in Coulton's index, which has not a few omissions and errors, e.g. he confuses John the Evangelist's residence in Patmos with a non-existent author named Joannes in Pathmon.

[77] Cowan & Easson, *Medieval Religious Houses*, 178, gives St Thomas but not St Anne; the altars are the Lady altar (same as parish altar), St Andrew, Holy Cross, St Catherine, St John Baptist, All Saints, St Sebastian (references in 'Holyrood Ordinale', *Book of the Old Edinburgh Club* (1916), ii, 23; xi, 13; xv, 74, 78; xxii, 168, 204; *Protocol Book of James Young*, ed. G. Donaldson and H.M. Paton (SRS, 1952), nos. 89, 194, 371, 558, 1255, 1412; the unprinted references are in Edinburgh City Archives, *Charters of the Commendators of Holyrood* (Transcripts), nos. 185, 214.

[78] See Ross, *Musick Fyne*, 90.

[79] See J. Cranstoun (ed.), *Satirical Poems of the Time of the Reformation* (STS, 1891–1893), i, 338; J. Paterson, *History of the Regality of Musselburgh* (Musselburgh, 1957), 77.

singer and organist in 1548, with the grant of a canon's portion.[80] In 1554 at Pittenween, sleeping accommodation was found for 'the boys and youths' in the canons' dormitory, a feature condemned in John Winram's visitation of that year.[81] It seems likely that Jedburgh had at least a reading and song school, for, as our Lists show, the first recorded master in the town was an ex-chaplain.

I.3.3 Cistercians

When we turn to Cistercian houses the position is more complex. Here we are once again bedevilled by the ambiguity of the term brethren (fratres or confratres), and the presence of layfolk with monks' portions – as at Coupar Angus, where Charles Rogers misunderstood the reference to six 'childer' of four 'brether of the place'. In 1536 these children were in the keeping of Mr Alexander McBreck, but because of his involvement in other business, were to be removed from his charge. Of McBreck, John Foxe records that when John Charteris, who favoured the Reformation, was deposed as provost of Perth, about 1543 (actually 1544), it was to make way for McBreck, a papist.[82] McBreck, agent at law for the abbey, was a married man, former sheriff clerk of Perth, dean of guild on occasion, provost in 1544 and 1553, tenant of the abbot's Perthshire lodge at Campsie, a notary and, at this point, acting as tutor or schoolmaster.[83] McBreck's letters of fraternity are not recorded, yet the issue of such letters to layfolk was an early development at Coupar Angus.[84] The abbey's lay porter had a monk's portion and his food came to him from the monks' kitchen until the Reformation, 'unto the tyme that the said abbey was demoleist', after which date the gatehouse remained but its chapel of St Catherine did not. This chapel was at the 'estir' or outer gate, and there the abbot occasionally held his court. The post-Reformation schoolmaster, John Tullis, occupied a monk's chamber in the gatehouse (the almoner's?) while the porter was accommodated above. The porter of that date could not write, so could not be responsible for the rental book, presumably kept by the almoner or the chamberlain.[85] Evidence of ample accommodation

---

[80] Retours, Perth, 1667; Fraser Papers, 225.

[81] NLS, Adv MS 29.4.2, vi, 106.

[82] Coupar Angus Rental, i, 317; J. Foxe, Acts and Monuments (London, 1858), v, 623; The Perth Guildry Book 1452–1601, ed. M.L. Stavert (SRS, 1993), 293, 349, 434, 1054.

[83] Coupar Angus Chrs., ii, 142.

[84] Ibid., i, xxx–xxxi.

[85] Coupar Angus Rental, ii, 100, 296, 394. The porter at the outer gate was 'principall' porter, ibid., i, 207, 293–4, 296, 305; Coupar Angus Chrs., ii, 240, 246–7. St Catherine's is the unnamed chapel in Fragmenta Scoto-monastica, ed. W.B.D.D. Turnbull (Edinburgh, 1842), p. xxvii (apud capellam sancte [blank]), which inform us that the abbot's court was otherwise held 'in pretorio' or 'in the great hall', pp. xxix, xxxi.

and the presence of the children of the 'brethren' mentioned above seems to argue for a school shared with outsiders at Coupar Angus.[86]

'Portionares seculares' are also found in 1564 at Melrose. Ralph Hudson, monk and notary there and keeper of the register, does not have his other offices in the monastery particularised, but, since he was occupying a cell in the 'infirmary', he may also have been the almoner.[87] Otherwise no school or lodging for scholars is recorded for Melrose. Newbattle certainly had an almonry, but the porter handed out the poors' doles in 1237 and 'the poors' infirmary' of 1293 looks like an external one. At the Reformation the monk George Richardson lived in Newbattle town, but had a piece of waste land adjacent to an unnamed chapel on the east of the great entry of the abbey, the usual site of an almonry chapel. Once again no school is specified.[88]

The remarkable educational scheme at Kinloss under Abbot Robert Reid, latterly – from 1540 – bishop of Orkney, has been dealt with elsewhere.[89] The teacher there was the Piedmontese Giovanni Ferrerio, who was thoroughly up to date and international in his interests. Though no outsiders are recorded among his students, he must have made some impact in nearby Elgin and in other Cistercian houses like Beauly and Deer.[90] He was on friendly terms too with the like-minded staff of King's College, Aberdeen, especially with Hector Boece, to whose *Historia* he was to make his own additions.[91] The regulations laid down by the visitor appointed by the Cistercian general chapter in 1537 envisaged a purely internal school at Deer.[92] No monk was to be ordained priest unless he had memorised the hymns, canticles and antiphons and was competently instructed in grammar. There was to be a learned and suitable reader, monk or secular, on ordinary days to instruct the brethren in grammar and the basic subjects, and in the higher subjects according to the capacity of his listeners who were bound

---

86 The reference in 1549 to a deed done in the 'infirmario' of Coupar Angus does not make sense. The correct reading must be 'infirmatorio', *Protocol Book of sir Robert Rollock*, ed. W. Angus (SRS, 1931), no. 188.

87 *Melrose Recs.*, iii, 139, 149.

88 *Newbattle Reg.*, 128, 142, 325, 339.

89 J. Durkan, 'The laying of fresh foundations', in J. MacQueen (ed.), *Humanism in Renaissance Scotland* (Edinburgh, 1990), 123–60; J. Durkan, 'Giovanni Ferrerio and religious humanism in sixteenth century Scotland', in K. Robbins (ed.), *Religion and Humanism* (Ecclesiastical History Society, 1981), 181–94; S. Holmes, 'The meaning of history: a dedicatory letter from Giovanni Ferrerio to Abbot Robert Reid in his Historia abbatum de Kynloss', *Reformation and Renaissance Review*, 10.1 (2008), pp. 89–115.

90 J. Durkan, 'Giovanni Ferrerio, Gesner and French affairs', *Bibliothèque d'Humanisme et Renaissance*, xiii (1980), 349–360.

91 See Dana F. Sutton's unfavourable comments in numbered paragraph 31 of his online Philological Museum edition of the 1575 Paris print of Boece http://www.philological.bham.ac.uk/boece/

92 *Illustrations of the Topography and Antiquities of the Shires of Aberdeen and Banff*, ed. J. Robertson (Spalding Club, 1862), iv, 10–16f.

to attend. For some hearers this will have meant going beyond the grammar course to study arts to university standard, and involved not only the junior monks but also such of their elders with the learning capacity or need of such studies. A copy of Aristotle's *Politics* in the medieval Latin translation survives, signed by the subprior of the time, who introduces a Greek letter into his signature.[93] Linked latterly with Kinloss and the Cistercians was the priory of Beauly whose seventeenth-century historian refers to the educating of Fraser, 'Master of Lovat, then tabled with the monks', in 1375, and in the same century we learn of sons and daughters 'all well educat' with the monks in Beauly, who were again responsible for a third Fraser son in the mid-fifteenth century. About 1505 Prior Dawson was 'most oblidging in educating gentlemen's children in the pryorie … The onely school in the north'. And in 1559, on the eve of the Reformation, 'young Lord Hugh' Fraser was 'left with the monks' and had learnt the catechism and how to construe in grammar as did 'many mo besides'.[94] All this teaching seems to have taken place in the prior's lodge. Abbot Robert Reid of Kinloss, who had become commendator of Beauly, is said to have educated Alexander, Lord Fraser, and to have kept noblemen's children with him for 'table and lodging'.[95] For a while Robert Reid's nephew Walter, future abbot of Kinloss, was under the tutorship of the Kinloss monk Adam Elder, who taught him Greek and Latin along with 'philosophy, rational, moral and natural' (that is, using the textbook of Hieronymus Wildenbergius). At Reid's desire, Adam Elder also taught the junior monks at both Beauly and Kinloss.[96]

At the other end of the country, arrangements similar to those at Beauly existed at Sweetheart Abbey; Maxwell, Lord Herries, declined the invitation to destroy it issued by the Privy Council, claiming that it was there 'quhair he was maist part brocht up in his youth'.[97] That there was a school at Culross Abbey in Fife is quite clear despite the loss of its monastic registers. About 1485 Thomas Crystal, a local boy, went with his brother Andrew to the school there. He first studied under Dene Thomas Peirson, a highly

---

[93] Described in N.R. Ker & A.J. Piper (eds.), *Medieval Manuscripts in British Libraries* (Oxford, 1992), iv, 250.

[94] *Chronicles of the Frasers: The Wardlaw Manuscript*, ed. W. Mackay (SHS, 1905), 76, 81, 84, 107, 124, 147.

[95] Ibid., 141. In earlier centuries, it seems, Beauly kept 'an academy' for the training of youth, ibid., 81–2.

[96] *Kinloss Recs.*, 66–7. There are two Acts of 1535 concerning Abbot Reid's attempt to help John Bad, portioner of Arbirlot, to pass through the school (NAS, CS/6, 174, 210).

[97] W. Huyshe, *Devorgilla, Lady of Galloway and her Abbey of the Sweet Heart* (Edinburgh, 1913), 87. A useful parallel is the appeal by the Protestant Anglo-Irish that Augustinian and Cistercian houses and nunneries in the Pale might be spared, since young men and children, both gentlemen's and others, girls and boys, were brought up in virtue, learning and the English language there; see *State Papers of Henry VIII* (Record Commission, 1834), iii (2), 130, 131. Pupils were not necessarily taught writing.

religious monk and, for the time, very learned in the elements of grammar. Under him, young Thomas advanced well ahead of his fellow pupils till, coaxed by their friends, his father and mother transferred him to learn the practice of music under an expert, William Rait, a layman and brother of the abbot, with whom he progressed so far in a few months that it was clear that nature had brought him there. He could produce at will a fine singing voice with a good range, and without any effort so harmonised with his fellow singers that he gained the appreciation of people of quality, including the abbot of Coupar Angus who wanted him to join his community along with Alexander Hetoun; but the abbot of Kinloss in the north prevailed upon Thomas's parents to persuade him to go there instead, though Thomas himself felt that he owed a debt to Culross. However, a visit to Kinloss won him over, and he took the habit there on Epiphany day, 1488. He speedily set out to memorise psalms, hymns and canticles under the music master there, Dene Patrick Wilson. Thomas was also noted as a keen student of letters, and in time he himself became abbot at Kinloss.[98]

I.4 Convents and the education of girls

It is likely that some daughters of good family or merchants were sent to be educated at nunneries, but information is both late and sparse. In 1487, a small convent of Third Order Franciscans, recently founded at Aberdour, was given permission to keep and instruct young girls of honourable parentage, willing to be brought up in letters and 'good arts'.[99] Initially this may have been possible, as the convent's first recruits had been Scotswomen trained in Grey Sister houses in France and Flanders, in Touraine, at Amboise specifically, whom their male counterparts, the Scottish Observant friars, considered to have more the status of laypeople than of genuine nuns. One can envisage these nuns teaching French, as well as habits of devotion and virtuous deportment. A decade or so later needlework and embroidery seem to be their speciality.[100]

Princess Margaret, the daughter of James III, was tutored by Dame Alison Maitland at the Cistercian nunnery of Haddington from 1464 to 1477 and is later found with the Cistercian nuns of Elcho, near Perth, from 1483 to

[98] Kinloss Recs., 20–2, 24.
[99] A. Theiner, Vetera Monumenta Historiam Hibernorum et Scotorum Illustrantia (Rome, 1864), 500.
[100] W.M. Bryce, The Scottish Grey Friars (Edinburgh, 1909), i, 391–7; ii, 267–73; F.M. Delorme, 'Olivier Maillard et le Tiers-Ordre régulier en Ecosse', Archivum Franciscanum Historicum, viii (1915), 353–8, where the name Clare Fotheringham has been misread; Bryce, Scottish Grey Friars, i, 398.

1503.[101] (The education of the Scottish royal household is a subject which awaits investigation.) The Elcho convent was largely destroyed in 1549, but we read that there had been 'many gentlemen's daughters at school' there, and the impression is that there was no limit on numbers boarded in such nunneries.[102] Another extant reference is to under-twelves Margaret and Elizabeth Sinclair, 'pupillis at the scule within the abbey' of Haddington. Their father, William Sinclair of Herdmanston, had, before his death at Candlemas 1531, appointed Robert Galbraith, the philosopher and lawyer, as tutor testamentar to the girls. He had placed them in the convent for schooling at his expense and in accordance with their social status, 'in all thingis efferand to their estait'. But Beatrice, Lady Herdmanston, their mother, in conjunction with some accomplices, abducted them and brought them to the residence of Crichton of Drylaw. Galbraith appealed to the Lords of Council who judged that they must be returned to the nuns' keeping 'to remane at the scule and for instructing of thaim in verteus' at their tutor's expense, and not to be transported therefrom to 'their perfite age' of twelve, without leave from the Lords.[103] Similar educational arrangements must surely have prevailed at other convents.

1.5 The friars

After their arrival in the thirteenth century, the orders of friars had a definite commitment to education, primarily, of course, that of their own members, young postulants as well as novices. It is likely that the famous thinker John Duns Scotus went to a grammar school in Scotland before proceeding to higher studies in England, France and Germany. Conventual Franciscans seem to have had no inhibitions about stating their university graduate status, as with Thomas de Rossy, doctor in theology in 1375, and Andrew Russell, professor in theology in 1492.[104] Since Observant Franciscans were reluctant to advertise their degrees, they are harder to pin down.[105] Knowledge of Scottish Carmelites is fragmentary and information about Augustinian friars even more so, on account of their short stay.[106] One great problem is assembling a list of their names. A Scottish master of theology and teacher in the University of Paris in 1281 is the Dominican Friar William, preacher there,

---

101   *Accounts of the Lord High Treasurer of Scotland*, ed. T. Dickson et al. (Edinburgh, 1877–1970), i, appendix to preface, p. cclxxxvi.
102   *Cal. State Papers Scotland*, i, 56.
103   Galbraith is given as their 'warder' in August and judgement given in November, NAS, CS5/43, 32, 67.
104   Watt, *Biographical Dictionary*, 168, 471; Bryce, *Scottish Grey Friars*, ii, 133.
105   Durkan & Kirk, *University of Glasgow*, 172–3.
106   For the English scene, W.J. Courtenay, *Schools and Scholars in Fourteenth Century England* (Princeton, 1987), 69–77.

whose sermons survive, as does one by the Scottish secular master, a master Renald.[107] A much earlier preacher in Paris had been Friar Clement, bishop of Dunblane from 1233.[108] In 1303 four Scots Dominicans, Friars Cuthbert, Hugh, Robert and Alexander, along with two Irish friars signed documents in Paris supporting Philip the Fair against Boniface VIII.[109] The executor of the will of a soldier in the service of Charles V of France in 1407 was a Dominican, Friar Gilbert of Scotland, presumably a student at the study house of St Jacques where the soldier was buried.[110] An English safe-conduct was issued in 1425 to a monk of Dunfermline and Friar William Wigton of the Edinburgh priory as they returned from studies in France.[111]

Theology was taught in various houses by rectors qualified for the purpose. These teachers had certain privileges like those of Friar James Gibson, the queen's confessor in 1477.[112] In Perth about 1269 Friar William Comyn of Kilconquhar was regent of theology; later, in 1375, there was Friar Adam of Brechin; and in 1477, Friar Thomas Dunning was rector there, seemingly in his case as a life appointment.[113] Friar Finlay Rede was rector at Edinburgh in 1479 and Friar Alexander Barclay at Elgin in 1545.[114] At Glasgow, Friar John Musselburgh was professor of theology in 1468, and David Craig was there about the same time, while John Mure was a bachelor in theology.[115] Our evidence for grammar teaching comes from late in the fifteenth century, at Ayr where an external student is involved, and at Glasgow where Friar Thomas Robison taught the liberal arts.[116] Yet in the other university town, St Andrews, there was only one small house by the 1440s in the charge of a *custos*, not a prior.[117] Even so, the Dominican interest in the schools is persistent.

---

[107] Paris, Bibliothèque Nationale, MS Lat 14947, 188v–189, 197v–198. Master Renald (not in Watt), ibid., 211–12.

[108] Watt, *Biographical Dictionary*, 99.

[109] G. Picot (ed.), *Documents relatifs aux Etats Generaux sous Philippe le Bel* (Paris, 1901), 381–2. Hugh's name, overlooked by Picot, is added by A. Dondaine in 'Documents pour servir à l'histoire de la Province de France: l'appel au Concile (1303)', *Archivum Fratrum Praedicatorum*, xxii (1952), 408.

[110] *Mélanges historiques*, iii, 456–7 (Collection de documents inédits pour l'histoire de la France, no. 83).

[111] *Rotuli Scotiae in Turri Londinensi et in Domo Capitulari Westmonasteriensi Asservati*, ed. D. Macpherson et al. (1814–1819), ii, 250.

[112] T. de Burgo, *Hibernia Dominicana* (Cologne, 1762), 73.

[113] Watt, *Biographical Dictionary*, 107; R. Milne, *Blackfriars of Perth* (Edinburgh, 1893), 36.

[114] *Laing Chrs.*, no. 177; NLS, Adv MS 34.7.2, 64.

[115] *Liber Collegii Nostre Domine*, ed. J. Robertson (Maitland Club, 1846), 183; Durkan & Kirk, *University of Glasgow*, 113; *Laing Chrs.*, no. 176.

[116] A.I. Dunlop, *The Life and Times of James Kennedy, Bishop of St Andrews* (Edinburgh, 1950), 5; Durkan & Kirk, *University of Glasgow*, 171.

[117] St Andrews University Muniments, Calendar of St Andrews Charters, no. 34. In 1446 Friar

The friars' schools need not detain us further, concerned as they were primarily with theology and philosophy. The Franciscans had links with Cologne and Paris and, if we find a Dominican in Cologne where their house had a notable *studium*, we may fairly conclude he was not there as a tourist: an instance is the last Dominican prior of Glasgow, John Hunter, 'outstanding theologian' according to David Chalmers, who noted a statue of an early saint during his residence there.[118]

I.6 Schoolmasters

I.6.1 Graduates

Like religious, secular masters also went to the universities abroad, especially Paris, Louvain and Cologne, even after the Scottish university foundations of St Andrews, Glasgow and Aberdeen. The foundation of Balliol College at Oxford had little Scottish relevance during this period, yet there was a trickle of students to English and even to Italian universities. D.E.R. Watt's *Biographical Dictionary of Scottish Graduates* does not confine itself to British sources of information, but its terminus is 1410. A continuation after that date, making even wider use of continental sources, would provide a basis for speculation about the number of probable schools at the foot of the educational pyramid, and might well upgrade the number of religious recorded, who form only a small proportion of the 1100 names the *Dictionary* lists for the 250 years preceding the founding of the first Scottish university. For instance, in 1420 Cambuskenneth always had one or two religious 'pensioners' on study leave.[119]

Exaggerated claims pushing the foundation of the Scots College in Paris back from 1603 to the fourteenth century are still made, but although there is every evidence that Scots in Paris often shared quarters and even books, the Scottish Grisy bursars were too few to constitute a college. The Book of Grisy often refers to a 'college of Grisy' or similar designation, but the bursars' petition to Queen Mary admits that they were constantly reproached for having no college body or college regulations.[120] A present intention to be a college is not tantamount to a present factual existence, but a Scots 'nation' at Orleans and an Anglo-Scots one at Padua are, of course, a different matter.

Andrew de Wedale was succeeded by Friar John Graham as *custos* of their oratory.

118   Bryce, *Scottish Grey Friars*, 180; Durkan & Kirk, *University of Glasgow*, 180, 211; J. Durkan, 'Heresy in Scotland: the second phase, 1546–1558', *RSCHS*, xxiv (1992), 331, 333.

119   *Cal Scot. Supp.*, 205.

120   Edinburgh, Columba House Archives, 'Book of Grisy'; J. Durkan, 'Grisy burses at Scots College, Paris', *IR*, xxii (1971), 50–2. Parisian late scholasticism was very much alive in early sixteenth-century Scotland, A. Broadie, *The Shadow of Scotus: Philosophy and Faith in pre-Reformation Scotland* (Edinburgh, 1995), 5–6.

Although a continuation of the *Biographical Dictionary* covering the years 1410 to 1560 would put us in a better position to estimate the number of schools postulated by the number of graduates recorded, the Highland area would still cause us problems. A Bartholomew of the Isles is known in 1360, and we find a 'scholar of the isles' and one 'of Sodor diocese' at Glasgow about a century later. Even in Dunkeld diocese, schools may have opened and closed: though James Williamson was an alumnus of that diocese, he studied at the Glasgow high school.[121] There are problems with identifying individuals as Highlanders, when we cannot even be sure that persons styled 'de Irewyn' actually came from Irvine, Ayrshire, or 'de Stramiglot' from Strathmiglo in Fife.[122] After all, the Dominican, Andrew 'of Cruden', reformer of his order in the fifteenth century, and student at St Andrews, Cologne and Paris, was actually an alumnus from Glasgow diocese.[123]

At parish level, there was a long-standing requirement that parish priests should provide a basic education for their flocks. But we cannot overlook the complaint made in 1410 by the Lollard, Quintin Folkhyrde (Folkhart) that priests neglected to pass on the rudiments of religion,[124] i.e. the articles of faith in the creed, the Lord's Prayer and the commandments in their own language. The parishes were often in fact manned by unbeneficed chaplains on whose shoulders in practice such duties would fall. Moreover, we should recall John Mair's comment that Scottish parishes were usually more extensive than English ones and that, since even the meanest laird kept one household chaplain, while magnates had as many as five or six, tenants would attend the laird's chapel in preference to their possibly rather remote parish kirk.[125] According to Mair, however, the lairds' household chaplains were at least as skilled in the arts of war as they were in the arts of peace, and the situation of education in letters and morals amongst the gentry was calamitous.

I.6.2 *Collegiate clergy*

Another of Mair's complaints is that priests were being ordained whose musical illiteracy precluded familiarity even with the normal Gregorian chant.[126] Musically illiterate clergy would have been of no use in staffing the collegiate churches, which must have had a certain educational function due to the presence of boy choristers. Some forty collegiate churches were

121   Watt, *Biographical Dictionary*, 285; *MAUG*, ii, 61, 85.
122   Watt, *Biographical Dictionary*, 284–5, 519–21.
123   J. Oehler, *Der akademische Austausch zwischen Köln und England-Schottland zur Zeit der ersten Kölner Universität* (Cologne, 1989), 291.
124   *Copiale Prioratus Sanctiandree*, ed. J.H. Baxter (Oxford, 1930), 231, 235.
125   J. Major, *A History of Greater Britain*, ed. A. Constable (SHS, 1892), 30.
126   Major, *History*, 30, 48, 129, 322.

established in the later medieval period.[127] Although their primary purpose
was prayer for the dead, they also served to mark the status of the founders.
A royal connection could be claimed for Kirkheugh (St Andrews), Stirling
and Trinity, Edinburgh, while the king shared with the bishop the patronage
of the shrine at Tain. One countess was involved (at Dumbarton), and about
ten earls (the earl of Angus inherited the patronage of Abernethy). Smaller
lairds also became founders, as did a few burgh councils and a few clerics.
While the standard of Latin in these colleges was related to understanding
the liturgy rather than writing Ciceronian prose, a high level of musical
attainment was essential.[128] Collegiate church inventories regularly refer to
books of 'precat sang', i.e. written scores of decorated music as opposed to
plainchant. The late fifteenth-century foundation charter of Seton Collegiate Church stipulates that the bairns and clerk were to be of sufficient
literature and 'cunnand in music and specielle in preccat sang',[129] and we find
a chaplain in Edinburgh's Trinity College being paid for a 'precett sangbuk'
in 1516.[130]

These churches were clearly homes of polyphonic music of high quality.
The fifth chaplain in the college in the Renfrewshire village of Lochwinnoch (now called Semple) was to be an organist and rule the song school
in the college bounds, teach the boys in Gregorian, pointed (that is, marking
a change in the chant) or 'precatus' music along with descant. At Lochwinnoch, 'cantus precatus, which others call curious', was performed daily, except
on ferial days. The sixth chaplain had likewise to be a musician, but his main
duty was to teach the two boy choristers the first two books of the grammar
of Alexandre de Villedieu, i.e. including advanced grammar (syntax) minus
versification, also a minimum requirement for entry to St Leonard's College.
The provost himself was expected to have musical training. This seems ambitious for Lochwinnoch, but the revenues pressed into service to pay for it
came not only from Glassford parish, but also two local chapels.[131] Parish
churches both large and small might be elevated to college status.[132] Even
a village like Darnley, boasting only a small chapel of St Ninian, would
seek, but fail to win, collegiate standing, though Bothans, Dirleton and
Dunglass succeeded.[133] While some minimum educational qualifications
were demanded of the chaplains, not all such churches allowed for founded
singing boys. It is probable that some extra local youths would get the benefit

[127] These choral foundations are discussed in Raymond White, 'Music of the Scottish Refor-
       mation' (St Andrews University PhD Thesis, 1972).
[128] Cowan & Easson, *Medieval Religious Houses*, 213–28.
[129] J. Durkan, 'Foundation of the collegiate church of Seton', *IR*, xiii (1962), 71–6.
[130] *Midlothian Chrs.*, 177.
[131] *Glasgow Reg.*, ii, 509–14; Herkless & Hannay, *St Leonard*, 146.
[132] Among the small, Strathmiglo might be a revival of a defunct Celtic site.
[133] Cowan & Easson, *Medieval Religious Houses*, 215, 218, 219.

of the instruction provided, though only Hamilton and Biggar mention such a concession.[134] The 'schools' of the collegiate churches of Lincluden and Maybole are mentioned in 1461 and 1464 respectively.[135] The boys' numbers in collegiate foundations ranged from one to six; even when multiplied by forty or so colleges, they make a modest total. Their real importance is in setting a standard for other schools, in education if not in comfort; significantly the term of the sacristan's duty was 'fra Allhollomes quhill Candelmas the quhilk is callit the deid of vinter'.[136]

I.6.3 Household chaplains

The subject of household education has a more central importance than has been hitherto realised, yet our evidence allows us only to touch on it briefly here. If John Mair's complaints are anything to go by, little schooling might be the norm in some aristocratic homes. But room could be found in a medieval noble's hall for a chaplain or a clerical kinsman giving formal literary lessons, while lessons in reading, music and dancing or a mother's introduction to speaking the language (Norman-French or Scots) were informal. The education of older girls and boys could be away from home with kinsfolk, the boys perhaps at court. The Dowager Lady of Lovet had her children taught according to 'their blood and birth', and her daughters Jean and Margaret were sent south to Wemyss in Fife.[137] Household schools might provide also for farmers' sons joining a noble household. In May 1526 we learn of aristocrats receiving their education in a school that has moved out of the castle hall into the market place. At that date William Murray of Tullibardine and his accomplices were summoned for hindering the earl of Huntly's 'brether', their schoolmaster Constantine Adamson and their servants from passing to the school, market, kirk and other places to do their lawful business. Adamson was not a simple tutor: he had a schoolhouse in Huntly.[138]

The Education Act of 1496 was an attempt to legislate more noblemen's sons into interesting themselves in grammar and law. In its sympathy for contemporary aristocratic ideals, Gavin Douglas's 1513 translation of Virgil's *Aeneid* would appeal to this new audience,[139] although of course its vernacular vigour would attract more than a blue-blooded readership. It was not the scarcity of schools that moved Ninian Winzet's later complaint about

---

134   J. Durkan, 'Medieval Hamilton', *IR*, xxviii (1977), 51–3; 'Miscellaneous Charters and Contracts', *Spalding Misc.*, v (1852), 296–308.
135   Rome, Archivio Vaticano, Register of Supplications, 535, 238; 571, 229.
136   D. Laing (ed.), *Registrum domus de Soltre necnon ecclesie collegiate S. Trinitatis prope Edinburgh etc.* (Edinburgh, 1861), p. 214.
137   *Chronicles of the Frasers*, 107.
138   NAS, CS5/36, 11.
139   C. Baswell, *Virgil in Medieval England* (Cambridge, 1995), 14.

lack of educational provision, so much as the reluctance of many of the great families to endow them, or send their sons to grammar school. The resulting ignorance was what the decisions of the church councils of 1549 were meant to rectify, as were the many government interventions over the next century. Yet the fact is that learned households did exist, such as that of the celebrated Maitlands of Lethington and the Humes of Wedderburn. The multiplication of pedagogues and tutors in late medieval households deserves investigation. At the highest social level, we find the Governor Arran employing Jacques Narrat for his eldest daughter, born about 1533. She was betrothed, if not married, to the eldest son of the earl of Huntly, Alexander, Lord Gordon, born about the same time. In 1548 Narrat was brought over from Hamilton or Glasgow to the court at Edinburgh, where he had charge of both of them in 1548 and 1549.[140] The governor himself occasionally made an offering to a poor scholar in Glasgow, following the example of some of our kings.[141]

A less exalted upper class milieu with a considerable interest in education is the lairdly family of the Humes of Wedderburn. David Hume of Godscroft, writing about his family's history, provides some information on household studies, though largely post-Reformation. All we learn of the early studies of the fifth laird of Wedderburn, David Hume, is that he had Alexander Manderston, an expert in law, to help him in his estate business, and got as far as logic in St Andrews. Here a fellow student called Montgomery, in the course of disputation, became annoyed with his opponent's denial of some point which Montgomery was sure was undeniable, and so, at a loss for a counter-argument, slapped him smack on the face, a type of debating technique which became notorious as 'Montgomery's proof'. In 1574, the fifth laird was succeeded by Godscroft's 22-year-old elder brother, Sir George Hume. His mother was a Johnstone of Elphinstone, and George's teacher up to the age of seven at his grandfather's house at Elphinstone had been one James Knox. His older cousin George Ker, a fellow pupil, also learned the rudiments under Knox. Ker excelled in music, and Hume in stature – so much that he was exhibited to the Queen Dowager as a boy prodigy. Godscroft tells us that at age eleven, George, who was used to reading to his mother, eased her inconsolable grief over her father's death by spontaneously reading her the fourth chapter of Paul to the Thessalonians. We will encounter George's post-Reformation studies at Dunbar in Section III.6.[142]

We are told of other Humes of Wedderburn that their mother educated her children with diligence, and that one daughter of Alexander Hume, then

[140]   *Treasurer's Accounts.*, ix, 243, 249, 250–1, 269, 271–2, 331.
[141]   Ibid., ix, 142, 272.
[142]   D. Hume of Godscroft, *De Familia Humia Wedderburnensi liber* (Abbotsford Club, 1839), 43, 59, 60.

a refugee from Scottish justice, was sent to the Dacre family in England for her education and returned home as Lady Samuelston.[143] And it is on behalf of Elizabeth Hume, Lady Hamilton of Samuelston, that we find John Knox, the future Reformer, executing a deed as apostolic notary, and, also at Samuelston about the same date in 1543, acting on behalf of an 'an elegant youth', William Brownfield, son of the laird of Greenlawdean, adjacent to Greenlaw in Berwickshire. Knox is described as Brownfield's 'maister'. It seems probable that Knox was chaplain of the St Nicholas chapel at Samuelston, which is clearly where he then resided. His other known pupils, such as Alexander Cockburn of Ormiston, may have attended the school we may presume he kept there.[144]

I. 7 Schools in towns

The foundation of the university at St Andrews curbed the activities of grammar masters in that town, and in 1430 the arts faculty decided to reduce the number to one, the future Glasgow Dominican John de Musselburgh: the archdeacon does not seem to have been involved in the decision.[145] Under the statutes for Elgin cathedral, the chanter of Moray was responsible for song and reading (i.e. elementary reading). In 1489, Elgin's chancellor was to take charge of the teaching of grammar in a 'general' school, and appoint a fit teacher. Indeed he was to cite the rector of Kincardine in Strathspey, whose responsibilities in the matter are not clarified.[146] Further north still, in Ross, the extant records allow us to find but a single schoolmaster, Laurence Mollison, MA, 'a man learned in the grammatical art', who died in the Chanonry on the 8 December 1558.[147]

What do the records tell us about the continuous existence of these schools? Such episcopal registers as we have are not registers kept by individual bishops, but selections of documents covering four or so centuries. Even so, though responsibility for schooling was in the first instance a church concern, little sign of that emerges in surviving records. Ordinations were also a church concern, yet no records of them are extant. There is nothing to show that Argyll, the Isles, Dornoch, the Chanonry of Ross and Whithorn kept registers, though copies were made from a Whithorn register in 15[04].[148] Glasgow, whose records are fuller than most, is dealt

---

[143]   Ibid., 33–4, 39.
[144]   D. Laing, 'A Supplementary Notice' and T. Thomson, 'Notices of the Kers of Samuelston', *Proceedings of the Society of Antiquaries of Scotland*, iii, 60, 62, 63, 66; the Kers of Samuelston were also close relatives of the Humes of Wedderburn.
[145]   *Acta Facultatis*, i, 31.
[146]   *Moray Reg.* 262–3, 270.
[147]   *The Calendar of Fearn*, ed. R.J. Adam (SHS, 1991), 121.
[148]   *Hist. MSS Comm., 11th Report*, Appendix, pt vii (HMSO, 1888), 159. The copies were made by a canon of the priory, Andrew Meligan, who was also a notary.

with in Appendix 2.2. In 1539 the expenses of some officials were met out of the bishop's teinds: the organist serving in the cathedral choir received ten merks yearly, twice the value of the 'pension' (settled payment) paid to the preceptor of the song school, while a chorister got £40. In 1562 there were three of them, and the grammar schoolmaster was collecting the allowance of the song school teacher.[149]

Our only evidence for pre-Reformation Dunblane, if such it be, comes from just after the end of the old dispensation. An annual pension of £20 by 'umquhil William, bishop of Dunblane' was paid to Duncan Nevay, MA, schoolmaster there at some date before 1564 when Bishop Chisholm died.[150] Nevay (or Nevin) may have been there before 1560; he was already school-master in May 1562 when he was party to a contract.[151] In 1562, he found his appointment by the Catholic bishop, William Chisholm, threatened by the change of religion in Dunblane. Nevay was clearly popular: three citizens contracted for the teaching of grammar in the grammar school with 'freindis barnis, utheris nychtbouris, and citienaris barnis of the toun', from funds supplied by these laymen but also supplemented from the city's common good.[152] The cost of education rose over the decades. In a 1561 rental of Dunkeld we find the cost for 'the upheld of tua sculls, and ther maister of grammer and sang 100 merkis', but fifty years earlier, in 1510, John Thomson, MA, 'rector of the scholars of the grammar school of the city of Dunkeld' and his successors were to be paid five merks out of episcopal land-rents.[153] In Brechin in 1486 the rector of the school was a cleric, sir Alexander Hog, a chaplain; in 1556, the master was the graduate William Laing.[154] And in Kirkwall in 1486, decades before Bishop Reid's elaborate refoundation in the next century, we have word of a school and a man adorned with the appropriate qualities for a schoolmaster being supported from land rents.[155]

In Aberdeen, the chancellor was responsible from the thirteenth century onwards for overseeing the teaching of grammar and logic. This would prob-ably mean the appointment of teacher-graduates. When Andrew de Syves died in 1418, he was replaced by a recent graduate of the new university

---

[149] A.L. Murray, 'The revenues of the bishopric of Moray in 1539', *IR*, xix (1968), 48, 50–1.
[150] NAS, CS7/38, 225.
[151] NAS, RD1/5, 190.
[152] Duncan Nevay subsequently became reader at Dunblane and then minister at Lecropt. He is entered in the King's College library borrowers' book in or before 1557, Durkan & Ross, *Early Scottish Libraries*, frontispiece; NAS, CS7/38, 190; RDI/5, 190v–192r; J. Kirk, *Patterns of Reform* (Edinburgh, 1989), 150. The kirk was 'within an stane cast to his scholle', *Stirling Recs*, 15. As cleric of Aberdeen diocese, Nevay was created apostolic notary (date torn off) and was thirty-two early in 1564. He was therefore probably born in 1531; NAS, NP2/1, 64.
[153] *Dunkeld Rentale*, 342; *RMS*, ii, 3482.
[154] *Brechin Reg*. ii, 119; NAS, CS7/13, 310.
[155] *Kirkwall Chrs.*, 4, 5, 7, 11.

of St Andrews, John Homill,[156] who had taken his degree in 1415. He was tested as to his 'sufficiency' (qualifications), his good living, his praiseworthy and honest conversation, his great skill in literature and learning generally and as to the taking of his well-deserved degree, and employed for his life-time. Both town and chancellor seem to have been well-pleased. The next appointment was not for another sixty years, in 1479 when Thomas Strachan was hired for ten merks yearly out of the town's common good fund. This appointment was at the king's request, side-stepping town and chancellor. On Strachan's death in 1509, the town presented John Marshall, MA, for a life engagement.[157] In 1521, Marshall having appealed to Rome for some undisclosed reason, the town authorities demanded to know by what authority he held the post, while Marshall only revoked his appeal on the condition that he could pursue the other grammar masters in the burgh to the limits of the law. In 1523 the burgh authorities again reminded him forcibly that he owed his job to them, and in 1527 the school needed and got urgent repairs.[158] The explanation of all this seems to be that Marshall believed his job was for life, but that in 1519 the town or the chancellor had appointed John Bisset, MA, with Marshall still in possession. The fact that their 'skuill is desert and destitut of barnis' in these years may be due to competition from other schoolmasters, as much as to plague.[159] In the event, Bisset went on to become university principal.

In 1538 the town experimented with a layman, Hugh Munro, MA, with the king's backing. Munro was presented to the chancellor who had other ideas, having already appointed another graduate, Robert Skene. But the town paid the piper, and the chancellor agreed to forego his choice if Skene were found incapable or unprepared to work in the town's interest. Munro's appointment won the day. It was for life and, although his movements were restricted in 1549 on account of plague affecting his kinsfolk, the town continued to pay him his 'pension' of ten merks. He resigned in April 1550 and received a redundancy grant of £40.[160] The records, alas, do not explain an incident of 1549 which might throw a sidelight on education in Aberdeen. Two doctors of the grammar school, David Anderson and John Robertson, found themselves under attack by some Aberdonians on the school premises, and responded by rallying the children to launch a counter-attack.[161]

---

[156] *Aberdeen Council Register*, i, 5; *Acta Facultatis*, i, 5.
[157] *Aberdeen Council Register*, i, 36, 80.
[158] Ibid., i, 97, 107, 120.
[159] *Cartularium Ecclesiae Sancti Nicholai Aberdonensis*, ed. J. Cooper (New Spalding Club, 1888–1892), i, 153, 171; ii, 136, 148.
[160] *Aberdeen Council Register*, i, 151, 186, 275, 276.
[161] Ibid., i, 265.

We might observe that the advantage of having a cleric as teacher was that his possession of a chaplainry could save the townsfolk from extra charges on the common good. When, in 1552, Cupar appointed a layman, Thomas Lawson, as master of the grammar school for life, he was to benefit from all its 'commoditeis, proffeitis and dewleis' of the bairns resorting thereto, except the poor at the consideration of the town, offering him a salary of 20 merks yearly to be paid out of an altar foundation, in part – till he was promoted to holy orders.[162] On the whole, it was in the interest of burgh and church to collaborate in spite of inevitable tensions.

Tension of another kind could arise between two church bodies with a say in the local church. This can be illustrated with reference to Dundee. In 1239 Gregory IX granted papal confirmation of the right of the monks of Lindores to have charge of the Dundee schools, in preference to Forfar, then the shire-centre of Angus, decades before Dundee had sheriffdom status.[163] In 1434 a forceful bishop of Brechin, John Crannoch, was determined to assert his own rights after Lindores had appointed Gilbert Knight to the 'rule of the scholars of the town' of Dundee. Knight appealed from the bishop to the abbot, but Crannoch compelled him to revoke his appeal and resign his right to him, and then claimed full authority to appoint his own candidate, Laurence de Lownan, MA. Lindores nonetheless retained its appointing rights thereafter.[164] Dundee's song school must have been just as ancient, and payments to choristers up to the Reformation and beyond confirm this.[165] The new forces for religious change in the 1550s caused problems for all the Dundee schools, as we shall see in Section I.10.

Lack of records for other towns makes it difficult to be definite about continuity. We know that Stirling had won its independence from Dunfermline Abbey by 1545. In that year the abbey still controlled schools in Perth, appointing sir Thomas Birrell for life to the 'principal grammar school' in succession to Simon Young, official of Dunkeld.[166] But Andrew Simson's appointment to Perth c.1550 is not recorded. Neither is Thomas Lister's at Haddington in c.1480, while at Wigtown, where the school exists in the earliest town records, the schoolmaster remains anonymous.[167] Our information on burgh schools depends on our having records to provide information about burghs, and today such records are simply non-existent for most towns at this period, though as recently as 1894, for example, a Kirkintilloch local historian obtained a list of masters from 1518 from a burgh court record

162 St Andrews University Library Special Collections, B13/10/1, 52.
163 *Lindores Liber*, 17.
164 *Brechin Reg.*, i, 62–3; Durkan, 'Education in the century of the Reformation', 149.
165 J. Thomson, *The History of Dundee* (Dundee, 1874), appendix, pp. xiii–xxx.
166 *Dunfermline Reg.*, 394.
167 Durkan, 'Education in the century of the Reformation', 158, 159, 163.

now lost.[168] In Ayr, we find various scholars signing an instrument of Gavin Ros, notary, in 1514, but he is recorded as chaplain-schoolmaster there only in 1526.[169] At Montrose, the records supply no names, but we know Andrew Melville studied there until 1557, not only under Thomas Anderson, but also under the Greek tutor Pierre des Marsilliers, a Frenchman, and we find scholars boarded in St Mary's hospital as far back as 1512.[170]

Some of the potential problems of maintaining schoolmasters from chaplainries can be illustrated by the situation in Linlithgow in 1539. James Brown, MA, the schoolmaster, complained that the curate held the bairns 'that he kennit in his schoule' in such subjection that they had to enter church on festival days for mass and 'evinsang' to sit down 'on cauld stanis' when they would be better employed learning their lessons. Some light can be thrown on this from an earlier foundation. The appointment of the schoolmaster at Linlithgow was in the hands of the priory of St Andrews, but at this date his maintenance came from his chaplainry of All Saints in the parish church, a chaplainry apparently founded by an abbot of Holyrood.[171] By a new foundation of February 1489, the chaplain at this altar was maintained by certain annual rents in order to pray for the souls of James III, his queen and his son, James IV, as well as for the kin of the founder, Robert Main (Mane). This chaplain was to be master 'of all schools and scholars' in the town. All scholars of higher and lower ages (*maiores quam minores*) were to sing or say on bended knee the antiphon to the Holy Spirit at six in the morning until the breakup for the holidays (*ante declinationem*), and at six in the evening before the psalm *De profundis* an antiphon in honour of the Virgin Mary, while on Fridays they had to pray the antiphon to the Holy Cross. But if the abbot of Holyrood and his monks were to appoint another chaplain or non-chaplain against the wishes of the townsmen, Main empowered the council to name whatever chaplain they pleased as schoolmaster. Main's own chaplain was to say the morrow mass in summer at five and in winter at six, obviously to chime in with the early school start. He had to see that anniversaries were celebrated by no less than twelve chaplains. All orphans and poor pupils were to be taught free of charge and in return the scholars had to pray their Latin prayers according to their proficiency in the language. Older pupils were obliged to say once a week and privately the *placebo* and *dirige* of vespers of the office for the dead; the middle age-group

168   T. Watson, *Kirkintilloch: Town and Parish* (Glasgow, 1894), 241.
169   Ibid., 167; *Protocol Book of Gavin Ros*, ed. J. Henderson and F.J. Grant (SRS, 1908), nos. 66, 70.
170   *Autobiography and Diary*, 39; J. Durkan, 'Hospital scholars in the Middle Ages', *IR*, vii (1956), 126–7.
171   *Protocol Books of Dominus Thomas Johnsoun*, ed. J. Beveridge and J. Russell (SRS, 1920), no. 177.

the seven penitential psalms with litany (of the saints); and the least advanced boys the Little Office of the Virgin Mary. Thus the requirements which the Linlithgow curate set in 1539, and which Brown objected to, exceeded these obligations.[172]

Young boys did not necessarily live at home while undergoing their schooling. There were substantial men living out of town who could well afford the school fees and have their sons educated at schools in towns. Attendance at school (in Edinburgh) was invoked as an alibi in a letter to the Lords of Council sent on behalf of an alleged juvenile criminal, William Twedy, said to have been involved in the slaughter of John, Lord Fleming; he petitioned the court in August 1525, stating that he dared not compear personally.[173] A few years later, we find the Browns of Colstoun under the obligation to provide a steading for the upkeep of the late laird's son, ensuring that it was 'plenissit' for his yearly maintenance at the schools from age ten 'to his perfect age'; nearby schools were at Haddington, Bothans and Samuelston.[174] Another example of upbringing away from home is the early life of Patrick Maule, eldest son of the family of Panmure, born in 1548 at Pitcur. With his brother William, he attended the school of Kettins, residing with the lady of Pitcur, a kinswoman who could oversee him. On her death he was sent to Dundee with his brother, the master being Thomas Macgie (Macgibbon), but he was taken out and sent to Montrose after the death of his grandfather. There he stayed until 1562, when, aged fourteen, he married a daughter of John Erskine of Dun, superintendent of Angus, and his French wife.[175]

Earlier, in the 1540s, we find a whole party of west coast scholars at school in the east; the remains of the correspondence of Patrick Waus of Barnbarroch, a boy from Wigtownshire, provide our first evidence for what must have been a long-established school at Musselburgh.[176] Waus would leave Musselburgh for further studies in Paris in 1549 but, even at this stage, the laird of Barnbarroch was slow to meet his son's school expenses. Patrick's correspondence reveals that a growing boy needed clothes, neckcloths and 'schankis' (stockings), and renders accounts for money already spent, partly laid out on a bow and six arrows: the tutor's son had broken the previous bow. A hat and string were needed and three pairs of blue hose (a uniform?). Patrick and Robert, presumably brothers, had gone to Edinburgh for books at the cost of £8. Twenty-three shillings went to another master that 'leiris

172   NAS, NRA(S) 1100, Bundle 1094.
173   NAS, Miscellaneous Justiciary Papers, no. 2.
174   NAS, CS5/34, 97.
175   *Registrum de Panmure*, ed. J. Stuart (Edinburgh, 1874), i, p. xxxvii.
176   *Correspondence of Sir Patrick Waus of Barnbarroch*, ed. R.V. Agnew, *Ayr-Galloway Coll.* (1887), 2–6.

me musik'. A psalm book and a New Testament were acquired (revealing Protestant commitment), and thirty-eight shillings paid for a *Silva* (probably an anthology), Caesar's Commentaries and Sallust, and once again Patrick and Alexander (another brother?) needed another half a dozen arrows for the physical side of education. Patrick had debts for his lodgings; the master had to be paid every quarter; the music teacher was again unpaid; and Patrick reminded the laird about William McLellan, the butler's son, a good scholar in need of help. Musselburgh is clearly a grammar school which we might have expected to be under the control of Dunfermline Abbey, like Musselburgh's hospital.

Paisley Abbey kept the Paisley school firmly under its own control. On 11 August 1554, in the name of the community of Paisley, two town officials approached Messrs John McQuhin, senior and junior, secular chaplains, notaries and schoolmasters, demanding the handing over of the key of their grammar school, a demand they both turned down, knowing they had the backing of their monastic master. The parties met on the bridge over the river Cart, with the abbey on one side of it and the town on the other.[177] This state of affairs persisted, for just before 1559 we find a later Paisley schoolmaster, Robert Maxwell, MA,[178] making the point to the archbishop of Glasgow that he, as 'moderator of Paisley's youth', had found it easy to get the abbot and convent to support him by furnishing their signatures, but had so far failed with Archbishop Beaton. Maxwell did move to the same post at Glasgow, but obviously did not then appreciate that it was harder for bishops to get signatures out of chapters of canons than it was for abbots dealing with monks.

Even for large towns, extant council records begin in the fifteenth century at the earliest, resulting in long centuries during which no hard information is to hand. Sometimes a private archive comes to the rescue. Thus on 4 December 1477, John Clydesdale is found as master of the school of the burgh (no longer 'church') of Edinburgh along with a Dominican, James Gibson, an influential friar at court.[179] In 1498 the town council ordered that 'all scuillis scail and nane to be haldin' because of plague. The high school was not Edinburgh's only school: in 1519 the master, David Vocat, MA, calls himself preceptor of the 'principal' grammar school. He acquired the prebend of St Vincent in the collegiate church of St Mary in the Fields, which the later masters retained, while from Vocat the townsmen got the 'hous of the Grammer Schule' in 1517. However, by the Reformation, the prebend of St Vincent was the song school at Kirk O'Field.[180] Vocat was succeeded by

177 NAS, NP1/199, 56.
178 Latin verses in Durkan, 'Education in the century of the Reformation', 166.
179 NAS, NRA(S) 1100, Bundle 1937.
180 *Edinburgh Burgh Recs.*, i, 75, 165, 481, 552; ii, 90; NAS, E48/1/135.

his friend and disciple, Henry Henryson, former master of the Canongate school, who had authority to suppress other grammar schools except simple reading schools. He was to appear in choir on solemn feasts. The patrons of the school continued to be the abbots of Holyrood.[181] Henryson's wife Mariota Gauye is described as his widow in 1557; her husband had left the country on account of heresy many years earlier.[182] The long courses at the Edinburgh school aiming at perfect grammar evidently seemed altogether too long to the Edinburgh merchants, and in 1531 Adam Mure, MA, promised to produce perfection in three years, before being snapped up by Cardinal Beaton as tutor to his kinsmen.[183] Mure, like Henryson, had been an Aberdeen student under John Vaus, the grammarian in King's College. It was a time when short compendia in grammar and logic were popular in Europe. When William Roberton, MA, a Paris graduate, took over, the three-year course to perfection was probably lengthened again to provide employment for at least one doctor. To ensure that the students did not follow cheaper courses in the neighbourhood, Roberton used his considerable powers to disperse the children of even the Canongate school.[184] There was always the grammar school in Leith, where in 1522 the master was a James Achinane, MA, a priest.[185] The song school underneath the curate's house at St Giles mentioned in 1496 (at the south-east corner of the church) would suffer damage along with the adjacent house in the 1544 English 'Rough Wooing' and again apparently in 1559/60, so that classes had to be held in the church. Its repair was not a priority of the new Reformit Kirk.[186]

I.8 Song schools

The song schools existed to train choristers (and composers) to supply the elaborate liturgical demands of the pre-Reformation church. The historian and St Andrews professor John Mair wrote of his conviction that in all Europe, the English were preeminent in music, but he could not deny that there were perfectly accomplished musicians in Scotland, if not in such numbers as in the south (we have already seen him complain that some ordinands to the priesthood were unskilled even in plainsong); and despite his view that Gaelic speakers were 'wild Scots', Mair acknowledged that

181   *Holyrood Liber*, 256–8; *Registrum Domus de Soltre*, ed. D. Laing (Bannatyne Club, 1861), 364.
182   NAS, NP1/14, 253.
183   *Edinburgh Burgh Recs.*, ii, 48; J. Durkan & W.S. Watt, 'Adam Mure's *Laudes Gulielmi Elphin-stonii*', *Humanistica Lovaniensia*, xxviii (1979), 199–233.
184   W.A. McNeill, 'Scottish entries in the *Acta Rectoria Universitatis Parisiensis*, 1519 to c. 1633', *SHR*, xliii (1964), 66–85; *RPC*, ii, 305–6.
185   NAS, Fragments from the Liber Sententiarum Officialis Laudoniae (1522–1544), fo. 1v.
186   *St Giles Reg.*, 180, 267–8, 273. Arrangements for its repair had been made in 1554, *Edinburgh Burgh Recs.*, ii, 192, 197.

the harpists of the Scottish Highlands were most pleasing to the ear.[187] Although this is not the place to attempt a detailed discussion of the place of song schools in pre-Reformation Scottish culture, a whole network of song schools probably existed, in both Highlands and Lowlands. Though the surviving repertory of what their pupils sang and what their products composed is too fragmentary to permit generalisation, its quality indicates that in some places, at least, the song schools achieved extremely high standards. We do not know what schools trained the polyphonists Robert Johnson 'of Duns' or Patrick Douglas, prebendary of St Giles, whose music survives largely in English sources. But the existence of fine music by John Angus, David Peebles, Robert Carver and John Black means that centres like Dunfermline, St Andrews, Scone and Aberdeen need to be taken into account, despite the implication in much current writing on the subject that artistic work of the highest calibre tended rather to focus on the royal court. In fact, Alexander Paterson's apparent policy of favouring plainsong at the Stirling Chapel Royal[188] from around 1525 is unlikely to have stimulated musical development there, although it was presumably revoked in favour of polyphony in April 1557, when Paterson was removed and replaced by Thomas Myrton, chaplain, as 'schuill maistir … of the bairnis'. The poet Alexander Scott got part of his income from the Cassillis lands in Ayrshire as a musician attached to the Chapel Royal.[189]

Town choirs such as that of Cupar had to be prepared to lose their expert singers, for example to the priory of St Andrews: in February of 1553, Alexander Bellenden, chorister, organist and servant of the parish clerk, contracted until the following Whitsunday, had to force an unwilling town council in Cupar to allow him to be 'prouidit ane chanon' before his contract ended.[190] The parish clerk's role here is like that at Inverness in 1539 when the provost and bailies presented James 'Auchlek', chaplain, to the town clerkship and parish clerkship. His duty was to govern the school with the scholars in attendance in the art of music, not only in singing but in playing the organ. Curiously, while teaching the boys to keep time, he was also responsible for municipal timekeeping in the shape of the town clock.[191] One of Andrew Myllar's books published in Rouen, but presumably with a Scottish market also in view, was an 'Exposition of Sequences and

[187] Major, *History*, 27, 30–50.
[188] See *Commentary on the Rule of St Augustine by Robertus Richardinus*, ed. C.G. Coulton (SHS, 1935), 81.
[189] NAS, CS7/15, 24–25; GD25191231D, endorsed 'Sande Scottis discharge'; T. van Heijns-bergen, 'The Scottish Chapel Royal as cultural intermediary between town and court', in J.W. Drijvers and A.A. MacDonald (eds.), *Centres of Learning* (Leiden, 1995), 299–313.
[190] St Andrews University Library Special Collections, B13/10/1, 117–18.
[191] NLS, Adv MS 29.4.2, vi, 71.

Proses according to the Sarum Use' (1506), obviously intended for teachers rather than students.[192]

One mystery music school was founded in Archbishop Forman's time in the parish of F (possibly for Forgan = Longforgan, though there are several parishes in St Andrews diocese with that initial). The master was to be chaplain of the Holy Cross, qualified to hold, by the wish of the parishioners, a public song school at the church for the teaching of scholars in Gregorian chant, the organ and descant. All the inhabitants of that parish, except, for the present, those in the barony of D., were to be stented annually from each ploughgate with eight plough oxen. This stent amounted to two firlots of barley from every cottar, and from others not having husbandlands two pecks of barley, payable only as long as the chaplain kept school. The parish went on to present a priest, sir A.B. (again, initials only are given).[193] This method of stenting by ploughgate later became routine. Such parish schools are hard to track down, unless elevated to collegiate status, but we know that in 1501 the laird of Carmyllie appointed a chaplain to serve in the local chapel and set aside an income for him. For this priest-schoolmaster, sir Malcolm Strubill, the rules emphasised continuous service and assiduity in holding a chapel school (not specifically for song, and therefore presumably a Latin school) for the instruction of the young.[194]

1.9 Schoolmasters' qualifications

The 1496 Act of Parliament required barons and freeholders of substance to put their eldest sons to the schools 'fra thai be aucht or nyne yeiris of age' and to remain at the grammar schools till they acquire a competent basis of learning and have 'perfite latyne'. The national conscience had been stirred during the fifteenth century, which saw the foundation of three universities.[195] Yet we have to scratch around for evidence of schools existing outside the urban centres; many of the latter were of course within easy reach for prospective scholars. For information as to levels of literacy among the chaplains who constituted the overwhelming majority of schoolmasters, we have to go to England, where a visitation of Lincoln diocese in 1576 found the Scot John Davison, the rector of Saperton, non-resident, celibate and knowing 'but little Latin [and] but little versed in sacred learning'. He had been ordained by the bishop of Dunblane in 1526, and in the year of visita-

192 He also printed a Latin vocabulary by John of Garland. Myllar may have had James IV's splendid new Chapel Royal in view. For a fuller account of sixteenth-century Scottish music, see Ross, *Musick Fyne*.

193 *St Andrews Formulare*, ed. G. Donaldson and C. Macrae (Stair Society, 1942), i, 185–7.

194 Ibid., ii, 263–7; the abbreviated version in *RMS*, ii, 3684, omits all mention of the school.

195 *APS*, ii, 238.

tion was an octogenarian. Another Scot, Thomas Maxwell, aged forty-two, was rector of Scrafield.[196] Unlike Davison, he was married, performed 'the sacred mysteries prescribed by public authority' and yet 'is ignorant of Latin [and] very little versed in sacred learning'; it is rather surprising to learn that Robert Reid, bishop of Orkney, that keen educationalist, had ordained Maxwell, as late as 1557. There are similarly unlearned incumbents among the English-born clergy listed, but evidently these two Scots were chaplains of a kind unlikely to be engaged in education.

Another type of chaplain altogether was Ninian Winzet, though he again was no graduate, unlike his predecessor at Linlithgow, Mr James Brown, a friend of Archbishop Hamilton of St Andrews. Winzet's birthplace in Renfrew (adjacent to Paisley, where Hamilton was commendator) may explain his succession to Brown.[197] Winzet first appears in Linlithgow records in June 1552.[198] If he was given the chaplaincy of All Saints, to which, as priest-schoolmaster, he was entitled, his patron would have been Hamilton of Kincavel.[199] In his 'Thrid tractat' of 1561, Winzet voices the high opinion of the office of schoolmaster characteristic of a much earlier age, before the university schools downgraded ordinary teachers. Schoolmaster in Linlithgow grammar school for 'about the space of ten zeiris', teaching the youth 'in vertew and science', Winzet placed the schoolmaster third in the hierarchy: the king and his government, the godly pastors and the teachers. He therefore had cause to 'marvell gretumlie' that while rich endowments had gone to other religious and learned foundations, little funding had gone to the grammar schools, to the extent that in many towns there was no community provision for a schoolhouse and 'in nane almaist of al' an adequate living for a teacher, although more than the availability of a salary might legitimately be demanded as requisite for the post. The result, he wrote, was that few children were kept at school in any branch of knowledge, especially grammar. For his own part, however, Winzet admitted to having under him gifted children to whom he proposed almost daily

---

196 *Lincoln Episcopal Records. Thomas Cooper, Bishop of Lincoln 1571–84*, ed. C.W. Foster (Lincoln, 1912), 196, 203.

197 Brown was given royal presentation to a vicarage in January 1548, and a few days later made rector of Kirknewton, *RSS*, iii, 1612, 1621.

198 *Protocol Books of James Foulis and Nicol Thounis*, ed. J. Beveridge and J. Russell (SRS, 1927), no. 165 of Foulis.

199 J. Ferguson, *Ecclesia Antiqua* (Edinburgh, 1905), 322–3. This chaplaincy is not found in the chits in the appendix, ibid., 336–57, or on p. 40, but there are several references in the *Protocol Books of Dominus Thomas Johnsoun*. It has been stated that the Hamiltons of Kincavel founded this altar, but there is no mention of them in the early deed we discussed earlier in connection with Brown's 1539 complaint against the curate, and the likelihood is that somehow Sir James Hamilton of Kincavel acquired the patronage from the town by virtue of his being sheriff of Linlithgow, and, as brother to the Protestant martyr Patrick, forfeited it temporarily for heresy.

some theme, argument or sentence for them to render in Latin prose, in oration or epistle form, including relevant contemporary subjects such as the recent chalking of the doors of Edinburgh Catholics. Linlithgow appears to be a school where Latin teaching went well beyond the basics, but not all schools would be so ambitious, nor all scholars so capable. A decade after the 1549 national church council which legislated for a school in all parishes, even in those with meagre financial resources, there is little sign that much headway had been made. Yet other evidence suggests that it was the fifteenth and sixteenth centuries especially that saw efforts made to start schools and to prevent the discontinuation of any existing ones threatened with closure. For Winzet, grammar was a necessary if small 'enteres to science', and it seemed to him that many of those theologising in the dawn of the Scottish Reformation not only knew no grammar but held it in contempt.[200] The godly pastors he speaks of would no doubt teach a few necessary prayers and articles of faith to the junior members of the parish, and schools with less stringent requirements than the grammar schools did of course exist.

There were, for instance, song and reading schools whose nature was preparatory, run sometimes by an unofficial or 'adventure' schoolmaster or mistress. In 1557 we find William Gullein, master of Stirling high school, insisting that no-one should poach on his territory: bairns over seven were his concern and nobody else's. David Ellis was not to teach any bairns over six unless Gullein licensed him, except those that had still to learn to read and write and do sums ('lay compt').[201] Writing is mentioned here, but many could read who could not write. In Edinburgh in 1520, schools other than the high school were permitted to teach only 'grace book, prymar and plane donatt'. The first was a prayer book, the second an elementary reader and the last the *Ars Minor* of Donatus, a basic Latin grammar, of which John Vaus of Aberdeen had produced a vernacular version. Any parents who patronised schools which did not obey this provision would be fined ten shillings, which would go to 'the maister of the said principal scule'.[202] The adventure schools could tailor their teaching to the children's or parents' specifications. In 1567 Ninian Swan, a post-Reformation schoolmaster, but a pre-Reformation chaplain and notary, took over the ancient Lanark school. The council allowed him to be sole master, charge ten shillings from each child, ascertain what he wanted to learn and then teach what 'ilk bairn pleissis'.[203]

Some distinction has to be made between Latin schools and grammar schools and, within grammar schools, those with short courses and those with a good complement of rhetoric and classical literature. Tradesmen

200   N. Winzet, *Certain Tractates*, ed. J.K. Hewison (STS, 1888), i, 24–5.
201   *Stirling Recs.*, i, 71.
202   *Edinburgh Burgh Recs.*, i, 194.
203   *Lanark Recs.*, 36; C. Haws, *Scottish Parish Clergy at the Reformation* (SRS, 1972), 315.

might be prepared to pay for a few years' basic Latin training for commercial purposes, and Adam Mure's offer to shorten the course for the benefit of Edinburgh burgesses was one they would have appreciated. A chaplain-schoolmaster might earn extra pence as a notary; the presence of scholars' signatures on a notarial instrument usually indicates a notary-schoolmaster. We in fact know from other sources that the Ayr notary sir Andrew McCormyll was schoolmaster there in 1501, but as far back as September 1485 an instrument made out by him was signed by a scholar – none other than the future Edinburgh printer, Walter Chepman.[204] In Dumbarton parish church, St Peter's altar supported the grammar master and the Rood altar the song schoolmaster, and in 1527 a chaplain transferring from the collegiate church had to pay maintenance for two boy choristers.[205] At Peebles in 1445, before the foundation of its collegiate church, a chaplain who could not sing plainsong was dismissed. After the foundation, the prebendary of St Mary had to be learned in Gregorian chant and descant – and also in grammar.[206]

I.10 The eve of the Reformation

The pluriform nature of pre-Reformation education makes its story a complex one. Matters would be drastically simplified in 1560, with the official abolition of monastic and friars' schools, cathedral schools, collegiate churches and education for girls in convents. A few friars would leave the country, but most would be pensioned off. Almonries which had supported the education of the poor would also disappear. Dunfermline almonry boys would in fact by that date have been sent for schooling to a non-abbatial town school, whose master was appointed by the abbot. The Abbey no longer controlled appointments in Stirling, but we have seen that the abbot could still have appointed Andrew Simson, a married layman, to a grammarian's post in Perth c.1550.[207] Holyrood still appointed in Edinburgh and Haddington, as will become clear in post-Reformation days. St Andrews appears to have no direct effect on Linlithgow appointments by the late fifteenth century. The late medieval struggle in Glasgow between the cathedral and the burgh over school appointments is referred to in our Glasgow

204 Durkan, 'Education in the century of the Reformation', 155; GUL, MS General 1483/1 (Boyd deeds).

205 J. Durkan, 'Chaplains in Scotland in the late Middle Ages', *RSCHS*, xx (1978), 93; F. Roberts, *The Grammar School of Dumbarton* (Dumbarton, 1948), 2–3.

206 *Peebles Chrs.*, 11, 410.

207 The abbot appointed his predecessor in 1545, *Dunfermline Reg.*, 394. Simson succeeded a priest, Thomas Burrell, 30 May 1550, when Simson was created a burgess in respect of his wife, *Perth Guildry Book 1452–1601*, ed. M.L. Stavert (SRS, 1993), no. 401. Burrell had a life-appointment, *Dunfermline Burgh Recs.*, 394. The reference to Simson at Perth in 1544 in Durkan, 'Laying of fresh foundations', 137, should, of course, read 1554.

Appendix. Extant sources are silent as to Dryburgh Abbey's influence on Lanark latterly, as they are for Kelso's on Roxburgh.

Dundee grammar school is a different matter. There was patently a struggle between the town and Lindores Abbey about authority to appoint. Given the strength of reforming opinion in the burgh from the 1540s onwards, it is tempting to depict this as a struggle on the town's part to appoint a Protestant master. It should be noted that two Dundee schoolmasters, John Fethy and Walter Spalding, became Lutherans and both left for Wittenberg in 1544.[208] The council's choice for training the bairns 'in gude manners and cumlie order' in a course of oratory, poetry, grammar and moral letters was Thomas Macgibbon, who certainly became minister of Moneydie in 1568, and was a man of some cultivation.[209] Although we have no evidence that Macgibbon was a Protestant in the 1550s, the Dundee historian Alexander Maxwell may well be right in surmising that religious issues lay behind Macgibbon's problems. Lindores Abbey objected to him, and appointed John Rolland whom in 1553 they had tried to appoint vicar of Dundee against the opposition of the bishop of Brechin, giving him power to appoint deputies. Several nominees were listed who threatened the school population under Macgibbon's control. In 1555 the council backed Macgibbon by inhibiting Robert Marshall and the musician Andrew Kemp[210] from teaching grammar, the vernacular or singing, whether openly or privately, except in association with Macgibbon and Richard Barclay, master of the song school. Parents whose bairns were not sent to Macgibbon were to be penalised. However, a school which attracted the support of at least twelve families was opened in the meantime by Henry Livingston, MA, a Paris graduate under the future St Salvator's and Sorbonne master Simon Simson.[211] Lindores and John Rolland then appealed to the church courts, where the official of St

208   Durkan, 'Heresy in Scotland', 347–9.
209   *Accounts of the Collectors of Thirds of Benefices*, ed. G. Donaldson (SHS, 1949), 251; Macgibbon also acquired the parsonage and had other churches in his charge. His library included a translation of the Greek historian Herodianus, bound with *Institutiones oratoriae*; the Roman historian Justinus; Andrea Alciati's *Emblems*; and *Scriptores rei rusticae*, featuring Cato, Varro, Columeila and other Roman writers (see Durkan & Ross, *Early Scottish Libraries*, 127; J. Durkan, 'Further additions to Durkan & Ross: some newly discovered Scottish pre-Reformation provenances', *Bibliotheck*, x (1980–81), 96; L. Witten, *Rare Books, Catalogue 7*, 24 November 1977, Connecticut, item 220).
210   Kemp became a chaplain in St Salvator's College; see Durkan, 'Education in the century of the Reformation', 149, 150. Several of Kemp's Reformed compositions appear in Thomas Wode's psalter, copied in St Andrews between 1562 and 1566, and some forty psalm harmonisations were recorded by the composer Duncan Burnett in his music book. Kemp himself was reader at Balmerino and Kilrenny, was involved in a dispute with various other Fife musicians (*RKSSA*, i, 338), and moved to Aberdeen as song-school master in 1570; at his death in 1571, he had been appointed minister of Fintray, although *Fasti*, viii, has him simultaneously at both the Aberdeenshire and the Stirlingshire parishes of that name.
211   McNeill, 'Scottish entries', 77. Simon Simson took refuge in Paris at the Reformation.

Andrews found for Lindores. Opposition continuing, Lindores got letters in four forms to be obeyed under pain of horning. The town then decided to appeal to the pope or his legate, Archbishop Hamilton, from whom it won a temporary victory in December 1557, but the litigation continued and in 1559 the case was still pending. In October 1559, the council insisted that no masters or doctors teaching bairns were to receive as their scholars any who had been withdrawn from Macgibbon's school. Meanwhile, Livingston was summoned for not paying the rent of his school (John Buchan, Macgibbon's predecessor, had experienced similar financial difficulties in 1553). At this stage, the religious civil war intervened, in which Lindores Abbey was so destroyed that by 1562 much of its timber could be set aside for the town's use.[212] In that year, John Buchan reappears as schoolmaster,[213] but he was soon replaced by the future grammarian and bishop of Ross, Alexander Hepburn, whom we will meet in Section IV.1.

In St Andrews, the priory did not control the city grammar school, which was still the archdeacon's privilege, but they did control St Leonard's College, and insisted that nobody could enter there who had not finished with at least the first and second parts of grammar (accidence and syntax, i.e. excluding versification and rhetoric): at the limit the entrant must know the greater part of the syntax section. Knowledge of music was restricted to plainsong, and ability to write was demanded, though overlooked in the original statutes. Keeping time with the others in choir was insisted on in Winram's visitation of 1545; 'difficult masses' were to be gone over in advance by students and by those unskilled in music.[214] At the principal's direction remedial lessons in grammar might even be necessary, or indeed the lessons in poetry and rhetoric omitted in some Latin schools.[215]

As regards the extent of pre-Reformation educational provision, my own belief is that the schools recorded in our lists as existing in 1560 represent

---

[212] A. Maxwell, *Old Dundee: prior to the Reformation* (Edinburgh, 1891), 152–5, 185–6; see also A. Maxwell, *History of Old Dundee, narrated out of the Council Register* (Edinburgh, 1884), 88–9. In 1564, another 'adventure' schoolmaster, John Soutar, was forbidden to keep school in Dundee any longer.

[213] The presence in Thomas Wode's psalter of two psalms harmonised by a John Buchan indicates that this Dundee master may well be the musician, later found at Haddington and then Glasgow as song schoolmaster. Wode says Buchan had borrowed his – evidently incomplete – part-books and simply inserted his own versions of psalms 67 and 128 on the appropriate pages – 'of my unwitting'.

[214] Herkless & Hannay, *St Leonard*, 146, 160, 200.

[215] Ibid., 147, 154, 163, 169, 172. A point of educational vocabulary can usefully be clarified here in connection with pre-Reformation St Leonard's. The suggestion has been made that the terms 'siege' and 'class' were new post-Reformation usages. But 'siege', in its Latin equivalent *sedes*, is used in that college's original statutes and repeated in the revision (the latter alone is printed by Herkless and Hannay). 'Siege' refers to a class from the presiding teacher's viewpoint. The Latin word *classis* appears too in the revised statutes, themselves of pre-Reformation composition.

only a proportion, albeit perhaps a significant one. A parish school like Kettins can scarcely have been a unique phenomenon, and after 1551 every priest-in-charge of a parish was duty-bound at least to teach the so-called catechism of Archbishop Hamilton.[216] There is a reference in 1589 to the existence of the grammar school at Culross 'since time immemorial', and at that date, it was still to be found in the abbey itself.[217] Ferrerio's biography of Thomas Chrystal, as we saw, attests to the previous existence of a song school in Culross, and in 1614 it was stated again that 'in all tyme bygane' there had been a grammar school in the abbey in which the local youth were instructed in grammar and 'tranit up' in virtue and letters.[218] In 1627, Ednam reported that 'their has ever mor beine a school heir', and Logie, Stirlingshire, at that time the site of a vernacular school, claimed to have had a grammar school of old.[219]

There is only one French school recorded, in Edinburgh in 1556, and one dame school there in 1499, but obscure schoolmistresses were not likely to make their way into medieval documentation.[220] And song schools may have been more widespread than extant records reveal: in 1536 'in a lytle univer-syte or study named Glasco, where I study and practyse physyk', the English xenophobe Andrew Borde recorded the Scots' failure to impress him with much they did – except their prowess and skill in music.[221] Yet in 1549–50, in that same educational environment and city which Borde so disliked, we find the university educated Glasgow canon Mr Thomas Hay seeking a servant 'that culd perfytely reid and writ'. Through the good offices of sir Andrew Hay, vicar pensioner of Rathven, one Andrew Reidfurth, then a student in Banff, duly left Banff for Glasgow. However, Mr Thomas moved to Edinburgh eight days after his arrival, fell ill, and 'skalit howss', dismissing Reidfurth and the rest of his household. He arranged with Mr George Hay, son of the laird of Tallo, then also in his service, to pay Reidfurth ten merks for a year's fee for his 'service studie', together with his expenses for himself and his servant on their journey from Banff, and also for his servant's return thither. This cash, Reidfurth claimed, was never forthcoming, and in 1556 he took his case to appeal. Reidfurth, whom we find in 1574 as a reader in

---

[216]   Issued in consequence of the 1549 national church council, but not until 1551; it was largely the work of a refugee English Dominican, Richard Marshall, on Hamilton's behalf.

[217]   NAS, PS1/59, 116–17.

[218]   NAS, CH4/1/4, 106.

[219]   *Reports on the State of Certain Parishes in Scotland*, ed. A. Macdonald (Maitland Club, 1835), 195, 201.

[220]   *Edinburgh Burgh Recs.*, i, 76; ii, 241. No man or woman was to keep a school while the plague lasted.

[221]   In his *First Book of the Introduction of Knowledge* (Early English Text Society, Extra Series no. 10, 1870), 137.

the kirk in his native north-east, cannot have been the only such educated youth in the service of the higher clergy.[222]

Banff was a royal burgh; pre-Reformation schools were still mainly town-based rather than 'landward'. To the list published in 1959 we can now add Trinity and the French school in Edinburgh, as well as Beauly, Cambuskenneth, Ednam, Elphinstone, Kettins, Kirkintilloch, the anonymous 'F', Hamilton, Huntly, Logie, Ross Chanonry, Samuelston, Scone, Strathmiglo and Sweetheart.[223] This excludes Highland schooling, which demands a different approach.[224] As we observed at the outset of this Section, whatever schooling existed (apart from women's schools), was by the sixteenth century mainly in the charge of chaplains, who preferred to designate themselves as such, a hard fact which impedes investigation of their work as schoolmasters and pedagogues. Nevertheless, at the level of education in music, reading and grammar, one can surely posit a minimum of a hundred schools, however precarious the life of some of them may have been.

---

[222]   NAS, CS7/13, 269–70; 'Register of Ministers and Readers in the year 1574', *Wodrow Misc.* i (1844), 342.

[223]   Durkan, 'Education in the century of the Reformation', 162.

[224]   There were about twenty notaries active (1530–1560) in Argyll alone: I. Bannerman, 'Literacy in the Highlands', in I.B. Cowan & D. Shaw (eds.), *The Renaissance and Reformation in Scotland* (Edinburgh, 1983), 220.

II. The Impact of the Reformation

II.1 The First Book of Discipline and roofless kirks

In the fateful spring of 1560, education was not the Reformers' first concern. A new church had to be established nationally, and matters of doctrine, policy and staffing called for prior attention. But it very soon emerged that an immense work of consolidation and re-education confronted the Reformed movement's leaders, and it was plain that rapid action was needed to consolidate their recent victory over the Old Church. It was important for the Reformed cause that ministers and readers be involved in education from the very start, to prevent the appearance of a generation of children who were either educated by surviving Catholic possessors or received no religious instruction whatever. An educational manifesto to match the demands of the times was contained in the *First Book of Discipline*, submitted to the General Assembly in December 1560, and presented to parliament in January 1561. At a late stage in the *Book*'s drafting, when it had become apparent just how massive the problems were, another two Johns were drafted in from St Andrews University to join the four Johns already working on the text: Winram, the new dean of theology in succession to Friar John Grierson, and Douglas, provost of St Mary's College. Johns Willock, Row and Spottiswoode were all graduates, and Knox himself had both actual schoolteaching experience, and (presumably) knowledge of how schooling was implemented in Geneva. It is worth noting, however, that none of the six Johns had experience of Highland education.

Under the heading 'For the Schollis', the *First Book of Discipline* bluntly observed that the 'office and dewtie of the godlie Magistrat' (i.e. the state) was to ensure that reformation was achieved and maintained 'to the posteriteis following'. The *Book* therefore calls on the 'Great Counsall of the Realm' to take full account of 'the necessitie of schollis', since 'God hath determined that his Churche heir in earth shallbe tawght not be angellis but by men; and seing that men ar born ignorant of all godlynes ... off necessitie it is that your Honouris be most cairfull for the virtuous educatioun, and godlie upbringing of the youth ... Off necessitie thairfore we judge it, that everie severall Churche have a Scholmaister appointed'. The *Book* laid down that while 'the riche and potent' were to pay for the education of their children, who were no longer 'to spend their youth in vane idilnes', the poor, their children, and teachers of the youth were all to be supported out of the church's patrimony. How this was to be achieved was far from clear. Little of the ecclesiastical patrimony was actually in the hands of the Kirk, and the help of the state, 'the godly Magistrate', was clearly essential in securing the requisite teinds and, in burghs, annual rents. The Council agreed in principle, but eighteen months later, little funding had actually been forthcoming. The General Assembly of July 1562, now faced with a Catholic queen, noted the general complaint from ministers, exhorters and readers that they had small or no stipends, repeated its 'supplication for the poor and their support' and for 'maintenance of schools for instruction of the youth in every parish' financed from the teinds 'and within burows' from the annual rents.[1] Chronic shortage of funding would be a problem for many years to come, and the visionary educational goals set out in the *First Book*, lacking parliamentary endorsement, would not be speedily realised. But there can be no questioning the significance of these visionary goals; once stated, they remained the point of reference for the future.

Given that in most parishes, education was intended to take place at the kirk, the prospects for education were far from bright in those parishes whose kirks were roofless or otherwise unusable, and where attached manses were in a similar sorry state or reverting to the lay patron's use. The evidence for the destruction of some parish kirks during the religious revolution is too strong to be overlooked. One of the most telling witnesses is a veteran of the Reformation, the minister, mathematician, judge and poet Robert Pont, whose *Against Sacrilege* was written and published as late as 1599.[2] His comments have been largely overlooked, but this founding father of the Reformit Kirk maintained that there were more sacrilegious men in Scotland than elsewhere in Reformed Europe, and, while he excused the original Scottish Reformers of 1560 on account of their pious motives, he observes that other impious contemporaries failed to differentiate 'many Parish Kirks' from monastic houses: 'of the lead that was taken off our kirkes and monasteries a greate part perished by sea'.[3] Moreover, he contended that the first Reformers, 'the most part of the Realme being in their contrarie', were hazarding their personal patrimony in the religious cause and thus they could be pardoned for helping themselves to bells, lead and jewels to ensure their victorious outcome. Yet there were 'a great many, not onely of the raskall sorte', but men of repute who enriched themselves unscrupulously at

[1]   *BUK*, i, 17.
[2]   Sig. B1, B2, B6, C2; other witnesses include Ninian Winzet in 1563, *Certain Tractates*, i, 128; David Fergusson, minister of Dunfermline, *Tracts by David Fergusson*, ed. Lee, 72, 73; an Act of Parliament of January 1573 (against private persons), *APS*, iii, 76-7; a satirical poem of 1573, 'The Lamentatioun of Lady Scotland', Cranstoun (ed.), *Satirical Poems*, 232; Nicol Burne ('kirks without cure, vindo or ruffe') 1581, *A Disputation* (Paris, 1581), fo. 59v; and Archbishop Spottiswoode, son of a superintendent of Lothian contemporary of these events, Spottiswoode, *History*, i, 372-3.
[3]   Pont, *Against Sacrilege*, sig. H1rv.

the Kirk's expense, whom Pont counted to 'haue bene the first sacriligious amongst us'.[4]

There is much else in Pont's treatise which provides a background to the sole surviving visitation record of this period, that for the Dunblane area as late as 1586. (In 1562, Pont had been appointed minister of Dunblane and then Dunkeld, and remained there several years before being transferred north to Elgin.) The 1586 visitation record shows how little had been achieved, a quarter of a century after the *First Book of Discipline*'s plea for the urgent repair of parish kirks.[5] The earlier and now lost visitation book of the bishop of Dunblane would doubtless have thrown further light on this central region: it is odd that, although the visitor was supposed to enquire about parish schools, the sole reference made in 1586 is to the school at Dunblane.[6] This does not mean there were no others; other sources name schoolmasters at Strageith and Muthill, both sited at kirks; about 1583, John Brown, schoolmaster at Strageith, acquired a degree and thereafter appeared as 'Mr'.[7] The kirk at Muthill was utterly decayed in 'thak and ruff' except for its choir: it is worth observing that 'thak' here does not necessarily mean thatch, merely roofing, and indeed, the parish was to contract with slaters for its repair.[8] The nave of Tulliallan kirk was 'thekit with hadder', but the choir was properly slated 'as of auld'.[9] Strowan kirk, which once had a reader, seems to have been uninhabitable, and had no minister or reader assigned.[10] Obviously, kirks that were not watertight were scarcely suited for daily schooling.

The General Assembly records show that even in the immediate Glasgow area there were kirks awaiting repair in 1576,[11] and as late as 1587, there were kirks in ruins in Fife.[12] In 1593, the records still talk of ruinous manses to be rebuilt, and of their erection where there were none.[13] The problem was not merely unplanted kirks, but 'displanted' ones forced on local inhabitants

4   Ibid., *sigs.* B2v, B7rv, B8v.
5   *Stirling Presbytery Records 1581-1587*, ed. J. Kirk (SHS, 1981), 117.
6   *Visitation of the Diocese of Dunblane and Other Churches 1586-1589*, ed. J. Kirk (SRS, 1982), 39.
7   *Stirling Presbytery Records*, 61, 77.
8   Ibid., p. xl; pp. 118, 44.
9   *Visitation of Dunblane*, 54. Reference to a proposal to 'theik' an Aberdeen steeple with lead in 1510 is only one of many of the wider use of this word, *Aberdeen Court Bk.*, i, 103. In 1572, William, Lord Ruthven, got a grant of 'the haill leid quhairwith the cathedrall kirk of Ros wes theikit', *RSS*, vi, 1653. The town of Edinburgh in 1581 constructed its tolbooth out of 'thaik stanes' from Inchcolm Abbey, *Edinburgh Burgh Recs.*, iv, 204, 210.
10   *Visitation of Dunblane*, pp. xxv, 79.
11   *BUK*, i, 348-9.
12   Ibid., ii, 719.
13   Ibid., iii, 812.

by the reduction in value of ministers' stipends.[14] The loss of the medieval chaplain's extras, 'corps presents', etc., could lessen the value of a minor benefice.[15] In some areas the parish kirk, an early medieval foundation, was now remote from the majority of the parishioners' homes; a change of site won the Assembly's blessing in 1593.[16] 'Spatious' congregations were still a problem in 1600, and indeed would continue to be so, because of the large spread of many of the country's parishes.[17] A new parish needed to be established in Ferryport-on-Craig, as it was too far from its parish kirk of Leuchars; in pre-Reformation days there had been a medieval chapel available in Ferryport. On the other side of the country, Stranraer, a new parish also came into being in place of the medieval chapel of St John.[18]

The problems faced by the new Kirk with regard to staffing its parish kirks provide us with some indication of the problems it faced in implementing its vision of a school in every several parish. While documentary evidence for schools is scattered and fragmented, there is an abundance of material relating to the Kirk. For the latter, there was a direct link between the ministry and education and, indeed, many of the first clergymen of the new Kirk were – as of old – also teachers. The Acts of the General Assemblies (which contain occasional specific references to schools and schoolmasters), therefore, allow us to follow the evolution of the attitudes taken and problems faced by the central authorities of the Kirk.

II.2 General Assemblies to 1567

The Assemblies of 1560–62 were sparsely attended, but this fact reflects the stipulation that no minister was to leave his flock to attend the Assembly unless he had 'complaints to make or else be complained on'. However, ministers were expected to have books 'in store' at the time of any visitation and had to show they had read them. As early as 1562 there was already one minister, Mr Robert Hamilton, threatened with removal; others were disheartened by non-payment of their stipends, and still others had to be pressed into service.[19] The arrangement whereby two thirds of a benefice went to old benefice-holders and only one third to the ministers meant they lived 'a beggar's life'. Many of them, like Andrew Melville's brother Richard

[14] Ibid., iii, 964.
[15] Ibid., ii, 660.
[16] Ibid., i, 281.
[17] Ibid., iii, 950.
[18] Ibid., iii, 1004; 950; for 'Chapeltoun' and 'Chapilbank' in Ferryport, see *RMS*, v, 2040, 2273; for St John's chapel in Stranraer, see P.H. McKerlie, *History of the Lands and their Owners in Galloway* (Edinburgh, 1870), i, 130.
[19] *BUK*, i, 16, 17.

Melville of Baldovie, could not even be sure of their manses,[20] detained as they were by the benefice-holders or local lairds. The difficult situation of the ministry may have discouraged some of those who had volunteered for service in the first flush of Reformation. Of the nine volunteers in the Assembly of 1560, of whom eight were to be readers and one an exhorter ('apt to teach'), only three survived: James Dalrymple, a former chorister in Ayr, later minister there, Rankin Davidson, former chaplain and notary in Wigtown, reader in Loudon and Galston, and Adam Landells, former chaplain-notary, later exhorter at Auchinleck. Richard Bannatyne, employed by the Ayr authorities to convoy their minister, Christopher Goodman, to and from Edinburgh, became secretary to John Knox but is not on record as a reader, and neither are the remaining volunteers, Robert Campbell, Hugh Wallace, Andrew and John Chalmer.[21]

In 1562, less than 'godly' schooling at Arbroath led the superintendent of Angus, John Erskine of Dun, to complain to the Assembly that the school-master, Mr Robert Cumming, continued a Catholic, 'infecting the youth … with idolatrie'. No mention of others doing the same was recorded by that Assembly; they existed nonetheless, as we shall see. Superintendent Erskine himself was accused of admitting as readers in his diocese many 'popishe preistis', unfit and of wicked life. Some were admitted as exhorters and even as ministers without having passed the tests required in the *Book of Discipline*. The Assembly lamented that 'sundrie ministers' did not live at their kirks, 'the zouth is not instructed', and the ministers did not come to the 'exer-cise' (the *Book of Discipline*'s scheme for the mutual education of ministers, involving discussion of theological and controverted issues). In spite of all this criticism, Erskine was deputed to visit the north, which 'for the most part was destitute of ministers', to establish ministers, elders and deacons.

In 1562 the Assembly spoke about 'this rarity of the ministry' when the laird of Pumpherston complained about the lack of preaching in his kirk of Calder.[22] How much the lack of preaching ministers was compensated for by the presence of readers, who were forbidden to preach, is difficult to gauge. The Assembly records say little about them. In 1563 it ordained that 'the instructioun of youth be committit to none … neither in universities nor without the samein, but to them that professe Chrysts true religioun'. Non-professors were to be removed. Schoolmasters were also to be placed in Moray, Banff and adjacent areas. Once again reference is made to 'the rare number of ministers', which made it impossible for 'everie kirk to have a

[20] Ibid., i, 22–3.
[21] *BUK*, i, 4; details of Dalrymple, Davidson, and Landells in Haws, *Scottish Clergy at the Reformation*, 264, 265, 287.
[22] *BUK*, i, 18.

severall minister'.[23] This has implications for schooling, although the educational role envisaged for ministers by the *Book of Discipline* could in some respects be supplied by readers.

Erskine of Dun was again criticised in 1563: he did not use discipline in many of the kirks; elders and deacons did not meet for correction of faults; he visited, but omitted to preach. The burden of visiting the north left him no leisure to attend to his charge.[24] Patently, reform was a slow process, and in such a context, schools were liable to get pushed into the background. The commissioner of the north, Mr John Hepburn, detailed to plant schools in Moray and Banff, could not observe his commission because of great sickness. Mr Donald Monro, commissioner of Ross, was not as apt to teach (i.e. preach) as his charge required. The sheer rarity of competent, high-quality ministers at this time is demonstrated by the fact that Mr Robert Pont, minister of Dunblane and Dunkeld, had already been commissioned to plant kirks in Inverness, and had taken over some of the Assembly's commission to John Hepburn. Unsurprisingly, Pont felt unable to continue, observing that he lacked Gaelic.[25] (At both Dornoch and Creich in Caithness, the exhorter and reader were said to speak the 'Irische toung' about 1567.[26]) The inhabitants of Calder were still unhappy with the new pluralism of the new Kirk where a man like Spottiswoode could hold two incompatible offices; unless rectified, 'we shall differ little frome the popish kirk'. The minister of Forres, David Rae, was admonished on account of his doctrine and 'maners'. Along with other colleagues in the north, he was complained upon and replaced, and his successor was only appointed with the caution that he avoid giving cause for such slander.[27] Many ministers did not reside where their charge was but in towns far distant, and the Assembly, while recalling that the old clergy might still detain their manses, insisted on ministers in residence when accommodation was available.[28] Sir Thomas Duncanson, a former chaplain and schoolmaster of Stirling, having committed fornication, was suspended, but he turns up later in Border towns like Bowden.[29]

In connection with the 1563 Assembly proposal that Mr Patrick Cockburn be appointed superintendent of Jedburgh, we would recall that the *Book of Discipline* laid down that a superintendent's seat ought to have a top tier college, though no medieval school is recorded for Jedburgh, unlike

[23] Ibid., i, 33–4.
[24] Ibid., i, 39.
[25] *BUK*, i, 34, 40. Pont had to plant kirks from 'Ness to Spey', *Register of Ministers*, 58, and Hepburn from the river Spey eastwards, *BUK*, i, 44.
[26] *Register of Ministers*, 53.
[27] *BUK*, i, 42; *Register of Ministers*, 58 and n.
[28] *BUK*, i, 44–5.
[29] Haws, *Scottish Clergy at the Reformation*, 30.

other suggested seats of superintendents at Aberdeen, Banff, and Dumfries.[30] Calderwood observes that in 1563, the Assembly 'aimed at a superintendentship in Teviotdaill, Nithisdaill, Annandaill and Selkirk, yitt could they never atteane to moe than five'.[31] The existing superintendents came under scrutiny in 1563: Spottiswoode of Lothian found the job too burdensome, as did Willock of the West (Glasgow area) who had only promised to do it temporarily, and blamed the slowness in extirpating 'idolatrie' on the duke of Châtelherault and the earl of Cassillis. Winram of Fife, we also learn, never preached in his visitations, but got a substitute.

In addition to all the other problems facing the new Kirk, opposition was still a factor to be reckoned with. The Assembly of 1564 wished the Lords of Council to point out to Queen Mary that transgressors of the proclamations against saying and assisting at mass in addition to 'abusers of the Sacraments' were now so common that a fearsome judgement on the situation was likely if not soon remedied. Complaints were also raised that many ignorant men 'of bad conversation' were being admitted as ministers, exhorters and readers, and nation-wide visitors were appointed to suspend or depose these guilty or unqualified persons. The closeness of the links between educational provision and the Kirk in 1564 can be demonstrated by the situation in central Fife: Robert Montgomery, then stationed at Cupar, served Largo as minister on alternate Sundays while the schoolmaster of Cupar was to read and exhort there in his absence. Thomas Jameson, the minister at Largo and Newburn, is described as 'instructar' as well as minister.[32]

Despite the Assembly's desire to purge the unworthy elements, it is not clear that many suspensions or depositions actually occurred. By the June 1565 Assembly, two superintendents had still not carried out their enquiries. The Assembly decreed that uniformity of worship was to be ensured by all ministers, exhorters and readers having a copy of the recently printed psalm-book.[33] The queen's evil example in hearing mass was denounced, and attention was again drawn to the failure of ministers to obtain possession of their manses and so to reside in their localities. Like the need to repair kirks, this was a matter that affected schooling. But as far as educational provision is concerned, most significant was the Assembly's reiteration of the *Book of Discipline*'s demand that the lands and rents formerly of friars and priests be used to maintain the poor and for the 'uphald of the schooles in the townes and uthers places wher they lie'.[34]

---

[30] *BUK*, i, 25–30.

[31] *History*, ii, 224.

[32] *Register of Ministers*, 23; R. Lindsay of Pitscottie, *The Historie and Chronicles of Scotland*, ed. A.J.G. Mackay (STS, 1899–1901), ii, 138–9. Jameson was himself originally from Cupar.

[33] *BUK*, i, 53–4, 57.

[34] Ibid., i, 60.

The supervision of the ministry continued to present obstacles; in 1565 Superintendent Erskine of Angus alleged that at visitation time he had to lodge with friends who were often the very people in most need of discipline and correction, while Alexander Gordon of Galloway excused his not visiting on account of 'the building of his nephew's house'. The problem of benefices and their control was raised with the queen again, but no answer satisfying to the Kirk resulted.[35] Mr John Row of Perth was commissioned to visit kirks, schools and colleges in Ayrshire 'to remove offending or unqualified ministers and others, and eradicate idolatrie'. Knox was to draw up a letter to encourage officers not to forsake the ministry and get parishioners to supply their needs.[36] As for provision of schooling in the west by 1567, Mr John Raes, a former prebendary of Hamilton collegiate church,[37] is described as 'exhorter and teycher of the zouth' at Hamilton; and we find the schoolteacher in nearby Lanark, Ninian Swan, exhorter, admitted to minister the sacraments at Carmichael. In Annandale, there was only one minister, a non-graduate; the rest were readers, with one exhorter. Fife, unsurprisingly, was much better provided for.[38] A more thorough enquiry is clearly necessary, based on *Thirds of Benefices*, the *Register of Ministers*, and the *Books of Assumption*.[39]

The overthrow of the Catholic queen in the spring of 1567 meant major changes in all spheres. At the June 1567 Assembly the new moderator was George Buchanan, a man of learning with wide experience as an educator. However, educational matters were not discussed, the Assembly being more worried about the ministry, still 'frustrat of all lyfe and sustentatioun'.[40] The Assembly of December 1567 did address the educational issue nonetheless, for the problem of Catholic schoolmasters was still impeding the accomplishment of the Kirk's educational manifesto. The nobles and others promised

> faithfullie to reforme schooles, colledges, and universities throughout the whole realme, and expell and remove the idolaters that has charges therof and uthirs quho hes not zet joynit themselfe to the true kirk of Chryst, and plant faithfull instructors in ther rowme, to the effect that zouth be not infectit be poysonable doctrine at the beginning, quhilk afterward cannot be well removit away.[41]

Queen Mary's fall had changed the situation of non-professing school-

35 Ibid., i, 65, 67–71.
36 Ibid., i, 73–4.
37 NAS, RH6/1376.
38 *Accounts of the Collectors of the Thirds of Benefices*, 264, 266; R. Renwick (ed.), *Records and Charters of the Burgh of Lanark* (Glasgow, 1893), 36; *Register of Ministers*, 23–5, 46–7.
39 *The Books of Assumption of the Thirds of Benefices*, ed. J. Kirk (Oxford, 1995).
40 *BUK*, i, 93, 94.
41 Ibid., i, 110–11. On p. 84, we read that in 1567, schools were 'decayand and kirks falland to the ground'.

masters quite dramatically. On 17 August 1567, parliament had explicitly excluded Catholic schoolmasters, enacting that 'nane to be permitted … to have charge in tyme cumming, nor instruct the zouth privautlie or opinlie, but sic as salbe tryit be the Superintendentis or visitouris of the Kirk'.[42]

II.3 The situation under the godly regents

The fall of Queen Mary and the succession of the Protestant earl of Moray created a new situation for Catholic schoolmasters, although as we have just seen, their exclusion was often merely theoretical in the burghs. But kirk sessions, which often took a patronising attitude towards their employees, would not tolerate them in the parish schools. In the terms of the Assembly's letter of January 1568, recalling John Willock from England, there was 'sufficient provision made for ministers' and God had brought about a 'most wonderfull victory for his evangell', although vigilance was still called for.[43] Willock duly returned as superintendent for the west and was elected moderator in 1568.[44] With the new regime of the Regent Moray, negotiations could now proceed much more swiftly and profitably than hitherto with Queen Mary. Unfortunately for our purposes, much business concerning readers and others would henceforth be settled locally, and thus no longer reach the assembly and its records. Small numbers attended the Assembly in July 1568, because of the evil weather as well as rumours of plague, and they were accommodated in the 'nether counsell-house' (lower tolbooth) of Edinburgh.[45] (But we should recall that some earlier and indeed later meeting places were no more commodious: the June 1567 Assembly had been held in the Magdalen chapel in Edinburgh's Cowgate, while an Assembly in St Andrews was held in 'Sanct Leonards school' in 1572.[46])

However, in spite of the more favourable turn of events under Moray, the problems of the Kirk's collectors of teinds continued. Non-payment was universal, 'as well be Protestants as Papists'.[47] The question of the creation of doctors of divinity in St Andrews and of drawing up a degree procedure was referred to the members of the colleges there, with revision by the next assembly, without which the procedure would not be fixed. It has been claimed that the temporary statutes for the theological faculty had been drawn up c.1560, but they probably date from as late as 1567, since they refer to John Douglas, 'formed bachelor', and also to James VI, who was

42 *APS*, iii, 24.
43 *BUK*, i, 120–1.
44 Ibid., i, 131.
45 Ibid., i, 132.
46 Ibid., i, 237.
47 Ibid., i, 139.

not born until that year.[48] Under the new government, it would now be possible to go ahead with deposing the staff of King's College in Aberdeen, who persisted in their Catholic ways despite Moray's personal intervention. More superintendents were envisaged by the assembly in 1569, but the Kirk's jurisdiction was to be kept separate from the civil. The regent was prepared to collaborate to help ministers get their stipends and manses, and wrote a careful reply to the Assembly's appeal, making much of his goodwill to the reformed Kirk. He pointed out, however, that as regards vacant chaplainries, some petitioners desired life appointments, some 'for infants that are of the schooles', some for seven years, so that he was pressed sometimes to confirm the assignation or demission of such benefices, in which there was already some involvement in corruption. The Kirk agreed with the arrangement that such chaplainries should go only to the colleges or to the poor, and found it hard to forgive the earl of Huntly on whose lands the ministers lived in great poverty while the abbot of Deer had 'debursed his money to the enemies of God'. Further progress, however, was shortly thereafter impeded by the assassination of Moray on 23 January 1570.[49]

The impediments can be illustrated with reference to the aforesaid 1567 theology statutes of St Andrews, which are of some importance for the training of ministers. At that point there were doctors of theology about.[50] But following Moray's death, it was not until 1574 that the earl of Morton's visitation was able to make up for 'the iniquitie of the tyme' which had caused education to falter. Some who had 'studyit of lang continewance' in theology had not been made doctor, and this was to be delayed no longer. In view of the scarcity of ministers, the statutory intervals between the degrees of bachelor, licence and doctor were to be dispensed with, to allow these men to take examinations by the following year. However, the degree procedure 'ordinarlie institute' (as reformed in the statutes, at that point in the hands of John Winram, dean of faculty) was still to be observed.[51]

At the March 1570 Assembly, several cases of ministerial neglect were reported, apparently without effectual action being taken: the minister of Kilconquhar who was seldom in Kilconquhar, the exhorter of Monkland

---

[48] *BUK*, i, 140; *The Statutes of the Faculty of Arts and the Faculty of Theology at the Period of the Reformation*, ed. R.K. Hannay (St Andrews, 1910), 112, 130, 134. If the revision followed on from this appeal by the Assembly, the changes are remarkably light. The chancellor (Hamilton) is also envisaged as being present.

[49] *BUK*, i, 153–5.

[50] *Statutes*, 184; that is what *magistri nostri* means. They have been capped but very recently: *nuperrime birretati*. In the printed text, Hannay (seemingly unaware of the technical sense of *magistri nostri*) has altered the manuscript phrase to *nostro nuperimme birretato*, as though John Douglas would be already capped as doctor while still only a 'formed bachelor'. Neither manuscript authorises Hannay's alteration of *nostri* to *nostro* and *birretati* to *birretato*.

[51] *Statutes*, 82–3. In other words, Morton did not reform them, but accepted the reforms made since Winram took over as dean.

who refused discipline despite double fornication, the vicar of Ayton who administered the sacraments without authority. All three were still in office in 1574.[52] Adam Bothwell, bishop of Orkney, was alleged to have committed simony in arranging an exchange of Orkney for Holyrood with the Lord Robert Stewart; two kirks attached to Holyrood, Falkirk and Whitekirk had had no ministers since the Reformation, while the ministers of Liberton and St Cuthbert's near Edinburgh had to give up their charges 'for meer poverty'; some kirks in Lothian and Galloway were even being used as sheepfolds for lack of repair. There may be some exaggeration here, as the ministers of Edinburgh were displeased with Adam Bothwell, the new commendator of Holyrood, and his criticism that in their public teaching they had 'past the bounds of Gods word'.[53] In his own defence, Bothwell argued that most of the roofless kirks had been pulled down 'at the first beginning of the Reformation' and had not been repaired since.[54]

Under such circumstances, it is not evident how teachers, if they existed, could be supervised or even appointed in fulfilment of the demand for a school in 'every severall kirk'. A more modest requirement was exacted meantime: that universally in Scotland the children should be examined as to their knowledge of religion, for which the parents rather than the ministers were to be held responsible. The young were henceforth to undergo three tests, set by the ministers and elders of the parish, to examine how they were advancing 'in the schoole of Christ': the first at age nine, the second at age twelve and the third when they reached fourteen. There were problems of language in conducting such tests, however: in Ross some spoke only Gaelic and others only the Scots vernacular. The then commissioner of Ross got an assistant because he was 'not prompt in the Scottish tongue'.[55] Sales of the kirk's printed literature were so inadequate to cover costs that Robert Lepreuik, who had printed most of it, had to plead poverty and ask for a Kirk grant.[56]

By 1570, the Assembly had decided to support the authority of the young king, rather than his exiled mother: any minister impeded by threats in this obedience was to have the Assembly's support. Earls, lords, barons and gentlemen who had refused to accept the king (i.e. Queen Mary's supporters) were to be persuaded to do so. There was still a problem with ministers not residing in their manses, and they were now threatened with

[52] *BUK*, i, 158–9; for Ayton, Kilconquhar and Monkland, Haws, *Scottish Clergy at the Reformation*, 18, 123, 182.

[53] *BUK*, i, 162–3; Haws, *Scottish Clergy at the Reformation*, 84, 246. It is not clear who the deserting ministers were, ibid., 161, 214.

[54] *BUK*, i, 167.

[55] *BUK*, i, 175–6.

[56] Ibid., i, 164.

excommunication. There is mention of giving 'answer to my Lord Regents Grace to Makquhyn and his companions' and also of maintaining the lead on the roof of the kirk of Glasgow and preserving that building. This seems to be an obscure reference to John Makquhyn (McQueen), former school-master of Paisley, Catholic adherent of Archbishop Hamilton, whose activi-ties disturbed the ministry in Paisley. Dunkeld was another location infected with 'idolatry'; Erskine of Dun was mandated to proceed there and visit its schools and colleges as was his custom in Angus. Aberdeen was yet another area where there was no obedience to ministers, so much so that its commis-sioner wished to resign.[57]

Mr Patrick Adamson was asked by the Assembly of 1570 to re-enter the ministry both because he was a gifted person, and because of the 'scarce-ness of ministers in diverse countries [i.e. regions]'.[58] These Assembly records evince a certain monotonous repetitiveness; the same points arise again and again, indicating that problems were too tough for instant solution. Infor-mation about particular places is scanty in such generalised proceedings, yet as far as schools and schooling are concerned, visitation and synod records, where they survive, actually add little.[59] The Assembly of 1571 was clearly keen to win over a prominent lawyer like Mr Robert Lumsden of Clova. To make up for the pre-Reformation perquisites he had previously enjoyed ('corpus presents, upmost cloaths, and pasch fynes') as vicar of Logie-Buchan and Cushnie, the deficit was, surprisingly, subtracted from his payment of thirds.[60] Yet, shortly after, the Catholics of Aberdeen also cultivated the self-same man with a grant of lands to him and his heirs, which was to fail if they fell from the Catholic faith into heresy 'in contumely of our Creator and of the unity of holy church'.[61] Lay patrons of benefices were still a problem, if, the parsonage teinds being at the Kirk's disposal, they insisted on presenting a man fit to be a reader only, where the Kirk had to refuse admis-sion. Superintendents and commissioners knew this problem at first hand. As Knox acknowledged, 'This battell, I grant, will be hard.'[62] The Kirk needed a sympathetic voice in the College of Justice for this and other purposes, and gave Robert Pont licence to act as a senator of the College provided he

57   Ibid., i, 188–190; Durkan, 'Education in the century of the Reformation', 161. For Catholics associated with Dunkeld, see J. Durkan, 'William Murdoch and the Jesuit mission in Scotland', *IR*, xxxv (1995), 4–5.
58   *BUK*, i, 193.
59   *Visitation of Dunblane*; *Synod Records of Lothian and Tweeddale 1589–1596 and 1640–1649*, ed. J. Kirk (Stair Society, 1977).
60   *BUK*, i, 194.
61   *RMS*, iv, 2313; *History of the Society of Advocates in Aberdeen*, ed. J.H. Henderson (New Spalding Club, 1912), 254.
62   *BUK*, i, 197–9.

also served his parish. Commendators of abbeys were henceforth to consider themselves 'senators for the spiritual estate' in the College of Justice.[63]

There was a danger that universities themselves would lose their endowment in this envisaged re-disposition of benefices. Within them there was 'exercise of liberall Science', and they were to continue as patrons of annexed kirks and chaplainries, provision being made for appointing qualified persons to the kirks, while the chaplainries could maintain the college bursars.[64] These arrangements included bursars and students in grammar, arts, theology, the laws, or medicine, and rental books were to be kept. The value of such burses was graded. Seven years, from age seven to age fourteen, was the duration specified for grammar bursars. Arts bursars must be above fourteen and could hold the bursary for five years; previous study in arts as far as MA in a Scottish university was required, a condition that was unlikely to be fulfilled. Grammar burses could only be enjoyed in university grammar schools or another famous school in a chief burgh or town.[65] An attempt was also made to restrict the bursars to universities within their own regions (the word 'diocese' is used in its old sense, clearly not synonymous any longer with a superintendent's area of control). Formularies to deal with these requirements were provided.[66]

A new note of boldness entered the Assembly proceedings after the 1572 Assembly at Leith. The Acts of Parliament against Catholics were to be strictly enforced and their assemblies at places like Old Aberdeen, Dunkeld, Paisley and Eglinton to be confronted by counter-assemblies to prevent mass-saying or mass-hearing. John Forrest, vicar of Swinton, had been accepted as reader, though still acting as priest in 1569, and had been allowed to minister by John Douglas: whatever Forrest's convictions, he was still reader in 1574.[67] Catholic controversialists like Winzet and Nicol Burne targeted the quality of the early recruits to the ministry and readership, key functions in respect of the *Book of Discipline*'s programme for education. The needs of congregations were hard to meet. A key burgh like Edinburgh required no ordinary minister, and it would face a special problem on the death of Knox in November 1572, for example.

The 1572 Assembly appointed a minister to visit 'colledges and schools' in Moray, two others were subsequently to visit colleges and schools in Caithness and Sutherland and 'plant' Reformed schoolmasters. The University of Glasgow, 'new erectit' on post-Reformation lines, had no endowments comparable to universities elsewhere and needed provision, while men of

[63] Ibid., i, 206, 210.
[64] Ibid., i, 212.
[65] Ibid., i, 214.
[66] Ibid., i, 226–32.
[67] Ibid., i, 255; Haws, *Scottish Clergy at the Reformation*, 251.

good 'ingyne' ought to be further trained in foreign lands: the rationale for this was that this was the one way to produce qualified ministers, the schools being the 'fountaine fra the quhilk Ministers must flow'.[68] With this came a renewed effort to win aristocratic support; the imperfections of the Reformed nobility had resulted in the Kirk's patrimony being misapplied, to the great hurt 'of the ministeris, the scullis and poore'.[69] The synod of Lothian in 1573 complained that a select few decided weighty Assembly business, and that 'as in foir tymes' the Assembly would be more respected if nobles and barons were present as well as ministers.

It was noted that the mutually educative occasion of the 'exercise' was not likely to succeed if ministers had not the wherewithal to buy books; the solution suggested was to subtract the cost of them from their stipends.[70] The tricky question was raised as to who should enjoy the benefit of the glebe; though the ruling favoured preference for ministers, the judgement was left to superintendents. The Assembly noted that in St Andrews, John Douglas, the bishop, neglected to be present at the exercise, to the extent that it was likely to decay. Superintendent Robert Pont of Moray never made his residence there, and had visited no kirks for the past two years except in the towns (Inverness, Elgin and Forres). Complaints regarding readers exceeding their function by making the sacraments available were incessant.[71] A 'more speciall article', no longer extant, dealt with the sustaining of schools in burgh and countryside ('to landward'). The Act of Parliament of 1567 had laid down that 'all scoles alsweill to burgh as land and colleges be reformit', which at least points to the existence of a number of rural schools.[72] In 1573, with the new insistence on membership of the Reformed Kirk, the authorities thought that former canons regular, monks and friars, otherwise liable to lose their pensions, should be ordered to serve as readers.[73] How committed would such recruits be?

II.4 Readers

From an early stage, school doctors and masters supplemented their income by working as readers in the kirk; we have already met a good example in Section I.10, the composer Andro Kemp, in Dundee before the Reformation and in St Andrews afterwards, who worked as reader in two Fifeshire parishes before going to Aberdeen as song school master, and died as minister desig-

---

[68]   Ibid., i, 233, 311, 329.
[69]   Ibid., i, 253.
[70]   Ibid., i, 265–6.
[71]   Ibid., i, 268, 270, 276 (1573); ii, 438 (1579).
[72]   Ibid., i, 279; *APS*, iii, 37.
[73]   *BUK*, i, 280.

nate of Fintry in Aberdeenshire in 1572. Our Ayr and Glasgow Appendices reveal just how common it was for graduate schoolmaster readers, as the decades passed, to go on to become ministers. Initially, however, there were many non-graduate readers. There were probably more readers than lists based on the Books of Assignations allow; at least two, Michael Gray and John Drummond, are not included in published lists. This was acknowledged in 1577: 'diverse readers are not entered in the Books of Assignation', partly due to the negligence of commissioners, but also because there were more posts than candidates to fill them.[74] The Regent Morton admitted that, for time being, ministers simply had to be placed, until it was God's pleasure to raise up worthier and better qualified persons. Lairds, when they did not attempt to officiate themselves, treated readers rather as they had chaplains, expecting them to marry them or, in emergency, do other services for them in view of the current scarcity of ministers.[75]

Some members of the Assembly thought the remedy was to abolish the readers, while others thought to control them by suspension or deprivation, and others again, to reward them with benefices.[76] Some ministers deprived by the Assembly were allowed by the state to keep their benefices; decisions of bishops and superintendents were not always consistent with Assembly policy.[77] Problems came from non-payment of stipends, and some ministers and readers had to tap ale, beer or wine to eke out their funds.[78] One of the Assembly's dress requirements was aimed at Gaelic-speaking readers and ministers; there was a ban, at least in the time of the exercise of their functions, on the wearing of the plaid.[79] The Assembly queried whether a minister could remain a provost of a college and master of a school simultaneously, and whether one reader should serve different kirks, and even whether the readers then in place should be dismissed.[80] It is interesting that though readers exceeded ministers over the whole country, in 1576 there was only one in Edinburgh and none at St Cuthbert's outside its walls.[81] The 1576 Assembly eventually decided that all readers should be re-examined by local synods, and that if they lacked the qualities laid down in the *Book of Discipline*, they were liable to be removed. Old customs died hard, and some were still celebrating Easter and Christmas, while some confined

---

[74] Not in Haws, *Scottish Clergy at the Reformation*; *BUK*, i, 287, 388.
[75] Ibid., i, 370. See the cases of George Boyd at Kilbirnie House, and of James Blackwood, reader at Saline, ibid., i, 276, 386, 397. Emergency was no excuse for defaulting readers, ibid., ii, 439.
[76] Cases have already been cited. Abolition was aired in 1576, *BUK*, i, 371.
[77] Ibid., ii, 424; i, 264, 269, 286, 287.
[78] Ibid., i, 378.
[79] Ibid., i, 325.
[80] Ibid., i, 370–2.
[81] *Register of Ministers*, 72–3. There was also a reader at Holyrood.

themselves solely to simple reading, yet their presence for the time being remained necessary.[82] However, the Assembly records now reveal a new sense of urgency, untypical of earlier years, i.e. before Andrew Melville's arrival from Geneva in 1574.

The Assembly of 1579 admitted that at first God's word was sown in this country by feeble and weak instruments.[83] If the young King James harked back to customary practice in arguing against accepting the *Second Book of Discipline*, the Assembly made it clear that it expected more of him as a modern Constantine or Theodosius.[84] In 1580, the Assembly discussed readers at some length, concluding that their only gift was for simple reading of the Bible, and their present status extraordinary, for their office was 'no ordinar office' in the Kirk. Thus no simple reader was entitled to a benefice or to have the use of a manse or glebe, that is, in kirks where there was a minister as well. Some light is thrown on this by the complaint that the Sunday afternoon 'exercise and doctrine' was neglected over a great part of the country, and thus people got no instruction in catechism and religion.[85] The weekly 'exercise' itself, on which basis it was hoped to found the new presbyteries, was neglected even in some central areas; in 1581 it was noted that there had been no exercise in Linlithgow for years.[86] The Assembly also distinguished sharply between the 'pastoure' and the 'doctor', noting that the latter title was used of university teachers as well as of ordinary teachers (many of whom were at this stage, as we have seen, ministers or readers) who taught the catechism and the rudiments of religion; it was stressed that while a minister 'may teache in the scoles', his task of preaching, marrying, and administering the sacraments 'pertenis not unto the doctour, onles he be utherwyis ordourlie callit'.[87]

II.5 Recruitment of ministers: a pattern for recruitment of schoolmasters?

Since recruitment was uneven for ministers and readers, we can speculate that the same may well be true of schoolmasters, whose names are excluded from the Books of Assignation, and who may in many places have been identical with the readers anyway. We should always bear in mind that while the Assembly records do provide an overall view, they have to be checked against other more local or more secular evidence, especially when a pessi-

[82] *BUK*, i, 372, 455.
[83] Ibid., i, 278; ii, 445.
[84] Ibid., ii, 428, 448.
[85] Ibid., ii, 455, 457, 460.
[86] Ibid., ii, 523.
[87] *The Second Book of Discipline*, ed. J. Kirk (Edinburgh, 1980), 187–90, 211n. See also *BUK*, ii, 495.

mistic picture is painted by the records of a body that is not only a national policy-maker but a court of final appeal, which inevitably means that disagreeable features acquire such prominence as to skew our perception of the true situation.

By 1562, it had been decided that the legitimate status of ministers already in position was to be accepted, unless they were found to be criminal or to have been privately forced into service, no doubt often by the private enterprise of lairds.[88] (Similar 'private enterprise' can be postulated of lairds and gentlemen helping to re-establish schools.) We have seen Erskine of Dun, superintendent of Angus, accused of admitting as readers 'manie popishe preistis, unabill and of wicked life', and some were 'rashlie' received as ministers and exhorters without proper testing. Some who were formerly found 'slanderous' in doctrine had not yet been cleared. Indeed, many ignorant men and 'of bad conversation' were by 1565 said to have been admitted. Robert Ramsay, active in Angus, had affirmed that there was 'a mid way betwixt papistrie and our religion'; certainly he had neither been elected nor admitted, but similar views must surely have been held by a few of those who had.[89] This negative perception of the earliest post-Reformation years has been disputed, yet in 1562 it is clear that many first recruits had 'an imprecise understanding of reformed practice'.[90] Furthermore, the 'beggar's life' that these initial church officials endured would scarcely be calculated to attract fresh young recruits from the universities or even retain those already in office, not to speak of problems of access to manses and glebes as well as to church funds.[91]

Catholic writers paint the early ministers and readers in dark colours. Nicol Burne speaks of Andrew Brebner and Paul Methven as 'new cummit fra the keiping of the scheip or the geise', which certainly did not apply to Methven. John Hamilton was nearer the truth in styling Methven a 'priuat baxter' in Dundee and William Harlaw a tailor in Edinburgh.[92] Ninian Winzet asked why in the first years there were admitted as preachers and ministers 'young childring of na eruditioun', except the reading of the vernacular, and with 'small entressis' in grammar – men, that is, qualified as simple readers, unable to teach Latin but able to read the new vernacular liturgy. But others, as Winzet admitted, were monastic recruits and must have known some Latin, and others were chaplains who were themselves teachers of Latin. The 'exercise' required officials who had enough Latin, as most contemporary Bible commentary and theology was in Latin. Many

88   *BUK*, i, 27, 44, 54.
89   Ibid., i, 44.
90   J. Kirk, *Patterns of Reform* (Edinburgh, 1989), 96–153.
91   *BUK*, i, 22.
92   *Catholic Tractates*, ed. Law, 151, 228.

pre-Reformation parishes had no ministers 'planted' in them as yet; though readers were fairly widespread, they were not supposed to take on sacramental duties. Winzet tells us that Knox himself opposed those Protestant lairds who wanted to continue their private house oratories as in times past, ministering communion to their own household servants and tenants.[93] This would explain the Assembly's reluctance to give recognition to any centre of worship apart from the parish kirk. The earl of Huntly cannot have been the only gentleman objecting to the 'mean' company he might have to associate with in the parish kirk. Reluctantly, and by way of exception, the Assembly granted the Catholic lairds temporary minister-chaplains to counter the influence of resident Jesuits and seminary-trained priests.[94]

The collapse for a time of the 'exercise' may have reflected the frequent lack of worthy, qualified persons to serve as ministers and the 'too light' admission of candidates, including some without Latin, indispensable for leaders in the exercise. Due to the absence, or decline in value, of receipts from the thirds of ecclesiastical benefices, ministers were found in trades considered unfit for their calling.[95] Ministers were also faulted for not ensuring provision for schools within their bounds.[96] But the very 'burrogh townes' might find themselves destitute of pastors, at least momentarily.[97] And if in parts of central Scotland, in 'mid country and inhabited and peopled land', as well as on the Borders, there were no pastors to be found, there was little likelihood of parish schools as such in these areas. Even some pre-Reformation schools, as at Kirkwall, were apparently in abeyance.[98] Whether it was permissible for a pastor to take a school was a doubt eventually settled.[99] Though family households and ministers were accountable for imparting basic religious teaching to the very young, some left this chore to readers or neglected the duty.[100] Because of the inadequate supply of recruits, it was even suggested that some kirks should be allowed to decay.[101]

Given that schools were often held at kirks or chapels, a proposal made by the civil authorities in 1581, is revealing of the state of educational provision about this time: namely, to reduce the number of kirks, many of which were either unmanned or had remained unrepaired after the English invasions or the stormy days of 1559/60. The church rentals for Argyle and the Isles had never been given up, and so its kirks were left out of consideration, but the

93   *Certain Tractates*, i, 100–101.
94   *BUK*, iv, 112; cf. ibid., iii, 965.
95   *BUK*, i, 278; ii, 583; iii, 864–6.
96   Ibid., iii, 1051.
97   *BUK*, iii, 959.
98   Ibid., iii, 801, 812.
99   Ibid., iv, 1123; cf. ibid., iii, 965.
100   Ibid., i, 176; ii, 165; iii, 1051–2.
101   Ibid., ii, 508.

reckoning of 1581 was that there were about 924 kirks, some of them pendicles attached to bigger kirks and some of them small parishes; but many kirks had been demolished, so it was proposed to reduce the number to 600. Lay patrons remained, but benefices were to be given out on the principle that young newcomers to the ministry from the schools would have those of lowest value, while the top ranking benefices ought to go to the eldest or most experienced, or those of greatest learning and judgement.[102] Prebends originally founded for the upkeep of schools and schoolmasters were to be rediverted from courtier recipients to meet the needs of the instruction of the youth.[103]

Something of the problems caused by the shortage of recruits to the underfunded ministry can be seen in the case of the Dalkeith minister Gilbert Taylor, who appeared before the presbytery on 21 June 1587 for not attending the exercise. When summoned a second time, he excused himself on the grounds that Canongate had summoned him for necessary action in 'writing their besynes', so that he was forced to resign his teaching there, 'quhilk culd not be left without ane scowling of the youth', and that he often supplied for Mr David Lindsay when he was absent in his parish of Leith.[104] Taylor was also minister at Penicuik, and presumably eked out his income by teaching in Canongate. His stipend is not mentioned, but his successor, James Davidson, initially appointed like Taylor by the Commendator of Holyrood Abbey, got £20 stipend in 1580 from the town council, plus 10 merks out of the abbey's petty commons.[105]

The parallels between the school and kirk situations notwithstanding, the relationship should not be pursued too closely. As the old possessors of benefices died off and a new generation of university-trained men replaced them, the situation must have eased, but, in any event, the absence of kirk funding for kirk schools as such could have proved providential for venturesome masters setting up non-parochial establishments. An example is Thomas Liston, a former St Andrews Dominican whose testament was registered on 23 October 1583.[106] 'Sumtyme ane of the freiris predicators of the city of St Andrews', Liston was incorporated in St Andrews University in 1544 with his colleague Henry Mason, reincorporated in 1574 and 1576 in St Mary's, Mason as *oeconomus*.[107] Liston died in August 1583, leaving to a chaplain an English bible, a dictionary 'callit Eliot' (Sir Thomas Elyot) and

[102] Ibid., ii, 480–1.
[103] Ibid., ii, 536.
[104] NAS, CH2/424/1, 2v.
[105] H.M. Anderson, 'The Grammar School of the Canongate', *Book of the Old Edinburgh Club*, xx (1935), 6.
[106] CC8/8/12, 282–3.
[107] *Early Records*, 250, 284, 288.

a Latin bible. In October the king's lawyers, naming Liston as 'scolemaister and bukebinder' in St Andrews, were objecting to the executors, including Henry Mason. The title bookbinder suggests that Liston may have bound the friars' books before their priory was destroyed.[108] About a fortnight later, Mason produced an inventory of Liston's gear, which gives the distinct impression that adventure schoolmastering was not a wealth-creator in itself.

There were lairds who made their own arrangements with readers and schoolmasters; in Section I we encountered the 'secularisation' of Duncan Nevay's school beside Dunblane cathedral by private individuals in 1562. Nevay subsequently became reader there and minister at Lecropt, so it is likely that his school returned to the kirk. An aspect of private arrangements for the education of the children of the upper classes which had concerned the General Assembly of 1578 was the way in which 'diverse persons within this realme' got round the lack of Catholic schoolteaching by sending their children, 'beand within age, furth of the countrey over sea to places quher superstitioun and papistrie is maintained, under pretence of seiking farther instruction and learning'. The assembly decreed that 'the parents of sick children … salbe chargit be their awin ministers respective to call back their children … vnder the paine of excommunicatioun'. The Assembly noted that the problem of studying in places 'quher the said papistrie is teachit and mantanit' also involved 'vthers beand of perfyte age', who plainly chose to attend Catholic universities, 'quherthrow, for the most part, they become corrupt in religioun, as be evident experience is daylie sein'.[109]

The absence of kirk funding for schools may have encouraged the flourishing of worryingly uncatechistical household education among the better off. In addition to the constant dread of a Catholic revival, there was fear of indifference and even alleged atheism, the last based on an education that included pagan literature: in the gentry houses there gathered 'cunning followers of the dissolute ethnike poets, both in phrase and substance', that is, individuals who admired classical love poems as something more than simple stylistic models.[110] We hear of lairds in the Merse and Teviotdale who 'vilipend' the Word',[111] and 'in the houses of greate men, and at the assemblies of yong gentilmen and yong damesels', Alexander Hume wrote in 1594, 'the cheif pastime is, to sing prophane sonnets, and vaine ballatis of loue, or to rehearse some fabulos faits of Palmerine, Amadis, or such like raueries'.[112] In 1595 there was a fresh policy of exercising more control over

---

[108] NAS, CC8/2/12.
[109] *BUK*, ii, 425–6.
[110] *The Poems of Alexander Hume*, ed. A. Lawson (STS, 1902), 6.
[111] *BUK*, ii, 720.
[112] *Poems of Alexander Hume*, ed. Lawson, 6.

the town grammar schools.[113] Yet in 1600 David Black attacked the 'manie wanton nobles of this worlde, who abuse and disgrace the worthie facultie of Poetrie, with uncleane Sonnettes, to satisfie their louse mindes with a kinde of contemplative fornication'.[114]

What there is of General Assembly evidence recognises the place that the secular authorities had in education, but insists above all on its own religious input from childhood to university and on the primacy of training for the ministry. The General Assemblies did not always see the state as a reliable source of aid in their push to establish and staff kirks and schools. In the early days, Mary, Queen of Scots, found it expedient to demonstrate a certain collaborative spirit, in the shape of the significant grant of the minor benefices to the Kirk. Under the four regents, from Moray to Morton, collaboration, in varying degrees, was more positive. By the 1580s it seemed possible to begin to take stock and consolidate. Yet while the Kirk was in the process of getting a firmer grasp on the old possessors' revenues, the value of these was being frittered away: 'idle bellies' who took the fruits and gave no return were still about in 1587.[115] The Kirk had its internal problems, such as the conflict between the bishops (sponsored by the Regent Morton, and then by royal authority) and distrustful elements in the Assembly, and these problems continued to divert the Assembly's attention. In 1584, on account of the so-called 'Black Acts', some of the Assembly's leading figures were forced to flee to England. Not for the last time: foreign exile would later become a regular experience for radical ministers. In spite of the so-called 'Golden Acts' of 1592, warmly welcomed in the Assembly, the previous state controls were only held in suspension, to be revivified in 1597.

The minister's involvement in child education was expected to be, like that of the medieval parish priest, a purely Sunday affair. The first Scots version of Calvin's catechism was not available until 1564; it was a method of religious teaching 'wherein the Minister demandeth the question and the chylde maketh answere'.[116] This catechism was at first usually bound up with the *Book of Common Order* of 1565, and was presumably meant at first as the minister's book. The Gaelic version of the *Book of Common Order* excludes the catechism, which would not appear in Gaelic until about 1630.[117] The *Parvus Catechismus carmine iambico* or shorter catechism in verse (1573) of

[113] *BUK*, iii, 896.
[114] David Blak, *An Exposition upon the thirtie two Psalme* (Edinburgh, 1600), 2.
[115] *BUK*, i, 714.
[116] R. Dickson & J.P. Edmond, *Annals of Scottish Printing* (Cambridge, 1890), 219–20.
[117] John Carswell's 1567 *Foirm na nu-urrnuidheadh*, published by Lekpreuik, includes a short, strongly anti-Catholic catechism by Carswell himself, discussed in the introduction to R.L. Thomson's edition (SGTS, 1970), pp. lxxv–lxxvi. Calvin's Catechism in Gaelic was printed by Wreitton c.1630, as is proved in the introduction to R.L. Thomson's edition thereof, *Adtimchiol an chreidimh* (SGTS, 1962), pp. xiii–xiv.

Robert Pont, meant as a preliminary test before communion for juniors of age fourteen at Latin schools, has some long as well as short answers (one, admittedly, being the creed). John Craig's *A short Summe* (1581) is written 'in few wordes, for the greater ease of the commoune people and children'.[118] It was important that the price be kept down. Two hundred and forty-four copies of Pont's Latin catechism were being sold at sixpence a dozen in 1577, in contrast to a so-called 'fyne' catechism costing twelve pence at the same date.[119] Similarly so-called 'single' catechisms were going at a hundred for six shillings and eight pence, less than a penny each: the printer stocked over two thousand of these. Mr James Lawson's catechism, of which no copy now exists, cost sixpence, whereas John Craig's went for sixteen pence; the latter was warmly recommended by the Assembly, which advised its use in 'lecture schools' instead of the little catechism.[120] Copies of the catechism were often sold with the metrical psalms and this added to the price. It looks as though the cheaper catechisms were sold in bulk to parishes. In 1580 fifteen gross of unbound single catechisms were selling for eleven shillings a gross, just under a penny each.[121] The demand seemed to have increased by then, and by 1599, one bookseller's stock held as many as 5,406.[122] Not all ministers were neglecting the catechising of youth, as the Assembly would suggest in 1608.[123]

Ever since 1567 parliament had authorised superintendents to keep an eye on the licensing of teachers, and the Assembly probably left the matter to kirk visitations conducted by the presbyteries; we might note that in 1615, schoolmasters who opposed King James's settlement of bishops in presbytery would be threatened with dismissal.[124] The regulations on catechising were probably more easily enforced in parochial schools under the minister's direct eye than in remote rural schools where the master benefited from no parochial subvention. At the far ends of the land, especially where local lairds were unsympathetic to the Kirk, there were problems. There were areas where it was long ere a parish kirk was planted. In 1587, the Assembly recorded that twenty-four out of twenty-eight kirks in the Lennox were without ministers.[125] In 1608 the Assembly was still noting the want of preachers in remote areas: seventeen churches were vacant in Nithsdale, twenty-eight in

[118]   Pont's text is in *Wodrow Misc.*, 303–18; John Craig, *A shorte summe of the whole catechisme* (Edinburgh, 1581).
[119]   Dickson & Edmond, *Scottish Printing*, 300, 302.
[120]   Ibid., 303; Lawson's is mentioned in Robert Gourlaw's testament of 1585, *Bannatyne Misc.*, ii, 209; for Craig's, ibid., ii, 212, *BUK*, ii, 788.
[121]   Dickson & Edmond, *Scottish Printing*, 330.
[122]   Ibid., 353.
[123]   *BUK*, iii, 1051.
[124]   Ibid., iii, 1130.
[125]   Ibid., ii, 722.

Annandale and thirty-one in one unnamed province.[126] So it is no surprise that some schools had ceased to exist by 1601, when the Assembly records speak of the decay of schools and the education of youth in knowledge of good letters and godliness 'speciallie on landwart', for lack of provision suffi-cient to entertain a qualified schoolmaster in places needful.[127] Schools were not necessarily permanent fixtures, and could have a mere casual existence; there were better prospects of continuity where support was available from a kirk session whose own continuity was assured.

II.6 Post-Reformation schools as university feeders

Historians could read the General Assembly records as evidence that the provision of wider national education was pushed to the back burner in the face of other pressing concerns. On the other hand, the Assembly's notable concern with the universities could be proof that the innovative idea of a detailed national education plan (as in the *First Book of Discipline*) must inevitably have generated the establishment of the schools it prefigured.[128] Impressions gained from the Assembly records need to be corroborated by solid facts, obtainable only by systematically counting named schools and schoolmasters. But the evolving situation at tertiary level can throw consid-erable light on what was happening in terms of secondary schooling, and not merely in terms of numbers.

The Assembly may have had little to say about schools, but it had plenty to say about the universities they fed. The Assembly urgently wished to see its own members staffing the universities and training a new generation of ministerial recruits, and this is of importance to us in estimating the increase in school numbers postulated by the growth in university education. We find the Assembly defending Glasgow against the state,[129] and winning the state's collaboration in replacing the Catholic rulers of King's College, Aberdeen, in 1569. Three decades later, the Assembly encouraged the new foundation of Marischal College there.[130] Another proposed new northern foundation, c.1600, at Fraserburgh, was abortive, but this concern for the north is paral-leled in an earlier failed proposal in 1581 for a college at Orkney.[131]

The Assembly also had much to say about Edinburgh. The pre-Reformation bishop of Orkney, Robert Reid, had bequeathed 8,000 merks

---

[126] Ibid., iii, 917, 1058, 1061.
[127] Ibid., iii, 965.
[128] R. O'Day, *Education and Society 1500–1800: The Social Foundations of Education* (London, 1982), 217–37, 'Education for Scottish Society, 1450-1800'.
[129] *BUK*, i, 315, 337–40; ii, 583.
[130] Ibid., i, 127–9, 141–3; ii, 624.
[131] *APS*, iv, 147; *BUK*, iii, 958; *APS*, iii, 214.

for a foundation in the capital, half of it set aside for the purchase of a site in south Edinburgh. The Reformation blocked both this foundation and a parallel one for royal lectureships on the French model set up by Queen Mary of Lorraine. The Reid proposal envisaged principally the academic training of lawyers in a school of law, but was to include three schools: a grammar school, a school devoted solely to literature and literary theory (poetry and oratory), and a third for civil and canon law.[132] The traditional medieval core training in philosophy was thereby sidelined, in tune with the contemporary mood. The first indication of this subsequently was in 1576, in the Regent Morton's time, when the foundation by Reid was taken up again, modified where its terms now appeared unsatisfactory. In spite of its critique of Aristotle (echoing some medieval doubts on his adequacy as a foundation for Christian education), the Assembly still felt that not only grammar and rhetoric, but also physics and logic were 'necessar instruments to come to the true meaning and sense of the will of God as revealed in his word'.[133] Thus the curriculum would be retained, but updated.

For our purposes, the notable fact is the sense of an imperative need to increase the number of university places, which means a concomitant increase in school places. The Kirk's core concern was to replace the initial (and inevitably, variably qualified) ministers of 1560 with a more standard 'seminary' functionary, thoroughly trained for the job. However, apart from St Mary's College, St Andrews, the 'seminary' aspect should not be over-stressed. The first-named and last-named Edinburgh graduates of 1587 are given as 'apostate'; out of forty-seven, there were but fifteen future ministers, and in 1633, only four, out of a total of thirty-two.[134] There was no notable predominance of students for the ministry, and it is worth noting that these were expected to add 'scriptures, and course of theologie in the original languages of the same' to their arts course.[135] Alongside the ministry and schoolmastering, the legal profession was a major destination for university graduates. However, in Scottish universities, legal studies, as is well known, lagged far behind. We have just seen that there was an awareness of the need to rectify this situation in the new college in Edinburgh. As for St Andrews, the problems experienced there by the author of *The Sea Law of Scotland* have been analysed in detail by John W. Cairns.[136] Edinburgh also had problems; King James overruled the university and appointed law lecturers, but

[132]   J. Durkan, 'The royal lectureships under Mary of Lorraine', *SHR*, lxii (1983), 73–8; *RPC*, ii, 528–9; iii, 472–4.
[133]   *BUK*, ii, 638–41, 723.
[134]   D. Laing (ed.), *A Catalogue of the Graduates in the Faculties of Arts, Divinity, and Law, of the University of Edinburgh* (Edinburgh, 1858), 7–8, 48.
[135]   *BUK*, ii, 723.
[136]   J.W. Cairns, 'Academic Feud, Bloodfeud and William Welwood: Legal Education in St. Andrews, 1560–1611', *Edinburgh Law Review*, 2:1–2 (1998), 158–79, 255–87.

ultimately failed in his attempt to fulfil Bishop Reid's pre-Reformation vision of a college which provided a legal education.

Bishop Reid had foreseen that law teaching would involve a revival of oratory. We find Glasgow apparently making provision at school level for just such a revival, in its reformed high school programme, quite probably of a piece with the revision of its university requirements post-1600, which included a scheme for law.[137] The university's plan foundered, but the new school curriculum (involving five classes, and more than one schoolmaster, even if aided by a single doctor) was regularly available after 1600. Perhaps it brought about an improvement in the quality of grammar teaching at Glasgow. Some simple Latin translations by Glasgow schoolboys c.1587 have survived in mutilated scraps formerly fortifying the binding of town clerk Archibald Hegate's protocol book, whose last entry is dated 1587.[138] Andrew Hamilton, William Dunlop major, Alexander Douglas, John Dunning, Robert Cunningham, Claud Hamilton, Robert Herbertson, William Johnstone, James Lawson, William Livingstone, John Lorne, Robert Lindsay, Hector McCaig, David Mathie, James Provan, Patrick Shields, William Spang, Thomas Walker, Archibald Wilson and John Young were all apparently in the same class. Six specimens as printed by the modern editor show the juvenile errors marked off by the schoolmaster. The results call to mind what one modern commentator has to say about Latin verses composed by beginners at Edinburgh University: 'the Latin varies from the incompetent to the perplexing'.[139] It is revealing that in 1588, grammar was still being taught at the country's most ancient university, in St Leonard's College, though in 1580 the state visitors had deemed grammar schools neither necessary nor convenient in the colleges.[140] By 1616, however, perfect grammar was a compulsory entry qualification.[141] Such requirements and regulations mean, of course, that the quality of the teaching of 'oratory' in schools had had to improve.

In 1610, we find a positive light shed on the quality of school education by a letter in Latin written by a Dunfermline schoolboy. William Dundas, the future laird of Blair Castle, wrote in March that year to his father, the laird of Dundas, about studies and the time devoted to rehearsing an oration delivered before the local gentry on speech day, to the glory 'of our learned

[137] J. Grant, *History of the Burgh and Parish Schools of Scotland* (London, 1876), 336–8.
[138] *Glasgow Prot. Bk*, ix, no. 3013, long footnote.
[139] C. Upton, 'The teaching of poetry in sixteenth century Scotland', in R.J. Lyall and F. Riddy (eds.), *Proceedings of the Third international Conference on Scottish Language and Literature, Medieval and Renaissance* (Stirling/Glasgow, 1981), 416. Hegate's son Archibald was a more than competent Latin poet.
[140] *Evidence, Oral and Documentary … for the Universities of Scotland, iii, The University of St Andrews* (London, 1837), 190, 191, 194, 195.
[141] *Evidence, Oral and Documentary*, iii, 200.

teacher and our ancient and distinguished school'. Young Dundas and four other young orators addressed the tough job teachers had in teaching untamed youths, while the last boy orator praised music by way of introduction to some choral pieces for bass, tenor, treble and counter-tenor. The idea of the letter was to show to a critical parent how far young Dundas had advanced in the art of writing epistles in Renaissance Latin.[142] By 1610, young William Dundas could have had the help of Buchanan's *De Prosodia*, the first edition of which only appeared in 1595 or thereabouts.[143]

This rhetorical practice continued at university. George Dundas attended St Leonard's College in St Andrews, and his letters sometimes feature verse epistles, with the comment that it was easy to find time to turn verses while studying Ramus in the rhetoric class, but that Aristotle demanded absolute concentration. The verses included one to his brother at school in Dunfermline, and an epistle in Greek to his old schoolmaster there, James Dalgleish. One of the eight to George's father apologises for the way its shortcomings might offend 'aures peritae tuae', indicating that the older Dundas was himself something of a poet. His son's Latin verses have been called 'pedestrian enough', and he has been shown to be an unsubtle borrower from Buchanan's New Year epigrams – as an impoverished student, he sent his father New Year verses instead of gifts, in the hope of extracting gold from his 'reverend genitor'. His rhetorical training at St Leonard's clearly left its mark, since George Dundas continued to write verse in Latin later in life. It is therefore interesting that he acknowledged he could not compose verse in the vernacular, presumably never having been trained in such an activity.[144]

II.7 Universities, the Kirk and the state

While the General Assembly saw schools and universities principally as seminaries for future ministers, the state had its own ideas, not always in harmony with the Kirk's. The state soon began to interpose its will in the higher stages of education, notably in St Andrews, ignoring for the moment Aberdeen, where the staff was still Catholic. As we saw, the English ambassador Thomas Randolph, reporting on Queen Mary's progress to Old Aberdeen, said there were only fifteen or sixteen scholars in King's College there; it is uncertain if that means bursars or students in general.[145] No matriculation or graduation records become available until those of 1600 when, as we shall see, King's

---

142 'A Schoolboy's Letter, 1610', ed. J.S. Ritchie, *SHR*, xxxvii (1958), 35–7.
143 J. Durkan, *Bibliography of George Buchanan* (Glasgow, 1994), 239; Grant, *Burgh and Parish Schools*, 336–8.
144 Upton, 'The teaching of poetry in sixteenth century Scotland', 418–20.
145 *Cal. State Papers Scotland*, i, 648.

had nine graduates.[146] Queen Mary's regulation in 1563 lamented the poor state of Glasgow University, when founding places for five poor bursars.[147] As has been said of the Reformers' scheme for St Andrews, the university was reorganised on the basis of the college and the college on the basis of the faculty. The really revolutionary feature of the policy was the new role of the Scottish Privy Council in university affairs.[148] The 'opinion' of George Buchanan was sought on the reform of St Andrews of which its college of humanity was the most interesting feature, laying much stress on drama and dialogue, on Terence and Cicero. In the college of philosophy, the bachelor stage of the MA degree was maintained as well as the regent system, and Aristotle was still principally envisaged as the basic text. The academic staff in the divinity college included a jurist and one divine as principal who doubled as Hebrew teacher. Of the other members of the 1563 commission of visitation, whose opinion might have been interesting had it survived, one was the Catholic Henry Sinclair, bishop of Ross.[149] The 1574 visitation under the Regent Morton makes provision for the Buchanan curriculum, without disturbing the actual college organisation, pinning down the lecturers in theology, Hebrew, Greek, mathematics, rhetoric and law, but insisting on the attendance at the weekly divinity lesson of the St Andrews grammar school-masters.[150] It was hoped thereby to raise not only the educational standard of ministers, but also of the country's lawyers (a matter already the object of state intervention in 1496); an Act of 1567 had already made provision, out of college provostries and minor benefices, for bursars debarred from education by poverty.[151]

The university college at Glasgow was refounded by the city in January 1573 until its 1577 *nova erectio* by state and Kirk in tandem, under Andrew Melville, the state appointee until his transfer to St Andrews in 1579.[152] The university rector's book had been removed to Tarrie in Angus by the last Catholic rector, James Balfour, and this may have motivated the exclusively collegiate view embodied in this refoundation.[153] Melville kept no records of matriculands and graduates, and he continued not to do so at St Mary's College, St Andrews, whither the Regent Morton translated him

---

[146] See tables on pp. 207–9.

[147] Durkan & Kirk, *University of Glasgow*, 356. Universities were already regulating themselves. Aristotle dominated, but not exclusively; Plato, Xenophon and Cicero passed muster in 1562, *Acta Facultatis*, ii, 418.

[148] R.G. Cant, *The University of St Andrews: a Short History* (St Andrews, 1982), 52–3.

[149] Durkan, 'The laying of fresh foundations', in J. MacQueen (ed.), *Humanism in Renaissance Scotland* (Edinburgh, 1990), 134–6, 155–6; P.H. Brown (ed.), *Vernacular Writings of George Buchanan* (STS, 1892), 8-15; *APS*, ii, 544.

[150] *Evidence, Oral and Documentary*, iii, 187–8.

[151] *APS*, iii, 25.

[152] Durkan & Kirk, *University of Glasgow*, 272ff.

[153] Durkan, 'Paisley Abbey and Glasgow archives', *IR*, xiv (1963), 51.

in 1579. However, he taught with relentless assiduity and breathed new
life into the place. His emphasis on the tongues Greek and Hebrew, with
their related languages, was not altogether novel, as William Ramsay and
John Davidson had been brought in on the eve of 1560 by Archbishop
Beaton, engaged as Greek and Hebrew scholar respectively.[154] Melville's
adoption of Ramist logic had no parallel within Scotland, however.[155] (At
school level, some of this, along with textbook lessons in civility, is visible
in the 1559 projects of William Niddrie.)[156] Melville went to St Andrews
as the result of the complete overhaul of St Mary's College in 1579, trans-
forming it into a college of theology pure and simple. Here again, state
and Kirk seemed at one. However, what the state does it can undo, as
Melville would personally experience later: 'St Andrews was now to know
the strength of the arm of Government control as never before.'[157] Melville
had hoped to attract two leading English puritans, Thomas Cartwright and
Walter Travers, to teach part of the divinity course but, failing that, the posts
were left vacant, while a single survivor from the old St Mary's regime, John
Robertson, and two Melville kinsmen were introduced.[158] The dismissal of
older staff and refoundation of King's College, Aberdeen, along with the
erection of Marischal College there, owed something to Melville's Glasgow
experiment, and Marischal's first principal, Robert Howie, was a convinced
disciple of Ramus. Another Ramist, Robert Rollock, became first principal
of the new University of Edinburgh, the 'Tounis College' later styled King
James's College, whence Ramist influence was expected to enter the abortive university planned for Fraserburgh.[159] By that date Melville had been
discredited in the king's eyes, apart from a brief honeymoon around 1592,
the date of the so-called 'Golden Acts' favouring the Kirk. Melville's final
fall could not be indefinitely postponed.

Before we leave the universities, the place of St Salvator's and St Leonard's
colleges in the 1579 refoundation deserves attention. The two humanity
regents at each college were to begin with Greek grammar and its use in
the text; the first year was divided between Latin and Greek composition;
the second occupied with invention, disposition and elocution, while parts

154   For Ramsay, see Durkan, 'The royal lectureships', 73–8; for Davidson, see Durkan & Kirk,
      University of Glasgow, 248.
155   Durkan & Kirk, University of Glasgow, 279.
156   Durkan, 'Laying of fresh foundations', 133.
157   J.K. Cameron, 'Andrew Melville in St Andrews', in D.W.D. Shaw (ed.), In Divers Manners:
      a St Mary's Miscellany (St Andrews, 1990), 59.
158   For Cartwright and Travers, see Durkan & Kirk, University of Glasgow, 270.
159   D. Stevenson, King's College, Aberdeen, 1560-1641: from Protestant Reformation to Covenanting
      Revolution (Aberdeen, 1995), 14–18; in King's College respect for the original foundation
      made the path of university reformers an uphill one. For Howie and Cameron, see p. 66.
      The General Assembly, following medieval precedent, listed the errors of Aristotle, BUK,
      ii, 638.

of rhetoric were likewise to be explored in the texts.[160] To be investigated later are the numbers coming from the schools to these university institutions, old and new. Meantime, it is worth drawing attention to the sort of declamatory composition in Latin or Greek envisaged in the humanity class, examples of which survive in the St Leonard's College 'Orator's Book'. In June 1592 David Lindsay discussed 'the weekly exercises in poetry and oratory to be set up by all classes and groups'. Whereas the 1562 regulation of John Rutherford had called for philosophy to be taught from purely philosophical textbooks, Nathaniel Carmichael in February 1593, helped 'by the breath of God's spirit', spoke of 'joining eloquence with training in philosophy', a Ramist aspiration insofar as it seems to call for a rhetorical philosophy, and as such, remote from Rutherford's design. In April of the same year, David Sinclair, a future regius professor of mathematics at Paris, treated of the misuse of epicycles and 'eccentrics' by those who are ignorant of astronomy, and later in December produced a Greek oration. There are long elegies by James Wilkie and Archibald Dunmore and a Greek verse by an Adam Bruce. A more political note is struck by William Penman in 1594, maintaining that 'no republic or city can be ruled without King, emperor or magistrate'.[161] Rhetoric had ascended from the grammar school to the university, to the temporary detriment of philosophical studies. The best outcome might have been a higher level of grammar teaching in the schools and of literary expertise in the wider society, but it may also be no accident that accusations of pedantry become more prevalent at this time.

A phrase about stupid pedants twice employed by King James VI in the 1590s shows how a word originally neutral in sense was beginning to attach itself to the phenomenon of academic pedantry.[162] The new curriculum had not removed the underlying suspicion of higher education entertained by king and aristocracy. The old complaints about the complexity and esoteric quality of scholastic logic might be revived on the subject of the complexity of rules in rhetoric, as categorised in the *Institutiones Rhetoricae* of George Cassander,[163] an author taught to James Melville at St Andrews in 1571.[164] Some sons of the nobility did not stay long at university. George Douglas,

---

160 *Evidence, Oral and Documentary*, iii, 184. The principal of St Salvator's had to profess medicine and the principal of St Leonard's, the philosophy of Plato.

161 St Andrews University Archives, SL320, fos. 191 (Lindsay), 231 (Carmichael), 224, 290, 370, 399 (long poem, all Sinclair), 163 (Dunmore), 176 (Wilkie), 50 (Bruce), 316 (Penman).

162 In J. Craigie & A. Law (eds.), *King James, Minor Prose Works*, separately paginated *Daemonologies*, p. 7 (STS, 1982); *Basilicon Doron*, ed. J. Craigie (STS, 1944), i, 1 80.

163 The first edition of this simple rhetoric textbook (G. Cassander, *Tabulae breves et expeditae in praeceptiones rhetoricae* (Antwerp, 1544), revised in 1550) was in catechetical form, treating of invention, disposition and elocution (the art of finding the right word), with examples of tropes like synecdoche and hypallage, and of classified figures of speech. This was rounded off with a short summary of the rules of composition.

164 *Autobiography and Diary*, 23.

an illegitimate son of the late Regent Morton, entered St Leonard's College
in November 1585 and left in August 1586; while David Wood, son of the
laird of Boniton, entered in late 1587 to leave the following January. Others
whose stay was brief were Walter Stewart, heir apparent of Minto, and John
Henderson, heir to Fordell. On the other hand, John, son of the master of
Lindsay, remained for some years.[165] A royal visitation of 1588 complained
of 'this confused tyme quhen all folkis ar loukand to the weltering of
the warld', and this is a sentiment which may have been shared by these
gentlemen students. In St Salvator's, because of plague, we find one regent
unemployed and so using his time teaching the earl of Cassillis and others
their grammar.[166] Clearly, post-Reformation secondary education had still
not attained its goal of producing university entrants with 'perfect grammar'.
But as we have already seen, by 1616 perfect grammar would indeed be a
compulsory entry qualification.[167]

---

[165]   EUL, Laing MSS 11, 3, 'Nomina commensalium in Collegio Leonardino', fo. I (Douglas);
        fo. Iv (Wood, Stewart, Henderson); fos. 1, 7v, 18 (Lindsay).
[166]   Evidence, Oral and Documentary, iii, 195. The fact that St Salvator's buildings were in a
        particularly ruinous state and its title deeds were only found by accident, buried under-
        ground, is further evidence of the lack of money for the upkeep of ecclesiastical (and
        educational) buildings after 1560.
[167]   Evidence, Oral and Documentary, iii, 200.

III. Schools after the Reformation

III.1 Schoolmasters affected by religious change

Recent scholarship has started to highlight the fact that, despite all the ideological and political upheavals of the 1550s and 1560s, one of the most striking features of Scottish culture throughout this period is continuity with the past. It is therefore worth observing that as far as schools are concerned, there is no observable change in many places. But religious change did affect some schoolmasters. We have seen the possible religious element in the troubles of Thomas Macgibbon in Dundee before the Reformation.[1] In post-Reformation Linlithgow, the prompt dismissal of the staunchly Catholic Ninian Winzet is well known. But at Aberdeen Mr John Henderson, who was schoolmaster in July 1559, when he was presented by the town to the chaplainry of St Michael in the parish church of St Nicholas, had his salary raised in March 1560. And he was still in office in January 1569, when he was opposed by schoolboys resenting the loss of their Christmas holidays.[2] Henderson had originated in Glasgow diocese and studied arts in Paris in 1542, later turning to theology in 1547–49 at Aberdeen. Two books owned by him have survived in King's College library.[3] In 1569, central government started taking a serious interest in the religious situation in Aberdeen. One result was that King's College was purged of Catholicism. Henderson, whose heart was not in the imposition of the new Kirk's discipline, soon disappeared to France with his fellow Catholic and former pupil James Cheyne of Arnage, whose monument at Tournai described Henderson as 'theologian, prefect of the school of Aberdeen, buried at Paris in the church of S. Hilaire'.[4]

But even in the godly epicentre, four years after the Reformation, we find an excommunicated cleric, sir John Scott, working as a less official schoolmaster in the Canongate in 1564. Called before the session in October, he was found recalcitrant, maintaining that the queen had given him her protection and that the authorities were powerless against him and could not prevent him 'teche anie schoale quhair he plesit'. The laird of Fordell and the

---

[1] See above, Section I.10.

[2] *Bon Record*, 17–18.

[3] W.A. McNeill, 'Scottish entries', 76; *Aberdeen Fasti*, 264, 271. Henderson signed the third part of the *Doctrinale* of Alexandre de Villedieu (the versification section) on 21 Aug. 1536, and on 3 May 1563, the *Syntaxis linguae Graecae* (Cologne, 1550) by the Belgian, Jan van der Varen of Mechlin.

[4] G. Mackenzie, *Lives and Characters of the Most Ancient Writers of the Scottish Nation* (Edinburgh, 1708–1722), iii, 459.

Justice Clerk (Sir John Bellenden) employed Scott in their houses and were ordered to remove him in 1566. His doctor had also offended.[5] (Lairds living in towns were prepared to make their own arrangements for the education of their young families during a critical period, as in 1562 in Dunblane.[6])

The case of Mr William Roberton in Edinburgh high school is documented in detail. He had graduated from St Salvator's in 1537, and studied in Paris about 1541, taking his master of arts degree the following year.[7] At the date of his appointment to the high school by the competent authority, 10 January 1547, the administrator of Holyrood was Alexander Mylne, abbot of Cambuskenneth, the commendator, Lord Robert Stewart, being a young man.[8] To safeguard his books and certificate of appointment during the religious civil war, Roberton had sent them outside the town to a safe place, no doubt fearing his post was under threat, though his Martinmas term fee was duly paid in 1560.[9] On 8 April 1562, the town council wanted to fire him as 'ane obstinat papist', calling on the earl of Moray to persuade his half-brother, the commendator of Holyrood, to cancel Roberton's appointment. On 11 April, the council demanded to see Roberton's letters of appointment, but he was able only to produce his predecessor's, his own papers being out of town. The issue having become Roberton's qualifications, the schoolmaster got himself a lawyer to guide his moves, as the council had its own. The council was looking to London for a new schoolmaster of the Reformed faith, James White, who had great profit of his school there and was excellent at Latin and Greek. But this came to nothing, except that White got a decree against the council for 300 merks.[10]

Roberton petitioned Queen Mary and had himself reinstated in February 1564, though the document was not registered till the following year. After Mary's fall, a fresh effort was made to replace Roberton with Thomas Buchanan during the regency of the earl of Moray.[11] This again failed, and in 1575 we find Roberton at his post, borrowing books, as many schoolmasters did. In William Stewart's memorandum book under 3 June 1575, we read 'lent to Mr William Robertoun the offices of Cicero de amicitia senectute et paradoxa with the commentareis Gottin agane', and under 1576, 'Mr W Roberton the metamorphoses in Inglische lent to him since anno 1576 gottin agane'. We also learn from this source that on 13 April 1575 'John Dike pate Robert Stewart sone to my lord of Orkney to Mr Williame

5   *The Buik of the Kirk of the Canagait, 1564–1567*, ed. A.B. Calderwood (SRS, 1961), 8, 11, 41, 64, 74; Scott may later have married, and may have been a minor cleric, ibid., 58, 74.
6   NAS, RD1/8, 190–1.
7   McNeill, 'Scottish entries', 79.
8   *Edinburgh Burgh Recs.*, iii, 141–5.
9   *Edinburgh Records: the Burgh Accounts*, ed. R. Adam (Edinburgh, 1899), 305.
10   *Edinburgh Burgh Recs.*, iii, 157, 209.
11   Ibid., iii, 250–2, 259.

Robertoun to bed, buird and scolage for ane yeir' for £32 yearly, with £8 delivered to Roberton for the first quarter, and Stewart to stand surety for the rest and to furnish a pair of sheets, etc. if Robert died or ran away from the schools, or if his father sent for him, or if pest or war should take him away, there would be no payment.[12] Roberton in fact continued to hold office till old age forced his resignation. The council could not leave him destitute, so in April 1584 they granted him a yearly pension of 200 merks and fixed the number of pupils he could teach in his retirement, so as not to damage the prospects of his successor, Hercules Rollock.[13]

A serious case from the Kirk's point of view was that of Ninian Dalzell, schoolmaster of Dumfries from 1558 until 1587. Over this period, he was also reader or minister at several kirks: besides Dumfries itself, he was at Colvend, Troqueer, Lochrutton, Caerlaverock, Tinwald, Trailflat and Torthorwald.[14] In July 1579, Dalzell, a former regent at St Andrews,[15] was called before the General Assembly for corrupting the youth of his school 'with papistrie', which he had taught generally in the countryside around. More specifically, he is said to have taught the Roman catechism. Later in the same Assembly he made the Confession of Faith concerning 'the heids of the religioun quhilk are in controversie'. He was deposed from office. One of his doctors was to take over and, though the evidence is confusing,[16] Mr David Glen would seem to have been in charge. But this may not have protected the youth in Dumfries, for Glen's kinsman, Mr Robert, owned a copy of a work of Cardinal Cajetan (i.e. Thomas de Vio), claiming that he had it 'from Mr David Glen, schoolmaster in Dumfries in the time that I bought it, 1582'.[17] In his will, Dalzell left his books to the 'trafficking' Catholic abbot of New Abbey (Sweetheart); and the succeeding master, Herbert Gledstanes, was accused in 1601 of harbouring the Catholics John Hamilton and Abbot Brown.[18]

Preaching to the Scots nobility at Leith in 1572, the Dunfermline minister David Ferguson complained that the kirks 'ar mair like to scheip cottis then the houssis of God' and the schools, the seed of church and common-wealth, 'utterlie neglectit and ouersene'.[19] Dunfermline itself did have a

---

[12] NLS, small memo book of an Edinburgh notary, MS 19312, fos. 144, 150v.

[13] This saga can be followed in *Edinburgh Burgh Recs.*, iii, 131, 133, 135, 139, 149, 150, 190, 193, 196–7, 215, 227; iv, 104–5, 179, 330, 342, 346.

[14] Haws, *Scottish Clergy at the Reformation*, 265; on some of these men, see M. Sanderson, 'Catholic recusancy in Scotland in the sixteenth century', *IR*, xxi (1970), 194.

[15] *Acta Facultatis*, ii, 405–13.

[16] *BUK*, ii, 432–33, 435; Spottiswoode, *The History of the Church of Scotland*, ed. M. Napier and M. Russell (Spottiswoode Society, 1847–51), ii, 269.

[17] Thomas de Vio, *Evangelia cum commentariis* (Paris, 1543), fo. 290v.

[18] G.W. Shirley, 'Fragmentary notices of the burgh school of Dumfries', *Dumfriesshire Trans.*, xxi (1939), 105–79.

[19] J. Lee (ed.), *Tracts by David Fergusson, Minister of Dunfermline, MDLXIII–MDLXXII* (Bannatyne Club, 1860), 72–3.

schoolmaster, but he did not meet with Ferguson's approval. John Henryson was a former monk, one of three novices, 'professed religious', who had obtained an ordination licence from Archbishop Hamilton in April 1552.[20] Later, when registering as a notary on 26 October 1573, as 'maister of the grammer schoole of dunfermling', he claimed to have passed a great part of his youth in studying letters. Born in St Andrews, Henryson was then forty-two and a married man.[21] Before the Privy Council twelve days previously, on 14 October, Henryson had raised letters as master of the grammar school in the abbey where he and his predecessors 'hes continewit maisters and teichearis of youth in letters and doctrine to their grit commoditie within the said schole past memor of man'. He had been admitted by the abbot, the legal authority. But David Ferguson, alleging an order from the Protestant archbishop, John Douglas, had charged Henryson to cease teaching under pain of excommunication. Henryson, however, unlike Roberton in Edinburgh, was content to abide by the judgement, not only of those he taught, but of honourable and famous persons. In his defence, he maintained he had never taught anything scandalous and had given his confession of faith as a professed member of the 'trew kirk'. Ferguson and Douglas, as kirkmen, had no authority over him; the issue was more a civil and profane matter, and no new law had given them the power they were claiming. Henryson argued for the charge against him to be dropped, and, in the absence of the kirkmen, the regent and Lords of Council found that no case had been made on the basis of the law as it stood, though they allowed for a right of appeal on other grounds.[22] As for Henryson's claims, we might note that he was still signing monastic deeds in October 1580, the year in which a Jesuit visitor to Dunfermline found the monks still about the place saying their office, keeping their garden and teaching, some of them in private houses. There were also some secular priests who 'teach the boys to read, to sing, and to play musical instruments'.[23]

In Reformation Glasgow, Bishop Leslie's *History* informs us, the schoolmaster Robert Maxwell, formerly of Paisley, was emboldened to dispute publicly with John Willock, superintendent of the west.[24] And even in Linlithgow, where Winzet was so speedily replaced, private houses did not necessarily patronise the new master. As late as 1604, Stirling presbytery was forced to summon a suspect Catholic, Mr Robert Thomson, 'petegog' to

[20] NAS, NP1/200, under April; day not specified.
[21] NAS, NP2/2, 28.
[22] *RPC*, ii, 288–9.
[23] NAS, *Yester Writs*, no. 828; W.J. Anderson, 'Narratives of the Scottish Reformation, 1: Report of Father Robert Abercrombie, SJ, in the year 1580', *IR*, vii, 31–3.
[24] Durkan, 'Education in the century of the Reformation', 165–6. Maxwell seems to have been a regent at St Leonard's college in St Andrews, *Acta Facultatis*, ii, 402.

Alexander, master of Linlithgow, teacher of the youth of the earl of Linlithgow.[25] Other suspects were to be found at Seton in that noble family's home. Stephen Bannatyne, schoolmaster to Seton's bairns in March 1593, was referred to as 'ane papist or atheist' and therefore to be blocked from schoolmastering till 'he embrace the trew religioun', while Robert, Lord Seton, was himself rebuked as an 'ill frequenter of the kirk'. He was excommunicated for 'obstinat continuation in papistry'. Stephen Bannatyne claimed that his faith was biblical, 'bundit within the auld and new Testaments'. If he followed that creed, said his prayers and kept the decalogue, including not committing adultery, he did not deserve to be fired: 'I know not that confessioun set out by your kirk.'[26] As our List shows, Bannatyne escaped to schoolmastering in Edinburgh. Presumably he had made some compromises in the interim. These various instances of specific religious resistance to the changeover by schoolmasters aside, however, the transition appears to have been swift and much smoother. No such problems are on record for Perth, Stirling, Haddington, Hamilton, Ayr or Montrose

III.2 A case-study in early Reformed schooling: James Melville at Montrose

James Melville, son of Richard Melville of Baldovie and nephew of the reformer Andrew Melville, provides many details of his education in his *Autobiography*. His career is probably still the best way of illustrating the new era in education, in the early years of which old ways were intertwined with new. James was born in 1556, and so his schooldays bridge the years.[27] He tells us that at age five or thereabouts, the grace book (prayer-book) was put into his hands. But he had learnt little of it by the time he was seven, at which stage his father sent him to school with his elder brother David, who was already eight. Richard Melville, a small laird, was the minister of Maryton, and his sons went to the school in nearby Logie-Montrose, conducted by the local minister, their kinsman William Gray, MA. Attending this school were a good number of 'gentle and honest men's berns' from the surrounding countryside, expecting to be trained in letters, virtue and honest games. Under Gray, they learnt their catechism (not just having it read to them, but also learning it by rote), prayers and bible (the last with added notes similar to the marginal notes in the Geneva Bible). They afterwards went on to the rudiments of Latin grammar, with vocabulary in Latin and French, concentrating in the latter on passages of French prose, to be read out and properly pronounced. This would be in 1563.

---

[25] NAS, CH2/722/4, under dates 14 Oct. and 28 Nov. 1604.
[26] G. Seton, *History of the Family of Seton* (Edinburgh, 1896), i, 212; Sanderson, 'Catholic recusancy', 94–5.
[27] For most of what follows, see *Autobiography and Diary*, 18–23.

The boys were then introduced to Latin grammar, in the shape of the 'etymology' (declensions and conjugations) of John Lily, whose work was the prescribed grammar for use in England. This was followed by Lily's syntax, and a little of the more difficult syntax of Thomas Linacre, another Englishman. (We might observe that it is odd to find no mention of the native Latin grammar of John Vaus, or of Buchanan's Latin version of Linacre, not the syntax but the rudiments.) Along with their grammar books, the boys used the following: Johann Honter's *Nomenclatura*, a classified list of names of things, usually subjoined to Honter's rudiments of cosmography; the lesser Latin colloquies of Erasmus; some eclogues of Virgil and verse epistles of Horace, with Cicero's epistles to his wife, Terentia. The absence of a Latin dramatist is noteworthy.

The boys went to the fields for recreation, where the minister taught them archery, how to hold a golf club and to use the batons in fencing, plus running, jumping, swimming and wrestling. However, this 'happie and golden tyme' was foreshortened. The minister saw his class numbers fall and, in about 1568, the school was dismissed when the plague came to nearby Montrose where 'contempt of God's gospel' was rife. After five years' schooling, the brothers went back home to Baldovie or Maryton, a mile from Montrose. On questioning both boys, their father found they had made reasonable progress. Richard Melville was not a graduate himself, but he had been 'brought upe in letters from his youthe'. In his early twenties he had been pedagogue to James Erskine, heir of Dun, with whom he travelled, visiting Dr Machabaeus (the former Perth Dominican John MacAlpine) at Copenhagen and Melanchthon at Wittenberg, and even attending Greifs-wald University for a time in 1546.[28] The whole family took an interest in books: the reading of Sir David Lindsay was not beyond his eldest sister, who may have attended a dame school. Reading and singing went hand-in-hand in medieval education, and she 'wald reid and sing' the passages from Lindsay. During the winter James spent at home after leaving primary school, she showed him a ballad one day, denouncing ministers who had already abandoned their charge because of non-payment of their stipends. What was to happen to those stipendless ministers, her father, or her uncle Mr James Melville (minister of Arbroath) and Mr James Balfour (this last also a visitor to Machabaeus and Melanchthon)?[29] Richard Melville himself passed that winter reading from Marcellus Palingenius (an anagram for the real name of Piero Angelo Manzoli, an Italian moralising satirist and critic

---

[28] For Machabaeus and Richard Melville, see Durkan, 'Heresy in Scotland', 326, 333–4. After the father's appointment to Maryton, the boy continued residing at Baldovie, *Autobiography and Diary*, 24.

[29] Durkan, 'Heresy in Scotland', 325.

of the Catholic clergy), telling the children to learn lines from this work by heart. When spring came, young James was put to the school at Montrose.

There, the sister of the minister at Logie-Montrose had taken up a dame's school, and in her house he lodged. The schoolmaster, Mr Andrew Mylne (not a graduate, the title was honorary) had been the member for Montrose in the first General Assembly, and afterwards was minister for Stracathro, Pert and Dunlappie. In the first year, he put James through the rudiments all over again, thereafter proceeding to the first part, 'etymology', of the grammar 'of Sebastian'.[30] After that they passed on to Terence's *Phormio*, began the second part, the syntax, of Despauterius, and with that Virgil's *Georgics* and other books not named. Melville tells that he escaped punishment from either of his schoolmasters, though on one occasion he set the 'bent' on fire (that is, the rushes on the school floor). The minister, Mr Thomas Anderson ('Mr' again by courtesy), a pious man 'of mean gifts but singular guid lyff' who limited his teaching to the Sunday, got Melville to rehearse Calvin's catechism in front of the congregation, 'because the peiple lyked weill of the clearnes of my voice, and pronuncing with sum feiling'. James observes that the reader, John Beattie, read distinctly and 'with a religious and devot feilling, whereby I found myselff movit to giff guid eare'. Beattie had the psalms in prose almost by heart, but James preferred the metrical psalter. A blind man, lodged in Montrose with Erskine of Dun and taught to sing the metrical psalms by the doctor in the school, sang so well that Melville took to them at once.[31]

A 'post' or messenger from Edinburgh brought psalm books to the school, and also ballads, especially Robert Semple's, and thus James learned to appreciate versification and rhetorical effects in Scots (and would himself later become a prolific vernacular poet). Wedderburn's *Gude and Godlie Ballatis* were shown him, and he learnt off many of these, and the 'great diversitie of toones' that accompanied them. The 'post' also taught him how to follow the calendar. After two years in Montrose, Andrew Mylne's departure to full-time ministry left the school much altered, and James returned home to Baldovie, in August 1571, where his father needed him to help with the harvest, 'wherein I had litle pleasour, for I lyked the scholaris lyff best'. He went up to St Andrews that November.

---

[30] i.e. Sebastian Novimola, who edited the versified the humanist grammar of Johannes Despauterius, found in use at, for example, Deer Abbey in 1537, and the standard Scottish grammar for years to come. For Andro Mylne's career, see Haws, *Scottish Clergy at the Reformation*, 296.

[31] Melville would, in later years, make at least two very fine, metrical versions of psalms, to be sung to the quirky, catchy tune of Alexander Montgomerie's 'Solsequium'; they were printed at the end of Melville's *Fruitfull and Comfortable Exhortatioun anent Death* (1597), pp. 111–12.

While much of James Melville's subsequent career at the University of St Andrews – and later – does not concern us here, we should note that on arrival at university, as he tells us, his grammar was so deficient, despite his school training, that he could not follow the regent's Latin at St Leonard's College and had to be tutored privately. He also relates how under Alexander Smith, musician and servant to the principal, James Wilkie, he learnt the scales, plainsong and the tenor part of the psalms, although he was dependent on a good ear for music, being unable to read the notes. Some fellow-students would play on the virginals, one played the lute and cithern, and Melville himself made some use of the spinet in the regent's chamber. There was also time for archery and golf; Melville's purse could not stretch to the 'catchpull' (tennis court), but he did learn something of handball and the use of a racket. At academic level, no Greek or Hebrew was available, other than the Greek alphabet and how to decline some nouns.[32] Afterwards, in 1574, he had the opportunity of thorough revision with his uncle, Andrew Melville, who visited their home in Baldovie on his return from Geneva, after a brief sojourn at court. Richard Melville committed James to Andrew's charge. His uncle had different views from the regents at St Leonard's on what it was proper to know. He began to tutor him afresh, in George Buchanan's Latin psalms, Virgil and Horace, particularly Virgil whom young Melville had already enjoyed at the grammar school where he had delighted to hear him read and 'sung' (which presumably here means 'declaimed in a chanting voice'), but never a line of which he had understood.

They studied the *Phormio*, and so his uncle revealed the 'fyne Latin langage' of Terence to him, and for the first time he appreciated the author's wit. He studied the Greek grammar of Nicolaus Clenardus (evidently his *Meditations*) by himself, while his uncle read Bodin. The Greek was not just theory, but practice on the epistle of Basil the Great to St Gregory Nazianzen on the solitary life. James's uncle got him to memorise it and went through the text with him for content as well as language. They then turned to the Greek New Testament, going through 'sum chapters of Mathew, and certean comfortable places of the Epistles, namlie the Romans'. Finally the young man took up Hebrew, where he covered the declension of nouns and pronouns and some conjugations of verbs. The texts used were his uncle's own, Johann Reuchlin's Hebrew dictionary and the grammar of Petrus Martinius. There does not seem to have been time to displace the rhetoric of George Cassander that James learnt as a young university student alongside the Ramist rhetoric of Omer Talon. James comments that Andrew

[32] *Autobiography and Diary*, 25, 29–30.

carried out 'all this, as it war, bot pleying and craking; sa that I lernit mikle mair by heiring of him nor ever I lernit of anie buik'.

But the books that Andrew used with James give a glimpse of the future as well as echoes of the past, although there is reason to think that Reuchlin at least had been known to John Vaus in Aberdeen,[33] and William Niddrie had his own grammatical 'meditations' ready for publication in the days of Mary of Lorraine.[34] Melville's school career was typical of many, and we can sum it up as follows. He had had some household education up to the grace book stage before going to school; at seven he went to a reading school conducted by a minister seeking to enhance his income, but given up when the numbers dropped. He learnt some very basic Latin along with some French, and enough syntax to serve as an introduction to Virgil and Horace and the prose of Cicero, though, by his own account, this was all superficial. Religious instruction confined itself to Calvin's catechism, prayers and selected Bible texts together with the master's gloss. Apart from the new Protestant religious orientation, all this would have been characteristic of much of medieval schooling. James's sister carried on his education at home in more popular literature, as relatives must have done in other families. Even his father, when he had more time on his hands in the winter, read to the family. James was by then eleven or twelve. Come the spring, David was withdrawn from education, and Andrew went to school in Montrose, where there were fewer games but more adolescent mischief, and where a new schoolmaster insisted on a harder text, the more up-to-date Despauterius. James wrote proses, but not Latin verses, as he had not gone beyond book two, the syntax, when the teacher left to devote himself to the ministry full time (he already had charge of churches while still teaching school).

We should be conscious that James Melville's low opinion of his own achievements in grammar and literature at this stage may well reflect a wish to highlight the change for the better wrought by his uncle Andrew. However, till he went to university, the young schoolboy was happiest when singing: the song school tradition would die hard. At the age of fourteen, he expressed his joy at receiving assurance, in prayer, that God would allow him to continue his studies, by 'praising my God, singing sum Psalmes'. A few days later, his father did indeed decide to send him to university. Some years later, talking about his love of instrumental music, 'quhairof my hart was verie desirus', James cites an interesting example of a household school in Glasgow, where a gentleman's town house he frequented in 1578 and

---

[33] Durkan & Ross, 'Early Scottish libraries', 156; other references: 3, 106, 142, 151. There is a Latin translation of Basil's letter in Censorinus, *De die natali*, of which Andrew owned only the 1597 edition.

[34] Durkan, 'Laying of fresh foundations', 133.

1579 was the resort of expert singers and players. These included the eldest daughter of the house, to whom Melville, 'a young man nocht unlovelie, and of nature verie loving and amorus' found himself 'verie extreamlie' attracted, to his great perturbation.[35] Although he sought salvation in betrothal to someone else, James would retain his love of music all his life.

III.3 The school day

James Melville does not go into details of how schoolboys passed the individual school day. Details can be provided, however, from the statutes of King's College grammar school in Old Aberdeen under Theophilus Stewart.[36] (These statutes may already have applied under his predecessor John Vaus, who died in the 1530s, for we find them included in the 1553 Paris version of Vaus's *Rudiments*, reprinted in 1566 by Lepreuik as a suitable grammar book for Scottish schools.)

The school day began at seven o'clock. First, on coming into school, the boys, on their knees, recited a short morning prayer inspired by one composed by Erasmus.[37] Parsing practice followed. Parsing over, the schoolmaster (*preceptor*) punished any delinquents with a telling off, or, if need be, with some strokes of a cane. That done, at eight there was an assembly of all classes (*lectiones*) addressed by the schoolmaster himself. Thereafter the boys scurried off for a hurried break and a snack (*ientatum*), before ten o'clock and the start of individual classes under their individual *hypodidascali* (a Greek borrowing), a term used for doctors or under-teachers. At eleven or half past the poor pupils had leave to go out into town, shortly followed by town students going home (if there were any, there being a town grammar school in New Aberdeen, after all). However, not all were free to go, for at this point, the *archididascalus* (the top teacher or preceptor) held his second class of the day on Terence, Virgil or Cicero, for those obliged to attend. The bell for lunch for those eating in college went at noon.

By two, all had to be ready for lessons in their different classes. The doctors were to be present at all times in school to mark mistakes, correct bad Latin, and also deal with any boys less determined to learn, i.e. idlers. The doctors themselves were to set a good example in these matters. At four a bell would sound, and the boys would check over with their instructors the schoolwork done that day. Boys feeling the call of nature could leave class in pairs, with a permit – some token or perhaps a rod kept for the purpose – in their hands, but nobody else could properly leave before the return of the first pair, except in an emergency. When the master (*gymna-*

---

35 *Autobiography and Diary*, 79–80.
36 The fullest text is in *Spalding Misc.*, v, 397–402.
37 J. Durkan, 'The cultural background in sixteenth century Scotland', 326.

siarcha) had a mind to do so, he might personally inspect any class besides his own top class. From five to six in the evening disputations took place, and thereafter scholars were obliged to be present to sing their psalms (*preces*). A Pythagorean (total) silence was laid down for scholars studying the elements and for newcomers. The 'table of confession' (the articles of the creed?) and a modicum of arithmetic were obligatory. Only Latin, Greek, Hebrew, French (or Gaelic, this being Aberdeen), were to be spoken, never the Scottish vernacular – at least, this would apply to all those who knew some Latin. Each boy was to carry his own ruler (*ferula*, which here may stand for all writing materials). The college was banned to outsiders, and no scholar doing grammar was to have anything to do with anyone doing logic (often a part of the grammar course in some schools).

Outside schoolwork, there was to be no attempt at barter, or to purchase somebody else's property, nor freedom to get rid of one's own property without leave from the master or his deputy. Games seem to have been less physical than those experienced by the young Melville: no bets were to be laid on the promise of a schoolbook, money, items of clothes (or even one's lunch). The stakes which were permitted, at least to older boys, were shoe-laces and pins (*aciculis*). Games of chance for money were forbidden; the poor would be glad of any coins available for such games. No gaming was allowed out of sight of the doctors. Nobody was to hurt another by word or deed. If a boy who had not replied in kind lodged a complaint, the offender was to be punished. If insults were mutual, and it came to a fight, only those who used physical force were to be punished. A double penalty faced senior pupils who set a bad example. The statutes then list punishments for not listening to the teacher, coming to school late, being unable to parse during the lesson on the text, moving about needlessly in class, running away or up and down the schoolroom,[38] returning late from meal break and lunch, taking excessive time over the call of nature, speaking in the vernacular, absenting oneself from class for protracted periods, and finally for being 'authors of evil' – which must have covered a multitude of sinners.

The Aberdeen statutes conclude by stating that 'these laws (*nomothetae*) have been set forth in print, and henceforth there can be no excuse for ignorance ... those who "soldier under our ferule" can now seek to be more dutiful in monitoring their behaviour (*nomophylaces*)'. Selected passages from Quintilian, Cicero and Terence buttressed the authority of these laws with the authority of the ancients. The course appears to have been of three years' duration, with two doctors in assistance, as advised for the Edinburgh school in 1530 by Adam Mure, himself an Aberdeen student.

---

[38] H.M. Simpson, in *Bon Record*, 108, translates *discurrentes* as truants.

III.4 Buchanan's plan for St Andrews in 1563

Mure's Edinburgh school scheme was not exactly the 'college of humanity' envisaged by George Buchanan in his St Andrews project of 1563. Here we find six classes with six regents, a public rector, and a principal. The students are required to bring their own paper and ink, and classes are subdivided into *decuriones* in the charge of juvenile monitors ('nomenclatouris') who may be punished themselves for overlooking the mistakes of their charges. Terence is to be in use from the start, at first only in snippets, and the daily exercise is a short prose composition. The easier letters of Cicero follow in the next class, alternating with the reading of Terence. Next year Ovid's verse epistles and elegies are added, along with the construing of the eight parts of speech. Greek begins in the fourth year, with some prosody and rhetoric and some of Linacre. The fifth and sixth years see pupils initiated into the rhetoric of Cicero (rhetoric had in the later middle ages been acquiring the status of a university subject), with Virgil and Horace (at last), as well as Ovid and some Homer and Hesiod.

In Buchanan's scheme, disputations were no longer a daily but a weekly matter, taking up four hours on Saturday. The school day was longer in summertime: students rose at five and the public lecture in assembly was at six; before eight there was room for two ordinary classes punctuated by a bell; at ten the bell sounded, and again at half past ten; the dinner bell went at eleven; at the grace again a bell; at the 'repetition' after grace, presumably a revision class, another bell; at three the bell rang twice; at four-thirty another bell, and finally a last bell at five. Not all would remain in college after this, as some pupils were lodged in town. Buchanan did not believe in forcing the three youngest classes to attend the sermon except on Sundays, thus echoing the practice of James Brown in pre-Reformation Linlithgow. Buchanan's plan would have conformed to the *Book of Discipline*'s project for colleges in the cities where superintendents were resident, and reflects not only the practice in his own college in Bordeaux, but also at Nîmes and Geneva.[39]

III.5 Terminology: schoolboys, schoolmasters and doctors

The age at which those who went to school actually did so seems to vary somewhat, but the norm is expressed in the will of Janet Gordon, registered in 1599, where she lays down that 'efter the expyring of sevin yeiris of his age compleit', her boy is to be put to school and 'hald him thairat quhill he have euaidit fourtene yeiris of his age complet'.[40] This is the age we saw

---

39   *Vernacular Writings of George Buchanan*, ed. Brown, 8–11 and the editor's note, 66.
40   NAS, CC8/8/34, registered 29 Nov. 1599.

James Melville go to school at, but how far this norm was adhered to, we have insufficient evidence to tell. The usual term for schoolboy is *scholaris*, though that could have the technical meaning of 'schoolboy bursar', as at King's College in the first years of the Reformation when the English ambassador, Thomas Randolph, estimated fifteen or sixteen scholars in residence in 1562.[41] The term 'student' in most of the examples found is the equivalent of scholar or schoolboy. But it does sometimes clearly refer to higher studies, and we have a student helping out with teaching in a school, as was John Ironside at Edinburgh high school.[42] On the other hand, the usual sense seems to apply to John Anderson, 'student' at Broughton in 1631.[43] But when we find two references to Gilbert Keith, 'student', at Rathen in 1620,[44] we need to remember that Rathen was not a school that mushroomed up overnight. Keith was an assistant. The Rathen school had been first mooted in 1610, and referred to again in 1614, when a public reader and schoolmaster were specified, for whom there were many parishioners willing to make a voluntary contribution. In 1617 a school was in existence, as were a school and schoolmaster for reading and training up the youths, for which a private person promised the presbytery of Deer to build a schoolhouse to be held without cost for five years to come.[45]

Individuals like Gilbert Keith were probably theology students, but an example of a student at the law schools can be found as early as 1508, when Coinneach, son of William, the judge or lawman in Trotternish, Skye, was to go to the schools to study the king's laws of Scotland; significantly, he belonged to a hereditary family of lawmen.[46] In university towns, 'student' witnesses have to be disregarded in the search for pointers to the existence of schools, yet elsewhere their presence, like that of 'scholars', can indicate a school when there is otherwise a blank in the record: a passing mention of 'students' can be a welcome testimony to the continuity of schooling. In a very few cases, a fine line exists between acceptance and rejection of evidence of this kind; in 1563 we find an Adam Hucheson, scholar, witnessing a document at the Chapel of Ferme; his presence as witness is ambiguous, because Ferme lay on the outskirts of Glasgow, though 'chapel' does suggest a possible school site.[47]

---

41 *Cal. State Papers Scotland*, i, 549.
42 NAS, CC8/8/52, 214.
43 NAS, CC8/10/9.
44 NAS, RD1/325, 371; SC1/60/41, 11.
45 NAS, CH2/89/1(1), 135; CH2/89/1(2), 159; ibid., 251.
46 *RSS*, i, 1654, commented on in J. Bannerman, 'The Scots language and kin based society', in D.S. Thomson (ed.), *Scots in Harmony: Proceedings of the Second National Conference on the Languages of Scotland* (Glasgow, 1990), 13.
47 NAS, RH6/1924.

A schoolmaster can be a 'master of schools', as in the early Middle Ages, a *scholearcha*, a *ludimagister*, a *praeceptor* or just plain *scholemagister*. The word 'teacher' is seldom used unless qualified by some addition like 'teacher of the youth'; otherwise the man concerned could be a minister or preacher. Schools might be held at the kirk or near the big house. Of the former there are examples at Drymen, Fyvie and Fetteresso;[48] of the latter there is Mr Alexander Balcanvall, schoolmaster at the 'castle of Grinlaw' in 1630.[49] If an individual appears as schoolmaster at a university grammar school, he is a regent, like John Vaus in pre-Reformation Aberdeen. A master, despite his already heavy duties, frequently acts as a notary, and even as a minister on occasion, as we saw with Andrew Mylne at Montrose, and will see with Mr James Carmichael of Haddington. The old link between schoolmasters and chaplains is preserved in the traditional word 'dominie', from *domine*, the vocative of *dominus* used when addressing priests and other grades of cleric. Both forms are used in a description of a visit paid by William Rhynd, schoolmaster, to Perth's first minister, John Row: 'the master of the gramer schoole, commonlie called Dominie Rind …' is then called 'Domine' when Row addresses him. Row had close links with the school, and 'many noble and gentle men [who] sent their eldest sonnes to be educat there'. Numbers of them 'were tabled' (lodged) with the minister, who compensated for compulsory Latin at school and in the fields of play by insisting on French only in his household! It is worth remembering that much learning was extra-curricular, as we saw in the Melville household at Baldovie: at meals Row would read the Old Testament in Hebrew and the New Testament in Greek, Latin, French or the vernacular.[50] A certain Robert Salmond is found as 'scuill domine' at Balhall in 1623, an early witness to the persistence of the title in country places down into the seventeenth century.[51] The terminology *scholearcha* is used of Dysart's schoolmaster, *gymnasiarcha* of Irvine's. From the 1553 statutes for the grammar school at King's College, other such Renaissance-type designations can be inferred, but, as often happened in other spheres, the older terminology survived.

It was customary for the master to choose his own teaching assistants, generally known as 'doctors'. In 1605, we find John Aird confusingly stated to be 'servant' and schoolmaster of Whitekirk; it is not clear whether he was the laird's servant or the schoolmaster's.[52] Some men styled 'servitors' are also styled 'doctors', and these have to be carefully distinguished from men

---

[48] NAS, RD1/209, 363; RD1/325, 268; RD1/345, 3.
[49] NAS, SC60/56, 4.
[50] J. Row, *The History of the Kirk of Scotland*, ed. D. Laing (Wodrow Society, 1842), 455–6.
[51] NAS, RD1/396, 253. See the twentieth-century poetry of W.D. Cocker, J.M. Caie, Walter Wingate, J.C. Milne, etc., for the persistent use of the term.
[52] NAS, RS1/14, 188; RS12/3, 588.

who were servants to lairds, or apprentices – for instance, to notaries. The only school-related entry in the official register of apprentices is Andrew Ker of Duddingston, apprenticed to Robert Mullikyne, schoolmaster, in 1639.[53] These doctors were usually paid by their schoolmaster employer, and could eke out their income by acting as notaries or scribes; the latter employment was not uncommon, with the document in which the doctor's name occurs often stating that it was he who drew it up. This is also true of rural schoolmasters (self-employed 'doctors' hired by the kirk session), as with one who is 'notar' and schoolmaster 'at the kirk' of Greenlaw in 1627.[54]

Country schoolmasters are very often styled 'doctors', one suspects because they only taught the rudiments of reading and spoken Latin. The phrase 'at the kirk' does not necessarily mean *in* the kirk, just as 'at the castle', as we saw in medieval Huntly, could be outside the castle; Mr Alexander Balcanvall is described as schoolmaster 'at the castle of Grinlaw', where we know there was a kirk parish school.[55] Some contemporary Latin usage echoes Castellio (whose secular titles for sacred offices annoyed Calvin and Beza), as where a man is described as clerk to the 'senate' (i.e. kirk session) of Belhelvie.[56] The title 'doctor' may be a clue to the status of a school; one might have expected better than 'doctor of the abbacie' at Melrose,[57] an educational location seemingly not on a par with Culross, another former abbey site. It is not clear what the significance is of 'instruckar' of the youth of Stracathro, seemingly equivalent to 'doctor', though youth implies adolescence more than boyhood (James Melville's 'age of bernheid').[58] There is a lower category than doctor, 'subdoctor', recorded in 1633.[59] The doctor must on occasion have replaced the schoolmaster, unless we are to envisage pupils being boarded in the schoolhouse, as in 1591, when Allan Lochhead was schoolmaster at Kilmarnock while simultaneously active as pedagogue to the earl of Eglinton.[60]

III.6 Pedagogues and aristocrats

When compiling our lists of schoolmasters, we encountered many men who styled themselves schoolmasters, but were quite obviously pedagogues attached to a laird's household, rather than schoolmasters attached to schools. (On the other hand, a genuine schoolmaster, Mr Andrew Simson, is described

---

53   *Edinburgh Apprentices*, 104.
54   NAS, SC60/56, 2.
55   NAS, SC60/56, 4.
56   NAS, CH2/30/1, 42.
57   NAS, RD1/29, 12.
58   NAS, RD1/254, 179; *Autobiography and Diary*, 20.
59   NAS, RD1/468, 189.
60   NAS, RD1/40, 65.

as 'pedagogue' of the Perth grammar school in 1557,[61] and at Dunkeld in 1572, Simson's fellow-grammarian Alexander Hepburn was *pethagogus ludigrammaticalis*.[62]) Pedagogues have been excluded from the lists, even though their educational importance is undeniable. Generally, schoolmasters 'of' or 'to' named individuals have had to be rejected, whereas schoolmasters 'at' a place have been accepted. For example, among hostages held by the English at Newcastle in 1562, we find 'Lord Claude Hamilton, his schoolmaster ...' and 'Mr George Grayme, the Earl of Monteith's son, his schoolmaster ...'.[63] In the case of 'Mr Robert Gray *ludimagister* and *hypodidasculus* of the Earl of Sutherland' in 1618, the second title contradicts the first, since it means under-teacher.[64] However, one can also find Mr Gilbert Gordon, schoolmaster at Dornoch and servitor to the earl of Sutherland, which suggests a school outside the castle.[65] Yet Mr Robert Park, 'servitor to Walter Stewart, Lord Blantyre', only later went on to become schoolmaster in Paisley.[66] Pedagogues might have several members of a family in their keeping and hold a household school, for example 'Mr James Crawfurde pedagogue of the boys of the said Sir William Mentaithe' (of Kerse, Knight) in September 1620.[67]

Some of these pedagogues were Catholics and suffered the attention of the Kirk. In 1604 Mr Robert Thomson, 'petegog to Alexander, master of Linlithgow', suspect Catholic, 'teacher of the zouth of ane nobill man My Lord Erll of linlithgow', was summoned to appear and give his confession of faith to Stirling presbytery.[68] There are many pedagogues attached to gentlemen's sons for whom we have no subsequent record of a university career. St Andrews University's medieval records are remarkably uninformative about lairds' sons in attendance there, until in 1553 the earl of Eglinton and his brother matriculated in St Mary's College, along with the young laird of Drumlanrig.[69] Later, in post-Reformation times, the laird of Drumquhassill's son was maintained by a burse out of a church benefice.[70] Glasgow's records are more satisfying. In its opening year it had the laird of Caerlaverock's son; in 1473 and 1492 sons of the earl of Lennox; in 1466, Andrew Hay, son of the Lord of Yester and so on.[71] In 1628, Glasgow had three sons of the earl of

---

[61] *Laing Chrs.*, no. 673.
[62] NAS, CH2/621/69.
[63] *Cal. State Papers Eliz. 1561–2*, no. 818.
[64] NAS, RS37/1, 118.
[65] NAS, RD1/35 1, 538.
[66] NAS, RD1/156, 7.
[67] NAS, RS58/2, 88.
[68] NAS, CH2/722/4, under that year.
[69] J.M. Anderson (ed.), *Early Records of the University of St Andrews* (SHS, 1926), 257.
[70] Ibid., 299.
[71] *MAUG*, ii, 56, 72, 81, 92.

Eglinton in its roll, along with their pedagogue, and the earl of Linlithgow with his pedagogue and servant in the following year.[72] There were, of course, also lairds' sons at university who are not on record as such. All of these young men must have had pre-university grammar training some-where, possibly in landward schools. It is possible that many gentlemen's sons did not patronise rural schoolmasters, preferring, like the city merchants, the more distinguished city graduate masters; moreover, city schooling provided them with ready access to the archery masters and fencing schools required to live up to the still vigorous chivalric ideal. However, it is likely that such schooling started in local households (as at Dunblane), and with the support of lairds in local schools, even grammar schools.

In Section I, we encountered the Humes and the school they attended at Elphinstone. In the pages of *De Familia Humia*, David Hume of Godscroft has provided us with an unusually detailed glimpse of a cultured aristocratic Scottish household. Unlike the highly polished Godscroft, his elder brother, Sir George Hume of Wedderburn, had little formal education though he lived in a cultured household. Born at Elphinstone where his mother lived (she died in 1564), George's educators were James Knox at Elphinstone and William Lamb and Andrew Simson at Dunbar. Also at Elphinstone was his cousin George Car, more proficient than himself at music. Godscroft tells us that hardly was young George out of his adolescence,[73] than he went to stay with the Regent Morton in the company of Archibald Douglas, eighth earl of Angus, whose tutor was an Edinburgh burgess, John Provand. Provand introduced the earl to John Rutherford's logic, which he himself might have been taught in St Andrews, for it did not see print in Edinburgh till 1577.[74] But, Hume tells us, the earl considered the study of letters too base an occupation, and viewed those 'that affects them pedantick', until his friendship with Sir Philip Sidney changed his mind during his exile in England in 1581–83.[75] We might note that a phrase about stupid pedants, twice employed by King James VI in the early 1590s, shows how a word originally neutral in sense was beginning to attach itself to the phenomenon of pedantry in schoolmasters.[76]

Though George Hume never evinced the eighth earl's literary interests,

---

[72] Ibid., iii, 80, 530. Mentions of pedagogues are frequent in the manuscript Registers of Deeds.

[73] George's father, Sir David, died in 1574, George himself in 1616, *Hist MSS Comm., Report on the Manuscripts of Colonel David Milne-Home*, 6–7.

[74] There was a Paris edition of 1555. Archibald Douglas studied at St Andrews; he too studied rhetoric under Provand 'with such success as is customary to Youth and Nobility', D. Hume, *History of the House and Race of Douglas and Angus* (Edinburgh, 1743), i, 288.

[75] Ibid., ii, 288–9.

[76] In King James, *Minor Prose Works*, ed. J. Craigie and A. Law, separately paged *Daemonologies*, 7 (STS, 1982); *Basilicon Doron*, ed. J Craigie (STS, 1944), i, 180.

he could, 'according to court custom', sing (including psalms to the music of the harp), as his father could, and was a good and modest dancer. He picked up some French, of which he was a passable speaker, and had a good passive knowledge of the spoken language. He read histories and, though he never went abroad, was familiar with foreign place-names. Without having been taught, he managed to measure heights with the use of a triangle. He canvassed opinions at table and elsewhere, tried to fathom the message of ancient philosophy and took part in philosophical argument. Once he had learnt something, he never forgot it. His other accomplishments, more predictably, were hunting with the hare and hounds and horse-riding (he was apparently an expert in horse-management), along with hawking and falconry. He did not neglect domestic economy, and he was not only interested in farming, but in law and 'empiric' medicine. In the field of sacred letters, he read, wrote and meditated, like many of his contemporaries, on the Book of Revelation, and studied religious polemics, seeking information on the soul, the love of God and the catechism. He even made a Scots translation of the mass to point out its 'follies' (*ineptia*) to his wife. He was humorous by nature, and got the name of being a wit, although his presbyterian brother did not always appreciate his satirical humour.[77]

Less devout, but clearly not devoid of minimum cultural interests, was the household of Robert Logan, laird of Restalrig. During the litigation following the Gowrie conspiracy against King James VI, Logan was alleged to have conducted a correspondence that revealed his involvement in the crime, and associates of his were called as witnesses. One was Alexander Watson, former schoolmaster and by the date of trial (1609), minister of Coldingham. He analysed the orthography of the letters produced in court and agreed they were Logan's. Logan never wrote 'z' (i.e. yogh), always 'y'; never wrote 'w' at the beginning of the word, always 'v'; in the middle of a word, however, never 'v', always 'w'; never wrote 'quhen', always 'qhen'; never wrote 'con' out in full, always abbreviating it; and never at any time did he cross his 't's. Although the evidence adduced hardly seems decisive in view of current variations in spelling styles, one who agreed was Mr Alexander Smyth, minister at Chirnside, aged thirty or thereabouts and very well acquainted with the young laird 'be ressoun he vas petagog to his barnis'.[78]

While many pedagogues remained obscure, others had successful public careers. One such was William Struthers, who died Dean of Edinburgh in November 1633. He was the son of an eponymous pre-Reformation chap-

---

77   Hume, *De Familia Humia*, 43, 60–2.
78   *APS*, iv, 422–3; Logan's accomplice, George Sprott, schoolmaster notary, added that Logan was 'voyd of Religioun', although he used Christian salutations in his letters. Sprott's own piety was revealed when in 1608, as a penitent on the scaffold, he led the watching crowd in the singing of the sixth psalm; see Pitcairn, *Trials*, ii, 261.

lain presented to the canonry of Moneydie in Dunkeld diocese by Queen Mary and Darnley, probably in view of his musical abilities; but somehow he failed to get possession of the benefice.[79] Oddly, this man was given the graduate title 'Mr' in 1562 when, as prebendary of Bothwell collegiate church, he was also exhorter at Stonehouse; we later find him, now with no graduate title, still at Stonehouse. By 1569 he was reader at Glasgow and on Sundays exhorter at Lenzie.[80] Styled 'sir', Struthers was master of the Glasgow song school in 1576/7 and in 1584, by which time he was again styled 'Mr'. As master of the song school in 1587 and 1588 he was expected to sing in the cathedral.[81] His son William graduated MA at Glasgow in 1599 and was admitted as minister of Lenzie in 1607; his father had been exhorter there from 1569 to 1571.[82] This Lenzie connection led to a link with the patron of Lenzie, the sixth Lord Fleming, earl of Wigtown, who c.1586 took as his first wife Lilias Graham, whose piety Struthers would later recall. William Struthers became schoolmaster to John, the future seventh Lord Fleming, who was born in 1589, and he described himself as 'director of your Lordship's studies', which may mean no more than grammar and music.[83] These studies probably took place in the Fleming household in Cumbernauld. In 1611 Struthers demitted the vicarage of Lenzie on returning to Glasgow as cathedral minister for the west quarter, having a collegiate charge there from 1612, whence he moved to St Giles, Edinburgh, in 1614.[84] Initially a keen supporter of James VI in church matters, later a critic of royal policy, but finally a fervent adherent of Charles I, Struthers was appointed Dean of Edinburgh a few months before his death in November 1633. He was a man of some learning who published several substantial devotional works. Some printed poetry is also extant from his pen.[85] That he left both books and a bursary foundation to Glasgow University in 1633 reflects the improved economic position of ministers.[86]

---

[79] *RSS*, v, 3029, 3158.

[80] *Accounts of the Collectors of the Thirds of Benefices*, 150, 261, 264; *Register of Ministers*, 31.

[81] *Glasgow Recs.*, i, 462, 472; *Wodrow's Biographical Collections upon the Lives of the Reformers*, ed. W.J. Duncan (2 vols., Maitland Club, 1834–48), ii, 22–3.

[82] Haws, *Scottish Clergy at the Reformation*, 148.

[83] William Struther [sic], *Christian Observations and Resolutions: Centurie II* (Edinburgh, 1629), dedication. A copy of this work, handsomely gold-stamped, with the initials of the Earl, is in Glasgow University Library: there are several references in *Glasgow Prot. Bk* to father and son as 'sir' or 'Mr'.

[84] His complete career is set out in *Fasti*, iii, 56.

[85] Poems by him in Latin and Greek appear in John Adamson (ed.), *The Muses Welcome* (Edinburgh, 1618) and he has a Greek poem and its translation into a vernacular sonnet in John Adamson (ed.), *Eisodia musarum Edinensium in Caroli Regis, Musarum Tutani, ingressu in Scotiam* (Edinburgh, 1633).

[86] *Fasti*, iii, 453, 481–2; W. Thomson (ed.), *Deeds Instituting Bursaries, Scholarships and Other Foundations in the College and University of Glasgow* (Maitland Club, 1856), 23.

Pre-1633 foundations at Glasgow owe surprisingly little to the nobility, for, apart from the laird of Jordanhill, Captain Thomas Crawford, other benefactors were the Morton regency, John Howieson, minister of Cambuslang, and Michael Wilson, merchant of Eastbourne.[87] But the nobility was interested in education. In the early 1560s some Reformed lords like Lord Ruthven, whose sons were hostages, wanted the boys, not to have 'tynt tyme' at Berwick, but to 'pass to the scole in Cambreche',[88] and some English lords agreed that the young hostages should be sent to Oxford or Cambridge as requested by their parents. They included Claud Hamilton (aged sixteen); Alexander Campbell, son of Argyll; Mr Robert Douglas, an adult; Mr James Cunningham, another adult, Glencairn's son; Mr George Graham (aged five), son of the earl of Menteith. Later in 1562 a special appeal for study at Cambridge was made on behalf of the young laird of Calder, Sandilands, a well travelled, 'prettilye learned … proper young gentleman of eighteen'. Naturally, the English ambassador in Scotland favoured such requests.[89]

We glean some idea of what aristocratic pupils studied from lists of expenses drawn up in 1600 and 1602 by Mr Andrew Dalrymple, teacher at Newmilns, with whom the extremely young John Stewart had been placed by Jean Campbell, duchess of Lennox.[90] The boy's expenses are mostly for clothes and laundry, but books are mentioned: in 1600, Jeremias Bastingius's catechism (basically the Heidelberg one), printed in Edinburgh 1591; the select epistles of Cicero; the first part of the grammar of Despauterius; the second part (syntax) of Ramus; and two paper books. (The mixture of Despauterius and Ramus must have been quite confusing to the young pupil!) With his teacher the boy visited Glasgow to buy a new hat. In 1602 he went on to acquire Terence, Buchanan's Psalm paraphrases, Buchanan's 'third part' (i.e. *De Prosodia*) and the *Metamorphoses* of Ovid. Added to these were 'tua bund paper buikis to writ his authors on'. Unfortunately these commonplace books do not survive.

An outstanding example of an educated aristocrat, and a somewhat unusual one, in that she was a woman, is the poetess Elizabeth Melville (fl.1599–1632). Daughter of the courtier, diplomat and memoirist Sir James Melville of Halhill, she must have received her clearly excellent education at home. Unfortunately, we do not know who the Melville family pedagogue was. Elizabeth was a prolific writer, but her only signed publication is the impressive long poem *Ane Godlie Dreame*, published in 1603 in Scots, and

---

[87] Ibid., 1, 6, 8, 13.
[88] *Cal. State Papers Scotland*, i, 325.
[89] Ibid., i, 334, 344, 627, 644.
[90] NAS, GD220/6/2006/8. Their home at the time seems to have been at Loudon. This is a unique source of information about Ludovic Stewart's son by his second marriage; no printed source even knows his name.

frequently thereafter in anglicised form. It relates the journey of a suffering member of the Elect beyond the bounds of this world, guided by Christ himself to the bourn of heaven and then to the depths of hell. A best-seller through into the 1730s, this poem almost certainly inspired John Bunyan's *Pilgrim's Progress*.[91] To date, another 3,500 lines of her skilful, wholeheartedly Calvinist verse have been identified in manuscript and print. She employed a wide range of verse forms with real skill, her sonnets being particularly fine, while her twelve extant letters reveal a forceful character, capable of using Latin tags to make her point. Much esteemed by her fellow-poet Alexander Hume, minister of Logie, she married John Colville of Culross, heir to the former commendator of the abbey there.[92] Their eldest son, Dr Alexander Colville, was a Hebrew scholar, professor at Sedan and principal of St Mary's College at St Andrews, and their youngest son, Samuel, was a minor satirical versifier of some coarseness.[93]

Another educated aristocrat, of rather higher rank than Lady Culross, was Margaret Cunningham, a daughter of the seventh Earl of Glencairn. Her younger sister Anna was the formidable Covenanter Marchioness of Hamilton. Like Lady Culross, Margaret came of a literate family with a tradition of making use of the written word; the fifth earl's anti-Catholic satirical verse epistle 'fra the Hermeit of Allareit', was preserved by his friend John Knox.[94] Margaret's long, articulate and deeply religious letter of May 1607, pleading with her errant and abusive first husband to mend his ways, includes a short sonnet sequence. While it failed to reform James Hamilton of Evandale, whom she divorced in 1610, it clearly circulated widely. The central sonnet, 'What greater wealth than a contented mind?', was printed (anonymously) as the final item, marked to be sung to the tune of the 110th Psalm, in the great harmonised Psalter edited by Edward Millar and published at Edinburgh in 1635.[95]

---

[91] In D. Laing (ed.), *Early Metrical Tales, including the history of Sir Egeir, Sir Gryme and Sir Gray-Steill* (Edinburgh, 1826), 252. Also in A. Lawson, *Poems of Alexander Hume* (STS, 1902), appendix.

[92] J. Reid-Baxter, 'Elizabeth Melville, Lady Culross: 3500 new lines of verse', in S. Dunnigan et al. (eds.), *Women and the Feminine in Medieval and Early Modern Scottish Writing* (Basingstoke, 2004), 195–200; 'Robert Bruce, John Burel and Elizabeth Melville', *RSCHS*, 2004; 'The songs of Lady Culross', in G. Munro et al., *Notis Musycall* (Glasgow, 2005); and *Elizabeth Melville, Lady Culross: Poems and Letters* (forthcoming).

[93] For Alexander, much embarrassed by Samuel's antics in St Andrews, see *Dictionary of National Biography*. Samuel's substantial *Mock Poem, or, the Whiggs Supplication* went through several editions from 1681; three other shorter manuscript poems (in NLS and NAS) are included in Reid-Baxter, *Elizabeth Melville Poems and Letters* (forthcoming).

[94] *Historie*, i, 72–5. Also reprinted in David Laing (ed.), rev. W. Carew Hazlitt, *Early Popular Poetry of Scotland and the Northern Border* (London, 1895), i, 175–8.

[95] *A Pairt of the Life of Lady Margaret Cuninghame, Daughter of the Earl of Glencairn, that She had with her First Husband, the Master of Evandale. The Just and True Account Thereof, as it was at First Written with her own Hand. Including a Letter to Her Husband, the Master of Evandale, and another*

The activism evinced by these and quite a number of other noble ladies on behalf of proscribed radical ministers, such as John Welsh, John Livingstone, David Dickson and Samuel Rutherford, show that they belonged to an altogether different class of aristocrat from the nobility whom David Fergusson, in a printed sermon of 1572, had denounced for making the ministers a laughing-stock: 'we ar now maid zour tabill talk, quhome ye mock in zour mirrines, and threaten in zour anger'.[96] Appropriately enough, Fergusson's sermon was endorsed in Latin liminary verses both by a minister, John Davidson of Prestonpans, and by a schoolmaster, Patrick Auchinleck of St Andrews.

to *My Lady Marquess of Hamilton, with Her Last Will Sent to the Said Lady Marquess, Inclosed therein*, ed. Charles Kirkpatrick Sharpe (Edinburgh, 1827), 12–17 (letter), 17–18 (sonnets); manuscript sources are NLS, MS 874, fos. 363–84, 906. For the 1635 Psalter, see the modern reprints ed. N Livingstone (Glasgow, 1864) and R.M. Terry (London, 1936).

[96] *Tracts by David Fergusson*, ed. Lee, 73, in 'Ane Sermon preichit befoir the Regent and Nobilitie', delivered 1572.

IV. Schoolbooks, Grammarians and Schoolmaster Poets

IV.1 Alexander Hepburn of Dundee and his grammar

Dundee is the first town known to be interested in producing its own grammar, written by Alexander Hepburn and published abroad by Christopher Plantin in Antwerp in 1568; Plantin was a correspondent of George Buchanan, who wrote the introduction to Hepburn's book.[1] Alexander Hepburn is known to have been master in Elgin, near Kinloss where Giovanni Ferrerio taught.[2] We do not know Hepburn's dates in Elgin, but he had graduated from St Andrews in 1533 (although if this is indeed our schoolmaster, he held the canonry of Rhynie in Moray for a time, though certainly not by the Reformation).[3] He was schoolmaster in Dundee by 1562, and made a burgess there in 1565. By 1571, Hepburn was in the grammar school at Dunkeld, and by 1574 he was minister at Little Dunkeld. In 1575 he was confirmed as Protestant bishop of Ross, and died in 1578.[4]

The final page of his 1568 *Grammaticae artis prima rudimenta* bears commendatory verses initialled HR, the work of a student at Dundee, the distinguished future poet and schoolmaster Hercules Rollock. Buchanan wrote in his introduction that Hepburn's book was a distillation of Despauterius (then and for many decades to come the leading Scottish grammar). He approved Hepburn's clarity and brevity, for he knew that the ocean of information to be found in Despauterius was too prolix for most schoolboys. It is strange that Buchanan himself did not reprint his own Latin rendering of Linacre's English language grammar; perhaps its association with Mary Tudor and her tutor, Juan Luis Vives, was politically incorrect by that date. Buchanan would have other ways of imposing respect for Linacre, by presiding over the reform of grammar begun in the discussions convened by the Regent Morton in 1575 with a view to producing a Latin grammar for universal use in Scottish schools.[5] The idea of a monopoly goes back at least to 1568 and the production of Hepburn's grammar.

In 1565 two school Latin readers were issued by Lepreuik in Edinburgh.

---

1   *Grammaticae Artis Rudimenta breviter et dilucide explicata* (1568).
2   'Gymnasiarcha elginensis'; later he owned an Angelo Poliziano of Ferrerio's, see Durkan & Ross, *Early Scottish Libraries*, 96 (Ferrerio, item 5), 116 (Hepburn seems to be the same as the 'benefactor of the Aberdeen Franciscans', entered separately).
3   J.M. Anderson (ed.), *Early Records*, 232; *Acta Facultatis*, ii, 376; Kirk (ed.), *Books of Assumption of Thirds of Benefices*, 486.
4   Durkan, 'Laying of fresh foundations', l 34; D.E.R. Watt, *Fasti Ecclesiae Scoticanae medii aevi ad annum 1638* (SRS, 1969), 270–1; *Fasti*, vii, 35s.
5   I.D. McFarlane, *Buchanan* (London, 1981), 44–6, 269; Durkan, *Bibliography of George Buchanan*, ix–x.

One was *Pasquillorum versus aliquot*, mostly a reprint of pasquils of an anti-Catholic nature edited by Celio Secondo Curione, but with some short pieces added by Buchanan, who probably also had urged the reprint that same year of the satirical *De vita monachorum* of Lelio Capilupi, propaganda all the more effective for being Italian in origin.[6] Although these rather sophisticated publications were probably aimed more at countering Italian influences at Mary's court, the *Rudimenta* of John Vaus, as reprinted in 1566, met the needs of the market more directly. In January 1567 Lepreuik was granted the privilege of reprinting Donatus for boys (Vaus), Pellisson's *Rudimenta*, and the as yet inexistent grammar to be 'callit the generall grammer to be usit within sculls of this realme'.[7] It was at this point that Hepburn brought out his *Grammaticae artis prima rudimenta*.

But it failed to catch on, and in December 1575, Hepburn now being bishop of Ross, the Regent Morton convened a conference of 'certane of the maist leirit Scolemaisteris', including the royal tutors George Buchanan and Peter Young, along with William Roberton (Edinburgh), his erstwhile rival Thomas Buchanan (Stirling), Andrew Simson (Dunbar), James Carmichael (Haddington), Patrick Sharp (Glasgow) and Patrick Auchinleck (St Andrews). The hope was that 'thar be onelie ane forme of grammar teachit in all the grammar scuillis'.[8] Almost twenty years later, an Act recalling their deliberations, and seeking to implement their recommendations, was finally passed in Privy Council in December 1593, which noted that 'maisteris of scoillis and pedagogis have, thir mony yeiris bigane, chosin to thameselffis' the books recommended to them by the printers or booksellers (who might have stocks to dispose of), or such as they had learnt from themselves or were used to. The result was that the texts utilised were not the best, but those that came most easily to hand, so that children moving from one school to another were 'chargeit to forget nor repeit that quhilk they have leirnit [to the] grite hindering of their procedingis, and confounding of their memoreis and ingynes', being compelled 'newlings to begyn that arte'. The 1575 conference of schoolmasters, the Privy Council recalled in 1593, had declared that no current textbook met pupils' needs, and a new grammar to be taught by public and private teachers was needed. The masters had 'devydit that arte in severall portionis amangis thamesalffis', but, as the Privy Council noted, the negligence and oversight 'quhilk oftymes fallis upoun commoun caussis and werkis' meant that the scheme had never been followed through to completion, although parts of it were in circu-

6   W. Beattie & J. Durkan, 'An early publication of Latin poems of George Buchanan in Scotland from the press of Lepreuik', *Bibliotheck*, xi (1983), 77–80.
7   Dickson & Edmond, *Annals*, 202, 224–5.
8   *RPC*, ii, 478.

lation.[9] And indeed, books by Simson, Carmichael and Buchanan himself had emerged from the conference convened in 1575. Buchanan's *Prosodia* was printed only in 1595, but like Andrew Simson's *Rudimenta* (based like Pellison on Despauterius), it had a long life ahead.

IV.2 Andrew Simson of Dunbar and texts used in teaching

There are a few printers' inventories in existence which may point to what schoolbooks were available in Scotland in the late sixteenth century, when Despauterius was quite clearly the leading Scottish grammar book. It is reassuring to see how the Aberdeen tradition in grammar begun by Vaus was to be developed by Andrew Simson, who had been an Aberdeen student just prior to 1537. He appears in a class list[10] scribbled in the King's College copy of John Vaus's edition (Paris, 1522) of Alexandre de Villedieu's Latin grammar. The names are: 'Jacobus gray, Vilelmus pendrech, Jo. haleburton, Alexr. haleburton, Tho. haburne, Simo steil norvigensis, Gavinus dunbar, Andreas symsoun.' Of these students, Gavin Dunbar is found subsequently at St Andrews in 1537, with the two Haliburtons and Thomas Hepburn there two years later.[11] Simson himself is next found in 1550, as we have seen, as schoolmaster in Perth. He was minister of Dunning about 1562, and later at Dunbar from 1564 to c.1580 or 1582, and he may have acted as schoolmaster there during the whole of that period, though documentary proof is only available for 1575. From 1582 till his death about 1590 he was at Dalkeith, where he is not known to have kept school; but while at Perth he seems to have taught James Lawson (later subprincipal at King's College) and the proverb-collecting grammarian James Carmichael; and at Dunbar, Simson taught both the long-lived grammarian Alexander Hume and David Hume of Godscroft.[12] This last relates how, at the school in Dunbar, even a talented latinist might find the yoke of the Muses of grammar and rhetoric a bit hard to endure under Simson.[13] But Hume also informs us that Simson's generally intimidating expression softened when he found his young scholar shared his enthusiasm for Latin versifying, and, for the time being, the ever-

[9]   Ibid., v, 110–12.
[10] Sig. mviii, copy in Aberdeen University Library.
[11] Anderson (ed.), *Early Records*, 239, 242. Hepburn is listed as in Lothian nation, the others, however, in Angus nation as one might expect.
[12] For James Lawson, see *Selections from Wodrow's Biographical Collections: Divines of the North-East of Scotland*, ed. R. Lippe (New Spalding Club, 1890), 193–4; for Carmichael, see *Wodrow Misc.*, 442; Carmichael recalls Simson's early enthusiasm for the Reformed cause, presumably while still schoolmaster at Perth.
[13] Durkan, 'Laying of fresh foundations', 136–7. The reference there to Vaus's grammar should read 1522, not 1511.

present tawse faded into oblivion.[14] Simson fathered seven sons, six of whom entered the ministry; Archibald, who succeeded his father at Dalkeith, was a Latin poet and prolific vernacular writer, while William, of Burntisland and Dunbarton, also a poet, wrote a Hebrew grammar published at London in 1617.[15] Of the 1580 and 1587 editions of Andrew Simson's *Rudimenta*, nothing now survives. His book, however, dominated Scottish schools till the early eighteenth century. The sole surviving copy of the *Second Rudiments* said to be by M(r) A(ndrew) S(imson) and dated 1607, does not conform to later editions of what are called the complete Simson *Rudiments,* in which Simson's *First Rudiments* are indeed his, but the Second have been consistently replaced by Andrew Duncan's *Studiorum Puerilium Clavis*, of which we will hear in due course.[16]

If Simson was born about 1526, he may have missed Vaus at King's College and studied rather under his successor, Theophilus Stewart.[17] Simson's classmate William Pendrech was, by 1544, a monk of the Abbey of Deer, which possessed the 1537 print of Johannes Despauterius.[18] It is likely that Despauterius was also beginning to be used at Aberdeen, judging from the written marginal comments in the Vaus *Rudimenta* of 1531.[19] Moreover, Despauterius was recommended in the epitome of Latin grammar published in Lyons in 1544 by the Aberdeen graduate Florence Wilson.[20] And the grammarian Alexander Hume of Dunbar tells us that as a pupil of Andrew Simson he had learnt the grammar of Despauterius.[21] A cursory examination of the *Short Title Catalogue of English Books published up to 1640* shows that all editions of Despauterius bar one are confined to Scotland. Copies could, however, be purchased from continental sources. Others have stressed the availability in Scotland of books published in England, overlooking the possibilities of continental importation; the grammars listed in Thomas Bassandyne's inventory after his death in 1577 were most probably imported directly from Antwerp through Christophe Plantin, or indirectly through agents like Thomas Vautrollier and Hercule François, Huguenots in

---

[14] C. Upton, 'The teaching of poetry in sixteenth century Scotland', in R.J. Lyall & F. Riddy (eds.), *Proceedings of the Third international Conference on Scottish Language and Literature, Medieval and Renaissance* (Stirling/Glasgow, 1981), 417.

[15] W.J. Couper, 'The Levitical family of Simson, 1: The founding of the house, 1529(?)'; '2: The family of Adam Simson, 1594–1771'; '3: Alexander, 1570(?)–1638, and his descendants', *RSCHS*, 4 (1932), 119–37, 208–66; '4: Families that failed', *RSCHS*, 5 (1935), 117–39.

[16] The opening phrase of Simson's 1607 edition is 'Secunda Rudimenta Constructionum. (Chartula). Lector habet totem syntaxeos artem'.

[17] Durkan & Ross, *Early Scottish Libraries*, 165. On Vaus, see *Bibliographia Aberdonensis*, ed. J.F.K. Johnstone et al. (Third Spalding Club, 1929), 1, 11.

[18] Durkan, 'Laying of fresh foundations', 136.

[19] Vaus, J., *Rudimenta* (Paris, 1531), sig. Lv and lvi verso.

[20] *Bibliographia Aberdonensis*, 1, 43.

[21] *Grammatica nova* (Edinburgh, 1612), dedicatory letter to Alexander Seton.

the English book market, who certainly had contacts with the Edinburgh bookseller Robert Gourlaw, of whom later.[22] The Bassandyne inventory of 1577 lists only four Linacre Latin grammars; this is probably his *Syntax*, as the price was eight shillings,[23] and in the Leipzig edition, as it was no longer being printed in England; but if it was the Latin *Rudiments* as translated by George Buchanan, these were older stock, the last issue being a French edition of 1559.[24]

The provincial council of Mechlin had laid down that an abridged form of the grammar of Despauterius should be the only one used in schools. This explains the initially discomfiting reference to 'ane Mauchline grammer, price xiiii s' in the Bassandyne inventory, i.e. not some textbook from rural Ayrshire, but the volume as printed in 1571 by Plantin. It had four books: Rudimenta, Etymology, Syntax, Prosody, but was an epitome; the rudiments occupied about 105 pages, the etymology about 160 (a simplified 'prima pars'), the syntax about 127, the versification or prosody about 63 pages.[25] Alongside his single copy of this, Bassandyne held twelve of Despauterius's *De figuris*, twenty of part three (prosody) and later 732 copies of the second part (syntax), with another 407 added to make 1,139 in all. There were also 620 copies of the rudiments and six of 'grammeris Sebastian', that is, of a compendium of Despauterius edited by Sebastian Novimola of Cologne and Duisburg, published by Plantin in 1568. There were several Cologne editions of this compendium of Novimola.[26] Another follower of Despauterius was Jean Pellisson, head of the college at Tournon, and Bassandyne held 74 copies of his Rudiments and eight of his grammars (the last, probably the Orleans edition of 1568), while 'ane Grammatica Cheperin' is likely to be a scribal error for a work discussed above, Alexander Hepburn's *Grammaticae artis prima rudimenta* (Antwerp, 1568). The time lag since publication in both cases would explain the relative fewness of the copies available for sale in 1577; however, Hepburn's *Rudiments* seem expensive at 18 pence compared with Pellisson at 3 pence.[27] Titles under which Despauterius was printed vary, but it might be worth noting that the 1579 Edinburgh publication by John Ross for Henry Charteris has the same wording as the 1573 Antwerp edition of G. van den Rade, who would print Buchanan's *History* for Alex-

---

22 C. Clair, 'Christopher Plantin's trade connexions with England and Scotland', *Library*, 5th series, xiv (1959), 32–4.

23 Dickson & Edmond, *Annals*, 294.

24 Durkan, *Bibliography of George Buchanan*, 29; Dickson & Edmond, *Annals*, 294.

25 Printed in separate sections 1571–1572 and reprinted 1573–1576, L. Voet, *The Plantin Press, 1555–1589* (Amsterdam, 1980–1983), ii, 1074–8.

26 Dickson & Edmond, *Annals*, 295, 296, 300, 301, 303.

27 Voet, *Plantin*, iv, 1756. Dickson & Edmond, *Annals*, 300; for Hepburn, see Durkan, 'Laying of fresh foundations', 134, 136, and Voet, *Plantin*, iii, 1309.

ander Arbuthnott in 1583.[28] Interestingly, the 1579 edition has the Scots equivalents of some Latin words added to it. Along with this work the Edinburgh publishers issued Johann Spangenberg's treatise on letter-writing.[29] The seven books of Despauterius included some attention to rhetoric and matched the seven years that grammar bursars were given to master the whole subject.[30]

As for the bookseller John Ross, who died in 1580, we can assume that the grammars in his inventory are the Despauterius from his own press. They include 460 Rudiments at 3 pence each, 800 unbound First Parts, 700 Second Parts unbound, and finally 400 Third and Fourth Parts, unbound, of Duisburg (i.e. Novimola).[31] The bulk of this printing must have been taken over by Henry Charteris; on his death in 1599 he still had 384 First Parts, 623 Second Parts and 350 Third Parts. But he also had 3,072 'Dunbar' *Rudiments*, at 2 shillings apiece, as Andrew Simson's grammar was popularly known. This 1580 printing by John Ross was apparently reprinted by Charteris in 1587, though again no copy is extant.[32]

The first edition of Andrew Simson's Dunbar *Rudiments* has been tracked down to Antwerp.[33] At the end of July 1580 Plantin was about to ship in a barrel to Scotland 2,000 *Rudimenta Scotica* destined for Charteris in Edinburgh. Each copy had six leaves, in total making twenty-four reams of paper at 4 Dutch florins a ream. Two hundred copies were, on instructions from Charteris, also shipped for sale at Frankfurt.[34] The *Rudiments* thus appeared when Simson was considering leaving Dunbar for Dalkeith, where we find him in 1582. The date and place of printing of the *Second Rudiments* by Simson are not known, but one copy at 4 pence appears in the will of Robert Gourlaw, who died during the plague of 1585.[35] In 1599, Robert Smyth had a royal licence to print the Dunbar *Second Rudiments*, alongside the four parts of Sebastian (i.e. Novimola, as editor of Despauterius).[36] In 1599 again, Charteris held 3,092 Dunbar *Rudiments* costing 2 shillings which seems excessive, unless both parts were bound together.[37] Presumably Smyth printed Simson's *Second Rudiments*, because he had 538 copies at his death

[28] *Grammaticae institutionis libri septem*, edited by Sebastian, see Durkan, *Bibliography of George Buchanan*, 219.
[29] *De conficiendis epistolis liber* (Ross for Charteris).
[30] *BUK*, i, 229.
[31] Dickson & Edmond, *Annals*, 330–1.
[32] Ibid., 519–20.
[33] Clair, 'Plantin's trade connexions', 44.
[34] Voet, *Plantin*, v, 2157.
[35] *Bannatyne Misc.*, ii, 215.
[36] Dickson & Edmond, *Annals*, 480.
[37] Ibid., 353.

in 1603. Once sold, they must have been well used, for not a single copy is now extant.[38]

It is not easy to extrapolate the number of schools (and still less of scholars) from figures such as these. Obviously it is inevitable that each schoolmaster would require his own personal copy, but one copy might serve several family members or even be shared at school within a class group. An introductory book such as the *Rudiments* would be used by a larger number of scholars than would more advanced textbooks: in Smyth's inventory the First Parts of Latin grammar (presumably Despauterius) ran to 2,860 copies, the Second Parts to 1,820 copies, the Third with Fourth Parts to 840 copies.[39] This suggests that some grammar scholars were failing to finish the full course. John Row, the minister, mentions three hundred and more schoolboys of Simson's in Perth about 1556 hissing a friar in church, but later we hear of a 'penurie' of scholars under him at Dunbar. He also offers a valuable tool for identifying Simson's *Rudiments*: the opening words were 'Quum literarum consideratio'.[40] Simson's First and Second *Rudiments* were in use in the first class in Edinburgh in 1598, and are presumably identical with the 'common rudiments' professed in all other schools and taught by Alexander Yule at Stirling in 1602. By this time Pellisson had temporarily replaced Novimola as an interpreter of Despauterius in both towns.[41] At her death in 1603, the wife of Robert Charteris, son of Henry, held 150 *Rudiments* (presumably Simson), had run out of First Parts, but had 500 Second Parts and 500 Third (with Fourth) Parts, these being of Despauterius either in the Pellisson or Novimola editions. Subsequent inventories are less useful for our purposes, being in general form under headings like Divinity or Humanity and thus not presenting specific titles as earlier, but in 1642 one printer held 4,000 First Parts, 2,000 Third and Fourth of Despauterius.[42]

The policy of creeping anglicisation adopted by post-Reformation Scottish printers, possibly more with an eye on the English market than any conscious intention of eliminating the Scots tongue, has obscured the fact that these same printers purchased from and were dependent on continental firms like Plantin, even when using English agencies. We have seen that the *Rudiments* of Andrew Simson and Alexander Hepburn were both Plantin productions. Robert Gourlaw in 1585 held many English books, yet almost all were single copies and the preponderant subject matter divinity, making one wonder whether their readership was not largely confined to minis-

---

38 Ibid., 483.
39 Ibid., 483.
40 J. Row, *The History of the Kirk of Scotland*, ed. D. Laing (Wodrow Society, 1842), 8, 9, 422.
41 *Edinburgh Burgh Recs.*, v, 225; *Stirling Recs.*, i, 102.
42 *Bannatyne Misc.*, ii, 257. There were only 2,000 *Rudiments*.

ters.[43] In his fairly detailed study, F.S. Ferguson assumed too easily that book-sellers' stocks of classical texts, as opposed to English translations, stemmed from English presses.[44] In the decade after 1580, we find John Davidson, James Bell, John Angus, Robert Smyth, John Small of Edinburgh, Henry Charteris and James Robertson constantly referred to as clients of Plantin. Among the 1583 purchases of Robert Smyth in Antwerp we find six copies of the *Dialectic* of Petrus Ramus, another six of his *Rhetoric*, alongside works of Virgil, Terence, Cicero, Horace, Ovid and Homer, as well as George Buchanan's *Psalm Paraphrases*.[45] Moreover, though we have no information on this, it is fairly certain that our booksellers also bought supplies on the French book-market. Another field of enquiry is opened up by entries in 1579 like 'Dialoge Massalani', that is, Petrus Mosellanus, *Paedologia: Dialogi* or 'thrie Brandelinus de conscribendis epistolis', that is, Aurelio Lippi Bran-doline, *De ratione scribendi*, which in some editions also contained Vives and Erasmus, and in others, *De conscribendis epistolis*: hence the verbal formulation of the inventory entry.[46]

Works like Andrew Simson's *Rudiments* were of course designed for grammar schools. It is less easy to envisage the schoolbooks used in reading and vernacular schools, apart from the simple, question-and-answer Donatus and the likely use of books of moral advice or proverbs like 'Cato, Inglis'. It is tempting to think of David Lindsay, John Rolland or Robert Henryson as possible reading texts. Eight ABC boards at 10 pence each may have sold to pupils in such schools.[47] Current grammar school programmes, however, would appear to have been adequately served by Scottish booksellers. In 1598, the high school in Edinburgh had four classes in the charge of a principal 'regent' (a term used because it was considered a college of arts) and three more 'regents'. There was ample provision for the first class in the number of Dunbar *Rudiments* on sale. In 1599 Robert Smyth had licence to reprint the *Second Rudiments* of Simson, as used in the Edinburgh high school.[48] The demand for the Protestant Mathurin Cordier's *Colloquia* rose from the seventeen in Gourlaw's inventory (1585) to over a thousand in that of Robert Smyth (1602).[49]

Used by the first two regents in Edinburgh on Sundays, the Heidel-berg Latin catechism of the Palatinate by Jeremias Bastingius was printed

[43]   M.A. Bald, 'The anglicisation of Scottish printing', *SHR*, xxiii (1926), 107–15; Gourlaw's inventory is in *Bannatyne Misc.*, ii, 209–15.
[44]   F.S. Ferguson, 'Relations between London and Edinburgh printers and stationers', *Library*, viii (1927), 145–98.
[45]   Clair, 'Plantin's trade connexions', 43–5.
[46]   Dickson & Edmond, *Annals*, 296, 302.
[47]   *Bannatyne Misc.*, ii, 214.
[48]   *Edinburgh Burgh Recs.*, v, 224–6.
[49]   *Bannatyne Misc.*, ii, 212, 214; Dickson & Edmond, *Annals*, 483.

in tandem with the vernacular version by Robert Waldegrave in 1591.[50] It is often referred to as the double catechism, and this too Smyth had a royal licence to reprint in 1599, though as far back as 1568 Robert Lepreuik had been licensed to print the psalms 'with the inglis and latine catechismes les and mair'.[51] In 1599, when Henry Charteris died, he held 557 catechisms in large type and 502 in small. This was obviously not the same printing as the 416 double catechisms from Waldegrave's press present in this very inventory. Of these Smyth issues, none has survived. At the Edinburgh high school, again, three parts of the Pellisson adaptation of Despauterius were preferred to the grammar of Ramus in years two to four. We find Pellisson along with Donatus, as far back as Lepreuik's printer's licence of 1568, like the proposed 'generall grammer' to be agreed for the whole realm, already discussed.[52] At Stirling in 1602, the pupils of Alexander Yule had the problematical pairing of Pellisson with the Syntax of Ramus. Yule even allowed those already grounded in Ramus to continue using him, which must have led to confusion, especially as Yule seems to have hoped to complete a full grammar course with the help only of a single doctor.[53]

Turning now to what these various rudiments were preparing the pupils for, the second year at Edinburgh provided for letter-writing with Cicero's *Familiar Epistles*, a thrice weekly translation exercise and Ovid's *Tristia*. Pellisson's syntax was supplemented by Erasmus in third year, and it was not till then that the plays of Terence were introduced along with Ovid's *Metamorphoses*. Buchanan's *Psalms* were for Sunday reading in the two final years, and the same author's *Prosodia*, recently published, eked out Pellisson on versification. Talon's *Rhetorica* and a section of Linacre's *De emendata structura* on 'figures of construction' were to be tested out in Virgil and in Ovid's *Epistolae*, in company with the prose writers Sallust, Caesar and Florus, all of them historians. As yet, Greek was postponed till university entry, with authors unspecified, but there was much declamation based on Cicero, with the bairns memorising a whole oration for public performance. For verse there was Juvenal and Horace (whose verse-forms would be familiar from Buchanan's *Psalms*) and the plays of Plautus to supplement those of Terence, which had formed a staple of the school curriculum since the early Middle Ages. We shall see that it is unlikely that, at Edinburgh, Alexander Hume enjoyed teaching a course in which Ramus did not figure at all, except

---

50   *Edinburgh Burgh Recs.*, v, 225; Dickson & Edmond, *Annals*, 416.
51   *Edinburgh Burgh Recs.*, 480; Dickson & Edmond, *Annals*, 202.
52   *Edinburgh Burgh Recs.*, 353; Dickson & Edmond, *Annals*, 202. Donatus was 'for boys', for reading schools or song schools, not a high school text.
53   *Stirling Recs.*, i, 102. What reading matter they had at Stirling is not made explicit. Yule had a rival master in Stirling, the pedagogue to Forrester, laird of Garden, Alexander Grieve (Greif), who offended Yule by taking in other pupils as well.

through his disciple in rhetoric Omer Talon, whom the university's humanity teacher avoided in favour of the more traditional rhetoric of Cassander, as used by James Melville in St Andrews three decades earlier. Neither Plautus nor Juvenal, oddly, figure on extant booksellers' inventories.[54]

We have a useful point of comparison with the 1614 Edinburgh school curriculum, in the shape of Glasgow high school's teaching programme for a five-year high school. The Glasgow and Edinburgh courses are remarkably similar, especially in the dependence on Despauterius throughout. The first year at Edinburgh relied on Simson, as Glasgow doubtless did too, with the memorisation of ancient saws in Cato and the *Dicta Sapientium* at Edinburgh and similar practice on proverbs and ancient saws at Glasgow. The dialogues of Cordier and Erasmus[55] are common to both, with Glasgow also adding Castellio (an author forced to leave Protestant Geneva for differently Protestant Basle). The common letter-writing model was Cicero, and Terence's plays were postponed in both till third year. Ovid's verse epistles *De Ponto* and his *Tristia* (published in Edinburgh in 1612) were common to both towns; Buchanan's psalms were introduced in Edinburgh a year earlier than Glasgow. The fourth class in both towns was devoted to Latin verse, with practice in versifying (elegiac, lyric and heroic) if pupils had the gift for it. In both, fourth year moved on to Ovid's *Metamorphoses*, and to Virgil, with Horace and Buchanan's Horatian psalms at Glasgow and an introduction to history (Quintus Curtius, Caesar and possibly Suetonius) at Edinburgh. The fifth year at both was devoted to speech-making, with much attention to Cicero again (at Glasgow his *Pro Archia*), and with Glasgow alone specifying the use of Talon (a Ramist text) as well as of Cassander on the side of theory. Glasgow had no more drama, where Edinburgh had Plautus, but Glasgow was then able to accommodate the historians (Caesar and Sallust, the latter also in use at Edinburgh). The stylistic models in both towns appear to be Cicero, Caesar and Terence, with Edinburgh alone venturing to read Juvenal and Persius. The course at Edinburgh ended with the verse-texts of Hesiod and Theognis as an introduction to Greek, strangely omitted at Glasgow.[56] The almost contemporary university course at Glasgow, it must be said, does not postulate any previous Greek grammar at school.[57]

Grant's proposed dating in *Burgh Schools and Schoolmasters* of the Glasgow course document as c.1573 is impossible. The university records, first

[54] *Edinburgh Burgh Recs.*, v, 224–6.

[55] Erasmus's *Colloquia* figure in Bassandyne's inventory of 1579 (615 copies), Dickson & Edmond, *Annals*, 294.

[56] *Edinburgh Burgh Recs.*, vi, 121; J. Grant, *History of the Burgh and Parish Schools of Scotland* (London, 1876), 340 (he misreads Talon as Tully); *MAUG*, ii, 307–9.

[57] Ibid., ii, 45; at Edinburgh too in 1628, the first year at university introduced Greek, A. Morgan (ed.) with introductions by R.K. Hannay, *University of Edinburgh: Charters, Statutes and Acts of the Town Council and the Senatus 1583–1858* (Edinburgh, 1937), 110–12.

mentioning it in 1643, do indeed state that the course was formerly agreed (*prius firmata*) by university and town, and 'formerly' here must certainly mean some time before 1643, but it is plainly at some date after the publication of Buchanan's *Prosodia* (c.1595), to which the course makes reference. The Glasgow course would also imply the existence of a doctor or teaching assistant, and the earliest given in our Glasgow lists is the notary John Allanson (1576). The next mention of a doctor is John Buchan in 1600, when the school was undergoing a physical overhaul and perhaps a curricular one too.[58] Motives for change spurring Glasgow into looking for state patronage around 1600 could well be a desire to exploit the opportunities for expansion offered by educational troubles in rival Edinburgh, where James VI was anxious to implement Bishop Reid's plan for a school of law. With the help of the law lords, James made two successive appointments resisted by the town and the body of advocates, namely Adrian Damman (the Dutch ambassador, translator into Latin of *La Sepwaine*, by the king's favourite poet, Du Bartas), and then Adam Newton. When the scheme collapsed in 1597, John Ray, banned from teaching in the town in May 1597 but having graduated in the meantime, took over the appointment – but as a professor of humanity, not of law.[59]

In Glasgow, it is quite unlikely that a five years' course of the quality desired could have been achieved without the hiring of extra doctors, as a single master could not have been expected to teach five such courses concurrently. The curriculum may as yet have been little more than a programme, and is more probably assignable to the post 1600 period when Glasgow was revising its university requirements as well.[60] The idea was floated that in many ways Glasgow was a good place (if not a better place than Edinburgh where the king had tried to overrule the university by appointing law lecturers) to restart law teaching. Such a restart would, as Bishop Reid had foreseen, call for a revival of oratory: hence the town's grammar programme must be contemporaneous with the university's law scheme. The latter foundered; the former, involving five classes, also involved more than one schoolmaster, even one aided by a single doctor, as regularly available after 1600.

---

[58] For these repairs, *Glasgow Recs.*, i, 216–17, and debate on curriculum, Durkan & Kirk, *University of Glasgow*, 429; *MAUG*, ii, 307–9 (Grant, in *Burgh and Parish Schools*, was unaware of this).

[59] Morgan (ed.) with Hannay, *University of Edinburgh Charters*, 99–100; *Edinburgh Burgh Recs.*, v, 95, 137, 188, 207; W.C. Dickinson, 'The advocates' protest against the institution of a Chair of Law in the University of Edinburgh', *SHR*, xxiii (1926), 205, 212; Laing, *Catalogue of Graduates*, 14.

[60] Grant, *Burgh and Parish Schools*, 336–8.

IV.3 John Ray of Edinburgh

John Ray was an Angus man, born in 1567. He was 'well stept in age' when he was appointed, as a recent Edinburgh graduate, to the post of humanity professor at Edinburgh in 1597; he had previously had a number of private pupils including the son of the town clerk, Alexander Guthrie. Ray was 'well seen' in humanity; in the university he defended the dignity of his humanity post against his peers, the regents in philosophy, though his previous experience fitted him better for the high school post which he duly took over on Alexander Hume's demission in 1606.[61] Ray wished to uphold established tradition in Scottish schooling, and would be resolute in his oppositon to his predecessor's ideas: he had no intention of allowing Hume's *Grammatica nova* of 1612 to inaugurate a new age of Ramus-inspired grammar in the schools. The Edinburgh programme of 1614 would lay down that Simson's Dunbar Rudiments alone were to be taught as 'maist approved and ressavit in the cuntrie', the first and second parts being introductions to Despauterius's own first and second; indeed Despauterius would have been at the heart of all grammar teaching till fourth year.

Like several other schoolmasters, John Ray did try his hand at original Latin verse, but the extant remains, both printed and manuscript, are scanty. He appears to have preferred to concentrate on editorial work, his most famous work being his 1615 edition of Buchanan's *Opera Omnia*. He is also found sponsoring many standard school editions. This is not the place to discuss Scottish Latin verse although, in schools, the works of Buchanan were not the only native models to be set alongside classical writings as models of good diction; we might cite Alexander Yule (Julius) at Stirling, who concentrated on slim volumes, some dealing with Old Testament prophets, others for social occasions like weddings. Yule could show his pupils how to cultivate powerful patrons, from the king down.[62]

As we saw, exercises putting theory into practice at Edinburgh would utilise the memorable pointed sayings of ancient wisdom in the *Dicta sapientium* and Cato's *Distichs*. There is every likelihood that it was Ray who got the Edinburgh printer Andrew Hart to reissue these texts, although his initials do not appear in Hart's 1620 reprint of the John Ross publication of Erasmus's version of the *Dicta* (whose printing William Niddrie had already proposed in 1559).[63] Hart's publication of Cato's *Disticha de Moribus* (1620),

---

[61] T. Craufurd, *History of the University of Edinburgh* (Edinburgh, 1808), 41.

[62] Yule's verses, sacred and secular, are reprinted in his *Poemata sacra* (Edinburgh, 1614). He also wrote an early poem on the Gunpowder Plot in 1606, and made a school edition of Buchanan's Psalms published at London in 1620; see http://www.philological.bham.ac.uk/yule/ and http://www.philological.bham.ac.uk/ecphrasis/

[63] Durkan, 'Laying of fresh foundations', 133.

in Joseph Scaliger's version, does bear Ray's initials. A third Hart publication, Sulpizio's *De moribus et civilitate puerorum carmen* (1619), had lengthy Scottish antecedents. As long ago as 1503, an Edinburgh man, David Lowis, had been involved in the publication, in Paris, of the grammar of Giovanni Sulpizio.[64] In 1523 one of John Vaus's former students, Robert Gray, advised him as a friend to abandon the outdated Villedieu grammar and turn to Sulpizio, among other grammars more modern.[65] Although John Ray's initials are again absent from Andrew Hart's 1619 publication of Sulpizio, the school-master seems likely to have been the sponsor.

The selection of the letters of Cicero published under Ray's supervision in 1618 was originally compiled by the Strasbourg Reformer Johann Sturm, and Ray fittingly dedicated it to two Edinburgh ministers. Ray was also likely to have been behind the reprinting of Mathurin Cordier's *Colloquies*, with his preface dated at Geneva.[66] The Edinburgh programme of 1614, master-minded by Ray, follows closely the John Ross publications of 1579 and 1580, which might have been those recommended by the schoolmasters' conference on uniformity in grammar convened in 1575: two items have dropped out, the anonymous 'Concordances' and the Spangenberg book referred to earlier.[67] Judging from the 1618 edition of Simson, Ray also had replaced the so-called *Second Rudiments* of Simson with the *Studiorum Puerilium Clavis* (1597) of Andrew Duncan, discussed below. (The 1618 and 1633 editions of Simson claimed to be more perfect than any previous ones, but this claim does not seem to be justified.) Ray also produced the first complete edition of all the poems sacred and secular of Buchanan, claiming to be working from manuscript.[68] It was published by Andrew Hart at Edinburgh in 1615. In that same year, we find evidence that Ray was involved in the early stages of Sir John Scot of Scotstarvit's project to bring out an anthology of Scottish poetry, the *Delitiae Poetarum Scotorum*. In April 1615, Scotstarvet[69] wrote to the bibliophile Sir David Lindsay of Balcarres that 'at the desire of Sir William Alexander of Menstrie, and mine, Mr John Rea, our auld maister, has undertaken the collecting and setting togidder of our Scottish poets, in the imitation of the French and Italians, whereof we have gadderit a good number already'.[70] Ray's involvement seems to have been

---

64 J. Durkan, 'David Lauxius', *Edinburgh Bibliographical Society Transactions*, iii (1952), 78–80.

65 In a letter in the 1523 edition by Vaus of Villedieu, February 1522, old style, thus 1523, misprinted as 1543 in Durkan 'Laying of fresh foundations', 132.

66 *Colloquiorum scholasticorum libri quatuor*, 1618.

67 *Breve compendium de concordentiis grammaticalibus* (Edinburgh, 1580).

68 McFarlane, *Buchanan*, 307, 367.

69 In December 1612, he had been a witness to the baptism of Ray's son John. See W. Steven, *History of the High School of Edinburgh* (Edinburgh, 1849), 53.

70 See A.W.C.L. Crawford, *Lives of the Lindsays* (3 vols., London, 1849), ii, 5. Crawford calls Ray 'minister', clearly having misread the abbreviated word 'maister'.

shortlived and the *Delitiae* would in fact appear only in 1637, long after Ray's death in 1630. He must have been an inspiring teacher of generations of Edinburgh schoolboys, to judge from the fulsome epitaph written by his former university student William Drummond of Hawthornden: 'Bright RAY of learning which so cleare didst streame, / Fare well Soule which so many soules did frame.'[71]

IV.4 Hercules Rollock of Edinburgh

Hercules Rollock, Ray's predecessor but one at Edinburgh, was perhaps the finest scholar-poet to work as a schoolmaster in our period.[72] Of Scottish towns, Edinburgh had the greatest drawing power for the upwardly mobile young and their ambitious parents and the town council's wish was to respond to their demands. As we saw earlier, the council failed to dislodge the Catholic incumbent William Roberton at the Reformation, but when he finally resigned, Hercules Rollock was appointed in May 1580 as principal master, his duties being to teach the youth piety, good manners, doctrine and letters – the order is surely interesting.[73] It was a life appointment (dated in May 1584) terminable only for good reasons or fault on the master's part, with £50 yearly payable at Candlemas in February and Lammas in August. All the scholars had to pay each 40 pence quarterly at Candlemas, Beltane (May), Lammas and All Saints (November); to their doctor half that sum; and to the 'rotator' or janitor 4 pence. These charges applied to Edinburgh children (if able to pay), but those outside the town were to pay whatever Rollock could discreetly exact. The council also promised to exclude anybody else, except his under-doctors, from teaching a grammar or Latin school in the town, but Rollock was personally responsible for minor repairs to the school building. One seemingly innocuous stipulation in his contract was to have unforeseeable consequences for this distinguished scholar, namely that his employment depended upon his keeping good order in the school.[74]

Rollock had come from Dundee and, as we have seen, made his first appearance with Latin liminary verses to the 1568 *Grammar* of the then master there, Alexander Hepburn, a work prefaced by George Buchanan himself.[75] Rollock, law student at Poitiers in 1576 and seemingly at St Maixent two years later, was known not only for his Latin scholarship (to which the still unprinted lists of books surviving from his library testify),

[71] L.E. Kastner (ed.), *The Poetical Works of William Drummond of Hawthornden* (2 vols., STS, 1913), ii, 249.

[72] See *Delitiae Poetorum Scotorum* (1637), ii.

[73] Steven, *High School of Edinburgh*, 44–6.

[74] Steven, *High School of Edinburgh*, appendix, 44–6.

[75] Durkan, 'Laying of fresh foundations', 134.

but also as a more than competent writer of Latin verse.[76] More detailed treatment of Rollock's life and work has to be reserved to another place, but his friendship with Buchanan no doubt helped his advancement; we find his name was mentioned alongside Buchanan's in connection with translation from the Spanish.[77] He is also mentioned in a letter of 1579 from Daniel Rogers to Buchanan and again when Buchanan recommended him to King James in connection with a judicial post.[78] However, although initially recommended for the Edinburgh job by Andrew Melville's friend James Lawson and by the Edinburgh ministry, Rollock somehow incurred the disfavour of the Melville party.[79] The town council's appreciation of their schoolmaster, however, is shown by their promising to add the value of Roberton's retirement pension to his salary, and they drew heavily on Rollock's literary gifts for the ceremonial surrounding James's Danish marriage with Queen Anna in 1590, when the town laid on a splendid 'Joyous Entry' for the new queen.[80] Indeed, the presence of a Danish pupil boarded with Rollock, about 1591, demonstrates that his school enjoyed a national and even international reputation.

But on 13 September 1595, disaster struck. Some of Rollock's more unruly pupils, vexed by the cancellation of school holidays, barricaded themselves in the school. They stood siege till 15 September, when a bailie was sent to force an entry – and in the mêlée, was shot dead. The pupils involved, 'being all, for the maist parte, the sonis of baronis and gentilmen', included one from Spinningdale, near Dornoch, one from Whitebank, Selkirk, one attached to the laird of Cessford (Morebattle parish), one from Chesters (Ancrum parish) and another from Kinhilt, Wigtownshire.[81] The incident destroyed Rollock's credit with the town authorities and made it inevitable that he would be replaced, but Rollock had also annoyed the council by sidestepping them and secretly acquiring a gift of the grammar school from the (titular) abbot of Holyrood.[82] He was dead by February 1600, when we find the council generously making provision for his widow and bairns.[83]

---

[76] T.C. Smout, *Scotland and Europe* (Edinburgh, 1986), 40–1.

[77] Ibid., 212.

[78] McFarlane, *Buchanan*, 471.

[79] Steven, *High School of Edinburgh*, 26.

[80] Ibid., 26. The most detailed account of the Entry, including translations of the Latin texts composed by Rollock, is Danish, available in English in D. Stevenson, *Scotland's Last Royal Wedding* (Edinburgh, 1997).

[81] *RPC*, v, 236–8. Another from 'Kirktoun of the Tour' is unidentified, unless it is the Tour near Kilmarnock.

[82] Steven, *High School of Edinburgh*, 27.

[83] Ibid., appendix, 27.

IV.5 Alexander Hume of Dunbar and the grammar monopoly

Alexander Hume was a notable choice as Rollock's successor on 3 May 1596.[84] Born in 1550, presumably in Dunbar, he was fortunate, when he reached grammar school age, to have as his teacher the grammarian Andrew Simson, author of the Dunbar *Rudiments*. In 1633, the 82-year-old Hume would write his own epitaph: 'Lancinaui vitam Barodunum semina, flores Sanandris [sic], fruges Oxoniumque dedi. Contempsi vanes vulgi spes, remque traducaui [sic], excolui ingenuis artibus ingeniatus, ad rectum methodum rectaque exempla vocaui grammaticum, logicum rhetoricarumque chaos.' That is, 'I squandered my life, produced the seeds at Dunbar, the flowers at St Andrews and the fruits at Oxford. I have scorned the vain hopes of the vulgar, and showed up the reality, with my natural gifts I have cultivated the liberal arts and called to order grammatical, logical and rhetorical chaos with the right method and right examples.'[85] At the end of a very long career, Hume still had no doubt that his crusade for the reform of these basic subjects of the Renaissance curriculum was the right one, but, he commented sadly, he had encountered nothing but envious opposition to all his efforts.

Under Simson, Hume learnt his Despauterius,[86] the grammar text he would spend so much of his adult life combatting. From Dunbar he went up to St Andrews, where his teacher was the interesting figure John Hamilton, regent in St Mary's College, who converted to Catholicism and fled abroad c.1575.[87] Hume's studies in St Mary's finished either in 1571/2 or 1575/6.[88] As a master of arts of St Andrews, Hume was incorporated in Oxford University in January 1581; a copy of his work presented to Dr Rainolds, now in the Bodleian Library, has four Latin lines addressed to the earl of Essex.[89] He tells us he spent two years at Oxford tutoring a noble youth, and we next find him in the *Accounts of the Chamberlain of Bath* as schoolmaster in the town. The entries cover 1589 to Michaelmas term 1592[90] (though the scribe there had difficulty with his name: Hunie, even Hunies, presumably from 'Humius'). On 28 February 1590, Hume was present at Chippenham when a minister preached a sermon on Christ's descent into hell. Hume

---

84 *Edinburgh Burgh Recs.*, 157.
85 GUL, MS General, 362, fo. 114, '83 annos et quinque menses natus anno 1633: finivit mense aug.', thus born in March. Much of the epitaph is in a faded hand (fo. 1), 'lancinaui' has an alternative reading, almost invisible.
86 Dedication of his *Grammatica nova* (Edinburgh, 1612), written in 1608.
87 He last appears in *Acta Facultatis*, ii, 443, in Nov. 1574, but was present on 17 Jan. 1575 and again on 2 Apr. when Alexander Hamilton was promoted from Orator to Bachelor in St Mary's, St Andrews University Archives, SM.B. 15.10 and SM.B. 16.1.
88 *Acta Facultatis*, ii, 438, 460.
89 A. Wood, *Athenae Oxonienses* (London, 1813–1815), i, col. 624; ibid., ii, col. 217.
90 *The Accounts of the Chamberlains of the City of Bath, 1568–1602*, ed. F.D. Wardle (Somerset Record Society, 1923), 109, 110, 117, 121.

replied in May, though the arrival of his response was delayed as he had to go home, he tells us, to meet his 'natural friends'. The minister Adam Hill, from Westbury in Wiltshire, replied in due course, in *The Defence of the Article: Christ descended into Hell* (London, 1592), and Hume's rejoinder to Hill appeared in Edinburgh in 1594,[91] having passed the censorship of the Edinburgh and Prestonpans ministers Robert Rollock and John Davidson on 12 February that year.[92] Hume displays some acquaintance with Greek and Hebrew and considerable theological learning, irrelevant to present considerations, in both this and a later work (dedicated to the provost and bailies of Edinburgh).[93] A further dedication to John Hamilton refers to him as Hume's former master, 'who hath a hearte at one time capable of contrarie persuasions of your saluation', that is, before his conversion to Catholicism.

While tutoring his noble adolescent in Oxford, Hume had been using Sulpizio, Melanchthon, Aldo Manuzio, Valla and above all Linacre. The compulsory use of William Lily's textbook at Bath gave him further reason to explore grammar theory: Lily's work had long secured a monopoly in England. Yet on his appointment to Edinburgh, as he tells us in the Address to the Reader in his *Grammatica nova* of 1612, Hume 'found that popular opinion and local custom forced him back on his old textbook, Despauterius, wherein he now found the versified grammar obscure, barbarous and void of method'. There remained Petrus Ramus, whose method had penetrated many schools in the realm but, as Hume carefully turned over the pages of his grammar, he still found no rest for his enquiring mind. Ramus seemed to him to have worked out not so much a grammar as a logic. Nevertheless, with him as model, Hume began to change some things, not neglecting authority in Varro, Quintilian, Priscian, Valla, Linacre and others. The way to a satisfactory method was still far from clear, but with experience he grew bolder and changed many things, either by addition or omission, at last showing his finished work to Andrew Melville and other friends. Where some praised, some did not condemn, while some disliked so much novelty. 'Da. Baik' (a misprint for David Black, the minister) advised him to complete what he had begun, lest another using his starting point should claim the honour due to Hume; he should not fear novelty; others make changes, so, if he can shed some light and still cover all that has to be covered, he is quite as authorised to change things as any other; the terminology of the art of grammar was quite different before Priscian, who himself was not followed in everything by later writers. On the strength of such advice,

---

[91] *A rejoynder to Doctor Hil concerning the descente of Christ into hell* (Edinburgh, 1594).
[92] NAS, CH2/121/2, ii, 30.
[93] *A diduction of the true and Catholik meaning of our Saviour his wordes, This is my bodie* (Edinburgh, 1602), dedication.

Hume says, he began to make greater changes.[94] However, we might observe that having friends like David Black and Andrew Melville would not have commended Hume to many of those in authority!

As principal master of Edinburgh he must have found his colleagues (four 'regents') less than enthusiastic for his new thinking. The old arrangement in the high school suited him better, with a single doctor of his own choice capable of carrying out his wishes, and in 1601, he obtained this. But the town council was not happy to rescind its recent new arrangements for the school and, at the beginning of the new academic year in October, the council rather hesitantly found it expedient to 'make an assay' of him for another year as master of the high school.[95] Also opposed to Hume was Mr John Ray, then humanity professor at the university, though his previous experience fitted him better for the high school post, and indeed, on Hume's resignation in 1606, Ray duly took over.[96] Glasgow's eagerness to exploit the crises in Edinburgh's university and school doubtless encouraged Ray to lose no time in reverting to more ample staffing arrangements.

From Edinburgh, Hume went to the country, to the school founded at Prestonpans by the minister, poet and polemicist, John Davidson. Hume's appointment there was approved by the Haddington presbytery on 8 July 1606, and after he was heard teaching by the presbytery visitors and the parishioners he was admitted on 28 July to teach Hebrew, Greek and Latin, according to Davidson's trilingual foundation.[97] In 1607, the Scottish Parliament noted that 'the latine townge is greatlie diminischit within this Realme, to the heavie prejudice of the commoun weale', and issued a 'Comissioun anent grammer and teacheris thairof' to the chancellor, Alexander Seton, earl of Dunfermline, stating 'that their shall be ane satlit forme of the best and maist commoun and approvin grammer and all pairitis thairof collectit, establischit and prentit to be universallie teacheit in all the pairtis of this realme be the haill maisteris and Teacheares of grammer'.[98] We have seen that the idea of a monopoly grammar went back at least to 1568, and that the schoolmasters' conference convened by Morton in 1575 had stated that since no current textbook met pupils' requirements, a new grammar to be taught by public and private teachers was needed, an opinion reiterated by the Privy Council in 1593. In the rural peace of Prestonpans, Hume set about

---

[94] A. Hume, *Grammatica nova* (Edinburgh, 1612), address to the reader. His defence of Mr Robert Bruce, the former minister of Edinburgh, against the Catholic controversialist at Louvain, William Reynolds, would be construed as loyalty to Calvin rather than as friendship with the king's ecclesiastical *bête noire*, at that time living in forced internal exile in Inverness.

[95] *Edinburgh Burgh Recs.*, v, 291–2.

[96] Craufurd, *History of the University of Edinburgh*, 41.

[97] T. McCrie, *Life of Andrew Melville* (Edinburgh, 1819), ii, 503.

[98] *APS*, iv, 374.

providing Scotland with that long-desired new grammar, in the shape of his *Grammatica nova*. (Rural and peaceful Prestonpans might be, but the school's reputation was high: James Simson, son of Patrick, minister of Stirling, and grandson of the grammarian, Andrew, attended the school in 1607.)[99]

Hume's *Grammatica nova*, unsurprisingly, bears a dedication to the chancellor, Alexander Seton, in which Hume claims that he first considered a revised grammar as early as 1598. The dedication was written in October 1608, but the delegates appointed to examine his work were not named till March 1610. We have no details of their deliberations, but when they finally reported in 1611, they were favourable.[100] We do know that Patrick Sandys differed with Hume about the definition of person, the concept on which, on his own admission, the whole of Hume's grammar turned, 'persona in quo cardo totius grammaticae vertetur'. Hume noted that Sandys, after eight years as a regent in Edinburgh, had gone abroad to France, Italy and Germany and had come back with a good name in literary matters. Hume, abandoning the more formalistic definition of Ramus ('a special termination of the verb'), defined person as 'the subsistence of a thing as indicated in a word' ('subsistentia rei voce notata'). Sandys did not altogether acquiesce. It was better, from a logical viewpoint, to define person as 'something subsisting demonstrable by I, thou, or he'. Since Hume deemed the idea of person to be of the highest consequence, he left the issue open to discussion, observing that he believed the Sandys definition applied to Linacre's dual definition, which he calls syntactical and verbal.[101] In his dedicatory address, which expresses the hope that Alexander Seton will prove to be a new Maecenas, Hume states that Linacre is a major influence on him: 'while I turn diligently to Linacre, as far as I can judge the prince of grammarians,[102] I

---

99 RD1/157, 381. Although Hume left in 1613, the school retained its fame, but by 1620, costs at Prestonpans were inordinate. In a letter to Alexander, sixth earl of Eglinton, Robert Seton, servant to Margaret, countess of Winton, who had looked into matters at Prestonpans, reported unfavourably. The schoolmaster of the time charged boarders tabled with the master 200 merks, whether at the top of the table or the foot, total cost per year 900 merks. Other payments were made at entry, each scholar paying a 'dolor' a quarter, plus clothes, laundry and candle silver at Candlemas. The parents must also provide a change of clothes for bedding. The servant's advice was against coming east for schooling. 'I think if there be ane guid grammar scoul in Glasgo, your bairns can be no wors there than at the Panes, and I think lairge cheipper', and moreover they would be near their father, where once a week either he or his servant could visit them, *Hist. MSS Comm., 10th Report: Eglinton* (HMSO, 1885), 45.

100 *RPC*, viii, 445; ibid., ix, 272–3, 276, 429.

101 *Grammatica nova*, second section, 107, referring back to 6–7 in first section, 14 (second section) while 13 (second section) points out that grammar does not use 'person' in the same sense as theology. This second section, called 'Schola grammatica' is separately paginated.

102 On comparatives, Hume rejects the common view for that of Varro and Linacre, 'whose

put his precepts into order as far as I understand them, following his example I observe all the changes authors have made: while I bring into line what is out of line, I explain the knotty points, and whatever is not sufficiently worked out I return to the anvil'.[103]

Some discussion of Hume's grammar theory can be found elsewhere; its originality cannot by doubted, but there was universal resistance to the adoption of his *Grammatica nova* as the sole acceptable textbook, and the commissioners, who were supposed to suppress Despauterius and to defend Hume's interests, failed to do so.[104] In November 1612, Hume wrote a long letter of complaint to his friend Andrew Melville, who, after his imprisonment in the Tower of London, had gone into exile at Sedan in France.[105] Hume wrote that Archbishop Gledstanes of St Andrews was opposed, and although Chancellor Seton was in favour, Hume was unwilling to seek any favours from him. John Ray, his successor at Edinburgh, was prepared to tolerate the Privy Council's edict, but was basically unwilling to teach from Hume's book: he would lead the opposition among the schoolmasters, as he would among the Edinburgh councillors who had already found Hume quite a handful. Thus Archbishop Spottiswoode, who had already given Hume's book his blessing, now went as far as to persuade James VI and I to write to the Privy Council to cancel the monopoly in letters proclaimed at Edinburgh cross. Seton was unwilling to do so, as the commission had deliberated for a year and more, and felt its mature decision should not lightly be set aside. But the bishops, while not all that interested in Ramus, did not like friends of Andrew Melville. Hume had appealed to John Johnston, principal of St Andrews, to protect Melville's part of the revenues of St Mary's College during his enforced absence, but both the principal of St Leonard's and Melville's own kinsman, Patrick, concurred in preventing this. However, Hume wrote to Andrew, Johnston lined up with Gledstanes and Robert Howie ('who had deserted Christ for the world'), both of whom plotted against Melville ('you who fought so strongly for Christ'). Hume tells Melville that Howie found this neglected correspondence of

---

name in this matter I regard as almost saintly', ibid., 42. He cites Grocyn as following Varro, p. 15 (second part).

103   Ibid., dedication to Alexander Seton, earl of Dunfermline. In the *Prima Elementa Grammaticae*, 1612, he mentions that his patron (Maecenas) is in great honour with the king, but does not name him. It is worth noting that the verso of the title page of the *Grammatica nova* bears – alongside a quotation from Isocrates – the arms of Henry, Prince of Wales, whose patronage Hume seems to have looked for.

104   Durkan, 'Laying of fresh foundations', 140–2; G.A. Padley, *Grammatical Theory in Western Europe, 1500–1700* (Cambridge, 1976), 112–17.

105   Summarised in Durkan, 'Laying of fresh foundations', 141, from EUL, MS Melvini Epistolae, D.c.6.45, p. 309. This letter, dated on the 6th Ides of November, is misdated in December in McCrie, *Andrew Melville*, ii, 300.

Hume's after Johnston's death,[106] and Archbishop Gledstanes had retained it, threatening to accuse Hume of treason against King James. Hume writes to Melville that he had nothing against the king, but was not averse from harming the bishop's majesty. He simply hoped King James might be better advised, and would hate the evil that the bishops did. The letter is followed by some lines by Hume on his hoped-for patron, Prince Henry, who had died shortly before.

We do not have the letter in which Hume sought the support of Isaac Casaubon, the Genevan scholar then at the court of King James. The king had passed his grammar on to Casaubon, and Hume seemed unaware of the opposition of Beza and others in Geneva to Ramus for his overly democratic ideas of church government. Ramus was therefore excluded from Geneva, so that Melville and others had to go to Lausanne to hear him. Casaubon shared this Genevan suspicion of Ramus, and replied from London on 31 March 1613, 'The findings of Ramus which you approve don't please me and never have. There is the appearance of novelty to be found in Ramus, and among his creations, a new vocabulary of the art of grammar, a new arrangement of the rules. When I once looked over his booklets, I did not observed a single novelty that added anything to Latinity as such. Wherefore, then, so much innovation?' He mentioned that Joseph Scaliger (another critic with Genevan affiliations) also took the same view. Casaubon said that he appreciated Hume as a man of ideas, but saw in him a man conned by Petrus Ramus.[107]

Novelty was no objection to Hume. In his address to the reader in the *Grammatica nova*, he drew the attention of his patron, Chancellor Seton, to the fact that a former chancellor of England, Sir Thomas More, had stood by William Lily, whose zeal for the new grammar led him to his ejection from Oxford. Lily had gone to Colet's school at St Paul's, and a few years' experience had proved the value of the new grammar. Thomas More, by his authority, 'and no less against the will of the public than what I am now experiencing', had brought it about that Lily's grammar should be publicly accepted in all schools, to the exclusion of the old grammar that everybody learnt then. 'I cannot sufficiently praise the zeal of those men who look after the republic of letters in the midst of the business of state, nor could any future age give such men all the thanks they deserve.'[108] In that revealing letter to Melville at Sedan in November 1612, Hume indicated that Seton continued to support his monopoly. But he himself was unwilling to make peace with his episcopal opponents and we have seen that in 1614 Edin-

---

[106] Johnston died in Oct. 1611, leaving some writings of John Davidson of Prestonpans to Hume; *Maitland Misc.*, i (2), 343.

[107] I. Casaubon, *Epistolae* (Rotterdam, 1709), 526–7.

[108] *Grammatica nova* (part 2), fo. Al, 'Ad lectorem'.

burgh and its principal master, John Ray, would have nothing to do with
the *Grammatica nova* in their revised curriculum. Hume, however, remained
a tireless propagandist in his own cause, even after moving from Prestonpans
to his home town of Dunbar in 1613. There is a fragment of a letter in a later
manuscript which suggests something of Edinburgh's problems with Hume;
as the letter has been severely trimmed, only a few words can be read. '… I
fynding this not done address my … made it because Edinb. wald not suffer
… me to a fewe disciples of my awne procure[ment] … The frute of it his
maiestie being absent, I offerd … [t]ryares of the learnedest that our cuntrie
… licence to print it; and with the sound of … aded it onlie to be taucht.
Quhairupon … above the capacitie of barnes procured … hearing that his
m[ajesty] had delivered it to [?Casaubon] … understand his opinion. He
wrote to me … and I was certefyed in other ways that … [Not]withstanding
that these divisiones be as … grammares; I tooke it in hand agayne.'[109] The
reference is clearly to the neglect of the royal privilege of monopoly in
Hume's *Elementa Grammaticae, in usum iuventutis Scoticae* of 1606, and to the
opposition Hume had encountered in Edinburgh. In a later manuscript, he
would mention how impoverished he was on coming to Edinburgh, and
infer that since his salary was reduced from 1601 onwards, he was forced to
go elsewhere.[110] Although he seems to have issued his *Prima Elementa Grammaticae* in 1606, only the edition of 1612 survives; the address 'ad lectorem'
calls the book Hume's 'Rudiments',[111] and tells the reader that the rules of
grammar are certainly learned from use, just as the rules themselves teach
us how to use them; Ascham's *The Schoolmaster* proves this with many arguments. Yet Hume says he does not altogether agree; a middling acquaintance
with Latin would not be enough for the serious Latin scholar.

In his *Grammatica nova*, Hume had set out his very interesting approach
to the question of schooling, which we can summarise as follows. Ideally
no apprenticeship to learning should be complete before age twenty-five:
this is reflected in the English colleges where entry is at age eighteen and
the MA degree takes seven years. No youth should be in charge of his
own life till he can manage it virtuously. Any severity called for should be
administered at home, so that as soon as the child speaks he can learn to love
school: his teachers ought to be able to correct him with diligence instead
of the whip. Starting in the 'Inglis' school, he has to learn to read and write
well, something that will take him up to age nine: he is not wanted in the
grammar school till he can do both without mistakes. Learning how to
decline nouns and conjugate verbs should not be made painful for tender

---

[109] GUL, MS General 362, pasted down on fo. 86a.
[110] NLS, MS 17998, *Virtutes grammaticae*, fo. 5v.
[111] He also refers to the *Prima elementa* as rudiments in his *Grammatica nova* (part 2), 25,
       observing that it is futile to repeat what he has already said there.

minds, but should advance step by step, with the pupils mastering the rudiments word by word, confirming what they have learnt in the past, rather
than being confronted with the new and unknown. Care is to be taken to
ensure that whatever they know, they know it exactly. The whole process
is to be achieved by examples rather than by rules. The vocabulary used in
teaching ought to give prior place to examples, lest anything in the art is
left. Examples should progress in difficulty, till the pupils can decline any
word following the prototype. Similar care applies to syntax. Thereafter the
class should proceed to Mathurin Cordier and the dialogues for the best
Latin expressions taken from the best authors used in the school. Turning to
Terence, whose *Adelphoe* Hume quotes, each word must be construed, with
all the schoolboys exercising both mind and lips, so that they realise the
sterility of the common practice, that is, 'Give the rule, give the exception'.

Immediately on beginning grammar proper, they may begin to speak
Latin, but not before: Quintilian says it is madness in the extreme to learn
what must be unlearnt. The choice of authors should be left to the teachers
(i.e. not, presumably, to the council). They must beware of anything old-
fashioned. The best texts are the easiest and tritest, as long as the Latinity is
pure. The first virtue is to speak clearly. Let them practise their grammar on
authors, in that way they will be happier to commit things to memory than
by learning word by word. This memory will grow together with judgement. Commit poetry only to memory. In everything translate prose till they
teach the tongue to 'speak Roman'. Let English give place to the cultivation
of Latin so that anglicisms are put to flight: 'I would rather the pupils were
taught what ought to be said rather than grow accustomed to anglicisms and
barbarisms.' Once familiar with Latin, they may begin to compose in verse.
Consequently it is fittest that some better known poem be used, so that they
may analyse the poem's context. After they have already striven to interpret
it, let them restore it once more to poetic form. Once this is done, dictate
the poem itself at the end of this and let them also memorise it when they
have the expertise to restore the poem without further ado. That way they
will get so used to it that they will not stray far from the poet's own words.
Thereafter give them some theme, or Aesop's fable, to practise on and render
into verse. Prescribe the exercise each day. Expose the slower ones to the
example of the rest. Do the same with prose-writers. When they reach that
point, admit them to university. 'I warn parents not only not to pick unripe
fruit, but also to wait till they [their offspring] have passed the storms of
adolescence and are able to take charge of their own lives.'[112]

Although all this was, in part, a criticism of unenjoyable and unthinking
rote-learning, and certainly displayed a healthily critical attitude to corporal

[112]   Paraenesis, in *Grammatica nova* (1612).

punishment, it does appear that the Latin texts were not studied primarily as literature: linguistic mastery was the main aim. For instance, Hume's scheme hardly touches on Terence as a writer of plays, rather than as a source of correct Latinity; it would produce clever versifiers rather than inspired ones. One wonders about the anti-papal play Hume put on in 1598, when the participating students found it such dry work that there was a run on their consumption of ale.[113] One also wonders whether this religious drama was related in any way to the performance in Edinburgh of more profane dramas by a company including Laurence Fletcher, English player, once in 1594 and again, to the kirk session's dismay, in 1599.[114] It is instructive to note Hume the theologian recording his furious objections to Ovid in 1593: 'of all vaine poets, the vainest [amongst] manie filthie and vaine workes, he wrote a book entituled Metamorphosis. In it he sets the edge of all his wits (which he had as sharp as ever had anie Poet) to the painting of lies in all colours.'[115] (The school at Glasgow, c.1620, clearly had no such scruples about Ovid, studying at least thirteen books of the *Metamorphoses*.) We can imagine Hume's discomfiture on his arrival at the Edinburgh high school, where he found himself expected to teach this multicoloured mendacity as a set text, on top of the use of Despauterius for grammar. The sheer seriousness of Hume's grammatical passion is revealed by a remark in the *Grammatica nova*: when pointing out that people do not commonly differentiate between quantity and accent, Hume roundly states that he was born and educated in that error and so had lived for most of his life. What had changed his view, he writes, was coming upon Melanchthon's grammar, 'one not all that common with us'.[116]

Hume had to wait till 1617 to meet King James, when the latter was on his way north from Berwick after fourteen years' absence in England. As soon as he crossed the Scottish border on 13 May, James called at Dunglass Castle, the seat of the Lords Hume. There Alexander was present to greet him with a set speech, beginning with a preliminary flourish: 'You are Priam, we are the sons of Priam. The Scots came from Ireland, their king was Fergus, who killed the Pictish ruler. The source of our monarchy is there.

---

[113] *Edinburgh Burgh Recs.*, v, 223, 365, 'ane galloun sell quhilk the scholleris drank'.

[114] J.C. Dibden, *Annals of the Edinburgh Stage* (Edinburgh, 1888), 20–7.

[115] A. Hume, *A Reioynder to Doctor Hil* (Edinburgh, 1593), 158.

[116] *Grammatica nova* (part 2), 4. Yet Florence Wilson, who originated in Moray, recommended in his own grammar the fuller grammars of Despauterius and Melanchthon (Durkan, 'Laying of fresh foundations', 133). Giovanni Ferrerio, the Piedmontese tutor at Kinloss, as we saw, used Melanchthon, and even after the Reformation, his influence cannot be ruled out in Moray, where Mr John Robertson was reader in Lhanbryde. His signature has been scored out on the St Andrews UL copy of Melanchthon's grammar (Mor PA 2075. M4), but the name appears as 'rector de Lhanbryd' on a *Catena in Exodum* (Paris, 1550), in the same library. He is recorded at Lhanbryde in 1574. Perhaps Melancthon remained commoner in the north than in Hume's southern stamping ground.

God approved the treaty or covenant following on this.' In rapid succession, Hume reviews the Roman Agricola, Kenneth McAlpine, and those fleeing for refuge to England to escape extirpation; Malcolm marries Queen Margaret, their sons Edgar and David are fleetingly sketched in and followed by Wallace and Bruce who 'restored our pristine liberty'. Having thus jolted our memories, Hume hurls us almost at once to James's own century. Hume also offered the king a Latin poem on the joy and sorrow of the Scots, and another addressed to the Muses. Whether this stage appearance helped Hume's cause is not clear; it could scarcely have damaged it. He was clearly an advocate of union under a British flag, but was keen that the Scottish element should not be steam-rollered out of existence.[117]

Hume seems to have lost no time in composing a manuscript treatise for the Royal Library, which is still there, 'Of the orthographie and congruitie of the Britan tongue'.[118] In an address to 'the maest excellent in all princelie wisdom, learning, and heroical arts, James of Great Britain, France, and Ireland, King', he tells us he had completed it about 'a yeer syne' when he learnt that he had had a predecessor, Sir Thomas Smith, which information he had gleaned from John Garret's *Alvearie* or quadrilingual dictionary. He alludes to the meanness of his own person while castigating the ignorance of printers and his fellow schoolmasters, whose silly brains will reach no further than the compass of their cap, and who are content to repeat 'My master said it', a clear reference to the Scots' devotion to Despauterius. Recalling an incident during the king's visit to Scotland when he took part in an academic disputation in Edinburgh, Hume notes that the courtiers' speech prompted the monarch to say that he 'wald cause the universities mak an Inglish grammar to repres the insolencies of sik green heades'. Hearing of this remark, immediately, Hume sought the means to convey his treatise to where the king could read it. He wanted a nationally received pronunciation, 'not to deal with impossibilities', but 'to conform … the south and north beath in latine and in English'.[119] This would indeed prove an impossibility, as the story of the doctor of divinity Hume had once met at dinner in Bath might have told him: 'the assumption is Scottish and the conclusion is false'.[120] (This divine might well have been that Dr Adam Hill with whom Hume as 'schoolmaster of Bath'[121] had debated about theology many years earlier.) One modern exponent of the 'received pronunciation', having re-examined Hume's orthography of the 'Britan tongue', concluded

[117] John Adamson, *The Muses Welcome* (Edinburgh, 1618), 1–4, 16.
[118] Edited under that title for the Early English Text Society by Henry R. Wheatley (1865, 1870, repr. Oxford, 1965).
[119] Ibid., 2, 9.
[120] Ibid., 18.
[121] A. Hill, *The Defence of the Article: Christ descended into Hell* (London, 1592), 33.

that 'Hume's book in truth is amusing rather than useful'; yet the same critic finds the elementary outline of English grammar 'concise and tolerably complete', unaware that it contained doctrine heretical even in Scotland.[122]

When Chancellor Seton died on 16 June 1622, with him died any hope Hume had of patronage in high places. Hume wrote to the Privy Council,[123] pointing out that in former times the concept of the grammar monopoly had not only been approved by the Council, but that the decision had been ratified twice in parliament, yet nothing had been done for years. However, when he had produced an officially approved textbook for universal use, discontent and complaints about its obscurity, beyond the grasp of young minds, had reached his Majesty's ears, and King James had halted the process till further tests could be made of Hume's book: 'whilk haveing now lyne deade for the space of ten yeiris', Hume had been working it over, 'and hes provin by tryall, as the colledgeis will testifie, that the worke is very effectuall to leade to the speakeing and writting not *Latinum* bot *Latine*' (i.e. as the Romans themselves would speak and write). Hume was now asking that a fresh look be taken at his work. All this was noted in council on 17 July and at the end of the month a new commission was set up. The commissioners had interviewed not only Hume, however, but also his old adversary, John Ray. Presumably it was Ray who made the foxy suggestion that not only should the masters foregather for judgement, but this time also two or three scholars of theirs and of Hume's. Inevitably, of course, the schoolboys would be baffled by Hume's novel terminology and turn it down. Besides Ray's own scholars, they included groups from Aberdeen, Dundee, St Andrews, Perth and Glasgow (with nobody from Stirling on this occasion). No conclusion is recorded, but the appearance of rival grammars shows that Hume's appeal had failed. Though as yet no rival won the monopoly from Hume, the field was still open.[124] Robert Williamson of Cupar brought out a new edition of his *Elementa linguae latinae* in 1624 (reissued the following year), based on the old favourites, Donatus and Despauterius. George Lightbody, at Langton, in Berwickshire, produced his *Quaestiones grammaticae* in 1628, but this, the grammar of a logician by training, was not reprinted until 1660.

In 1623, when Hume resumed his campaign for the acceptance of his national monopoly, he prepared for printing a statement on the virtues of his grammar, *Virtutes grammaticae*, listing over fifty of them. The text is preceded by an address to the reader (fo. 2) and another to the commissioners chosen to examine the project (fo. 3). There must have been those who wondered why a master in a small country school should dictate the teaching programme for large town schools, and at one point Hume breaks

---

122 E.S. Dobson, *English Pronunciation, 1500–1700* (Oxford, 1968), i, 316–21.

123 *RPC*, xi, 264–5. The original of Hume's petition is mentioned in ibid., xiii, 805.

124 *RPC*, xiii, 264–5, 318–19.

off with an obscure interjection to meet this: 'From boyhood, the weight of poverty, heavier than Mount Etna, has ground me down most heavily. When first I came to the grammar school in your city here, with the benevolence of schoolboys whose books I had in my keeping, I endured the life for more than four years [phrase omitted due to tight binding]. When I had no strength to struggle any longer with my lack of means, I was compelled to embrace a modest post, teaching small country boys.' This passage both raises questions and suggests possible answers. Does it mean that when Hume returned to Scotland in 1593 he was seemingly without a job; or does this period of unemployment refer to his English stay of sixteen years? He seems to have studied some theology at Oxford, concurrently with his tutorship, but he fails to explain the years 1583 to 1589. The four years or so at Edinburgh require explanation, since his actual stay was for ten. The reference to keeping of schoolboys' books appears to mean more than it says, probably referring to the books laid down in the 1598 order, including the Despauterius of which Hume disapproved. Was the schoolboys' 'benevolence' lost when he felt the need to change the course? Parents might have objected to the reduction of classes when Hume got rid of the 'regents' and thereby lost the goodwill of parents and boys both. Teaching at Prestonpans, however ambitious that school may have been, was a comedown for an Edinburgh principal schoolmaster.[125] And, indeed, he did not remain long at John Davidson's foundation, for in 1613 he was in Dunbar, where he soon became the highest paid schoolmaster in the land, earning £400 Scots per annum.[126]

Addressing the reader of the *Virtutes grammaticae*, Hume makes great claims for his own approach. 'All of us who teach this art teach the same thing, yet we do not all teach it in the best way. Any art has two requirements: one, to proceed methodically along a certain path, which once known, no matter whither you go, may lead you straight to the fountainhead; and second, to teach the causes of things, because things are known only by their causes … Everybody teaches that the verb must agree with the noun in number and person, but they agree because they are of the same person.' Hume was the first to centre his grammar on person, as he observed, for 'prior to Linacre, nobody did so, and his teaching is not definite enough'. Let those who want to praise Despauterius do so; for his part, Hume 'would three times over rather follow the example of Terence than the rule of Despauterius'. He ends by calling for Despauterius to be proscribed, and himself to

125 NLS, MS 17998, *Virtutes grammaticae*, formerly owned by Thomas Ruddiman, bound with two printed books of his. See also T. Ruddiman, *A catalogue of a rare and valuable collection of books … to be sold by auction.… 1st February 1758* (Edinburgh, 1758), 51.
126 *Maitland Misc.*, ii (1), 43.

be prescribed.[127] But this was unlikely to happen, since, as Hume noted, the commissioners themselves 'think ill of my grammar, since you have, all of you, learnt Despauterius'.

1623 did not see the end of the matter, so Hume had to have recourse once again to the powers that be. On 15 July 1629, we find King Charles I writing from Windsor, having clearly received representations either from Hume or his friends. The king wrote that Hume had apparently been robbed of his monopoly by some objectors who thought his work difficult and obscure, and that the truth of these objections required testing; a committee of learned and indifferent persons, men of no *parti pris*, was needed to hear the pros and cons of Hume's case.[128] Finding such a disinterested group took some time, and there is reason to think that it was replaced by the commissioners for the Scottish burghs, who then reported back to the Privy Council. By July 1630 a committee existed, appointed to meet in Edinburgh on 13 July and summon the burgh schoolmasters of Edinburgh, Dundee, St Andrews, Montrose, Stirling and Glasgow to appear by 22 July and state their case against Hume's grammar.[129] It must have seemed sensible to this committee to delegate the task to representatives of the Convention of Royal Burghs, who did not decide immediately, although they had already excluded Hume's work in favour of that of the schoolmaster of Aberdeen, David Wedderburn. Yet before committing themselves, they called for 200 copies to be dispersed to schools up and down the country for their animadversions. The outcome was that the choice fell on Wedderburn's work, which was then approved for use nationwide in Scotland in 1631.[130] Hume was no longer on offer, the final blow to the old man's long cherished hopes.

Hume insisted on some arrangement for compensation from Wedderburn, who went off home after the Privy Council's decision. Furthermore, he had no intention of teaching from Wedderburn's book, nor of allowing his son, Mr John Hume, to do so. The exceptions were to be allowed 'within their awne schooles allanerlie', and after some haggling, Wedderburn agreed to pay a composition fee of 1,000 merks.[131] Nevertheless, Hume started to revise his own manuscript of *Grammatica nova*, as if he were still hoping for a printer, and here and there made alterations which necessitated the pasting in of scraps of paper over the text. The result sees *scholia* glosses scattered throughout the work, whereas in the 1612 edition, the 'Scholia'

---

[127]   *Virtutes grammaticae*, fos. 2, 12, 14.
[128]   *RPC* (series 2), iii, 597.
[129]   Ibid., 596.
[130]   *RPC* (series 2), iv, 163; J.D. Marwick (ed.), *Extracts from the Records of the Convention of Royal Burghs of Scotland* (Edinburgh, 1880), iv, 527, 532.
[131]   *RPC* (series 2), iv, 172, 176, 242, 488.

section had been completely separate, following on the first section, devoted to etymology and syntax.

We began by quoting the epitaph Hume wrote himself when he was eighty-two,[132] but on the last leaf of his *Grammatica nova* text he wrote 'Alexander Hume with his hand, 83 years and five months old 1633. He finished it in the month of August.' This last leaf states that with regard to the use of the noun substantive, Hume had maintained it had only one gender. 'At that point, John Ray, over-reacting as was his wont, shouted "This is utterly disgraceful. A substantive can also contain three genders like the word *penus*" ...', a claim Hume denied, saying that even Priscian only taught two genders for that word. Hume further noted that since Ray had recently died, he was not prepared to speak of the dead, except to observe that Ray had bequeathed his argument to one who resembled him – presumably Thomas Crawford, his successor in the Edinburgh school.[133] Interestingly, a Sibbald manuscript which treats briefly but knowledgeably of Scottish grammars mentions that Hume, at the age of eighty-one, had written a dissertation on grammatical theory with Wedderburn and Thomas Crawford, which manuscript Sibbald had then in his possession. If this is not the present Glasgow manuscript, it would appear to be one written at the time of the Privy Council's decision in 1631, not two years later in 1633.[134]

We hear nothing further of Alexander Hume. We do know that he failed to persuade printers to bring out his 'Rerum Scotorum Compendium ad usum Scholarum' (a shortened version of Buchanan's history),[135] or his revised version of Andrea Guarna's *Bellum grammaticale*. The latter, 'ad exemplar Mri Alexandri Humii in Gratiam eorum, qui amoeniores Musas venerantur, Editum', was published by Christopher Irvine at Edinburgh in 1658 and Glasgow in 1678, with a fulsome dedication to Sir Robert Sibbald.

IV.6 Andrew Duncan of Dundee and his grammar

While the grammarian Alexander Hepburn had been a product of St Salvator's College, Andrew Duncan studied at St Leonards where he graduated in arts in 1575, and acted thereafter as regent and in other official capacities.[136] While there, he went on to study theology and changed his views under the influence of Andrew Melville, presumably c.1580.[137] In 1598, the presbytery of St Andrews appointed him as an arbiter in a case involving another St

132 GUL, MS General 362, fo. 1.
133 Ibid., fo. 114.
134 NLS, Adv MS 33.3.19, fo. 34. Sibbald also notes an earlier 1606 edition of *Elementa prima*.
135 Hume here is said to be 'of the ancient, noble race of Humes in Scotland, sprung from the first line (*stirpe*) and the fifth offshoot (*sobole*)'.
136 *Acta Facultatis*, ii, 444, 453, 454.
137 *Autobiography and Diary*, 124.

Andrews teacher, William Welwood, the author of *The Sea Law of Scotland*; he is found in other presbytery minutes, but never on the St Andrews kirk session.[138]

He was appointed to the Dundee school in 1591, and four years later published his *Prior Pars* (or *First Rudiments*).[139] Echoing Buchanan, whose Latin adaptation of Linacre had been addressed to Gilbert Kennedy, earl of Cassillis, Duncan addressed his work to the then earl, John Kennedy, and went on to speak of its readers being able to 'visit and stroll about the fruit gardens of grammar', while claiming, in another echo of Buchanan, to avoid the prolix and the unclear. Modern grammars, he wrote, abounded in rules, a 'vast and immense sea' of them, which most would find offputting. The subsequent dedication to the Dundee council returns to this theme in connection with Despauterius (clearly the textbook used at Dundee), saying that its mnemonic verses were here being avoided. Only what was necessary for writing good Latin was being offered; disquisitions on Graecisms were omitted. What relevance had they, after all, to those turning their thoughts to jobs as merchants, sailors, farmers, tailors and shoemakers? (Much religious literature was still in Latin, and this Duncan may have had primarily in mind, rather than the reading of classical literature.) The book contains liminary verse by Principal Robert Wilkie of St Leonard's, Thomas Ramsay, Duncan's predecessor and now minister of Rossie, David Lindsay and John Johnston of St Mary's, but their verses add little. John Echlin, professor of philosophy and eloquence at St Leonard's, speaks with scorn of Despauterius and Villedieu: 'Why should anyone wish to grow old any more in the dismal school of Despauterius?' John Johnston, on the other hand, invokes ancient grammarians like Varro and Festus, and moderns like Joseph Scaliger and Justus Lipsius.

If Duncan's *Prior Pars* was intended to replace Simson's *First Rudiments*, it failed. But, as we saw, his *Studiorum Puerilium Clavis* of 1597 displaced Simson's *Second Rudiments* in most seventeenth-century editions.[140] Duncan's *Key to Boys' Studies* was less wordy and, revealing its dependence on Buchanan's recently issued *Prosodia*, it made room for a short section on versification as the final stage in the schoolboys' pre-university learning – a stage the dominie might choose to skip. Typical of Duncan's pious turn of mind is his injunction to the youth to model their lines on Buchanan's Latin psalms, with which they were acquainted from their earliest days at school. The book's epistle dedicatory, dated at Dundee on 13 April 1597, is addressed

138   *RKSSA*, ii, 860, 877, 882, 909, 912.
139   *Latinae grammaticae pars prior* (Edinburgh, 1595), reprinted at Menston by the Scolar Press in 1968.
140   *Studiorum Puerilium Clavis, miro quodam compendio ac facilitate, Latinae linguae ac Poeticae Rudimenta complectens* (Edinburgh, 1597).

to Andrew, eldest son of Patrick, Lord Gray, whom he warns against the enemies of the mind, namely error and, worst of all, lack of knowledge. Teachers fight to reclaim youth from these faults, which bar the path to those teachers who wish to rescue youth from its enemies and restore it to primitive liberty; yet over and over again teachers are compelled almost to agree and come to terms with the enemy's evil intentions. All this seems to be an excuse for not piling on the agony by demanding too much from young students.

The work itself cites no authors, and the influence of Ramus, while still present, is largely limited to the book's trend towards oversimplification. The anti-Ramist John Ray could use it with a clear conscience. (It is notable that when Ray was Edinburgh's university regent in humanity in 1598 both Ramus and Talon were absent from his programme, in favour of the more traditional Cassander. Yet it looks as though the other university classes made use of Ramist logic, and were still doing so when the university 'recalled its old laws' in 1628.[141] One suspects that Alexander Hume might have had more supporters for his Ramist addiction among the philosophy regents than among the humanists!)

Duncan's *Rudimenta pietatis* of 1595, dedicated to Andrew Leslie, fifth earl of Rothes, had been the first to appear. Its frequent reprints contained some additions, but always retained his original forty-one questions and answers, followed by his scholia. The penalty for Duncan's stormy ecclesiastical career after 1600 was that, like the *Rudiments of Piety*, reprints of his *Key to Boys' Studies* were anonymous, omitting the author's name. Indeed, in the introduction to the reprint of the 1653 edition it is mistakenly suggested that it was the work of Andrew Simson; the original work has no prayers, and the Latin prayer (for docility) in that 1653 edition is by Erasmus.[142] In 1595, Andrew Duncan also published an *Appendix to Etymology*.[143] This includes a short dictionary of Latin words with their equivalents not only in Scots but also in English. The Latin term 'edax' is followed immediately by the English 'a great eater', and then the vigorous Scots 'a greedie Gutte'. This was only eight years away from the Union of the Crowns of 1603, and Duncan was offering his own contribution to the anglicising process which had probably entered the Scottish schoolroom before his time.[144] But it may be significant that this *Appendix* was never republished, although in 1596 his printer,

---

[141] Morgan (ed.) with Hannay, *University of Edinburgh Charters*, 60–1, 110–11. Glasgow recalled its 'old laws', with details of the new curriculum, in 1643; see *MAUG*, ii, 307ff.

[142] H. Bonar (ed.), *Catechisms of the Scottish Reformation* (London, 1866), 287–8.

[143] *Appendix Etymologiae, ad copiam exemplorum, una cum indice interprete* (Edinburgh, 1595).

[144] The English Dialect Society reprinted the Duncan glossary, *Series B: Reprinted Glossaries*, ed. W. W. Skeate (London, 1874), 65–7.

Waldegrave, an English refugee in Scotland, published English word-lists by John Stanbridge in Edinburgh.[145]

We do not know exactly when or why Duncan moved from the school at Dundee.[146] Ordained minister in 1596 and presented to Crail by James, Lord Lindsay, he became minister there in 1597. He lost the post when he declared his support for the rebellious General Assembly at Aberdeen in July 1605, thus incurring the wrath of King James, who was rapidly moving towards the imposition of episcopacy.[147] In 1605 Duncan and several other irreducible ministers were warded in Blackness Castle and tried at Linlithgow in January 1606. Forced into banishment, he sailed to France,[148] soon becoming a candidate for posts at the Protestant academies of Die and La Rochelle. In 1607 he accepted the post of professor of theology at the latter, in the teeth of opposition from a former fellow inmate of Blackness, John Knox's son-in-law, John Welsh, who felt himself superior, being 'of greiter accompt nor ever he was'. Having reconciled himself with King James over Aberdeen by declaring that he had been unaware of the king's opposition to that Assembly, Duncan returned home in 1613.[149] However, after clashes over the Articles of Perth in August 1618, Duncan was back in James's bad books, to the extent that in 1621, since he declined the authority of the Court of High Commission, it was decided to keep him out of Crail and Edinburgh, but to allow him to settle elsewhere. He finally opted for Berwick-on-Tweed, and died there in 1626.

His involvement in kirk affairs cut short Duncan's work on grammar. But despite his probable contribution to anglicisation in schools, he used good round Scots terms to remind his great opponent Archbishop Spottiswoode that there were dangers in playing the courtier in the king's service: 'Hall binks are slidderie ... and earthlie courts are kittle', the first phrase an echo of an old Scots proverb.[150] Similar language is found in his will, drawn up in April 1626 just before his death, when he looked forward to angels bearing him upwards, and painted all human ambition – such as John Welsh had once accused him of harbouring – as being just so much 'baggadge and clathrie'.[151]

145   Dickson & Edmond, *Annals*, 435.
146   Maxwell, *Old Dundee*, 93, neglects to mention Duncan, but records problems in the grammar school in June 1594.
147   *Fasti*, v, 192.
148   D. Calderwood, *The History of the Kirk of Scotland*, ed. T. Thomson and D. Laing (Wodrow Society, 1842–1849), vi, 287, 292, 347, 449, 590; vii, 364, 470, 564.
149   Wodrow, *Lives of the Reformers*, ii, 289, 294, 295; ibid., i, 272; the visit of 1610 must have been a flying one, since Duncan's petition to the king was dated 1 July 1613.
150   Calderwood, *History*, vii, 564; *The James Carmichael Collection of Proverbs in Scots*, ed. M.L. Anderson (Edinburgh, 1957), 73 (no. 627).
151   *A last will and testament of Mr Andrew Duncan, Minister of Crail*, ed. W. Peterson (Montreal, 1919); Durkan, 'Laying of fresh foundations', 142–4.

IV.7 James Carmichael of Haddington and his grammar

James Carmichael was born about 1546, and we first meet with him as a student at St Leonard's in 1561. By July 1570, he was schoolmaster in St Andrews, when he criticised the local minister for not denouncing the murderers of the Regent Moray.[152] The following month he was appointed minister of Haddington, where he also became schoolmaster two years later. Schoolmasters were clearly difficult to come by in the town. The schoolmaster in November 1557 had been Mr John Lowis, whose name is associated also with Elgin and Peebles.[153] On 12 October 1559, the town found it 'expedient' (probably because he had already been presented by the patron, the commendator of Holyrood, Lord Robert Stewart) to appoint Mr Robert Dormound, with 24 merks yearly, payable from the burgh's common good fund, with other fees of £120 for himself and the doctor payable each term by parents and friends 'as the use and wont was of befor', and the council to find him 'chalmer' and school 'maill' fee. Dormound (as 'Dormounht') is found witnessing a deed 'in the place of the Friars Minor' on 7 December 1560, but is otherwise unrecorded.[154] On 17 February 1564, a contract was signed between the town and its new schoolmaster, Mr Thomas Cumming, for a lifetime appointment to instruct 'in grammatick lettres in latyne toung and moralle uertu'. Reference is made to his honest conversation and 'exempell to utheris' (his predecessor may not have lived up to expectations). His period of office was to begin on 14 September 'called Beltane' and he was to agree not to absent himself beyond three days without council licence. His wage was raised to 60 merks and no rural school was to be permitted; 4 shillings yearly for scholage were also promised.[155] His wage receipts show 4 merks only on 1 December 1564, but that can scarcely cover the whole period Martinmas to Whitsunday, as in June of the next year he got £23,[156] a sum repeated at Martinmas, and so on till 1569.

There appears to have been a lack of volunteers to take over the post. When, on 16 April 1572, the town council made Mr James Carmichael the schoolmaster, he was to combine this office with his duties as minister of the town.[157] The council stressed the fact that his appointment was totally a matter for the town, and could be terminated at the town's discretion.[158] The provost and council took the precaution of writing to King James,

152 *RKSSA*, i, 1, 334–5 and note.
153 Durkan, 'Education in the century of the Reformation', 156; NAS, B30/13/1, 36.
154 NAS, B30/13/1, 22; Protocol Book of Robert Lawder, 1540–1562, B56/1/1, fo. 219.
155 NAS, B30/13/1, under that date.
156 These receipts are in NAS, B30/21/52, Schoolmasters' receipts.
157 *The James Carmichael Collection of Proverbs in Scots*, ed. M.L. Anderson (Edinburgh, 1957), 31.
158 NAS, B30/21/52.

explaining that their school being destitute of a master, they had pressed
Carmichael to take on the post. The king (or rather the Regent Morton on
his behalf) summoned them to Leith for 12 June 1572.[159] The trouble was
that Thomas Cumming had the gift of the school from the commendator
of Holyrood and, indeed, as late as 1576 he would still not have renounced
it.[160] In 1575, we find Morton calling on Carmichael's services as one of the
schoolmasters requested to provide for a new national grammar, along with
his relative by marriage, Andrew Simson of Dunbar, and the equally bookish
Mr Patrick Auchinleck, schoolmaster in St Andrews – the latter apparently
Carmichael's own immediate successor in that post.[161]

The first extant Haddington receipt of wages for the post of schoolmaster
is for the Martinmas term in November 1573, when Carmichael received
£20 in the presence of Mr Walter Balcanquall, minister at Bothans, then
doctor in the school; another exists for November 1574, for 40 merks in
total. Balcanquall was to take up his duties at Martinmas 1573, acting as
reader and session clerk as well as doctor.[162] No Haddington receipts for 1572
or 1576 remain, but Carmichael was evidently paid £40 for the first term
of 1576 before the 'ourgevin' of the school, a payment covering his 'Scule
hous fie' and his rented schoolhouse, quite an advance on the payment to
the pre-Reformation master, Lowis, who got 20 merks in 1557 plus 40 shillings for his rented schoolhouse, but who probably also held a chaplaincy
in addition.[163]

By May 1574 the Haddington council could not have been too happy
with Carmichael, laying down that 'in na tym cumin the minister of the kirk
sall not be admitted to be scolemaister'.[164] The matter was further complicated in February 1576, when another claimant materialised, namely the
minister of North Berwick, Mr Patrick Creich, presented as schoolmaster
in the town by the patron, the commendator of Holyrood, with the proviso
that if he should leave the country, the post was transferable to Carmichael,
preacher in Haddington.[165] Like Creich, Carmichael had resorted to the
ancient patron, which meant sidelining the town; yet it is not easy to see how
he could satisfactorily have discharged both duties, besides having charge
of the parishes of Bolton, St Martins in Nungate and Athelstaneford.[166] In

159   NAS, B30/21/53.
160   NAS, B30/13/1, 53.
161   There are several works which were owned by Auchinleck in St Andrews University
       Library.
162   NAS, B30/13/1, 70; Balcanquall got 50 merks.
163   The common good accounts for Scottish burghs relating to education are in *Maitland
       Misc.*, ii (1), 45.
164   Ibid., fo. 78.
165   Edinburgh City Archives, Charters of the Commendators of Holyrood, no. 60.
166   *Wodrow Misc.*, 371.

August 1576, the Regent Morton actually ratified the gift to Carmichael of the 'scolemaisterschip' for his lifetime, with all the perquisites already granted in February, and also approved his election by the provost and council and his admission by the official – or more probably, superintendent – of Lothian (i.e. the choice made in 1572, which the town had now begun to regret).[167] This arrangement was not to last, for in November 1576 the town required Carmichael, in consideration of his great burden in the ministry (i.e. the charge of four churches), to allow them to replace him with a master from outwith the ministry. Carmichael responded by defending his title and diligence in the post, that 'bairns were abstractit fra his schole', less through neglect on his part than through the council's own failure always to maintain a doctor-assistant, and because other schools were allowed to operate in the town. Yet the council could not clear Carmichael of the 'maist part' of the disorder or inconvenience, and determined to choose another, 'onsuspectit of ony kynd of heresy, papiestrie or idolatry'.[168]

One suspects that Haddington suffered from Carmichael's frequent absence on Assembly business in Edinburgh, and that, as would happen in 1589, the council found his teaching like his preaching – sound enough, but 'overleirnit above the commoune pepillis capaciteis'.[169] The saga of his appointment in Haddington shows that despite appearances, the transition from old to new, magnified by the problem of conflicting jurisdictions, was far from painless for him. There is a constant refrain throughout this schoolmaster's later career: accusations of neglect, springing partly from too many kirk responsibilities which took him off to Edinburgh on Assembly affairs. When attacked in 1579 for the spread of 'superstition' and 'the singing of carrolis and yool sangis', he claimed he had rectified the situation on his return from a 'plat' committee in the capital dealing with the planting and manning of kirks. However, Carmichael was not wholly against people dressing up for plays, for example, since, in 1574, the town council had subscribed 10 pounds out of the common good fund for those participating in a theatrical representation, to be spent by the schoolmaster on costumes 'and other necessaries for the play'. Again, in 1583, when complained against for neglecting the Thursday sermon and Sunday catechism (the latter a part of the educational programme), Carmichael's excuse was the impossibility of gathering an audience because of the harvest. In 1591, when he had neglected to hold kirk sessions, the synod found his excuses unsatisfactory.[170]

[167] NAS, B30/21/54, incorporating the provost's letter of 1572; *RSS*, vii, 687, abbreviated slightly.
[168] NAS, B30/13/1, 87.
[169] *Second Book of Discipline*, ed. J. Kirk (Edinburgh, 1980), 95.
[170] *Records of the Synod of Lothian and Tweeddale*, ed. J. Kirk (Stair Society, 1977), 4, 12, 67; J. Miller, *The Lamp of Lothian* (Haddington, 1900), 129.

On two occasions he was found to neglect the exercise, and at one point in 1594 the town sent a deputation to demand that he be made either to reside in the town or to leave Haddington and go elsewhere.[171] He took on the copying of General Assembly acts, as well as the *Second Book of Discipline*, but progress was slow.[172]

Nonetheless, Carmichael seems to have benefited from some leisure afforded him in 1584–87 by his enforced exile in England for supporting Andrew Melville's party against King James and his favourite, James Stewart, earl of Arran. Melville does not seem to have been familiar with Carmichael when he was at St Leonard's College in St Andrews in 1561, but their later joint travels in exile led Melville to style him a 'profound dreamer' when enquiring after him in 1612.[173] Carmichael was certainly a bookish person. He acquired his *Pasquine in a trance* (London, 1584) while at Honey Lane in London in 1585, noting it as no. 426 of his private library. When preparing a paper for his English allies, he consulted books in libraries and borrowed them from Sir Robert Bowes and others. Some years earlier he had made a copy of the *Second Book of Discipline* for Bowes, as English ambassador in Edinburgh, and in 1582 he had sought Bowes' aid in reconciling another Carmichael to the earl of Angus.[174] James Carmichael's friend and former fellow student John Colville was an important collaborator at this time. Sir Francis Walsingham invited him to Richmond Palace for consultations, and with the help of Paul Methven, once banished by the Assembly for adultery, he was introduced to the earl of Leicester at St James's Palace, where he also encountered Sir Philip Sidney.[175] The influence of Carmichael's English contacts can perhaps be seen in the two fine sonnets he later addressed to Melville's nephew James, in the latter's *A Spiritual Propine of a Pastour to his People* (Edinburgh, 1589).[176] Open to English influences Carmichael may have been, but during his London exile he used a striking Scots phrase in a letter to his father-in-law, Andrew Simson (whose wife Violet, sister of Patrick Adamson, gave her Christian name to her daughter, Carmichael's wife). As schoolmaster of Perth, Carmichael wrote, Simson went before the others in 1560 'with the reade [ready] knapska' (steel bonnet), but had in the meantime lost his early militancy and subscribed to the king's acts. Intriguingly, the idea of covenant is also aired in this letter from London.[177]

171   *Records of the Synod of Lothian and Tweeddale*, ed. Kirk, 67, 71, 89.
172   Ibid., 57, 96; *BUK*, i, xxvi, xxvii, xxxi.
173   McCrie, *Andrew Melville*, ii, 426.
174   *Cal. State Papers Scotland*, vi, 73; *Correspondence of Robert Bowes* (Surtees Society, 1842), 246, 402.
175   *Wodrow Misc.*, 414, 421, 425.
176   Reprinted in *James Carmichael Proverbs*, 41.
177   *Wodrow Misc.*, 441–2. Cf. 'meit for scapperars' on 443.

Carmichael stayed on in England, moving to the house of Thomas Thomas, the printer, in Cambridge. Here he published his *Grammaticae latinae liber secundus* in 1587. It was providential that Thomas was about to bring out a Latin dictionary, and therefore doubtless had at his disposal a library of classical sources which would be available to Carmichael too. Thomas Dempster went so far as to claim Thomas's Latin dictionary as Carmichael's own, sold to Thomas at little cost, Dempster promising to keep silent as to the work's real authorship; this information came from papers in Carmichael's autograph found in his 'museum' or study.[178] This 'museum' must have been at Cambridge rather than Haddington. Back in 1576, by royal invitation, Carmichael had already discussed suitable Latin texts, and, along with the royal tutor Peter Young, Simson, Patrick Auchinleck and Thomas Buchanan, he had drawn up a list of school texts for printing in Scotland. In order, they were: Cicero, Virgil, Terence, Ovid, Horace, Livy, Julius Caesar, colloquies or dialogues by Mathurin Cordier, Vives and Erasmus, 'ane onomastik', certain select sentences (Cato and Sulpizio, one presumes), along with the catechism for 'young bairns'.[179] Later curricula would feature all of these, barring only Livy.

The title page of Carmichael's Cambridge grammar states that it follows 'that method which the council of the learned held at Stirling decided was easiest for Scottish youth', that is, the 1575 conference convened by Morton. However, there is little that is specifically Scottish about the few vernacular words Carmichael uses; the latter half of the work is exclusively in Latin. Yet he tells us that the first syllable of the Greek 'eta' is pronounced like the Scots 'a' in 'father', something between the sound of 'a' and 'e'. For a person writing among the Cambridge Ramists, it is striking that the only reference to Petrus Ramus is to his *Scholae grammaticales*, while Talon is ignored altogether in the fairly ample bibliography. In a verse dedication to James Wilkie, Carmichael lives up to his claim that his grammar is what he was taught himself at St Leonard's when he was a student and Wilkie (by 1587 its principal) was a regent there. Carmichael observes that much of the contents is too detailed for Scots schoolboys in a hurry to master the subject,[180] and he puts this in smaller type for the fast workers, while warning off slow learners. On one page he cites the Hebrew and Syriac equivalents of *cornu*, a horn; he also prints a Greek alphabet.[181] The latter has Hebrew equivalents in transliteration, and this may have been as far as the boys at St Leonard's went with learning Greek in Carmichael's younger days, although as the

178 *Thomae Dempsteri Historia Ecclesiastica Gentis Scotorum: sive De Scriptoribus Scotis*, ed. D. Irving, i (Bannatyne Club, 1829), 173. This is a reprint of the 1627 edition.
179 *RSS*, vii, no. 828.
180 *Grammaticae latinae liber secundus*, title page: 'ex intimis artis penetralibus'.
181 Ibid., 27, 1.

student advances through the pages the vernacular disappears from the text and the odd Greek word is inserted.

Medieval grammarians are totally absent from Carmichael's long list of authorities, replaced with names like Flavius Sosipater Charisius and, above all, Varro. Plautus and Terence are lavishly represented, as is the author's fellow-countryman Buchanan. Late medieval writers are also absent, apart from the Carmelite Giovanni Battista Mantuano. 'Vasius Scotus' is John Vaus, but Hepburn and Andrew Simson are not mentioned, although the latter's *First Rudiments*, as we saw, had been published in 1580. Nonetheless, Latin and Greek lines by Simson's son William preface the grammar. Linacre is cited, 'he whom our poet [Buchanan] translated into Latin, with a commendation to the Earl of Cassillis, and wished to dedicate to Mary, Queen of England [the future Mary Tudor]'. In a long preliminary letter invoking the patronage of James VI, Carmichael mentions the meeting of grammarians at Stirling some years before, and foreshadows the words of the Privy Council in 1593, complaining about the way Scots youngsters wasted valuable time in a situation where teachers could teach any grammar they liked and so, out of the great variety of books available, chose not the best, but whatever they themselves had learnt or were accustomed to teach, or appealed to the greed of booksellers.[182] This meant that every time parents saw fit to change the youngsters' teacher, the children had to unlearn what they had already learnt and start afresh, which was not only a hindrance to their progress but also a waste of their talents. Instead of the three hundred grammars on the market, the Stirling council had decided to have something new, and part of its making was assigned to Carmichael, with Buchanan present and presiding. At Stirling a method had been prescribed, the first lineaments set out, and tasks assigned to the schoolmasters in attendance. Carmichael's words here are echoed in the 1593 state regulations on the grammar monopoly, but his book itself was probably anticipated by Andrew Simson's 1587 *Second Rudiments*; Carmichael's grammar is not to be found in booksellers' inventories of the time, nor was it ever reprinted. The lines dedicated to Melville as the master-poet whose criticisms Carmichael feared ('iudicium metuens, Archipoeta, tuum'), would scarcely help his cause with the king.[183]

Yet it is doubtful whether the book would have sold in England either; although Carmichael avoids 'ane' as the article, Scots forms are regularly used, for example: 'pleuch', 'quhisperer', *Ambae* equals 'baith the twa', and *enchiridion* is 'a quhingar' or 'hilt'. Modern translators of contemporary documents will find it useful to see *architectus* glossed as merely 'a maister of wark'. No attempt is made to Latinise Haddington, but 'Taodunum' (a favourite

---

182   See pp. 98–99.
183   There are also lines addressed to Archibald, earl of Angus, Mr Richard Cockburn, son of the laird of Clerkington, and to Sir Patrick Lindsay.

form with Buchanan) is used for Dundee.[184] Though a short morning prayer before studies is included, there are few references to Reformers, apart from poets like Beza. Valla is drawn on, and Priscian much more so. Citations from Buchanan range from the *Baptistes*, *Jephthes* and *Fratres Fraterrimi* to the elegies, *Sphaera* and *Rerum Scoticarum Historia*, and, of course, the psalm paraphrases. Catullus is often mentioned,[185] alongside more familiar Latin authors. But nonetheless, the most important name in Carmichael's literary roll of honour was probably still Despauterius.

Like Duncan, Carmichael seems to have seen the learning of grammar as moral training; Roger Ascham's *The Schoolmaster* (1570) had stressed the barbarousness of the language of friars and others which, in his view, led to a divorce between tongue [language] and heart.[186] In actual fact, so called 'barbarous' language abounded in his contemporaries and even in Thomas Thomas's great Latin dictionary, which Thomas issued in the same year and month as he published Carmichael, as mentioned above. We can well believe that they collaborated to some extent while Carmichael was living and working in Thomas's printing house, but while existing papers show Guillaume Morel's influence on Thomas, the documents Dempster claimed to have seen pointing to Carmichael's collaboration, not to say his publisher's wholesale plagiarism, are not now extant.[187] Carmichael's fascination with words is undeniable: his word-lists are copious in a way Duncan's are not. Their vocabulary is less anglicised than Alexander Hume's; although Carmichael remained longer in England than his fellow exiles, he had not become naturalised, as Hume had in 1590.[188]

Nor, for all his talents, had he grown rich. His regret is voiced in the poem addressed to his old teacher, Wilkie, in the *Grammaticae latinae liber secundus*. If only, Carmichael writes, he could lay his hand on the gold found in the sands of Pactolus, which takes its rise under the summer sun in the fertile ground of Mount Tmolus, or enrich himself from the goldbearing waters of the river Hermus: 'If only our freezing Dunpender [Traprain Law] would proffer those precious things wherewith fertile Tmolus nourishes its folk, or that the ebbing Pactolus would flow back into the waters of the Tyne [at Haddington], or if rich Hermus would add thereto its golden waters, I might then be able with a far costlier gift the more liberally to manifest my gratitude to my master. Fate denies me these, or waters down what foreign

---

184   Ibid., 3, 6, 12, 23, 32. The older form for Dundee was 'Deidonum'.
185   For example on 33, 34 and 35.
186   See the reprint edited by L.V. Ryan (Amherst, USA, 1974), 118.
187   D.T. Starnes, *Renaissance Dictionaries* (Austin, Texas/ Edinburgh, 1954), 42, 114–38; G. Stein, *The English Dictionary before Cawdrey* (Tübingen, 1995), 313–14; T. Thomas, *Dictionarium Linguae Latinae et Anglicanae* (Menston, 1972), a reprint of the 1587 edition, ed. R.C. Alston.
188   W. Page (ed.), *Letters of denization and acts of naturalization for aliens in England* (Huguenot Society Publications, 8, 1893), 128.

soil gave. Here I present what my talent can give: do accept it.' Later, in 1609, in a long poem appended to Sir John Skene's *Regiam Majestatem*,[189] the vernacular version, Carmichael returned to the theme of prospecting for gold in the context of suggesting that the *Regiam Majestatem* is a golden work. Here, the addressee is James VI, 'unconquered King, adorned with titles proud'. Carmichael states that Crawford in Lanarkshire produces fine gold as good as anybody's. Again, there is a reference to the Pactolus, to whose golden sands, Carmichael writes, Croesus owed so much. Gold is also drawn from the Tagus in Spain, while the classical Hermus continues to throw up gold from its 'metal-bearing waves', but Scotland has its own rivers like the Esk (whose role here is not clear). The gold deposits of the famed 'rocky height' of Dunpender [Traprain Law] are at least implied, if not mentioned. 'Verdant Garioch' is celebrated, perhaps for its fertility but also for its silver, while Dunnydeer and Menzies are specifically gold-mining centres. Though the worst of Carmichael's financial crisis seems now to be over, gold is much on his mind.[190] Carmichael then styled himself 'ecclesiae quae Hadinae est, pastor', and in 1608 the Haddington presbytery willingly gave him two months off from his pastoral duties to see Sir John Skene's *Regiam majestatem* through the press. The Privy Council explained that there was 'none so meete for this purpose' to act as proof-corrector for every page coming off the press. At first Carmichael was 'loath to undirtak' the task without his presbytery's express leave, but Skene's book would redound not merely to its author's but to his country's reputation.[191] Obviously Carmichael's experience with his printer friend Thomas Thomas in Cambridge had stood him in good stead.

Much of Carmichael's work was on 'helps' for scholars, or specifically directed at interested parties, like the high-placed Englishmen he cultivated for a time; for example, 'The manner of the coronation, set furth by Mr James Carmichael, minister at Haddington' was dispatched through Bowes, the English ambassador, to Cecil, Lord Burghley, in May 1590, soon after the crowning of Queen Anna of Denmark at Holyrood.[192] Carmichael had been one of the book censors appointed back in 1576,[193] at which time he was a tireless compiler and circulariser of Presbyterian, not to say anti-episcopal, documentation. When Robert Montgomery, archbishop of Glasgow, was being forced to submit to a General Assembly, held in the restricted ambi-

---

[189]　A poem by a James Carmichael, junior, presumably a son, features at the start of the book. Carmichael's own verse is at the end, on signatures Hh2 to Hh3.

[190]　S. Atkinson, *The discoverie and hystorie of the gold mynes in Scotland* (Bannatyne Club, 1825), 76 (Tagus), 81 and 85 (Menzies, gold and silver), 82 (Dunpender Law); Menzies is in Foveran parish: *Regiam Majestatem*, sig. Hh2 verso.

[191]　*RPC*, viii, 534–5.

[192]　*Cal. State Papers Scotland*, x, 307.

[193]　Calderwood, *History*, viii, 206.

ence of St Mary's College, Carmichael recorded his submission, something noted by Calderwood with the words 'as I find in Mr James Carmichael his manuscript'.[194]

After 1600, although Carmichael was still closely linked to his local colleagues in the ministry, other external links seem to be broken. When there was a national appeal after the town suffered a great fire in 1598, Carmichael received £16 by way of his son, Nathaniel, from the burgh of Linlithgow, but got no account from him.[195] In 1610, with royal approval, moves were made to elevate the authority of the bishops, and some commissioners, including Carmichael as sole delegate from his presbytery, possessed authorisation to prevent the Assembly from adopting conclusions prejudicial to earlier Assembly decisions. These limitations and directives were, however, largely ignored. The archbishop wished to hold a diocesan synod for Lothian in Haddington, presided over by the bishop. There was 'gentle protestatioun in the fairest termes' from the presbytery, pointing out how the king himself had protected their rights and had accepted the *Second Book of Discipline*; the smooth words of the presbytery's protest were followed by words even smoother in Carmichael's harangue, which referred to 'my lord bishop'.[196] In 1612 Andrew Melville, who had travelled together with Carmichael in 1584 during their English exile, wrote home from his second exile in France, 'What is the profound dreamer …, our Corydon of Haddington, about? I know he cannot be idle: has he not brought forth or perfected anything yet after so many decades of years?' Later, in 1616, he wrote again 'I cannot tell whats becum of Mr James Carmichells labours, or whether he be yet alive.'[197] This makes it clear that Carmichael was not keeping in touch with his old friend; but it is simply incredible that he could have become and died a Catholic convert after a visit from Fr Patrick Anderson, the Jesuit.[198] Whatever lies behind Dempster's assertion, there is no evidence of Carmichael's dying until after Dempster's own death in 1625, while Anderson pre-deceased Dempster, and could not have been present at Carmichael's deathbed in 1628!

A fascinating pedagogical manuscript in Carmichael's hand is an alphabetical list of Scots proverbs.[199] The idea may well have been to replace the traditional Latin saws in books like Cato's *Disticha* or Erasmus's *Adagia*, not useable in most of the new vernacular schools. The manuscript records 1,868 proverbs. While Carmichael's English contacts may have made his

[194]   Ibid., viii, 215.
[195]   J. Robb, *History and Guide to Haddington* (Haddington, 1891), 11.
[196]   Calderwood, *History*, vii, 98, 106, 124, 127, 129.
[197]   McCrie, *Life of Melville*, ii, 286, 529.
[198]   *Thomae Dempsteri Historia Ecclesiastica*, i, 173.
[199]   *James Carmichael Proverbs*.

Scots anglicised in parts, it cannot be claimed that anglicisation in his case made him any more genteel, to judge from some examples of country crudity.[200] Of Scots poets his favourite is Alexander Montgomerie.[201] There is one disparaging proverb about Haddington ale; another Haddington reference is to the public humiliation about 1560 of Friar John Auchinleck, driven about the town to suffer the taunts (and quite possibly missiles) of the hostile mob: 'God mak yow reward as Freir Flek said, when he was cairted through the toun'[202] (we might note that normally Carmichael uses the Scots form 'quhen'). There had been Franciscan conventual friars in the burgh, but the indications are that Carmichael did not like friars, priests or popes, though the theme does not dominate these proverbs.[203] There is a reference to the saying of mass in an obscure corner of a large church, which is probably a saw older than Carmichael himself.[204] Brought up on the Proverbs of Solomon at St Leonard's College, he cites a number from that source, and he has consulted two sources of sacred adages, including a Lutheran work printed in Leipzig in 1601 by Joachim Zehner, and a Jesuit collection published in Lyons in 1612 by Martino Delrio.[205] Among the proper names in the proverbs we find that of Thomas Ross, whose condemnation in 1618 is adverted to,[206] providing a terminal date for the compilation as it stands. It was natural for a schoolmaster to believe 'Better unborne nor untaucht', though 'Sillie bairns are eith [easy] to leirne' is not every teacher's experience.[207] However, both these proverbs seem to have been inherited from his predecessor in proverb-collecting, David Ferguson, minister of Dunfermline.[208]

Carmichael's work provides some insight into contemporary schooling, in spite of his occasional neglect of his own scholars. It is interesting to see that he felt that all children of grammar school age should know the Greek alphabet as a foretaste of things to come, and even more interesting that he should tease the bright children into thinking it might be worthwhile turning sometime to Hebrew and Syriac, citing the name of Angelo Canini (or Caninio), author of *Institutiones linguae syriacae* (1554). In James Carmichael we have an example of a schoolmaster poet widely read in classical and vernacular literature. Some of his own verse has echoes of

---

200   Ibid., for example nos. 343, 423, 465, 667, 708, 718, 812, 865, 1079, 1491, 1502, 1584, 1672.
201   Ibid., p. 28.
202   Ibid., nos. 607, 755.
203   Ibid., nos. 557, 558, 585, 1247
204   Ibid., no. 1630.
205   Ibid., pp. 60, 65.
206   Ibid., p. 28 and no. 1753.
207   Ibid., 321, 1333. 'Sillie' here may, however, mean 'sickly'.
208   Circulating either in manuscript or in a lost print; first known printing 1641. STS edition, 1924, ed. E. Beveridge.

George Buchanan, especially the *Jephthes*, but he adapts his borrowings for his own individual purposes.[209]

IV.8 *George Lightbody of Haddington and his grammar*

Another figure connected with Haddington is George Lightbody, whose *Quaestiones grammaticae in compendium digestae*, published at Edinburgh in 1628, the year of Carmichael's death, took up a challenge flung down by Alexander Hume. Hume had remarked on the absence of logic from the current grammarians of his time. In reply to a critic objecting to his own deployment of logic, he said 'But you'll say, this is logic. Indeed it is. And it is necessary in teaching grammar, for there is no art (skill) without logic, which is the instrument whereby all arts are taught and learnt; without it, no art can be taught. And so the popular grammarian Despauterius, in particular, who offers no definitions, offers no teaching either. He teaches, it is claimed, by natural logic, which is rough and unpolished. But if you use rough thread you'll get rough cloth.'[210] Lightbody, while still adhering to Despauterius, nonetheless took up the challenge, providing 'rules of syntax from Despauterius' at the end of the syntax section in his *Quaestiones*.[211] The very title *Grammatical Questions* suggests a programme.

Lightbody is found at Haddington in the spring of 1607, whence he left for St Leonard's College. Though we find him amongst the matriculands of 1608–09,[212] he managed to graduate as early as the session which ended in 1610. By the spring of 1611 he is found teaching at Oldhamstocks, but he returned to Haddington, where he was paid £20 in 1617 for his 'lang, gude and thankfull service' as doctor of the grammar school, being minded to remove himself.[213] By July 1627 he was at Langton, and his book of *Quaestiones* was dedicated to Sir William Cockburn, knight, as a lover of letters and good friend, and because of his children, brought up in all kinds of honest discipline, especially philosophical studies.[214] Unlike Despauterius, Lightbody does not avoid definition: 'What do you profess? Grammar. What is grammar? The art of correct writing and correct speech' (*recte loquendi*, not *bene*, as in Carmichael). And what is that? A letter is the 'element, and just as the body is made up of four elements, we have syllables and "dictions"

---

[209] See *George Buchanan's Tragedies*, ed. and tr. P. Sharrat & P.G. Walsh (Edinburgh, 1983), 37 (11.396–7) and 55 (11.1101–3) for references to the Tagus, Croesus and Hermus. See also notes on pp. 252–3 and 263.

[210] GUL, MS General 362, fo. 64v.

[211] Op. cit., sig. G2–G4 verso.

[212] These details are in St Andrews University Archives, UY305/3, p. 142.

[213] Haddington Burgh Court Book, transcript in Wallace James Notebooks, NAS, GD1/413/2, p. 27.

[214] *Grammaticae Quaestiones*, dedication, verso of title page.

[words] made up of letters'. Lightbody's etymologies can be distinctly odd, for example: 'Why is it called a verb? From striking [*verberando*]. Why? Because it is formed from the striking of the air, as its sound strikes the ear. What do others say about its origin? From verity, the truth. Why? Because we ought always to speak the truth.'[215] When defining what a verb is, Lightbody stands in a well established line. Andrew Duncan's 1595 definition of a verb had echoed Linacre: 'A verb is a conjugated word; and it is personal or impersonal.'[216] Not too dissimilar would be David Wedderburn's definition in his vernacular grammar of 1632: 'A verbe is conjugated by Moods, Tymes, Numbers and Persons', which slightly shifts the emphasis.[217] Lightbody leaves out the person: 'A verb is a part of speech, which has inflections for moods and tenses, and signifies to act, to suffer, or to be.'[218]

Like Carmichael, Lightbody likes to point out differences in other languages which the pupil may encounter later on: for declensions, Greek is said to have three terminations, Hebrew only one. As in Linacre, the potential mood figures here alongside the others.[219] While literary citation is nothing like as copious as in Carmichael, Lightbody seems partial to Plautus as well as Terence, and he quotes Persius, Sallust and Tacitus, Ovid, Ausonius and Horace. Lightbody is fascinated by words like *quorsum*, and quotes *sinistrorsum* (i.e. left-wards) and other examples. He informs us that 'ex'or 'e' signifies the material cause, while 'a' is the efficient cause, as in 'ut a puero sit sermo, that there may be a talk by the boy'; and wry humour, too, is not lacking: 'the urinator lasts wonderfully well under the water'.[220] As it happened, Lightbody's book had just finished printing by the time its royal privilege, granted by Charles I at Whitehall on 11 July 1628, arrived. The privilege is therefore to be found not in pride of place on the title page, but tacked on at the end amongst the errata. This fortuitous positioning is an amusing foreshadowing of Lightbody's ecclesiological allegiance ten years later, when he attacked King Charles' Scottish service book in a vigorous tract, *Against the apple of the left eye of Antichrist* of 1638, apparently printed in Holland.

IV.9 *Robert Williamson of Cupar and his grammar*

Our penultimate grammarian and poet, Robert Williamson, takes us north to Fife, and back a few years from the Year of the Covenant. The timing

215 Ibid., fos. 2, 15.
216 Duncan, *Latinae grammaticae pars prior*, 58.
217 D. Wedderburn, A *Short Introduction to Grammar* (Aberdeen, 1632).
218 G. Lightbody, *Quaestiones Grammaticae* (Edinburgh, 1628), 15.
219 Ibid., 8, 21.
220 Ibid., 32. The grammar was reissued in Edinburgh at the Restoration in 1660.

of Williamson's grammatical publication is striking. The first edition was in 1609, before Alexander Hume was granted the monopoly, and the second was in 1624, just after Hume had failed to have his grant renewed. The full title of Williamson's rudiments, *Elementa linguae latinae praemia Despauterianae grammaticae, seu introduction ad ipsum*, states them to be an introduction to Despauterius. Williamson's liminary verses include eight lines to Sir John Scot of Scotstarvet, and the epistle dedicatory of the first surviving edition, the *Editio altera et limatior* of 1624, is addressed to John Preston of Airdrie in Fife. It describes this new edition as both larger and freer of errors than the first, which had been published fifteen years earlier. On the flyleaf of the copy held in Edinburgh, there is a note of gift to Mr James Dalgleish, minister of the second charge in Cupar (and formerly schoolmaster of Dunfermline).

If our Williamson was the man of that name who was one of the five candidates for the master's post at Aberdeen in 1580, when the local man Thomas Cargill was appointed,[221] he was a St Leonard's College student at St Andrews from 1574 to 1578. Williamson was certainly a native of Cupar.[222] His first appointments were perhaps as doctor in various Fife schools; he was schoolmaster in Cupar by 1609. In his will, registered 31 May 1649, he is still designated master in Cupar.[223] William Christison, a burgess of Cupar, prior to his death (between 1623 and 1625) had resigned an annual rent in the town to the schoolteacher 'in respect of his son'.[224] In 1627 Williamson was being paid £100 out of the town's common good fund, like the music schoolmaster, and had a single doctor as assistant.[225]

The 1625 third edition of his book follows the text of the second edition, apart from the opening leaves.[226] Grammar is here defined as 'the art of speaking congruously [*congrue*, as against *recte* or *bene*]'. A noun is a 'diction [part of speech] made variable by number and cases, signifying a thing, but without tense'. The detailed explanation of some things, says Williamson, has to be left to the preceptors, if they are real teachers; 'otherwise the art of grammar will freeze and its profession languish, if all is handed down in too precise and wordy a form'. His rudiments, he claimed, could be rushed through in a single year, by methodically following, as it were, the thread of Ariadne through the labyrinth of grammar. Williamson reveals some debt to Linacre, for instance when he refers to 'the circumstance of the thing' with

---

221   *Bon Record*, 22n.
222   See his verses on the town, printed on reverse of title page of his *Paedagogia moralis* (1635).
223   *Commisariot Record of St Andrews. Register of Testaments, 1549–1800*, ed. F.I. Grant (SRS, 1902), 375.
224   RS1/19, 5.
225   *Maitland Misc.*, ii (1), 42.
226   *Elementa linguae latinae, e grammaticorum imprimis Donati, Despauterii, etc., cornucopiae grammaticali excepta* (Edinburgh, 1625).

regard to prepositions, or when he gives space to enallage and attention to ellipsis, for example, when parsing ('in resolutione grammaticali'). The 1632 fourth edition of his *Elements* (a copy of which is in Trinity College Library, Dublin), claims to follow primarily Donatus, Despauterius, Erasmus, Lily, Linacre and the Spaniard, A.A. Nebrija. It cites Vives on its title page, where it is described as the third corrected edition, and is dedicated to the new chancellor of the realm, George Hay, baron of Kinfauns.[227]

Williamson's work is referred to in a letter of Charles I from Greenwich to the Privy Council in June 1632, by which time David Wedderburn of Aberdeen was competing with Alexander Hume in the quest for a monopoly. Williamson was clearly also competing. It seems that his positively adhesive schoolmastering in Cupar was at times against the townspeople's wishes: perhaps they resented his frequent absences in Edinburgh and other Scottish towns, and even, it seems, in London, lobbying on behalf of his grammar. In the third corrected edition he included Latin lines by John Boyle, minister, and by Mr Patrick Sibbald of Cupar, as well as lines addressed to Charles I and to the rectors and churches, city and schools of Edinburgh. The king's letter from Greenwich mentions that Williamson's grammar had the approval of the learned in both Scotland and England; that Williamson himself had borne the printing costs; that, if approved by the Council, it ought to have twenty-one years' licence with the expedition of a royal patent 'under our lachet and sealls' and subject to the necessary restrictions.[228] The Edinburgh University copy has four manuscript lines of Latin verse in Williamson's fine italic hand, offering the book to Principal John Adamson, whose patronage he desired. On the verso of the title page we have testimonials from no fewer than eleven schoolmasters, including three from London,[229] including John Turing[230] and Thomas Farnaby, whose commendation had some value. Obviously, unlike Alexander Hume, Williamson had backers. How far the town of Cupar supported him is far from clear; other schoolmasters, whether assistants or rivals, are on record in the town. Williamson was forced to

---

227　*Grammatica Latina ad artium methodum, et unius anni stadium, e grammaticorum cornucopiae, praecipue Ioh. Despauterii et Linacri commode concinnata. Jam tertio limata, 1632* (Edinburgh, 1632).

228　*The Earl of Stirling's Register of Royal Letters relative to the Affairs of Scotland and Nova Scotia 1615 to 1635*, ed. C. Rogers (Grampian Club, 1885), ii, 597.

229　Namely Thomas Farnaby, John Turing and Henry Bonner; the others are Thomas Crawford of Edinburgh, John Durward of Perth, William Wallace of Glasgow, David Will of Stirling, A. Rind of Linlithgow, James Ready of Dunfermline, Thomas Christie of Burntisland and Samuel Tullidaff of Culross, who had formerly been music master at Ellon.

230　A witness regarding the teinds of Rutherglen in 1633, where Turing 'continually dwelt till within this tua yeir', was another Scot who had moved south, Mr Robert Riddell, described as a 'scolemaster at rodeberrie [Rodborough, Glos.] in Ingland' and, in the same document, as schoolmaster in 'Beucastell [Beaucastle, Worcs.] in Ingland'; NAS, Teinds Records, TE5/32, 1.

fight the prospect of a monopoly for Wedderburn, submitting his objections to the Council in February 1632. Wedderburn promptly replied, and Williamson responded forthwith on 1 March. In June, however, Williamson is styled 'sometyme schoolemaster' at Cupar. Further consideration of King Charles's letter took place in parliament in July.[231]

Williamson proposed the following order of study: a crash course for one year in the rudiments, mostly declensions and conjugations, with word lists and writing up to age ten, unless the pupils were precocious. Thereafter syntax should take one year; practice based thereon a further year; year three could be devoted to verse-composition; year four (and possibly five) extended to rhetoric. The Londoner Farnaby had not exaggerated the grammar's virtues; he had read it and 'with the author's leave, freely corrected it', adding that 'In it I like the method, and if my vote is of any value, I praise its brevity and lucidity, and prefer it to others which I have happened to see.' Most of the Scottish masters praised its clarity of exposition, including Crawford of Edinburgh, who also liked the abundant examples; Durward of Perth thought teachers as well as scholars could benefit from it; Wallace of Glasgow liked the section on figurative speech, and added 'I would be lying if I claimed to have read anything of this sort more free from error, more perfect, or showing greater evidence of diligence'; and Christie of Burntisland appreciated its usefulness to the young.

The book takes the form of question and answer. There are, of course, quotations from such as Terence and Livy. As the grammar proceeds, Williamson increasingly cites the rules of Despauterius's versified grammar to the extent that his work becomes a commentary on the latter. Williamson notes that teaching had to relate both to the uncultivated minds of the young and to the 1597 decree of the Three Estates of the realm; this had laid down requirements for a clear, short and methodical approach to teaching, which was to take account of youthful capacity, the talents and memory of that tender age, and not to overburden it with advanced matter. Though verse-form memorisation often leads to obscurity, it can help (as with Despauterius) the answers to come more readily to pupils' minds, and the dialogue method helps to clarify the ideas. Improvements, Williamson adds, have been effected as a result of the comments of British grammarians.

David Wedderburn's victory in obtaining the monopoly, however, soon put paid to Williamson's grammar. Defeated in one direction, the Cupar schoolmaster then turned to the production of a Latin *Moral Pedagogy*, perhaps to replace Andrew Duncan's *Rudiments of Piety*, mentioned earlier.[232]

---

231   *RPC* series 2, iv, 432, 436, 437, 493, 500, 514.
232   *Paedagogia moralis tertia R Williamsoni Cuprensis cura aucta et limata in gratiam juventutis Christianae* (Edinburgh, 1635), NLS copy. The earlier Cambridge copy, listed on Early English Books Online as Edinburgh, c.1635, is defective.

The new work, however, would include, under its new title, not only basic piety but also the elements of civility. The date of the first edition is uncertain; an edition of 1635 is said to be issued 'with additions and corrections for the third time'. An undated copy of Williamson's *Paedagogia* from Emmanuel College Cambridge is dedicated to John and Walter, sons of Preston of Airdrie, and to Robert and James Arnot, sons of the laird of Fernie. We would recall that in 1624, the patrons of Williamson's grammar had been Sir John Preston of Airdrie (baronet of Nova Scotia from 1628), as well as Bruce of Earlshall, whose sons George and John were mentioned. The undated edition of the *Paedagogia* includes some prefatory Latin verses by Williamson himself, as well as four lines by a minister, James Spens, and verse by Williamson at the end. It would therefore seem to precede the 1635 edition, in which Spens has six lines, there is prefatory verse by the poet Robert Fairlie, and the list of dedicatees is extended to include James Preston and John and William Arnot.

The first part of Williamson's *Paedagogia* comprises a rudiments of piety: 'The scholarly upbringing of boys is their lawful training in good letters and morals and is chiefly grammatical or moral.' As far as grammar is concerned, it is 'formation in knowledge of the principal tongues, Latin, Greek and Hebrew, etc., and concerns congruity of speech [grammar], modulation [verse], and ornamentation [rhetoric]'. Moral training is training in the precepts of God and civil manners, and Williamson adds that 'He who progresses in letters and lags behind in morals is more a failure than a success.' A morning meditation addressed to the 'blessed Jehovah' includes the young scholars' promise of obedience to their parents and schoolmasters. There follows the 'Morning Hymn for Sundays to be sung to Christ by the scholars, from Buchanan'. In printed editions of Buchanan, part of this hymn is given after the text of the psalms, but the unique version in Williamson is closest to those in some of the Plantin and Herborn editions of Buchanan. The Sunday singing of the hymn, as presented by Williamson, is stressed by a textual reference: 'Lo, the night has gone, now shines the dawn of the holy Sabbath, which you ordain to be solemnly dedicated to your worship … let us pass this day in holiness, leaving aside play and worldly affairs. Let us worship you from within, in truth and in spirit, giving thanks to the Holiest with our unceasing praise.'[233] It is not too much to believe that this was a

---

233   En nox recessit, iam nitet
    Aurora sancti sabbathi
    (quod tu lubes sacratier
    Cultu tuo solenniter) …
    Fac transigamus hunc diem
    Sancte abdicatis ludicris,
    Negotiisque saeculis.
    Fac te colamus intimo

version made by Buchanan personally for use in Scottish schools, which some native composer may have set to music (now, alas, lost).[234] Williamson follows it with four versified prayers of his own, to be said before lessons, before the midday meal and before leaving school.

In this 1635 edition, Williamson gives (in Latin) the catechism of William Scot, minister of the first charge at Cupar. Scot's was a name strongly associated with opposition to King James's ecclesiastical policies, and therefore one unlikely to commend the book to his son, possibly even nullifying the dedication to Robert Ker, earl of Ancrum. At the close are edifying verses dedicated to Dr George Sibbald, Mr Robert Douglas, William Monteith, laird of Ranchford, and Mr Henry Magill, preacher. The earlier, undated edition does not use Scot's catechism, and begins rather with an admonition to be mindful of God and to love one's neighbour, a process which would be followed in later revisions of Andrew Duncan's *Rudimenta Pietatis*. In the undated copy, the discussion of the Lord's Supper attacks the theology of 'transmutation' of the species put forward by the mass-mongers, while in the 1635 edition, the grace after meals includes a prayer seeking protection for the flock in the face of the 'cunning of Antichrist'. The first part of the *Moral Pedagogy* is saturated with Calvinist doctrine. Hypocrites and infidels will be punished with hellfire. Moral knowledge comes from acquaintance with scripture, and it is summarised in the Decalogue, the Apostles' Creed, the Lord's Prayer and the sacramental teaching. One's election is triple: first in one's calling; secondly in one's adoption; and finally in one's justification. Williamson's teaching was anchored in the Calvinist understanding of revelation, where there existed deep initial scepticism regarding 'merely natural and rational beliefs'.[235]

In veritate et spiritu
Congratulantes Numini
Indesinenter laudibus.

234 There are printed musical settings of Buchanan's psalm paraphrases; relatively complex polyphonic versions of Pss. I to XLI, for up to eight voices, by Jean Servin, published in 1578, and, more relevantly, from 1582, a set of four part homophonic settings made by Statius Olthoff, suited to the thirty metres employed by Buchanan. These settings were long used by the boys at the Gymnasium in Herborn and the students at the University of Rostock; it is by no means impossible that they could have been used in some Scottish schools. See G. Bell, 'Notes on some music set to Buchanan's paraphrase of the psalms', in *George Buchanan, Glasgow Quatercentenary Studies* (1906), 333–45, and McFarlane, *Buchanan*, 266–8. On Olthof and Servin, see also Margaret Duncumb, 'Buchanan's psalms and the musical settings by Statius Olthof' and James Porter, 'The historical importance of Jean Servin's settings of Buchanan's psalm paraphrases', in P. Ford and R.P.H. Green (eds.), *George Buchanan: Poet and Dramatist* (Swansea, 2009).

235 R.L. Emerson, 'Calvinism and the Scottish Enlightenment', in Joachim Schwend et al. (eds.), *Literatur im Kontext: Literature in Context, Festschrift fur H.W. Drescher* (Frankfurt/ Bern/New York/Paris, 1992) , 19–28. One wonders whether Williamson's school still possessed Balbi's medieval textbook *Catholicon*, left to the schoolmaster in Cupar by Mr

It is against this background that we must read Williamson's teaching on the need for schoolboys to learn 'civility', social conduct and good manners. Civility was not new in Europe in the sixteenth century,[236] but the word only starts appearing in Scottish sources during that period, with the suggestion that the courtly tradition which it was to replace was still acceptable in some measure:

> I luff modest sobir civilitie
> Mixit with gentill courtess hamlyness.[237]

And indeed, Principal Alexander Arbuthnott of Aberdeen's ideal of 'sobir civilitie' is precisely what Williamson aimed at. Another Scots poem of the same era calls the earl of Northumberland

> That paragon of trew nobilitie
> And perfect patroun of civilitie.[238]

There are earlier antecedents for this; in 1505 we find reference to human elegance (as distinct from Valla's verbal elegance) in a deed of Robert Shaw, abbot of Paisley, granting a holding in Stockwell, Glasgow, to the 'elegant and honourable man, Alan Stewart of Cardonald', and in 1543, a notarial deed drawn up by the Reformer John Knox makes a similar reference to his pupil William Brownfield as 'an elegant youth'.[239] Although by the time of James VI it was considered highly undesirable to be 'reput rusticall and rude',[240] rusticity was not easily put down. Williamson tells the boys that the way to get rid of moisture from the nostrils, mucus, was not by wiping it with your arm or the sleeve of your tunic; moreover, in the presence of more distinguished people, you should turn your back when blowing your nose. Teeth are not to be cleaned with a knife or your nails; remove the plaque with mouth washes (*oraculis*) or the point of a pen. You are not to uncover your private parts (*pudenda*) unnecessarily; in cases of urgent need, you should do so modestly (*cum reverentia*), for even if there is no witness present, the angels are always there (*nunquam enim non adsunt angeli*). Boys sharing beds with older boys should speak only rarely. Pupils should not prolong their presence at table, but eat just enough. When at table, the head should be kept covered, French-style, when answering or toasting someone, since the cap will prevent hair from making its way into the food. Placid, cheery, modest conduct was to be the norm. Regulations follow, concerning bodily cleanli-

John Bonar of St Andrews in his will dated 31 Mar. 1527; and if so, whether he was aware that Bonar's purpose had been that the school might pray for his soul and that of Master Walter Lawson (St Andrews University Archives, St Andrews Burgh Deeds, Box 8).

236   M.V. Becker, *Civility and Society in Western Europe 1300–1600* (Bloomington, Indiana, 1988).
237   *Maitland Folio Manuscript*, ed. W.A. Craigie (STS, 1919), i, 51.
238   *Maitland Quarto Manuscript*, ed. W.A. Craigie (STS, 1920), i, 51.
239   *Registrum Monasterii de Passelet*, 433; Durkan, 'Scottish reformers', *IR*, xiv (1994), 21.
240   John Burel, *Pamphilus speakand of lufe* (Edinburgh, c.1590), line 824.

ness, clothes, attending kirk, and (in some detail) table manners, not cheating at games, civility and regard for others (*morigeratio*) in human 'conversation' where the word retains the classical meaning of 'social intercourse',[241] as in the medieval requirement that men be 'of good conversation' if they are to be employed as chaplains. Verbal exchange is only part of the meaning! Williamson's rules, with their echoes of Erasmus,[242] bring the inside of a Cupar school vividly to life for a modern reader; grammar, it seems, was not the only civilising influence.[243]

IV.10 David Wedderburn of Aberdeen wins the grammar monopoly

Both Williamson and James Glegg of Dundee opposed the Aberdonian David Wedderburn's application for a grammar monopoly in 1632. But Williamson could not match Wedderburn's literary patrons and ability as a theorist or poet. All Wedderburn's productions were of a consistently high standard. His extant poetry is far from negligible, including a celebration of the now lost Latin verse of his Aberdonian predecessor William Carmichael (d.1580) who was also celebrated by the St Mary's College poet John Johnston. The latter held David Wedderburn in high regard, bequeathing him an unpublished volume of poetry 'quhilk I desyir to be reveist, and if thocht worthie, it may be published be the said Mr David Wedderburne'.[244] The Aberdeen schoolmaster's poetry includes significant elegies on the deaths of Prince Henry in 1613, the notable medical writer Duncan Liddell in 1614 and King James in 1625[245] – by which time a local printer, Edward Raban, had established himself in Aberdeen. This eased publication of Wedderburn's works. In his fight for the grammar monopoly, he would enjoy the full support of his town council, and he could call on the help of friends in high places: Thomas Reid, secretary to King James, who had been his colleague at the grammar school, and that outstanding son of the north east, Arthur Johnston, not only a major Latin poet but also physician to Charles I.[246]

By 1630 Wedderburn was clearly determined to outpace both Alexander Hume and Robert Williamson in the race for a grammatical monopoly. When Hume's monopoly was under reconsideration in July 1630, the Aber-

---

241 *Paedagogia moralis* (1635), C1 verso to D2 verso.
242 His *De civilitate morum* occurs in the sixteenth-century Scottish book inventories cited above, pp. 99, 102.
243 See Durkan, 'Laying of fresh foundations', 147–8.
244 *Musa Latina Aberdonensis*, ed. W.K. Leask (New Spalding Club, 1910), iii, 123, poem XX, and 368, 1.191; *Maitland Misc.*, ii (2), 343.
245 All to be found in *Musa Latina Aberdonensis*, iii.
246 *Bon Record*, 28; Arthur Johnston commended the early edition of Wedderburn's Latin grammar. See *Musa Latina Aberdonensis*, iii, for Wedderburn's reply to Johnston (after 1622), 392–8, and his elegiac 'sighs' on his friend's death in 1641, 432–5.

deen town council decided to pay Wedderburn's expenses in Edinburgh to the tune of £40;[247] by March 1631 this had risen to over £66 on account of a long stay in the capital.[248] As early as December 1630 the council noted that Wedderburn had a reformed grammar ready, which he would not put into print without the agreement of the Lords of Council; hence the need to lobby Edinburgh, and financial aid from Aberdeen to the value of £100.[249] By the end of March 1632 success was Wedderburn's; he had lobbied the councils and 'clergie' of the kingdom at the cost of a further 100 merks. In 1633 he got £100 to help cover printing costs.[250] In June 1633 his case had reached parliament, which referred the granting of his monopoly to the Lords of Council committee appointed for the purpose.[251] It is clear that Wedderburn had by 1632 managed to get the backing of the commissioners of the royal burghs, each one contributing to the cost of the printing, towards which Edinburgh had paid £120 on their behalf.[252] His 1632 vernacular grammar, referred to earlier, was an astute innovation, for vernacular schools had flourished and needed to lay down more stable foundations, especially where the teaching was being done by graduates.

The second edition of his Latin grammar, dated 1633, must have followed closely on the first. On the verso of the title are Wedderburn's verses to his patrons, the commissioners of the burghs, followed by a dedication to Paul Menzies of Kinmund, and the council of Aberdeen, dated 1 May 1633, where he claims he has taught in Aberdeen for thirty years, and mentions 'the remainder of my already encroaching old age'. Then come Latin lines by Arthur Johnston, which state that by Wedderburn's craft the huge bulk of Despauterius is both improved and halved in volume. There follows a long commendation in prose by Alexander Lunan, minister. A hint of the influence of Linacre's grammar is the long section on enallage (p. 96), while the influence of Valla and his followers is seen in the 'formula of some elegances' (p. 99), first in nouns, then in other parts of speech. The three main sections are (1) etymology (2) syntax and (3) orthography and prosody with a brief supplement on rhetoric. Like Carmichael, Wedderburn envisages Greek at a later stage, for this Latin grammar goes into much greater detail than its vernacular predecessor of 1632. Prosody is treated at a length (pp. 113–36) which goes well beyond the 'figurative syntax' of Williamson. Here again, Greek usage is invoked. Wedderburn is more thorough than

247   J. Stuart (ed.), *Extracts from the Council Register of the Burgh of Aberdeen* (SBRS, 1871), 29. This is a continuation of the earlier Spalding Club volumes, *Aberdeen Council Register*.
248   *Spalding Misc.*, v, 147, 148.
249   Ibid., v, 149; *Aberdeen Extracts*, ed. Stuart, ii, 32.
250   *Aberdeen Extracts*, ed. Stuart, ii, 35; *Spalding Misc.*, v, 104.
251   *APS*, v, 48.
252   L.B. Taylor (ed.), *Aberdeen Council Letters* (Oxford, 1942), i, 348, 350.

Buchanan, whose *Prosodia*, however, the Aberdonian's work never displaced. In the main text, Wedderburn cites Cicero, Virgil, Terence, Plautus, Pliny, Caesar, Boethius (not quite an Augustan, of course), Cato, Juvenal, Livy and Quintus Curtius. In the section on versification, examples are culled from Virgil's *Eclogues* and *Aeneid*, Ovid, Horace, Tibullus, Ausonius and Martial. The vernacular explanations fade out as the text proceeds, and rules are cited at length, apparently from the verse of Despauterius. Before the close, a few lines of Melanchthon warn against prolixity.[253]

Wedderburn's career after 1633 hardly concerns us. His thematically arranged *Vocabula* I have seen only in the 1685 edition; the first edition of 1636 appears not to have survived. He also produced an edition of Persius, *Persius enucleatus*, published at Amsterdam as late as 1664. Wedderburn follows the Aberdeen tradition that had started with Vaus and was continued by Simson, which placed value on the verse mnemonic as used by Villedieu and classicised by Despauterius.

---

[253] *Institutiones grammaticae. Editio Secunda* (Aberdeen, 1633). An extant 1634 edition seems very similar.

V. Subjects Other than Grammar

V.1 Music and song schools

At the Reformation, monastery, collegiate church and cathedral choirs, and the complex liturgical life which they had existed to serve, were declared redundant, along with altars and images. This called into question the future of the network of song schools which had existed to supply the requirements of the Catholic rite. In terms of praise in worship, the Reformers' aim was quite straightforward: it should be provided by the congregation, not by a small body of professional singers. To make this possible, choral polyphony was replaced by metrical psalmody. The model was Geneva, where the congregation sang the impressively varied and poetic versions made by Clément Marot and Théodore de Bèze (Beza), 'all together in a plain tune' – of which the splendid French psalter had no fewer than 125, each assigned to a specific psalm (or, in twenty-five cases, to two). In 1549, Thomas Sternhold had laid the foundations of an English metrical psalter, which would eventually appear in complete form in 1562.[1] The brand new Scottish Kirk took some time to provide itself with a complete metrical psalter, closely related to, but far from identical with, the English *Whole Booke of Psalms* of 1562.[2] When the Scottish psalter was finally printed in 1564–65, it contained 105 tunes for the 150 psalms, as opposed to the 68 tunes of the English *Whole Booke*, which included twenty-seven hymns and canticles in addition to the psalms.

In Scotland, for some time after 1564, the editions of the psalter featured only psalms, but later editions of the psalter gradually introduced a number of canticles and suitably didactic 'hymns', apppointed to be sung to specified psalm melodies, taken from the English *Whole Booke*.[3] It is important to stress that the Scottish metrical psalter was by no means identical with the *Whole Booke*. The English and Scottish books did share a large amount of material; but while in no way poetically superior to the impressively unpoetic English volume, the Scottish book displayed a far greater range of metrical schemes,

---

[1] See B. Quitslund, *The Reformation in Rhyme: Sternhold, Hopkins and the English Metrical Psalter, 1547–1603* (Aldershot, 2008).

[2] See J.M. Patrick, *Four Centuries of Scottish Psalmody* (London, 1949). For a complete harmonised psalter, see N. Livingstone's edition of the 1635 *Scottish Metrical Psalter* (Glasgow, 1864), reissued (minus its substantial prefatory matter) by R.R. Terry as *The 1635 Scottish Psalter* (London, 1936). K. Elliot, 'Scottish music of the early reformed church', *Transactions of the Scottish Ecclesiological Society*, xv (2) (1961), 18–31, is essential reading in this field.

[3] The exceptions are James Melville's 'Song of Moses', first added in Andro Hart's 1615 edition, and Margaret Cunningham's sonnet which joined the Melville 'Song' in Hart's 1635 psalter. For Cunningham see Section III above, p. 95.

thanks to its retention of all the 'Anglo-Genevan' versions jettisoned by the *Whole Booke*. These had been written to mostly French tunes by William Whittingham and the Scot William Kethe, as were a substantial number of entirely new texts by the Scottish divines Robert Pont and John Craig.[4]

Choral arrangements of the psalms had existed in Huguenot circles from early on, and the decision that there should be harmonised (but not polyphonic) settings of the new Kirk's psalms was taken by 'my Lord Jamis (wha efter wes Erle of murray and regent) being at the reformation pryour of sanctandrous'. Lord James's parish minister in St Andrews was the Geneva-trained Englishman Christopher Goodman (Knox's closest male friend), whom Lord James would have consulted along with various local musicians.[5] These appear to have included a former monk of Lindores, Thomas Wode (who would conceivably have wished to continue his former monastic practice of singing the psalms daily). Lord James commanded one of his canons, David Peebles (described by Wode as 'ane of the cheiff musitians into this land'), to arrange the psalm tunes for four voices, but to 'leave the curiositie of musike [i.e. polyphony] and sa mak plane and dulce'. Wode, it appears from his own marginalia, began immediately to make fair copies of whatever psalm texts and tunes he had available, but was told to stay his hand until the whole psalm book published in Geneva in 1562 should arrive. From that year onwards, Wode, now living in St Andrews, set about copying out Peebles' harmonisations, which were not very rapidly forthcoming from the composer. Wode notes that 'he wes nocht earnest', and adds 'but I … wes evir requeisting and solisting' until all the tunes were arranged in four parts.[6]

It is unlikely that the bulk of the congregation sang more than the tune, but in church the harmonisations were sung by song school pupils when these were available. In the post-Reformation song schools, however, training in song itself would henceforth be overshadowed by coaching in reading. Whatever the boys might be learning in terms of musical technique, the song schools were also vernacular reading schools: when Mr Andrew Stewart was appointed to the music school in Ayr on 28 August 1583, he obliged himself to teach sufficient theory 'and learne thame to sing … and

4   Some twenty of these psalms are now available on disc. See n. 9 below for details. In 1650, the 1564 texts were replaced by the present metrical psalms in standardised, common metre, in a publication devoid of any music at all. See also J. Reid-Baxter, 'Metrical psalmody and the Bannatyne Manuscript: Robert Pont's Psalm 83', *Renaissance and Reformation*, 30.4 (2006/7), 41–62.

5   See J. McQuaid, 'Scottish Musicians of the Reformation' (University of Edinburgh Ph.D. thesis, 1949), 13–18.

6   See J. Reid Baxter, 'Thomas Wode, Christopher Goodman and the curious death of Scottish music', *Scotlands* (Edinburgh University Press), 4.2, 1997.

to learne the barnis that singis to read and write Inglis and sall sing in the kirk the four partis of musik beginning ilk Sunday at the second bell'.[7]

Wode completed copying out the psalms in 1566, adding no fewer than eighteen canticles whose texts he had taken from the English *Whole Booke*.[8] Perhaps because of Peebles' dilatoriness in carrying out a task which he seems to have regarded as unworthy of his compositional skills, Wode called upon other musicians to help. Certain psalms were set by John Buchan and others by Andrew Blackhall, a former canon of Holyrood Abbey, who also contributed to the settings of the Canticles, alongside dene John Angus, one of the conventual brethren of Dunfermline, and Andrew Kemp, song schoolmaster in St Andrews (over forty of whose own three- and four-part psalm harmonisations survive in another manuscript source).[9] As time went on, Wode began adding other 'godlye songs' (including a number of pre-Reformation Latin motets!); these included a polyphonic setting of a penitential sonnet by Knox and Goodman's close friend Mrs Anne Locke, made by Kemp at the English pastor's specific request.[10] Kemp himself added marginal notes to metrical canticles by John Angus, to the effect that the written note-values needed to be halved, otherwise the effect would be too 'hevy and doylit' – and, by implication, dull.[11]

The reservations of composers trained before 1560 as to the musical value of simple four-part harmonisations may also be reflected in the wealth of instruction in vastly more complicated compositional and performing techniques contained in the anonymous manuscript treatise *The Art of Music*

---

[7] Carnegie Library, Ayr, B6/11/1(1), 162v. For detailed discussion of Scotland's post-Reformation music schools, see Gordon Munro, '"Sang Schwylls" and "Music Schools": Music Education in Scotland 1560–1650', in R.E. Murray (ed.), *Music Education in the Middle Ages and Renaissance* (Indiana, 2010).

[8] For details see H.P. Hutchinson, 'The St Andrews Psalter' (University of Edinburgh Ph.D. thesis, 1957), vol. 1. Vol. 2 contains a complete transcription of the entire contents of the *Psalter*; several of the psalms, canticles and other music can be found in K. Elliot & H.M. Shire (eds.), *Music of Scotland 1500–1700* (3rd edn, London, 1975) and K. Elliott (ed.), *Fourteen Psalm Settings of the Early Reformed Church* (London, 1960).

[9] Duncan Burnett's Music Book (c.1615), NLS, MS 9447, fos. 140v–161r. Examples of Kemp's work are printed by Elliott (see previous note). Modern editions of Kemp's work can also be found in Raymond White, 'Music of the Scottish Reformation 1560–1650' (University of St Andrews Ph.D. thesis, 1972). Settings by Peebles and Angus from Wode's collection can be heard sung by Cappella Nova on *Sacred Music for Mary Queen of Scots* (CD ASV Gaudeamus), and, along with works by Kemp, Blackhall and Buchan, by Edinburgh University Renaissance Singers on *Psalms for the Regents of Scotland* (CD, 1998).

[10] 'Have mercy, God' is from Locke's *The Meditation of a Penitent Sinner*, a sonnet sequence which explores Ps. 51, the Miserere, verse by verse; it was published in London in 1560. Modern editions by K. Morin-Parsons (Waterloo, Ontario, 1997) and in S. Felch (ed.), *The Collected Works of Anne Vaughan Locke* (Arizona, 1999).

[11] See McQuaid, 'Scottish Musicians', p. 175.

collectit out of all antient doctouris of musick (c.1580).[12] This musical textbook
is thought to have been written in response to King James VI's 'tymous
remeid' of the deplorable state of musical education, a statute issued on
11 November 1579 reinstating the burgh and collegiate song schools on a
civic basis. *The Art of Music* clearly reflects both pre- and post-Reformation
practice, since it covers the learning both of Gregorian ecclesiastical modes,
ornate polyphony in the style of Robert Carver, and faburden (harmonised
plainsong), and of metrical psalms, both in simple four-part harmony and 'in
reports' (a kind of primitive fugal technique using imitative counterpoint);[13]
the book contains an example believed to be the work of Andrew Blackhall.
Complex 'lessons upon psalms', thought to be the work of John Black of
Aberdeen, also appear, polyphonic pieces in which the church psalm tune
appears in the tenor voice, surrounded by flowing counterpoint; these may
well have been purely instrumental pieces for performance in godly households.[14]

The work of this first generation of post-Reformation musicians had a
long life ahead of it. The editor of the 1635 *Psalter*, Edward Millar, acknowledged that the plain note-against-note four-part harmonisations of that
volume were indebted to the most principal musicians of Scotland, and he
named dene John Angus, Andrew Kemp, Alexander Smith, David Peebles,
a certain Sharp and John Buchan, without, alas, specifying which hand had
been responsible for each psalm.[15] It is indicative of the steady decline in
creative musicianship since 1560 that much of these composers' work must
have been over fifty (and even seventy) years old in 1635. Millar's *Psalter* also
included a number of psalms in reports; since in these works the polyphony
makes it difficult to understand the text, they may have been intended for
domestic singing and not for church services, but the 'provost and prebends
of the Chapel Royal did sing the 21 psalme of David according to the art
of musique to the great delectation of the noble auditorie' at the baptism of
Prince Henry Frederick in 1594.[16]

More elaborate music, if not heard in kirk, would nevertheless continue

---

[12] Edited by J.D. Maynard as 'An Anonymous Scottish Treatise on Music from the Sixteenth
      Century, British Museum Additional Manuscript 4911, Edition and Commentary' (Indiana
      University Ph.D. thesis, 1961).

[13] An anonymous Ps. 6 in reports can be heard on Paisley Abbey Choir's *Cantate Domino*
      (Abbey Records).

[14] They can be heard played as such by D. James Ross and Coronach on *A Scottish Mass
      of 1546* (cassette CMF 004). The pieces are printed in Elliot & Shire, *Music of Scotland
      1500–1700*.

[15] Elliott, 'Music of the early reformed church', 22. Sharp is unidentified; the others were all
      connected with music in St Andrews: Alexander Smith was James Melville's music teacher
      there, while Buchan and Angus contributed to Wode's *Psalter*. Elliott also shows just how
      creatively Millar edited the manuscript sources in preparing his 1635 Psalter.

[16] C. Rogers, *History of the Chapel Royal of Scotland* (Edinburgh, 1882), lxxxiii.

to be cultivated – in private households, such as the city houses visited by
James Melville in Glasgow, in the homes of lairds and ladies like Forbes of
Tolquhon and Lady Margaret Wemyss, and, as evidenced by the manuscript
books of teachers themselves, in schools. Duncan Burnett was song schoolmaster in Glasgow until his death c.1652, and presumably taught the forty
or so Andrew Kemp psalm settings which he transcribed. His own fine
keyboard music has somewhat sombre overtones, but he also transcribed
colourful pieces by the Scot William Kinloch[17] and even a pavane by the
great William Byrd. Indeed, the music of Orlando Gibbons also seems to
have been popular with Scots; Edinburgh made him a burgess in 1617 on
his arrival with King James.[18] As far as that other keyboard instrument, the
organ, is concerned, in pre-Reformation times it had been customary for
the song schoolmaster to be not only a qualified singer, but to be able
to play and teach the organ, as at Inverness in 1539.[19] No liturgical organ
music appears to have survived,[20] but despite the Reformation's destruction
of kirk organs,[21] secular performance of keyboard music clearly continued
to be prized. One of the requirements of the Ayr council in 1583 was that
Andrew Stewart should teach the bairns to play 'upoun the pynatis' (from
the French, *épinette*, a spinet),[22] an instrument upon which James Melville
had entertained himself as a St Andrews student in the early 1570s, while in
Edinburgh in 1627 the council hired a Frenchman, Claud Bucellis (obviously of Italian ancestry), to teach instrumental music;[23] and we might note
that in 1617, when two musicians had attempted to open a music school
there, without success, the council had insisted on a preliminary test of their
abilities.[24] The poet Alexander Hume (1557–1609), minister of Logie near
Stirling, enjoyed instrumental music; his poetry makes several references to
it, and to his own lute playing to accompany his domestic psalmody, while
his testament indicates the presence of instruments in his manse.[25] We find

---

[17] Both Kinloch and Burnett can be heard played by John Kitchen on *Kinloch his Fantassie*
      (CD ASV Gaudeamus). Many pieces are printed in K. Elliott (ed.), *Early Scottish Keyboard
      Music* (London, 1967), and the complete works of Kinloch and Burnett, edited by K. Elliott,
      are to appear in the *Musica Scotica* series (Glasgow University).
[18] T. Dart, 'New sources of virginal music', *Music and Letters*, xxv (1954), 101–3; C.B.B. Watson
      (ed.), *Roll of Edinburgh Burgesses and Guild-brethren* (SRS, 1929), 202.
[19] NLS, Adv MS 29.4.2, vi, 71; the consent of the previous parish clerk was required.
[20] Probably because there was very little music specifically written out for organ; standard
      practice seems to have been to improvise on plainchant, as seen in the Trinity Altarpiece.
      A plainsong gradual 'for the use of the organist' is recorded in Aberdeen; F.C. Eeles, *King's
      College Chapel, Aberdeen* (Edinburgh, 1951), 42–3.
[21] See Ross, *Musick Fyne*, 98–101.
[22] Carnegie Library, Ayr, B6/11/1(1), 167v.
[23] *Edinburgh Burgh Recs.*, vii, 20.
[24] Ibid., vi, 163–4.
[25] He had borrowed a lute from the lady of Menstrie, wife of the poet Sir William Alexander,
      and had two other unidentified instruments. Hume, *Poems*, ed. Lawson, 213.

instances of whole families of musicians, like the Tilliedaffs, some of whom
were clearly qualified grammarians as well. When Mr Samuel was in the
'gramer and musik' school at Ellon, Mr Alexander was a doctor in the
school there, but later went on to teach music at Dunfermline and Cupar.
Mr Samuel moved to Culross as grammar schoolmaster in 1623. Mr John
can be traced at Kirkwall, Tain, Kiltearn and Tarbat.[26] Finally, Mr Stephen
Tilliedaff is found in Dunfermline and Edinburgh. As far as musical training
in the Highland area is concerned, different arrangements continued to exist;
and, as in John Mair's day a century earlier, even Lowlanders continued to
appreciate Highland harping as 'most pleasing music'.[27]

Song schools were not a pressing requirement in the eyes of the first
Scottish Reformers. In Ayr in May 1559, the song schoolmaster, George
Cochrane, was discharged from the post of organist at Ayr parish kirk and
forced to hand over his key to the organ loft. Cochrane protested that
because of this discontinuation of service, nobody should allege his departure from the cure had been 'of benevolence' (i.e. willingly), but solely
because he had been fired.[28] Some of these teachers may have found a place
in the new Kirk, as did Andrew Kemp at St Andrews, while others may
have found other employment or gone abroad, as John Black of Aberdeen
did for a time, being replaced by the same Andrew Kemp in 1570.[29] Some
went to England, as the priest-composer Robert Johnson of Duns had done
some decades earlier when he found himself accused of heresy by the then
Catholic authorities.[30] One of those who left Reformed Scotland for the

---

26 RD1/460, 63.
27 Major, *History*, 50. Wode included a selection of clarsachs amongst the instruments with
    which he embellished the pages of his partbooks; see Ross, *Musick Fyne*, 144–7, for the
    full extent of evidence of Lowland appreciation of Highland harping. Both Alexander
    Hume and John Burel appear to celebrate this instrument in the context of municipal
    music making during public celebrations. In Burel's, 'Description of the Queen's Entry',
    in *Watson's Choice Collection*, ed. H.H. Wood (STS, 1977), part ii, 1–16, there is a mysterious
    reference to 'clarche pipe and clarioun' (line 138). This may concern three instruments, not
    two, the first being a mispelled 'clarsach'. Further evidence that (some) Lowlanders liked
    Highland music, and that Burel's *clarche* and *pipe* should be separated, is found in Alexander
    Hume's demand that in the celebrations of the defeat of the Armada 'On hieland pypes
    Scots, and Hybernik/ Let heir the shraichs of deadly Clarions' (*Poems*, ed. Lawson, VII:
    58–9), and perhaps also in 'heauenly harmony/ Of instruments accorded in a kie/ Maist
    musicall and delicate to get […] As clarshons cleare, douce friddoning of flutes/ The viols
    swift, and finest Venus lutes' (ibid., 203–8), where *clarshons* could well be 'clarsachs' rather
    than a wind instrument.
28 Livingston (ed.), *Scottish Metrical Psalter*, 16
29 When Kemp arrived, there was 'na exercitatioun of musick usit in the said scoill', *Aberdeen
    Extracts*, ed. Stuart, i, 370.
30 See Ross, *Musick Fyne*, 71–2 and note; several pieces by Johnson are to be found in Elliot &
    Shire, *Music of Scotland 1500–1700*, and much of his Latin church music has been recorded
    by Cappella Nova (CD ASV Gaudeamus). Our sole source for his flight into England 'lang
    before reformation' is Thomas Wode. Robert may have been a kinsman of John, 'humble'

south was the composer Patrick Douglas, formerly of St Giles, naturalised on 10 November 1565.[31] In London in 1565 we find James Caldwell, Scot, minstrel, sharing a house with the composer William Kinloch as tenants to the parish of St Foster, and John Linde and John Philips, Scots musicians, living in the parish of St Martin's in the Fields and frequenting St Paul's and the 'Quenes Majesties Chappell'.[32] The impact of the Reformation on the song schools had enormous implications for musical life. In the 1570s, Thomas Wode noted of the harmonised psalms and canticles he had recorded for the use of the Reformed Kirk, 'God grant we use them all to his glory; but notwithstanding of this travell [travail] I have taken, I can not understand bot musike sall pereishe in this land alutterlye.'[33]

In pre-Reformation times, a burgh parish school in remote Inverness could attain respectable if modest levels of achievement in terms of choral training.[34] After the Reformation, and more particularly after the 'tymous

professor of theology, whom I have proposed as being the former guardian of the Glasgow house of Observant Franciscans, recorded in 1512–13 (*Diocesan Registers of Glasgow, Protocol Book Simson* (Grampian Club, 1875), ed. J. Bain & C. Rogers, ii, 432, 436, 486). John Johnson's treatise *An Comfortable Exhortation* appeared in 1535, allegedly in Paris (the imprint may be false). Dr Kenneth Elliott has informed me that handwritten music by Robert Johnson has been found on a single leaf of *In hoc volumine haec continentur Aristotelis …* (J. de Colines, Paris, 1524), sig. bbbb vi verso. It is likely therefore that Robert, as well as John, was in England by 1535, for this volume has two English signatures on it. Robert is identified only in York and Windsor, and survived into Queen Elizabeth's reign. His compositional style continued to develop, and one of his late pieces, *Gaude Virgo Maria*, shows that in England, Reformed views and traditional Marian devotion could sometimes co-exist, not to mention the cultivation of complex polyphonic music for church use. The possibility has been raised by Dr David Skinner, of Sidney Sussex College, Cambridge, that Robert Johnson was an Englishman, originally from a clan of musical Johnsons who worked at the great royal collegiate foundation at Fotheringay. This does not explain why Thomas Wode thought he came from Duns.

[31] *Calendar of Patent Rolls Elizabeth I, iii (1563–1566)* (London, 1960), 198; the same source states that Henry Lough (i.e. Loch), Scottish subject, also formerly at St Giles, was naturalised on 20 January 1565. This information is also in W. Page (ed.), *Letters of Denization and Acts of Naturalization for Aliens in England* (Publications of the Huguenot Society, 1893), 81. It appears that Douglas did not find England congenial; in 1584 he was in Paris as a student in theology (W. Forbes-Leith (ed.), *Narratives of Scottish Catholics* (London 1889), 196), and at his death in 1597 he is found recorded at the Scottish monastery in Regensburg as 'Patricius Douglass noster philosophiae rector' (M. Dilworth, 'Two necrologies', *Innes Review*, ix (1958), 183). Only one complete work of Douglas is now extant, in several English sources, *In convertendo*, published in the Musica Scotica series in an edition by Gordon Munro (Glasgow, 1997). In *Musick Fyne*, 97, Ross makes the point that post-Reformation Scotland, unlike England, was not 'conducive' to large-scale musical endeavour.

[32] R.E.G. & E.F. Kirk (eds.), *Returns of Aliens in the City and Suburbs of London* (Publications of the Huguenot Society, 1907), iii, 353, 398.

[33] Tenor part book of the St Andrews Psalter, p. 166.

[34] S. Allenson, 'The Inverness Fragments: music from a pre-Reformation parish church and school', *Music and Letters*, lxx (1989), 1–45. A faburden processional psalm from Inverness can be heard on *A Scottish Mass of 1546*, cassette CMF 004. See also Atholl Murray, 'The Parish Clerk and Song School of Inverness', *Innes Review*, 58 (2007), pp. 107–15.

remeid' restoring the song schools, the kirk usually employed the parish song schoolmaster as 'taker-up' of the psalms (preceptor), while the town contributed his salary from its common good fund. The fact that training in singing was not the sole requirement is obliquely confirmed by the fact that in 1598 the Aberdeen council hired John Leslie, a 'qualifeit musician, albeit he can not instruct his scholers in playing', and the appointment lasted only a month or two.[35] In 1619 we find a boy at Monkton being paid to take up the psalm,[36] and at Stirling in 1621 the council issued instructions to 'mak commodious seatttis' under the pulpit ('about the fit thairof') for the master of the song school and his bairns singing the psalms.[37] As we saw earlier, the native contribution to the use of psalms in worship was not limited to harmonising the Genevan tunes; not only were many of the metrical versions of the texts the work of Scots (writing in English), but new tunes by Scottish composers were added to the repertory.[38] In his *Some helpes for young schollers* of 1602, the church leader and poet John Davidson provided a variant from the usual musical diet when he included his own metrical version of Psalm 130, set in four parts by his neighbour Andrew Blackhall, sometime collaborator in Thomas Wode's psalter, and now minister of Musselburgh, where he kept a music school, thanks to a pension from James VI in 1589.[39]

With no printed Scots music yet available, song schoolmasters had to depend on imported publications from England or continental Europe, though manuscript copies were almost certainly in wide circulation. In the library built up from 1619 onwards by Andrew Melville, song schoolmaster in Aberdeen, the music collection extends from dance music (pavane and galliards) to four psalters, along with a distinct set of 'Gloria Patris' (i.e. concluding doxologies) to the psalms. In 1575, Bassandyne's printed psalter had included only one such doxology; by 1596 Charteris had thirty-two. Quite a number of them feature as opening items in 'Ane Buik off Roundells' collected by David Melville, apparently a kinsman of Andrew, and music teacher likewise at Aberdeen.[40] Most of the rounds in this manuscript are taken from the collections of the Englishman Thomas Ravenscroft, such as his *Pammelia* of 1609; one native round (no. 95) is from the pen of James Melville the diarist, poet and minister. The roundels are set for three to five and even more voices, and are followed by other song material.

35   *Aberdeen Extracts*, ed. Stuart, ii, 174.
36   NAS, CH2/809/1, 231.
37   Quoted in Patrick, *Four Centuries of Scottish Psalmody*, 135.
38   See M. Frost, *English and Scottish Psalm and Hymn Tunes, c.1543–1677* (London, 1953).
39   K. Elliott, 'Some helpes for young schollers: a new source of early Scottish psalmody', in A.A. Macdonald, M. Lynch & I. Cowan (eds.), *The Renaissance in Scotland* (Leiden, 1994), 264–76. For the music school at Musselburgh, see *Reports on the State of Certain Parishes in 1627* (Maitland Club, 1835), 76, and NAS, *Register of the Privy Seal*, Ix, fo. 69v.
40   *The Melvill Book of Roundels*, ed. G. Bantock & H.O. Anderson (Roxburghe Club, 1916).

The library of Andrew Melville of Aberdeen included half a dozen 'arts of music' expounding musical theory, including, it has been argued, the manuscript entitled *The Art of Music* mentioned earlier, often referred to as 'Scottish Anonymous', which is in fact the oldest Scottish theoretical text now extant. Besides a theoretical work of Ravenscroft, another Englishman, W. Bathe, student in Oxford, features with a transcript of his lost publication of c.1590.[41] In it, Bathe recommended as musical models Fairfax, Tallis and Byrd, although the first was by this time many decades dead.[42] The Roundels collected by David are listed in the song school library as 'ane singing book Robert Ogilvie'; the original, now in the Library of Congress, has Robert Ogilvie's stamp on the binding, which is otherwise similar in style to that of Alexander Forbes of Tolquhon's 'Cantus Part Book', now in the Fitzwilliam Museum, Cambridge;[43] the Tolquhon family worked in close harmony with the Melvilles, as David's closely related 'Bassus Part Book' also serves to demonstrate.[44] It contains much contemporary English printed music, madrigals by Byrd and Thomas Morley published in the 1590s, and by Michael East (1604). There are also Italian songs by Bernardino Mosto and Ruggiero Giovanelli. Of the six metrical psalms included, only one is found in the Scots metrical psalter of 1635. Also listed in the library are 'four Italian books', clearly a set of part-books. When we further recall that Andrew Melville, teaching like David in the town's music school, has been credited with composing the 'common tunes' in the metrical psalter, and that a later Aberdeen song schoolmaster, the second Patrick Davidson, actually lived in Italy for some time, we begin to see how the basic psalm singing that everybody had to be taught was supplemented by courtly dance music, and that vocal music was complemented by instrumental.[45] When George Douglas, the son of a stonemason from Old Aberdeen, was hired at Elgin in 1597, he was to play on all musical instruments, especially virginals, monochords, lute and cittern ('seister'); again, however, we find that he was also to teach reading, writing, manners and courtesy.[46]

Further variety in the musical diet might conceivably have been provided by the simple four-part settings of Buchanan's *Psalm Paraphrases* made by

---

[41]   A transcript by Dr Kenneth Elliott of Melville's own transcript of Bathe has been placed at my disposal.

[42]   Fairfax (d.1528) appears in the Carver Choirbook, and is cited in both the *Art of Music* and Thomas Wode's partbooks as a supreme musician; three pieces by Tallis also appear in Wode.

[43]   H.M. Shire & P.M. Giles, 'Scottish Song-book, 1611', *Saltire Review*, i (2), 46–52.

[44]   British Library, Add. MS 36484; see Shire & Giles, 'Scottish Song-book'; also H.M. Shire, 'Court Song in Scotland after 1603: Aberdeenshire', parts i and ii, *Edin. Bibl. Soc. Trans.*, iii (1957), 161–8, and part iii, ibid. (1960), 3–12.

[45]   *Gideon Guthrie: a monograph written 1712 to 1730*, ed. C.E.G. Wright (Edinburgh, 1900), 122–3. But note that K. Elliott, in '*Some helpes*', claims the common tunes as perhaps the work of Andrew Blackhall, who also wrote secular music for the Court.

[46]   *Elgin Recs.*, ii, 392.

Statius Olthoff, which were included in all the Herborn printings of the texts up till 1702, and apparently infiltrated Lutheran hymnals in Germany, being commonly used into the eighteenth century; in the 1570s, French composers had also set Buchanan.[47] French music must certainly have been familiar on account of the Scots attending the French Protestant academies. We are told that the earl of Mar's son Alexander, in 1618, 'playis prattilie weill upon the lutt' at Saumur; a year was spent in dancing lessons, eight months in fencing classes.[48] In 1591, the earl of Cawdor paid a lute player for his performance in Glasgow.[49] The lute was clearly enormously popular in Scotland. A number of seventeenth-century lute manuscripts survive, assembled by various aristocratic households. Their contents include many extremely fine native pieces, often distinctively Celtic in character, alongside much music from England and mainland Europe.[50] In 1612, we find lutes made in Venice more highly valued than those made in Cologne, and valuations given also for imported citterns, clavichords, viols and virginals.[51]

Literary evidence about musical instruments has to be used with caution, for its distant source may well be a foreign literary work, but two fifteenth-century texts show familiarity with instrumental music, namely Richard Holland's *Book of the Howlat* and the anonymous metrical romance *Clariodus*. Besides the expected organ at a church wedding, and trumpets and clarions linked with heralds, we find a short list which includes the lute, harp, viol, clarsach and gittern, and we hear of timpani accompanying a sung mass, of forty children playing at a banquet, and also of twenty not so young, being aged fourteen; there are also references to part-singing.[52] In the real world, towns needed pipes and drums for proclamation purposes. In pre-Reformation Edinburgh there is a reference to the playing of shawms (ancestor of the oboe) before the image of St Giles in 1555.[53] Alexander Hume's poetic call, in post-Reformation times, the 'praise of God to play and sing/ with cornet and with shalme' cannot, however, refer to playing in kirk, but to sacred music in the home.[54]

In his poem celebrating the ceremonial entry of Anna of Denmark into her new capital on 19 May 1590, John Burel listed the following instruments: organ, regal (small organ), hautbois (oboe), harp, clarsach, pipe, lute ('of

---

[47] F. Blume, *Protestant Church Music: a History* (London, 1975), 145. See also p. 146 above.
[48] *Hist. MSS Comm., The Manuscripts of the Earl of Mar and Kellie* (London, 1930), ii, 83.
[49] C. Innes (ed.), *The Thanes of Cawdor* (Spalding Club, 1859), 204.
[50] See Ross, *Musick Fyne*, 144–7.
[51] *The Ledger of Andrew Halyburton*, ed. C. Innes (Edinburgh, 1827), xxxi, cxiv, 295, 308, 321, 332.
[52] *Clariodus: a Metrical Romance*, ed. D. Irving (Maitland Club, 1830), ii, 915, 1712, 1754; iv, 1159, 1210, 2416; v, 734, 927, 990, 1769.
[53] *Edinburgh Burgh Recs.*, ii, 220.
[54] Hume, *Poems*, ed. Lawson, 32.

instruments the onely king'), seistar (cittern), and sumphian (i.e. 'symphony' or hurdy-gurdy).[55] This last also appears in John Rolland's list of instruments in his evocation of a *Joyeuse Entrée* in his *Sevin Seages* (626–627), published in 1577. Alexander Hume provides quite a list of instruments taking part in his (idealised) municipal celebrations of the defeat of the Spanish Armada, in his 'Triumph' dated October 1589.[56] A century earlier, instruments like the unidentified 'bumb' or 'boume' had been available for the Corpus Christi processions of the hammermen craft of Edinburgh, with a child playing on the 'gret bumbart' (bombard, an ancestor of the bassoon), in 1496, 1497 and 1499.[57] Earlier still, *The Buke of the Howlat* had listed over twenty instruments, while folk-dancing to the flute and a bagpipe in the Ayrshire village of Cockelbie was cited early in the fifteenth century in *Colkelbie Sow*, and a whole list of instruments accompany the rustic merrymaking in the *Complaynt of Scotland* of 1550.[58] Playing techniques may have had less to do with schooling than with family traditions in musical households, necessary also to support the more sophisticated musicianship of the better schools. Merchants must have imported new types of instrument such as the 'almany quhissil' or fife met with in Edinburgh in 1532 and subsequently.[59] Civility required restraint in the use of the pipes to rouse the sleeping workers in Aberdeen; in 1630, the city banned their use as an 'uncivill forme to be met with in sic a famous burghe'.[60]

As for the organ, it had been banned from the kirk since 1560. But in 1617 we find record of a Mr Dalam, organ-maker, at the Chapel Royal in Edinburgh, apparently lured thither by Bishop William Cowper, although in 1631 the institution had to acquire both an organist and an organ book.[61] Organ lofts originally existed at Falkland, Stirling and Edinburgh, and an additional annexe was slapped onto Holyrood for a violar's chamber.[62] There was an organ-maker, Humphrey Datsone, in Edinburgh in 1611, and indeed as early as 1578 the king had his own organist, John Robesone.[63] There is some ambiguity here between music for the court and music for the

---

[55] See 'Danish Account of the Coronation and Entry', in D. Stevenson, *Scotland's Last Royal Wedding* (Edinburgh, 1997); Burel, 'Description of the Queen's Entry'. For Burel's clarsach, see n. 27 above. See also Munro, '"Sang Schwylls" and "Music Schools"'.

[56] See n. 27 above.

[57] A.J. Mill, *Mediaeval Plays in Scotland*, (Edinburgh, 1927), 326–7.

[58] F.J. Amours (ed.), *Scottish Alliterative Poems* (STS, 1897), 73ff; *Colkelbie Sow and the Talis of the Fyve Bestis*, ed. G. Kratzman (New York, 1982), 62, 64; *The Complaynt of Scotland*, ed. J.A. Stewart (STS, 1979), 51–2.

[59] Mill, *Mediaeval Plays*, 233; J. Smith, *The Hammermen of Edinburgh* (Edinburgh, 1907), 87, 114, 144.

[60] *Analecta Scotica* (Edinburgh, 1834), ii, 322.

[61] Rogers, *History of the Chapel Royal*, cxxv, clxvii.

[62] H.M. Paton (ed.), *Accounts of the Master of Works* (Edinburgh, 1957), i, 318, 327.

[63] *Edinburgh Marriages*, 36; *Treasurer's Accounts*, xiii, 250.

church; sacred music on cornet and sackbut (trombone) seemed suitable for
the Chapel Royal in 1631, as cornet and cittern had once seemed to the
minister of Logie.[64] Royal endowment for music offered a possible career
for musicians, but endowments could be alienated, and even the Chapel
Royal's revenues had a chequered career. In 1619, James VI and I wrote
home pointing out that before 1603 he had provided funds for a music
school out of the rents of the Maison Dieu hospital at Elgin, and asked his
Scottish treasurer to assure continuing payments; this foundation went back
to 1595 and covered a school for music and other liberal arts,[65] including
some reading and writing with a modicum of grammar. In August 1610,
a similar foundation for £100 yearly to a song schoolmaster was made at
Dunfermline by Anna of Denmark.[66] No doubt passing patronage of individuals persisted in the post-Reformation period, echoing that afforded to
the countess of Crawford's harper in 1505, Lord Fleming's 'taubronar' in
1507 and the earl of Bothwell's minstrel in 1508; but such appointments
may have been of restricted duration.[67] Finally, it is curious to note that, out
of charity, Edinburgh council gave a blind man a 'symphonion' in 1582.[68]

After the Reformation, the humble 'taker-up' of the psalms, the preceptor,
was often the basis of the nation's acquaintance with what we may call art-
music, and this fact could be a limiting factor on the range of music available, for not all these men could read music, and their repertory of tunes
was unlikely to encompass all 105 of the 'proper tunes' (i.e. for specific
psalms) of the 1564 psalter; by the early seventeenth century there is a
clearly discernible trend, even in terms of harmonised psalm tunes, towards
concentrating on the so-called 'common tunes', that is, a limited repertory
of melodies which could be used interchangeably for any of the numerous
psalms written in common metre. Another limiting factor was the 'funda-
mentalism' of many ministers and presbyteries in matters of worship. In
the 1560s, Thomas Wode had copied harmonised versions of no fewer than
eighteen canticles and hymns, and even Cranmer's prose *Te Deum*, into his
harmonised psalter. But in February 1596, the Glasgow presbytery banned
John Buchan, its composer-preceptor, from non-scriptural hymn singing,
declaring 'that their be na thing red or sung in the new kirk be Johne

[64] Rogers, *History of the Chapel Royal*, clxvii; Hume, *Poems*, ed. Lawson, 32.
[65] *Hist MSS. Comm., Report on the MSS of the Earl of Mar and Kellie* (London, 1904), 87; *RMS*,
      vi, 349.
[66] E. Henderson, *Annals of Dunfermline* (Glasgow, 1879), 267–70.
[67] *Treasurer's Accounts*, ii, 467; iv, 75, 93. Lady Barbara Gordon, daughter of the regent Arran,
      later wife of Alexander, earl of Huntly, was given a gittern (a guitar-like instrument) in 1552,
      ibid., x, 50.
[68] *Edinburgh Burgh Recs.*, iv, 564. The 'symphonion' is the same as Burel's 'sumphian' (cf.
      English 'cymphan' in 1506); the word hurdy-gurdy is eighteenth-century, and the instru-
      ment was originally called an 'organistron'.

Buchan reidare their, bot that quhilk is contenit in the word of God'.[69] At Monkton, as we saw, a boy was paid to take up the psalm in 1619, and at Haddington in 1610 the master of the music school was to teach not only children, but 'men and bairnis to sing and play'.[70] South Leith thought Aberdeen was the best place to learn musicianship, for in 1610 it hoped to acquire a reader and a 'musicianer' from that town.[71] One pre-Reformation centre for music, Paisley, had re-started its song school by 1618, but this reverted to being a schoolhouse for the grammar school, only to reappear again by 1648.[72] Ecclesiastical endowments for music schools were usually alienated. Kirkwall complained in 1627 that 'their is few or nane can be hard to praise God in his hous' and 'their is necessitie of ane sang schoole for musick, being taucht their of auld' – when it had been supported by St Augustine's 'stouk' which was now in royal hands.[73] Two years later, 'both vocall and instrumentall music' cost pupils 40 shillings a quarter.[74]

We have seen James Melville's account of his acquaintance with music, vocal and instrumental.[75] The pre-Reformation musical training of his teacher Alexander Smith may have been largely in sacred vocal music, but the students, their psalms apart, probably had a more secular repertory. (Indeed, Melville suggested as much with his account of the music-making in a Glasgow gentleman's house, which proved too seductive for the religiously minded youth, executed as it was by specially invited and 'maist expert singers and playaris'.[76]) Melville does not mention learning faburden improvisation on a given tune, but John Davidson of Prestonpans was familiar with it when he excoriated the anti-Melville 'libellers' of c.1584, accusing the initial libeller of improvising on top of other lies, and thereby encouraging others 'to hold in a baise of plaine sang unto his discant'. Davidson's later collaboration with Andrew Blackhall has been mentioned, and his musical metaphor is paralleled by the Catholic convert Nicol Burne's accusation that 'Lene, the false loun sings the bass to Blackhall'.[77] The beauty of

---

69 *Maitland Misc.*, i (1), 79. Thomas Wode, as reader in St Andrews, incurred a similar injunction to 'reid … without ony additioun of his awin brane, noit, or utherwyis', *RKSSA*, ii, 528.
70 Haddington, James Robb transcripts (c/o East Lothian Nat. Hist. Soc.).
71 D. Robertson (ed.), *South Leith Records* (Edinburgh, 1911), i, 9.
72 R. Brown, *The History of Paisley Grammar School* (Paisley, 1875), 43, 44, 55, 57. Paisley Abbey is the earliest known centre of polyphonic singing in Scotland; see K. Elliott, *The Paisley Abbey Fragments* (Glasgow, 1996).
73 A. Peterkin, *Rentals of the Ancient Earldom and Bishoprick of Orkney* (Edinburgh, 1820), iii, 35.
74 *Proceedings of the Orkney Antiquarian Society*, iv (1925), 33. The fee is already as high as it would be for the same tuition in Glasgow in 1646, *Glasgow Recs.*, ii, 96.
75 See Section III.2 above.
76 *Autobiography and Diary*, 22, 29, 79.
77 Calderwood, *History*, iv, 43; J. Cranstoun (ed.), *Satirical Poems of the Time of the Reformation* (STS, 1891–93), i, 338.

polyphonic music-making is celebrated for its own sake in the first version of Alexander Montgomerie's *The Cherrie and the Slae*:

> Quhair deskant did abound
> With treble sweet and tenor just,
> And ay the echo repercust
> The diapason sound
> Set with the C sol fa ut cleife[78]

The *Art of Music* manuscript seems, as we have said, to reflect a combination of pre- and post-Reformation musical studies. It suggests the following progressive curriculum: plainsong, pricksong, figuration, faburden, descant. 'Pricksong' involved singing in a measured way, memorising note values (breves, semibreves, etc.), with pupils practising keeping in time by singing canons. Figuration involved putting their new understanding of rhythm into practice, sometimes by alternating long and short notes.[79] Faburden followed logically on this, 'a very simple method of harmonisation springing from an improvisatory technique. … the *cantus firmus* (normally in the tenor) is set note for note according to a strict system of parallel and contrary motion'.[80] More accomplished singers could decorate their own parts in sophisticated ways, producing something verging on polyphony. It is doubtful that much of this could be done by ear without written or printed music, but little has survived, since such music was liable to disintegrate in the hands of boy learners – hence the music scratched on less perishable slates at Paisley.[81] Finally, descant was another way of harmonising a melody. All these elaborate rules were intended for choirs tackling complex polyphonic music designed to beautify the ritual of the liturgy. The musical architecture of such compositions was often on the largest scale, and the process of learning to sing and compose such music was lengthy.

Post-Reformation song schools could doubtless devote more time to learning to play instruments, since polyphony had been replaced by simple psalm tunes, harmonised note against note, but instrumental music as a form of high art was still in its infancy, and there was a serious decline in musical standards.[82] For all that the 1564 psalter offered a rich repertory of varied

---

[78] G. Stevenson (ed.), *Poems of Alexander Montgomerie (Supplementary volume)* (STS, 1910), 9. 'Ut' is still the French for 'doh'.

[79] Hence Gavin Douglas, 'In modulatioun hard I play and sing … Cant Organe, figuratioun and gemmell' (*Palice of Honour*, 11. 499–501); 'gemmel' (gymel) refers to dividing a given voice-part into two, i.e. 'twinning it' to enrich the harmony.

[80] Ross, *Musick Fyne*, 41.

[81] The 'Inverness Fragments' (see n. 34 above) are assumed to date from near the date of the Reformation precisely because they had not yet disintegrated; the sheets were used to stiffen the binding they were found in. For the use of slates, see Elliott, *Paisley Abbey Fragments*, 5.

[82] J. Flynn, 'The education of choristers in England during the sixteenth century', in J. Morehen (ed.), *English Choral Practice 1400–1650* (Cambridge, 1995), 180–99.

melodies, and harmonised versions for choirs were circulating in manuscript, as we have seen, there was always the temptation to simplify the musical element in worship further still. By about 1620, the Edinburgh Chapel Royal found the attendance of choir members so poor that 'only they sing the commone tune of a psalm', although by 1631, an energetic 'new broom' master there spoke of his Holyroodhouse chamber as being set up with an organ, two flutes, two pandores, viols and English, French, Dutch, Spanish, Latin, Italian and 'old Scotch' music, vocal and instrumental.[83] However, Charles I's attempt to impose Anglican worship in 1637, leading as it did to the National Covenant, virtually silenced harmonised music in the kirk, and hence in the lives of the vast majority of the population.

Forty years earlier, however, choirs had sung harmonised psalms in the kirks and streets of Edinburgh to greet Charles's mother, Anna of Denmark, when she entered Edinburgh on 19 May 1590. In addition to his list of musical instruments, John Burel evokes the products of the song school, starting with the more accomplished and ending with the less skilled:

> Tennour and trebill with sweit sence,
> Ilkane with pairts gaff notes agane,
> With priksang and the singing plane:
> Thair enfants sang and barnelie brudis,
> Quho had bot new begun the mudis.[84]

The 'mudis' the young children had just begun to master were musical indicators of note duration such as minims and semibreves, as evoked in the later version of *The Cherrie and the Slae*:

> With treble, tenor, counter, meen:
> And echo blew a basse between
> With long and large at list,
> With Quaver, Crotchet, Semi-briefe
> And not a minim mist.[85]

Music clearly did not die out overnight after the Reformation. Although the simple psalm repertory in kirk meant that the high standards of pre-Reformation choral singing inevitably fell after 1560, it is quite clear that instrumental music was assiduously cultivated in the post-Reformation song schools, which were more numerous than has perhaps been appreciated hitherto. At different times between 1560 and 1633 the following towns allowed payments from their common good funds to music masters: Aberdeen, Ayr, Cupar, Dumfries, Dunbar, Dundee, Elgin, Inverness, Irvine,

[83] Rogers, *History of the Chapel Royal*, cxxxiii, clxviiii. The pandora is a mandolin-type instrument.
[84] Burel, 'Description of the Queen's Entry', 5.
[85] *Alexander Montgomerie: Poems*, ed. D.J. Parkinson (2 vols., STS, 2000), ii, 185 (lines 90–4).

Lanark, St Andrews and Tain.[86] Additional schools of varying duration and quality can now be added from our lists: Alford, Crail, Crichton, Cullen, Dalkeith, Dumbarton, Dunfermline, Edinburgh, Edinburgh Canongate, Fraserburgh, Glasgow, Haddington, Kiltearn, Kirkcaldy, Kirkcudbright, Kirkwall, Leith South, Linlithgow, Montrose, Musselburgh, Newbattle, Paisley, Perth, Peterhead, Rothesay and Stirling. And despite the triumph of the Covenanting party in the religious wars of the 1640s, and the consequent restriction of the psalms to the common metre and the twelve common tunes in the new metrical psalter of 1650, music schools survived in some major centres, sufficient at least to allow the flowering of concert life that took place in the eighteenth century.

V.2 Writing schools

Before proceeding to the question of the teaching of writing in our period, a concise history of Scottish handwriting of the period is in order. The writing of one's name as a facile test of literacy cannot easily be applied when writing is regarded as a semi-vocational accomplishment for men like notaries and scribes. When teachers were being hired, writing is not as constantly met with as a requisite as is reading. Yet many vernacular ('vulgar') schoolmasters must have taught writing. Medieval hands often varied with the nature of the work undertaken. An important text would require a clear bookhand, a hand often difficult to date because of its timeless regularity. Charter hand was a formal hand whose name indicates its purpose. Court hand, a more cursive style, originated in the law courts and with government, but was a popular hand with men of affairs. There are various transitional hands in the late fifteenth century, one of which has been characterised as 'pre-secretary' because it antedates secretary hand proper. Walter Small, treasurer and canon of Dunkeld, was credited with being the best penman of his time not only in that hand, but in every style of writing.[87] The Dunkeld scribes would learn styles by apprenticeship. In one parchment manuscript of John Fordun it is another Dunkeld scribe, Richard Stirling, who tells us that Bishop George Brown had several works transcribed.[88] Stirling was at Kinnell in 1509.[89] The Glasgow University arts statutes of 1452 are in the small, neat hand of Principal Duncan Bunch,[90]

---

86 *Maitland Misc.*, ii (1), 39–50.
87 G.G. Simpson, *Scottish Handwriting 1150–1650* (Edinburgh, 1973), 12, 13; the long decorated initial letter is characteristic. Attempts have been made to subdivide these Scottish scripts further and more specifically, but no results have so far been published.
88 British Library, Harleian MS 4764.
89 *Laing Chrs.*, no. 274.
90 Illustrated in H. James (ed.), *Facsimiles of National Manuscripts of Scotland* (Edinburgh, 1872), iii, no. vi.

while a strongly individual hand is that of Archibald Whitelaw, a royal secretary.[91] Bunch taught the young William Elphinstone, later bishop of Aberdeen, whose cursive hand is quite unlike that of his father, William senior, being more accessible and attractive to the modern eye.[92] Gilbert Haldane's signature of 1491 is in an italic hand, though his marginal notes are in the contemporary pre-secretary.[93]

Before coming to the prevalence of italic in Scotland, we should note that the earliest humanistic hands were learnt in Italy. A small roman hand of some beauty is that of the scribe George Kinninmonth, first found in a copy of Suetonius completed in 1453 for the *podestà* of Rieti, a learned doctor from Naples.[94] Kinninmonth moved to Bologna, presumably initially to study at its university. In that city he was scribe for a manuscript of Augustine's *Epistolae*, now in the Escorial in Spain.[95] While in Bologna, he entered the service of Filippo Calandrini, archbishop there, half brother of Pope Nicholas V, and completed his copy of Cyprian's Works for Calandrini in June 1456, and within the same decade, perhaps, almost all the orations of Cicero.[96] Kinninmonth had been a bachelor in arts in St Andrews in 1451, and in 1462 described himself as having been present in the Roman Curia for eleven years, by then a continual commensal member of Calandrini's household.[97] Compared with Kinninmonth, Robert Pringle, scribe of a manuscript from the library of the dukes of Urbino, had a less distinctive curial hand. Carefully executed, Pringle's copy of the New Testament *Postillae* of Nicholas of Lyra, finished in October 1458, nevertheless took four years to complete, while a Flemish artist was employed to decorate it in 1459. This is the sole survival of Pringle's work. He seems to be one of the thirty-four scribes attached to Federigo of Urbino, and lost his right hand when the Curia was resident in Ancona; in 1467 he applied for papal provision to the vicarage of Kilpatrick along with a prebend of Bothwell collegiate church.[98] The invention of printing largely pushed traditional

---

91 Simpson, *Handwriting*, 19.
92 Durkan & Ross, *Early Scottish Libraries*, 31–4, note some examples.
93 Ibid., facing p. 29. Cf. facing p. 36 (plates vi and vii).
94 Paris, Bibliothèque Nationale, MS 580s, fo. 124; C. Samaran et al. (eds.), *Catalogue des manuscrits en écriture latine portant des indications de date* (Paris, 1962).
95 G. Antolín, *Catálogo de los códices latinos de la Real Biblioteca del Escorial* (Madrid, 1910), i, 17–19, MS a.1.10.
96 Rome, Vat. Lat. 1744; M. Vattasso and P.F. de Cavalieri (eds.), *Codices Vaticani Latini* (Rome, 1902), i, and E. Pellegrini et al. (eds.), *Les manuscrits classiques latins de la bibliothèque Vaticane* (Paris 1991), iii (1), 356–8.
97 Durkan & Kirk, *University of Glasgow*, 10, 18; Glasgow University Scottish History Department, Ross Fund Transcripts from Rome, Archivio Vaticano, Register of Supplications, 502, 102; 511, 140; 528, 177; 555, 204.
98 Vatican, Urbinates Lat. MS 13; C. Scomajolo (ed.), *Codices Urbinates Latini* (Rome, 1902), 21–2; J. Dennistoun, *Memories of the Dukes of Urbino* (London, 1851), mentions Nicholas of

professional scribes into unemployment or into posts as minor law officers, humble notaries or, much later, writing masters. Elite scribes, however, could still find posts with the well-off.

The so-called pre-secretary transitional hands had their own stylish appeal: an example is to be found in the obituary calendar (1478?–1553) of the Aberdeen Observant Franciscans.[99] Exchanges of personal correspondence are not well documented, but ordinary chaplains wrote such letters on their parishioners' behalf and examples survive in the justiciary records. A letter of c.1526 exists from sir Thomas Russell, chaplain, to the parish rector of Carstairs, pressing a parishioner's claim to be rentalled as a tenant in the parish.[100] Doubtless ministers and readers of the Reformed Kirk made themselves available for the same purpose. It is interesting to note that Cuthbert Simson's notarial protocols appear in the same volume as Russell's letter. Before becoming chapter clerk at Glasgow cathedral, Simson had been in charge of pupils who witness his earlier instruments at Irvine, and later, concurrently with that post, he taught in Glasgow both at school and university.[101] A Paris graduate of 1496, he nevertheless used and probably taught a 'late mediaeval set hand' of the type Walter Small's contemporaries at Dunkeld so admired.[102] John Law, who also studied at Paris, was a schoolmaster at Ayr before joining the Augustinian canons at St Andrews, where he wrote his chronicle in a hand of the same transitional type as is found in the Aberdeen Grey Friars' obituary calendar.[103]

There is no certainty that either Simson or Law, unlike Kinninmonth, picked up their writing styles abroad. It is likely that many masters who taught writing used styles contaminated by features unconsciously repeated from other styles. Even when the new secretary hand was more generally in use (c.1540), elements inherited from older styles or borrowed from newer or less familiar hands (like italic) might interpose themselves. The

Lyra; J.A. Twemlow (ed.), *Catalogue of Entries in the Papal Registers relating to Great Britain and Ireland* (London, 1933), iii, 556. These Scottish humanist scribes had their contemporary English counterparts; see A.C. De la Mare, 'Humanistic Hands in England', in A.C. De la Mare & B.C. Barker-Benfield (eds.), *Manuscripts at Oxford: an Exhibition in Memory of R.W. Hunt* (Oxford, 1980), 93–101.

99   W.M. Bryce, *The Scottish Grey Friars* (Edinburgh/London, 1909), ii, 285–336. A similar hand can be found in the Cambridge copy of Fordun and in the Dunfermline Abbey copy in Fairfax MS 8 (Bodley).

100   *Liber Protocollorum M Cuthherti Simonis. Rental Book of the Diocese of Glasgow, 1509–1570,* ed. J. Bain & C. Rogers (Grampian Club, 1875), i, 55.

101   Ibid., ii, 6, 24 (Irvine 1500); 42, 154, 202, 342, 345, 389, 398 (Glasgow, 1503–1511); Durkan & Kirk, *University of Glasgow,* 174, show Simson was in Glasgow from 1501. But in 1507 he revisited Irvine, where a local scholar was present as witness to his protocol, *Glasgow Prot. Bk,* ii, 298.

102   Ibid., ii, frontispiece; Simpson, *Handwriting,* 14–15.

103   Durkan, 'St Andrews in the John Law Chronicle', *IR,* xxv (1974), 49–62.

lawyers were aware that every individual's hand had its own specific character. In 1474, a certain Scot, James of Duchir, broke his contract with a merchant of Bruges and denied that the hand on the document was his: the outcome was that his hand was ordered to be cut off in the market.[104] In post-Reformation times, as we saw, the minister who taught the bairns of the laird of Restalrig, Robert Logan, certified that his hand was 'the chap of his ordinar writing' and that he 'wraitt it without ane straik throw the "t"' (a feature of much secretary-style cursive handwriting). George Sprott, a schoolmaster-notary, confessed and was executed for forging the Logan letters in question.[105] One's writing style, consciously adopted or not, could clearly be a matter of great consequence. Entering his signature in a work of Marko Marulic (1519), the Dominican friar Alexander Barclay was at pains to point out that he did so 'vith the curt hand'.[106] One naturally looks to the court scribes for italic. Patrick Paniter, secretary to James IV, is one example,[107] and his son David employed a similar hand in 1537.[108] A later royal secretary and official of James V's court, James Foulis, likewise wrote in italic.[109] James IV's son Alexander, archbishop of St Andrews, signed his name in an italic hand while still a pupil of Patrick Paniter; he would perfect this later, understudying Erasmus.[110]

Though secretary remained the commoner and favourite hand, italic seems to have been popular with high-born ladies from the time of Mary Queen of Scots onward; a few pre-1600 practitioners are Katharine Oliphant of Arniston (1571), Margaret Leslie (1574), Margaret, Lady Elphinstone (1575), Margaret Abernethie, wife of Alexander Fraser younger of Philorth (1595), Lady Eleanor Bruce (1597), Grissel Scott, Lady Borthwick (1599), and, of course, Esther Inglis.[111] Male signatures with italic elements include those of the Franciscan friar John Scott, David Spens (1559), Henry Lord Darnley, John Maxwell younger (1563), John Bellenden, later of Auchnoull

---

[104] *Acta Dominorum Auditorum: Acts of the Lords Auditors of Causes and Complaints* (Edinburgh, 1839), 42.

[105] Pitcairn, *Criminal Trials*, ii, 288–289. Such a letter, said to be Logan's, is reproduced in James (ed.), *Facsimiles of National Manuscripts*, iii, no. lxxvi.

[106] J. Durkan & J. Russell, 'Further additions to Durkan and Ross, *Early Scottish Libraries*, in the National Library of Scotland', *Bibliotheck*, xii, 86.

[107] Simpson, *Handwriting*, 20, refers to an example of 1512. See also Durkan & Ross, *Early Scottish Libraries*, 44.

[108] *Registrum de Cambuskenneth*, cii.

[109] Fraser, *Stirlings of Keir*, vii, 567.

[110] Simpson, *Handwriting*, 20.

[111] W. Fraser, *Elphinstone Family Book* (Edinburgh, 1897), i, 106; *Frasers of Philorth* (Edinburgh, 1879), iii, 34; *Scotts of Buccleuch* (Edinburgh, 1878), i, 122; G.W.T. Ormond, *The Arniston Memoirs: Three Centuries of a Scottish House, 1571–1838* (Edinburgh, 1887), 4; C.D. Abercromby, *Family of Abercromby* (Aberdeen, 1927), 33; J. Anderson, *Oliphants of Scotland* (Edinburgh, 1879), 167.

and justice clerk (1551), William Maitland of Lethington (1569), Charles Lennox (1572), Nicholas Inglis (1574), Andrew Melville, John Maitland of Thirlestane (1586) and King James VI writing to the Shah of Persia in 1601.[112] Some of these signatories are quite calligraphic, others less so. The Auchinleck manuscript of Andrew of Wyntoun's poetical *Chronicle* bears a note informing us that 'Margaret Hammy[ltoun] vreittis not veill and spellis far war'.[113] There were those who could not write at all; in the Glasgow neighbourhood even in the seventeenth century, many wrote with their 'hand at the pen' directed by the notary.[114] Contemporary notaries used secretary, and occasionally italic, for headings, but neither, when cross-contaminated, is especially attractive. Peter Young drew up an italic alphabet as a model for the young James VI, and generally the elite classes adopted italic, at least for signatures. The prevailing style, however, remained secretary. Scottish secretary hand was in some measure different from English and Irish, and had to be so.

Scotland's most famous penman was a woman. Esther Inglis's date of birth is usually given as 1571, based on the age stated in her book of 1624, but this must be corrected to before 1569 if she is truly of French origin, as a 1571 entry in the register of aliens makes clear. It says that living in the parish of Blackfriars were Nicholas Inglishe, Frenchman, schoolmaster and householder, Mary his wife, David his son, with 'Yester', his daughter, 'coming into this realm about two years past for religion'.[115] Specimens of her calligraphy range in date from 1586 to 1624, her father being schoolmaster in Edinburgh from 1574. He was responsible for 'forming of his pupils hands to a perfyte schap of lettir'. His wife, Marie Presot, was also a calligrapher and wrote two little books for the library of James VI.[116] All that remains of Esther's mother's work, however, is a single sheet in the Newberry Library, Chicago, in several handwriting styles. Her daughter too mastered several styles, including a roman hand comparable with George Kinninmonth's. She left for England, but was back in Edinburgh by 1624, when she describes herself as fifty-three, the age that has misled her biographers.[117] Her brother

---

112   W. Fraser, *Sutherland Book* (Edinburgh, 1892), iii, 130; Durkan & Ross, *Early Scottish Libraries*, 117; *RKSSA*, i, 1, 27; W. Fraser, *The Lennox* (Edinburgh, 1874), ii, 261; W. Fraser, *Memoirs of the Maxwells of Pollok* (Edinburgh, 1863), i, 299.

113   *The Original Chronicle of Andrew of Wyntoun*, ed. F.J. Amours (STS, 1903–14), i, lxvi.

114   RH1/32/15.

115   Kirk & Kirk (eds.), *Returns of Aliens*, ii, 15; D. Laing, 'Notes relating to Mrs Esther Langlois (Inglis), the Celebrated Calligraphist', *Proceedings of the Society of Antiquaries of Scotland*, vi (1865), 283.

116   *Miscellany of the Scottish History Society* (SHS, 1893), i, li.

117   A.H. Scott-Elliot and Elspeth Yeo, 'Calligraphic Manuscripts of Esther Inglis (1571–1624): a catalogue', *Papers of the Bibliographical Society of America*, lxxxiv (1990), 19, 83, illustration no. 30. For another example of her roman hand, see James (ed.), *National Manuscripts of Scotland*, iii, no. xciii.

David also had a good hand, as can be seen from an entry in the album of Michael Balfour of Burleigh; his signature while a student at Edinburgh University confirms the accuracy of his statement that he was 'French by nation, Scots by education'.[118]

We know of only six writing schools in Scotland: Aberdeen, Ayr, Dumfries, Dunfermline, Edinburgh and Glasgow. The Englishman Edward Diggens came to Aberdeen in October 1607 with an offer to teach 'for the space of thrie moneths, promeissing in that space at farest to leirne the youthe a sufficient habite of a legible hand', as his testimonials 'at grit lenth' confirmed he had done in Glasgow, Dumfries 'and dyvers utheris pairtis'.[119] But writing skills were also imparted, less expertly, in many other schools. In the printed works of David Brown we get a glimpse of what might be taught. The first of his books, *The New Invention, intituled Calligraphia*, was published in 1622. Its aim was to provide the rules that would render the teacher unnecessary. It had the royal privilege, included a pious address to King James, had tetrasticha in English and a sonnet by D.A. and lines in praise of writing by I.S. It refers to diverse methods of writing taught by masters of university schools, each 'in some pretended manner his owne'. Students at Latin schools were required to attend vernacular schools at certain hours for writing lessons, an arrangement dismissed as incommodious. Pen, ink, paper and penknife were needed (the last to slit the quill). Pens had to be carefully chosen: raven and goose pens for any writing on paper and small writing on parchment, and swan or 'briszell' (an unidentified bird) pens for large writing on parchment. In his Fables, Robert Henryson had shown Aesop thus,

> Ane roll of paper in his hand he hair
> Ane swannis pen stikkand under his eir.[120]

Brown preferred the secretary hand, 'the most usuall characters in the world' and 'the most frequent in Europe', and his book was for the universal use of the youth and all who either lacked or neglected to learn writing when young. He described himself as 'His Majesties Scribe', but that must have been quite some time before, as the king's letter is signed at Holyrood. Brown occasionally taught writing to gentry, mostly ladies, in the countryside.[121] Some examples of secretary hand are given, but some spaces left for

---

[118]   Laing, 'Notes relating to Mrs Esther Langlois (Inglis)', 286; James (ed.), *National Manuscripts of Scotland*, iii, no. lxxi.

[119]   *Aberdeen Extracts*, ed. Stuart, ii, 293. Diggens was to be paid on the strength of the results he obtained, so the council gave him licence to teach writing and mathematics, the children having to be at least ten years of age.

[120]   G.G. Smith (ed.), *The Poems of Robert Henryson* (STS, 1906), ii, 101.

[121]   D. Brown, *The New Invention, intituled Calligraphia: or the arte of faire writing* (St Andrews, 1622); G.H. Bushnell, *From Papyrus to Print* (London, 1949), 75–8.

the printer to insert samples are not filled in. Brown went to England, but before that he is known to have taught in Ayr and Edinburgh.

David Brown's *Whole arte of expedition in teaching to write* of 1638 is interesting from many aspects.[122] It contains Latin lines by two Edinburgh academics, Thomas Crawford and Patrick Sands, and an English tetrastich by John Dick. Mention is made of 'the most rare and curious writs and works of one woman, Esther English by name, which are extant both in His Majesties librarie at St James, and in the Universtie of Oxford'. Praising his fellow Scots to the skies, Brown cites as excellent writers Mr Alexander Paterson, John Mathieson, Charles Geddy, John Peter, James Clerk and Hugh Wallace, 'some whereof are very exquisite also in many other hands than be used in Britaine'. He gives an example of a modified italic, 'the new mixt current, or speedy Italian writing'. By the time the book was printed, he had moved to a country house in Kemmington [sic], adjoining Newington Butts, a little above the sign of Jacob's Well, about a mile from London, and was available in the afternoon at the sign of the Spectacles over against the Royal Exchange. In vacation time he was invited to the countryside where Mary Stewart and her daughter taught by his help and direction. He probably also visited noble houses when he was in Scotland, the country whose prowess in the art of writing he extolled so highly.

V.3 Languages

The pre-Reformation Education Act of 1496 had laid down that children were to attend the schools from age eight or nine until they had acquired 'perfyte latyne', and after 1560 Latin remained the basis of all learning: 'the ground of all liberall artis and scienceis', as the Privy Council would put it in 1593.[123] An Act of 1563 enjoined St Andrews and other universities to employ those 'quha hes the toungis and humanitie'.[124] Despite the abandonment of the Latin liturgy, we find that when John Orr, a non-graduate, was hired by Ayr council on 20 November 1559 as most qualified and worthy to teach the grammar school, he was to teach all children coming to him grammar with 'maneris convenient', for a fee of £20 out of the town's common purse, plus 12 shillings from each child in the burgh.[125] But vernacular schooling was on the increase. In the same year, the master in

---

[122]   D. Brown, *The introduction to the true understanding of the whole arts of expedition in teaching to write in 6 hours* (London/Edinburgh, 1638). We also possess Brown's single sheet advertisement, *A speedy new way of teaching write* (Oxford, c.1640).

[123]   *RPC*, v, 111.

[124]   *APS*, ii, 238, 544.

[125]   W. Motherwell, *Memorabilia of the City of Glasgow* (Glasgow, 1835), 7; *Ayr Burgh Accts.*, 30 (there is a blank in the accounts 1560–74).

Peebles was to 'separat the Inglis redaris to the tolbuith fra the Latinists'.[126] In Glasgow in 1582, Thomas Craig was master of the vernacular school in the former collegiate church near the Tron.[127] In 1598, Thomas Mackie, sometime schoolmaster at Kintore, applied for a schoolmastering post in Aberdeen; qualified 'in religioune, vrettin and redinge', the town authorised him on probation to teach the Kintore bairns to read and write; in 1599, he was, with parish consent, allowed to hold an 'Inglische schole' at Kintore and to be session clerk. In 1604, Robert Forbes knew English but had no Latin, and it was therefore uncertain that he could be a minister.[128] Since 1560, the ministry had improved in educational quality; almost all were now arts graduates, but readers and clerks needed only to speak English. However, it was perhaps a bit exaggerated for parliament to claim in 1607 that for want of a common national grammar, 'the latine towng is greatlie diminischit within this Realme to the heavie prejudice of the commoun weal'.[129]

Grammar masters were tested before assuming their posts. Andrew Dishington, schoolmaster of Dunbar in 1594, had been turned down as both minister and grammar master after teaching a piece out of the first book of Virgil's *Georgics*.[130] A young applicant for the schoolmastership of Banff was brought to the presbytery of Fordyce in 1626 and there tested by being made to teach a 'lessone of humanitie' on the tenth ode from the first book of Horace's *Odes*,[131] while at Elgin in 1621, two newcomers had been tested on the third book, ode 10.[132]

As regards languages other than Latin, there cannot have been many grammar schools as fortunate as Elgin in 1566, where a new St Andrews graduate, Mr Patrick Balfour, was instructed that he 'sall reid and teiche Greik and Ebrew', since both were regarded as university subjects.[133] When John Callander was appointed grammar master at Haddington in 1591, however, he obliged himself to instruct 'the said school ... sufficiently in the latyne and Greek grammar and in all classic authors necessary'.[134] The classical languages were even useful in religious teaching, for when William Dunbar became Elgin schoolmaster in 1612, he was required to teach Calvin's catechism every Sunday 'baith in Latin and Greke'.[135] Some introduction to

126 *Peebles Recs.*, i, 257.
127 *Glasgow Prot. Bk*, viii, no. 3453.
128 J. Stuart (ed.), *Selections from the Records of the Kirk Session, Prebsytery and Synod of Aberdeen* (Spalding Club, 1846), 164, 170, 196.
129 *APS*, iv, 374.
130 J. Miller, *History of Dunbar* (Dunbar, 1830), 210.
131 *Banff Annals*, ii, 25.
132 *Elgin Recs.*, ii, 185.
133 *Elgin Recs.*, ii, 395–6.
134 W.F. Gray and J.H. Jamieson, *A Short History of Haddington* (Stevenage, n.d.), 30.
135 *Elgin Recs.*, ii, 400.

Greek might have been usual in other schools; we have already seen that James Carmichael's Latin grammar of 1587 contained brief notes on Greek and Hebrew, and that was probably as far as most grammar schools went. The universities certainly found they needed to start with the 'precepts' of Greek, while a brief introduction to Hebrew occupied the third or the fourth and last year of their course. Edinburgh University students were introduced to Greek in their first year, and to Hebrew in their third, while Glasgow likewise taught Greek in the first year, but Hebrew only in the fourth.[136] St Andrews in 1642 had a university policy of Greek in first year alongside the elements of Hebrew. Back in 1588 both St Salvator's and St Leonard's colleges had taught only Greek in the first class, while only at St Mary's did divines start with Hebrew, from 1579.[137] James VI's new foundation at King's College, Aberdeen, mentioned Hebrew in first and fourth years, while at Marischal College in 1593 Greek was available in the first class, with the principal himself teaching Hebrew and Syriac to the final year.[138]

One has the impression that Latin dominated the Renaissance curriculum, with Greek being more marginal; but when the pre-Reformation Banff grammar school was 'erected' in 1585 by David Cunningham, bishop of Aberdeen, it was laid down that the rector was to be skilled in Latin and Greek, and a later foundation of 1620 insisted on Latin and Greek grammar and the master's being 'weill versit' in such authors both in poetry and rhetoric as were customarily taught in other burghs.[139] In a manuscript dedicated to James VI and completed c.1617, Alexander Hume credits the king with reforming 'the grammar' and teaching Aristotle 'in his awn tongue, quhilk hes maed [sic] greek almost as common in Scotland as the latine'.[140]

As for French, there was probably more teaching than emerges from our records: a succession of French masters were present in Edinburgh from 1574.[141] Edinburgh also supplied a want for those intending to do further study in Holland, by providing David Phorbous, 'Dutche scoolemaister', to open a school in 1630.[142]

---

136   Morgan (ed.), *University of Edinburgh Charters*, 60, 61, 66; *MAUG*, ii, 45, 53; the grammar school taught the elements in its fifth year, ibid., ii, 309.

137   *Evidence … taken by the Commissioners … for Visiting the Universities of Scotland* (London, 1837), iii, 183, 188, 194, 195, 199, 205. Hebrew was taught at St Mary's by 1574: ibid., iii, 188.

138   *Aberdeen Univ. Graduates*, 338–40; also P.J. Anderson (ed.), *Fasti Academiae Mariscallanae Aberdonensis* (New Spalding Club, 1889, 1898), i, 63.

139   *Banff Annals*, ii, 166–7.

140   A. Hume, *Of the Orthographie and Congruitie of the Britan Tongue*, ed. H.B. Wheatley (Early English Text Society, original series, no. 5, 1863), 3.

141   *Edinburgh Burgh Recs.*, iv, 21. The first, Nicholas Langlois, father of Esther Inglis, unsurprisingly also taught calligraphy.

142   Ibid., vii, 71.

V.4 Dame schools, fencing schools

We can assume that the small number of dame schools recorded is an under-estimate, for the simple reason that they mostly appear when the authorities decide to close them. Those we have are found in Aberdeen, Dumbarton, Dundee, Haddington, Kirkcaldy, Leith North and South, Montrose, Paisley, Perth and Stirling. At Paisley and Kirkcaldy, they taught embroidery;[143] in Stirling, we find men teaching girls,[144] and by 1590 in Dundee there was an attempt to curb unlicensed men and women from taking boy pupils above eight years old.[145] In Aberdeen in 1598, dame schools were to teach 'madyne bairnis' only and not to employ a male doctor.[146] Janet Gordon there in 1622 was ordered to attend to her religious duties, being absent from sermon and communion.[147] At Peebles in June 1633, it was decided to have a spinning school with 'maistress and bairnes', but it is not found in action until 1634.[148] Fencing schools are likewise underestimated in our lists; they are recorded in Edinburgh from 1563, and later in the Canongate, with 'Roger's scule' there, complete with a reference to a doctor, achieving literary immortality in a broadsheet sonnet published by John Burel in 1601.[149]

V.5 Religious teaching

Religious education was of prime importance in all schools. The teaching involved Calvin's catechism, above all. This was the basic religious text used in the schools, as the booksellers' inventories bear witness. Even New Testaments are few in number before 1600: twenty-two are recorded in 1599.[150] By 1608 parents were encouraged to teach their children the Lord's Prayer, the articles of belief, the ten commandments, a short grace before meals and some short morning and evening prayers before they reached the age of six. Ministers were expected to test them on this, but sometimes seem to have failed to do so.[151] Formal education followed. It is surprising to find Robert Howie, principal of Marischal College, Aberdeen, writing to say that part

---

143 Brown, *History of Paisley Grammar School*, 41; *Kirkcaldy Recs.*, 145.
144 *Stirling Recs.*, i, 108.
145 A. Maxwell, *History of Old Dundee* (Edinburgh/Dundee, 1884), 93.
146 *Aberdeen Extracts*, ed. Stuart, ii, 171.
147 J. Stuart (ed.), *Selections from the Records of the Kirk Session, Presbytery and Synod of Aberdeen* (Spalding Club, 1846), 103.
148 *Peebles Chrs.*, 373, 419.
149 *Cal. State Papers Scotland*, xiii (2), 898. For a discussion of this sonnet, see J. Reid-Baxter, 'Poetry, passion and politics in the circle of James VI', in A.A. Macdonald and S. Mapstone (eds.), *A Palace in the Wilds* (Groningen, 1998).
150 Dickson & Edmond, *Annals of Scottish Printing*, 354.
151 *BUK*, iii, 1051–2.

of his time was taken up in lectures during which he dictated on Calvin's catechism.[152] Both the latter and adaptations thereof, such as John Craig's, the Heidelberg catechism, Robert Pont's and Patrick Adamson's, were in use. An otherwise unknown catechism of James Lawson is listed in a 1585 inventory.[153] In 1599, Principal Patrick Sharp of Glasgow issued a *Doctrinae Christianae brevis explicatio*. John Davidson's *Some helpes for young schollers in Christianity … partly At the examination before the Communion … And partly in the ordinarie Catechisme every Sabbothe day* of 1602 mentions the use made of schoolchildren, questioning and answering each other 'by cuples' publicly, and thus teaching the people.[154]

Sometimes, as at Edinburgh, catechism was eked out by George Buchanan's *Psalm Paraphrases*. Psalm books in various formats were in some demand; in 1579 fourteen bound copies printed by John Ross, plus 211 unbound, were inventoried.[155] Henry Charteris held over 400 of one edition, 'fyne print', another 216 likewise, and 264 in pica.[156] Passages from the Bible were probably taught, but the Bible itself (psalms apart) did not figure on school timetables till the seventeenth century, as book inventories reveal: by 1642 there were 5,000 Proverbs of Solomon, 700 New Testaments bound with psalms, another 5,000 Testaments, and 2,000 for bairns, as also 900 large psalms for bairns. Full bibles by that date ran to 300 copies.[157] The Proverbs of Solomon continued to be another favourite text.[158] In Prior Hepburn's original foundation of St Leonard's College there is no mention of Solomon but, by the time of the revision in Winram's time, the biblical wisdom books credited to Solomon could even replace Aristotle's *Ethics* for undergraduates.[159] However, the catechism and the psalms were the fundamental religious teaching texts in the decades following the Reformation.

152 J.K. Cameron (ed.), *Letters of John Johnston c.1565–1611 and Robert Howie c.1565–1645* (Edinburgh, 1963), 318.
153 *Bannatyne Misc.*, ii, 213.
154 Elliott, '*Some helpes*', sig D 8 verso.
155 Ibid., 302; described as 'of littell volume', ibid., 293.
156 Ibid., 353.
157 *Bannatyne Misc.*, ii, 259–60.
158 Ibid., iii, 259; cf. also iii, 213 (1586) and Herkless & Hannay, *College of St Leonard*, 1, 48, for pre-Reformation use of 'unum aliquem de Salomonis libris'.
159 Herkless & Hannay, *College of St Leonard*, 148; the original foundation statutes were unknown to the editors: see their comments, ibid., 91.

VI. Schoolmasters and their Status

VI.1 Burgh schoolmasters

The status of our schoolmaster and his doctor is not easily determined. It proved impossible to deduce it from the order of signatures to notarial documents: although a teacher is sometimes the first in the list of witnesses signatory, occasionally he even appears as the last. As more masters acquired degrees, and their economic situation improved, their standing in the eyes of their fellows must have improved, but we should not rule out a sense of status derived from the admiration teachers evoked in the minds of their pupils; when an Aberdeen 'committee of clairge [clergy]', including a lay advocate and his brother, examined a leet of five MAs following Mr William Carmichael's death in 1580, they chose the local man, Mr Thomas Cargill.[1] Acceptance of masters as burgesses of the town might be a sign of recognition, although it could also be dependent on relationships with deceased burgesses.[2] The master's status might be enhanced by his school, if it had a national reputation and was attended by scholars from all over the country. In Edinburgh in 1595, for example, we read of scholars from Caithness, Sutherland, Selkirk, Roxburgh and Wigtownshire – all, incidentally, reported for misconduct.[3]

The town schoolmaster had more than one source of income. Firstly there was his stipend, paid out of the common good fund. Then there were occasional gifts of money from the pupils: on entry, on special days, or for bent (grass or straw) to sit on. Thirdly, he might well be in receipt of fees for acting as reader, precenting at kirk or acting as session clerk. When David Black was appointed at Arbroath in 1564, he was to have £10 out of the chaplaincy of Our Lady, and 4 shillings from each 'freeman's barn', plus as much as he could get, 'his vantaig', of the landward children. In 1567 he was discharged, but no appointment is heard of till David Mitchell was chosen in 1573 as grammar schoolmaster, and the town scholars were henceforth charged 8 shillings. The schoolhouse was free.[4] In 1565, the Edinburgh headmaster was paid £20.[5] In 1566, the Elgin master got £10 and his meals in certain burgess houses.[6] In 1557 in Haddington, the master

1   *Bon Record*, 22n.
2   *Glasgow Burgesses*, p. 4, John Manson; p. 5, Thomas Craig; p. 82, Mr John Hamilton; p. 83, Mr James Anderston.
3   *RPC*, v, 236.
4   Hay, *History of Arbroath*, 259.
5   *Edinburgh Records*, ed. Adam, i, 479.
6   *Elgin Recs.*, ii, 396.

had been paid 20 merks (£13 6s 8d),[7] but he would be paid only 5 merks in Lanark in 1570.[8]

It was a period of inflation, a fact which the payments made begin to reflect. In 1582, the Elgin schoolmaster's fee was up to £20,[9] Aberdeen in 1574 was paying £33 6s 4d; Cupar in Fife £40 in 1570; while in 1577 £10 was added in Dumbarton 'becaus all things ar derar nor in tymes of auld'.[10] In Lanark, the master's fee in 1586 was given as £20.[11] Kirckcaldy two years later was paying £80.[12] In Edinburgh high school, the headmaster on appointment in 1584 received £50; it was found possible to double this sum on the death in 1588 of his predecessor, the Catholic William Roberton; as we saw, Roberton had not only outfaced all attempts to remove him, but had succeeded in retiring on a pension. The new appointee, Hercules Rollock, had complained that the income from the third category of master's payments, schoolboys' annuities, had been reduced by absence due to rumours of war and plague.[13]

By 1612 in Elgin the schoolmaster's wages had risen to 80 merks per annum (£53 62 8d), and by 1624 to 100 merks (£66 13 4d).[14] In Stirling, in September 1612, the burgh offered William Wallace, a native of Irvine, 100 merks (£66 13s 4d) with an expected extra 50 merks (£33 6s 8d) from the earl of Mar. He had a dwelling house free for three years and his transportation expenses were paid.[15] When, in August 1625, Mr David Will was hired, he got £100 of stipend, plus 6s 8d of scholage from each town bairn and 'libertie to tak of gentill mennes bairnes according to the discretioun of the gevares'.[16] Ayr paid £100 in 1627; Aberdeen £133 6s 8d in 1633. In 1628 Annan paid £40, Banff £54 6s 4d, Burntisland only £33 6s 8d, but since the master there probably doubled as reader, we can also double his fee. Cupar paid £100 in 1627, as did Crail in 1628. Dumfries paid £60 in 1627, in which year Dunbar paid its exceptionally well-qualified master, the grammarian Alexander Hume, no less than £400! Dundee paid £300 in 1628, Forres £80; in 1633 Haddington paid £200 and Irvine £53 6s 8d.

7 J. Dennistoun & A. Macdonald (eds.), 'Extracts from the accounts of the Common Good of various burghs in Scotland', *Maitland Misc.*, ii (1), 44.
8 *Lanark Recs.*, 51, 53.
9 *Elgin Recs.*, ii, 396.
10 *Maitland Misc.*, ii (1), 39, 41, 42–43.
11 *Lanark Recs.*, 91.
12 Beale, *Schools of Fife*, 42.
13 *Edinburgh Burgh Recs.*, vi, 517–18. His predecessor, Roberton, had a pension of 200 merks on his retirement in 1584.
14 *Elgin Recs.*, i, 400–1.
15 Ibid., i, 131.
16 Ibid., i, 160.

By 1628 Inverness was paying £80, and Lanark £100; Perth paid 250 merks (£166 13s 4d).[17]

These figures show that the cost of hiring a burgh schoolmaster was increasing throughout the whole period, though the real rise in the cost of living due to the ructions of the sixteenth century was offset by greater economic stability after 1600.[18] One slightly confusing instance of a school-master's double income is to be found in a contract signed between the elders and deacons of Bendochy kirk and Mr Francis Peirson, schoolmaster at Cupar Angus, on 3 October 1613. He was to instruct and 'learne' the chil-dren and bairns that 'cumis to the scoole' and undertake their guarding and ruling in both doctrine and discipline. Before and after Sunday preaching, he was to 'uptak' and sing a psalm in the kirk, and be scribe to the session on all occasions. His payment while remaining 'at the said scoole of Cowper' (Coupar Angus) was to be 80 merks. Marriages and baptisms would bring in £20 per annum, and the remaining 50 merks were payable at 'allhaliday' (1 November) and Candlemas (2 February), together with the termly payments, 1 merk per bairn per term, payable for the second term at Candlemas, for the third on Rood Day (3 May) and for the fourth at Lammas (in August). If, as expected, the Lord of Coupar was content to pay Mr Francis, this would be additional to what was agreed in the contract. Peirson's services at Bendochy would seem to have been purely ecclesiastical, his schoolmastering taking place at Coupar.[19]

Since smaller burghs paid less than larger towns, it is not possible to average out schoolmasters' salaries. Music masters generally got less, except at Cupar in 1627 where Mr Alexander Tullidaff was paid the same as the grammar master.[20] In most burghs, the master's schoolhouse was a separate charge, paid for by the council, and his doctor was sometimes paid for as well; in Dunfermline, from 1620, he got 50 merks (£33 6s 8d).[21] The master himself frequently hired the doctor, but in Stirling in 1620 the council hired him to teach English reading and writing under Mr James Edmeston, principal master, and to act as kirk preceptor, for 20 merks plus a further 20 merks from the presbytery, with 8 shillings a quarter for the scholage and board of each town bairn learning to read or write, and 6s 8d if learning music. 'Outlandis' (landward) bairns depended on what their parents were prepared to pay.[22]

---

[17] *Maitland Misc.*, ii (1), 39–45, 47.
[18] A.J.S. Gibson & T.C. Smout, *Prices, Food and Wages in Scotland, 1550–1780* (Cambridge, 1995), 5.
[19] RDI/232, 424.
[20] *Maitland Misc.*, ii (1), 42. From 1610, under Queen Anna's mortification, Dunfermline's music master was paid £100 annually; *Dunfermline Recs.*, 91.
[21] *Dunfermline Recs.*, 129.
[22] *Stirling Recs.*, i, 155, Cf. *Maitland Misc.*, i (2), 458.

Mr William Skene, Aberdeen's song schoolmaster in 1597, had to act as preceptor 'in bayth the kirkis'. His regular stipend was 120 merks (£80), but for precenting there was an additional 10 merks which could devolve on his doctor or a capable pupil.[23] In Fife, song schoolmasters were paid £100 in Dunfermline in 1610, £200 at St Andrews for precenting and teaching in 1620, and £100 at Cupar in 1627.[24] Mr John Moodie at Kelso was partly paid by the town and partly by the kirk; for 1635, he was paid £30 in the following January 'for the kirk sessiones part of my fie' as reader-schoolmaster, and the same the two following years.[25] Out of his salary, the schoolmaster might have to pay for his house (which was also the school-house), usually rented from a citizen: at Ayr, as in some other burghs, the town's treasurer paid for this expense.[26]

VI.2 Parish schoolmasters

The parish schoolmaster was in a less secure position than his burgh counterpart. Continuous employment was always doubtful where the parish was unable to afford the fees. In the case of John Christie at Drumwhindle in Ellon parish, teaching a vernacular school without licence or knowledge of the minister, the brevity of his employment was due to other reasons. A stranger, seemingly from Fyvie, he had failed to prove his status by supplying within the month a testimonial from a previous minister, and in February 1617 it was decreed that his school was to be closed.[27] A parish school-master's salary was paid by the heritors generally, and this was based on the number of ploughgates, which varied from parish to parish; this appears to be a continuation of the pre-Reformation arrangement we saw earlier. One merk per ploughgate was common, or sometimes a firlot of meal. From 1610 we have a contract between Alexander, bishop of Caithness, and various heritors of Fettercairn who have to assist and concur in searching and 'finding furthe' a qualified man for education of the youth of the parish. The bishop led with a promise of £24, and others promised other sums.[28] In September 1617, at Newburgh, we find the bishop of Aberdeen ordaining 13s 4d or a firlot of meal from each ploughgate for the maintenance of the school, with which arrangement the minister, elders and parish there were content.[29] The Synod of Fife stented Abdie and Forgan in 1611 for one merk

23 *Aberdeen Extracts*, ed. Stuart, ii, 157.
24 NAS, CH2/264/1, unfoliated, under date 2 April 1628.
25 NAS, CH2/1 173/1, under dates 17 January 1636, 1 January 1637, 26 November 1637.
26 *Ayr Burgh Accts.*, 216, 281.
27 NAS, CH2/146/2, 125v.
28 RDI/214, 281.
29 NAS, CH2/146/2, 133.

on every plough; and at Ceres the fee was fixed at two merks per plough, but this seemingly included payment for session clerking and uptaking the psalm.[30]

It has been shown that a stent of about three and a half merks was common in Fife by 1636. The heritors were not anxious to pay, nor even always able to do so in some cases. Presbyteries and kirk sessions had to support the schoolmasters against defaulters. The bairns' parents were also called upon to pay, and the kirk session covered the expenses of poor scholars,[31] generally out of fines. As these were variable, so were the numbers of poor scholars. In 1611, the parish children of Forgan were charged 4s 8d a term, which was the fee for town bairns in Ayr, while in 1626, Ceres charged 20s for Latin and 13s 4d for the vernacular, according to the standard set by the Cupar presbytery.[32] At Ellon in 1620, Mr Samuel Tullidaff and his brother, masters of the grammar and music school, complained about the uncertainty of their maintenance. Named heritors were to contribute a firlot of meal (a frequent substitute for cash payment). As to 'routhis collegde' (quarter's scholage) of the said school, payment was fixed as follows: those learning to read and write, 13s 4d every 'routh' or quarterly term; grammar school pupils 20s every term; music pupils 20s per term, and those learning to play and sing, 40s per term.[33] In 1626 at Newbattle, the session provided for a set rent for the schoolmaster, naming those who were to pay (the maximum was £20, the minimum 5 merks); this was in addition to his quarterly stipend. Every scholar was ordered to pay 10 shillings for learning to read and write Scots, 6s 8d for music, 13s 4d for Latin (fees applicable only to parishioners of Newbattle). In 1627 those lairds who failed to pay were to be poinded and there was a list of contributing parishioners, the highest paying 20s, the lowest 2s.[34]

The master was paid extra if he also served as session clerk and preceptor. Fees for these extra posts were payable out of baptisms (in Ayr the doctor kept the baptismal register), marriage contracts and burials. At Lasswade, the provision for the schoolmaster, who was also session clerk and kirk officer, varied from £5 from the earl of Roslin to the 2 merks paid by the mother of a laird.[35] At Menmuir in 1628, the reader-schoolmaster, Patrick Brokas, was finding it difficult to get a 'gryt part of the stipend appointed to be payit till him' by the parish 'viz ane merk the pleuche yeirlie', and stated

---

[30] Beale, *Schools of Fife*, 51.
[31] Newbattle had always seven or eight poor scholars to maintain, J. Lee, *Lectures on the History of the Church of Scotland* (Edinburgh, 1860), ii, 432.
[32] Beale, *Schools of Fife*, 51–6.
[33] NAS, CH2/146/2, 155.
[34] Lee, *Lectures*, ii, 431–2.
[35] Ibid., ii, 437.

that he had already served for one and a half years. The session demanded pro rata payment by Whitsunday and failing that, 'ilk landit gentilman till gif his justice', poinding the tenants for payment.[36] The fact that schoolmasters often discharged kirk duties makes it difficult to estimate exactly what they received. The Maybole schoolmaster Mr John Hume's receipt of £20 in 1631, paid by the earl of Cassilis, was only part of his fee for serving the school and reading the prayers daily in Maybole kirk. However, another receipt, for 1633, reads 'I Mr Jhone Hume, scholemastere of Maybole be thir presentis grants me to have receaved the soume of tua hundrethe pundis form the potent and nobell Earle of Cassils Lord Kennedie and that in the name and behalf of my La. Uchiltrie his L. mothere. In testimone whereof I have writtene and subscrived thir presents at Cassils the fift of August anno 1633.'[37]

Parish schools in country parishes were almost always held 'apud ecclesiam' or 'at the kirk'. Other schools might be sited at or a near a castle, or indeed at a convenient point in the village. In one instance, at Fintry, Stirlingshire, it was customary to hold the school at the bridge: it was decided in 1641 that the school would be held month about at Fintry bridge and at the kirk. However, the previous year, the master related how he took up school at the bridge end at Martinmas 1640, having only three bairns in his charge after New Year; thereupon, moving to the kirk, he had never more than eight and only three 'abides'.[38]

VI.3 Doctors

The doctor was, in the burgh schools, the assistant to the schoolmaster, who might on occasion hire him personally and pay him out of his own pocket. As the foregoing would lead us to expect, stipends were low: 50 merks in Dunfermline from 1620, and £53 6s 8d in Cupar in 1627. In Falkland in 1649 the doctor's wage of £83 16s 4d was made up from common good, kirk session and casual fees.[39] Henry Cunningham, doctor in Anstruther Wester, thought all the local children should have compulsory education, including the poor, who in 1595 'sall be furnished upon the common expences'; if any poor refused, they should be denied other aid. Those who had children and kept them off school should nevertheless pay the term's payment, as well as the cost of their meal. A month later, the poor were given time off to seek their food, though the latter requirement was soon withdrawn.

---

[36] NAS, CH2/264/1, unfoliated, under date 2 Apr. 1628.
[37] NAS, GD25/9/44/5.
[38] NAS, CH2/438/1, 14v, 19. A parish visitation of 1642 shows his school desolate, and a woman, unfit to teach, at work there, ibid., fo. 45.
[39] Beale, *Schools of Fife*, 59.

In 1600, the campaign continued. However, it was decided that schooling could not benefit some, and if they could not read or write for 'want of injyn', or because the teacher could not spare the extra hours 'to await on' them, they must at least learn the Lord's Prayer, commandments, articles of faith and main points of the catechism.[40] Obviously, a note of cold realism had persuaded the session that universal education in the humanities was not possible. On the southern shores of Fife in 1596, the 'honestest men' of Burntisland were ordered to provide the schoolmaster with bed and board in their houses in turn. But it was usually the doctor who was housed in this fashion. In 1619, Kirkcaldy ordered the school doctor to have 'his meatt about', but in Dysart in 1626 the doctor complained that he got no food from scholars or their parents 'as was the custom in the grammar schools'. The practice continued after 1638,[41] and is redolent of pre-Reformation custom. In 1616, William Dyet was doctor in Peebles for 10 merks per term, but his replacement from Ayrshire in 1627 got 20 merks quarterly plus ordinary term fees of children. Back in 1565, a previous doctor was to have had his 'meit about'; this situation still obtained in 1627.[42]

VI.4 Schoolmasters' circumstances: some evidence from testaments

We saw in Section II.5 how the 1583 testament and inventory of the 'adventure schoolmaster' Thomas Liston, a former Dominican, showed that he died a poor man in St Andrews.[43] In 1594, we find sir George Calland, a former Catholic chaplain, dying intestate as schoolmaster at Kilconquhar in Fife. An inventory by his brother shows his comparative poverty, his total wealth being £43, £40 in the keeping of a citizen of Kilconquhar, and no debts owing to or by him.[44]

This is in striking contrast to the circumstances of Mr William Bowie, schoolmaster in Haddington, at his death in October 1623. His widow, Esther Quintin, as his executrix, handed in his will, drawn up in September. Bowie had a farm, the income from which was (along with his house furnishings) £1,084. George Barron of Kinnaird owed him 203 merks; a lady called Carmichael, spouse of Sir John Home of Huttonhall, owed £100 plus three bolls of meal at £8 per boll, for boarding of their son John. Lady Fallside, for boarding of James Edmeston, brother to her husband the laird of Edmeston, owed 100 merks, £7 10s for 'furnishing', and three bolls of wheat promised as a bounty and also for his board, at 19 merks the boll: a total of £112 3s 4d.

---

[40] Lee, *Lectures*, ii, 432–4, citing the kirk session minutes.
[41] Beale, *Schools of Fife*, 47.
[42] *Peebles Chrs.*, pp. 299, 361, 367.
[43] See Section II.5 above.
[44] NAS, CC20/4/2, 363.

Patrick Carkellie of Morkill owed £30, while a late Mr Bowie in Whitekirk owed £15 for the board of his son Adam. Moving next to the Highlands, where Bowie had formerly taught, we find him owed 100 merks yearly by Sir Duncan Campbell of Glenorchy, conform to a contract from Martinmas 1593 to Whitsunday 1623, a thirty-year debt rising to 3,000 merks. Bowie's own debts included 50 merks to the laird of Lauderdale for his ground; of three female servants, two were to get 10 merks and one £4 10s. The most striking item in all this is the huge debt owed by the laird of Glenorchy, whose sons Bowie had continued to teach at Haddington.[45]

The will of James Dalzell, an Edinburgh schoolmaster, gives some indication of extra monies received from pupils' parents; on his death in October 1624, Dalzell was also reader at Greyfriars kirk.[46] He taught the eldest son of the laird of Blackbarony, for which he was owed 5 merks. John Macronald, agent, owed him £3 12s for furnishing him with paper and ink and teaching him as an 'extraordinar scholar' for one term. Mr Patrick Forrest owed £4 for his two sons for two years' teaching in John Matheson's school (St Giles Upper Tolbooth), and one term in Dalzell's (Greyfriars). For teaching a boy called James Galloway for half a year and supplying paper and ink, the wife of Robert Porteous owed him £48; the two children of Andrew Michelson, stabler, owed 52 shillings for six months; Thomas Andrew, merchant, had a son who owed 32 shillings for the same period as did Harry Forrester, stabler, for his son; John Kennedy, fishmonger, owed 15 shillings for his bairn. For the term up to Martinmas, his servant, Jonet Mitchell, was owed 4 merks.

VI.5 Endowment of schools

Mortifications and endowments for the upkeep of schools are few. The last pre-Reformation example was at the collegiate church of Hamilton, where the earl of Arran's song school taught boy singers plus all the poor not having the wherewithal to buy education, yet wishing to attend school.[47] The years 1560 to 1600 were difficult years for the aristocracy, or indeed any other possible school benefactors: prices rose steeply, wages lagged somewhat behind, and plague and famine were constant. 'Recurrent pestilence and famine held up development [and] between 1560 and the early 1600s the top-grade craftsmen of Edinburgh seem to have enjoyed a threefold increase in money wages … the unskilled increased their money wage by no more than sixty percent.'[48] The first recorded foundation (actually a refounda-

---

45 CC8/8/52, 291–292.
46 NAS, CC8/8/54, 12v.
47 J. Durkan, 'Mediaeval Hamilton: Ecclesiastical', *IR*, xxviii (1977), 51–3.
48 S.G.E. Lythe, *The Economy of Scotland in its European Setting 1550–1625* (Edinburgh/London, 1960), 28–30.

tion) of our period was a royal one, when the Regent Moray refounded the grammar school of Dunkeld, in February 1568; revenues from various parishes in Dunkeld diocese were assigned to the schoolmaster's stipend. An annual rent was diverted from the 'blew freris', choristers of the cathedral, to the new foundation, an endowment repeated in the same terms in 1588.[49] After 1600, aristocratic finance was simply not up to the demands made on it, as many noble families were in debt.[50] We saw in Section III that Glasgow University endowments between 1576 and 1633 owed little to the nobility. Benefactors included John Howieson, minister of Cambuslang, and Michael Wilson, merchant of Eastbourne.[51] What is rather surprising is the fact that the university population rose steadily over the same period.[52]

At Cambuslang, the first mention of Mr John Howieson's support for the school there is found in 1602, but it clearly antedated this,[53] for in an action before the Lords of Council in April 1603, Mr Andrew Hamilton, schoolmaster, mentions it as existing 'dyvers yeris bygane'. It was to the value of 500 merks with schoolhouse, dwellinghouse and kirk, with, in a later addition, the vicarage pensionary of Cambuslang and the Lady Chapel of Kirkburn. In Fife, we find the king confirming a charter by William Scott of Abbotshall on 25 July 1593,[54] for building a school to teach the youth of Pittenweem, on the site of a former Augustinian house. At Preston-pans, there was clearly some difficulty in collecting the money set aside for the school John Davidson had founded. He died in 1604; no less than £466 13s 4d which he had 'mortefeit … to the skole of Prestonpans' was owed by Richard Lawson when he died in Edinburgh in September 1622.[55]

A similar delay in the implementation of a mortification by Sir Thomas Menzies of Durn to the grammar school at Fordyce seems to be posited. Consisting of three land annuities, two of them worth 12 merks, plus a feu duty in Fordyce, as a stipend for the schoolmaster, the owner had not handed it over by May 1627; yet an old inventory speaks of certain tenements and yards in Fordyce being mortified to the grammar school on 1 September 1599.[56] In 1611, the Aberdeen-born poet and academic John Johnstone, of St Andrews University, left 200 merks to be mortified to poor scholars at

[49] *RSS*, vi, 160; NAS, PS1/57/146.
[50] K. Brown, 'Aristocratic finance and the origins of the Scottish Revolution', *English Historical Review*, civ (1981), 46–87.
[51] Thomson (ed.), *Deeds Instituting Bursaries*, pp. 1, 6, 8, 13, 23.
[52] Lythe, *Economy of Scotland*, 29.
[53] T. McCrie, *Life of Andrew Melville* (1824 edn), ii, 414n; NAS, CS7/212, 97.
[54] *RMS*, v, 2356.
[55] *Bannatyne Misc.*, iii, 202.
[56] D.G. McLean, *History of Fordyce Academy* (Banff, 1936), 29; W. Cramond, *The Church and Churchyard of Fordyce* (Banff, 1886), 15; NAS, GD248/1/137 (no number).

the Aberdeen grammar school.[57] Another benefactor of that school was Mr James Cargill, a medical man, who in 1614 left 500 merks to pay the scholage and school dues, both in vernacular and Latin schools, with grammar books, authors and English books used in the same schools, 'and that for the use of my puir freyndis'. Part of this was used to rebuild the school in 1623.[58] In fact, Aberdeen town has the best record for mortifications, but only from 1613, when Dr Duncan Liddell left 12 merks to the poor scholars in college and at grammar school. In 1628, an anonymous neighbour of the burgh mortified 500 merks to found a yearly rent for the upkeep of a school doctor. In 1629, Alexander Irvine of Drum left enough money to maintain four masters at the school, and in 1631 Dr Patrick Dun gave the lands of Ferryhill to Aberdeen grammar school.[59] Down the east coast, at Monimail in 1632, Lord Melville mortified sums of money for the school and for the kirk reader; other heritors promised to help so that the total for the school-master's stipend would be £100 Scots.[60] Even allowing for mortifications that have not so far come to light, the endowment of schools and scholars in Scotland seems pretty slim. The prevalence of debt among the aristocracy may well have been the major factor here.[61] The most important single endowment was the royal gift of chaplainries for the upkeep of bursars in the early days of the Reformation.

VI.6 Schoolmasters in the courts

Schoolmasters frequently held office in the kirk as reader, session clerk or preceptor; if not, their contracts might stipulate the duration of their employment, although life-appointments were often promised to those who lived without scandal (*ad vitam aut culpam*). Whether discharging kirk duties or not, masters were expected to be moral exemplars, but misbehaviour by schoolmasters is occasionally recorded. Thomas Duncanson in Stirling, allowed as a reader in 1560 to keep a school in addition to Stirling grammar school, is found not long afterwards making public repentance for his fornication, reported to the General Assembly in 1563. As a reader, Duncanson was vulnerable and had to go; he was suspended until he married the woman, and was reinstated at the request of the local church.[62] Gilbert Taylor, as minister of Penicuik, formerly Canongate schoolmaster, was

---

57 *Maitland Misc.*, i (2), 337.
58 *Aberdeen Extracts*, ed. Stuart, ii, 332,384.
59 *Bon Record*, 109, 109–10, 111, 111–12, 112–22.
60 W. McCraw, *More about Monimail* (Cupar, n.d.), 12–13.
61 K.M. Brown, 'Noble indebtedness in Scotland between the Reformation and the Revolution', *Historical Research*, xii (1989), 260–75.
62 *BUK*, i, 44.

accused of drunkenness in 1586.[63] In 1617, we find the composer Duncan Burnett, music master at Glasgow, supplicating the presbytery; he had been suspended from reading and instructing the youth for abusing himself in drunkenness. Repentant, he asked to be restored, and was to appear before the archbishop, the bishop of Argyll and the presbytery in the bishop's castle. The archbishop imposed a penalty for his uncharitable words to Mr Joseph Lawrie, who forgave him.[64] Burnett can hardly have enhanced his standing as a moral exemplar by fathering his natural daughter Jonet two years later.[65]

In Elgin in 1597, George Annand, grammar schoolmaster, was forced to do public repentance and pay a fine for fornication with Barbara Jardine.[66] At Tulliallan Patrick Ramsay also suffered for fornication in 1607.[67] Five years earlier, in April 1602, William Norvell had quite a spectacular cata-logue of offences when his case came before the justiciary court. He had been at Torryburn as schoolmaster for three years, then went to Millburn or 'Futhies myle', a school within Dunfermline parish. Challenged for keeping Christian Douglas, he asserted he was married, but the contrary was proved true and he left the area. He had been married for seven years to Margaret Morrison, as well as keeping Christian Douglas, to whom he gave the use of his body about six months before his wife died. He took the poor-box of Cockpen on 11 April, broke it up on the 'water bray' beside Monktonhall, and removed £8 – the laird of Cockpen duly fined him that sum. Much earlier, about 11 November 1585, he had had his name registered as a notary, without royal presentation, and he had no protocol book. With regard to his serving woman, 'the young las betie lassels', he had been drunk at the time and knew not what he did to her, declaring that he had done nothing. On 21 May 1602, he was banished.[68]

In Edinburgh on 6 November 1590, the diarist Robert Burrell, school-master (and reader in the East Kirk), had less spectacularly been 'fund to half done wrang in uttering maist injurious and filthie speichis aganis the maistres of the Cunzie hous', and had to ask her forgiveness on his knees. Ordered to do likewise before the session, and 'discharget of his scole induring the touns will', he was nonetheless 'reponet' the following month. The lady in question was Isobel Abernethie, mother of the poet John Burel. At that point, Isobel had been married for some six months to Thomas Acheson, 'Maister Cunzeour to our Soverane Lord', who was her third husband in three years,

---

[63] NAS, CH2/121/1, 6v.
[64] NAS, CH2/171/35, under that date.
[65] For the 28 Dec. 1619 baptism of Jonet, begotten on Jonet Montgomerie, see the Jamieson Transcripts (Mitchell Library): Baptisms, High Kirk, vol. i.
[66] *Elgin Recs.*, ii, 53.
[67] Stirling Council Archives, CH2/722/4, under 3 November 1607.
[68] NAS, JC2/6/F/2.

no less.[69] Birrell's fame as a schoolmaster long outlived his disgrace; on 29 December 1637, we find a reference to Robert Birrell's school, now a workhouse, 'known as the schoolhouse' on the east side of Barclay's Close off the High Street and rather nicely, as late as 25 April 1691, Robert has actually turned into John Burel in a reference to the building 'formerly known as the schoolhouse'.[70] Across in Falkirk in 1594, it was continual fornication with Jonet Yule that got Mr Thomas Ambrose, schoolmaster there, deposed. Under promise of marriage he was debarred until he made public repentance, or till parishioners demanded his restoration – which they promptly did, and he duly married Jonet. He served as a minister in Alva and elsewhere till 1613, when the Assembly deposed him for marrying Lord Livingstone to the Catholic daughter of the marquis of Huntly. Reponed by the General Assembly in 1614, he was finally suspended in 1628.[71]

Slanderous talk had been the issue again at Stirling in 1614: a former school doctor, Mr James Brady, was caught calumniating and speaking evil of Mr William Wallace, appointed principal schoolmaster in 1612. He was found guilty of conversing and haunting with the schoolboys and drawing their affections away from Wallace; he confessed, but was told a repeat offence would lead to his banishment from the burgh.[72] Troubles of a different kind had afflicted the Canongate grammar school in 1612, when Mr William Henry, a teacher there, 'brak the haill inward noble pairtis' of the body of a pupil and left him in a state from which he was unlikely to recover: called before the courts and failing to compear, he was denounced rebel.[73] And in 1617, the Canongate master, Mr Robert Steven, was summonsed, with many others, for the crime of usury (charging interest at more than 10%); he too failed to compear and was denounced rebel.[74] Also in 1617, the doctor in Ayr, Hugh Tran, and his wife were in trouble for sinning with their tongues. They were accused of 'flyting and scalding mutuallie'; if the offence were

---

[69] *Edinburgh Burgh Recs.*, iv, 457, 479; v, 29, 30. Robert Birrell was almost certainly related to Isobel Abernethie, by her first marriage to the wealthy flescher Harry Burrell (d.1587). The poet John, her son, is found alongside 'Robert Burrale maister of ane woulgare scull', as witness to a discharge made by Isobel on behalf of the late advocate, Mr Edmond Hay, her second husband, on 16 Dec. 1589 (SRO, RD1/36, fo. 12v). She was engaged to Thomas Aitcheson by 4 Mar. 1590. Robert is later found witnessing transactions involving Thomas and other Cunzie House personnel, so the difficulties must have been resolved (e.g. NAS, NP1/183, fo.17; RD1/58, fo.127r).

[70] Edinburgh City Archives, Moses Bundles Misc Papers, vol. 1, bundle 21, no. 851, and vol. iv, p. 132, bundle 97, no. 4155.

[71] *Fasti*, i, 227; J. Love, *The Schools and Schoolmasters of Falkirk* (Falkirk, 1898), 5.

[72] *Stirling Recs.*, i, 136.

[73] *RPC*, ix, 322.

[74] *RPC*, xi, 44. Steven had been in trouble with Edinburgh town council in 1608, when he was placed in ward until he paid a fine; he had 'contravenit his ayth of burgesscchip in the taking up of ane rammer schole in the Kannogaitt and in drawing the burges bayrnes from their hie schole to himself', *Edinburgh Burgh Recs.*, vi, 37.

repeated, they were to be put in the 'brankis'. Tran was accused again the following year, imprisoned in the tolbooth and had to 'satisfie laich', that is, do repentance on a low stool in kirk.[75]

A more distinguished offender was Mr Samuel Rutherford, the future author of *Lex Rex* and spiritual correspondent of many aristocratic and other ladies. As humanity regent in the University of Edinburgh, he was deprived of office on 3 February 1626 because he had 'fallin in furnicatioun with Euphamie Hammiltoun, and hes committit ane grit scandle in the colledge'.[76] Mr William Spence, master in Leith, was removed from office for adultery in 1629.[77] The previous year, George Sinclair, formerly reader at Beith kirk in Fife, and teacher of 'young childrene als weill laidis als lassis at Keltieheuch', had been found to have committed adultery seven years before, and 'incest' a year or so earlier with 'tua young damosellis baith being sisters … his scolleris and young virganes'. Sinclair had also drawn up a false testimonial for a Keltieheuch man, and he was sentenced to be drowned.[78] Less chillingly, in Linlithgow in 1629, Mr Alexander Rynd was removed from his mastership for inefficiency, though this must have been a temporary suspension, since he survived as master till later.[79]

We have already had cause to refer to the rather different case of the Edinburgh schoolmaster William Roberton. In 1568 he was a Catholic schoolmaster in a Protestant burgh, appointed by the abbot of Holyrood and in possession for twenty-three years, being paid 20 merks by the town. Nevertheless, the provost 'masterfullie eiecit' him on 29 August 1568, and barred him from the school. The burgh's lawyers produced a decree on 3 October 1562 ordering him to desist from teaching; Roberton repelled the decree, since after its grant he had continued to teach. His reply was accepted by the Lords of Council and he was continued in office; this then created the problem of Mr Thomas Buchanan's having a contract dated 25 July 1568. Buchanan demanded indemnity and called for payment of £100 Scots within two days, which demand the Lords also concurred with.[80]

Another master who took his case to the Lords of Council was Mr John Bonar, schoolmaster at Inverkeithing before his move to Ayr. On 10 February 1603 he purchased letters against the council. He had a contract going back to 1585, for reading the common prayers and teaching the grammar school for 14 merks per quarter (56 merks annually), the council to provide at its own expense a schoolhouse with a room for himself. He

75 Ayr District Archives, CH2/751/1(2), 330, 353v.
76 *Edinburgh Burgh Recs.*, vi, 296.
77 *RPC*, 2nd series, iii, 157.
78 S.A. Gillon et al. (eds.), *Select Justiciary Cases, 1624–1650* (Stair Society, 1951), i, 95–6.
79 A. Bain, *Patterns of Error* (Edinburgh, 1989), 92.
80 NAS, CS7/45, 36v, 236–257, 260.

was owed £74 up to August 1601, and there had been no room provided for six years, constraining him to pay 10 merks for one. On 17 June 1603 the case continued. In the meantime, various inhabitants of the town had met on 11 April to pay the £154 they owed Bonar for the 80 merks per annum owing; they imposed a stent on the townspeople. They also 'have the burden' of paying Bonar as reader 13 chalders of victual yearly, and said it was not right to impose on them, most of whom were poor and indigent, the sum of 10 merks. However, the Lords of Council found the letters of horning against the council to be in order, notwithstanding allegations to the contrary.[81]

Few cases went as far as the Lords of Council. Our final example is a case that threatened to do so, and concerns the master of the writing school in Aberdeen, Gilbert Leslie.[82] On 5 December 1612, he was attacked by Patrick Gordon of Birsmuir, who on the king's highway drew his sword on Leslie and pursued him. A burgess was found cautioner for him not to repeat the offence. The same day, Leslie complained to the council about his dread of further attack, and the council gave him an indemnity of 500 merks, for which his cautioner gave him security. On 8 February following, however, several accomplices of the attacker renewed the assault on Leslie, giving him 'many bluidie and best straikis … to the great effusione of his bloode'. It was proposed to complain formally to the Privy Council. Two days later, the council paid for letters to be raised against Gordon by the Privy Council, while the offenders were summoned on 19 February. The cautioner for the attacker reappeared on 24 February, promising satisfaction and the payment of any fines due. The outcome was that the cautioner was made to pay 200 merks, one half to the town, the other half to Leslie. Furthermore, the offender and his accomplices were also requested to appear in the burgh kirk and before the pulpit crave God's pardon, thereafter the magistrates' pardon and finally, forgiveness from Gilbert Leslie himself. The town of Aberdeen had taken decisive action in support of its writing master.

[81] NAS, CS7/207, 9v–10v, 345v.
[82] *Aberdeen Extracts*, ed. Stuart, ii, 312–13, 314–15, 318, 319.

VII. Schooling in the Highlands

When we turn to the Highland area, we have to bear in mind that schooling there was of a different type and is hard to quantify, since bards, harpists and pipers were attached to the homes of clan chiefs, as were leeches and medicos. Some Highland children were occasionally sent to the Lowlands for education. As far back as 1542, we find John Elder informing Henry VIII that he had been 'educat and brought up, not onely in the West Yles … named the Sky and the Lewis, but also, being a scholer and student in the southe partis … called Sanctandrois, Abirdene and Glasgow, for the space of xii yeares'.[1] Earlier still, we have Donald McLean, scholar of the Isles, as rector of a church in Islay, incorporated in Glasgow University in 1461, as was a certain 'scholar of Sodor'.[2] We also find James Macdonald, eldest son of Alexander of Islay, having his 'burd and lair' at royal expense under dene William Henderson, canon of Holyrood. After the Reformation, Hector Munro, later dean of Ross and in 1588 laird of Foulis, was to be sent to St Andrews in 1570, to profit there in letters and 'learing of the trew Word'. The chief of the Dewart clan 1578–1598, Lachlan Mór MacLean, spent his childhood at court till he was of age to manage his affairs, the king taking charge of his education. Archibald Campbell, son of the provost of Kilmun, was a student in Glasgow in 1582, while in 1615 Sir Ruari Mór McLeod visited his children at school in that city.[3]

Schools in the Highlands which tried to follow the Lowland pattern destined themselves to a short life, and the best solution was to send the pupils directly to school in the Lowlands. We have already encountered the Haddington schoolmaster William Bowie, who was owed a huge sum by Donnchadh Dubh, seventh Campbell of Glenorchy. A former servitor of 'Black Duncan', Bowie was tutor to his grandsons, acted as his notary, and dedicated his eulogistic family history (the Black Book of Taymouth) to him in 1598. Bowie's name occurs as a student at Perth in June 1587; he had become 'Mr' by Candlemas 1597.[4] He continued to teach Donnchadh Dubh's grandsons at Haddington, and in 1619 we find him worrying about the children. John would be a scholar, he thought; young Duncan, 'God saiff

---

[1] *Bannatyne Misc.*, i, 10.
[2] *MAUG*, ii, 61.
[3] *Notes and Queries of the Society of West Highland and Island Historical Research*, nos. 7, 8, 18; J. Bannerman, 'Literacy in the Highlands' in I.B. Cowan and D. Shaw (eds.), *Renaissance and Reformation in Scotland* (Edinburgh, 1983), 127.
[4] GD112/5/10, 79–80; *Black Book of Taymouth*, ed. C. Innes (Edinburgh, 1855), 253–4; M.D.W. McGregor, 'Political History of the McGregors before 1571' (University of Edinburgh Ph.D. thesis, 1989), 255.

him', began well, but 'ye wald say he wearis his belt as men sayis Mr George
Buchanan did weare his', so short was his doublet, up to his breast. Clearly
concerned on this point, Bowie adds after his signature at the end of the
letter, 'Duncan mon haiff ane uther dowblet'.[5]

Looking beyond Glenorchy to the Islands, it was presumably within our
period that Catriona, daughter of Donald Gorm Òg of Sleat, had as her
tutor the great exponent of bardic verse, Cathal MacMhuirich, but whether
he also taught others we are not informed.[6] There is other evidence of
Gaelic learning in the second half of the sixteenth century and beyond,
despite the Statute of Iona of 1609, and the 1616 Privy Council order that
English be made the universal language, with the 'irische' language being
castigated as one of the main reasons for the continuance of barbarity and
'incivilitie' in the Highlands and the Isles.[7] Nobody was to be served heir
to his father who was not trained in the 'inglis tung', and after the age
of nine children should be sent to inland schools to learn it.[8] This policy
was soon applied to Sir Donald Gorm of Sleat, who in 1617 was ordered
to send his bairns to the Lowland schools to be 'trayned up to write and
reid and to speake Inglishe'.[9] However, some time earlier, in June 1599, Mr
John Blackburn, Glasgow schoolmaster, was being urged to report on 'quhat
Irische men ar in his schule, and of their religioun'; the previous year, he
was already being asked to catechise his 'Irish scholars' so that they might
understand the grounds of their religion.[10] The bishops were instructed to be
active in promoting the cause of establishing such English schools; in their
visitations they were to see whether schools had been established in such
places 'as should be thought most fitting for the ease of the said children',
and by settling suitable stipends to attract schoolmasters. They were also to
ensure that every week the minister did indeed catechise his parishioners on
the grounds of religion, as required.[11] Again, in 1629, the question of planting
schools in the Islands was to the fore.[12]

The problem for schools in remote areas was that of paying the stipend
deemed necessary by candidates of the period. At Kiltearn in 1612, a contract
with Mr Alexander Hossack was signed by Robert Munro of Foulis and
others. Hossack was to teach the youth committed to him in the grammar
school in grammar and other sciences according to his knowledge, 'quhairin
he wes hiderintills imployit', from Whitsunday 1612 till Whitsunday 1613,

5   *Black Book*, 441–3.
6   Bannerman, 'Literacy in the Highlands', 218.
7   *RPC*, x, 671–2.
8   *RPC*, x, 775–6.
9   *RPC*, xi, 192.
10 'Extracts from the registers of the presbytery of Glasgow', *Maitland Misc.*, i (1), 90, 93.
11 *The Earl of Stirling's Register of Royal Letters*, i, 75.
12 *RPC*, 2nd series, iii, 172.

and thereafter yearly till transported elsewhere by the presbytery of Tain. They offered to pay him 32 bolls of 'bere' yearly, and to furnish a sufficient chalmer, with schoolhouse. He was to be entitled to take from each bairn of the said country of 'Ferindull' 6s 8d for entry fee during the period of his residence; 16 bolls of his fee were deliverable between 20 October and 15 November 1612, and the remaining 16 between 1 and 30 April the following year. For every undelivered boll they promised him £6 money of 'North Britain'. The bere was to be delivered 'within ony kiln or girnell' appointed by the master in Alness parish. The contractual deed was to be registered in the sheriff's books of Inverness.[13] Hossack may have had a separate arrangement with the Alness session for kirk duties; the advantage of being paid in kind at a time of inflation is obvious.

A later master at Kiltearn was Mr John Tillieduff, a member of the musical dynasty we encountered earlier. He can be traced at Kirkwall, Tain, Kiltearn and Tarbat, being obliged by contract 'to hauld ane grammar and musick schoole' in Kiltearn 'but intervall or break of lerand' for two years from November 1631. The heritors, including some in Lemlair, to which Kiltearn had recently been conjoined, were to pay him in kind 11 bolls of victual for 11 davachs, and failing payment, they obliged themselves to pay him 10 merks for each boll undelivered.[14]

A contract dated at Cromdale (Upper Banffshire), 28 November 1628, is witnessed by 'Mr Williame Dunbar scholemaster at Cromdell',[15] but schools in Strathspey seem to be few.[16] Further north, there were hopes in 1626 of developing the grammar school of the Chanonry of Ross into a Protestant college. A letter from London, suggesting this to the bishop of Ross, spoke in terms of removing the barbarity from the northern Highlands. The bishop was to deal with the project, get a voluntary supply for it and write each person's contribution in a book, choose a site in the Chanonry, keep London informed about its building, and see to the upkeep of masters and regents, the public professors and maintenance of poor students. The bishop was also asked to report how much was collected, so that London might lend a helping hand.[17] Despite all these references to barbarity, it has been suggseted that phraseology such as 'that unChristian language … of that unhallowed people' did not necessarily mean the Stewart kings waged an all-out war against Gaelic culture, such as would characterise Hanoverian policy in the Jacobite period.[18]

---

[13] RD1/213, 232v.

[14] RD1/460, 63.

[15] NAS, GD248/431.

[16] L. Shaw, *History of the Province of Moray* (1775), 306.

[17] *Earl of Stirling's Register of Royal Letters*, i, 76.

[18] D. Withrington, 'Education in the 17th century Highlands', in L. MacLean (ed.), *The Seventeenth Century in the Highlands* (Inverness, 1986), 60–9.

Contacts between the Highlands and Lowlands had always, of course, existed. But in the Lowlands there was nothing comparable to the learned orders as they existed in the Highlands and the Isles, where the Scots vernacular was of no use. The planting of schools may have been hindered by the fact that late sixteenth-century heritors in the Highlands were suffering from the same problems of debt as their Lowland counterparts, and their lands were more remote and less profitable. Orkney, however, had seven schools in this period, at Kirkwall, Stromness, South Ronaldsay, Orphir, St Margaret's Hope, Birsay and Butray, while in Scotland's northernmost isles, we find that on 22 August 1612, the noble gentlemen and commons, possessors and occupiers of land in Shetland, signed a contract with Mr William Humphrey to teach a school at Scalloway Banks. (A levy of 3 shillings was to be imposed on each 'last' of land, various lairds and ministers being appointed to collect the stent, but the following year the new schoolmaster appears as minister of Birsay.[19]) This was at a time when no school is recorded in Stornoway, though schools are found at Kilberry (1617), Inverary (1619), Campbeltown (1622), Kilmichael Glassary and Lochhead (1629). In Caithness schools exist in Dornoch (1585), Thurso (1621) and Reay. As for the central Highlands, it has been noted that there is reason to think there was a good supply of schools in Perthshire as the century proceeded.[20] At Kingussie in Invernesshire in 1642, the minister conceded that there had been a school, now deserted for lack of maintenance. The presbytery ordered a formal stent of every plough according to the 1633 Act, and that letters be raised thereupon to ensure that the school be 'againe opened'.[21] The fact is that the real expansion of English schooling in the Highlands came after 1633. Although this is therefore outwith our period, it merits some discussion.

Our Supplementary List of schools from 1634 to 1660[22] reveals several additional schools in the Highlands, including Ardchattan, Croy, Kilmorack and Urquhart (Ross) among parishes; and among non-parochial schools we find Duntulm (Skye), Foulis (Ross), Strathnaver (Sutherland) and Toward (Argyll). We would also draw attention to the school at Unyeasound in Shetland. It may well be the case that some of these schools preceded 1633; what is recorded in the Supplementary List is the earliest mention found. The centrally situated school at Inverary was already in existence when, in 1639, its lack of grammar school status led to the decision that each minister

---

[19] 'Seventeenth century landlords asserted their new powers', *Shetland Times*, 21 March 1986; RD1/211, 277–8; RDI/232, 256–7.

[20] Withrington, 'Education', 64–5.

[21] CH2/271/1, 239.

[22] Largely the work of John Ballantyne, who noted these names while working on the Registers of Deeds subsequent to 1633. No special effort has been made to expand the Supplementary List from other sources.

should pay 10 merks yearly (out of kirk penalties) to provide for the master's maintenance.[23] Thomas Young MA was master at Kilmichael Glassary in 1640, but one minister was failing to support him and the Argyll Synod took up his case. The Isle of Skye was unwilling to be troubled with payment of such exactions; it was enough to pay those imposed nationally. Sir James Macdonald in 1649 proposed that the money from vacant parishes might go to the maintenance of a master in Duntulm (Kilmuir parish, Skye), and the Synod voted him £100 with no guarantee of continuance.[24] In 1648 it was proposed to found nine parish schools in the presbyteries of Inverary, Dunoon and Kilmore, each school to have 1,000 merks to provide an annual rent for the master, and Inverary grammar school to have 2,000 merks provided. In Cowal, besides Dunoon which was already maintained, schools were to be opened at Kilfinan, Kilmodan and Lochgilphead; in Argyll they were to be sited at Kilmichael Glassary (but meantime at Kilmartin till a building was erected), at Castleswine, and in the district of Loch Awe; and in Lorne, one in Kilmore, one in Kilmoluag on Lismore, and a third apparently undecided.[25] The earlier school at Lochhead (Campbelltown) could not have been very successful, as it was decided in 1649 to ask the marquis of Argyll to establish one there; in 1643, its master, Thomas Neere, had not been paid.[26] In 1650 it was decided that when the parish schools were erected, they should teach certain subjects: the reading and writing of English, and the rudiments of Latin.[27]

In 1656, a school on Iona was proposed, with the heritors willing to subscribe; this seems to be the school on Mull that some 'gentill men' had supported. A school in Morven was not to prejudice the Mull-Iona foundation.[28] A school at Kingarth was proposed in 1657, but this repeated an earlier order, as our lists show.[29] It was the custom of boys to visit houses to teach people the catechism, and this custom was to be applied to the Catholic isles.[30] Mr John Lindsay complained in 1654 that he could get no maintenance in Kilmichael, so he was transported to be schoolmaster at Kilchrenan and help the minister there. In 1656 we find exceeding slackness shown in setting up Kilchrenan school, the Synod threatening to transfer the foundation fund to Kilmartin.[31] In 1658 several students were paid allowances to attend schools and colleges; the Synod admitted progress had been

[23] *Minutes of the Synod of Argyll 1639–1651*, ed. D.C. McTavish (SHS, 1943), i, 11.
[24] Ibid., i, 32, 155.
[25] Ibid., i, 129–130.
[26] Ibid., i, 80, 135.
[27] Ibid., i, 184.
[28] Ibid., ii, 126, 142, 153.
[29] Ibid., ii, 156.
[30] Ibid., ii, 52, 140.
[31] Ibid., ii, 186.

made, 'but it is yet small'. The money was allocated only to those who already knew some grammar, unless good things were expected of them or the maintenance was not such as to prejudice more advanced scholars.[32] It would appear therefore that there was some success in establishing schools, though the impression is not so much one of schools established as of schools proposed.

[32] Ibid., ii, 186–7.

VIII. Final Considerations and Conclusions

VIII.1 Royal interference in education

Apart from the long drawn out efforts to establish a monopoly in grammar, reviewed above, there is little evidence of royal interference in the school curriculum (or indeed by way of helping the establishment of a school in every parish!) until 1615, when King James threatened teachers in schools, colleges or universities with punishment for 'teaching or speaking against the present established order of the Kirk or Estate'.[1] More specific was the Act of Privy Council of 1616.[2] This Act required that in order that the true religion be advanced, the 'vulgar Inglishe toung' be universally planted, and the Irish (i.e. Gaelic) be abolished; and to further his Majesty's purpose of establishing schools in particular parishes where the young might be taught at least to write and read and learn the catechism, schools must be established in every parish. But there was an escape clause, viz. 'whair convenient meanes may be had for interteyning a scoole'. The nature of the school would depend on the quantity and quality of the parish. The stress on writing is new, as also on the secular value of 'civilitie'. It might be that the parishioners were favourable and the lay patrons less so, although many poor parishioners were reluctant to release their children from paid work, especially at harvest time. At Urie in the Mearns in 1618, all the tenants of the barony were compelled to pay 1 merk for every plough owned towards the schoolmaster's stipend, and an officer was appointed to poind non-payers.[3]

1618 was the year of the fateful 'Five Articles of Perth'. Between the submissive General Assembly in Aberdeen in August 1616 and the Perth Assembly which adopted the Articles, there arrived from England, by direction of King James, a little catechetical work, a dialogue between Theodidactus and Philalethes, written by the warden of All Souls College, Richard Mockett. It was called *God and the King*, or, in Latin, *Deus et Rex*, and had been published in both tongues at London in 1615, with special editions 'pro regno Scotiae' and 'for the kingdome of Scotland' the following year.[4] It was to be made compulsory in all schools and colleges in Scotland. In Perth in 1617, money was not paid for a large number of copies of *God and the King* which the Perth baillies ordered for the use of the town and school.

---

[1] *BUK*, iii, 1111–12.
[2] *RPC*, x, 671.
[3] *The Court Book of the Barony of Urie, 1604–1707*, ed. D.G. Barron (SHS, 1892), 28. Urie lies in Fetteresso parish.
[4] The Scottish editions were published by E. Allde, and were in the hands of the Scottish bishops in May 1616; see *RPC*, x, 521–2 for an account of the work.

According to the arrangement made, Mr James Primrose took possession of copies printed in London, of which every schoolmaster was to ensure that every scholar had a copy.[5] The Perth bailies were put to the horn for their failure to pay up. In July 1619, it was pointed out that Primrose had distributed his copies to presbyteries, the moderators of Linlithgow and Forfar presbyteries receiving 400 and 200 copies respectively. The copies had indeed been distributed, but not paid for, and the distributors refused to account for them.[6]

In November, again Primrose reminded the council that although the king commanded the book to be publicly taught in all colleges and schools universally throughout the kingdom, there was 'verie grite oppositioun' to its distribution by undutiful subjects; a citizen of Paisley had struck him with a baton and an officer of the Crown was also attacked.[7] The presbytery of Blackford was visited by Primrose in 1620; the moderator there had received 300 copies three years earlier, promising to distribute them and pay Primrose. Instead he returned the money he had collected for them.[8] In his efforts, Primrose made use of more than just council officials and presbyteries. In October 1619 he made a bond, whereby the Ayr schoolmaster, Mr John Bonar, took 70 copies of *God and the King* and 34 of *Deus et Rex*, for which Bonar promised to pay a total of £41 12s by 25 November. If Bonar used 'his exact dewitie and diligence in putting oute of the saidis buikis to the skolleris of his skoole', Primrose was to charge him only for what had been sold, and accept the return of the remainder. Two years, Primrose complained to the Privy Council, had now elapsed, and no payment had been made nor reckoning received. A messenger in Clackmannan was also at fault over 40 copies. Neither he nor Bonar had paid nor returned their unsold copies, nor did they obey the summons to compear in court, and the Lords ordered them to be denounced rebels.[9] Clearly, a book preaching passive obedience to the king as the voice of God was not going to be a marketable commodity in a Scotland where the battle lines were slowly being drawn for the conflict which would eventually be unleashed by the signing of the National Covenant in February 1638.[10]

---

5   *RPC*, x, 530; xi, 392.
6   *RPC*, xii, 42, 55; letters were sent to presbyteries by Primrose.
7   *RPC*, xii, 118–19.
8   *RPC*, xii, 229.
9   *RPC*, xii, 601.
10   One 1616 edition, 'to the onely use of J Primrose, for the kingdom of Scotland', was printed in London. Glasgow and Edinburgh University libraries hold copies.

VIII.2 Growth of educational provision to 1633

Less unwelcome royal interference in matters educational came in 1627, when the heritors of parishes were summoned to report on the state of their parishes to the commissioners for planting kirks. Some of these reports have been published,[11] others will doubtless turn up in other sources. We learn that Logie in Stirlingshire, for example, had an 'Inglische schoole', but because of the many people living in the parish, 'it var requisit that thair suld be ane better provisioun for ane grammer schole as their vas of old', which had been set in feu since the Reformation.[12] Some parishes fail to record whether they had a school or not, some merely the bare fact that they had none. Of forty-nine lowland parishes, twenty-nine had no school, thirteen had one, and seven had two. Currie is recorded as having no school, though schoolmasters are listed between 1607 and 1626.[13] It is clear from these reports that some schools had no continuous history. Some, like Oldhamstocks, were anxious to have a foundation and not depend on parish upkeep.[14] Some had a school but no founded rent, like Tillicoultry. In Mordington parish, nobody could read or write except the minister. In Ednam, there had been a school, 'but very poorlie preservit'. Nearly 120 bairns were capable of learning, 'but maist pairt of the parentis is not able to pay their school waidgis'.[15] At Bothans collegiate church, of which Lord Yester was patron, there was a school, but the 50 merks promised by Lady Yester for its maintenance were not forthcoming. In Pencaitland, the school 'is sustainet by the labouraris of the ground'. At Tranent there was no school or schoolhouse, 'excep an voluntar quha is Reider', paid by the parishioners.[16] In July 1627 it was reported that Hawick had no school, though it was a populous town, with no common fund to sustain a master, since there was great ignorance of the grounds of religion because of its remoteness.[17] In the same month, the commissioners found that in Wilton, Roxburghshire, 'their is no foundatioun for hospitall or schooll, albeit they war necessar',[18] while in the previous month, Wandell or Hartside reported that there was no school

---

[11]   *Reports on the State of Certain Parishes in Scotland* (Maitland Club, 1835).
[12]   *Reports on the State of Certain Parishes*, p. 202.
[13]   NAS, GD1/509/17, notes in chronological order on Currie.
[14]   *Reports*, 101.
[15]   Ibid., 22, 27, 175.
[16]   Ibid., 106, 127, 135.
[17]   J.R. Oliver, *Upper Teviotdale and the Scotts of Buccleuch* (Hawick, 1887), 286; J. Wilson, *Hawick and its Old Memories* (Edinburgh, 1858), 115, 119; some groups would not subscribe to an article promising £100 for the upkeep of a school.
[18]   NAS, GD157/340.

in this forty-pound land, but the parishioners wished for one 'fra their hert' and wanted the royal commissioners to help them get one.[19]

In 1633, the Scottish Parliament went a little further, ratifying the 1616 Act of Council, but pointing out that the bishops could establish schools, with the parishes' consent, with or without the heritors' approval. Where schools existed, they were to be maintained, and where they did not exist, they were to be established by a tax levied on every ploughgate and husbandland, to ensure that income was available. It would be possible to appeal to the Privy Council, and letters were to be sent ordering the payment of these dues.[20] Naturally, the entries in our Lists will, in most cases, precede this form of extra compulsion. As we saw in Section III.5 on terminology, the description 'student' against a witness signatory is one way of identifying the presence of a school in a given locality.

The availability of schooling in general can likewise be demonstrated by the growth, or otherwise, in numbers of university places. This is not unproblematic: it is not always easy to find out what year the name entries are to be assigned to, while some years are missing. As we saw earlier, the Glasgow rector went off with the matriculation book at the Reformation, and neither John Davidson nor Andrew Melville kept entries of matriculands or graduates at Glasgow. Melville was equally negligent at St Andrews.[21] King's College lists have been lost. Glasgow matriculation lists do not start till 1590, though graduate lists are available from 1580. Graduates from King's College, Old Aberdeen, are available from 1600, and matriculations from the following year, and for Marischal College from 1605.[22] Significant numbers of students went to universities abroad, but these are omitted. The actual figures are set out for each university (and college) in tabular form in Appendix 1. When considering these statistics, we have to remember that they include all graduations (or matriculations) in arts, including those of foreigners, mostly Protestant refugees from France, who, however, make no difference of substance. Where only graduations are recorded, it should be borne in mind that there would have been a larger number of matriculands who did not complete the course. The absence of early figures for King's

---

[19] NAS, GD237/200/3.

[20] *APS*, v, 21.

[21] St Andrews matriculations 1580–1633 kindly compiled by R.N. Smart, former university archivist there. On the eve of the Reformation, the total for 1550–59 was 351; few came in 1559 because of religious turbulence.

[22] For St Andrews matriculations before 1580, see J.M. Anderson (ed.), *Early Records*, for Glasgow graduates, *MAUG*, iii, 3–8, 60–86; for Aberdeen, *Aberdeen Fasti*, 449–62, and P.J. Anderson (ed.), *Fasti Academiae Mariscallanae*, ii, 186–208 (the Marischal entries are sometimes difficult to follow: for instance in 1620 we have 24 bajans, to whom we have to add eight names when we compare entries with the index in volume iii); and for Edinburgh, Laing, *A Catalogue of the Graduates of the University of Edinburgh*.

College and Glasgow, apart from the mention of fifteen or sixteen 'scholars' alleged to be at King's in 1562, is regrettable. However, taking the figures as we have them, there is a remarkable fivefold increase in total university numbers during these seven decades, from around 329 to 1,671. How the figures relate to feeder schools can only be guessed at, but there must clearly be an increase in such schools between 1560 and 1633, more especially in the north east and south east, with the new universities in Aberdeen and Edinburgh.

VIII.3 The school day c.1630

In Section III.3 we gave a detailed description how the school day would have been regulated at the beginning of our period, using the Aberdeen statutes of 1553, reprinted by Buchanan in 1566. Just beyond the end of our period, from 1640 or earlier, we have a document concerning Dundonald. (The reader can compare these two accounts with that of the Glasgow high school day under the regime (1649–81) of Francis Kincaid, given in Appendix 2.2.)

One immediate difference is that the Dundonald regulations were not drawn up in Latin, but in Scots.[23] The master was to be in school with his children at all times, and not to be out drinking, playing or doing another job (masters were commonly also notaries). If any unavoidable necessity drew him away for a whole day, or a large part thereof, somebody had to be left in charge of the children. If necessity of business demanded absence beyond one day, he must inform the kirk session or, should his absence be urgently required, at least the minister. During the winter months from October till February, lessons would begin at sunrise and end at sunset, except for certain very young pupils or those living at a distance from the school. The rest of the year they were to gather at seven and 'skaill' at six. An hour was allowed for breakfast at nine, returning at ten, with lunch at twelve, returning at one or as near as might be. The master was to lead the prayers 'gravelie and religiouslie' in the morning and before dispersal into classes. Every evening, a task was to be prescribed in the Lord's Prayer, articles of belief, Commandments, graces or catechism, according to the pupil's age and progress in learning, and then be heard the following morning before the ordinary lesson. On the Lord's Day, the scholars were to attend in silence, listening modestly and reverently, and give a ready account of what they observed; on Monday morning, and on Saturday evening before they went home, the master was to address them on the fundamentals of religion.

The document then sets out the regulations for Latin scholars: each morning they were to repeat a piece already learnt, and be examined on it,

---

[23] J. Paterson, *History of the County of Ayr* (Paisley, 1852), ii, 8–9.

before proceeding to their lesson on an author's text or in grammar, if they were so far advanced, with difficulties being explained. As much of the lesson as the pupil could manage was to be heard in the forenoon, the remainder at one in the afternoon. Pupils were to be given a theme to translate into Latin every day between eleven and twelve, which was the common writing hour for the whole school. Each day's lesson had to be covered before the children 'skailt', so as not to prejudice the morning piece. Regulations for classes in the vernacular are different, as they depended on the time of year (harvest might cause many to be absent), and on the number of students and their varying levels of proficiency. The master was to do what was feasible. At every visitation, both the minister and the best-skilled gentlemen were to be present, measuring the time spent on each subject with a sand glass, so as to direct the master as to how many lessons he should give in the morning and afternoon. The minister and gentlemen were also to inspect the state of the school, the children's proficiency and the master's diligence in faithfully carrying out his duties, and report thereanent to the session so that the master might be commended or otherwise. Should the master deceive the examiners, he might be removed.

For the good of the children, the Dundonald regulations laid down that those more advanced in Scots should have charge of the more backward, the eldest pupil asking the master to explain words they did not know. With regard to writing, special care was to be taken with those 'who are meit for it'; the writing time from eleven to twelve could be extended for some. The master himself would make the quills or mend them, rule their paper, cast their copies and inspect the writing of all, teaching improvement by demonstration. He was to lead the hands of young beginners, stand over them and direct them for their advancement in writing practice. They must also be taught good manners, how to carry themselves 'fashionablie' towards all as well as courtesy to the master in school, to their parents, to gentlemen, the elderly and others of 'honest fashion' elsewhere. The master was to put in their mouths styles of address suitable to the status of the person addressed; teach them how to compose their countenance, eyes, hands and feet when addressed by others or otherwise; and persuade them to abandon all 'unciveill' gestures, like scratching their head or arms.

Recreation days were Tuesday, Thursday and Saturday, for an hour in the afternoon in winter and two in summer. The pupils were not to indulge in any unlawful or obscene pastime, or such as would dirty their clothes or harm their bodies. A convenient place for playing was to be chosen: this was not the kirkyard, 'the dormitory of the saints'. Since without discipline no company could be kept in order, least of all unbridled youth, there ought to be a secret censor to report any ill doing to the master. For some, punishment should be meted out on the hand with a 'birk wand', belt, or 'pair of tawse', and for others on the hips; but none on head or face. Indeed, the

master was to encourage the young by mildness, allurements, commenda-
tions, fair words and 'some little rewards', gaining their confidence by his
own example rather than by strokes of the cane – but not neglecting the
rod where it was necessary.

VIII.4 Final conclusions

The manuscript Registers of Deeds, on which our Lists of Schools and
Schoolmasters are based, also increase in number over this period. The
earliest cover one or two years, the latest only a few months. Some are so
damaged as to be largely unreadable, such as RD1/82, where the outer half
of every page is eaten away. Most of these registers of deeds have about 400
folios, but whereas RD1/1 covers two whole years, from November 1554 to
November 1556, RD1/468 covers only October to December 1633. Again,
RD1/72 runs from August 1599 to February 1600, and has 463 folios as
against the 435 of RD1/1. While the period 1554 to 1599 is contained in
72 volumes, there are 396 for the period 1599 to 1633. It is possible therefore that, had there been as many documents registered before 1599 as after,
we would have records of many more schools, or of schools of earlier date.
Other registers, like the General Register of Sasines and Particular Registers
for the Shires start only from 1599. This also helps to skew the evidence. As
it is, we are able to record, up to 1633, over 500 schools at parish level, and
a further 300 odd which were presumably more independent of parish and
kirk session, but not necessarily free from presbytery visitation. Kirk records,
where available, tell us little of schools and schoolmasters. The non-parochial
schools must, in some instances, be the heirs of the old lairds' chaplain-
schools of medieval times, and where not, they may have got accommodation or some encouragement from the local gentry, especially when the kirk
was in a remote situation.

There is good reason to suppose that what the *First Book of Discipline*
meant by 'a school in every parish' was a parish school, supervised by the
minister and kirk session and supported by the session as necessary. Yet
almost half of the 800 schools listed here are independent of the session, and
in fact represent the continuation of a tradition of lairds' chaplain schools
from the middle ages, more discontinuously than the kirk session schools
at times. The General Assembly records show that the ministry was not
satisfied with its own efforts, impeded as they were in 1560 by the destruc-
tive violence of that year and by the abolition of certain medieval schools
because of their links with monks, nuns or chaplains. Yet our figures show
that the numbers of those attending university steadily increased (even
though lack of matriculation and graduation records makes earlier figures
less than certain). Moreover, the founding of new colleges and the fact that
the older clergy joined the Reformation movement made greater numbers

of schoolmasters available. Nonetheless, there were a thousand parishes in Scotland. Those remote from lowland Scotland's central belt often had no ministers, and the need to fill that gap took precedence over the need to appoint schoolmasters.

By the time our period ends, all of the various impediments to fulfilling the scheme of a school in every parish were in the process of being removed. The new educational policy of 1560 had slowly produced results: a quarter of a century after the Reformation, no fewer than 21 poor scholars are found 'remaning and abyding at the schoill and having the tounis mark taken [token] on their arm' at Perth in 1588.[24] On the other hand, a decreet arbitral drawn up at Edinburgh in 1583, and a common indenture in Aberdeen in 1587, both reveal that none of the craft representatives could sign their names. Yet by 1610, a Canongate document shows that while forty craftsmen were still unable to sign, no fewer than thirty were now able to do so.[25] So clearly there had been some progress in the intervening two decades. The teaching of music, however, had suffered grievously from the massive simplification of religious worship as part of the Reformed programme, and only with James VI's maturity were music schools salvaged for the future. And while good music could be heard in aristocratic households and in schools fortunate in their masters (like Aberdeen, or Glasgow with Duncan Burnett), there was no national career structure for professional musicians, culminating in employment in a cathedral or the Chapel Royal. The result, in lowland Scotland, was that new, original composition became almost entirely extinct.

Highland schooling had its own ways, and the 1616 Privy Council Act set out to establish English schools, abolish Gaelic, and adapt Highland education to Lowland requirements. Such efforts were bound to encounter resistance. Schooling for girls remains an area of research where the very lack of status of female teachers, unlikely to make it into the records, means that we can only speculate that more schools must have existed than we have evidence for. As regards the development of the curriculum, vernacular education had achieved prominence, and while the basis for a new Renaissance culture of civility existed well before 1616, it was now fortified by a series of grammar manuals. Latin (and to some extent Greek) were available, even in villages, and divines would study Hebrew at university. An achievement painfully accomplished, it was one to be proud of.

The Scottish towns could not produce the funding required to maintain the long years of study which were aimed at by colleges in Geneva or in

24 E. Smart, *History of Perth Academy* (Perth, 1932), 12; GD79/3/35 is a decreet by the minister, elders and master of the hospital to pay 4s weekly to the twenty-one poor scholars who have the town's tokens.

25 A.I. Cameron, 'The Canongate crafts: an agreement of 1610', *Book of the Old Edinburgh Club*, xiv (1925), 35, 42–4.

the Reformed towns of France. This clear goal of the *First Book of Discipline* could only be achieved in places like Edinburgh, where the town grammar school was in fact a national school. In the country parishes, not all the lairds took their duties to ensure the provision of education seriously, even if they could afford such duties. The 1616 Act laid down that the bishop was to authorise schools 'where convenient means might be found', a loophole with which many heritors would be well content. The Act of 1633 was designed to increase pressure on these reluctant sponsors while ratifying the Privy Council motion of 1616. Parliament enacted that the heritor, being warned to appear, was to ensure the schoolmaster's stipend; if he failed to appear, the bishop was empowered, where there was a local desire for a school, to stent every plough in the parish according to its value, and thus to set up a school despite the heritor. This would prove an important weapon in establishing parish education for the future.

APPENDICES

APPENDIX 1. Scottish University Matriculations 1560–1633

The following tables show all recorded matriculations at all the Scottish universities during our period. Under St Andrews, SS stands for St Salvator's College, SL for St Leonard's College, SM for St Mary's College, n.k. for not known. Under Aberdeen, KC stands for King's College, MC for Marischal College. The letter *g* stands for graduations, and *m* marks where matriculations begin.

| Year | St Andrews | | | | | Glasgow | Aberdeen | | Edinburgh | Decade Total |
	SS	SL	SM	n.k	Total		KC	MC		
1560	–	12	11		23					
1561	4	16	7		27					
1562	7	5	8		20		15/16			
1563	–	15	12		27					
1564	12	14	15		41					
1565	3	–	13		16					
1566	15	17	11		43					
1567	8	–	29		37					
1568	9	–	19		28					
1569	11	21	19		51					
Decade					313		15/16			328/9
1570	11	24	8		43					
1571	9	17	22		48					
1572	11	18	13		42					
1573	9	9	21		39					
1574	14	19	23		56					
1575	9	33	23		65					
1576	19	31	9		59					
1577	11	34	13		58					

Year	St Andrews				Total	Glasgow	KC	MC	Edinburgh	Decade Total
	SS	SL	SM	n.k						
1579	18	41	17		76					
Decade					**528**					**528**
1580/1	11	27			38	g5				
1581	17	43	–		60	8				
1582	29	32	–		61	10				
1583	21	39	–		60	18				
1584	13	28	–		41	15				
1585	–	22	–		22	15				
1586	–	20	7		27	6				
1587	16	19	–		35	9			g47	
1588	–	–	–		–	12			30	
1589	29	23	6		58	9			–	
Decade					**402**	**107**			**77**	**586**
1590	10	35	–		45	m35			13	
1591	16	19	2		37	–			14	
1592	–	27	3		30	–			28	
1593	16	22	–		38	27			22	
1594	–	–	–	33	33	22			20	
1595	–	–	–	40	40	25			29	
1596	–	–	–	46	46	–			24	
1597	–	–	–	38	38	–			34	
1598	10	13			23	77			32	
1599–1600	29	36	17		82	–			35	
Decade					**412**	**186**			**251**	**849**
1600/1	18	21	–		39	–	g 9		35	
1601	16	38	9		63	38	m14		20	
1602/3	27	28	4		59	19	12		32	
1603	24	24	–		48	–	14		23	
1604	28	29	–		57	30	38		26	
1605	22	4	2		28	43	11	31	24	

Year	St Andrews					Glasgow	Aberdeen		Edinburgh	Decade Total
	SS	SL	SM	n.k	Total		KC	MC		
1606	33	49	4		86	11	21	25	28	
1607	26	28	1		55	26	14	6	28	
1608	32	21	1		54	23	32	19	–	
1609	30	43	6		79	29	17	28	32	
Decade					543	219	182	109	248	1301
1610	17	43	5		65	28	14	15	27	
1611	31	51	1	2	85	30	17	15	22	
1612	29	41	7		77	30	25	10	24	
1613	47	59	5		111	13	20	17	31	
1614	35	32	–	1	68	26	23	21	28	
1615	41	15	7		63	30	29	22	35	
1616	31	48	11	4	94	32	11	18	28	
1617	55	28	7	3	93	44	16	16	47	
1618	37	29	5		81	33	14	18	34	
1619	27	25	13		65	27	14	10	33	
Decade					802	293	183	162	309	1749
1620	18	24	–	–	42	31	16	32	36	
1621	28	29	17	–	75	41	24	19	42	
1622	26	18	5	–	49	26	22	22	36	
1623	28	31	13	–	72	37	12	21	34	
1624	45	29	10	–	84	34	18	22	29	
1625	–	–	–	29	29	33	23	22	36	
1626	24	22	14		60	23	30	15	26	
1627/8	39	30	5		74	27	22	27	26	
1628	28	41	8		77	44	20	23	16	
1629	29	–	–	–	25	33	20	22	38	
Decade	265	224	72	30	587	329	207	225	319	1667
1630	17			4	21	50	22	24	29	
1631	38			14	52	42	23	33	43	
1632	20				20	43	21	13	33	
1633	36				36	30	14	26	31	
4 year					129	165	80	96	136	606

APPENDIX 2. Pointers for Local History Research

The evidence used for the compilation of our Lists of Schools and School-masters has come mainly from national documentation. But local historians with access to regional archives could add further names, particularly for the decades after 1633. By way of illustration, and to provide pointers for further work, there follow two studies of particular localities.

2.1 Schoolmasters in Ayr

2.1.1 Grammar school

The first post-Reformation master at Ayr was appointed on 20 November 1559: the council appointed John Orr to teach 'maneris and the airte and science of the Lating tongue and grammar'. The council not only 'thocht and thinkis [Orr] maist wirthie and qualifiet to teiche the airte of grammar', but 'in absence of Christofer Guidman (quhilk sall be but viii or ix dayis at the maist at aneis, sall say and reid the common prayaris, and minister the sacrament, sua the said Cristofer was nocht to be oft absent and him self thairfra'. For this, Orr was to be paid £20 out of the common purse per year, and 12 shillings in the year fir 'ilk bairne of this burcht, by his wantage to be had for lerning of landwert menis soneis. And na uther grammar scole to be teiched within this burcht, be na person nor persounis'.[1] Orr was still in office in January 1563, but the records thereafter are missing until 1574, in which year we find there was difficulty about the payment of certain church revenues. The minister, James Dalrymple, complained in 1574 that the town failed to pay him his dues from chaplainries and obits. The town maintained that £20 each was paid to two chaplains, £20 to the reader (James Davidson), 8 merks to the clerk of session for his services, £10 to the 'sangster that takis up the psalmis', and other small payments.[2]

From 1574, Ayr continued to look to St Andrews for its schoolmasters, as in pre-Reformation times. Many of these university trained burgh schoolmasters would proceed to the ministry, starting with the St Salvator's product Laurence Dalgleish, despite the fact that (unlike John Orr) he was a late convert. The St Andrews kirk session records of 1 July 1569 state that he was 'desyrit to imbrace and resave the religioun offerit to us be the grite favour and mercy of God', and did so, 'renuncing idolatrie superstitioun and Papistrie, befoir authorized in tyme of the Paip and the Antechristis

---

[1] 'Conductio Johannis Or', Carnegie Library, Ayr, B6/12/3 (unfoliated). Reproduced in *Memorabilia of the City of Glasgow* (Glasgow, 1835), 7.

[2] W.S. Cooper (ed.), *Charters of the Royal Burgh of Ayr* (Edinburgh, 1883), 109.

kingdome'.[3] For Martinmas term 1575 Dalgleish was paid £10, his annual stipend being the same as Orr's, £20. From 1586 till 1591, his successor was paid £26 13s 4d for both schoolmastering and acting as reader.[4]

When Dalgleish became minister of Craigie in 1580, he was succeeded by a Glasgow graduate, Mr Ninian Young. In 1583 Young supplicated for 'ane skillit doctour' as 'success of learning hes nocht followit in tymes bygane as necessitie requiris' (although Dalgleish had been assisted by a doctor, Thomas Greig).[5] This would be 'conformit to uther burrowis', and the bailies agreed the doctor would be paid as follows: burgh children 12d per term, landward bairns 2s. They also agreed that no separate school should exist except the common school, and all children were to have access to it for both the vernacular and Latin. In that same year, Young is found complaining about the provost and bailies, calling for £20 salary for his work as reader, as the collectors and 'Lordis modifears' had assigned him. Since these annuals were given to the burgh by Queen Mary, the bailies suspended the letters raised by Young, deciding in the meantime to pay him what they owed him. He got £20 for one and a half years' reading, and a gratification of £20 for 1594–95.[6] Young was succeeded by Mr William Murray, recruited from St Andrews. His stipend, allowed on 5 May 1595, was to be £40 from the common good; the town children were to pay 20s yearly, and 8s to his doctor, while landward children were to pay 40s yearly and 13s 4d to the doctor. At his first entrance, each child had to pay for a term of his scholage, continuing termly thereafter. The boarders of the landward children were liable for the scholage due, and 'an honest man' was to collect the payments from each quarter of the town, those failing to pay being charged double. Young appeared before the council in July and told them that he was 'to direct himself to his functioun of the ministerie'. The town decided to add a further £20 to his term's stipend of 20 merks as 'ane rememberance' of his good service. On the same day it was decided to send a boy to St Andrews to seek out a qualified schoolmaster, as the town was without one; this would suggest that William Murray had already left his post.[7]

Murray's successor, Mr Archibald Dunmore, seems to have been a St Andrews graduate, recommended by the ministry of that town and appointed on 28 August 1595.[8] His engagement was for five years. Every week he was to introduce the youth to 'the principall heidis of religioun', read in the kirk

---

3   *RKSSA*, i, pp. xix, 218, 323.
4   *Ayr Burgh Accts.*, 139, 142, 143, 153; index references for pp. 148–67 should be to Ninian Young.
5   *Ayr Burgh Accts.*, 139.
6   Carnegie Library, Ayr, B6/11/1(1), 117; B6/11/2, 257; *Ayr Burgh Accts.*, 175, 183.
7   Carnegie Library, Ayr, B6/11/2, 435, 441, 468v.
8   Ibid., fo. 480.

both on Sundays and on the weekdays appointed for reading, and support the minister in the kirk session in writing up the session book. The new master was to be paid £40 out of the common good at two terms in the year. Each town bairn was to pay 20s in scholage per annum, and each landward child 40s, as well as the customary casualities, with the boarders of the landward bairns again being responsible for the dues, collectable by an honest person for each quarter of the town. No other school teaching Latin or English was to be allowed. The doctor was to have 13s 4d yearly from town children and 26s 8d from landward. Mr Henry Danskin, a future poetic member of staff at St Andrews, was inducted as doctor and also obliged to read the Sunday morning prayers and to read before the preaching on Sunday forenoon and afternoon.[9] In 1596, William Dunmore was hired as doctor for a year with similar payment and reading duties as Danskin.[10] These years were notable as years of plague. In December 1596, Dunmore was paid £10 extra in respect of the 'seasoun of the tyme very skerss', but warned that this was not 'ane preparative dewtie'. He was also helped with the rent of the schoolhouse. The doctor was given £10 in respect of the dearth in September 1597, and in November of that year William Wallace of Barnwell was chosen doctor on William Dunmore's death, presumably of the plague.[11] A like fate may have befallen Mr James Landells, appointed as doctor in September 1602, at 20 merks with 40d each term from town bairns and 6s 8d from landward; he died in June 1603. His total estate was over £140; his brother, Mr Robert, had three sons who were to have his books 'except scapula and grit dictioner quhilkis I leif to my brother mr archibabld dynmure in taikin of my luff to him'; Jonet Shaw, wife of Dunmore, had provided him with certain furniture.[12] In 1603 the doctor was Mr Henry Stewart,[13] who seems to have been acting as master on Mr Archibald Dunmore's becoming minister of Colmonell, for in 1604–05 he was paid £30, plus £7 10s of support. His date of appointment was 16 August 1603, under the usual conditions.[14]

Another St Andrews graduate, Mr Alexander Dunmore, was appointed as schoolmaster on 10 May 1605, with the same duties as Mr Archibald. His payment was to be £60, with two merks from each town bairn yearly, and four from each landward bairn. No other schools were to exist but the grammar and music schools.[15] On 9 July it was decided to pay the master in

9   See Danskin's prefatory verses to John Abernethy, bishop of Caithness, *A Christian and Heavenlie Treatise* (London, 1630). Dunmore was the 'new' schoolmaster, paid £40 in 1595/6, *Ayr Burgh Accts.*, 187; both he and the doctor got £10 for reading in 1598/9, ibid., 196.
10 Carnegie Library, Ayr, B6/l 1/13, 10v, under date 11 Aug. 1596.
11 Ibid., 52v, 78v, 157, 158.
12 Ibid., 481; NAS, CC8/8/38, under 12 Sep. 1603.
13 *Ayr Burgh Accts.*, 218.
14 Ibid., 218; Carnegie Library, Ayr, B6/11/3, 551.
15 Ibid., 627.

advance of his Martinmas term, although he entered only at Whitsunday, 'in respect he has ado thairwith'.[16] In October 1607, Dunmore got a rise: the council, considering his 'travellis and panes', augmented his salary by £20 to £80 annually, the fee also covering his reading duties.[17] A new doctor, Mr Hugh Tran, was appointed at £20 yearly from the common good fund, plus the usual extras obtainable from the pupils. His initial contract, unlike Alexander Dunmore's, was for one year, not five; in 1608 his stipend rose to £30.[18] He had been admitted as a burgess on 17 November 1607, whereas Dunmore was admitted only on 12 June 1610 by right of his wife, daughter of a burgess.[19] On 6 July 1612 we find Dunmore present at the Ayr kirk session, who had paid £7 6s 8d to the repairing of a 'chalmer' in his school-house in 1607.[20]

The last appointee in our period was John Bonar of Inverkeithing, Alexander Dunmore having been presented to the parsonage of Girvan by James VI.[21] An indenture between the council representatives and Bonar was drawn up on 2 June 1612, whereby Bonar became their schoolmaster.[22] He was to teach the youth of the school and 'sum utheris gentilmenis and landwart menis barnis resortand thairto' for five years, entering the post on that day. His duties were reading on the Sabbath before the preaching forenoon and afternoon, reading the prayers daily at convenient times and acting as session clerk; he was to furnish a musician to take up the psalms on the Sabbath and weekdays in time of preaching, but he was not to study theology, which would 'hinder him in discharging his cure of the scule'. For all this, the payment was £80 as before. Scholage was payable termly by the town's bairns at 6s 8d and by landward bairns at 13s 4d. In addition, he was to be paid twenty merks for psalm-singing and another twenty as session clerk, both payable by the kirk session. Once again, all schools other than the grammar and music schools were forbidden. The Ayr folk bore the costs of moving Bonar's gear and books from Inverkeithing.[23] Subsequent session records of Ayr are in John Bonar's fine handwriting, both italic and secretary. He was also a skilled mathematician and technician, building sundials for various aristocratic families in Ayrshire and Galloway, and even at Bangor in Ireland: he wrote a verse account of a journey from Bangor to the port of

[16]   Carnegie Library, Ayr, B6/18/1, under 9 July 1605.
[17]   Carnegie Library, Ayr, B6/11/4, 72.
[18]   Carnegie Library, Ayr, B6/18/1, under 25 June 1605; ibid. under 12 Jan. 1608 (it was a time of plague).
[19]   Carnegie Library, Ayr, B6/11/4, 76v, 219v.
[20]   Ayr District Archives, CH2/751/1/1, 113v; CH2/751/1(2), 222v.
[21]   *Fasti*, iii, 41.
[22]   Carnegie Library, Ayr, B6/11/4, 337v.
[23]   *Ayr Burgh Accts.*, 249 (1610–11), 252 (1611–12), 256 (1612–13).

Ayr.[24] He was still at Ayr at the end of our period. His first doctor, Hugh Tran, is found at Wigton as schoolmaster from 1621. Bonar's other doctors included John Sawyer, Mr William Fullarton and Adam Ritchie; John Sheringlaw was an under-doctor.

2.1.2 Music school

The masters of the Ayr music school are less easy to put names to. The first, paid in 1583–84, was probably Mr Andrew Stewart, who received £17 and a further £10 in December 1584 'in respect of his present necessitie',[25] although a certain William Mont is mentioned in 1584–85.[26] The next recorded appointee comes years later, Mr Alexander Spittal, hired on 26 April 1601 to be master from Whitsunday. His salary was £40, plus 10s termly from town bairns learning to sing and play, and 5s from those learning to read and write. He was also to act as psalmist in the kirk.[27] Before beginning at the music school he had already been psalmist in the kirk for part of Martinmas term, being paid £5, and his payment for being available from then till 1602 was £26 13s 4d; in 1603 he was paid £40 plus £14 on account of the 'dearth', the extra being reduced to £6 13s 4d in 1604, with no extra recorded for 1605.[28] In May of that year, the contract made with the new grammar schoolmaster, Mr Alexander Dunmore, specifically states that all lasses were to be subject to 'gang to the Musik' according to the agreement with the song schoolmaster.[29] The next musician recorded is Alexander Fiddes 1610–11, who was paid £13 15s 8d.[30] He was followed by James Lawrie, paid up to Martinmas 1613, with part payment for 1613–14, totalling £39 13s 4d in all. A suit of clothes for him had cost £20 in 1612–13, and by 1614–15 his stipend had risen to £80, which included taking up the psalm in kirk.[31] In September 1616, the kirk session declared his post vacant 'throuche the negligence of James Lawrie maister thairof and his leaffing the Toun towards Irland', without leave of council or session. In February, however, Lawrie had had a fortnight's leave to look for a replacement for himself in Edinburgh.[32]

Ayr's next music master, William Smyth, was born in Dunfermline, producing testimonials from that town and its presbytery as to his capacity

[24] A.R. Somerville, 'The sundials of John Bonar, schoolmaster of Ayr', *Antiquarian Horology*, xvi (1986), 233–42; Paterson, *History of the County of Ayr*, ii, 344n.
[25] *Ayr Burgh Accts.*, 149; Carnegie Library, Ayr, B6/11/1(2), 235v.
[26] *Ayr Burgh Accts.*, 151.
[27] Carnegie Library, Ayr, B6/11/3, 381.
[28] *Ayr Burgh Accts.*, 204, 209, 214, 218, 223.
[29] Carnegie Library, Ayr, B6/11/3, 627.
[30] Ibid., 249; RD1/318, 244.
[31] *Ayr Burgh Accts.*, 252, 254, 256, 257, 260, 263.
[32] Ayr District Archives, CH2/751/1(2), 312, 324.

to act as a 'ful reader' as well as music master. He appeared in August 1617, and John Bonar was henceforth exonerated from reading, though not from keeping the kirk session record, while Hugh Tran had to hand over the baptismal records to Smyth as well.[33] His own transfer and his gear cost the burgh £40 in 1617. The treasurer paid him £40 for that year, and £19 10s for hiring a horse and for travelling expenses from Dunfermline to Edinburgh and Glasgow. He got £100 in 1617–18 (which included 50 merks from the kirk). His services from 1 August to 10 November 1617 cost the town £23 6s 8d.[34] Thereafter the regular fee was £100, though £10 extra support was needful in 1624. Meantime, the grammar schoolmaster was still paid £80, while a writing master whom we have already met, Mr David Brown, 'profesour of the art of ortografie and fair wryting', was paid a mere £13 6s 8d for a whole year,[35] but he would also have given private lessons to supplement this.

One fact emerges from all these financial arrangements. The drastic inflation between 1560 and the early 1600s is the main cause for the fourfold rise in wages between Dalgleish's time and Bonar's. Moreover, the extras payable by the pupils were not always available in times of famine and plague, when they absented themselves. Ayr council had to take account of this, although sometimes they paid in advance.

2.2 Glasgow down to 1700

2.2.1 Pre-Reformation masters

Almost as soon as there was a cathedral chapter, we can posit the existence of both a grammar schoolmaster and a song schoolmaster. In 1259 we learn that according to the Salisbury (Sarum) model Glasgow followed, the chancellor's office involved him in 'ruling the schools', while to the preceptor pertained 'the instruction and discipline of boys' for the choir, with the subchanter having 'to rule the songschool through his officer'.[36] Since a chancellor existed from at least 1258, a preceptor from 1179 to 1221, and a subchanter from 1455 to 1471, we can be sure that schools existed from that time,[37] although we have no names of schoolmasters till much later. In fact, since Glasgow was following the Salisbury model prior to 1164, a school of some sort must also have been in existence.[38] Scholars living with the chan-

[33] Ibid., 340v, 343.
[34] *Ayr Burgh Accts.*, 262, 263, 267, 268, 272, 274, 276, 278, 289, 281.
[35] Ibid., 277. It was unusual for a song schoolmaster to have a doctor, but in Glasgow, 'archibald mcKellar, doctour in duncan bumets skuill' is found in 1615: NAS, CC9/14/4, 166.
[36] *Glasgow Reg.*, i, 169–70.
[37] D.E.R. Watt & A.L. Murray (eds.), *Fasti Ecclesiae Scoticanae Medii Aevi Ad Annum 1638* (SRS, 2003), pp. 203, 208, 219.
[38] *Glasgow Reg.*, i, 26.

cellor signed a deed of his in 1458.[39] After the foundation of the university, scholars were accommodated in the Old Pedagogy or the university until 1461, when a chaplain, Mr Alexander Galbraith, was granted a schoolhouse by the preceptor, Mr Simon Dalgleish, on a site facing the university on its High Street site. The burgh council, not the Church, was to act as patron of this building and as governor of the donation. The following is a list of recorded schoolmasters of the grammar school:

Galbraith, Alexander, MA: 1461 Jan 20 (*Glasgow Charters,* i (2), 436)

Lorne, George, chaplain: 1477 Oct (*MAUG,* ii, 87)

Simson, Cuthbert, MA, chaplain: 1507 Jul 6 (*Liber Protocollorum Cuthberti Simonis,* ii, 202; scholar is witness to his protocol. Cf. also ibid., ii, 42, 154)

Reid, John, MA, chaplain: 1508 Jun 19 (*Liber Protocollorum,* ii, 267); 1511 Jan 11 (ibid., ii, 389)

Reid, Matthew, MA: 1521 Oct (*MAUG,* ii, 139); 1525 (ibid., ii, 150)

McNesche, James, MA: 1547 Apr 29 (NAS, Acta Dominorum Concilii, xxiii, fo. 60)

Crawford, Alexander, MA: 1549 Oct 25 (*MAUG,* ii, 170); as 'Archibald', 1555 (ibid., ii, 299)

Maxwell, Robert, MA: 1560 n.d. (McRoberts, *[Essays on the Scottish Reformation],* 162)

The appointment by Simon Dalgleish looks very like an attempt to give the secular burgh authorities more say in the grammar school. However, in 1494, Mr Martin Wan, chancellor, reminded the authorities of his power over such appointments and over the schoolboys, both in grammar and the rudiments, by objecting to David Dun MA, who that year taught both openly and on the quiet in the city or university.[40] Again, when Mr John Reid was appointed by the chancellor, Mr Martin Reid, the latter referred to his position as chancellor as his authority for making the appointment, as he was master of Glasgow school; the provost and citizens pointed to the Dalgleish charter as their entitlement as Dalgleish's heirs to make appointments, at least with regard to Reid's possibility of admission to such walled schools (*scolas murales*) and buildings as were assigned to them for teaching.[41]

For masters of the song school, there is much less information:

---

[39] Durkan & Kirk, *University of Glasgow,* 25; NAS, Glasgow Registrum MS, liber ruber, fos. iv–v; H.A. Ashmall, *The High School of Glasgow* (Glasgow, 1976), 5, suggests 1136.

[40] Durkan & Kirk, *University of Glasgow,* 174; *Glasgow City Chrs.,* i, part ii, 89; *MAUG,* i, 37.

[41] *Glasgow Prot. Bk,* ii, 267; scholars witnessed a notarial deed of his in Oct. 1509, *Paisley Reg.,* 396.

Brown, Hugh: 1476 Oct 25 (*MAUG*, ii, 86)
Panter, John: c.1507 (McRoberts, *Essays on the Scottish Reformation*, 147)[42]
Unnamed master: 1539 Nov 5 (*Glasgow Prot. Bk*, iv, no. 1318, 118)

2.2.2 Post-Reformation masters

At the Reformation, Glasgow had a Catholic schoolmaster, Robert Maxwell MA, who chose to debate with the Reformer John Willock in the town. Maxwell was succeeded in 1567 by Thomas Jack, exhorter in Rutherglen in 1563 and minister there in November 1567, later serving also Carmunnock and Rutherglen. In his *Onomasticum poeticum* of 1592, Jack records that it is eighteen years since he began teaching in Glasgow, giving a date of 1574. But he was in the city in 1569, and is presumably the schoolmaster who, in 1573, was given the All Saints chaplaincy without payment of thirds by the city magistrates.[43] Robert Rollock's liminary verses in the *Onomasticon* describe Jack as 'that former teacher of mine', which must have been before 1574 when Rollock, future first principal of Edinburgh University, enrolled at St Andrews.[44] Jack himself is presumably more exact when he claims that he demitted his grammar school charge on '5 Cal. Sep.' 1574 (i.e. 24 August). His surname indicates that his origins were in the north east. The earl of Atholl referred to him in c.1584 as 'our cowsing' who had been attacked by Ninian Stewart of Castlemilk.[45] Jack would rebuild Eastwood church in 1577, but in May 1573, as grammar schoolmaster and vicar of Eastwood, he had found Robert, Lord Semple, intruding a Catholic as vicar.[46] The case went to the Privy Council, who decided in Jack's favour. The intruder was John Hamilton, 'a papist preist', but by 1592 Jack was at peace with the Hamiltons, for his *Onomasticon* is dedicated to James, son of Lord Claud Hamilton, commendator of Paisley. He presented Glasgow University library with two books, one of which had belonged to Archbishop John Hamilton,[47] and some other books went to the library of Paisley presbytery.[48]

Jack was succeeded by Mr Patrick Sharp, of the Sharps of Houston, sometime in 1574. According to Andrew Melville's nephew James, 'the schoolmaister of the town, Mr Patrik Scharpe, was his ordinar heirar and contubernal, whome he instructed, and directed in the maist commodious bringing up of the youthe in grammer and guid authors; whom I hard often-

---

[42] Panter is first mentioned as 'preceptor of the song school' alongside his duties as organist in 1567, i.e. after his death: *Glasgow Recs.*, iii, 535, 562.
[43] *MAUG*, i, 77.
[44] The Rollocks had property in Glasgow at the time. In his *Onomasticon*, Jack also refers to Gabriel Maxwell as his relative (*nepos*, i.e. son-in-law).
[45] Fraser, *Memoirs of the Maxwells of Pollok*, ii, 157.
[46] *RPC*, ii, 229.
[47] Durkan & Ross, *Early Scottish Libraries*, 41.
[48] *Fasti*, ii, 133.

tymes profes that he lernit mair of Mr Andro Melvil craking and pleying, for understanding of the authors quhilk he leached in the scholle nor be all his commentares'.[49] Sharp was one of the masters convened by the Regent Morton in 1575 to discuss the idea of a grammar monopoly for all Scotland. By 1590, after becoming university principal, Sharp had recovered the rector's mace – missing since the Reformation – from its Catholic owners. He seems to have supported the king on policy against Melville, and wrote a short, simple Latin summary of Christian doctrine (1599). From his will we learn that his second wife was Elizabeth Jack, his predecessor's daughter, widow of Walter Maxwell of Pollok. Among his pupils was John Cameron, theologian and follower of Petrus Ramus. Sharp resigned his teaching post on 13 November 1582, when his successor John Blackburn was appointed.[50]

Son of a local burgess, Blackburn had graduated at Glasgow in 1578, when he appeared as reader and exhorter at Cathcart. He was vicar of Cardross from 1603 till appointed minister of the Barony kirk in 1615. He held the chaplainry of All Saints, valued at 8 merks 6s 8d yearly, and had the chaplainry of St Michael from 1600, which paid £4 3s 4d per year. His salary as master included the annual rents of the school lands, two burgess fines each year (commuted to a money payment of 40 merks), plus the chaplaincy of St Ninian's hospital chapel in the Gorbals.[51] In June 1606, he was presented by James VI to the archdeaconry of Down, Ireland, an appointment confirmed in 1609 and lasting till 1622.[52] In April 1610, he got leave of absence to visit Down as he was liable to lose the benefice if he did not present himself there in person.[53]

It was under Blackburn that the school was rebuilt around 1601. He served the university as dean of arts, just as Jack had served it as quaestor in his day. He presented a copy of Onofrio Panvino's *Fasti et triumphi Romani* (Venice, 1537); the present university library also holds a copy of Aristophanes which belonged to him. He had to be replaced in 1617 as he was too old to be an effective headmaster, but he had been a gifted teacher in his day,[54] before being weighed down with a plurality of church benefices in Ireland and Scotland. Around 1614, the elderly Blackburn had obtained the assistance of a new graduate, Mr Robert Blair, who writes as follows: 'Having now finished my course of philosophy under the discipline of my brother, Mr William Blair, I took only some few days to refresh myself

[49] Melville, *Autobiography and Diary*, 50.
[50] Durkan & Kirk, *University of Glasgow*, 303; *RPC*, v, 110, gives Sharp's name in 1593, omitted in the 1575 list of ibid., ii, 470.
[51] Ashmall, *High School*, 116–17.
[52] J.B. Leslie & H.B. Swanzy (eds.), *Biographical Succession Lists of the Clergy of the Diocese of Down* (Enniskillen, 1930).
[53] *Glasgow Recs.*, i, 311.
[54] Ashmall, *High School*, 7–8.

hawking and hunting in the country, with my friends, before I immediately entered upon a most laborious duty; for I had been engaged beforehand to be an assistant to the aged and decayed schoolmaster of Glasgow, who had under his discipline above three hundred children, the one-half whereof were committed to my charge, where I remember no remarkable things, save that, being outwearied with the toil of the day, I often went to bed without supper, not for want but for sheer tiredness, conscientiously mindful of my employment.'[55] One doctor hardly seems enough for such numbers, and we can scarcely be surprised to find that by 1615 Blair had abandoned his career as school doctor.

Blackburn's successor was William Wallace MA, said to have become master in 1617; he certainly became a Glasgow burgess on 8 January 1618.[56] He had been a schoolmaster at Irvine and then at Stirling when the poet Alexander Yule was persuaded to resign due to age. A former pupil of Wallace's at Stirling from 1613 to 1617, John Livingstone, wrote that during his first year he profited not much and was often beaten by Wallace. One day the beating left a mark on his cheek which his father complained about. The complaint was effective: Wallace gave up beating Livingstone, which caused the boy to learn a lot more! In September 1616, having gone through all the Latin and Greek taught at Stirling, Livingstone was persuaded by Wallace to stay another year. For the most part, as a member of a small group, he was allowed 'ane little chamber' above the school, where they read mostly choice Latin works furnished by Wallace. He described his former teacher as 'a good man and a learned humanist',[57] and Wallace's prowess as a poet is clear from his Latin verses welcoming King James to Stirling in June 1617.[58] As the Glasgow town records are missing from 1613 to 1623, we have no copy of his contract of appointment. However, when it was up for renewal in 1630, the council maintained him on the original contract, being content with his service. His stipend appears to have been £80, paid from Michaelmas to Michaelmas, at least for 1624–25, but this may not represent all his earnings. He died early in 1642, for in February a messenger was sent to Stirling to hire Mr David Will as his successor. Will was in Glasgow by March, when he was made a burgess.[59]

Some of William Wallace's assistants, like Mr John Hamilton and James Anderston, in 1629 and 1632–39, were evidently expectant ministers called

55   R. Blair, *The Life of Robert Blair* (Wodrow Society, 1848), 9.
56   *Glasgow Burgesses*, 51.
57   R. Wodrow, *Select Biographies*, ed. W.K. Tweedie (Wodrow Society, 1845–47), i, 130–1, which volume also contains letters to Livingstone from his close friend the poetess Elizabeth Melville.
58   J. Adamson, *The Muses Welcome* (Edinburgh, 1618), 134–6. See also Section IV.3.
59   *Glasgow Recs.*, i, 376, 437, 477.

to help with the preaching,[60] while in 1617 the ex-doctor, Robert Blair, had been one of those who provided Latin verses to welcome King James to Glasgow.[61] In 1631 we hear of 'umquhill Robert Scott, schoolmaster', but are not told where he practised.[62] Another schoolmaster who had burgess status was the writing master James Clerk, who had gifted to the town 'ane brod' with the town's arms and a covenant very well written upon parchment in lieu of his burgess fine in 1641.[63] In 1652, he found his writing school had been burnt down, and he was allowed to occupy the kirk session house in the Trongate.[64] Half a century earlier, in 1603, the song schoolmaster, John Buchan, musician and reader at the Tron kirk, had sources of income not revealed in the accounts, for he complained that his pension of Maybole had recently not been paid to him: this was presumably the vicarage of Maybole, united to the collegiate church of St Mary of Loreto and St Anne (the predecessor of the Tron kirk), and set aside as revenue for the archpriest, first prebend after the provost.[65] One Walter Duncan was allowed to continue a school on 19 October 1644, his salary being increased from 200 merks to £100.[66] In September 1646 John Cant was appointed for five years to keep 'ane musick schoole … teaching the tounes bairns vocall musick for threttie schillings in the quarter and both vocall and instrumentall musick for fourtie schillings', and he is described as master of the music school in 1648 when he was created burgess.[67]

Council visitations of the grammar school feature prominently in these decades; and Scots schools independent of the session, including 'poor' schools, also attracted the council's attentions, with a view to learning by what warrant such schools were kept. In June 1649, a master from Govan school, Mr John Anderson, joined the staff of the high school as doctor for 200 merks, an appointment probably related to the discussion between Mr David Will and the council earlier that month. There was trouble with the appointment of Mr Francis Kincaid in 1649 on Will's death. In 1652 we hear of a controversy between him and the doctor, Mr Robert Speir, who was soon removed by the council, but of Mr David Will himself, very little is to be learned from Glasgow's records.[68] In 1655, Mr John Stewart

[60] *Glasgow Recs.*, i, 372; ii, 9, 14, 19.
[61] *The Muses Welcome*, 250–4.
[62] *Glasgow Recs.*, ii, 3.
[63] *Glasgow Burgesses*, 105, 107.
[64] *Glasgow Recs.*, ii, 239; in 1655, Clerk had a room in Hutcheson's Hospital, ibid., ii, 321.
[65] *Glasgow Recs.*, i, 243; *Liber Collegii Nostre Domine*, ed. J. Robertson (Maitland Club, 1846), 13–24, 61–2.
[66] *Glasgow Recs.*, ii, 74.
[67] *Glasgow Recs.*, ii, 96; *Glasgow Burgesses*, 127.
[68] Visitations in 1636, 1644, 1646, 1657, 1662, *Glasgow Recs.*, ii, 43, 73, 92, 361,485; for Scots schools, ibid., ii, 96, 159, 254. Mr John Anderson, ibid., ii, 168; Robert Speir, ibid., ii, 239, 240.

was admitted doctor with the consent of the high schoolmaster. Vernacular schools were spreading in the town. In April 1654, councillors were to visit John Paterson's school, and, if he had too many poor, they were to be sent to other schools.[69]

James Selkrig replaced James King as 'scoolmaister within the toune' in December 1651, being made burgess in 1658.[70] Robert Forrest, preceptor in Blackfriars church, was also a schoolmaster when he was created burgess in 1659.[71] In 1655, James King was re-employed as master of a vernacular school, as he had been before; in 1657, William Brock was allowed to teach a school, provided it was in the Saltmarket; a woman who had a school at the head of the Saltmarket had to give it up in 1658; early in 1659, Alexander Dunlop kept a reading and writing school in the city's north quarter and shortly after, Alexander Wilson kept one in the Gallowgate; in 1660, two men, James Adam and James Frissall, were licensed to open schools in the Gallowgate, but once again there was worry about women taking up Scots schools.[72] When Robert Inglis offered to teach music, a report was required in April 1663; in the same year, James Bernardon offered to teach as a professor of French language, dancing and fencing at an annual fee of 40 shillings sterling and with a five-year licence; and in 1669, the council was anxious to employ an able musician, the bishop promising £100 Scots and the town 350 merks.[73]

Suspicion that vernacular teachers had no licence from the council led to the decision to authorise the following seventeen teachers in November 1663: Jonet Ramsay in Drygate, Elizabeth Miller, William Bogill, Marion Watson (wife of William McNab), Alexander Wilson, George Steinstouns's wife, Mr John Morison and his wife, John Paterson, Margaret Murray, George Fussall, William Brock, Robert Forest, Agnes Hutcheson, Elizabeth Boyd, Jean Mauchen and James Hadden. The William McNab in question was a tailor, and his son had become a burgess in 1618 through marrying Marion Watson. Some of those keeping Scots schools did not frequent the kirk, and three citizens including McNab had to remove from the town for that reason. It was required that the rest henceforward have certificates from the bishop or their ordinary ministers.[74]

An account of the scholastic day at the high school under Francis Kincaid's rule (1649–81) has been preserved.[75] The morning was spent as follows: from

---

[69] *Glasgow Recs.*, ii, 286.
[70] *Glasgow Burgesses*, 149; *Glasgow Recs.*, ii, 216.
[71] *Glasgow Burgesses*, 158.
[72] *Glasgow Recs.*, ii, 317, 391, 410, 415, 453. King was schoolmaster in June 1649 (Glasgow, Mitchell Library, B10/15/1, 56).
[73] *Glasgow Recs.*, iii, 12, 24, 120.
[74] *Glasgow Recs.*, iii, 22–3.
[75] J. Cleland, *The History of the High School of Glasgow* (Glasgow, 1878), 2–3.

six to seven, all schoolboys learnt what they had to repeat at eight. All five classes had two repetitions. The three top classes would then proceed to lessons for over an hour. All classes together were to expound till 9 a.m. Breakfast followed. An hour of exposition and parsing ensued, and themes were given out every other day, on Mondays and Wednesdays. The corrected Monday theme was to be redrafted which took an hour. An hour and a half was spent learning by heart, and the same length of time spent testing this; only half an hour thereof to be devoted to repeating by rote. On Friday from six to eight they repeated the grammar learnt that week, and then underwent a test on it from eight to nine. From nine to three was devoted to an author, except ten to noon, devoted to a theme or versification, not omitting parsing. From three to five, the pupils repeated all they had learnt, and from five to six they were to prepare the debates for the Saturday morning. These would have ended at nine, and from ten to noon was writing time. Saturday afternoon saw the lowest classes taught the vernacular catechism and the higher classes the Heidelberg catechism of Zacharias Ursinus. On the Sunday, this was explained in the morning and examined in the afternoon, with tests on the Monday morning. These arrangements were later modified somewhat; on Friday from eight to nine, after hearing grammar, the headmaster heard the reports of the censors of conduct, 'that discipline may be keeped up'. On Saturday forenoon, shortly after eleven, Friday's themes were examined and corrected out of a print book which the pupils copied out and learnt by heart. On Saturday afternoon, the two top classes got Buchanan's psalms dictated to them; the Heidelberg catechism was taught to the fourth class, Sebastian Castellion's *Dialogi sacri* to the third. As there was insufficient seating in the kirk to accommodate all the scholars, the catechism was explained after both sermons and examined on the Sunday, and on Monday, after their study of the Psalms, Dialogues and Catechism, the pupils were asked to give an account of the sermon. There is no mention here of studying the Bible, apart from the psalm paraphrases.

Mr Robert Park took up a school in the Trongate in 1668, and Walter Winning in Stockwellgate two years later.[76] In 1674, Mr George Ward got six rex dollars, or £29, to encourage him to continue with his writing school. He seems to have been succeeded by Mr Samuel Heslett the following year.[77] The cost to the council in 1664 of payments to the high school staff was £540 altogether; the master of the music school and preceptor received £200.[78] In place of Mr John Anderson, deceased, Mr George Glen became doctor in the grammar school in 1672, but when on 8 October 1681 his learning was certified as adequate for his accession to the post of grammar

---

[76]   *Glasgow Recs.*, ii, 11, 148.
[77]   *Glasgow Recs.*, iii, 194, 497, 499.
[78]   *Glasgow City Chrs.*, ii, 334, 347, 349.

schoolmaster, his other qualifications were deemed doubtful. He had apparently no control over his scholars, as the authorities in Paisley subsequently found too. He was dismissed in Glasgow in November 1690, and forbidden to teach anywhere in town. However, in 1717, soon after dismissal from Paisley, we find him made a city burgess by right of his wife.[79] Mr John Wingait was the son of a burgess and doctor in the high school when created burgess in 1671; he was dead by October 1676, and replaced by Mr Hugh Muir.[80] There is mention of the need to appoint a third doctor the next year. Mr George Adam, received as preceptor of the high kirk in 1679, was to teach a music school in town in place of the late William Innes, and to receive the same fee.[81]

An arrangement of 1685 between the town and university during George Glen's tenure laid down a programme for the school.[82] The first year was to continue with current practice, learning the Latin rudiments with vocabularies, *Dicta sapientium*, Sulpizio, etc. In second year, the larger half of the first part of Despauterius, with Mathurin Cordier, Erasmus's *Colloquia minora*, and selected epistles of Cicero and Cato. In third year, more Despauterius, along with Ovid's *Epistulae*, another work by Ovid and Buchanan's psalm paraphrases (such as were in elegiac or sapphic metres) and themes mainly out of Cicero. In fourth year, the syntax of Despauterius, with Caesar's *Commentaries*, Justin's *History*, Ovid's *Metamorphoses* and Virgil. In the fifth year, the remainder of Despauterius, Buchanan's *Epigrams*, *Jephthes* and *Baptistes*, selections from Horace and Juvenal, with prosody.

Mr John Campbell appears to have been the last doctor appointed under the Kincaid regime, though he seems to have felt he was underpaid. In 1674 a certain Mrs Cumming was appointed to teach manners, doubtless to gentlewomen in the town; she informed the council at that date that she was thinking of leaving, but to encourage her to stay she was paid 100 merks plus the rent of her school.[83] In 1681, Hugh Jaffrey, professor of navigation, was to be paid £4 sterling in addition to his current payment of 10 dollars, and in the same year he was also paid £77 to discourage him from leaving, although in later years this was reduced to £48 Scots.[84] In 1682, Mr Hugh Muir complained about the small numbers of scholars in his school; he was granted £30 Scots and a small salary as preceptor at the town's expense; but in 1688, there were complaints against him for abusing a bailie and striking high school pupils too severely: the tradition of the former rector, Patrick

[79] Ashmall, *High School*, 176; *Glasgow Recs.*, iii, 265, 471; *Glasgow Burgesses*, 332.
[80] *Glasgow Burgesses*, 191; *Glasgow Recs.*, iii, 227.
[81] *Glasgow Recs.*, iii, 236, 261.
[82] Cleland, *History of the High School*, 4–5.
[83] *Glasgow Recs.*, iii, 180, 289.
[84] *Glasgow Recs.*, iii, 308, 505.

Sharp, 'of belt wielding fame', had clearly not been forgotten,[85] though there was less excuse for Muir when school numbers were down. In 1682, the school library was given a book press.[86]

Outside the high school, we find Mr John Porterfield teaching reading, writing and arithmetic in a schoolhouse of his own provided by the town in 1687–90,[87] while in September 1689, Mr George Skirvane was appointed to the high school; he had hitherto been master in Hamilton. He lasted till 1715, having been created a city burgess in 1691.[88] High school doctors in 1690 included Mr Mungo Lindsay and Mr John Mclleran; both were called to the ministry that same year, and were replaced by Mr Thomas Lawrie and Mr William Brisbane. In 1692, Mr Archibald Marshall from Cairns in Galloway was engaged as doctor, but he left in 1697 to become minister at Kirkmaiden in Galloway where his enthusiasm for witch hunting necessitated his removal to Kirkcolm in 1700. His powerful voice must have proved daunting as it could be heard across Loch Ryan quite distinctly.[89] Three years before he left the high school, a third doctor was appointed because of high pupil numbers, Mr Thomas Findlay. He had not turned up by 20 May 1695, however, and Mr John Walker, a master from Dumbarton, was appointed. He was dismissed in 1697, but later reinstated.[90] From Whitsunday 1696, Mr William Marshall was hired as doctor for £100 Scots and £40 for acting as preceptor in the Tron kirk. Mr Alexander Peers was also doctor from about this date.[91]

French teaching was available in the town, conducted in 1690 by M. Jean Pujolas, a French Huguenot with a gift of £5 sterling towards the publication of his French grammar, and, for his encouragement meantime as a schoolmaster, he was paid £100 yearly. There was also a M. Louis de France, who was to teach music, and to take only 14 shillings per month for one hour each day, and teach the poor for nothing: he too was offered £100 Scots annually.[92] A school for navigation was held by Robert Whytingdale in 1695, and in 1697, Mary Young came from Ireland to teach young gentlewomen.[93]

A 'reidar or scoolemaister' was deemed necessary at the Hutcheson's Hospital in April 1648; John McLay taught from 28 October 1648 till 1652

---

[85]   *Glasgow Recs.*, iii, 309, 41 1; Ashmall, *High School*, 60.
[86]   *Glasgow Recs.*, ii, 317.
[87]   *Glasgow Recs.*, iii, 399, 402–3, 458.
[88]   *Glasgow Recs.*, iii, 433; *Glasgow Burgesses*, 225.
[89]   *Glasgow Recs.*, iv, 61, 75; *Fasti*, ii, 339; *Glasgow Recs.*, iv, 37.
[90]   *Glasgow Recs.*, iv, 1 67, 242, 275.
[91]   *Glasgow Recs.*, iv, 223; *Glasgow Burgesses*, 237.
[92]   *Glasgow Recs.*, iii, 475; iv, 36–7. Louis de France's MS music book is in Edinburgh University Library.
[93]   *Glasgow Recs.*, iv, 187, 253

when he demitted due to the lack of funds to pay him.[94] In 1654, we find Mr Alexander Forrest seemingly schoolmaster there.[95] Robert Forrest succeeded him, apparently in 1660, but did not satisfy the town, and lost his post as preceptor in the Tron Kirk, although he was later reinstated. Eventually he was suspended for criticising the government under William and Mary in September 1690, and was replaced in May 1691 by Peter Reid.[96]

2.2.3 Other Glasgow parishes

The post-Reformation parish of Glasgow Barony was already in existence by 1600. The prodigiously energetic and productive writer Zachary Boyd (1590–1653), twice rector of the university, was incumbent from 1623.[97] Unfortunately, the kirk session records for most of the seventeenth century have been lost, and the first extant book of minutes covers 1673–98 (NAS, CH2/173/1). On 14 February 1674, we read of Gardner, the schoolmaster in Shettleston; but the previous year another record notes payments of a marriage fine to him for teaching his poor scholars, one of whom from Sandyhills applied to the session in his own name.[98] Gardner continued at Shettleston at least until 1686.[99] In 1677, John Graham is listed as schoolmaster, as is also James Luke, but their whereabouts is not identified.[100] We find John Lennox recorded in Provan in 1692, where James Young had been found as schoolmaster in 1684, although otherwise noted as in Ruchazie, where, however, the master was Richard Kirkland in 1686. In Possil, James Stewart is listed as schoolmaster in 1686.[101] In 1701, we find that the barony agreed to support four schoolmasters, one at Ruchill or Lambhill (this latter taking the place of Possil), the others at Shettleston, Provan and Clayslap.[102] How far this school extension scheme reflected the increasing population of Glasgow's rural hinterland is arguable, though the Shettleston school is found in our pre-1633 lists, and may well have existed longer than surviving records allow. There was one schoolmistress only, Isobel Sharp, who taught

---

94 *Glasgow Recs.*, iv, 130, 132, 153, 227

95 *Glasgow City Chrs.*, ii, 32.

96 W.H. Hill, *History of the Hospital and School Founded in Glasgow, 1639–41, by George and Thomas Hutcheson of Lambhill* (Glasgow, 1881), 144, 147, 282; *Glasgow Recs.*, iii, 228, 458, 502.

97 Much of his work was published, but far more remained in MS, and was bequeathed to Glasgow University, as was half his estate.

98 CH2/173/1, p. 712; General Register Office for Scotland, OPR 622, under that year; CH2/173/1, p. 23.

99 CH2/173/1, p. 34.

100 Ibid., pp. 9–10, 20.

101 Ibid., pp. 60, 34.

102 Ibid., pp. 34, 59.

reading with the support of the session.[103] The first schoolmasters at Cathcart and Gorbals are recorded in 1603 and 1621 respectively. Robert Park was master at Possil before he moved to Trongate in 1668, and Mr George Hutchison at Cadder in 1673.[104] John Lennox had moved to become master at Monklands by 1694 and Patrick Stewart was schoolmaster at Port Glasgow two years later.[105]

For Govan, we can establish a succession of masters. The kirk session records survive only from May 1651. There is, however, a presbytery record of 12 February 1606, where there is mention of the lack of 'ane to teiche the zouthe of the parochin of govane dwelland besyde the kirk thairof' (i.e. apart from the teacher at Brigend in Gorbals, apparently).[106] On 15 November 1655, the schoolmaster at Brigend was Robert Kelso, who petitioned the session for payment in view of some poor children he taught, a grant duly made with the addition that the same arrangement should apply to the school at Meikle Govan. On 15 July 1639, John Stewart, fiar of Rosland, had made an obligation concerning the mortification by George Hutcheson of Lambhill to the minister and session of the parish kirk of Govan for the schoolmaster there. This mortification of 1,000 merks was to provide an annual rent for the master's stipend to 'learne and instruct the poor young ones'. For the two half years following, 40 merks would be paid, that is, £26 13s 4d annually.[107] The schoolmasters at Govan Kirk from 1646 are as follows:

Mr John Anderson: 1646–49 (GUA 35089, 35122, 35123; also GUA 26734, fo. 76)

Robert Forrest: 7 May, 9 Dec 1652 (RD1/579, 265 and CH2/1277/1 under those dates)

Mr John Vernon: 1653–54 (GUA 26734, fo. 98); Vernon was later schoolmaster at Renfrew 1655–56 (ibid., fo. 125)

Robert Mair, doctor: 13 Jul 2 Nov 1654 (CH2/1277/1, under those dates)

Mr William Cochrane: 27 Mar 1656 (CH2/1277/1, under that date)

Thomas Kelso: 14, 21 May 1657 (CH2/1277/1 under those dates)

Thomas Young, reader and schoolmaster: 11 May 1664 (GUA 35241), 1688 (GUA 26652, fo. 187)

Mr William Reid: 1691 (GUA 26652, fo. 203)

On 27 February the session ordained that the East Sheills and other 'tounes nixt adjacent' must send their bairns to the Gorbals school if they

---

103   CH2/173/2, p. 39; cf. p. 63, where 200 merks Scots are stented on the parish for the four masters under the provisions of 1696.
104   *Glasgow Recs.* iii, 111; *Glasgow Burgesses*, 197.
105   *Glasgow Burgesses*, 234; *Glasgow Recs.* iv, 207.
106   NAS, CH2/171, fo. 307.
107   RD1/609, fos. 513–15.

are 'abill and of capacitie'. The session seems to have found it difficult to lay their hands on foundation funds.[108] Finally, there was a teacher of French in Govan in 1708, M. François Delavilla. And in 1709, the school at Partick is noted.[109] With that reference we conclude this overview of the local situation in the Glasgow area, which was not in any case intended to go beyond 1700.

---

[108] CH2/1277/1, under that date; and under 12 Nov. 1657.
[109] Glasgow District Archives, Collector's Accounts, Govan parish, unfoliated and out of order.

Unless otherwise stated references are to the General Register of Deeds, so that 84, 299 means RD1/84, fo. 299. Other manuscript references are in the NAS unless stated.

ABBEYGREEN, *see* Lesmahagow

ABDIE (par), Fife

Johnston, Robert	1599 Mar 27 (67, 394)
Burrell, David, MA	1624 Jul 1 (438, 255)
Laing, William, MA	1624 Jul 10 (RS31/5, 266v) 1631 Feb 26 (RS31/9, 98)

ABERCORN (par), West Lothian

Taylor, Thomas	1620 Jun 3 (445, 93v) 1623 Jan 10 (359, 331)
school	1630 Aug 19 (A. Bain, *The Education Act of 1696 in West Lothian*, Dept of Educational Studies 1974, 24)

ABERCROMBIE (par), Fife
(united to St Monans 1646)

Hasson, Robert	1602 Mar 4 (89, 94)
Mudie, Robert, MA	1617 Oct 9 (*RMS*, vii, 1781) 1619 Jun 18 (CC20/11/3)

ABERDALGIE, *see* Dupplin

ABERDEEN, Aberdeenshire
King's College, Grammar School

Stewart, Theophilus, MA	1539 Apr 17 (*Aberdeen Univ. Graduates*, 45) *died* 1576/7 Mar 20 (ibid.)
Rait, David, MA, pr, later reg	1580 Oct 30 (*Aberdeen Univ. Graduates*, 45) 1581 May 27 (ibid.)

Udney, Peter, MA, later reg 1583 Aug 14 (*Aberdeen Univ. Graduates*, 45)

Clark, David, MA, later reg 1584 Jul 12 (*Aberdeen Univ. Graduates*, 46)

Guthrie, John, MA, later reg 1585/6 Mar 15 (*Aberdeen Univ. Graduates*, 46) 1587 Dec 21 (ibid.)

Erskine, John, MA 1585/6 n.d. (*Aberdeen Fasti*, p. lxxxiii)

Rait, William, MA 1587 Aug 12 (*Aberdeen Univ. Graduates*, 46)

Sibbald, James, MA, later reg 1589 May 24 (*Aberdeen Univ. Graduates*, 46)

Barclay, Alexander, MA 1590 n.d. (*Aberdeen Univ. Graduates*, 46) 1598 Jul 22 (*RPC*, 1st ser., v, 77)

Arbuthnott, Robert, MA 1600–1602 n.d. (*Aberdeen Univ. Graduates*, 46)

Rait, James, MA, later reg 1604 n.d. (*Aberdeen Univ. Graduates*, 46) 1610 Mar 12 (*RPC*, 1st ser., viii, 717, 723)

Dunbar, Robert, MA, later reg, later min of Skene 1610 Dec 15 (*Aberdeen Univ. Graduates*, 46)

Forbes, William, MA, reg, later subprincipal 1613 n.d. (*Aberdeen Univ. Graduates*, 46)

Cant, Andrew, MA (the elder), later reg, min of Alford c.1617 1614–1615 n.d. (*Aberdeen Univ. Graduates*, 46)

Leslie, William, MA (AbK 1615), 'doctor', later reg, later principal of King's College c.1615–16 (G. Garden, 'The Life of John Forbes of Corse', *Opera Omnia*, Amsterdam 1703, p. 25)

Lunan, Alexander, MA, later reg 1619 Jun 12 (*Aberdeen Univ. Graduates*, 46)

Ross, John, MA 1621 Jun 7 (334, 15) 1622 n.d. (*Aberdeen Fasti*, p. lxxxiv)

Harvie, James, MA, min of New Machar 1625 Jul 5 (*Aberdeen Univ. Graduates*, 46) 1626 Aug 15 (ibid.)

Lundie, John, MA, prev reg 1628 May 2 (*Aberdeen Fasti*, 283) 1648 Oct 6 (ibid., 163)

Mylne, George, MA 1628 Nov 11 (*Aberdeen Univ. Graduates*, 46)

schoolmaster, unnamed 1633, 1634 n.d. (*Common Good*, p. 39)

Music School (also known as Public School)

Meldrum, William, sir, p 1574/5 Feb 10 (*RMS*, iv, 2360) 1593 Apr 6 (*Aberdeen Fasti*, 134)

Lindsay, William, pr 1604 Nov 11 (C.S. Terry, 'The Music School of Old Machar', *Miscellany of the Third Spalding Club*, ii, Aberdeen 1940, 232) 1608 Feb 12 (*RS4/6*, 329)

Ross, Gilbert, MA, r, ch, 1628 Jun 29 ('Music School', p. 232) 1640

cl, *see also* New Aberdeen Nov 30   (ibid.)
English School
Doctors

Walter (Watter), Patrick, b,   1604 Sep 21 ('Register of Burgesses of
d, cf. Alford   Guild and Trade of the Burgh of Aberdeen',
                                 ed. A.M. Munro, *New Spalding Misc.*, i, 1890,
                                 99) 1619 Jun 24 (291, 182v)
Mow, John; d   1606 Jun 13 (166, 414)
Melville (Meling), Andrew,   1619 May 21 (RS5/1, 414) 'master' 1627 Sep 6
b, d   (428, 168v) 'doctor' 1629–30 (*Aberdeen Burgh
                                 Accts.*, 147)

NEW ABERDEEN
Grammar School

Henderson, John, MA, c   1559 Jul 3 (*Bon Record*, 17) 1569 Jan 9 (ibid.,
                                 18)
Carmichael, William *or*   1573 (*Aberdeen Council Register*, xxviii, 127)
                                 1580 Jul
James, MA, p   30 (*Bon Record*, 22n.)
Cargill, Thomas, MA   1580 Aug 30 (*Bon Record*, 22n.) 1601 Sep 22
                                 (ibid., 27)
Reid, Thomas, d, conjoint   1602 Feb 6 (*Bon Record*, 28) *resigned* 1603
   master, later reg at   Oct 12 (ibid., p. 34)
   Marischal College
Wedderburn, David, MA,   1602 Feb 6 (*Bon Record*, 28) *demitted*
   conjoint master, later reg   1640 (ibid., 67)
Chalmer, George   1616 May 25 (267, 55)
Doctors

Moir, John, d   *died* 1579 Jun 6 (*Analecta Scotica*, ed. J.
                                 Maidment, Edinburgh 1834, 280)
Mackie, George, MA, s   *before* 1602 Feb 10 (*Bon Record*, 31)
doctor, unnamed   1603 Oct 12 (*Bon Record*, 34)
Wallace, William, MA, d   1604 Jun 7 (RS15/2, 138)
Leslie, Gilbert;, b, d, r,   1611 May 18 (*Aberdeen Court Bk*, ii, 170)
   see also Writing School   1633 Dec 14 (DI21/34, 217)
Wedderburn, William, d,   1616–17 (*Aberdeen Burgh Accts.*, 96) 1617
   later reg, min of   Jun 4 (*Bon Record*, 51)
   Bethelnie by 1633, min
   of Strathdon by 1651
Petrie, Robert, MA, d   1619 Nov 4 (294, 12)
Dascore (Destore), Robert,   1619 Nov 25 (SC1/68/6)
   d, *see also* Writing School
Fraser, Alexander, MA,   1628 Jul 23 (*Bon Record*, 59) *demitted* 1630

(AbM), second doctor, u   Jul 28 (ibid., 61) *usher* 1632 Sep 19 ('Aberdeen
                            Burgess Register 1631–1700', ed. A.M. Munro,
                            New Spalding Misc., ii, 1908, 370)

Chalmer, Thomas, MA,   1630 Jul 28 (*Bon Record*, 61) *resigned* by 1636
  (AbM), second doctor   Apr 27 (ibid., p. 64)

Music School (also known as Public School)

Black, John, sir, MA, c   1558 Oct 8 (*Bon Record*, 16n.) *died* c.1587 Aug
                            14 (*Aberdeen Council Register*, ii, p. 60)

Kemp, Andrew   *in John Black's absence abroad* 1570 Oct 6
                            (*Aberdeen Council Register*, i, 370)

Anderson, John   1587 Aug 14 (*Aberdeen Council Register*, ii, 60)

Skene, William, MA   1595 Nov 20 (104, 39v) *died before* 1599 Nov
                            13 (*Aberdeen Burgh Accts.*, 125)

Leslie, John, of Kyntor   1599 Nov 13 (*Aberdeen Burgh Accts.*, 125)

Davidson, Patrick, MA   1601 May 30 (RS4/1, 136) 1633–34 n.d.
                            (*Aberdeen Burgh Accts.*, 150)

Doctors

Simpson, James, d, *under* 1577 Oct 4 (*Aberdeen Council Register*, ii, 29)
  sir John Black

English School

two English schools, taught 1605 May 1 (*Bon Record*, 39)
  by readers

Gray, Alexander, r   1621 Jun 30 (319, 116v) 1623 Jun 25 (*Aberdeen
                            Council Register*, ii, 387)

Ross, Gilbert, MA, r, ch, cl, 1628 Jun 29 ('Music School', 232) 1640
  see also Aberdeen Music Nov 30 (ibid.)
  School

Doctor

Brabner, Alexander, d   1628 Nov 24 (487, 101)

Writing School

Diggens, Edward   *school of writing and arithmetic* 1607 Oct 7 (*Bon
                            Record*, 40)

Dascore (Destore), Robert, 1625 Jan 1 (428, 101v)
  d, *see also* Grammar
  School

Leslie, Gilbert, b, r, *see* 1612 Dec 4 (*Aberdeen Council Register*, ii, 312
  also Grammar School   1639 Oct 23 (*Bon Record*, 66)

Howat, Andrew   1628 Feb 13 (*Bon Record*, 59)

Adventure Schools

Cumming, John, n	1586 Apr 29 (*Bon Record*, 24)
Kanzie, David, MA, p	1593 Mar 22 (*Bon Record*, 25) *died* 1598 n.d. (*see* 'David Makynius' in Dempster, *Historia*, ii, 408–9)

Fencing School

Ballantyne (Bannatyne, Bellenden), Thomas	1598–9 (*Aberdeen Burgh Accts.*, 72)

Dame Schools

Thomson, John *and* Forbes, Margaret, *spouses*	1598 Oct 25 (*Aberdeen Council Register*, ii, 171)
Cheyne, Marion	1598 Oct 25 (*Aberdeen Council Register*, ii, 171)
Gordon, Janet	1622 Jun 2 (*Selections from the Records of the Kirk Session, Presbytery and Synod of Aberdeen*, ed. J. Stuart, Spalding Club 1846, 103)

ABERDOUR (par), Aberdeenshire

Ramsay, Alexander, c, r	1563 n.d. (*Fasti*, viii, 578) 1613 n.d. (ibid., vi, 209)
no school	1614 Jun 23 (CH2/89/1(2), 162) 1616 Aug 29 (ibid., 200v)
school	1617 Jun 26 (CH2/89/1(2), 209) Aug 7 (CH2/89/1(2), 211)
Tullidaff, John	1617 Oct 17 (RS5/1, 61v)
no reader or schoolmaster	1619 Jul 1 (CH2/89/1(2), 233v) 1620 Jul 13 (ibid., 249v)

ABERDOUR (par), Fife

Bonar, James, MA	*1600 Jan 18* (114, ?[1]) 1602 Mar 27 (90, 336) 1604 May 11 (137, 187)
Wallace, William, MA	1612 Nov 23 (216, 218) 1613 Jul 13 (229, 86)
Fenton, William, MA	1613 Nov 1 (216, 172v)
Brown, James, MA	1614 Dec 12 (NP1/188, 148) 1623 May 8 (349, 35)
Wemyss, James, MA	1629 Apr 8 (418, 93) 1641 Feb 26 (533, 433)
Graham, Charles	1631 Nov 18 (544, 155)
Beverage, George, MA	1631 Jul 2 *and* 6 (496, 1)

---

[1]   Reference missing: see Preface.

ABERLADY (par), East Lothian

Todd, William	1607 Apr 29 (RS24/8, 220v) 1615 Jun 16 (239, 114)
Kinross, Colin, n, r	1620 Jun 8 (304, 304v) 1620 Jul 7 (ibid.)
Pringle, William	1625 Jun 15 (391, 365) 1637 Sep 17 (516, 4)

ABERLEMNO (par), Angus

Dickson (Dikiesone), David	1612 Apr 25 (CC3/9/4) 1614 Jun 8 (CC3/9/4)
Petrie, Robert, MA	1615 Mar 7 (CC3/9/4) 1616 May 7 (CC3/9/5)
Duncan, Thomas	1625 Jan 18 (380, 80)
Mylne, John	1628 Jul 22 (408, 419v)

ABERLETHNOTT, *see* Marykirk

ABERNETHY (par), Perthshire
Grammar School

Ross, Daniel	1601 Jul 13 (93, 270) 1607 Dec 15 (RS50/4(2), 272)
students	1616 Nov 17 (329, 310)
Ross, Archibald, MA	1623 Mar 1 (RS50/4(2), 186) 1640 Mar 4 (530, 558)

ABERNYTE (par), Perthshire

Anderson, Adam, MA	1602 Jun 9 (RS48/1, 263v) 1603 Feb 22 (RS48/2, 167)
Young, Alexander, MA	1614 Jul 5 (288, 179) Dec 20 (306, 99v)

ABERUCHIL, Perthshire MRf NN7421
Comrie par

Inglis, David, MA	1625 Mar 19 (383, 159v) Dec 30 (RS50/2, 78v)

ACHAVOULIN, Argyll MRf NS1169
Dunoon par

Wilson, Silvester	1612 Aug 7 (288, 160v)

ADAMSTON, Aberdeenshire MRf NJ5637
Drumblade par

Fisher, Thomas	1617 Aug 14 (295, 52)

AIRLIE (par), Angus

Alexander, Thomas, r	1609 May 24 (160, 408v) 1623 Jun 10 (CC20/4/8, 54v)

AIRTH (par), Stirlingshire

Row, William, MA; (Ed 1616), min of Forgandenny 1624, cf. Stirling	1620 Feb 2 (RS25/3, 94)

ALFORD (par), Aberdeenshire

Wedderburn, George, MA	1613 Jul 9 (265, 344)
student	1620 Nov 10 (SC1/60/6, 36v)
schoolmaster, unnamed	c.1625 (I.J. Simpson, *Education in Aberdeenshire before 1872*, London 1947, 12)
Anderson, George, MA	1632 May 6 (SC1/60/9, 66)
school	1633 (*Bon Record*, 15)

Music School

Walter (Watter), Patrick, cf. Aberdeen	1618 n.d. (461, 213)

ALLOA (par), Clackmannanshire
(united to Tullibody 1600)

Ayson, Duncan, i, n	1602 Nov 9 (174, 241)
Tullis, William, MA	1610 Sep 29 (230, 16)
students	1613 (215, 410v) 1614 (228, 204)
Keirie, Andrew, MA, n, r	1618 Aug 2 (CH2/942/5, 30v) 1633 Aug 31 (ibid., unfoliated)

ALNESS (par), Ross and Cromarty
Grammar School

Hossack, Alexander, MA, min of Kilmuir Easter 1618	1612 Whitsun (213, 232v) 1616 Apr 2 (GD125/5, unnumbered)
Ross, William	1615 (GUA NRAS2808/78)
Ross, David, MA	1618 May 25 (RS37/1, 108)
Munro, John, MA	1623 Jun 30 (390, 425)
Ross, Andrew, MA	1628 Nov 5 (460, 24) 1633 May 1 (486, 25)

ALVAH (par), Banffshire

Mortimer, Thomas, MA	1626 Apr 19 (463, 199)

ALVES (par), Moray

Spens, James, MA	1628 Aug 27 (418, 48v)

ALYTH (par), Perthshire

Simpson, James	1604 Jan 13 (RS48/2, 438v) 1610 Feb 14 (194, 311)
Crichton, David, MA	1616 Jun 19 (252, 428v) 1616 Jul 8 (320, 188)
Donaldson, Thomas, MA	1623 Feb 17 (340, 312) 1630 Mar 10 (RS50/4, 395)
Strachan, James, MA	1631 Dec 26 (CC3/3/5, 75) 1632 May 17 (RS50/6, 73)

AMISFIELD, Dumfriesshire MRf NY0082
Tinwald par
Doctor
Kessan, George, b of Ayr, d 1601 Apr 28 (383, 64v)

ANGELROW, Berwickshire MRf NT7445
Greenlaw par
Gray, John   1600 May 16 (CC8/8/40, 36)

ANNAN (par), Dumfriesshire

Neill, Simon, MA	1624 Jun 20 (RS22/2, 165)
schoolmaster, unnamed	1628 n.d. (*Common Good*, 40)

ANSTRUTHER (uncertain), Fife

Thomson, James, MA	1595/6 Mar 18 (54, 163)

Doctors

Hailes, Robert, d	1614 Feb 22 (226, 377v)
Carmichael, David, d	1629 Jun 25

ANSTRUTHER EASTER (par), Fife

Smith, Simon	1624 Apr 4 (M.F. Connolly, *Fifiana*, Glasgow 1869, 164, 196–7) 1636 May 19 (536, 349)

Doctor

Bowsie, Thomas, d	1631 Jun 12 (RS31/9, 172v) Jul 5 (445, 144)

ANSTRUTHER WESTER (par), Fife
(disjoined from Pittenweem 1588)

school	1595 Oct 26 (J.M. Beale, *A History of the Burgh and Parochial Schools of Fife*, Edinburgh 1983, 6, 66)
Cunningham, Henry	1600 Sep 7 (Beale, 6, 66)
Lindsay, Robert, MA	1613 Oct 1 (229, 80v) 1614 Aug 16 (229, 209)
Watson, Andrew, MA, s	1613 Dec 30 (254, 324v)

Sibbald, James, MA	1619 Mar 2 (338, 306) 1620 Feb 14 (332, 260)
Cunningham, Robert, MA	1624 Nov 19 (382, 313) 1637 Feb 17 (543, 13)
Mitchell, David, MA	1627 May 11 (413, 257) 1635 Sep 29 (509, 334)
Morris, John	1620 Mar 2 (335, 442) 1621 Feb 10 (334, 84)
Doctors	
Cunningham, Henry, d	1595 Oct 26 (J. Lee, *Lectures on the History of the Church of Scotland*, ii, Edinburgh 1860, 432) 1600 Sep 7 (ibid., 433)
Black, Robert, MA, d	1620 Jul 20 (302, 141v) 1621 May 28 (324, 84v)
Carmichael, David, d	1629 Jun 25 (421, 312v)

APPLEGARTH (par), Dumfriesshire

Broom, Robert	1629 Apr 2 (417, 127)

ARBIRLOT (par), Angus

Glover, Thomas, MA (SA 1591)	1598 Jul 21 (CC3/9/1) 1607 Jan 9 (*RMS*, vi, 1830)
Wood, David, MA	1607 Jan 5 (176, 69v) 1610 May 8 (CC3/9/3)
Auchterlonie, John	1612 Jul 14 (214, 19)
Cumming, Alexander, MA	1617 Jul 6 (317, 140v)
Irving, James, MA	1619 May 27 (306, 354)
Wood, Andrew, MA	1620 Dec 22 (305, 456)
Mudie, Thomas, MA	1631 Feb 20 (RS33/8, 4v) 1631 Feb 21 (NP1/71, 260v)

ARBROATH (par), Angus

Cumming, Robert, MA	*deposed* 1562 Dec 28 (G. Hay, *History of Arbroath*, Arbroath 1876, 259)
Black, David	*elected* 1564 Nov 10 (Hay, 259) *discharged* 1567 Jun 20 (ibid.)
Mitchell, David	1573 Oct 27 (Hay, 259)
Kinneir, Alexander, MA	1600 May n.d. (81, 176v) 1604 Aug 31 (199, 120)
Durward, John, MA	1610 Mar 6 (177, 396)
Guthrie, James, MA	1613 Nov 12 (CC3/9/4)
Philp, James, MA	1615 Dec 2 (260, 16) 1622 Sep 17 (389, 80)
Mudie, Thomas, MA	1625 Jul 11 (389, 372)
Granger, Arthur, MA	1623 Aug 6 (RS31/5, 2v) 1626 Dec 13 (404, 254)
schoolmaster, unnamed	1633, 1634 n.d. (*Common Good*, 40)

Doctor

Hill, James, d	1621 Dec 12 (321, 223v) 1638 Jun 19 (520, 266)
doctor, unnamed	1633, 1634 n.d. (*Common Good*, 40)

ARBUTHNOTT (par), Kincardineshire

Beddie, James, MA	1610 Dec 20 (182, 191) 1611 May 7 (250, 415)
Irving, John, MA	1625 Jun 25 (CC3/9/7)
school	c.1630 (*Fasti*, v, 453)

ARDESTIE, Angus MRf NO5034
Monikie par

Noble, James, MA	1631 Feb 18 (444, 212)

ARDOCH, Perthshire   MRf NN8409
Muthill par (later a parish on its own)

Harbertson, Robert, MA	1632 Aug 30 (RS50/6, 143v)

ARNGASK (par), Perthshire

Melville, Andrew	1618 Mar 26 (304, 98)

ARTAMFORD, Aberdeenshire MRf NJ9048 (New Deer)
Deer par before 1622, thereafter Auchreddy

Davidson, William	1624 May 15 (360, 442v)

ASHKIRK (par), Selkirkshire

Cuthbertson, Robert	1618 Jan 27 (CH2/327/1, 143) 1629 Mar 28 (420, 271)

ATHELSTANEFORD (par), East Lothian

Adinston, William	1616 Sep 28 (252, 411v)
Fowles, James	1619 May 18 (296, 39)

AUCHENCROW, Berwickshire MRf NT8560
Coldingham par

Strachan, William	1616 Jan 16 (262, 129)
Lindsay, Adam	1633 Jul 30 (RS1/37, 152)

AUCHINDOIR (par), Aberdeenshire

Douglas, William, MA	1633 Jun 25 (464, 343v)

AUCHINDOWN, Banffshire MRf NJ3437
Mortlach par

Glass, William, MA	1633 Jun 25 (RS1/37, 73)

AUCHLANE, Kirkcudbrightshire MRf NX7458
Kelton par

Williamson, Nathaniel, MA (Ed 1623)	1628 Feb 26 (436, 328)

AUCHMACOY, Aberdeenshire MRf NJ9930
Logie Buchan par

Watson, Robert, MA	1610 Jan 31 (CH2/146/2, 63) Mar 28 (ibid., 66v)
Innes, Alexander, MA	1610 Feb 28 (CH2/146/2, 65v) 1613 Feb 5 (214, 75v)

AUCHREDDY (par), Aberdeenshire
(later called New Deer)

Gordon, Thomas, MA	1623 Sep 30 (SC1/60/6, 155)

AUCHTERARDER (par), Perthshire

Leckie, William	1613 Apr 18 (CC6/12/1, 103v)
Balnevis (Bannewis), John	1623 Mar 16 (351, 216v)

AUCHTERDERRAN (par), Fife

Gow, Alexander	1610 Dec 17 (RS31/1, 103) 1613 Dec 1 (CC20/4/5, 425)
Stenhouse, John, MA	1619 Jul 13 (298, 47v) 1623 Nov 20 (RS1/14, 248v)

AUCHTERHOUSE (par), Angus

Wemyss, James, MA	1620 Feb 27 (301, 147v)

AUCHTERLESS (par), Aberdeenshire

Lind, John	1626 Apr 20 (SC1/60/7, 66)

AUCHTERMUCHTY (par), Fife
Grammar School

Robertson, Thomas, prev r at Collessie	1595/6 Feb 23 (*RMS*, vi, 798) 1597 Aug 10 (CC20/4/3, 240)
Balvaird, John	1606 Feb 8 (RS30/7, 140) Jul 15 (123, 387)
Bennet, James, MA, later min	1607 Jul 17 (RS30/10, 53, 54)
Blair, Patrick, MA	1609 Aug 4 (NP1/53A, unfoliated) 1610 May 8 (180, 29)
Carswell, Patrick, n	1611 Feb 1 (*RMS*, vii, 489) 1624 Aug 26 (NP1/69A, 115)

AUCHTERTOOL (par), Fife

Balvaird, John, MA (SA), min of Hoy	1631 Nov 25 (W. Stevenson, *The Kirk and Parish of Auchtertool*, Kirkcaldy 1908, 116) 1642 Nov 9 (ibid., 117)
Thrift, William, MA	1642 Nov 9 (Stevenson, 117)

AULDEARN (par), Nairn

schoolmaster, unnamed	1582 Jul 12 (*RSS*, vii, 886)
Smyth *or* Sleigh, David	1620 Dec 21 (RS28/1, 235v) 1631 Jan 12 (NRA 3094/338)

AYR (par), Ayrshire
Grammar School

Orr, John	1559 Nov 20 (B6/12/3, unfoliated) 1561–1562 (*Ayr Burgh Accts.*, 134)
schoolmaster, unnamed	1574–1575 (*Ayr Burgh Accts.*, 135)
Dalgleish, Laurence (student at SAS 1557), min of Craigie 1580	1575 Martinmas term (*Ayr Burgh Accts.*, 139) 1579–1580 (ibid., 144)
schoolmaster, unnamed	1580–1582 (*Ayr Burgh Accts.*, 146, 148)
Young, Ninian, MA (Gl 1578), r, min of Monkton 1594	1582/3 Feb 5 (B6/11/1(1), 117) 1592–1593 (*Ayr Burgh Accts.*, 175)
schoolmaster, unnamed	1593–1594, 1595–1596 (*Ayr Burgh Accts.*, 179, 187)
Murray, William, MA	1595 May 5 (B6/11/2, 435) May 7 (ibid., 437)
Dunmore, Archibald, MA (SA), r, later min of Colmonell	1595 Aug 28 (B6/11/2, 480) 1605 May 13 (CC8/8/40, 225v)
Mure, Robert, MA, cf. Maybole	1602 May 11 (Pitcairn, *Trials*, iii, 128)
Stewart, Henry, MA, d	1603 Aug 16 (B6/11/3, 551) 1604–1605 (*Ayr Burgh Accts.*, 223)
McQueen (McQuhyn)	1604 Oct 18 (RS11/3, 3v)
Dunmore, Alexander, MA, (SAL 1604), r, later min of Girvan	1605 May 10 (B6/11/3, 627) 1612 Jul 6 (CH2/751/1(2), 222)
Bonar, John, later MA, cl, r	1612 Jun 2 (B6/11/4, 337) 1633 Oct 19 (RS1/38, 216)

Doctors

Greig, Thomas, d, r	1575–1576 (*Ayr Burgh Accts.*, 139)
Danskin, Henry, MA (SA), d	*before* 1596 Aug 11 (B6/11/3, 10)

Dunmore, William, d	1596 Aug 11 (B6/11/3, 10)
Wallace, William, d	1597 Nov 9 (B6/11/3, 158)
doctor, unnamed	1598–1599 (*Ayr Burgh Accts.*, 196)
Landells, James, MA, d	1602 Sep 15 (B6/11/3, 481) *died* 1603 Jun n.d. (CC8/8/38)
Tran, Hugh, MA, d, r	1605 Jun 25 (B6/18/1, unfoliated) *before* 1619–1620 (*Ayr Burgh Accts.*, 273)
Sawyer, John, d	1615 Mar 17 (366, 15) 1619 Feb 12 (301, 47)
Fullarton, William, MA, d	1620 Aug n.d. (*Ayr Burgh Accts.*, 273) 1625 Aug 7 (CH2/751/2, 73)
Sheringlaw, John, under-doctor	1620 Sep 7 (325, 23) 1632 Feb 1 (CH2/751/2, 189)
doctor, unnamed	1627 n.d. (*Common Good*, 40)
Ritchie, Adam, MA, d	1627 Nov 14 (RS12/4, 177v) 1628 Mar 20 (B6/7/1, 240)

Music School
'Sang School, known also as the Scots school or English school'

Stewart, Andrew, MA	1583 Aug 28 (B6/11/1(1), 162) 1584 Dec 3 (B6/11/1(2), 235)
Mont, William	1584–1585 (*Ayr Burgh Accts.*, 151)
Spittal, Alexander, MA	1601 Apr 22 (B6/11/3, 381) 1605 Feb 4 (186, 366)
Fiddes, Alexander	1610–1611 (*Ayr Burgh Accts.*, 249) 1611 Nov 18 (318, 244)
Lawrie, James	1613 Jan 12 (B6/11/4, 393) 1617 Feb 24 (CH2/751/1(2), 324)
Smyth, William, MA, r	1617 Aug 1 (*Ayr Burgh Accts.*, 268) 1633 Nov 4 (CH2/751/2, 235)

Writing School

Brown, David, MA	1621–1622 (*Ayr Burgh Accts.*, 277)

AYTON (par), Berwickshire
(incorporating Lamberton 1627)

Craig, David	1583 May 4 (NP3/75)
Richardson, John	1602 Mar 2 (*Hist. MSS. Comm., Report on the Manuscripts of Colonel David Milne-Home*, 215) 1603 Feb 9 (227, 390v)
Litster, John	1610 May 29 (*Milne-Home*, 216)
Hamilton, Arthur	1608 Nov 25 (222, 331v) 1609 Apr 14 (RS18/2, 3)

Todrig, George   1615 Mar 24 (242, 96v) 1616 Aug 31 (392, 337)

Fairlie, James   1622 Aug 5 (RS18/2, 43v)

Houston, Leonard, MA,   *before* 1624 (*Fasti*, ii, 26)
  later min of Ellem

Fairlie, James   1622 Aug 5 (RS18/2, 43)

Doctor

Heriot or Hewat, Thomas, d 1623 Jan 14 (393, 409) 1623 Mar 16 (SC60/56/2, 45)

BACHILTON, Perthshire MRf NO0023
Methven par
Drummond, Daniel, MA   1607 Sep 28 (206, 116)

BALDAVIE, Banffshire MRf NJ6261
Boyndie par
Imlach, Robert   1629 Jul 10 (455, 87v)

BALGAVIES, Angus MRf NO5451
Aberlemno par
Petrie, Robert, MA   1620 Jan 31 (293, 289v) Sep 21 (326, 191)

BALHALL, Angus MRf NO5184
Menmuir par
Salmond, Robert   1623 Jul 11 (396, 242)

BALKEERIE, Angus MRf NO3244
Eassie-Nevay par
Fortune, Samuel   1597 Aug 10 (CC8/8/32) 1601 Apr 21 (86, 24)

BALLAGGAN, Dumfriesshire MRf NS8301
Penpont par
Blaik (sic), Thomas   1622 Jun 5 (318, 395)

BALLANTRAE (par), Ayrshire
Mure, Thomas   1632 Feb 16 (452, 220v)

BALLECHIN, Perthshire MRf NN9353
Logierait par
Stewart, Walter   1624 Mar 12 (356, 264) 1641 Oct 4 (*Clan Campbell*, iv, 283)

BALLENCRIEFF, East Lothian MRf NT4878
Aberlady par

Smyth, David   1602 Jul 3 (89, 43) 1606 Jul 15 (125, 190v)
Anderson, Patrick   1611 Feb 8 (217, 430) 1619 Jul 4 (313, 279)

BALLINDALLOCH, Banffshire MRf NJ1736
Inveravon par
Grant, Alexander   1617 Feb 26 (279, 407v)

BALLINTON, Perthshire MRf NS6898
Kilmadock par (later in Kincardine-in-Menteith par)
Newton, Thomas, n   1609 Nov 30 (CC21/13/2) 1618 Jan 7
                                (RS58/1, 58)

BALLOCH, Perthshire MRf NO2649
Alyth par
Crichton, David, MA   1618 Jun 29 (RS1/2, 24)

BALLOGIE, Aberdeenshire MRf NO5795
Birse par
Lumsden, Patrick, MA   1624 May 8 (RS5/4, 405)

BALLUMBIE (par), Angus
(later in Murroes par)
Petrie, John   1610 Dec n.d. (223, 111)

BALMACLELLAN (par), Kirkcudbrightshire
McClellan, Robert   1621 Nov 13 (361, 219v)

BALMUIR MILL, Angus MRf NO4138 (Tealing)
Tealing par
Duncan, James   1619 Jan 10 (464, 56)

BALQUHAIN, Aberdeenshire MRf NJ7323
Chapel of Garioch par
Strachan, John, MA   1618 Jul 8 (324, 319)

BALTERSAN, Ayrshire MRf NS2809
Kirkoswald par
Nairn, David, MA   1587/8 Mar 6 (33, 357)

BANCHORY-DEVENICK (par), part Aberdeenshire, part
                                Kincardineshire
Gray, Andrew, MA   1618 Feb 4 (SC1/60/3, 45) 1620 Apr 24
                                (RS7/1, 150)
Irving, William *or*   1621 Nov 13 (462, 409v) 1622 Dec 27 (342,
    Alexander   73v)

Downie, Robert, MA	1625 Jul 20 (376, 347)
students	1626 Mar 13 (SC1/60/7, 62) 1631 n.d. (I.J. Simpson, *Education in Aberdeenshire before 1872*, London 1947, 40)
schoolmaster, unnamed	before 1633 (Simpson, 12)

BANFF (par), Banffshire

schoolmaster, unnamed	1612 n.d. (*Common Good*, 41)
Abernethie, William, MA	1615 Oct 25 (262, 309v) 1617 Jun 19 (SC2/56/1)
students	1618 Nov 19 (352, 259) 1619 May 10 (423, 67)
Chalmer, George, MA, r	1620 Whitsun (*Banff Annals*, ii, 167) 1624 Aug 10 (ibid., 23)
students	1625 May 16 (530, 74); 1625 Nov 7 (407, 123); 1625 Dec 18 (SC2/56/1)
Chalmer, Thomas, MA	1626 May 17 (*Banff Annals*, ii, 25) *removed* Jul 19 (ibid., 26)
students	1626 Sep 1 (SC2/56/1) 1626 Oct 17 (SC2/56/1)
Anderson, Robert MA	1626 Michaelmas (*Banff Annals*, i, 59) *demitted* 1628 Whitsun (ibid., ii, 168)
no schoolmaster	1628 Jul 1 (*Banff Annals*, ii, 168)
Thomson, Thomas, MA	1628 Dec 2 (RS1/25, 173v)
Strachan, William	'continued some years' (*Banff Annals*, ii, 168)
Brown, Robert, MA, cl, r	1632 n.d. (*Banff Annals*, ii, 169) 1635 n.d. (ibid., 170)

BARRAS, Kincardineshire MRf NO8378
Dunnottar par (later in Kinneff and Catterline par)

Cargill, Thomas, MA	1616 May 8 (CC20/4/6, 123v) before 1623 Apr 29
(AbK1610), later min of Catterline	(*Fasti*, v, 476)

BARRY (par), Angus

Chrystal, James	1598 May 31 (*RMS*, vi, 760)
Anderson, John	1607 Mar 27 (195, 155v)
Bairdie, Andrew	1616 Aug 14 (CC20/4/6, 182v)
Bisset, Patrick, MA	1619 Jan 8 (292, 386v) 1620 Feb 18 (311, 432)
Blair, George, MA	1621 Mar 4 (320, 137)
Ferguson, James, MA	1622 Oct 26 (342, 350) 1630 Oct 11 (NP1/71, 256v)

BASSENDEAN (par), Berwickshire MRf NT6245
(later in Westruther par)
Sinclair, Daniel   1601 Dec 6 (142, 335v)

BATHGATE (par), West Lothian
Cassells, James   1611 Jul 23 (190, 322v) 1619 Jul 3 (310, 68)
Burn, John   1622 Jul 22 (332, 189)
Binnie, John   1630 Aug 10 (A. Bain, *The Education Act of
                                  1696 in West Lothian*, Dept of Educational
                                  Studies 1974, 32)

BEATH (par), Fife
Sinclair, George   1626 May 18 (469, 469)

BEDRULE (par), Roxburghshire
Mather, James   1608 Dec 28 (CH2/198/1, unfoliated) 1609
                                  Feb 28 (ibid.)

BEITH (par), Ayrshire
Lang, Archibald, d, r   1613 Feb 24 (215, 318) 1633 Jun 11
                                  (CC9/7/26, 114r)

BELHELVIE (par), Aberdeenshire
school   1624 Nov 8 (CH2/32/1, 16v)
Thomson, Robert, MA,   1628 Dec 30 (CH2/32/1, 33) 1632 Apr 22
  cl, r   (SC1/60/8, 166)

BENDOCHY (par), Perthshire
Peirson, Francis, MA, pr,   1613 Oct 3 (232, 424)
  sc, simultaneously at
  Coupar Angus
McLaren, George   1631 May 17 (RS50/5, 272v)

BENHOLM (par), Kincardineshire
Scrimgeour, Robert   1592/3 Mar 20 (CC3/9/3)
Watt, James, MA   1601 Apr 25 (CC8/8/36) 1602 May 28
                                  (CC8/8/44, 362v)
Melville, William, MA   1610 May 31 (182, 150) Jun 12 (182, 150)
Johnston, William, MA   1613 May 29 (247, 223v) 1614 May 3 (233,
                                  106)
Allardyce, David, MA   1615 Mar 27 (235, 360v) *1616 Jun 19*[2]

---

[2] Reference missing: see Preface.

Sibbald, James, MA   1617 n.d. (299, 86v) 1619 Aug 3 (472, 41)
Bairdie, Andrew   1620 Jun 13 (308, 169) Nov 24 (304, 178)
Barclay, John, MA   1632 May 23 (458, 321)

BENVIE, *see* Inchture

BERVIE, *see* Inverbervie

BIGGAR (par), Lanarkshire
Fleming, William   1605 Mar 13 (114, 431)
Brown, James, n   1608 May 24 (193, 162) 1619 Dec 2 (RS1/5,
                           29v)
Greig, William   1617 Dec 2 (315, 155)
Brown, William   1629 Jan 30 (25, 250) 1633 Aug 7 (37, 248v)

BIRGHAM, Berwickshire MRf NT7939
chapel, Eccles par
Hamilton, Patrick   1620 Apr 27 (341, 34)

BIRSAY (par), Orkney
Whyte, Andrew   1633 Jun 25 (RS43/4, 407) 1633 Jul 6
                           (RS43/4, 406)

BIRSE (par), Aberdeenshire
Forbes, Duncan, MA   1629 May 31 (463, 347) 1630 May 31 (476,
                           374)

BISHOP'S CRAMOND, *see* Cramond

BLACKFORD (par), Perthshire
(formerly called Strageath)
Toward, Malcolm, r   1613 Sep 6 (CC6/12/1, 58v) Dec 17 (239,
                           216)
Given (Govan), John, MA,   1627 Nov 20 (RS50/3, 232v)
  min 1655

BLACKWOOD, Lanarkshire MRf NS7843
Lesmahagow par
Campbell, Matthew   1614 Mar 23 (232, 86v) 1614 Apr 9 (235, 145)

BLAIR ATHOLL (par), Perthshire
McKay, Robert   1617 Nov 22 (268, 122) 1620 May 22
                           (RS49/3, 243)

BLAIR CASTLE, Ayrshire MRf NS4236 (Riccarton)
Riccarton par
Miller, Robert   1625 Aug 30 (RS12/3, 478v)

BLAIRGOWRIE (par), Perthshire
Paton, John   1630 Jan 13 (438, 349)
Guthrie, Henry, MA   1616 May 5 (379, 362v) 1622 Nov 5 (379, 372)
Christison, John, MA   1616 Feb 27 (262, 386v) 1616 May 31 (273,
                                    47v)
Walker, John, MA   1602 May 21 (RS48/1, 271v)

BLAIRYFEDDON, Angus MRf NO4454
Oathlaw par
Morris, David   1622 Feb 28 (CC3/9/6)

BLANERNE, Berwickshire MRf NT8356
Bunkle and Preston par
Wallace, Cuthbert   1606 May 10 (124, 338)

BLANTYRE (par), Lanarkshire
student   1611 Jan 9 (199, 219)
Glassford, John   1611 Nov 20 (B64/1/1, 103)
Forest, William, MA   1622 Jul 17 (RS40/26, 27v)
  (Gl 1612)
Semple, Robert   1624 Apr 4 (366, 94)
Nisbet, William   1632 Jun 6 (526, 402)

BOARHILLS (Byrehills), Fife MRf NO5614
St Andrews par
Mitchell, David, MA   1619 Mar 23 (356, 329)

BOLD, Peebleshire MRf NT3636 (West Bold)
Innerleithen par
Wilson, Thomas   1606 Dec 6 (SC42/28/1)
Turnbull, Adam   1621 Jan 17 (RS1/7, 209)

BOLESIDE, Selkirkshire MRf NT4933
Lindean par (called Galashiels 1622)
schoolmaster, r, unnamed   1617 Aug 14 (CH2/327/1, unfoliated)

BO'NESS, West Lothian MRf NS9981
Carriden par
Wilson, Adam   1603 Apr 25 (101, 469)

Winram, John, MA   1612 Jul 13 (213, 311) 1621 May 3 (400, 94)
Adinston, David, MA, p   1624 May 6 (359, 159v) 1640 May 14 (533, 1)

BONSKEID, Perthshire MRf NN8961
Blair Atholl par
Carmichael, John   1621 Oct 8 (*RPC*, 1st ser., xii, 581) 1625 May
                            29 (RS50/1, 223)

BORTHWICK (par), Midlothian
Oswald, John, n   1612 Aug 9 (256, 438) *broken service* 1620 Aug
                            19 (309, 33v)
Hay, William   1618 May 6 (285, 140)
Cochrane, James   1620 Jan 5 (313, 132v)
Douglas, Andrew   1629 May 17 (424, 222v) 1650 Mar 20 (605,
                            124)

BOTARIE (par), Aberdeenshire
(later called Cairney)
Watson, John, MA   1622 Nov 7 (347, 273v)

BOTHANS (par), East Lothian
(later called Yester)
Brown, William   1606 Feb 23 (*Yester Writs*, no. 1031)
Hay, William, *see below* 1615 Nov 11 (CH2/377/1, 22v) 1617 Jan 5
                            (CH2/377/1, 22v)
school   1627 (*Reports*, 106)
Hay, William, *see above* 1628 Jul 11 (421, 377)

BOTHWELL (par), Lanarkshire
Young, Allan, n   1612 Jul 23 (CC9/14/3, 380v)
Gray, Archibald   1618 Dec 5 (395, 496) 1630 May 27
                           (RS40/3A, 283v)

BRACO, Perthshire MRf NN8211
Muthill par (later in Ardoch par)
Cranston, William, MA   1629 May 23 (RS50/4(2), 1v)

BRANSHOGLE, Stirlingshire MRf NS5285 (Killearn)
Killearn par
Mushet, Archibald;, r at   1620 Nov 27 (483, 107v) 1621 May 9
   Campsie   (CC9/14/10, 59)

BRECHIN (par), Angus
Leach, Andrew, MA, min, p 1580/1 Jan 13 (*RMS*, v, 82)

Lindsay, John, MA   1590 Jun 27 (*RPC*, 1st ser., iv, 499)
Walwod, Charles, MA   1593 Nov 6 (52, 374)
Bisset, Alexander, MA, min 1606 Aug 14 (*RPC*, 1st ser., vii, 650)
Skinner, Laurence, MA, min 1611 May 15 (CC3/9/3) 1616 Sep 18
  of Dunlappie   (CC3/9/5)
Petrie, Robert, MA   1623 Mar 5 (CC3/9/7) 1629 May 22 (442,
                       288)
Marshall, William, min   1633 n.d. (*Fasti*, v, 379)
Doctor
Watt, James, d, r   1615 Nov 13 (CC3/9/5) 1628 Jun 5
                       (CC3/9/7)

BRIDGE OF EARN, Perthshire MRf NO1318
Dunbarney par
Duncan, Gavin   1621 Jul 19 (315, 130)
Wilson, Andrew   1625 Oct n.d. (404, 12)

BRIGHALL, see Hailes

BRIG OF LYNE, Peebleshire MRf NT1648
(later called Romanno Bridge)
Newlands par
Dyet, William   1614 Aug 17 (241, 298)

BROOMHOUSE, Berwickshire MRf NT8056
Edrom par
Strachan, William   1620 Apr 12 (306, 325v) 1621 May 23 (323,
                       183v)

BROUGHTON (par), Peebleshire
Chisholm, Archibald   1630 Jul 3 (490, 423)
Forest, Laurence   1630 Dec 7 (442, 84)

BUCHTRIG, Berwickshire MRf NT7714
Morebattle par
Wood, George, p   1605 Sep 23 (*RMS*, vi, 1674)
Haistie, John, MA   1622 Feb 19 (338, 375)

BUITTLE (par), Kirkcudbrightshire
Gibson, John   1631 Jun 7 (471, 156) 1651 Dec 27 (585, 326)

BURNTISLAND (par), Fife
Grammar School
student   1587 Jun 23 (B9/1/1, 52v)

Martin, David, MA   1597 April 10 (B9/1/1, unfoliated) 1602 Apr 9
                           (136, 324)
Bonar, James, MA   1605 Apr 10 (106, 393v) 1607 Dec 17 (141,
                           144)
school   1612 n.d. (*Common Good*, 41)
no grammar school, but   1613 Apr 13 (J.M. Beale, *A History of the Burgh*
  'ane who teichis the   *and Parochial Schools of Fife*, Edinburgh 1983, 5)
  bairnes to reid and wreitt'
order for grammar school   1614 May 30 (Beale, 8)
Adamson, James, r   1616 Jul 3 (254, 346)
school   1620 (Beale, 8)
school and schoolmaster   1621 n.d. (*Common Good*, 41)
Christie, Thomas, MA   1621 Aug 8 (382, 132) 1630 Mar 15 (*RMS*,
                           viii, 1572)
schoolmaster, unnamed   1633 n.d. (*Common Good*, 41)
Doctor
Bonar, Robert, d   1605 Apr 18 (169, 302v) 1606 Jul 26 (172,
                           361v)

BURRAY (par), Orkney
Hayne, James, MA, s   1631 Nov 20 (NP1/75B, 285) 1631 Nov 25
                           (RS43/4, 254)

BUTTERDEAN, Berwickshire MRf NT8064
Channelkirk par (later in Coldingham par)
Gray, Patrick   1592 May 30 (61, 229v)

BYSBIE, Wigtownshire MRf NX4735
Whithorn par
Edgar (Edzer), John   1631 Apr 17 (490, 184)

CAIRNEY, *see* Botarie

CALDER, *see* Midcalder

CALLANDER (par), Perthshire
Ferguson, John   1627 May 28 (454, 395v)

CAMBO, Fife   MRf NO6011
Kingsbarns par
Robertson, Patrick, MA   1616 Oct 12 (326, 79)

CAMBUSLANG (par), Lanarkshire

Home, John, MA	1597 May 3 (57, 463) 1597/8 Jan 27 (B64/1/1, 44)
endowment for school	c.1602 (J.A. Wilson, *A History of Cambuslang*, Glasgow 1929, 69)
Hamilton, Andrew, MA, later min of Kilbarchan	1604 Feb 29 (CS7/212, 97) May 19 (*RPC*, 1st ser., vii, 553)
Neilson, John, MA	1607 Feb 20 (B64/1/1, 90)
Nicoll, Robert, MA	1612 Jul 23 (CC9/14/3, 380v) 1616 n.d. (Wilson, 69)
Andrew, Robert	1618 Mar 2 (CC9/7/15, 121)
Forest, William, MA	1621 Jun 16 (437, 203)
Baxter, Edward, r	1628 Mar 29 (CC9/14/4) 1632 Jun 14 (465, 50)
Glasgow, Archibald	1632 Jun 29 (CC9/14/13, 74) 1633 Jun 29 (CC9/16/1, Bundle of Writs for 1633)

CAMBUSNETHAN (par), Lanarkshire

Couper, John	1627 Jun 27 (CC9/14/13, 42v) 1633 May 25 (DI75/4, 213)

CAMPBELTOWN, *see* Lochhead

CANONGATE, *see* Edinburgh

CAPRINGTON, Ayrshire MRf NS4036
Riccarton par

student	1625 Oct 18 (437, 167)

CARBIESTON, Ayrshire MRf NS3920
Coylton par

Adam, John	1621 May 19 (349, 287)

CARFIN, Lanarkshire MRf NS7758
Bothwell par

Steven, Roger	1622 Dec 26 (351, 542) 1630 May 10 (CC9/14/13, 269v)
Davidson, Richard	1631 May 3 (446, 69) 1632 Dec 1 (468, 235v)

CARGILL (par), Perthshire

Anderson, Robert	1619 Apr 23 (RS49/2, 294v)

CARLINGWARK, Kirkcudbrightshire MRf NX7662
(later known as Castle Douglas)
Kelton par
Doctor
Thomson, Paul, d   1611 May 14 (222, 258v)

CARLUKE (par), Lanarkshire
Arneil, John   1607 Feb 15 (223, 18v)
Greig, John, MA   1615 May 6 (235, 408)
Aird, John   1618 Dec 1 (300, 88v) 1620 Apr 30 (304, 316v)
Hamilton, James, MA   1620 Jun 16 (380, 304v) Nov 10 (RS40/2A, 23)
Somerville, John, MA   1622 Sep 13 (CC14/5/2) 1623 Apr 17 (387, 415)
Somerville, Thomas, r   1631 Jul 3 (RS40/3B, 133v) 1632 Jul 3 (458, 274v)

CARMUNNOCK (par), Lanarkshire
Cook, George   1607 Aug 18 (B64/1/1, 90)
Sawyer, John   1611 Jan 23 (181, 313v)
Warnock, John   1632 Jul 6 (CC10/11/5, 35v) Nov 5 (CC9/14/13, 39)

CARMYLLIE (par), Angus
Herries, John, MA, min of   1574 Apr 5 (Inscription in C.T. Suetonius,
   Ormiston 1576, min of   *Duodecim Cesares*, Lyons 1548, now in NLS)
   Newbattle 1583

CARNBEE (par), Fife
Dalgleish, David, MA   1613 Apr n.d. (*RPC*, 1st ser., x, 131)
Rule (Roull), James, MA   1607 Apr 29 (134, 62v) 1610 Aug 17 (215, 121v)

CARNOCK (par), Fife
Thomson, James, MA   1628 Jun 23 (459, 421)

CARNWATH (par), Lanarkshire
Brown, Walter   1590 Jul 17 (40, 300) 1592 Jun 15 (41, 415)
Veitch, John, MA   1614 (RS1/1, 70) 1617 Aug 17 (357, 89v)
Ballantyne (Bannatyne,   1622 Jul 9 (RS40/2A, 86) 1629 Dec 24 (425,
   Bellenden), William,   165)
   MA, p, sc

Anderson, Alexander, MA, r 1631 Jan 2 (GD124/17/625)
Wiseman, James, MA   1631 Oct 29 (RS1/32, 172)
Wiseman, Thomas, MA   1632 Jan 24 (Lockhart of Lee and Carnwath
                         Papers, NLS)
Allison, Robert MA   1633 Jan 23 (469, 130)

CARRIDEN (par), West Lothian
Craigie, James, MA   1629 May 1 (RS1/26, 1v)
Hamilton, William   1632 Jul 25 (RS1/34, 242v)

CARRINGTON (par), Midlothian
Symonton, Michael   1628 Jun 28 (452, 352v)

CARSTAIRS (par), Lanarkshire
Stark, John, n   1619 Jan 16 (291, 136v) 1624 Apr 18
                         (CC14/5/2)
Somerville, Thomas   1628 Mar 31 (RS40/2A, 36v) 1630 Jun 9
                         (442, 353)

CASHOGLE, Dumfriesshire MRf NS8604
Durisdeer par
Thomson, John   1610 Apr 16 (*RPC*, 1st ser., viii, 727)

CASTLE DOUGLAS, *see* Carlingwark

CASTLEHILL, *see* Lanark

CATHCART (par), Renfrewshire
Stein, Robert   1603 Mar 30 (CC9/14/3, 49v) Sep 23
                         (CC9/14/2, 103)

CAVERTON, Roxburghshire MRf NT7527
Eckford par
Ker, John   1613 May 11 (302, 14)
Ainslie, John   1617 Feb 5 (CH2/198/1, unfoliated) 1617 Apr
                         16 (ibid.)
Davidson, John   1617 Sep 21 (272, 236v)
Stewart, John   1619 Nov 4 (299, 363v)

CERES (par), Fife
Baxter, Henry   1600 Jun 10 (90, 165v) 1601 Aug 15 (86, 275)
Anderson, Andrew, MA   1612 Jul 5 (208, 41v)

stent for school   1619 n.d. (J.M. Beale, *A History of the Burgh and Parochial Schools of Fife*, Edinburgh 1983, 8)

Craig, James, MA   1620 Feb 2 (RS1/5, 93v) 1636 Dec 7 (504, 378)

Thomson, John   1629 Oct 30 (RS31/8, 208v)

Bennett, George, MA   1631 Aug 28 (Beale, 15)

CHANONRY, *see* Ross, Chanonry of

CHAPEL, Dumfriesshire MRf NX8684 (Dunscore)
Dunscore par
Doctor
Wells, Andrew, d   1629 Jun 13 (418, 371)

CHAPEL OF GARIOCH (par), Aberdeenshire
(also known as Logie-Durno, united with Fetterneir 1599)
Mutray, George, min   1613 Apr 1 (219, 95v)
Cargill, Nicol, MA, r   1617 Oct 28 (281, 4)
Ker, Archibald, MA   1619 Nov 17 (SC1/60/4, 165)
Strachan, Alexander, MA   1629 May 29 (533, 250) 1631 Jun 4 (454, 54)

CHAPELHILL, Lanarkshire MRf NS8354 (Chapel)
Cambusnethan par
Williamson, David   1622 1627 (RS40/26, 18v)

CHAPELTON, Lanarkshire MRf NS6848
Glassford par
Gibb, John   1600 May 7 (75, 176v)

CHIRNSIDE (par), Berwickshire
Edgar (Edzer), Edward   1599 May 2 (89, 372)
Mylne, John   1611 Mar 29 (189, 247)
Simpson, Bartholomew   1616 Apr 25 (287, 19) 1620 Jun 4 (313, 8)
Strachan, William   1619 Apr 5 (SC60/56/2, 279) 1624 Mar 26 (424, 167)
Houliston (Houlatstoun),   1629 Mar 29 (SC60/56/3, 167) 1630 Jul 22
   William   (SC60/56/4, 16v)

CHOICELEE, Berwickshire MRf NT7451
Langton par
Cook, William, MA   1606 May 6 (145, 239) 1609 Feb 9 (157, 134v)

CLACKMANNAN (par), Clackmannanshire

Penny, Andrew	1600 May 19 May 19 (105, 36v) 1611 May 11 (245, 67v)

Doctor

Minister's servant, doctor, unnamed	1590 Jul 14 (CH2/722/2, unfoliated)

CLAVERHOUSE, Angus MRf NO4134

Mains par

Inglis, Patrick, MA	1597 Sep 20 (87, 429) 1598 Dec 3 (75, 276v)

CLIEN, Perthshire MRf NO2023

Kinfauns par

Smith, Simon	1599 Jul 7 (116, 169)

CLEISH (par), Kinross-shire

Drummond, Daniel	1600 Sep 9 (NP1/61, 16)
Christie, Thomas	1633 Nov 18 (RS31/10, 294v)

COCKBURNSPATH (par), Berwickshire

Inglis, James	1609 Apr 21 (168, 210)
Matheson, David	1618 May 19 (311, 173) 1619 Sep 17 (RS1/4, 175)
Hewat, Alexander, MA	1621 Aug 21 (380, 356v) 1626 Mar 3 (504, 209)

COCKPEN (par), Midlothian

Norvell, William	1602 Apr 11 (Pitcairn, *Trials*, ii, 387) Jun 9 (ibid., 389)
no school	1627 (*Reports*, 45)

COLDINGHAM (par), Berwickshire

Watson, Alexander, MA (SAS, 1582), min of Coldingham 1593	1587 Jun 12 (RH6/209) 1590 Sep 12 (36, 260)
Hart, James, MA	1598 May 15 (71, 408)
Oswald, John	1600 Mar 1 (332, 114) 1602 Apr 12 (*Hist. MSS. Comm., Report on the Manuscripts of Colonel David Milne-Home*, 183)
Dalzell, Mungo, MA	1613 Nov 16 (255, 379)
Adamson, William	1618 Apr 6 (RS18/1, 34)
Matheson, David	1621 Nov 16 (330, 99v) 1623 May 21 (343, 49v)

Aitken, Edward, MA   1624 Dec 31 (400, 119) 1632 Mar 11 (RS1/33, 152v)

COLINTON, *see* Hailes

COLLACE (par), Perthshire
Boyd, William   1602 Mar 28 (99, 119v) 1613 May 24 (272, 401v)

COLLESSIE (par), Fife
Gardiner, James, MA   1631 Jan 23 (34, 265v)

COLMONELL (par), Ayrshire
Elliot, Thomas, MA   1630 Mar 30 (463, 103) 1632 Aug 3 (34, 242v)

COLMSLIE, Roxburghshire MRf NT5139
Melrose par
Brown, James   1622 Aug 20 (*Melrose Recs.*, iii, 379n.) 1623 Aug 20 (RS56/3, 192)
Chalmer, James   1622 Oct 26 (369, 229)

COLQUHALZIE, Perthshire MRf NN9117
Trinity Gask par
Rollok, William, MA   1618 Feb 18 (320, 153v)

COMRIE (par), Perthshire
Haggart, James   1621 Apr 8 (369, 2v) Jul 21 (342, 322)

CONGALTON, East Lothian MRf NT5480 (Congalton Mains)
Dirleton par
Merrilees, Robert   1604 Jun 16 (109, 340) 1604 Dec 11 (105, 249)

CORSBIE, Berwickshire MRf NT6044
Legerwood par
McClellan, Patrick, MA   1627 Jan 29 (404, 324)

CORSTORPHINE (par), Midlothian
Alexander, Walter   1589/90 Feb 3 (NP1/52, 15)
Denny, Patrick   1593/4 Mar 20 (54, 100)
presbytery order   1596 Aug 22 (CH2/121/2, 243)
  appointment
Cockie, William   1602 Feb 1 (162, 164v)

Denny, Patrick	1610 Jun 15 (210, 48)
Lawson, Robert, MA	1622 Oct 24 (351, 550) *before* 1628 Jul 19 (437, 243)
Dewcat, John, MA, r	1624 Dec 21 (424, 148)
Greig, William	1632 Mar 29 (RS25/18, 312v) 1636 Jan 9 (521, 75)

COSSANS, Angus MRf NO3949
Glamis par

Bisset, William, MA	1630 Jan 31 (441, 116)

COULTER (par), Lanarkshire

student	1620 Sep 11 (RS40/2A, 19)
Kello, Hugh	1621 Apr 5 (DI75/3, 42v)
Nisbet, David	1624 mid Apr (CC9/14/12, 201)
Sharp, James, MA	1627 Dec 8 (412, 14)
Shaw, James, MA	1628 Oct 20 (25, 75)

COUPAR ANGUS (par), Angus

Tullis, John, MA	1579 Dec 2 (176, 30v) 1603 Aug 1 (105, 258)
Scheves, Patrick, MA	1608 May 5–6 (RS48/6, 421v)
Adamson, Patrick, MA;	1611 Jun 6 (197, 187)
Peirson, Francis, MA, pr, sc, simultaneously at Bendochy	1613 Oct 3 (232, 424) 1621 Apr 12 (318, 298v)
Lindsay, Robert, MA (SA 1611), min	*before* 1625 Jan n.d. (*Fasti*, v, 258)
Jack, William, MA	1626 Jun 9 (388, 155v) 1629 Jun 14 (462, 181)

COUPAR GRANGE, Perthshire MRf NO2342
Coupar Angus par (later in Bendochy par)

Crichton, James	1627 Jun 8 (RS50/3, 76)

COVINGTON (par), Lanarkshire

Rule, John	1620 Jun 17 (RS40/1, 139v) 1621 Sep 13 (321, 10v)
Young, Gavin	1609 Jul 23 (203, 343)

CRAIG, Angus, *see* Inchbrayock

CRAIG, Ayrshire MRf NS4340
Kilmaurs par

Batie *or* Battie, James	1632 Jun 27 (RS12/5, 306) Jul 21 (RS12/5, 292v)

CRAIGEND, Kirkcudbrightshire MRf NX9269
Troqueer par
Gibson, John   1632 Jun 30 (446, 438r and v)
Doctor
Hunter, Robert, d   1630 Mar 16 (RS22/3, 86)

CRAIGHALL, Fife MRf NO4010
Ceres par
Rule (Roull), James, MA   1613 Jul 22 (255, 204v)

CRAIGIEBURN, Dumfriesshire MRf NT1105
Moffat par
Donaldson, Robert   1622 Feb 3 (335, 139)

CRAIL (par), Fife
Grammar School

Bowman, John, sir, MA (SAL), p	1542 Oct 5 (J. Lee, *Lectures on the History of the Church of Scotland*, i, Edinburgh 1860, 334) *died* 1564 Jun n.d. (CS7/30, 275)
Buthill, John, MA (SAL), *frequent disputes over his tenure*	1564 Dec 19 (CS7/30, 275) 1582 May 29 (Lee, 336)
Kinneir, Thomas, MA (SAL), min	1566/7 Feb 25 (Lee, 336–7) never took up the charge (J.M. Beale, *A History of the Burgh and Parochial Schools of Fife*, Edinburgh 1983, 65)
Bennett, John, MA (SAM)	1571 Sep 1 (Lee, 337)
Herries, John, r	1571 Nov 14 (Lee, 337) *renounced in favour of Buthill* 1576 Dec 4 (ibid., 338)
Edmeston, John, MA (SAM), min, *disputed by Buthill*	1579 Dec 8 (Lee, 338) 1580/1 Feb 18 (ibid.)
Maxwell, David, MA, n, r	1584/5 Jan 29 (Lee, 336) 1605 May 8 (113, 294)
McDuff, Alexander, MA	1612 Oct 14 (204, 120) 1613 Nov 6 (RS31/5, 227)
Heggie, William, MA, cl	1622 Jun 29 (344, 97v) 1648 Apr 15 (Lee, 340)

Doctors

doctor, r, unnamed	1568 Oct 12 (Lee, 337)
Gibb, John, d	1571 Dec 11 (Lee, 337)
Dansken, Patrick, d	1605 Jun 1 (146, 88)

Music School

King, George, sir, c, *disputed by Buthill*	1567 Nov 25 (Lee, 337) *discharged* 1582 May 29 (ibid., 339)

CRAMOND (par), Midlothian
(also known as Nether Cramond or Bishop's Cramond)

Coiss, John	1586/7 Mar 6 (CS1/3(2), 328v)
Strang, William, MA	1599 Aug 21 (CH2/121/2, unfoliated)
Anderson, William, n	1610 Oct 18 (198, 184) 1611 Jun 1 (233, 223v)
March, Francis	1622 Nov 18 (RS25/7, 91v)
Ballantyne (Bannatyne, Bellenden), William, MA, r	1632 Mar 14 (RS25/18, 349) Jun 4 (RS25/19, 183v)

CRAMOND REGIS, Midlothian MRf NT1070 (Barnton)
(also known as Over Cramond or King's Cramond)
Cramond par

Christison, Alexander	1600 Oct 2 (116, 389v) 1601 Dec 17 (CC8/17/14)
Cranston, Thomas	1630 Jun 20 (RS25/16, 118v)

CRANSTON (NETHER), Midlothian MRf NT3865 (Cranstoun Riddell)
Cranstoun Riddell par

Kennedy, William	1628 Jan 25 (426, 109) 1629 Sep 4 (431, 13)
Liddell, John	1631 Jan 5 (405, 40) Mar 22 (452, 447v)
Craig, John	1631 Jun 23 (432, 325v)

CRAWFORD (par), Lanarkshire

Craig, John	1632 Jan 13 (486, 272) 1633 Jan 18 (RS40/3B, 191v)

CRAWFORDJOHN (par), Lanarkshire

Purdie, Arthur	1599 Jun 29 (*RPC*, 1st ser., vi, 22) 1601 Oct 30 (ibid., vi, 221)
Watson, Archibald, MA	1627 Nov 27 (418, 132) Dec 4 (465, 83)
Adamson, Patrick, MA	1632 Jun 5 (452, 327)

CREICH (par), Fife

endowment for school	c.1630 (J. Lee, *Lectures on the History of the Church of Scotland*, ii, Edinburgh 1860, 429)

CRICHTON (par), Midlothian
Grammar School

Wilson, James	1623 Jul 22 (426, 195v)
Anderson, Thomas;	1620 Jul 20 (330, 10)
Nisbet, George;	1627 Nov 11 (469, 54)

Music School

Kene, Richard	1584/5 Feb 16 (CH4/1/1, ii, 131v)

CRIEFF (par), Perthshire

Rawson, Robert	1601 Dec 15 (272, 469)
Ayson, Patrick	1602 Sep 10 (RS48/2, 107v)
students	1606 Jun 6 (206, 10) 1610 Apr 14 (221, 383v) 1615 Feb 6 (239, 405v) 1617 Feb 24 (311, 371v) 1623 Jun 12 (345, 333v)

CRIMOND (par), Aberdeenshire

school	by 1601 (I.J. Simpson, *Education in Aberdeenshire before 1872*, London 1947, 12) 1609 Sep 14 (CH2/89/1(1), 126)
no school	1613 Sep 2 (CH2/89/1(1), 150v)
school	1614 Jul 21 (CH2/89/1(1), 164) 1620 Sep 7 (CH2/89/1(1), 254)
Young, John	1621 Apr 5 (CH2/89/1(2), 262v) 1622 Apr 22 (SC1/60/5, 23)
Noble, Andrew, MA	1626 Jun 7 (RS5/5, 351) 1642 Jan 6 (CS7/504, 246)

CROMARTY (par), Ross and Cromarty

'lye schule'	1564 Mar 27 (NP1/25, 5)
schoolmaster, unnamed, c in Ross	1573/4 Jan 30 (CH4/1/1, i, 101)
grammar school	1580 Sep 9 (*RSS*, vii, 2505)
student	1610 May 27 (215, 411v)
Harvie, Francis	1626 Apr 26 (RS37/3, 206)

CROMDALE (par), Moray

Peter, John, MA	1626 Jan 31 (390, 5)
Smart, Thomas, MA	1626 Nov 1 (401, 180v) 1627 Jan 28 (454, 55v)
Dunbar, William, MA	1628 Nov 28 (RS28/3, 184v)

CROOKSTON, Midlothian MRf NT4251
Heriot par (later in Stow par)

Lawrie *or* Lowrie, William   1621 Jul 15 (RS25/5, 15v) Sep 21 (GD350/1/120)

CROSSMICHAEL (par), Kirkcudbrightshire
Doctor

Reid, William, d   1624 Jan 7 (371, 294)

CRUDEN (par), Aberdeenshire

Alexander, John, MA, simultaneously at Ellon   1602 May n.d. (*Records of the Parish of Ellon*, ed. T. Mair, Aberdeen 1846, 51)

no school   1605 Jul 17 (CH2/146/1, 131)

schoolmaster, unnamed   c.1606 (I.J. Simpson, *Education in Aberdeenshire before 1872*, London 1947, 11)

CULLEN (par), Banffshire
Grammar School

Hay, George, sir;   1566 n.d., 1567 n.d. (*Exchequer Rolls*, ix, 351, 391)

Leslie, William, MA   1586 May 8 (CH4/1/1, ii, 154v)

student   1603 Jul 3 (100, 241)

Sharp, William, MA, s   1604 Jan 16 (RS15/2, 93) 1616 May 16 (305, 129)

Clark, George, MA   1606 Nov 14 (RS15/3, 171v) 1607 May 2 (RS15/3, 195v)

Guthrie, Richard, MA   1610 Jun 7 (192, 19v)

student   1611 Apr 19 (226, 476v)

Seton, Alexander, MA   1613 Nov 16 (RS16/1, 150) 1618 Nov 9 (SC2/56/1)

schoolmaster, unnamed   1619 n.d. (W. Barclay, *The Schools and Schoolmasters of Banffshire*, Banff 1925, 86)

Garioch, Alexander, MA   1620 Jul 28 (356, 286v) 1625 Jul 31 (400, 141)

Brown, William, MA   1626 Jan 5 (SC2/56/1) 1628 Sep 23 (435, 68)

Leslie, Norman, MA   1632 May 1 (479, 391) 1633 Dec 25 (505, 386)

Music School

Lawtie, William or James, MA (Gl 1543), n, min of Banff, Cullen, Deskford, Fordyce and Inverboyndie 1563   n.d. (J. Durkan and J. Kirk, *The University of Glasgow*, Glasgow 1977, 200)

CULROSS (par), Fife (previously in Perthshire)

Home, William, MA, later min of Crombie and Torry	1585 Jun 17 (24(1), 94v) 1589 Apr 1 (PS59, 116v)
Ewing, David, MA	1601 Jan 28 (PS1/71/349v–350) Nov 14 (84, 299)
Fairfull, John, MA (SAL 1570), exh, n, min of Aberdour 1587, min of Dunfermline 1598, min of Anstruther Wester 1610	1603 Feb 2 (*Fasti*, v, 27) 1613 Jan 2 (377, 11)
Edmeston (Edmonston), James, MA	1614 Feb 22 (CH4/1/4, 106) 1617 Feb 25 (NP1/61, 138v)
Rollok, William, MA	1619 Mar 22 (324, 22) Apr 21 (RS1/3, 158v)
Greig, Walter, MA	1621 Jun 12 (310, 142)
Tullidaff, Samuel, MA, p	1623 Nov 16 (*RPC*, 1st ser., xiii, 382) 1633 Sep 5 (514, 203)

Doctor

Thomson, John	1617 Nov 20 (273, 94)

CULTS (par), Fife

Heriot, Patrick	1629 Jul 6 (421, 38v)

CULTYBRAGGAN, Perthshire MRf NN7619
Comrie par

Fernie, Robert	1618 Jul 31 (RS49/2, 119)

CUMBERHEAD, Lanarkshire MRf NS7734
Lesmahagow par

Whyte, Thomas	1623 Aug 3 (351, 6)

CUMNOCK (par), Ayrshire

Paterson, Isaac, MA	1599 Sep 2 (73, 338v)
school	1625 Mar 21 (*Clan Campbell*, v, 195)
Mure, William, MA, n	1627 Apr 28 (RS12/4, 26v) 1628 Jan 11 (RS1/23, 165v)
school	1629 Aug n.d. (*Clan Campbell*, v, 200)
Wallace, William, MA	1632 Apr 12 (RS12/5, 260v)

CUPAR (par), Fife
Grammar School

schoolmaster, unnamed	1564 Jun 26 (*BUK*, i, 46)
Fraser, David, MA, r	1566/7 Jan 22 (*RKSSA*, 287)

schoolmaster, unnamed	1575, 1579, 1581 n.d. (*RKSSA*, 287)
Balcomie, David, MA	1595 Aug 5 (49, 506) c.1619–20 (RS31/2, 254)
Williamson, Robert, MA, p	1609 May 29 (310, 264) *demitted* 1628 May 9 (B13/10/2, unfoliated) *readmitted* 1638 Feb 28 (ibid.) 1649 May 31 (*St Andrews Testaments*, 375)
Christie, Thomas, MA	1628 May 9 (B13/10/2, unfoliated)
Scott, Alexander, MA, b	1628 Nov 25 (B13/10/2, unfoliated) 1637 Jun 15 (507, 269) 1637 Jun 15 (507, 269)
Gleg, James	*before* 1632 Jun 26 (*RPC*, 2nd ser., iv, 500)

Doctors

doctor, unnamed	1579 n.d. (*Common Good*, 41) 1581 n.d. (ibid., 42)
Miller, James, MA, d	*before* 1613 Nov 11 (295, 269)
Sibbald, Henry, MA, d	1623 Jul 7 (447, 363v) *'last doctour'* 1626 Nov 3 (B13/10/2, unfoliated)
Lindsay, Robert, MA, d	1625 Mar 25 (418, 8v) 1626 Nov 21 (RS50/2, 337v)
Morris, John, MA, d	1626 Nov 3 (B13/10/2, unfoliated) 1633 Aug 26 (RS37/5, 112)

Music School

schoolmaster, unnamed	1581 n.d. (*Common Good*, 42)
Sibbald, James, MA, d	1613 Aug 21 (226, 56v) 1614 Aug 2 (307, 85)
Tullidaff, Alexander, MA	1626 Dec 18 (393, 80v) 1628 Mar 1 (410, 409)

Doctor

Mitchell, John, d	1627, 1628 n.d. (*Common Good*, 42)

CURRIE (par), Midlothian

Graham, John	1607 Apr 6 (RS24/8, 188v) 1609 Aug 13 (190, 330v)
Napier, Alexander	1620 Mar 5 (293, 312)
Moffat, George	1626 Dec 12 (RS25/11, 345v)

DAILLY (par), Ayrshire

Mure, Thomas	1628 Sep 22 (416, 321v) 1630 Feb 25 (RS60/2, 87v)

DALGINROSS, Perthshire MRf NN7721
Comrie par

Riddoch, William	1603 Aug 4 (RS48/2, 315v)

DALKEITH (par), Midlothian
Grammar School

Haistie (Hastings), George, MA (Ed 1587), later min of Temple	1589/90 Feb 16 (GD150/2212) 1602 May 26 (ibid.)
Nimble, Alexander, MA	1602 Dec 21 (98, 176) 1603 Feb 18 (94, 5)
Douglas, John, MA	1604 Feb 21 (RS24/3, 345)
Johnston, David	1607 Nov 28 (148, 352)
student	1608 Jan 4 (195, 194v)
Wilkie, John, MA	1612 Feb 15 (NP1/68, 36) 1613 Mar 1 (206, 440)
Abercrombie, Robert, MA	1618 May 28 (308, 124) 1641 Jul 7 (538, 261)

Doctors

Calderwood, James, d	1597/8 Feb 15 (62, 338)
Livingstone, David, d	1614 Dec 8 (243, 48)
Austin or Ogston (Oisteane), George, d	1630 Jul 4 (452, 442)

Music School

Blacklaw, Daniel, r	1601 Jun 1 (in error given as master of grammar school, RS25/4, 241) 1608 Apr 22 (CC8/8/44, 44v)

DALMENY (par), Midlothian

Graham, Charles	1630 Apr 28 (435, 145v)
Marshall, James	1612 Jul 2 (203, 113v)

DALRY (par), Ayrshire

schoolmaster, unnamed	1612 Oct 12 (CC9/7/14, 79v) 1617 May 3 (CC9/7/14, 46)
Bell, Patrick, MA	1623 Feb 10 (RS12/2, 473)
Forest, William, MA (Gl 1612)	1625 Dec 27 (RS12/3, 524)
Garven, James, MA	1630 Jun 7 (442, 261v)

DALRY, ST JOHN'S CLACHAN (par), Kirkcudbrightshire
(later called Dalry par)

Crawford, George	1605 May 18 (108, 254v)
Cauldcleuch, William	1618 Nov 1 (348, 362)
Mar, Andrew	1619 Nov 2 (307, 240) 1626 Dec 1 (447, 448v)
Smith, Abraham	1628 Dec 8 (RS1/25, 122v) 1631 Jun 2 (449, 344v)
Cairns, Alexander	1632 May 16 (491, 198)

Doctors

Newall, John, d	1608 Apr 25 (CC8/8/45, 84)
Herries, Robert, MA, d	1622 Mar 17 (390, 487) May 16 (366, 168v)

DALSERF (par), Lanarkshire

Good, Stephen, n	1618 Nov 21 (377, 128) 1621 Jun 11 (348, 418)

DALVEEN, Dumfriesshire MRf NS8806

Durisdeer par

Latimer, Andrew	1624 Dec 4 (370, 98v)

DEAN VILLAGE, *see* Edinburgh

DEER (par), Aberdeenshire

Pettindreich, Alexander, sir	*died before* 1574 Jun 24 (*RSS*, vi, 2556)
Roche (Richie?), William, MA	1606 Apr 19 (209, 262v) 1607 Jan 12 (137, 168v)
order for school	1608 May 5 (CH2/89/1(1), 103v)
school vacant	1609 Jun 15 (CH2/89/1(1), 122) 1610 Jul 5 (ibid., 133)
schoolmaster	1613 Jul 5 (CH2/89/1(2), 148)
'na schoull throw want of provision to the maister of it', i.e. probably no settled master in charge, cf. Davidson (*below*)	1614 May 19 (CH2/89/1(2), 160)
Brown, John, MA, later min of New Deer	1615 Jan 22 (SC1/60/2, 118v) 1619 Oct 19 (RS5/2, 97v)
student	1620 Nov n.d. (SC1/60/4, 66v)
school	1621 May 3 (CH2/89/1(2), 264) June date torn (ibid., 266v)
Smyth, William, MA	1622 n.m. 3 (341, 312) 1622 Jul 11 (357, 318v)
Clark, George, MA	1631 Oct 12 (449, 380v) Oct 27 (SC1/60/9, 152)

Doctor

Davidson, Robert	1611 May 23 (215, 117) 1625 Jun 22 (386, 330v)

DINGWALL (par), Ross and Cromarty

Adamson, Donald, exh	*before* 1569 Jun 21 (*RSS*, vi, 657) 1580 n.d. (W. Macgill, *Old Ross-shire and Scotland*, Inverness 1909, no. 39)
schoolmaster, unnamed	1573–4 (CH4/1/1, i, 101v)

DIRLETON (par), East Lothian
(incorporating Gullane 1612)

Nicolson, George	1602 Dec 15 (116, 200v) 1605 Nov 8 (114, 58v)
Duncan, Thomas	1605 Apr 10 (112, 428v) *before* 1606 Jul 11 (123, 250)
Donaldson, Robert	1608 Jun 20 (151, 303v) Nov 12 (RS24/10, 295)
Marshall, James	1616 May 20 (311, 305) 1623 May 17 (333, 150)

Doctor

Nicolson, Roger *or* George, d	1630 Dec 6 (CC8/8/55, 18v)

DOLPHINTON (par), Lanarkshire

Wilson, Archibald, MA	1623 Jan 18 (RS1/12, 208v)
Somerville, John, MA	1624 Apr 29 (RS1/13, 170v) May 8 (RS40/2A, 193)
Young, Thomas	1631 Jul 19 (RS1/31, 241v)

DORE, Shetland MRf HU2176
Northmaven par

Bruce, Alexander, n	1582 day and month torn off (NP3/1, 41) *demitted* 1582/3 Jan 23 (CS1/3(1) *'in Yetland'* 1640 Oct 13 (533, 30)

DORNOCH (par), Caithness

Pape, William, MA (SA 1587), min of Dornoch 1588, min of Nigg 1613	1585 (C.D. Bentinck, *Dornoch Cathedral and Parish*, Inverness 1926, 169) before 1600 (D. Mathew, *Scotland under Charles I*, London 1955, 172)
student	1628 Dec 28 (466, 400)
Gordon, Gilbert, MA, s	1621 Nov 7 (336, 212) 1623 Nov 25 (351, 538)
Hossack, John, MA	1625 May 12 (RS37/3, 106)
Innes, Robert	1632 (472, 160) 1633 Dec 6 (497, 244)

DORNOCK (par), Dumfriesshire

Rae, Nicol	1633 Sep 13 (489, 259)

DOUGLAS (par), Lanarkshire

Brown, William, n	1606 Apr 23 (157, 372v)
Brown, John	*before* 1613 Feb 28 (217, 392)
Good, John	1613 Jan 20 (217, 374v) *May 8*[3]

---

[3] Reference missing: see Preface.

Good, Stephen   1616 May 8 (263, 35v)
Wilson, John, MA   1613 Dec 23 (259, 225v) 1614 Jul 23 (239,
                           293v)
Rule, John   1619 Jan 6 (359, 124)
Stark *or* Spark, James   1629 Dec 24 (429, 356v) 1633 Dec 20 (476,
                           39)

DOUNE, Perthshire MRf NN7201
Kilmadock par
Leckie, William   1607 Feb 27 (139, 270)
Newton, Thomas, d, n   1625 Aug 15 (RS58/3, 361) 1634 May 30
                           (523, 150)

DOWHILL, Kinross-shire MRf NT1197
Cleish par
Murray, William or   1616 Feb 20 (245, 261v) Dec 22 (CC/20/4/6,
  Robert, MA   408)

DRAFFAN, Lanarkshire MRf NS7949
Lesmahagow par
Fairie, James   1623 Feb 18 (CC10/5/5, 23)

DREGHORN (par), Ayrshire
Doctor
Simpson, William, d   1619 Jul 9 (328, 161)

DREM (par), East Lothian
Edmeston, William   1629 Oct 5 (452, 145)

DRUMBANE, Ayrshire MRf NS2617
Maybole par
Doctor
Shillinglaw, John, d   1605 Dec 12 (230, 185)

DRUMELZIER (par), Peebleshire
Greig, William, MA   1622 Apr 20 (RS1/10, 112)

DRUMEND, Perthshire MRf NN9920
Findo Gask par
Rae, Alexander   1613 Jan 28 (210, 53)

DRUMLANRIG, Dumfriesshire MRf NS8600 (Drumlanrig Woods)
Durisdeer par
Black, John   1619 Jun 30 (RS1/3, 309)

DRUMLITHIE, Kincardineshire MRf NO7880
Glenbervie par

Sibbald, Alexander, MA	1610 Nov 27 (191, 57)
Steven (Stewin), Andrew, MA	1615 Jun 15 (248, 398)
Petrie, Alexander, MA	1617 Jun 26 (336, 212) Aug 25 (294, 358)
Sibbald, James, MA	1619 Jul 17 (RS7/2, 199)
Rait, William, MA	1620 Mar 24 (333, 108v) 1621 Nov n.d. (328, 225)
Chalmer, John, MA	1630 May 30 (540, 101) 1633 Jun 8 (RS7/3, 306v)

DRUMELLAN, Ayrshire MRf NS3110
Dalry par

Miller, John	1631 Jun 28 (RS12/5, 133v)

DRUMNAGAIR, Kincardineshire MRf NO6868
Marykirk par

Innes, John	1616 Jul 3 (CC3/9/5)

DRUMRASH, Kirkcudbrightshire MRf NX6871
Parton par

Bell, John, MA	1614 Jan 12 (237, 92)

DRUMWHINDLE, Aberdeenshire MRf NJ9235
Ellon par

Christie, John	1617 Feb 26 (CH2/146/2, 125v) *discharged* Mar 12 (ibid.)

DRYBURGH, Berwickshire MRf NT5932
Mertoun par

Wighton, Patrick	1608 Mar 1 (147, 124)

DRYMEN (par), Stirlingshire

Jackson, John	1610 May 25 (209, 363)
Leckie, William, r	1622 May 8 (RS58/2, 321) 1623 Feb 7 (345, 250v)
Ferguson, Allan, MA	1624 May 18 (480, 251)
Boyd, Robert, MA	1625 Nov 19 (444, 388) 1628 Jun 15 (451, 331)

DUDDINGSTON (par), Midlothian

Graham, George	1620 Jan 18 (RS1/5, 235v)
Frank, Andrew	1621 Apr 17 (347, 280)

Lynn, John   1622 Feb 1 (320, 64v) 1635 May 22 (491, 428) 1662 n.d. (W. Baird, *Annals of Duddingston and Portobello*, Edinburgh 1898, 249)

DUMBARTON (par), Dunbartonshire
(school in parish church)

Maxwell, Robert, MA	before 1576 Apr 7 (GUL, MS Murray 623, 232, *cited from* Acts and Decreets, CS7/62, 141)
Drummond (Dormond), Robert, MA, c, n	1576 Apr 7 (GUL, MS Murray, 623, 232) 1580/1 Mar 8 (GUL, MS General, 643, 623)
Cunningham, James, MA, c, n	1583 Apr 21 (B16/1/4, 61) 1605 Jan 19 (158, 70)
Watson, Robert, MA (Gl 1610)	1613 Dec 4 (228, 522v) 1615 Mar 25 (320, 200)
Semple, Andrew, later min of Bonhill	1616 (F. Roberts, *The Grammar School of Dumbarton*, Dumbarton 1948, 15) 1620 May n.d. (*Dumbarton Common Good Accounts 1614–1660*, ed. F. Roberts and I.M. MacPhail, Dumbarton 1972, 26)
students	1619 Dec 20 (333, 265)
Stirling, William, MA (Gl 1616)	1620 May 2 (300, 221) 1629 May n.d. (Roberts, 15)
Semple, Henry, MA (Gl 1627), later min of Killearn	1629–1639 Aug (Roberts, 15)

Doctors

Biggar, Robert	1599 Nov 13 (B16/1/4, 172)
Dalzell, Kentigern, MA	1603 Oct 6 (B16/1/4, 264) 1604 Mar 3 (B16/1/4, 271v)

Music School

Fiddes, Alexander	1618 Nov 23 ('Protocol Book of Robert Brown' *Ayr-Galloway Coll.*, ix, 79)

Dame School

Abernethie, Isobel	1623 n.d. (*Dumbarton Common Good Accounts*, 35)

DUMFRIES (par), Dumfriesshire

Dalzell, Ninian, MA, n, min of Dumfries 1567 min of Caerlaverock 1574	1558 Nov 8 (G.W. Shirley 'Fragmentary Notices of the Burgh School of Dumfries', *Dumfriesshire Trans.* xxi, 1939, 112–13) 1587 Apr 21 (55, 60v)

Glen, David or James, MA (1585)	1582 n.d. (*inscription* in Thomas de Vio: Commentary on the Gospels, Paris 1543, *c.18.26, 290v, EUL)
Sinclair, Archibald	1590/1 Mar 24 (PS62, 22)
Gledstanes, Herbert, MA (Gl 1590), n, min of Caerlaverock c.1612, min of Troqueer 1613	1601 Nov 13 (CC8/8/37) 1618 May 26 (300, 40)
students	1620 Jun 15 (308, 168) 1620 Jul 24 (330, 333) 1621 Feb 13 (306, 60) 1621 May 29 (385, 366) 1622 May 20 (357, 239v) 1622 Jun 17 (386, 222)
schoolmaster, unnamed	1627, 1628 n.d. (*Common Good*, 43)
MacGeorge (McIvir, McJorr, Makjore), James, r, also taught Music, prev student	1629 Dec 5 (436, 253) 1638 Sep 11 (542, 68)

Doctors

Thomson, John, d	1617 Oct 2 (Shirley, 118) 1624 Dec 15 (*Lanark Testaments*, 119)
McKinnell, John, n, d, under teacher, prev student	1619 Aug 15 (294, 25) 1621 Apr 21 (316, 1v)
Armstrong, John, d, under teacher, prev student	1622 Nov 11 (RS1/2, 241v) 1630 n.d. (466, 240)

Music School

schoolmaster, r, unnamed	1612–13 (Shirley, 117) 1633, 1634 n.d. (*Common Good*, 43)

Presumably **Adventure School**

Ellem *or* Altem *or* Aitken, John, MA (SA 1580 or 1581)	1623 Mar 3 (355, 268) 1626 Jun 3 (405, 315v) 1630 Sep 9 (Shirley, 118)

Writing School

Diggens, Edward	*before* 1607 Oct 7 (*Bon Record*, 40)

DUN (par), Angus

Jameson, John	1615 Feb 27 (CC3/9/4) 1617 Feb 1 (269, 337)

DUNBAR (par), East Lothian
Grammar School

Simpson, Andrew, min 1564	1575 Dec 15 (*RPC*, ii, 478)
Home, Alexander, MA	*succeeded* Simpson (J. Miller, *The Lamp of Lothian*, Haddington 1844, 445n.)
school and schoolmaster	1581 n.d. (*Common Good*, 43)
Dishington, Andrew	1594 Apr 3 (*Records of the Synod of Lothian and Tweeddale 1589–1596, 1640–1645*, ed. J. Kirk, Stair Society 1977, 74) *found unsuitable to be minister or schoolmaster* Oct 1 (ibid., 77)
Manuel, John, MA	1597 Jun 21 (*RMS*, vi, 713) 1606 Jun 30 (RS24/5, 82)
Dalrymple, James, MA	1607 Oct 17 (NP1/58, 50) 1609 Jul 6 (181, 4v)
Hume (Home), Alexander, MA	1616 Dec 2 (NP1/55, 103v) 1633 Jun 8 (B18/1/1, 204v)
Foirbrand, Thomas	1631 Apr 29 (445, 264)

Doctors

Kellie, John, MA (SAM 1578), d	1582 n.d. ('Ane forme of sindrie materis to be usit in the elderschip', *Wodrow Misc.*, i, 537–8) 1591 Oct 22 (*RMS*, vi, 1952)
Anderson, William	1598 May 22 (68, 157v) 1603 Dec 8 (272, 122v)
Fairlie, James	1612 Aug 12 (202, 29v) 1614 Mar 17 (B18/1/1, 37v)
Home, Nathaniel, d, pr, r	1614 Feb 21 (B18/1/1, 36v)
Miller, Alexander, MA, d	1616 Feb 5 (B18/1/1, 55)
Rewit, Alexander, MA	1621 May 23 (RS40/2A, 61v)

Music School

Lawrie (Lowrie), James *'teicher of the Inglische Schoole and musick'*	1607 Oct 12 (146, 21) 1620 Jun 1 (294, 337) 1621 n.d. (*Common Good*, 43)

English School (also known as the 'Scottis Skuill')

Forrester, James	1618 Jul 13 (287, 418) 1620 May 22 (RS25/3, 140)
'teicher of the Inglische Schoole and musick'	1621 n.d. (*Common Good*, 43)
schoolmaster, unnamed	1627 n.d. (*Common Good*, 43)
Christie, Alexander	1633 Sep 1 (468, 325)

DUNBENNAN (par), Aberdeenshire MRf NJ5040

schoolmaster, unnamed   1631 n.d. (I.J. Simpson, *Education in Aberdeenshire before 1872*, London 1947, 12)

DUNBLANE (par), Perthshire
Grammar School

Nevay (Nevene), Duncan, MA (AbK), r   1562 May 12 (5, 196v) 1591/2 Feb 10 (PS63, 174v)

Young, Andrew, MA, min   *made contract with Duncan Nevay to teach Grammar School in return for granting Nevay a pension* 1593 Apr 18 (CH2/722/3, unfoliated)

Buchanan, William, MA   *before* 1594 Jul 3 (CH2/722/2, unfoliated)

Clark, Thomas, MA, *see below*   *before* 1594 Jul 3 (CH2/722/2, unfoliated)

Niven, James, MA, n, son of Duncan Nevay   1598 n.d. (CH2/722/3, unfoliated) 1605 Jul 29 (RS43/4, 165)

student   1607 Jun 5 (135, 207v)

Clark, Thomas, MA, *see above*   1627 Jan 10 (RS50/2, 376v)

Doctor

Barbour, John, d   1605 Jun 10 (146, 16) 1606 Aug 26 (125, 366)

DUNDEE (par), Angus
Grammar School

Buchan, John   1553 May 26 (A. Maxwell, *Old Dundee: prior to the Reformation*, Edinburgh 1891, 152) *reappointed* late 1560 (ibid., 155)

Macgibbon, Thomas, MA   *before* 1555 Nov 15 (*Old Dundee*, 153) *dismissed* late 1560 (ibid., 155)

Hepburn, Alexander, MA   1562 Dec 23 (*Old Dundee*, 155)

school   1563/4 Mar 16 (A. Maxwell, *The History of Old Dundee*, Edinburgh 1884, 88)

schoolmaster, unnamed   1564 Jun 12 (*History*, 88)

Ramsay, Thomas   1566 Apr 6 (*History*, 89) *resigned by* 1591 Oct 21 (ibid., 92)

Nairn, David, MA;
Strachan, Alexander, MA;
Wallace, Robert, MA;
Stewart, Walter, MA   *all nominated* 1591 Oct 21 (*History*, 92)

Cheyne, Thomas   1579 Dec 2 (176, 30v)

grammar school   1594 Jun 25 (*History*, 93)

Duncan, Andrew, MA   1595/6 Mar 1 (dedication in his *Latinae Grammaticae pars prior*, Edinburgh 1595) 1597

	Apr 13 (dedication in his *Studiorum Puerilium Clavis*, Edinburgh 1597)
Hayne, Alexander	1595/6 Jan 24 (63, 396v) 1597 Jun 25 (61, 106)
Lindsay (Lyn), David, MA, later min, bishop of Brechin 1619	*appointed* 1597 n.d. (*History*, 324) *resigned* 1606 Mar 23 (ibid.)
Nairn, Robert, MA	1607 Apr 14 (*History*, 331) *dismissed* 1610 Dec 18 (ibid., 332)
Gleg (Glen, Greig), James, MA, reg	1610 Dec 18 (*History*, 332) *died* c.1653 (ibid., 335)
Goldman, Robert, b	1609 May 24 (165, 38)
Croal, John	1618 Sep 11 (337, 133v)
Yeaman, David, b	1624 Sep 14 (373, 385)

Doctors

doctors, unnamed	1560 May 28 (*Old Dundee*, 155) 1562 Dec 23 (ibid., 156)
Matthew, David *and two others, unnamed*	1564 Jun 12 (*History*, 88)
Duncan, William, d, b	1590 Sep 24 (36, 191)
Morgan (Morgound), David, d	1595 Mar 31 (51, 333) 1599 Dec 6 (GD48/727)
Sibbald, Archibald, d	1599 Dec 6 (GD48/727)
Dunmore, Alexander, d	1601 May 30 (136, 321)
doctors, unnamed	1603 Jul 12 (*History*, 324)
Dunmore, John, d	1603 Apr 29 (RS48/2, 212) 1605 Nov 14 (158, 162v)
Ferguson, James, MA, d	1604 Nov 8 (135, 268) 1606 Jul 30 (*RPC*, 2nd ser., vii, 206)
Wright, James, d	1605 May 20 (108, 285)
McLaren, George, d	1612 Jan 18 (280, 312v) May 14 (226, 244)
Dewar, George, d	1615 May 8 (242, 61) Jul 5 (277, 123)
Ramsay, Silvester, MA, d	1624 Apr 1 (CC3/9/7) Apr 17 (ibid.)
Busbie, Alexander, d	1624 Aug 4 (RS31/5, 253) 1626 Jul 14 (428, 240)

Music School

| Williamson, James or John, n | 1594/5 Jan 8 (67, 367v) 1603 Jul 12 (*History*, 336) |
| Mow, John, MA, b, pr, r in East Kirk and in West Kirk, *also taught reading and writing* | 1609 Oct 10 (*History*, 337) 1637 Aug 22 (ibid., 339) *died before* 1647 Nov 23 (ibid., 339) |

Doctors
Campbell, Archibald, d   1622 Jun 17 (364, 108v)

Dame School
school   1594 Jun 25 (*History*, 93)

Adventure Schools
Soutar, John   *prohibited* 1566 Apr 6 (*History*, 89)
schools   1594 Jun 25 (*History*, 93)
Spens, James, MA   1609 Sep 21 (173, 452v)

DUNDEE, HILL OF MRf NO3931 (Dundee Law)
Dundee par
Fithie, John   c.1563 (A. Maxwell, *Old Dundee: prior to the
                                Reformation*, Edinburgh 1891, 156)
Thomson, William   1623 Nov 8 (366, 161)

DUNDEUGH, Kirkcudbrightshire MRf NX6087
Apparently in Dalry, St John's Clachan par (later in Kells par)
McMichael, James   1615 Jun 18 (261, 52)

DUNFERMLINE (par), Fife
Grammar School
Henryson (Henderson),   1563 Aug 21 (CS7/51, 160–1) 1573 Oct 26
   John, n, monk   (NP2/1, 28)
Christison, John, MA, exh,   1573 Jun 11 (CS7/51, 160–1)
   in dispute with Henryson
school   1575 Oct 25 (*Dunfermline Recs.*, 13)
Fairfull, John, MA (SAL   1579 May 5 (NP2/2, 127) 1587 Apr 5 (*Parish
   1570), n, min of   Registers of Dunfermline, 1561–1700*, ed.
   Aberdour   H. Paton, SRS 1911, 85)
   1587, min of Dunfermline
   1598, min of Anstruther
   Wester 1610
Dalgleish, James, MA   1588 Sep 5 (102, 190) 1610 Oct 3 (*Parish
                                Registers*, 138)
Matheson, John, 'wrytter'   1608 Jan 14 (*Dunfermline Recs.*, 45)
student   1609 Nov 26 (181, 381v) 1623 May 31 (349,
                                138)
schoolmaster, unnamed   1610 n.d. (R. Brown, *The History of the Paisley
                                Grammar School*, Paisley 1875, 43)
Smyth, William, MA   *applied* 1610 Dec 12 (J.M. Webster, *Dunfermline*

	Abbey, Dunfermline 1948, 179) 1616 Mar 17 (*Parish Registers*, 160)
students	1617 Jan 11 (419, 226)
Sibbald, James, MA, min of Torryburn and Crombie 1629	1618 Apr 21 (*Parish Registers*, 168) 1628 Oct 30 (423, 145)
Ready, James, MA	1628 Oct 30 (423, 143) 1635 Dec 30 (516, 468)

Doctors

Durie, Robert, MA, d, i, min of Abercrombie 1588, min of Anstruther Wester 1592	1596 Dec 12 (CC8/8/30)
Walker, John, MA, d	1603 Dec 3 (109, 135v) 1604 Dec 19 (CC8/8/40, 16v)
Hislop, John, d, i	1608 Jul 13 (CC8/8/44, 358v) 1613 Apr 23 (213, 402v)
Anderson, John, d	1632 Jan 11 (*Parish Registers*, 252)

Music School

mortification for master	1610 n.d. (*Dunfermline Recs.*, 118)
Cullen, William, MA	1612 Feb 8 (321, 21v) 1616 Nov 16 (347, 279)
doctor, unnamed	1620 Nov 24 (*Dunfermline Recs.*, 129)
Tullidaff, Alexander	1621 Jul 11 (NP1/189, 33v)
Tullidaff, Stephen	*presented* 1626 Nov 27 (*Dunfermline Recs.*, 156) *demitted* 1630 Dec 20 (ibid., 166)
Anderson, Robert	1631 Feb 11 (*Dunfermline Recs.*, 166–7) 1637 Jan 25 (*Parish Registers*, 283)

Writing School

Matheson, John;	1607 n.d. (*Dunfermline Recs.*, 50) 1608 Jan 14 (ibid., 45)

DUNGLASS, East Lothian MRf NT7671
Oldhamstocks par
Grammar School (in Collegiate Church or at Oldhamstocks)

Hepburn, Thomas, MA	1577 May 25 (*RSS*, vii, 1042)

DUNINO (par), Fife

Killoch, Robert, MA	1631 Jul 7 (451, 366)
Watson, Charles	1624 Jul 5 (CS15/278)

DUNKELD (par), Perthshire

'King's school'	1567 (CH4/1/1, i, 5) 1587/8 Feb 22 (ibid.)
Hepburn, Alexander, MA	1572/3 Feb 29 (CH2/621/69)
school	1588 Jul 6 (PS1/57/146)
Glass, William, MA, min	1590 May 11 (PS60, 138)
Stewart, Walter, MA, n	1590/1 Mar 12 (NP1/54, 2v) 1605 Jul 9 (C.P. Stewart, *Memoirs of the Stewarts of Forthergill*, Edinburgh 1879, 114)
Glass, William, MA, prev student	1594 May 26 (PS66, 134)
MacLagan, Duncan, MA	1607 May 29 (146, 314)
students	1609 Dec 9 (203, 182v) 1610 Jun 5 (232, 311)
Anderson, Thomas, MA	1611 Jul 10 (192, 128)
students	1617 Aug 23 (RS49/4, 112) 1620 May 16 (RS49/3, 290) 1622 Apr 15 (341, 110v) 1623 Sep 20 (361, 44v) 1625 Apr 13 (RS50/3, 173)
Ireland, Alexander, MA	1628 Jul 14 (RS1/25, 268)
Crichton, Andrew, MA	1632 Oct 12 (RS50/6, 170v) 1636 Jun 3 (542, 153)

DUNLAPPIE, *see* Stracathro

DUNLOP (par), Ayrshire

Loudon, John	1622 n.d. (NP3/3, unfoliated)
Paterson, John, MA	1629 May 20 (CS7/535, 92)

DUNNIKEIR, Fife MRf NT2894
Kirkcaldy par

Davidson, Robert	1624 Jan 2 (NP1/189, 61v)

DUNNINALD, *see* Inchbrayock

DUNNING (par), Perthshire

Yett, John	1610 Nov 28 (*RMS*, vii, 434) 1617 Sep 14 (CC6/5/4, 234)

DUNNOTTAR (par), Kincardineshire
Steven, Andrew, MA   1621 Oct 20 (316, 400v)

DUNROBIN, Sutherland MRf NC8500
Golspie par

Gray, Robert, MA	1618 Apr 6 (RS37/1, 40) May 13 (ibid., 118)

DUNS (par), Berwickshire

Hamilton, Patrick, MA	1582 Aug 23 (21, 3)
Gates, James, MA	1596 Nov 29 (77, 144)
Crichton, George	1600 Aug 2 (RH6/3716)
Sinclair, Samuel, MA	1601 Jul 5 (107, 253) 1602 Sep 30 (97, 299v)
Houston *alias* Miller, Leonard or Bernard, later min of Ellem	1604 Dec 24 (CC8/8/39, unfoliated) 1614 Jun 8 (223, 201)
Wallace, Cuthbert	1610 Apr 13 (195, 67)
Swinton, Walter, MA	1613 Oct 9 (291, 284) 1621 Dec 11 (RS18/1, 226v)
Fairlie, James	1622 Jul 31 (463, 237) 1625 Mar 9 (SC60/56/2, 247v)
Wilson, William, r, simultaneously at Edrom	1630 Nov n.d. (*RPC*, 2nd ser., iv, 60)
Colville, Patrick, MA, later min of Beith	1633 Feb 9 (465, 181) Jun 27 (37, 204v)

DUNSCORE (par), Dumfriesshire

Hogg, Thomas, MA, r	1629 Sep 10 (423, 448) Nov 8 (458, 27v)

DUNSYRE (par), Lanarkshire

Barton (Bartrum), Robert	1622 Feb 4 (CC14/5/2) 1633 Sep 17 (RS1/38, 30)

DUPPLIN (par), Perthshire
(united to Aberdalgie 1618)

Henry, James	1633 Nov 22 (RS1/38, 200)

DURIE, Fife MRf NO3702
Scoonie par

Hayne, Alexander, MA, s	1610 Jan 31 (171(2), 290) Jul 3 (225, 351v)
Wedderburn, James, MA	1613 Aug 5 (219, 7) 1614 Feb 12 (229, 347)
Jameson, John	1614 Nov 11 (305, 314)

DURISDEER (par), Dumfriesshire

Black, Thomas	1624 May 2 (366, 146) Dec 4 (370, 98v)

DYSART (par), Fife

Strang, Henry, MA	1579 Dec 15 (*Notices from the Local Records of Dysart*, ed. W. Muir, Maitland Club 1853, 39)
Anderson, William, MA	1586 Apr *or* May n.d. (CH4/1/1, ii, 144v)
Peebles, Andrew, MA	1600 Nov 30 (87, 262v)

Simpson, James, MA   1605 May 24 (126, 144)
Melville, Thomas   1606 Dec 6 (135, 26)
Lamont, Allan, MA   c.1617–19 (RS31/4, i, 123) 1629 Jan 1 (RS31/7,
                            425)
Wells, William, d   1628 Sep 29 (RS31/7, 332v)
Littlejohn, John, MA   1631 Aug 8 (RS1/31, 313v) 1632 Jun 11
                            (RS1/33, 289v)

Doctor
order for doctor   1600 Nov 30 (87, 262v)
Gaw *or* Gow, John, b, d   1612 Dec 19 (208, 307v) 1633 Jul 10 (462, 423)

EAGLESHAM (par), Renfrewshire
Semple, John, r   1630 May 10 (RS1/28, 308)
Doctor
Drummond, John, d   1622 Apr 26 (356, 16v)

EARLSTON (par), Berwickshire
Hislop, William   1607 n.d. (239, 150v) 1619 May 27 (295, 133v)

EARNOCK, Lanarkshire MRf NS7153 (Meikle Earnock)
Hamilton par
Glassford, John   *before* 1619 May 8 (CC9/14/11, 270)

EAST BARNS, East Lothian MRf NT7176
Dunbar par
Brown, John   1582 Jun 5 (GD1/382/3)
Lowrie, Thomas   c.1600 (*Select Justiciary Cases, 1624–50*, ed. S.A.
                            Gillon et al., Stair Society 1953, i, 97–102)
Home, James   1608 May 22 (170, 307)
Inglis, James   1612 Apr 13 (248, 60) 1614 Jan 6 (230, 71v)
Morton, George   1620 Dec 23 (RS25/4, 70v) 1622 Nov 25
                            (RS25/7, 148v, 149)
Fairlie, James   1629 Jun 14 (A.I. Ritchie, *The Churches of St
                            Baldred*, Edinburgh 1881, 217)

EAST KILBRIDE (par), Lanarkshire
Broom, John   1591 Aug 17 (CH2/722/2, unfoliated)
Bryce, George   1601 Jun 25 (86, 328v)
Bogle, John, MA (Gl 1607)   1607 Dec 8 (147, 66)
Hutcheson, Robert, MA   1621 Oct 31 (RS40/1, 224, 224v) 1622 Dec 6
                            (408, 287)
school   1627 Jun 7 (GUA, 39520, Report of East
                            Kilbride parish)

Hamilton, John, MA, r   1630 Nov 14 (525, 20) 1633 Mar 13 (RS1/36, 125v)

EAST LINTON, *see* Prestonkirk

EAST RESTON, Berwickshire MRf NT9061
Coldingham par
Neilson, Laurence   1593 May 23 (*Hist. MSS. Comm., Report on the Manuscripts of Colonel David Milne-Home*, 235)
Methven, Alexander, MA   1609 Jun 3 (210, 46) Jun 17 (213, 21v)
Cook, William   1619 Aug 5 (305, 475)

EAST WEMYSS, Fife MRf NO3396
Wemyss par
Blackwood, Adam   1629 Aug 17 (368, 448v)

EASTER BROCKHOLES, Berwickshire MRf NT8263 (Brockholes)
Coldingham par
Todd, James   1616 Jan 16 (262, 129)

EASTER DREM, East Lothian MRf NT5079 (Drem)
Athelstaneford par
Young, William   1616 May 12 (255, 202v)

EASTER POWRIE, Angus MRf NO4234 (Pourie Castle)
Presumably Murroes par
Mollison, Thomas, MA   1629 Oct 27 (NP1/71, 240)

ECCLES (par), Berwickshire
Black, George   1618 Jul 12 (292, 308v) 1622 Mar 31 (SC60/56/1, 87, 88)
Courtie, David   1609 Nov 4 (184, 109) 1612 Jun 30 (343, 163)

ECCLESGREIG (par), Angus
Jamie or Jameson, John   1614 Nov 30 (273, 49v)
Whittet (White),   1616 Apr 29 (267, 403v)
   Thomas, MA
Innes, John   1619 Jun 3 (327, 158v)
Stratton, David, MA   1620 Jan 20 (CC20/4/7, 446) 1621 Dec 10 (313, 384)

ECCLESMACHAN (par), West Lothian

reader-schoolmaster, no *maintenance*	1630 Aug 26 (A. Bain, *The Education Act of 1696 in West Lothian*, Dept of Educational Studies 1974, 72)

ECCLESIAMAGIRDLE, *see* Exmagirdle

ECKFORD (par), Roxburghshire

Stein, Robert	*unlicensed* 1608 Dec 21 (CH2/198/1, unfoliated) 1609 Sep 13 (ibid.)
Jaffrey, Adam	1624 Feb 2 (395, 398)

EDDERSTON, Peebleshire MRf NT2439

Peebles par

Kirk, John	1619 Apr 1 (309, 404v)

EDINBURGH COLLEGE/UNIVERSITY
Grammarians, Humanists

Newton, Adam, MA	1594–5 (*Edinburgh Burgh Recs.*, v, 116) *appointment frustrated by Town Council*
Rae, John, MA (Ed), reg, *see also* High School	1597 Dec 28 (*Edinburgh Burgh Recs.*, v, 188) 1606 Sep 17 (ibid., vi, 23) *died* 1630 Feb (W. Steven, *History of the High School of Edinburgh*, Edinburgh 1849, 49)
Colt, Blaise, MA	c.1606 Dec 12 (*Edinburgh Burgh Recs.*, vi, 25) *died* 1611 Feb 13 (ibid., 71)
Burnett, Robert, MA	c.1611 Jan 16 (*Edinburgh Burgh Recs.*, vi, 69) *demitted* 1616 Sep 3 (ibid., 148)
Rutherford, Samuel, MA	*forced to resign because of fornication* 1626 Feb 3 (*Edinburgh Burgh Recs.*, vi, 296)
Crawford, Thomas, MA (SA), *see also* High School	1626 Mar 29 (*Edinburgh Burgh Recs.*, vi, 303) 1638 Jul 7 (547, 417)
Armour, John, MA	1630 Mar 17 (*Edinburgh Burgh Recs.*, vii, 71) *resigned* 1633 Dec 6 (ibid., 136)
Gibson, Alexander, MA	1633 Dec 27 (*Edinburgh Burgh Recs.*, vii, 136) *resigned* 1636 (ibid., 183)

EDINBURGH
High School

Roberton, William, MA (Paris)	1547/8 Jan 10 (CS7/45, 36) *violently ejected* 1568 Aug 29 (ibid.) *restored by Lords of Council* 1569/70 Mar 18 (ibid., 236) *pensioned off by*

	town 1584 Mar 27 (*Edinburgh Burgh Recs.*, iv, 330)
Buchanan, Thomas, MA (SAM)	1568 Jul 28 (*Edinburgh Burgh Recs.*, iii, 250)
Rollok, Hercules (studied Law at Poitiers)	1584 May 9 (*Edinburgh Burgh Recs.*, iv, 340) *dismissed* 1596 Mar 26 (ibid., v, 155)
Haistie (Hastings), George, MA (Ed 1587), *see below*, later min of Temple	1588 Feb 26 (*Fasti*, i, 348)
Peacock, Laurence	1596 Mar 26 (*Edinburgh Burgh Recs.*, v, 155) 1628 Jul 13 (407, 356) *doctor of the High School* 1636 Jun 19 (514, 384)
Hume, Alexander, MA (SAM)	1596 Apr 23 (*Edinburgh Burgh Recs.*, v, 157) *demitted* 1606 Jun 28 (ibid., vi, 22)
Rae, John, MA (Ed), *see also* College	*forbidden to teach grammar* 1597 May 18 (*Edinburgh Burgh Recs.*, v, 188) 1606 Sep 17 (ibid., vi, 23) *died* 1630 Feb (Steven, *History of the High School of Edinburgh*, 49)
Brown, David, MA, master of writing, *see also* Writing School	1618 Jan 28 (*Edinburgh Burgh Recs.*, vii, 172) *resigned* 1619 Dec 18 (Edinburgh City Archives, Moses Bundle 204, vii, 7416–17)
Crawford, Thomas, MA (SA), *see also* College	1630 Feb 26 (*Edinburgh Burgh Recs.*, vii, 70) still in office 1640 (ibid., p. xlix)

Doctors

Drummond (Dormond), Robert, MA, *see also* Canongate High School	1555 (*Edinburgh Burgh Recs.*, ii, 368) *committed suicide* 1574 Apr 11 (J. Durkan, 'Scottish Reformers: the Less than Golden Legend', *IR*, xlv, 27–8)
master complained of lack of doctors and instructors; henceforth the Town Council to intervene in appointments	1579 Apr 29 (*Edinburgh Burgh Recs.*, iv, 106)
Kirkwood, George	1582 Jul 2 (39, 47) 1601 Jul 31 (82, 90)
Duncan, Thomas	1582 Jul 2 (39, 47)
Hislop, Patrick, *see also* Vernacular Schools (unassigned)	1582 Jul 2 (39, 47) *left* 1597 Jun 24 (59, 314)
Hilston, Simon	1583/4 Jan 20 (22, 17)
Hall, William	1583/4 Jan 20 (22, 17)
Colville, David	1593 May 26 (382, 431)
Monypenny, Patrick, MA	1597 Apr 10 (74, 28)

Balfour, John, MA   1597 May 18 (*Edinburgh Burgh Recs.*, v, 188)
                                     1599 Jan 17 (ibid., 241)
Haistie (Hastings),   1598 Jan 9 (*Edinburgh Burgh Recs.*, v, 226)
   George, MA, *see above*   1601 Nov 11 (ibid., 292)
Haistie, John, d, *see also*   *removed 'bent' unlawfully* 1601 Oct 30
   Canongate High School   (*Edinburgh Burgh Recs.*, v, 294)
Steven, Robert, MA (Ed)   1599 Jan 24 (*Edinburgh Burgh Recs.*, v, 241)
   see also Canongate
   High School
Clark, Robert, *see also*   1603 Jul 29 (139, 163) *left to teach independently*
   Edinburgh Vernacular   1607 Nov 12 (*Edinburgh Marriages*, 135)
   Schools (unassigned)
   and Canongate
   Vernacular Schools
Watson, William, s   1607 Nov 17 (140, 41)
Kinloch, Patrick, MA (Ed)   1613 Jan 14 (209, 274)
Ironside, John, MA (Ed)   *also student in Theology* 1615 Feb 9 (234, 152)
                                     died 1616 Nov 16 (CC8/8/52, 52)
Logan, James, MA (Ed)   1617 Mar 12 (*Edinburgh Burgh Recs.*, vi, 155)
Reid, Alexander, MA   1618 Aug 15 (376, 260) 1619 Aug 4 (*Edinburgh
                                     Burgh Recs.*, vi, 194)
Lawson, Thomas   1618 Aug 15 (376, 260) 1625 Jul 3 (375, 375)
Will, David, MA   1619 Aug 4 (*Edinburgh Burgh Recs.*, vi, 194)
                                     1625 Jul 3 (375, 375)
Spang, William, MA   1625 n.d. (*Edinburgh Burgh Recs.*, vii, 65)
   (Gl 1625), later min of   1630 Feb 19 (ibid.)
   Campvere
Fairlie, Robert, MA (Ed)   *resigned* 1627 Aug 15 (*Edinburgh Burgh Recs.*,
                                     vii, 31)
Hodges, James, MA, d   1627 Aug 15 (*Edinburgh Burgh Recs.*, vii, 31)
                                     1638 Apr 29 (*Edinburgh Marriages*, 331)
Newton, Archibald, MA   1630 Feb 19 (*Edinburgh Burgh Recs.*, vii, 65)
   (Ed)   1634 Feb 7 (ibid., 139)
Bishop, David, MA (Ed)   1630 Mar 12 (*Edinburgh Burgh Recs.*, vii, 71)
                                     1635
Feb 5 (*Edinburgh Marriages*, 61)
Douglas, Archibald, MA   1632 Nov 30 (*Edinburgh Burgh Recs.*, vii, 116)
   (Ed)
Adamson, James, MA (Ed)   1632 Nov 30 (*Edinburgh Burgh Recs.*, vii, 116)
                                     demitted 1634 Mar 26 (ibid., 141)

Music School

(in East Kirk of St Giles until 1611, then new school built in Kirkyard)

Henryson, Edward, sir, c	1551 Jul 31 (*RSS*, vi, 487) *died* c.1579 Aug 15 (*Edinburgh Testaments*, i, 128)
Buchan, Andrew, MA, pr	1579 Nov 18 (*Edinburgh Burgh Recs.*, iv, 126) *demitted* 1582 Aug 1 (ibid., 239)
Henryson, James, pr	1582 Aug 1 (*Edinburgh Burgh Recs.*, iv, 239) *died before* 1585/6 Feb 25 (ibid., 450)
Henryson (Henderson), Gilbert, pr, *see also* St Cuthbert's *and* St Giles *and* Vernacular Schools (unassigned)	1585/67 Feb 25 (*Edinburgh Burgh Recs.*, iv, 450) *died* 1589/90 Feb 7 (CC8/8/1, 53)
Cumming, David, pr	1585/6 Feb 25 (*Edinburgh Burgh Recs.*, iv, 450 1592 Apr 14 (49, 606)
Chalmer, John, MA, pr	1593 Nov 3 (*Edinburgh Burgh Recs.*, v, 103) 1596 Apr 14 (ibid., 156)
Cumming, William, pr	1596 Apr 9 (*Edinburgh Burgh Recs.*, v, 156) Jun 9 (54, 91)
Henryson, Alexander, pr *in two kirks*	1597 Jun 10 (*Edinburgh Burgh Recs.*, v, 191) *resigned* 1602 Jul 13 (ibid., 309)
Henryson, Samuel, r, *see also* St Giles	*elected* 1602 Jul 13 (*Edinburgh Burgh Recs.*, v, 309) *died before* 1609 Mar 8 (ibid., vi, 50)
Henryson, Patrick, MA (Ed), pr, r, simultaneously at St Giles *and* Trinity, *see also* St Cuthbert's	1609 Mar 8 (*Edinburgh Burgh Recs.*, vi, 50) 1612 Jun 27 (199, 35)
Troup, Walter	1616 Jul 31 (*Edinburgh Burgh Recs.*, vi, 144) *pension payment ceased by* 1625 (ibid., 216n.)
Crichton, James	*unofficial, banned* 1617 Aug 6 (*Edinburgh Burgh Recs.*, vi, 163) *still teaching* 1628 Apr 22 (RS25/13, 286)
Keith, James	*unofficial, banned* 1618 Nov 13 (*Edinburgh Burgh Recs.*, vi, 184) 1623 Sep 17 (382, 259)
Crichton, Andrew, s	1628 Apr 11 (RS25/13, 232)
Buccellis, Claude (Frenchman) instrumental music	1627 Jan 26 (*Edinburgh Burgh Recs.*, vii, 20)
Tullidaff, Stephen, *licensed*	1630 Dec 8 (*Edinburgh Burgh Recs.*, vii, 85)
Ritchie, Andrew, *licensed*	1632 May 1 (476, 68) 1633 Nov 27 (*Edinburgh Burgh Recs.*, vii, 135)

Writing School

(in one of the rooms in the High School)

Murdoch, William, MA	1593/4 Feb 8 (*Edinburgh Burgh Recs.*, v, 109)
	1594 Dec 27 (ibid., 126)
Fleming, Alexander	1594 Dec 27 (*Edinburgh Burgh Recs.*, v, 126)
Drury, Erasmus (Englishman)	1601 Feb 20 (*Edinburgh Burgh Recs.*, v, 282)
King, David, *see also* Vernacular Schools (unassigned)	*demitted* 1618 Jan 28 (*Edinburgh Burgh Recs.*, vi, 172)
Brown, David, MA, *see also* High School	1614 Nov 16 (*Edinburgh Burgh Recs.*, vi, 122) *moved to High School* 1618 Jan 28 (ibid., 172)

Vernacular Schools, Unassigned Masters

(also known as 'Vulgar' or 'Inglis' Schools)

Turnbull, William	1579 Jul n.d. (*Treasurer's Accounts*, xiii, 275)
	1579 Aug 12 (D. Moysie, *Memoirs of the Affairs of Scotland*, Maitland Club 1830, 24)
West (Wast), Thomas	1580 May 19 (CC8/17/2, 315)
Wilson, Roger *or* Robert	1581 Dec 25 (CS1/3(1), i, 158)
Black, John	1581/2 Jan 26 (*Edinburgh Burgh Recs.*, iv, 229) *died* 1602 Jan 28 (CC8/8/36)
Gillies, John, d	1581/2 Jan 26 (*Edinburgh Burgh Recs.*, iv, 229) 1585 Mar 30 (24, 179)
Henryson (Henderson), Gilbert (*given in error as* Cuthbert Sanderson), r (filled in for Cairns, r at St Giles and St Cuthbert's), *see also* St Cuthbert's *and* St Giles *and* Edinburgh Music School	1584 Sep 30 (*Edinburgh Burgh Recs.*, iv, 352) *licence to teach vulgar school* 1585/6 Feb 25 (ibid., 450)
Johnston, Simon	1586 Sep 7 (*Edinburgh Burgh Recs.*, iv, 479)
Ralston, James	1586 Sep 7 (*Edinburgh Burgh Recs.*, iv, 479) 1610 Jan 13 (168, 429)
Lothian, John	1586 Sep 7 (*Edinburgh Burgh Recs.*, iv, 479) 1587 Aug 14 (25, 231)
Muirhead, James, MA (Ed 1596), later min of Leith	1586 Sep 7 (*Edinburgh Burgh Recs.*, iv, 479)
Oliphant, William	1586 Sep 7 (*Edinburgh Burgh Recs.*, iv, 479) 1587 Aug 9 (38, 33)
Robieson, Andrew	1586 Sep 7 (*Edinburgh Burgh Recs.*, iv, 479)
Paterson, Thomas	1589 Sep 5 (*Edinburgh Burgh Recs.*, v, 3)

Miller, William	1595 Nov 26 (56, 113)
Oliphant, John	1595 Dec 4 (CC8/8/29, 57)
King, David, *see also* Writing School	1596 Mar 30 (57, 113) 1624 Mar 3 (376, 125)
Good, Thomas, s	1596 Mar 30 (57, 113)
Forest, Archibald	1596 Sep 3 (61, 8)
Burrell (Birrell), Robert, b, r, *see also* St Giles	1597 (CC8/17/4) *died* c.1605 ('The Diarey of Robert Birrel [*sic*], burgess of Edinburgh, 1532 –1605', in J.G. Dalgleish, *Fragments of the Scotish* [*sic*] *History*, Edinburgh 1798)
Hislop, Patrick, MA, n, *see also* Edinburgh High School	1598 Jun 17 (75, 212) 1616 Jun 20 (258, 106)
Gray, John, *see also* St Cuthbert's	1598 Aug 19 (69, 11) 1613 Jul 2 (226, 499v)
Hamilton, Robert	1599 Jul 31 (75, 325) 1602 Jun 25 (90, 124)
Moffat, James, s	1599 Jul 31 (75, 325) 1602 Jun 25 (90, 124)
Armour, John	*before* 1599 Nov 20 (*Edinburgh Apprentices*, 8)
Donaldson, Robert, *see also* Potterrow	1599 Aug 29 (*Edinburgh Marriages*, 193) 1612 Jan 15 (86, 142)
Fiddes, Robert	1600 Aug 26 (*Edinburgh Marriages*, 29)
Mather, Patrick, *see also* Canongate Vernacular Schools	1600 Sep 4 (86, 362) *died before* 1626 Oct 18 (*Edinburgh Apprentices*, 122)
Purves, James	1601 Jan 4 (148, 220) 1612 Aug 29 (202, 206)
Lowrie, John, *see also* Magdalene Chapel	1601 Jul 11 (86, 116) 1604 Jun 12 (110, 363)
Scott, Robert	1601 n.m. 12 (81(2), 13) 1609 Jul 18 (*Clan Campbell*, Edinburgh 1918, 113)
Hamilton, Patrick	1602 Jul 8 (326, 81)
Balfour, James	1603 Mar 21 (159, 197)
Laing, James, *see also* Trinity	1603 Apr 21 (156, 195)
Kirkcaldy, James	1603 Jun 9 (95, 366)
Carrick, John	1603 Nov 8 (103, 120)
Merser, Thomas, s	1603 Nov 8 (103, 120)
Davie, Matthew	1604 May 5 (139, 99) 1623 Feb 24 (345, 275)
Burnside, James, s	1604 May 5 (139, 99)
Little, Patrick	1604 May 23 (124, 2) 1622 Nov 30 (CC8/8/54, 73)
Kinghorn, Robert	1605 Dec 7 (146, 47) 1633 Dec 16 (475, 59)
Clark, Robert, *see also* Edinburgh High School	*from High School* 1607 Nov 12 (*Edinburgh Marriages*, 135) 1620 Mar 25 (307, 302)

and Canongate Vernacular
Schools

Cunningham, Donald	1608 Apr 26 (*Edinburgh Marriages*, 165) 1610 Dec 20 (ibid.)
Porteous, John	1609 Nov 10 (*Retours*, Edinburgh, no. 285)
Lightfoot, Alexander, s	1612 Jun 29 (227, 454) 1614 Jan 5 (230, 289)
Pilmure, James, s	1616 Nov 5 (258, 293) 1632 Jun 12 (494, 224)
Forrester, William, r	1620 Mar 17 (*Edinburgh Burgh Recs.*, vi, 205)
Dalzell, Alexander, r subdoctor	1620 Mar 25 (307, 302) 1633 Jul 18 (CS7/476, 244)
Arthur, Neil, pr, r, *see also* Canongate Vernacular Schools	1620 Dec 6 (*Edinburgh Burgh Recs.*, vi, 216) 1629 Apr 3 (CC8/10/9)
Lowrie, Adam	1623 Jan 31 (*Edinburgh Burgh Recs.*, vi, 240)
Colt, Adam, MA (Ed)	1623 Jul 23 (*Edinburgh Burgh Recs.*, vi, 244)
Arnott, John, s	1626 Dec 20 (341, 69)
Moore, John	1627 Jun 5 (*Edinburgh Marriages*, 499)
Moir, Richard	1626 Jul 1 (411, 157) 1627 Dec 21 (427, 274)
Hamilton, Andrew	1628 May 3 (415, 147)
Beg, Archibald	1628 Dec 28 (427, 309) 1633 Oct 3 (514, 163)
Fisher, James, MA (Ed)	1629 Feb 21 (*Edinburgh Burgh Recs.*, vii, 53) 1638 Jul 9 (528, 71)
schoolmaster, unnamed	1629 May 4 (424, 112)
Rule, John	1630 May 12 (*Edinburgh Burgh Recs.*, vii, 74)
Harper, Andrew, s	1631 Sep 14 (CC8/10/9)
Kilpatrick, James	1633 Aug 15 (474, 389)

French School

Inglis (Anglois, Langlois), Nicholas	1574 Sep 3 (*Edinburgh Burgh Recs.*, iv, p. 23) 1614 Jul 23 (*Edinburgh Testaments*, ii, 210)
Beaugrand, Jean de, *resided in Canongate though school was in Edinburgh*	1616 Jul 12 (*Edinburgh Burgh Recs.*, vi, 143) 1620 Nov 14 (382, 252)

Dutch School

Phorbous, David	'*Ressavis David Phorbous, Dutche scoilemaistir, for teaching the Dutch language within this burgh*' 1630 Mar 5 (*Edinburgh Burgh Recs.*, vii, 71)

Fencing School

Henderson, Thomas	'*maister of the fence scule*' denounced for *non-compearance* 1563 Oct 30 (Pitcairn, *Trials*, i (2), 436)

Rodger, John, *see also* Canongate Fencing School	1590/1 Feb 25 (RH6 and RH7) 1593/4 Jan 23 (CC8/8/26, 271)
Bannatyne, Gilbert, *master fencer*	1610 Mar 14 (*Edinburgh Burgh Recs.*, vi, 60)
Cameron, John, *master of defence*	'*scule of fence*' 1630 Sep 8 (*Edinburgh Burgh Recs.*, vii, 80)

EDINBURGH, ST GILES, EAST KIRK (?vernacular)
(in the former medieval Choir)

Burrell (Birrell), Robert, r, *see also* Vernacular Schools (unassigned)	1583 Oct 2 (RH6/2682, 2684)
Grinton (Bryntoun), Henry, d, r, *see also* Trinity	1594 Oct 23 (*Edinburgh Burgh Recs.*, v, 123)

EDINBURGH, ST GILES, MID KIRK

Watson, Thomas, r in St Giles *and* Kirk O'Field, *see also* Kirk O'Field	c.1595 (*Edinburgh Burgh Recs.*, v, 166) *forbidden to teach grammar* 1597 May 18 (ibid., 188)
Henryson (Henderson), Gilbert, pr, *see also* St Cuthbert's *and* Edinburgh Music School *and* Vernacular Schools (unassigned)	1586 Feb 25 (*Edinburgh Burgh Recs.*, iv, 450)
Henryson, Samuel, r, *see also* Edinburgh Music School	1602 Jul 13 (*Edinburgh Burgh Recs.*, v, 309) *died before* 1609 Mar 8 (ibid., vi, 50)
Henryson, Patrick, MA, pr, r, simultaneously at Trinity *and* Edinburgh Music School, *see also* St Cuthbert's	1609 Mar 8 (*Edinburgh Burgh Recs.*, vi, 50) *reader 'at the grit Kirk'* 1629 Sep 9 (ibid., vii, 59)

EDINBURGH, ST GILES, UPPER TOLBOOTH
(School transferred to Greyfriars in 1620)

Matheson, John	1601 Oct 3 (202, 373) 1638 May 1 (513, 318)
Morton, George, s	1601 Oct 3 (202, 373)
Stewart, George, s, *see also* Canongate Vernacular Schools	1610 Apr 11 (CC8/8/47, 159)

Dalzell, James, MA (Ed   1620 Jun 7 (351, 360)
    1603), s

EDINBURGH, GREYFRIARS
(School transferred from Upper Tolbooth in 1620)
Dalzell, James, r   1624 Jul 23 (387, 199v) *date of will* 1626 Oct 4
                             (CC8/8/54, 12)
Hamilton, James, r   1626 Dec 8 (*Edinburgh Burgh Recs.*, vii, 17)
Doctor
Dalzell, Gavin, b, s, *see*   1624 Jul 23 (387, 199v) *schoolmaster in*
    also Canongate   *Edinburgh* 1641 Dec 9 (542, 213)
    Vernacular Schools

EDINBURGH, KIRK O'FIELD
(also known as St Mary's Collegiate Church)
Watson, Thomas, r in St   1595 Oct 29 (*Edinburgh Burgh Recs.*, v, 141–2)
    Giles *and* Kirk O'Field,
    see also St Giles

EDINBURGH, MAGDALENE CHAPEL
Lowrie, John, *see also*   1594 Dec 6 (70, 318) 1598 Nov 13
    Vernacular Schools   (CC8/17/4)
    (unassigned)
Nasmyth, John, *see also*   1595 Jul 4 (63, 142) Oct 10 (98, 7)
    Dean Village
Lawson, David   1599 May 24 (73, 345) Jun 13 (CC8/17/4)
Lawson, Peter, MA, s   1602 Jun 25 (90, 124v)
Johnston, Patrick   1594 Dec 6 (70, 318)

EDINBURGH, NIDDRIE'S WYND, St Mary Chapel
Lindsay, Robert, MA (Ed),   *possibly* 1602 Dec 29 (*Edinburgh Marriages*, 412)
    later min of Corstorphine 1611 Sep 25 (NP1/68, 29)
Draffin, Edward, s   1609 Jul 9 (172, 19)
Draffin, William, s   1611 Mar 23 (CC8 '8/47, 64) 1638 May 26
                             (512, 277)
Penman, John, s   1626 Aug 23 (390. 100) 1629 Aug 15 (527,
                             166)

EDINBURGH, TRINITY COLLEGE
Ballantyne, Stephen   1586 Sep 7 (*Edinburgh Burgh Recs.*, iv, 479)
                             1601 Nov 6 (83, 110)
Moffat, Eleazar, r   1586 Sep 7 (*Edinburgh Burgh Recs.*, iv, 479)
                             died 1620 Aug 30 (CC8/8/51, 6)

Miller, Robert, s, *see also* Canongate Vernacular Schools	1592 Aug 15 (54, 357)
Laing, John	1596 Jun 2 (53, 438) 1609 Jun 1 (CC8/8/45, 220)
Fairbairn, George, d	1596/7 Jan 19 (62, 165)
Laing, James, s, *see also* Vernacular Schools (unassigned)	1602 Aug 21 (181, 197) 1604 Dec 5 (105, 87)
Kiersen, Patrick, s, cf. Patrick Carswell in Canongate	1596 Aug 28 (55, 329)
Grinton, Henry, r, s, *see also* St Giles	1597 May 26 (79, 262) 1616 Feb 13 (281, 414)
Brown, Walter, n, r, *see also* Canongate	1600 Sep 5 (CC8/8/5, 10) 1628 Jan 31 (CH2/141/1, 10, 26)
Rodger, David, d	1616 Feb 6 (290, 92) *'elder doctor'* 1623 n.d. (392, 254)

Music School

Hamilton, James, d, r, s	1601 Jun 10 (102, 143) 1626 Dec 8 (*Edinburgh Burgh Recs.*, vii, 17)
Henryson, Patrick, MA, pr, r, simultaneously at St Giles *and* Edinburgh Music School, *see also* St Cuthbert's	1609 Mar 8 (*Edinburgh Burgh Recs.*, vi, 50)
Kirk, John, r	1616 Jan 20 (269, 411) 1626 Jun 15 (412, 93) *schoolmaster in Edinburgh* 1636 Dec 14 (506, 117)

EDINBURGH, ST CUTHBERT'S (par), West Kirk
(at the West Port)

Henryson, Gilbert, cl, pr, *see also* St Giles *and* Edinburgh Music School *and* Vernacular Schools (unassigned)	*died* 1589/90 Feb 7 (CC8/8/1, 53)
Maxwell, Tobias, cl, r	1590/1 Jan 20 (*Edinburgh Burgh Recs.*, v, 33) *dismissed* 1594 (P. Lorimer, *Precursors of Knox, or, Memoirs of Patrick Hamilton*, Edinburgh 1957, 13)
Brown, John, cl	1596 May 13 (Lorimer, *Precursors of Knox*, 91, 160)

Gray, John, *see also* Vernacular Schools (unassigned)	1590 Jun 24 (38, 422) 1603 Mar 9 (93, 340)
Henryson, Patrick, MA (Ed), pr, *see also* St Giles *and* Trinity *and* Edinburgh Music School	1600 Sep 3 (*Edinburgh Burgh Recs.*, v, 271)
Downs, James, r	1604 Jul 19 (108, 58) 1615 Feb 16 (CC8/8/48, 300)
Oliver, Thomas, s	1610 Feb 21 (207, 292)
West (Wast), Samuel, *see also* Potterrow	1612 May 12 (Lorimer, *Precursors of Knox*, 161)
Bowmaker, James, r	1622 Mar 1 (*Edinburgh Burgh Recs.*, vi, 230)

EDINBURGH, DEAN VILLAGE MRf NT2274
(also known as Water of Leith)
St Cuthbert's par

Nasmyth, John, *see also* Magdalene Chapel	1591 Nov 2 (NLS, Adv MS 29.4.2, xii, 148)
Horne, John, MA	1611 Feb 13 (214, 109)
Manuel, Robert, MA	1626 Sep 16 (CC8/10/8)
Lowrie, James	1631 Mar 14 (RS25/17, 144)

EDINBURGH, PLEASANCE
St Cuthbert's par

Moffat, John	*new school* 1631 (Lorimer, *Precursors of Knox*, 164)
Wanehope, Robert	1633 Dec 3 (468, 267)

EDINBURGH, POTTERROW
St Cuthbert's par

Donaldson, Robert, *see also* Vernacular Schools (unassigned)	1596 Apr 28 (53, 440) 1612 Jan 15 (86, 142)
Campbell, Archibald	1614 May 28 (225, 117)
West (Wast), Samuel, *see also* St Cuthbert's	1619 Aug 9 (CC8/8/50, 323)
Adamson, William	1621 Dec 29 (388, 14)
Semple, Robert	1625 Jun 25 (394, 163)
Steven, Alexander, MA	1630 Aug 9 (RS25/18, 36)

EDINBURGH, SAUGHTON HALL
St Cuthbert's par

Dungalson, John	*before* 1615 Sep 22 (29, 104)

Napier, Alexander   1626 Dec 1 (392, 176) 1629 Nov 17
(CC8/10/9, unfoliated)

EDINBURGH, CANONGATE (par)
High School (also known as the Grammar School)

Drummond (Dormond),   1554 Aug 10 (H.M. Anderson, 'The Grammar
   Robert, MA, *see also*   School of the Canongate', *Book of the Old*
   Edinburgh High School   *Edinburgh Club*, xx, pp. 4–5) 1568 Sep 13
                                       (ibid.) *absent briefly in Haddington*, q.v.

Panton, James, MA   *forced to desist* 1573 Apr 19 (CS7/76, 417;
                                       465–6)

Pitcairn, James, MA (SAL)   1575 (*Canongate Bk*, 35)

Taylor, Gilbert   1575 Nov n.d. (CS7/76, 465) *forced to desist*
                                by William Roberton of High School (ibid.)
                                re-appointed 1579 Oct 20 (*Canongate Bk*, 35)

Davidson, James, MA (SA)   1584 Jun 16 ('Extracts from the records of the
                                burgh of the Canongate', *Maitland Misc.*, ii,
                                345)

French, James *or* Robert,   1592 Oct 8 (44(2), 326) 1605 May 22
   MA (Ed), later min of   (RS24/5, 303)
   Penicuik

Haistie, John, *see also*   1603 Jul 23 (102, 190) 1606 Nov 14 (*Canongate*
   Edinburgh High School   *Bk*, 35)

Steven, Robert, MA; (Ed),   1609 Nov 18 (CC8/10/5) *died* 1618 Jan 17
   see also Edinburgh High   (CC8/8/50) *schoolmaster in Edinburgh* 1635
   School   Sep 4 (519, 38)

Miller, Alexander *or*   1617 Nov 22 (296, 81) 1619 May 28 (319, 215)
   Andrew, MA (Ed)

Douglas, George, MA (Ed)   1620 Mar 2 (299, 262) 1627 Dec 13 (411, 44)

Hart, John, MA (Ed),   1629 Jan 28 (RS25/14, 257) *called 'junior'* 1636
                                Jul 4 (500, 309) *died* 1633 Oct 21 (Anderson,
                                9)

Doctors
Henry, William, MA (Ed), d 1611 Dec 26 (*RPC*, 1st ser., ix, 322)

Carswell, Patrick, d,   1615 Jul 18 (246, 116) 1616 Jun 5 (332, 262)
   cf. Patrick Kiersen
   in Trinity

Balfour, Robert, MA,   1633 Mar 11 (468, 189) Apr 24 (RS25/20,
   under-teacher   256)

EDINBURGH, CANONGATE
Vernacular Schools
Scott, John, sir, c   1564 Oct 7 (*The Buik of the Kirk of the*

	Canagait, ed. A.B. Calderwood, SRS 1961, 8) 1573 Jun 27 (*RSS*, vi, 2009)
Lawson, Robert, r	1598 Sep 16 ('Visitations of the kirk of Holyroodhouse', *Wodrow Misc.*, i, 464)
Brown, Walter, n, r, *see also* Trinity	*possibly before* 1603 Aug 14 (CC8/8/40, 214)
Mather, Patrick; (*presumably assistant to* Robert Lawson); *see also* Edinburgh, Vernacular Schools (unassigned)	1605 Apr 8 (RS24/5, 172)
Clark, Robert (in association with Robert Lawson;), *see also* Edinburgh High School *and* Vernacular Schools (unassigned)	1605 Jul 31 (116, 11)
Stewart, George, *see also* St Giles	1611 Dec 14 (220, 231) 1612 Aug 15 (256, 369)
Johnston, David, d	1612 Jul 29 (204, 28) Sep 28 (207, 303)
Forrester, Adam, d	1612 Jul 29 (204, 28)
Arthur, Neil, pr, r, *see also* Edinburgh, Vernacular Schools (unassigned)	1620 Jun 22 (311, 129)
Miller, Robert, *see also* Edinburgh Trinity	1612 Mar 21 (313, 247) 1624 Oct 29 (CC8/10/8)
Anderson, William, MA, n	1625 Jun 27 (435, 3) 1629 Jul 11 (425, 253)
Thomson, Martin	1629 Nov 28 (460, 194)
Dalzell, Gavin, s, *see also* Greyfriars	1629 Nov 28 (460, 194)
Adamson, William	1633 Apr 24 (RS25/20, 256)
Robertson, James	1633 Aug 15 (474, 138)
Doctor	
doctor, unnamed	1565/6 Feb 2 (*Buik of the Kirk of the Canagait*, 38, 41, 74)

Music School

Cumming, David	1584/5 Feb 1 (CH4/1/1, ii, 122v) *'master of the sang schule of Edinburgh'* 1592 Apr 14 (49, 437)
Brown, John, d	1585 Mar 30 (24, 179)

Fencing School
Rodger, John, see also   1596/7 Mar 8 (144, 294)
  Edinburgh Fencing School

EDINGTON, Berwickshire MRf NT8955
Chirnside par
Crawford, Adam   1617 Apr 7 (288, 199)
Strachan, William   1619 Mar 2 (SC60/56/2, 200)

EDNAM (par), Berwickshire
Bulman, Peter   1622 Apr 1 (347, 276v)
school 'hes ever mor beine' (*Reports*, 195)
Sparke, Thomas   1630 Apr 16 (437, 158v)
Haistie, John, MA   1630 Oct 23 (RS1/30, 10v)

EDROM (par), Berwickshire
Wilson, William, r,   *before* 1630 Nov 10 (JC2/6/355) 1630 Nov
  simultaneously at Duns   n.d. (*RPC*, 2nd ser., iv, 60)

ELGIN (par), Moray
Grammar School
Balfour, Patrick, MA, min   1566 Sep 10 *contract for three years to begin Nov 11*
  of Alves 1567, min of   (*Elgin Recs.*, ii, 395) 1574 Dec 13 (W.
  Urquhart 1574   Cramond, *Municipal Life in Elgin in the*
       Sixteenth Century, Elgin 1899, 15)
Forrester, John, min of   1576 n.d. (*Elgin Recs.*, ii, 447, no more refs.)
  Forres 1585   1582 n.d. (*Fasti*, vi, 421)
Mogg, Thomas, MA   1582 Jun 21 (*Elgin Recs.*, ii, 396) 1585 Jun 21
       (Cramond, *Municipal Life*, 49)
Clark, William, MA   1590 n.d. (*Elgin Recs.*, ii, 447) 1595 n.d. (ibid.,
       397, no more refs.)
Annand, George   1596 n.d. (*Elgin Recs.*, ii, 447) 1597 Jul 15
       (ibid., 53, no more refs.)
Douglas, George, p, r,   1597 Sep 14 (*Elgin Recs.*, ii, 392) 1611 May 28
  simultaneously at Music   (213, 218v)
  School
Maule, Thomas, MA   1600 Jan 4 (*Extracts from the Records of the Kirk*
       Session of Elgin, ed. W. Cramond, Elgin 1897,
       64) May 21 (ibid., 68)
Leslie, Robert   1600 May 13 (*Kirk Session Records*, 68)
schoolmaster, unnamed   1600 May 30 (*Elgin Recs.*, ii, 81)
student   1605 May 18 (RS4/4, 261v)

Stewart, John, MA	1606 Jun 9 (119, 401v) 1609 Jun 24 (*RPC*, 1st ser., viii, 700)
student	1611 Jul 25 (285, 269)
Dunbar, William, MA	1612 Whitsun (*Elgin Recs.*, ii, 400)
Gordon, Alexander, MA	1615 n.d. (*Elgin Recs.*, ii, 447, no more refs.)
Turing, John, MA	1616 Sep 24 (*Elgin Recs.*, ii, 400) 1617 Feb 22 (275, 144v)
Allan, John, MA	1619 Apr 8 (*Elgin Recs.*, ii, 401) 1620 Feb 2 (328, 8v)
Rae, John, MA	1621 Aug 9 (330, 67) 1624 Mar 5 (RS1/17, 1v)
student	1624 Jul 3 (400, 176)
Anderson, Gilbert, MA	1624 Nov 15 (*Elgin Recs.*, ii, 401, no more refs.)
Murray, David, MA	1625 May 16 (*Elgin Recs.*, ii, 401) 1629 Jan 21 (430, 184)
Duff, John, MA, p	1627 Nov 12 (411, 162) 1632 n.d. (*Elgin Recs.*, ii, 448)
Strachan, James, MA	1633 n.d. (*Elgin Recs.*, ii, 447)

Music School (also known as the English School)

school	*founded* 1594 (*Elgin Recs.*, ii, 447)
Fraser, William	1595 (*Elgin Recs.*, ii, 447)
students	1600 May 13 (*Kirk Session Records*, 68)
schoolmaster, unnamed	1600 Dec 12 (*Elgin Recs.*, ii, 85)
Douglas, George, p, r, simultaneously at Grammar School	1597 Sep 14 (*Elgin Recs.*, ii, 392) 1622 (*Kirk Session Records*, 168)
Mow, John	1603 n.d. (*Elgin Recs.*, ii, 447)
Murray, David	1625 n.d. (*Elgin Recs.*, ii, 447) 1633 Feb 9 (RS28/3, 367v)
schoolmaster, unnamed	1632, 1633, 1634 n.d. (*Common Good*, 44)
Assistants	
Cowie, David	1620 Jun 25 (*Elgin Recs.*, ii, 164)
Schilps, John	1622 Feb 1 (*Kirk Session Records*, 168)

ELIE, Fife MRf NO4900
Kilconquhar par until 1641 (later a parish on its own)

Gleg, James, MA	1598 Nov 11 (66, 303) 1600 Jan 1 (73, 137)
McDuff, Alexander	1604 May 23 (RS30/5, 78) May 30 (*RMS*, vii, 1213)
Lamont (Lawmond), Allan, MA	1608 Dec 5 (178, 113v)
Duddingston, George, MA	1619 Oct 16 (335, 396v)

Craig, James, MA	1623 Jul 8 (381, 43) 1630 Oct 5 (RS31/8, 446v)
Doctor	
Peadge, Henry	1628 Nov 23 (431, 441v) 1629 Jun 26 (RS31/8, 87v)

ELLON (par), Aberdeenshire
Grammar School

Greig, John, r	1567–86 (J. Godsman, *A History of the Burgh and Parish of Ellon*, Aberdeen 1958, 284)
Mackie or Mathieson, George, MA	1603 Dec 14 (CH2/146/1, 107) 1604 Feb 12 (CH2/146/2, 27)
Alexander, John, MA, simultaneously at Cruden	1602 May n.d. (*Records of the Parish of Ellon*, ed. T. Mair, Aberdeen 1846, 51)
Ross, James or Henry, MA	*offer to teach* (CH2/147/1, 9) 1603 Oct 21 (*Records of the Parish*, 55)
schoolmaster, unnamed	1605 Sep 18 (CH2/146/2, 134)
no school	1605 Oct (Godsman, *Burgh and Parish of Ellon*, 285)
Leslie, William, MA	1606 May 30 (173, 361v)
Innes, Alexander, MA	1610 Apr 24 (*Aberdeen Court Bk*, ii, 156) 1613 Feb 5 (214, 75v)
no school	1616 Jun 19 (CH2/146/2, 122)
request for schoolmaster	1617 Mar 26 (CH2/146/2, 126)
students	1618 Nov 4 (SC1/60/3, 44)
Allan, John, MA	1619 Mar 2 (SC1/60/3, 84v)
Tullidaff, Samuel, MA, r, 'gramer and musik skuill'	1620 Dec 27 (CH2/146/2, 155) 1622 May 23 (SC1/60/5, 70v)
order for maintenance of master and reader	1622 Jul 24 (CH2/146/2, 213)
no school	1624 Sep 23 (CH2/146/2, 191v)
Merser, Robert, MA, pr, r, later min of Logie Buchan	1625 Aug 27 (CH2/146/2, 200v) 1628 Nov 30 (CH2/147/1, 100)
order for maintenance of master and reader	1627 May 29 (CH2/146/2, 213)
no schoolmaster	1627 Jun 26 (CH2/146/2, 214)
Panton, Anthony, MA	1627 (CH2/146/2, 211)
Doctor	
Tullidaff, Alexander	1620 Dec 27 (CH2/146/2, 155)

ELPHINSTONE, East Lothian MRf NT3970
Tranent par
Whyte, Nicol, MA   1624 Jul 18 (*RPC*, 1st ser., xiii, 845)
Cockburn, John   1612 Jan 16 (205, 348) 1622 Mar 11 (356, 178)

ELSICK, Kincardineshire MRf NO8894 (Elsick Ho)
Fetteresso or Maryculter par
Jack, John   1616 May 4 (SC1/60/5, 214)

ERROL (par), Perthshire
(united to Inchmartin 1628)
Grammar School
Welland, James, MA   1600 Jan 26 (84, 46) 1601 Oct 5 (RS48/1,
                          108)
Blair, Andrew, MA, r   1603 May 12 (RS48/2, 218v) 1629 Jul 20
                          (RS1/26, 271)
Gardner, James, MA   1632 May 19 (476, 397)

ERSKINE (par), Renfrewshire
Sharp, James, n   1606 Nov 30 (195, 305v) 1608 Apr 1 (168, 64v)
Urie, John   1617 Dec 24 (CC9/7/16, 24) 1620 Jan 7
                          (CC9/7/17, 5v)

EXMAGIRDLE (par), Perthshire
(also known as Ecclesiamagirdle, united to Dron 1652)
Oliphant, William, MA   1624 Dec 27 (RS50/1, 96)

EYEMOUTH (par), Berwickshire
(disjoined from Coldingham 1618)
Home, John, MA   1588 Dec 30 (48, 5v)
Sprott, George, n   1594 Dec 7 (*Hist. MSS. Comm., Report on the
                          Manuscripts of Colonel David Milne-Home*, 211)
                          1595 Jul 2 (ibid.)
Trench (Trynsche),   1598 Dec 4 (88, 197v) 1599 Jul 12 (*Milne-
  Thomas, MA   Home*, 214)
Smyth, Alexander, MA   1601 Apr 15 (107, 174) May 11 (107, 175)
Clark, Patrick   1603 Jun 30 (105, 153) 1614 Oct 17 (310, 252)
Brown, Robert, MA   1618 Aug 15 (309, 120v) 1619 Aug 10 (RS18/1,
                          91)
Bulman, Peter   1623 Sep 10 (400, 156)
Home, David, MA   1626 Apr 17 (SC60/56/2, 278)
Napier, Alexander   1628 Dec 20 (*Milne-Home*, 218)

FAIRNILEE, Selkirkshire MRf NT4532
Lindean par, called Galashiels 1622 (later in Caddonfoot par)
Erskine, Robert   1618 Dec 19 (299, 43v)

FALKIRK (par), Stirlingshire
Ambrose, Thomas   *deposed* 1594 (J. Love, *The Schools and*
                                     Schoolmasters of Falkirk, Falkirk 1898, 5)
Fraser, Alexander   1606 Jun 30 (140, 120)
Rankine, John, MA   1607 May 14 (143, 295)
   (Gl 1604)
schoolmaster, r, unnamed   1619 (A. Bain, *Education in Stirlingshire*, London
                                     1965, 72)
Johnston, James, r   *not qualified* 1628 (Bain, 52)
Dishington, John, MA, cl,   1631 May 27 (RS58/5, 197v) 1632 Dec 2
   pr   (466, 264)

FALKLAND (par), Fife
school   1589 Oct 18 (PS60, 78)
Paterson, Stephen, n   1590 Aug 10 (NP1/53A, i, 1)
Henryson, Alexander, MA   1606 Sep 5 (CC8/8/43, 293)
Ballvaird, David, MA   1607 Jun 26 (RS30/10, 11v) 1614 Feb 4 (232,
                                     198v)
Freebairn (poss. error for 1617 Jan 7 (262, 127v)
   Berwick), John, MA
Berwick, John, MA   1617 Jan 24 (326, 427) 1625 Feb 26 (539, 64)
Galbraith, Andrew, MA   1619 Mar 10 (282, 344)
Wilkie, Henry, MA   1629 Apr 4 (NP1/69A, unfoliated)

FALLSIDE, Kincardineshire MRf NO8182
Glenbervie par
Martin, Alexander, MA   1602 Nov 19 (94, 69v)

FENCE, Lanarkshire MRf NS8045 approx
Lesmahagow par
Fairie, James   1620 Aug 14 (315, 341)

FENWICK, Ayrshire MRf NS4643
At that time in Kilmarnock par (later a parish on its own)
Doctor
Calderwood, John, d   1628 Jul 8 (RS12/4, 279, 280)

FERN (par), Angus
Lyon, James, MA   1619 (RS1/3, 213v)

FERRYPORT-ON-CRAIG (par), Fife
(disjoined from Leuchars 1602, later called Tayport)
no schoolmaster   1611 Aug 13 (*Ecclesiastical Records: Selections
                         from the Minutes of the Synod of Fife*, ed. G.R.
                         Kinloch, Abbotsford Club 1837, 29)
Allan, Henry, MA   1604 Aug 25 (RS30/5, 226v) Sep 25 (ibid.)

FETTERCAIRN (par), Kincardineshire
Thom, John, r   1567–74 (A.C. Cameron, *History of Fettercairn*,
                         Paisley 1899, 215)
Simpson, Alexander, MA   1606 Jul 16 (149, 117v)
Davidson, William, MA   1611 Jul 2 (CC3/9/3)
Strachan, William, MA   1613 Jun 15 (221, 200v) Aug 18 (215, 209–10)
Anderson, James, MA   1614 Oct 8 (276, 389)
Irving, John, MA   1622 May 17 (329, 210)
Straiton, David, MA   1626 May 13 (RS7/2, 242)
Norrie, Robert, MA   1632 Jul 14 (RS7/3, 275v)

FETTERESSO (par), Kincardineshire
Mylne, James, MA   1597 Jul 5 (75, 443v)
Martin, James, MA   1604 Aug 25 (CC3/9/2)
Steven, Andrew, MA   1612 Nov 9 (345, 145) 1631 Nov 23 (457, 50)
Mylne, Andrew, MA   1619 Jan 14 (RS7/1, 69)

FETTERNEIR, *see* Chapel of Garioch

FIDDES, Aberdeenshire MRf NJ9524 (Mill of Fiddes)
Foveran par
Griff *or* Goiff, Thomas, MA 1622 Mar 26 (411, 155v)

FINDO GASK (par), Perthshire
(also known as Gask)
Donaldson, Thomas   1609 May 19 (CS7/243, 163)
Graham, James, MA   1625 Jun 7 (RS50/1, 283) 1627 Feb 23
                         (RS50/2, 413)

FINGASK, Perthshire MRf NO2227
Kilspindie par
Playfair, Andrew, MA   1609 Mar 15 (166, 337)

FINTRAY (par), Aberdeenshire
Andrew, John   1618 Jan 30 (RS5/1, 104v) Aug 28 (ibid., 299)

FISHERROW, Midlothian MRf NT3473
Duddingston par

Wallange, Matthew, n	1613 Apr 12 (228, 388v) 1617 May 14 (289, 161)
March, James, cf. Musselburgh	1622 Sep 24 (RS25/7, 59) 1628 May 22 (RS25/13, 334)
Doctor	
Dunlop, Robert	1618 Jan 9 (305, 103v)

FISHWICK, Berwickshire MRf NT9151
Hutton par

Murray, William	1624 Jan 16 (SC60/56/2, 127)

FLASKHOWGILL, *see* Howgill

FOGO (par), Berwickshire

Marshall, Robert	1618 Aug 24 (SC60/56/2, 251)
Lyall, Robert	1632 Aug 21 (RS18/3, 56v)

FORDOUN (par), Angus

Austin, Patrick	1605 May 29 (132, 61)
Sibbald, Alexander, MA	1608 May 14 (RS6/3, 88) 1609 Oct 13 (180, 424)
Pigott, John, MA	1610 Mar 1 (183, 190v) 1611 May 18 (238, 126v)
Wishart, James, MA	1612 Mar 8 (221, 379) 1613 Jun 14 (243, 447)
Beaton, Patrick	1613 Nov 24 (230, 450) 1617 Jan 24 (265, 225v)
Strachan, Alexander, MA	1618 May 28 (317, 315)
Walker, John, MA	1619 Aug 10 (RS7/1, 119) 1622 Nov n.d. (363, 337)
Thom, George	1631 Jul 20 (472, 88) 1633 n.d. (489, 399)

FORDYCE (par), Banffshire

school endowed and erected	c.1592 (W. Barclay, *The Schools and Schoolmasters of Banffshire*, Banff 1925, 22)
mortification for school	1599 Sep 1 (GD248/15, unnumbered, i, 137)
Sanders, William, MA, later min of Bellie	1601 May 8 (RS15/1, 87v) 1605 Jun 6 (RS15/3, 31v)
Gellie, John, MA	1609 Jul 16 (168, 96v)
student	1617 Nov 9 (SC2/56/1)
student (David Allardyce), later schoolmaster	1620 Jun 20 (333, 252)

Allardyce, David, MA, prev   1621 Mar 4 (SC2/56/1) Nov 14 (ibid.)
  student
students   1622 Jun 27 (340, 92v)
Darg, Walter, MA   1624 Nov 3 (W. Cramond, *The Church and*
  (AbK 1623), min of   *Churchyard of Fordyce*, Banff 1886, 14)
  Deskford 1627
Gordon, Adam   n.d. (Barclay, *Schools and Schoolmasters*, 22)
Douglas, George   n.d. (Barclay, *Schools and Schoolmasters*, 22)
Darg, William   n.d. (Barclay, *Schools and Schoolmasters*, 22)
Innes, John, MA   n.d. (Barclay, *Schools and Schoolmasters*, 22)
mortification for school   1627 May 30 (Cramond, *Church and*
       Churchyard, 15)
no schoolmaster   1627 Sep 14 (Cramond, *Church and*
       Churchyard, 15)
four years with neither   n.d. (Barclay, *Schools and Schoolmasters*, 22)
  school nor schoolmaster
Speed, George, MA   1633–1639 (*Fasti*, vi, 334)
  (AbK 1625)
Doctor
Moir, George, s   1621 Mar 4 (SC2/56/1)

FORFAR (par), Angus
Grammar School
school and schoolmaster   1576, 1577 n.d. (*Common Good*, 44)
Henryson (Henderson),   1600 May 16 (101, 155) 1603 Feb 14 (109, 197)
  Patrick
Allan, Andrew, MA   1603 Nov 30 (116, 368) 1607 Mar 9
       (CC3/9/2)
student   1612 Jan 30 (210, 430)
Pitcairn, Alexander, MA   1614 Jul 5 (CC3/9/4) 1616 Jun 7 (257, 205v)
Pigott, Thomas, MA   1619 May 12 (CC3/9/6) 1625 Apr 25 (412,
       136)
Doctor
Fithie, William, d   1629 Jan 20 (418, 100) 1633 Jun 1 (475, 201)

FORGAN (par), Fife
Cunningham, Samuel, MA   1598/9 Jan 25 (J. Lee, *Lectures on the History of*
       the Church of Scotland, ii, Edinburgh 1860, 441)
       1605 Jun 29 (110, 84)
school and schoolmaster   1611 Aug 14 (*Ecclesiastical Records: Selections*
       from the Minutes of the Synod of Fife, ed. G.R.
       Kinloch, Abbotsford Club 1837, 30) Sep 4
       (*Fasti*, v, 200)

FORGANDENNY (par), Perthshire
Brewhouse, David   1632 Dec 24 (RS50/6, 197v)
Carnegie, James   1600 Apr 19 (CC8/8/36)

FORGUE (par), Aberdeenshire
Whyte, Patrick   1622 Aug 13 (344, 179) 1628 Jul 21 (418, 370)

FORRES (par), Moray
Forrester, John, min   1582–99 (J.B. Ritchie, *Forres: its Schools and
                                 Schoolmasters*, Forres 1926, 263)
Duncan, Norman   *temporarily* 1590 (Ritchie, *Forres*, 263)
school   *re-opened* 1594 (R. Douglas, *Annals of the Royal
                                 Burgh of Forres*, Elgin 1934, 266)
Stratton, John, MA, min   1599–1608 (Ritchie, *Forres*, 263)
Dunbar, Gavin, MA   1603 Aug 29 (NP1/65, 15) 1604 Jun 28 (108,
                                 47)
Fraser, James   1608–16 (Ritchie, *Forres*, 263)
Dunbar, Thomas   1616–23 (Ritchie, *Forres*, 263)
Munro, Alexander   1623–24 (Ritchie, *Forres*, 263)
Spens, Alexander, MA   1624–27 (Douglas, *Annals*, 266)
  (AbK 1623)
Dunbar, John, MA (AbK   1627–42 (Douglas, *Annals*, 266) 1629 May 15
  1631)   (NRA 3094/330)

FORTINGALL (par), Perthshire
Simpson, John   1617 Dec 10 (RS49/1, 109)

FORTUNE, East Lothian MRf NT5579 (East Fortune)
Athelstaneford par
Anderson, Patrick   1604 Aug 18 (104, 75v)

FOULDEN (par), Berwickshire
(united with Lamberton 1616)
Ritchie, William   1619 May 29 (RS1/3, 178v)
Spens, John   1631 May 30 (SC60/56/4, 45)

FOVERAN (par), Aberdeenshire
grammar school   1605 Aug 26 (CH2/146/2, 132)
Tullidaff, Samuel, MA   1610 Jul 2 (*RPC*, 1st ser., ix, 647)
schoolmaster, unnamed   1617 Oct 9 (CH2/146/2, 133)

FOWLIS WESTER (par), Angus
Rollok, David   1597 May 11 (58, 213v) 1601 Jan 12
                                 (CC8/8/36)

Cook, William, MA	1616 Aug 27 (*RMS*, vii, 1973) Nov 30 (CC6/5/4, 119v)
student	1621 Jun 28 (354, 259)
Spens, William, MA	1623 Jun 6 (RS1/24, 241) 1630 Apr 15 (439, 92)

FRASERBURGH (par), Aberdeenshire
Grammar School

Bidie, Andrew, MA	1606 May 29 (136, 191) 1609 Oct 28 (*Aberdeen Court Bk*, ii, 151)
schoolmaster, unnamed	1613 Jul 5 (CH2/89/1(2), 148)
Martin, Alexander, MA	1614 Dec 2 (250, 194)
schoolmaster, unnamed	1615 Aug 3 (CH2/89/1(2), 184)
Dunbar, Patrick, MA, r	1616 Jul 25 (CH2/89/1(2), 199) 1617 Feb 11 (268, 128)
school	1617 Jul 24 (CH2/89/1(2), 211) 1619 Jul 15 (ibid., 234)
Jaffrey, William, MA, later min of New Deer	1619 Aug 26 (CH2/89/1(2), 237) 1622 Apr 6 (SC1/60/5, 133v)
Morrison, Hugh, s	1620 Jul 6 (342, 37)
Howieson, David, MA, p	1628 Oct 18 (RS5/6, 248v) 1630 Sep 30 (RS5/7, 215v)
student	1631 Aug 4 (*Select Justiciary Cases, 1624–50*, ed. S.A. Gillon et al., Stair Society 1953, i, 208)

Music School

| Reid, John | 1616 Jul 25 (CH2/89/1(2), 211) 1619 Aug 26 (ibid.) |
| Burnett, James | 1602 Mar 13 (RS4/1, 283v) |

FRENCHLAND, Dumfriesshire MRf NT0905
Moffat par

| Donaldson, Robert | 1620 Dec 31 (374, 546) |

FRENDRAUGHT, Aberdeenshire MRf NJ6241
Forgue par

| Massie, William | 1628 Nov 12 (RS5/6, 257) |

FRIARTON, Perthshire MRf NO1121
Perth par

| Boyd, William | 1606 Jun 3 (205, 335) |

FYVIE (par), Aberdeenshire
Lawson, Vedast, MA	1614 Jul 6 (418, 319v) Aug 8 (325, 268v)
Dovartie, James, MA	1621 May 17 (336, 70) 1623 Apr 4 (SC1/60/6, 29v)
Irving, Alexander, MA	1623 Oct 13 (RS5/4, 281v)
Clark, George, MA	1628 Oct 6 (RS5/7, 283) 1630 Apr 24 (RS5/7, 95v)
Urquhart, Walter, MA	1633 Dec 27 (*RMS*, ix, 54)
Doctor	
Mackie, Thomas, d	1607 Jun 13 (148, 159)

GALASHIELS (par), Selkirkshire
(formerly called Lindean)
Cunningham, William	1606 Apr 4 (118, 378)
Laing, William	1610 Apr 16 (206, 312) 1612 Dec 29 (206, 99)
Wright, James, MA	1629 Jan 23 (557, 228) Feb 27 (ibid.)
Urquhart, James, MA	1629 May 18 (RS25/4, 395)
Yett, John	1630 Dec 6 (RS1/30, 116v)
Brown, Adam	1631 Dec 9 (RS1/32, 303)

GALSTON (par), Ayrshire
schoolmaster, unnamed	1627 Mar 18 (CH2/1335/2, p. 30)
Doctor	
Brown, John, d	1604 Jan 9 (CC9/7/3, 92)

GARGUNNOCK (par), Stirlingshire
Smart, John	1622 Jul 11 (GRO OPR 481, 19) 1625 Mar 22 (ibid., 25)

GARLOGIE, Aberdeenshire MRf NJ7805
Skene par
Thom, John	1612 Dec 13 (SC1/60/4, 159)

GARTLY (par), Aberdeenshire
Middleton, Robert, MA	1626 Apr 3 (425, 157)

GARVOCK (par), Kincardineshire
Bairdie, Andrew, d	1614 Jan 5 (237, 270) Nov 14 (313, 3)
Irving, John, MA	1620 Aug 17 (346, 393) 1621 Aug 28 (390, 410v)

GASK, *see* Findo Gask

GATTONSIDE, Roxburghshire MRf NT5434
Melrose par
Wallace, Andrew   1611 Jun 16 (190, 285)

GIRVAN (par), Ayrshire
Primrose, Henry   1623 Apr 21 (348, 54v)

GLAMIS (par), Angus
Pigott, Abraham   1603 Apr 6 (98, 385)
Neish, Patrick   1603 Nov 18 (304, 112v)
Bruce, William, MA   1610 Mar 30 (200, 402) Jul 9 (176, 327)
Wilkie, John, MA   1614 Jul 14 (294, 108)
Brown, Robert, MA   1621 Apr 13 (358, 289)
Armour, John   1623 Feb 3 (343, 6) 1631 Sep 6 (RS33/8, 142)
Simpson, Alexander   1630 Jan 31 (441, 116)

GLASGOW (par), Lanarkshire
Grammar School (later known as High School)
Maxwell, Robert, MA   c.1560 (J. Durkan, 'Education in the Century
                              of the Reformation', in D. McRoberts (ed.),
                              Essays on the Scottish Reformation, 1513–1625,
                              Glasgow 1962, 162) *1563* (?, ii, 111[4])
Jack, Thomas, MA, min of   1567 n.d. (H.A. Ashmall, *The High School of*
  Eastwood 1570   *Glasgow*, Glasgow 1976, 116) *1574 Nov 12* (?[5])
Sharp, Patrick, MA, min of   1574 n.d. (Ashmall, *High School of Glasgow*,
  Paisley, Neilston and   116) *demitted* 1582 Nov 13 (*Glasgow Recs.*, 99)
  Kilbarchan 1584, min of
  Govan 1585, principal
  of the University 1585
Blackburn, John, MA, min   1582 Nov 13 (*Glasgow Recs.*, 99) 1616 n.d.
  of Barony par 1615   (Ashmall, *High School of Glasgow*, 116)
Wallace, William, MA (Gl   1617 n.d. (Ashmall, *High School of Glasgow*, 64)
  1607), b   1642 n.d. (ibid.)
Doctors
Allanson, John, cl, d   1576 May 17 (*Glasgow Burgesses*, 4)
Buchan, John,   1600 Dec 22 (*Glasgow Recs.*, 217)
  see also Music School at
  the Collegiate Church of
  St Mary and St Anne

---

[4] Reference missing: see Preface. The 'ii' suggests that, in any case, this may not be a
     reference to the Register of Deeds.
[5] Reference missing: see Preface.

Mure, Andrew   1607 Jun 10 (CC9/7/5, 43) 1627 Dec 26 (412,
                                95v)
Blair, Robert   1614 n.d. (Ashmall, *The High School of Glasgow*,
                                68)
Mure, John, MA   1615 Sep 8 (266, 71) 1617 Sep 8 (265, 99v)
                                1632 Sep 4 (509, 53)
Hamilton, John, MA, d   1623 Sep 17 (360, 304v) 1632 Feb 16 (*Glasgow
                                Burgesses*, 82)
Hill, John   1629 Apr 14 (CC9/7/23, 284)
Anderston (Adderston),   1629 Nov 14 (*Glasgow Recs.*, 372) 1632 Feb 16
  James, MA (Gl 1624), d   (*Glasgow Burgesses*, 83)

Music School at the Cathedral or High Kirk
Struthers, William, sir, r   1576/7 (*Glasgow Recs.*, 462) 1587 Sep 7
                                (*Wodrow Collections on the Lives of the Reformers*,
                                Maitland Club 1848, ii, 2, pp. 22, 23)
Crawford, Mungo, r   1630 Apr 30 (B10/10/1, 152)

Writing School
Diggens, Edward   *before* 1607 Oct 7 (*Bon Record*, 40)
Clark, James   1615 Jun 21 (CH2/171/35, p. 382) 1623 May 9
                                (359, 346v)

Vernacular School at the Collegiate Church of St Mary and St Anne
  (also known as the Vernacular School, Common School, Trongate or
  New Kirk School)
school   1570 Aug 2 (*Glasgow City Chrs.*, 142) Aug 10
                                (*Glasgow Prot. Bk*, vi, no. 1702)
Craig, Thomas   1575 Nov 11 (*Glasgow Burgesses*, 3) 1597 Apr
                                24 (*Glasgow Recs.*, 187)
Sanders, James, r   1626 Jul 15 (*Glasgow Recs.*, 354) *dismissed* 1638
                                May 5 (ibid., 388)

Music School at the Collegiate Church of St Mary and St Anne
Buchan, John, r   1592 Jun 8 (CH2/550/1, 174v) 1608 Feb 6
  see also Grammar School   (*Glasgow Recs.*, 274)
Burnett (Barnet), Duncan, r   1615 Jun 3 (CC9/14/5, 89v) 1620 Aug 18
                                (338, 413) *reappointed* 1638 May 5 (*Glasgow
                                Recs.*, 388)

Unassigned Masters
Dunlop, James or John, b, n   1608 Apr 20 (CC9/7/5, 193) 1620 Jul 21 (320,
                                234v)

Fleming, John   1626 Jun 8 (RS1/19, 342) 1628 Jul 8
                             (DI117/2) *1629 Jun 27* (?[6])

GLASSFORD (par), Lanarkshire
Bruce, Arthur   1596 Jul 13 (59, 5v)
Park, Humphrey   1620 Jun 2 (RS40/1, 122)
Miller, Alexander   1629 Apr 2 (CC10/13/1, 17)

GLENBERVIE (par), Kincardineshire
Sibbald, Alexander   1604 Sep 24 (RS6/2, 68) 1606 Dec 1 (RS6/2,
                             206v)

GLENCAIRN (par), Kirdcudbrightshire
Scott, James   1610 Nov 11 (264, 243)

GLENHOLM (par), Peebleshire
Small (Smaill), John   1625 Jul 18 (387, 355v)
Elliot, Archibald   1629 Jul 19 (433, 342v)
Brown, Alexander   1630 Nov 24 (447, 60) 1649 Oct 7 (592, 223)

GLENISLA (par), Angus
Salmond, Robert   1629 Feb 22 (CC3/9/7) 1632 May 9
                             (RS33/8, 260)

GLENLUCE (par), Wigtownshire
Dunlop, John   1632 Feb 7 (RS60/2, 150v)

GOGAR (par), Midlothian
(united to Corstorphine 1599)
Wallace, William   1619 Apr 29 (383, 31)

GORBALS, Lanarkshire MRf NS5863 (Hutchesontown)
Govan par
Graham, George   1621 Aug 20 (408, 407v)
Howie, James   1626 Dec 20 (428, 355v)
Mair, John   1633 Oct 14 (475, 441)

GORDON (par), Berwickshire
Sinclair, Daniel   1602 Aug 1 (93, 377v)
Hislop, William   1613 May 12 (222, 284)

[6]   Reference missing: see Preface.

GOVAN (par), Lanarkshire

schoolmaster, unnamed	1625–26 (GUA 26620, 231)
Thomson, George	1628 Nov 4 (CC10/5/5, 250v)
schoolmaster, r, unnamed	1633 (GUA 26620, 413)

GRANGE (par), Banffshire
(disjoined from Keith 1618)

Gardyne (Gairne), William, MA (AbK 1628), later min of Kinloss	1631 Aug n.d. (W. Cramond, *The Church of Grange*, Keith 1898, 7) 1632 Nov 19 (502, 79)

GREENLAW (par), Berwickshire

Falconer, Patrick	1605 Jun 23 (130, 282v) 1609 Nov 29 (176, 163)
Foster *or* Forrester, James	1613 Mar 28 (SC60/50/1, 165) 1616 Feb 27 (261, 217)
Harrat, Andrew	1619 Mar 24 (SC60/56/4, 18v)
Wilson, William, n	1622 Nov 10 (SC60/56/2, 45v) 1623 Jan 10 (ibid., 55)
Balcanvall, Alexander, MA	1630 Apr 18 (SC60/56/4, 40v)
Paterson, John	1632 Aug 3 (DI1/58) 1633 Sep 13 (RS1/38, 211v)

GRENNAN, Kirkcudbrightshire MRf NX6379
Dalry par

Adamson, Patrick	1631 Jan 31 (463, 38v)

GULLANE (par), East Lothian
(united to Dirleton 1612)

Wright, George	1598 Aug 26 (*RPC*, 1st ser., v, 702)
Wood, George	1598/9 Jan 6 (*RPC*, 1st ser., v, 713) 1602 Aug 12 (94, 27v)
Adinston, William	1610 Dec 3 (B56/1/5, 20)

GUTHRIE (par), Angus

Gray, Walter	1615 Sep 11 (250, 95v)

HADDINGTON (par), East Lothian
Grammar School

Drummond (Dormond), Robert, MA	1559 Oct 6 (B56/1/4, 219) 1560 Dec 7 (ibid., 219)
Cumming, Thomas, MA	*appointed by abbot of Holyrood* 1563/4 Feb 17

	(B30/13/1, 36) *still disputing his place* 1576 Jun 14 (B30/13/1, 85)
Carmichael, James, MA (SAL 1564), min	1572 Apr 16 (J. Miller, *The Lamp of Lothian*, Haddington 1844, 434) *discharged* 1576 Nov 15 (ibid., 435)
Creich, Patrick, MA	1575/6 Feb 7 (Edinburgh City Archives, Charters of the Commendators of Holyrood, transcripts, no. 60) *neglected his office* Feb 27 (GD1/413/6)
Panton, James, MA, d	1577 Apr 15 (B30/13/1, 90v) 1578 Jun 10 (ibid., 95)
Ker, John, MA, b, min of Haddington 1585, min of Aberlady 1587	1579 Jun 19 (*Fasti*, i, 369) *demitted* 1591 May 19 (Miller, *Lamp of Lothian*, 448)
Callander, John, MA	1591 Jul 29 (Miller, *Lamp of Lothian*, 448)
McGhee (Makghie), Andrew, MA	1594 Nov 9 (60, 42)
Bowie, William, MA, b	1600 Dec 27 (78, 99) *died* 1623 Oct n.d. (CC8/8/52, 291)
Greig, John	1606 Mar 24 (122, 48v)
Paterson, Thomas, MA	1617 Mar 10 (GD1/413/2) 1619 Nov 5 (Miller, *Lamp of Lothian*, 449)
Seton, Alexander, MA	1623 Nov 10 (Miller, *Lamp of Lothian*, 449) 1640 May 16 (531, 44)

Doctors

doctor	1559 Oct 12 (B30/13/1, 22)
Balcanqual, Walter, MA, b, cl, d, r, min of St Giles 1574, min of Edinburgh Trinity 1598	*appointed* 1571/2 Feb n.d. (Miller, *Lamp of Lothian*, 447) 1572/3 Feb 27 (B30/13/1, 70)
Chapman, Henry, MA, r	1578 Sep 10 (B30/13/1, 101v)
doctors	1579 Jun n.d. (Miller, *Lamp of Lothian*, 448) 1579 Nov n.d. (ibid.) 1580 Jul n.d. (ibid.) 1588 Jul 29 (CH2/185/1, 32r)
Sprott, George, d, pr	1592 Aug 9 (Miller, *Lamp of Lothian*, 448)
Lightbody, George, MA (1609–10), d	1607 Mar 7 (132, 384) *left* 1617 May 23 (GD1/413/2)
Paterson, John, MA, d	1630 Apr 12 (436, 94v) May 22 (516, 417)
Merser, John, subdoctor, *see also* Nungate School	1617 Mar 10 (GD1/413/2)

Music School

Buchan, John, pr, r	1583 Jun 17 (Miller, *Lamp of Lothian*, 459)

	1592 May 3 ('Ane forme of sindrie materis to be usit in the elderschip', *Wodrow Misc.*, i, 536–7)
Gray, Robert	1607 Mar 27 (GD1/413/2)
Dunbar, Patrick	1610 Dec 31 (GD1/413/2)
Dunbar, James	1619 Sep 13 (Miller, *Lamp of Lothian*, 460)
Lawrie or Lowrie, James	1623 Mar 29 (506, 14) 1629 Jun 22 (RS25/14, 391)

School in St Katherine's 1576 Dec 14 (B30/13/1, 88v)
chapel

Nungate School

| Burnside, John | 1606 Dec 26 (GD1/413/2) 1606 (*magistrates ordered closure*, W.F. Gray and J.H. Jamieson, *A Short History of Haddington*, Stevenage n.d., 130) |
| Merser, John, *see also* High School | 1617 (*closed by order*, ibid.) |

Adventure Schools

| Lamb, James | 1594 Dec 17 (D. Withrington, 'Schools in the Presbytery of Haddington in the Seventeenth Century', *East Lothian Trans.*, ix, 1963, 92) |

Dame School

Spence, Isabel	before 1586 (Gray, and Jamieson, *Short History of Haddington*, 131)
Lindsay, Marion	1586 (ibid.)
Haliburton, Jane	1600 (ibid.)
Redpath, Marion	1609 (*sewing and reading*, ibid.)

Dame School 2

| Donaldson, Elizabeth | 1609 (*her rival school later closed by the magistrates*, ibid.) |

HAILES (par), Midlothian
(also called Brighall, later called Colinton)

Denny, Patrick	1599 Aug 7 (CH2/121/2) 1604 May 29 (109, 325)
Crawford, Michael	1606 Jul 4 (110, 148)
Chirnside, James, r	1630 May 6 (435, 391)

HALLGREEN, Kincardineshire MRf NO8372
Inverbervie par
Sym, Alexander   1629 Feb 26 (RS7/3, 126)

HAMILTON (par), Lanarkshire
Grammar School
Rais, John, MA, c, exh, t   1563 n.d. (*Thirds of Benefices*, 264) 1569/70
                                  (RH6/2171)
Sangster, John, MA, min, n   1581 May 4 (CS1/3(1), 148) 1583 Dec 26 (49,
                                  343)
school refoundation   1588 Oct 30 (M. Mackintosh, 'Education in
                                  Lanarkshire up to the Act of 1872', Glasgow
                                  Ph.D. thesis 1968, xxv)
Mathie, David, MA, b, r   1599 Oct 29 (CC10/5/2) 1625 Jun 27 (408,
                                  205v) *1628 Aug 5* (?, 94[7])
Doctors
Bruce, Arthur, *underteacher*   1593 May 19 (47, 369v)

Music School
Bowmaker (Bowman),   1625 Jan 21 (447, 335) 1631 Nov 12 (458, 59v)
    James, d

HARDACRES, Berwickshire MRf NT7641 (Eccles)
Eccles par
Cheislie, John, MA   1620 Oct 18 (RS18/1, 151v, 156)
Haistie, John, MA   1620 Dec 31 (341, 86)

HARTREE, Peebleshire MRf NT0436
Presumably Coulter par (later in Broughton, Glenholm and Kilbucho par)
Jack, John   1614 Sep 3 (249, 230)

HARTSHAW, Clackmannanshire MRf NS2591
Clackmannan par
Penny, Andrew   1596 May 3 (58, 202) Nov 22 (58, 203v)

HASSENDEAN (par), Roxburghshire
Collace, Robert   1613 Aug 26 (237, 178) 1631 Jun 30 (516, 269)

---

[7] Reference missing: see Preface. This reference is not to be found at fo. 94 (or on nearby
     pages) of either RD1/408 or RD1/409, the volumes covering relevant years. RD1/408
     has blank pages where fo. 94 would be.

HASSINGTON, Berwickshire MRf NT7341
Eccles par
Haistie, John, MA   1622 Jan 24 (RS18/2, 118v) 1623 May 23
                                 (SC60/56/2, 37v)

HAWICK (par), Roxburghshire
Sword, Andrew   c.1592 (CH2/198/1, unfoliated) 1616 Nov 20
                                 (CH2/198/1, unfoliated)
Hay, William, n   1606 Mar 31 (129, 321v) Apr 18 (247, 9)
Scott, Adam, MA   1622 Aug 21 (CH2/198/2, 8)
no school   1627 (Jedburgh Kirk Session Archives, Report
                                 dated 1627, p. 115)
Carmure, James, MA   1631 May 18 (CH2/198/2, 43v) Jul 17 (ibid.)

Adventure School
Douglas, Archibald   1607 Jan 8, Jan 15 (CH2/198/1)

HEADSHAW, Selkirkshire MRf NT4623
Ashkirk par
Steven, Alexander, MA   1623 Dec 13 (374, 563)

HEATHPOOL, Peebleshire MRf NT2544
Peebles par
Doctor
Dyet, William, d   1620 Mar 2 (312, 126v)

HENDERLAND, Selkirkshire MRf NT2041
Yarrow par
Harper, James   1633 Aug 31 (RS56/5, 161v)

HESSILHEAD, Ayrshire MRf NS3852
Beith par
Doctor
Landells, Robert, d   1604 Apr 18 (RS11/2, 381v, 383)

HEUGHFIELD, Perthshire MRf NO1317
Dunbarney par
Duncan, Gavin   1617 Dec 10 (RS49/1, 116)

The HIRSEL (par), Berwickshire
(later in Coldstream par)
Wood, Thomas   1627 May 1 (SC60/56/3, 57)

HOBKIRK (par), Roxburghshire
Rutherford, William   1616 Dec 28 (354, 170)
Arbuthnott, James   1619 Apr 14 (CH2/198/1, unfoliated) May 5
                             (ibid.)

HOLMAINS, Dumfriesshire MRf NY0876
Dalton par
Armstrong, John   1620 Apr 11 (318, 128)
Martin, John   1631 Mar 14 (526, 10)

HOWGILL, Dumfriesshire MRf NY3789
(formerly called Flaskhowgill)
Annan par
student   1626 Aug 26 (RS1/20, 26v)

HOWNAM (par), Roxburghshire
Rutherford, William, r   1609 Sep 27 (CH2/198/1, unfoliated)

HUME (par), Berwickshire
Waugh (Waich), Thomas   1612 Jan 23 (237, 61v)
Neish, David, MA   1623 Jun 19 (355, 285v)

HUNDALEE, Roxburghshire MRf NT6418
Jedburgh par
Moffat, John   1608 Oct 19 (CH2/198/1, unfoliated)
Mather, James, cf. Jedburgh 1610 Dec 18 (*RMS*, vii, 581)
Mudie, Thomas   1611 Dec 3 (205, 290)

HUNTLY, Aberdeenshire MRf NJ5239
Presumably Dunbennan par (later a parish on its own)
Brown, William, MA   1603 Aug 18 (101, 400v)
Annand, William, MA   1613 Oct 2 (222, 61)

INCHBRAYOCK (par), Angus
(later called Craig, united to Dunninald 1618)
Ramsay, Thomas   1621 Nov 9 (357, 144v)

INCHINNAN (par), Renfrewshire
Handesoun *or* Herbesoun,   1623 April 14 (CC9/14/9, 42)
   Robert, MA

INCHMARTIN, *see* Errol

INCHTURE (par), Perthshire
(Inchture and Benvie under single charge at this date)
Armour, John, d   1605 Apr 3 (RS48/3, 454) 1619 Aug 17
                                 (RS49/2, 401)
Young, Alexander, MA   1627 Jul 23 (RS50/3, 119)

INNEROCHTIE (par), Aberdeenshire
(later called Strathdon)
Strachan, James, MA   1632 Jan 14 (RS5/7, 481)

INNERWICK (par), East Lothian
Kellie, John, MA   1609 Jul 15 (181, 78)
Cumming, Alexander   1619 Dec 23 (291, 127)
Mure, Robert, r   1630 Jan 20 (RS25/20, 175v) 1640 Mar 19
                                 (530, 518)
Kellie, George   1624 May 19 (420, 241v)

INSCH (par), Aberdeenshire
Galloway, Robert   1601 Aug 12 (102, 163)
Mitchell, Alexander, MA   1617 Oct 3 (383, 379) 1619 May 25 (RS5/2,
                                 2v)
Liddell, Francis, MA   1620 Feb 13 (300, 206v) 1621 Mar 1 (442, 281)
Whyte, Patrick   1630 Apr 10 (430, 202) May 19 (ibid.)

INVERARAY (par), Argyll
Riddoch, Duncan, MA   1619 Aug 6 (445, 394v) Nov 26 (307, 134)
Henderson, Robert, MA   1623 Oct 2 (359, 120) 1625 Oct 27 (379,
                                 355v)
Campbell, Donald, MA   1626 Sep 6 (RS1/20, 173) 1629 Apr 29
                                 (RS1/26, 63)
McIlvorie, John, MA   1630 Mar 6 (463, 135)

INVERAVEN (par), Banffshire
Anderson, Gilbert, MA   1624 Apr 15 (424, 235)
Gordon, Alexander, MA,   1633 (W. Barclay, *The Schools and Schoolmasters*
   cl, r   *of Banffshire*, Banff 1925, 161)

INVERBERVIE (par), Angus
(also known as Bervie, disjoined from Kinneff 1618)
Johnston, William, MA   1610 Sep 11 (271, 82) 1617 Dec 26 (315, 116v)
Rait, Robert, MA   1620 Jul 2 (311, 227v)

INVEREIGHTY, Angus MRf NO4345
Inverarity par
Ferguson, James, MA   1607 May 11 (143, 125v)

INVERESK (par), Midlothian
Wright, John   1607 May 13 (136, 419) 1629 Dec 4 (530, 544)

INVERKEILLOR (par), Angus

Kinneir, Alexander, MA	1601 Sep 11 (84, 187v) 1602 Feb 3 (89, 37v)
Henryson, Patrick	1604 Jan 28 (136, 6)
Robertson, Alexander, MA	1608 Apr 21 (162, 337v)
Pitcairn, Alexander, MA	1609 Nov 3 (274, 159v) *1611 Sep 22*[8]
Pitillok, Henry, MA	1614 Aug 14 (CC3/9/4) 1616 Nov 28 (CC20/4/6)
Duncan, James	1617 Dec 7 (309, 139) 1620 Dec 30 (RS49/4, 109)

INVERKEITHING (par), Fife

Angell, Adam, sir, c, r	1582 n.d. (W. Stephen, *The Story of Inverkeithing and Rosyth*, Edinburgh 1938, 68) *died after* 1593 Jul 20 (ibid., 389)
Bonar, John, r, later MA	1594/5 Mar 18 (CS7/207, 9–10v) 1611 Jul 16 (226, 275)
Ready, James, MA, r	1613 Sep 9 (216, 326v) 1629 May 14 (420, 49)
Haggie, James *or*	1630–32 (Stephen, *Inverkeithing and Rosyth*, 389)
John, MA, r	
Ready, David, MA, r	1633–42 (Stephen, *Inverkeithing and Rosyth*, 389)

INVERKIP (par), Renfrewshire
Urie, John   1626 May 3 (CC9/7/2, 111v) Jun 29 (390, 144)

INVERNESS (par), Inverness-shire
Grammar School

Howieson (Hewison), Thomas, MA, min	1562 Aug 1 (*Inverness Recs.*, i, 92) 1570/1 (ibid., 198)
Logie, Martin, MA	1564 Oct 4 (*Inverness Recs.*, i, 116)
schoolmaster, unnamed	1576 n.d. (*Common Good*, 45)
Howieson, John, MA	1613 Oct 11 (*Inverness Recs.*, ii, 116) 1617 Dec 22 (ibid., 151)

---

[8] Reference missing: see Preface.

Ross, William, MA	1615 Oct 14 (*Inverness Recs.*, ii, 141) 1618 May 23 (RS37/1, 58v)
Dunbar, Patrick, MA	1619 Aug 4 (288, 66)
student	1622 Aug 19 (347, 199v)
Annand, John, MA	1623 Aug 23 (359, 155v) 1626 Jun 16 (418, 192v)
Ross, Walter, MA	1627 Oct 30 (478, 117–118v) 1633 Nov 28 (475, 441)

Doctors

Anderson, Patrick	1565/6 Feb 2 (*Inverness Recs.*, i, 131)
McPhail, Andrew, min	1570/1 Feb 17 (*Inverness Recs.*, i, 198)

Music School

Cowie, John	1619 May 23 (296, 356) 1624 Mar 23 (432, 324)
schoolmaster, unnamed	1628 n.d. (*Common Good*, 45)

INVERUGIE, *see* Longley

INVERURIE (par), Aberdeenshire

school to be erected	1606 Oct 20 (J. Davidson, *Inverurie and the Earldom of Garioch*, Edinburgh 1878, 171)
Keith, Gilbert, MA	1607 Oct 19 (Davidson, *Inverurie*, 171)
Barclay, Adam, MA	1607 Oct 23 (Davidson, *Inverurie*, 172)
Keith, George, MA	1608 Dec 24 (Davidson, *Inverurie*, 172)
Mitchell, Alexander, MA	1612 Oct 10 (Davidson, *Inverurie*, 172) 1627 May 11 (RS5/5, 384)
school	1633 n.d. (*Common Good*, 45)

IRVINE (par), Ayrshire
Grammar School

founded	1572 Jun 8 (*RMS*, iv, 2071)
Fullarton, William, MA	1586 Sep 26 (CC9/14/1, unfoliated) 1589 Apr 29 (32, 447v)
schoolmaster, unnamed	1593 October n.d. (B37/12/1, 3) 1597 Jun 18 (ibid., 2v)
Girvan (Garven), John, MA, p	1599 Nov 19 (RS11/1, 5v) *before* 1605 Sep 11 (NP1/66)
Birrell, James	*before* 1601 Jul 29 (*Irvine Muniments*, ii, 239) 1609 Whitsun (ibid., 250)
Wallace, William, MA	*before* 1601 Whitsun (*Irvine Muniments*, 239) *before* 1609 Whitsun (ibid., 249)
Barclay, David, MA	*before* 1611 Jul 13 (*Irvine Muniments*, 251)

Ross, Hugo, MA	1615 May 27 (B37/1/1, 111v)
Ramsay, Robert, MA (Gl 1618)	c.1618 (J. Strawhorn, *The History of Irvine*, Edinburgh 1985, 62) 1626 Mar 16 (*RMS*, viii, 945)
Girvan (Garven), Thomas, MA (Gl 1624), b	1626 Jul 7 (B37/11/1, 82) 1633 Jan 15 (B37/1/2, 167v)

Doctors

Young, John, d	1601 Aug 22 (85, 165)
Mure, Thomas, d	1621 Jul 23 (348, 202) 1622 May 27 (RS1/10, 227)
'our Doctour and Musiciner'	1628 n.d. (*Common Good*, 45)
Miller, Robert, d	1630 Sep 8 (RS1/10, 227)
'our Doctour and Musiciner'	1633 n.d. (*Common Good*, 45)

Music School

Bell, Patrick, MA	1625 Feb 23 (B37/1/2, 61) 1626 Jul 7 (B37/11/1, 82)
'our Doctour and Musiciner'	1628, 1633 n.d. (*Common Good*, 45)

JEDBURGH (par), Roxburghshire

Johnson, William, sir	1569 May 15 (B38/1/1, 75v)
schoolmaster, unnamed	1591, 1592 n.d. (*Common Good*, 46)
Thomson, James, p	1594 n.d. (RH6/3306)
Monypenny, Henry, MA	1605 n.m. 5 (140, 391)
Johnston, James, r, *see also* Adventure School	1606 Nov 20 (CH2/198/1, unfoliated) *discharged* 1609 Oct 3 (ibid.) *occurs again* 1616 Aug 6
Scott, Walter, MA, later min	(ibid.) 1609 Oct 3 (CH2/198/1, unfoliated)
Mather, James, cf. Hundalee	1610 Dec 18 (*RMS*, vii, 581)
Bourleyis, Robert, MA, r	1616 Nov 6 (CH2/198/1, unfoliated)
Kirkton, Andrew, MA (Ed 1617), later min of Oxnam	1619 Dec 6 (RS1/12, 120v) 1623 Feb 6 (381, 387)
Jaffrey, William, MA	1624 Jul 6 (434, 136) 1625 Nov 7 (381, 472)
Steven, William, MA	1630 Jun 1 (432, 107) 1632 Aug 31 (457, 75)

Doctors

Wilson, Adam, d, r *'and to teitch a musik school'*	1609 Oct 3 (CH2/198/1, unfoliated) Nov 8 (ibid.)
Peacock, John, d	1619 Sep 6 (RS56/1)
Dalgardine, William, MA, d	1626 Jun 3 (423, 405v)
Miller, William, d	1632 Jun 22 (469, 11)

Rutherford, Andrew *or*   *before* 1634 Feb 15 (CH2/198/2, 48v)
  Archibald, d

Adventure Schools
Ainslie, William, MA   1606 Nov 20–27 (CH2/198/1, unfoliated)
Johnston, James, *see above*   1623 Sep 17 (CH2/198/2, unfoliated)

KAILZIE (par), Peebleshire
(later in Traquair par)
Dickson, William, MA   1624 Aug 24 (374, 54v)

KEIG (par), Aberdeenshire
Gardyne, George   1613 Aug 13 (280, 350v) 1614 Mar 9 (227, 285)
Brabner, Alexander   1630 May 24 (431, 195)

KEITH (par), Banffshire
Grammar School
Smyth, Walter, MA, min of   1605 Aug 3 (122, 140v) c.1620 (*Fasti*, vi, 402)
  Dipple 1625
Young, William, MA   1614 May 16 (296, 359v)
Anderson, Gilbert, MA   1619 Oct 23 (RS16/1, 154)
Munro, David, MA   1622 May 27 (372, 59) 1624 Jun 20 (362, 139v)
Speed, George, MA (AbK   1625–1632 (*Fasti*, vi, 334)
  1625)

Music School
Cumming, David   1583 Nov 22 (CS7/55, 268)

KELSO (par), Roxburghshire
Kirkwood, James   *after* 1593 (J. Miller, *The Lamp of Lothian*, Haddington 1844, 446n.)
Tait, William, n   1584/5 Mar 22 (NP3/1, 138)
Knox, John, MA, r   1614 Nov 14 (243, 452v)
Mudie, John, MA, cl, r   1619 Jan 28 (318, 287v) 1637 May 27 (516, 297)

Doctors
Craig, James   1606 Jul 2 (144, 36v)
Haistie, Thomas   1611 Dec 16 (238, 106) 1614 Feb 6 (248, 189)
Davidson, John   1623 May 25 (349, 247)
Sudane, Thomas, MA   1625 Nov 15 (384, 227v)
Grahamslaw, George   1631 May 18 (RS12/5, 125v)

KELTIEHAUGH, Fife MRf NO1494 (Kelty)
Presumably Kelty par (later in Beath par)
Sinclair, George, r at Beath 1627 (S.A. Gillon et al., *Select Justiciary Cases, 1624–1650*, Stair Society 1953, i, 95)

KEMBACK (par), Fife
Ganton, William, MA   1627 Mar 12 (439, 75)

KEMNAY (par), Aberdeenshire
Spark, Robert, MA   1619 Nov 7 (SC1/60/5, 112v)
Moncreiff, Alexander, MA   1626 Dec 1 (401, 66)
Steven, Alexander   1628 Feb 18 (463, 168v) Apr 4 (430, 28v)

KENNETHMONT (par), Aberdeenshire
Chessor, William, MA   1626 Feb 11 (SC1/60/7, 58v)

KENNETSIDEHEADS, Berwickshire MRf NT7241
Eccles or Hume par
Wood, Thomas   1628 Jan 19 (431, 320v) 1630 Apr 27 (RS1/28, 272v)

KENNOWAY (par), Fife
Simpson, John, min, canon   c.1575 (*Fasti*, v, 91)
   regular at St Andrews
Hayne (Hay, Hume),   1602 Mar 24 (92, 375) 1608 Apr 13 (143, 257)
   Alexander, MA
Miller, James, MA   1608 Dec 1 (225, 357)
Hasson, Robert, MA   1614 Jun 10 (234, 439v)
Hedderwick, Robert, MA   1617 Feb 9 (RS31/1, 229a) Aug 9 (RS31/1, 19v)
Lundie, Robert   1625 Sep 25 (380, 337v)
Paterson, Oliver   1626 Jun 26 (RS31/6, 125) 1627 May 28 (399, 190)
Dickson, John   1629 Jun 29 (RS31/5, 238v)

KENNY, Angus MRf NO3054
Kingoldrum parnot in 71 census
Brown, Robert, MA   1620 Aug 10 (160, 426)

KETTINS (par), Angus
Carnegie, James   1602 Jul 9 (200, 380v)
Bruce, William, MA   1614 Mar 23 (CC20/4/5, 171v)
schoolmaster, unnamed   1618 Apr 12 (GRO OPR 294/3, unfoliated) Oct 18 (ibid.)

Robertson, Thomas, MA   *schoolmaster of 'Calperis'* 1619 Mar 4 (GRO OPR 294/3)

Callander, Alexander, MA   1621 Sep 30 (GRO OPR 294/3)

schoolmaster, unnamed   1622 Jul 28 (GRO OPR 294/3) Sep 16 (ibid.)

Haliburton, William, MA   1625 Apr 24 (GRO OPR 294/3) 1626 Jun 11 (SC47/56/1)

Small, Andrew, MA   1628 Dec 7 (SC47/56/1) 1630 Feb 12 (428, 349)

school   1630 Jun 27 (GRO OPR 294/3)

schoolmaster, unnamed   1633 May 5 (GRO OPR 294/3)

KETTLE (par), Fife
(also known as Kingskettle)

Ballingall, Walter, MA   1591 Dec 30 (NP3/1, 265)

Morris, John, MA   1618 Nov 11 (295, 440) 1622 Dec 7 (RS31/4, 192v)

Seton, James, MA   1628 Aug 6 (RS31/7, 300v) Dec 11 (NP1/69A, unfoliated)

KILBERRY (par), Argyllshire
(united with Kilcalmonell before 1560, later in South Knapdale par)

Mudie, James, MA   1617 Aug 20 (*Argyll Sasines*, ed. H. Campbell, i, Edinburgh 1933, no. 3)

KILBIRNIE (par), Ayrshire

Mure, Thomas, d   1617 Nov 23 (278, 382v) 1619 Sep 23 (RS1/4, 256v)

KILBRIDE, *see* East Kilbride *or* West Kilbride

KILCALMONELL, *see* Kilberry

KILCONQUHAR (par), Fife

Calland, George, sir   *died* 1593/4 Jan 20 (CC20/4/2, 363)

Rankine, John, MA (Gl 1604)   1610 Mar 12 (171(2), 369v) *banished* 1628 Apr 1 (S.A. Gillon et al., *Select Justiciary Cases, 1624–1650*, Stair Society 1953, i, 92, no school is given in this reference)

Forrester, Adam   1603 Nov 20 (RS30/4, 261) 1608 Nov 20 (170, 349)

KILGRASTON, Perthshire MRf NO1217
Dunbarney par
Dysart, Andrew   1588/9 Feb 24 (CC20/4/2, 163) 1611 Oct 26
                                  (190, 392)

KILLEARN (par), Stirlingshire
Mushet, Archibald   1621 Dec n.d. (350, 359v)
Fisher, William, MA   1630 Nov 18 (489, 185) 1631 Jan 21 (466, 404)

KILLIN AND STRATHFILLAN (par), Perthshire
(united 1617)
school   *before* 1627 (*Reports*, 180)

KILMACOLM (par), Renfrewshire
Bonar, James   1623 Nov 10 (CC9/14/10, 91)
Ballantyne, James   1624 Apr 10 (365, 425)

KILMARNOCK (par), Ayrshire
Heriot, John, MA, r   1586 Apr 15 (CS1/3(2), 286v)
Lochhead, Allan   1591 May 18 (RH6/3125) *died before* 1604 Dec
                                  27 (CC9/14/2, 127)
Wallace, Michael, later   1595 Nov 25 (CC9/14/3, unfoliated) 1597/8
   student in Glasgow   Jan 27 (CC8/8/32)
Power, Edward, MA   1608 Jul 14 (338, 256v) 1610 Dec 8 (190, 10v)
Smyth, William, MA   1612 Sep 4 (229, 99) 1613 Mar 8 (241,
                                  incomplete foliation)
Burding, James, MA   1622 May 13 (DI121/1)
Anderson, John, MA   1625 Jul n.d. (400, 75)
Taylor, James, MA   1631 Aug 18 (495, 229)
   (Gl 1627)

KILMAURS (par), Ayrshire
Calderwood, John   1614 Nov 25 (GD39/172)
Neill, John   1620 Jan 30 (350, 33) Jun 30 (328, 226)
Simpson, Adam   1623 Nov 19 (367, 49) 1624 Jun 6 (388, 207)
Acheson, Alexander   1632 Aug 7 (RH11/19/6) Nov 25 (492, 120v)

KILMENY (par), Islay
student (Martin McLachlan, 1622 May 29 (398, 103)
poss later min of Kildalton)

KILMICHAEL–GLASSARY (par), Argyll
Lindsay, William, MA   1629 Oct 26 (491, 397)

KILPATRICK (par), Dunbartonshire
Semple, Robert   1609 Feb 8 (348, 85v)
Hamilton, William   1622 May 28 (332, 418v) Dec 14 (CC9/14/10,
                              53v)
Blair, Hugh, MA   1624 Apr 25 (381, 216v) 1628 May 31 (*Argyll
                              Sasines*, ed. H. Campbell, ii, Edinburgh 1934,
                              no. 249)

KILRENNY (par), Fife
Thomson, John, MA   1612 Oct 1 (398, 145v)
Bowsie, Thomas   1633 May 9 (RS31/10)

KILRY, Angus MRf NO2255 (Little Kilry)
Glenisla par
Wilson, George, MA   1615 Jun 14 (275, 202v)

KILSPINDIE (par), Perthshire
(united to Rait before 1620)
Baxter, Henry   1614 Mar 17 (225, 401v) May 13 (*RMS*, vii,
                              1150)

KILSYTH (par), Stirlingshire
(previously known as Monyabroch)
Broom, John, later r at   *before* 1590 Jul 21 (CH2/722/2, unfoliated)
  Kilmarnock
Young, David   1620 May 9 (310, 150) 1627 Jun 13 (398, 391)
Russell, James   1633 Apr 6 (542, 432)

KILTEARN (par), Ross and Cromarty
Grammar and Music School
Tullidaff, John, MA   1631 Nov 11–1633 Nov 11 (460, 63v)

KILWINNING (par), Ayrshire
Harper, John, MA   1594 Sep 24 (CC8/8/28, 339)
Wrighton, Alexander,   1605 Feb 12 (*Fasti*, iii, 116) 1610 Dec 23 (235,
  MA (Gl)   6v)
Ross, Hugh, MA   1617 Jul 18 (267, 118) 1618 Jun 5 (331, 9)
Drysdale, John, MA   1619 Feb 4 (487, 308)
Anderson, John, MA   1621 Jun 28 (351, 156) 1622 Jun 11 (DI121/1)
Ker, Patrick, MA   1624 Jul 29 (RH11/45/5) 1630 Jan 1 (ibid.)
Mure, William, MA   1631 Mar 15 (RH11/45/5) 1632 Aug 1
                              (CC9/7/26, 7)

KIMMERGHAME, Berwickshire MRf NT8150
Edrom par
Cunningham, John   1609 Mar 7 (160, 406) 1623 Aug 21 (360, 16)

KINBATHOCH (par), Aberdeenshire
(later called Towie)
Scrogg, Robert, MA   1626 Sep 11 (437, 250v)
Gibson, Andrew, MA   1620 Sep 5 (RS5/2, 371v) 1621 Feb 8
                                (SC1/60/4, 58)

KINCARDINE, Fife MRf NS9387
Tulliallan par
Penny, Andrew   1611 May 10 (282, 326v) 1621 Feb 26 (RS1/7,
                                279)
Leckie, William   1618 Oct 23 (CC6/5/5, 7)

KINCARDINE O'NEIL (par), Aberdeenshire
Black, Nicholas, MA   1613 Jun 15 (SC1/60/8, 142)
Strachan, John, MA   1618 May 18 (318, 371)
Robertson, William, MA   *before* 1622 May 26 (326, 3)
Chalmer, John, MA   1625 Nov 29 (451, 433) 1628 Sep 18 (RS5/6,
                                344v)

KINCLAVEN (par), Perthshire
Clark, James   1604 Jun 4 (RS48/3, 98v)
Watson, James, MA   1609 Sep 13 (*RMS*, vii, 1782)
Christison, John, MA   1612 Apr 17 (194, 249)

KINEDWARD (par), Aberdeenshire
student   1601 Nov 8 (146, 113)
Geddes, Charles, MA   1609 Jun 8 (174, 28v)
Harvie, Francis, MA   1620 Jun 10 (RS5/2, 327)
Duncan, Alexander, MA   1622 Dec 29 (SC1/60/5, 180v)
Dalgarno, John   1632 Jan 1 (565, 172)

KINFAUNS (par), Perthshire
Carnegie, James   1604 Nov 21 (RS48/3, 326) 1636 Dec 24
                                (512, 274)

KINGHORN (par), Fife
schoolmaster, r, unnamed   1575 n.d. (*Common Good*, 46)
schoolmaster, cl, unnamed   1581 n.d. (*Common Good*, 46)
Biggar, Thomas, MA, r   1605 Dec 9 (RS30/7, 94) 1623 Apr 22 (405,

51v) *still reader* 1633, 1634 n.d. (*Common Good*, 46)

Doctors

Paterson, John	1604 May 26 (RS30/5, 61) 1606 Sep 28 (136, 242)
Wells, William, d	1612 Dec 22 (211, 250) 1627, 1628 n.d. (*Common Good*, 46)
Wemyss, William, d	1623 Apr 22 (405, 51v)
doctor	1633, 1634 n.d. (*Common Good*, 46)
Mackie, Henry, d	1634 Dec 16 (497, 197)

KINGLASSIE (par), Fife

Lyall, John	1619 Apr 28 (CC20/4/7, 64v)
Brown, Robert, MA	1629 Jun 3 (RS31/8, 67v) 1638 May 4 (511, 289)

KINGOLDRUM (par), Angus

Gray, Walter	1619 Nov 6 (CC3/3/4, 56v) 1629 Aug 5 (CC3/9/7)

KING'S CRAMOND, *see* Cramond Regis

KINGSKETTLE, *see* Kettle

KINKELL (par), Perthshire
(united with Trinity Gask 1639)

Donaldson, Thomas	1602 Jul 18 (*RPC*, 1st ser., vi, 738) 1605 Jul 2 (RS48/4, 137v)

KINLOCH, *see* Lundeiff

KINNAIRD (par), Perthshire

Hasson (Awsone), Robert, MA	1613 Mar 19 (222, 214) Sep 3 (G.R. Kinloch (ed.) *Ecclesiastical Records: Selections from the Minutes of the Synod of Fife*, Abbotsford Club 1837, 65)
Watson, James, MA	1614 May 12 (*RMS*, vii, 1084) 1617 Dec 27 (271, 23)
Wemyss, John, MA, min	1627 Jun 3 (J.C. Jessop, *Education in Angus*, London 1931, 49)

KINNEIL (par), West Lothian

schoolmaster	1623 Jan 15 (A. Bain, *The Education Act of*

1696 in West Lothian, Dept of Educational
Studies 1974, 39)

KINNELHEAD, Dumfriesshire MRf NT0301
Kirkpatrick Juxta par
Sharp, John, d   1610 Nov 16 (191, 105v)

KINNELL (par), Angusnot in 71 census
Smart, John   1617 May 9 (CC20/4/6, 251)
Guthrie, William, MA   1618 Oct 25 (CC20/4/7, 3)

KINROSS (par), Kinross-shire
Keltie (Kellie), Adam   1612 Dec 1 (232, 299) 1615 Jun 26 (245, 318v)
Barclay, Robert, MA   1617 Oct 20 (313, 13) Nov 8 (RS49/1, 105v)
Colden, John, MA   1620 Jun 13 (327, 449)
Colden, Robert, MA   1627 Jan 12 (RS1/20, 332) 1629 Mar 12
                                  (RS50/4(1), 55v)
Crawford, Thomas, MA   1622 Jun 12 (399, 391v)
Lightfoot, John, MA   1626 May 4 (RS1/19, 252) Aug 2 (RS1/19,
                                  369v)

KINTORE (par), Aberdeenshire
English School
Mackie, Thomas, cl   *before* 1598 Nov 17 (J. Stuart (ed.), *Selections
                                  from the Records of the Kirk Session, Presbytery
                                  and Synod of Aberdeen*, Spalding Club 1846,
                                  164) 1610 Apr 20 (*Aberdeen Court Bk*, ii, 156)
Meldrum, Arthur, r   1618 Oct 4 (SC1/60/3, 80v) 1619 Oct 24
                                  (SC1/60/4, 186)
Barclay, Adam, MA   1613 Jun 18 (273, 381) Nov 22 (325, 48v)
Sharp, Robert, MA   1621 May 31 (317, 168)
Watt, Andrew, MA   1624 Jan 24 (SC1/60/6, 179) May 22 (RS7/2,
                                  131)
Fraser, Walter, MA   1629 Jul 30 (SC1/60/9, 175)
Gardyne, Alexander, MA   1633 Nov 12 (483, 185)

KIRKBEAN (par), Kirkcudbrightshire
Thomson, Adam, d   1626 Feb 9 (405, 243) 1651 Apr 5 (576, 333)

KIRKBRIDE, *see* Traquair

KIRKCALDY (par), Fife
Grammar School
Spens, David, MA, min   1582 Jul 10 (*Kirkcaldy Recs.*, 71)

school	1582 Oct 8 (*Kirkcaldy Recs.*, 73)
school vacant	1584 Jan 18 (*Kirkcaldy Recs.*, 104)
Michelson, John, MA	1585 May 3 (*Kirkcaldy Recs.*, 106) 1586 Sep 10 (46, 197v) 1587 Oct 9 (ibid., 118)
Powtie, Thomas, MA	1591 Oct 29 (*Kirkcaldy Recs.*, 130)
Melville, Thomas, MA	1607 Aug 31 (NP1/57, 118) 1613 Jan 20 (282, 392)
Row (Reid), John, MA	1620 Jun 26 (346, 255v) 1622 Jul 8 (335, 87v)
Law, Mungo, MA (Gl 1627), min of Dysart 1636	1628 May 31 (RS1/23, 365) Oct 15 (471, 130)

Doctors

doctor, unnamed	1582 Jul 10 (*Kirkcaldy Recs.*, 71)
Morris, John, d	1608 Dec 8 (166, 144) 1627 Oct 11 (RS1/22, 199v)
Davidson, Robert, d	1613 Nov n.d. (291, 235) *'scholemaster'* 1624 Jan 2 (RS1/14, 221)
March, Francis, d	1617 Jul 19 (271, 212v) 1619 Jul 19 (271, 212v)
Thomson, John, d	1625 May 28 (RS1/17, 209) 1626 Jun 10 (395, 275v)

Music School

school	1582 Jul 10 (*Kirkcaldy Recs.*, 72) Oct 8 (ibid., 73)
Beverage, Henry, MA	1596/7 Feb 25 (*Kirkcaldy Recs.*, 145)
Malcolm, John, MA	1630 Dec 30 (*The Presbytrie Booke of Kirkcaldie*, ed. W. Stevenson, Kirkcaldy 1890, 22) 1636 Jun 23 (ibid., 96)

Reading School

Morrison, James, r	*discharged* 1587 Oct 9 (*Kirkcaldy Recs.*, 118)

Sewing School

Williamson, Margaret	*discharged* 1596/7 Mar 16 (*Kirkcaldy Recs.*, 145)

Adventure Schools

school	*discharged* 1587 n.d. (J.M. Beale, *A History of the Burgh and Parochial Schools of Fife*, Edinburgh 1983, 6)
school	*discharged* 1596 n.d. (Beale, *Schools of Fife*, 6)

KIRKCOLM (par), Wigtownshire

Rodman, John	1627 May 5 (411, 189)

KIRKCONNEL (par), Dumfriesshire
(united with Kirkpatrick Fleming 1609)
Whillis (Quhillous), Gilbert   1615 May 26 (265, 344) Jun 20 (265, 348v)
   or Cuthbert

KIRKCUDBRIGHT (par), Kirkcudbrightshire
Grammar School

McClennan, Ninian, MA	*before* 1576 (J.A. Russell, *History of Education in the Stewartry of Kirkcudbright*, Newton Stewart 1950, 119)
Dodds, James, MA, min of Dalry 1567, min of Kirkcudbright 1579	1576 n.d. (Russell, *History of Education*, 120) 1578 Dec 3 (*Kirkcudbright Recs.*, 46)
Aikman, John, MA	1582 Apr 14 (*Kirkcudbright Recs.*, 167)
Turner, William, MA (SAS 1579)	1582 Apr 30 (Russell, *History of Education*, 120) 1590 Oct 31 (*Kirkcudbright Recs.*, 257)
Dickson, James	1586 Apr 29 (*Kirkcudbright Recs.*, 208) 1591 n.d. (Russell, *History of Education*, 120)
Blyth, David, MA, min	1591 Oct 13 (*Kirkcudbright Recs.*, 268) *discharged* 1592/3 Feb 9 (ibid., 282)
Gledstanes, Herbert, MA	1592/3 Feb 9 (*Kirkcudbright Recs.*, 282)
Callander, John	1593 Sep 8 (*Kirkcudbright Recs.*, 287)
Sharpro, John, MA, later min of Tongland	1594 Oct 10 (*Kirkcudbright Recs.*, 304)
Thomson, John	1595/6 Jan 21 (Russell, *History of Education*, 121) 1603 Dec 29 (CC8/8/39)
Dalzell, Mungo, MA	1605 Aug 6 (CC8/8/43, 147v)
Thomson, Paul	1607 Jun 12 (151, 37)
Glen, James, MA	1607 Oct 26 (*Kirkcudbright Recs.*, 25) 1613 May 5 (ibid., 133)
Hay, William	1612 Apr 13 (211, 361v)
Brown, John, MA	1612 Nov 4 (*Kirkcudbright Recs.*, 123) 1618 Oct 26 (ibid., 219)
Crawford, George, MA	1619 Jun 15 (*Kirkcudbright Recs.*, 244)
Lamb, James, MA, also to *teach singing*	1620 n.d. *for three years* (Russell, *History of Education*, 122)
McClellan, John	1620 Oct 30 (311, 408)
Forrester, James	1621 n.d. (*Kirkcudbright Recs.*, 268) 1626 Feb 11 (RS22/2, 183)
Airdrie, William	1627 Feb 14 (*Kirkcudbright Recs.*, 345)
Rutherford, George, MA, r	1629 n.d. (Russell, *History of Education*, 122) 1633 Aug 20 (RS1/37, 323)

Doctors

order for doctor	1584 Oct 14 (Russell, *History of Education*, 120)
	Oct 28 (*Kirkcudbright Recs.*, 197)
order for doctor	1591 Oct 13 (*Kirkcudbright Recs.*, 268)
McCartney, William, d	*before* 1619 Oct 20 (*Kirkcudbright Recs.*, 250)
	1621 Mar 21 (344, 312v)

KIRKINNER (par), Wigtownshire
Williamson, Nathaniel, MA 1632 Apr 26 (RS1/33, 274)

KIRKINTILLOCH, Dunbartonshire
Lenzie par

Plaine, George	1599 ((T. Watson, *Kirkintilloch: Town and Parish*, Glasgow 1894, 242)
Fleming, Malcolm	1599 (Watson, *Kirkintilloch*, 241)
Gudine, James	1617 (Watson, *Kirkintilloch*, 241)
Dollar, John	1620, 1642 (Watson, *Kirkintilloch*, 242)
Ramsay, John, MA	1627 Apr 11 (451, 300v)
Bull, James	1627–8 (Watson, *Kirkintilloch*, 241)
Plaine, Malcolm	1627–8 (Watson, *Kirkintilloch*, 242)

KIRKMICHAEL (par), Ayrshire
Marshall, John   1633 Dec 17 (492, 423)

KIRKMICHAEL, Perthshire, *see* Strathardle

KIRKNEWTON (par), Midlothian

Rawson, Robert	1619 Dec 30 (354, 158v) 1620 Nov 16 (342, 406v)
school	1627 (*Reports*, 82)

KIRK OF MURE (par), Stirlingshire
Leach, William   1613 Oct 5 (RS58/4, 60v)

KIRK OF STEILL, *see* Ladykirk

KIRKPATRICK-DURHAM (par), Kirkcudbrightshire
Turner, James, d   1620 Mar 19 (315, 53) 1622 Feb 17 (418, 124)

KIRKPATRICK-FLEMING, *see* Kirkconnel

KIRKTONHILL, Kincardineshire MRf NO6966
Marykirk par
Stewart, Andrew   1616 Feb 10 (CC3/9/4)

KIRKURD (par), Peebleshire

Tweedie, John	1627 Mar 13 (402, 195v)
Moffat, George	1630 Jun 5 (SC42/28/2)

KIRKWALL (par), Orkney

Houston, John, MA, c, r	1554 May 27 (J.B. Craven, *History of the Church in Orkney 1558–1662*, Kirkwall 1897, 48) 1594 Sep 4 (NP1/36, 35)
Dishington, Andrew, MA, min of Sandwick and Stromness 1599, of Rousay and Egilsay 1601, of Hoy 1614, of Walls and Flotta 1617	1595/6 Feb 26 (CS7/196, 62) 1601 May 22 (ibid.)
Inglis, Patrick, MA (SA 1597)	1617 Sep 16 (Craven, *Church in Orkney*, 130)
Jack, James	1602 Apr 25 (130, 416)
Balfour, Robert, MA	1621 Apr 3 (RS43/, 47v)
Watson, David, r, later min of Rousay	1622 May 11 (RS43/2, 36) 1625 Jan 8 (RS43/3, 13v)
Sinclair, Hugh	1626 Mar 25 (RS43/3, 178)
Cargill, William, MA	1629 Apr 30 (CC17/5/2, 259) 1638 Jun 1 (529, 24)
Mudie, George, MA, pr, r	1629 Nov 20 (Craven, *Church in Orkney*, 157–8)

Doctors

Bonar, John, d	1593 Nov 23 (NP1/36, 31)
Ogston, George, d	1605 Feb 5 (178, 82v)
Tullidaff, John, MA, d	1623 Dec 30 (RS43/2, 155) 1624 Feb 19 (NP1/75B, 8)
Dishington, John, MA, d	1625 Jan 18 (RS43/3, 39v) 1626 Feb 4 (RS43/3, 196)

KIRRIEMUIR (par), Angus

Cabell, Patrick	1596 Apr 18 (110, 177) 1616 Jan 6 (289, 32v)
Haly (Hely), Robert, MA	1611 Mar 4 (259, 23)
Cumming, George, MA student	1619 Dec 7 (CC3/9/7) 1620 Jun 20 (387, 36) 1620 Aug 23 (RS33/1, 131)
Thomson (Henisoun), John, MA	1621 Dec 24 (341, 459) 1627 Feb 10 (401, 283v)

KNAPPERNA, Aberdeenshire MRf NK0431
Slains par

Scorgie (Scorgeauche), David	1628 Dec 13 (RS5/6, 323)

LADYKIRK (par), Berwickshire MRf NT8847
(also known as Kirk of Steill *or* Upsetlington)

Anderson, Alexander	1606 May 28 (CC8/8/42, 56v)
Cranston, Hugh	1621 Jul 29 (SC60/56/1, 242v) Dec 18 (SC60/56/1, 78)
Trotter, Andrew	1626 Feb 10 (SC60/56/3, 46)

LADYLAND, Ayrshire MRf NS3257
Kilbirnie par

Algeo, Robert	1600 Nov 26 (RS11/1, 39)

LAMBERTON (par), Berwickshire, *see also* Ayton
(united with Foulden 1616, Ayton 1627)

Houliston (Houlatstoun), William	1626 May 20 (403, 399)

LAMINGTON (par), Lanarkshire

Shanks, John	1606 Nov 18 (182, 223)
Wilson, John, MA	1622 Feb 5 (RS40/2A, 61v)

LANARK (par), Lanarkshire
(also known as Castlehill)

Grammar School

Swan, Ninian, r at Carmichael	1567 Oct 9 (*Lanark Recs.*, 36)
Mackie, David	1570 Aug 19 (*Lanark Recs.*, 51) *resigned* c.1571/2 Mar (ibid., 65n.)
Lindsay, Robert, MA, min	c.1575–6 (*Lanark Recs.*, 70) *demitted* 1581 May 13 (ibid., 79)
Weir, James, MA	*appointed* 1581 May 13 (*Lanark Recs.*, 79)
Wilson, Matthew, MA (Gl 1587)	c.1586–7 (*Lanark Recs.*, 91) 1588 Candlemas and Beltane (ibid.)
Hetton, Thomas	1588 Lammas and Hallowmas (*Lanark Recs.*, 92)
schoolmaster, unnamed	1588–90 (*Lanark Recs.*, 94, 100)
school	1590/1 Jan 15 (*Lanark Recs.*, 101)
Bannatyne, Robert, MA	1592 Nov 16 (*Lanark Recs.*, 108)

schoolmaster, unnamed	1599, 1600 n.d. (*Common Good*, 46)
Gleghorn, George, MA	1604 Aug 8 (101, 442v)
Cunningham, David, MA	1606 Dec 25 (126, 250)
Ogston, George	1611 Jan 30 (219, 69v)
Young, Gavin, MA	1616 Jan 9 (298, 262v)
schoolmaster, unnamed	1614–15 (*Lanark Recs.*, 122) 1621, 1622 n.d. (*Common Good*, 46)
Veitch *or* Welch, John, MA	1622 Apr 22 (324, 70) 1623 Nov 7 (359, 187)
schoolmaster, unnamed	1627, 1628 n.d. (*Common Good*, 47)
Young, Matthew, MA	1632 Mar 26 (DI75/4, 166)
Paterson, John, MA	1633 Mar 26 (490, 421) 1642 Feb 21 (547, 31)

Doctors

doctor, unnamed	1592 Nov 16 (*Lanark Recs.*, 108)
Lamb (Law), Thomas, d, English, Latin and Music	1615 Jun n.d. (*Lanark Recs.*, 122)

Music School

schoolmaster, unnamed	1627, 1628 n.d. (*Common Good*, 47)
Meiklejohn, Robert	1628 Aug 5 (421, 143v) 1632 Jun 25 (466, 337)

LANGTON (par), Berwickshire

Anderson, William	1595 Jul 1 (87, 299v)
Sinclair, Samuel, MA (Ed 1599), min 1608	1600 Jul 4 (77, 321v)
Cockburn, John, MA	1613 May 19 (215, 173v) 1614 n.d. (228, 452)
Kellie, William, MA	1620 Jun 14 (RS18/1, 150)
Lightbody, George, MA	1627 Jul 3 (RS1/22, 366v)

LARGO (par), Fife

Jameson, Thomas, i	1567 n.d. (*Register of Ministers*, 23)
Kingzo, Herman	1607 Jun 29 (304, 171)
Paterson, Oliver	1617 Jan 15 (278, 199v)
Duncan, David, MA	1623 Mar 21 (499, 196)
Davidson, George, n	1626 Mar 27 (RS31/6, 81v) 1633 Mar 7 (RS31/10, 144v)

LARGS (par), Ayrshire

Bennett, James	1595 Jun 12 (*RPC*, 1st ser., v, 654)
Mure, Thomas, MA, later min of Cumbrae	1605 Sep 11 (*RPC*, 1st ser., vii, 614)
Bogle, John, MA (Gl 1607)	1611 May 22 (CC9/14/3, unfoliated) Nov 16 (275, 27v)

Paterson, John   1619 May 1 (332, 189) 1628 Oct 19 (494, 129)

LASSWADE (par), Midlothian
Galbraith, William   1602 Sep 16 (94, 45)
school   1615 May 12 (J. Lee, *Lectures on the History of
                                        the Church of Scotland*, ii, Edinburgh 1860, 437)
                                        Aug 20 (ibid.)
Watson, Andrew, MA, r   1616 Nov n.d. (Lee, *Lectures*, 437) 1618 Dec 8
                                        (CC8/8/50, 175)
Big, Archibald   1623 Dec 8 (CC8/17/6, 42v)
Blacklaw (Blackhall),   1625 Sep 11 (Lee, *Lectures*, 437) 1650 Jan 4
    Daniel, MA, cl, r   (ibid.)
no provision for   1627 May 21 (GD90/2/59)
    schoolmaster

LAUDER (par), Berwickshire
Smith, John   1588 Jul 12 (GD350/1, 4)
schoolmaster, unnamed   1594 n.d. (*Common Good*, 47)
Edmeston, Andrew   1604 Dec 6 (124, 56) 1605 May 13 (118, 278)
Courtie, David, MA   1608 Jun 13 (197, 178)
Paterson, John, MA   1609 Jun 6 (162, 256)
Craig *or* Gray, Malcolm   1612 Jan 4 (208, 75) *'sumtyme'* Jun 22 (236,
                                        243)
Horne, John, MA   1613 Apr 29 (430, 112v) 1617 Sep 27 (266,
                                        139)
Lauder, James, MA   1618 Jul 22 (RS56/1, 120) 1620 Mar 7 (304,
                                        177v)
Allan *or* Ellem (Ewin),   1620 Aug 2 (333, 135v) 1633 n.d. (*Common
    George, MA, b   Good*, 47)

LAURISTON, Kincardineshire MRf NO7666 (Lauriston Castle)
St Cyrus par
Lindsay, David, MA   1602 Dec 10 (CC3/9/2)
Stewart, Thomas, MA   1630 Apr 4 (RS1/28, 206v) 1633 Apr 22 (462,
                                        466)

LAWS, Angus MRf NO4935
Monifeith par
Dunmore, Alexander   1597 Apr 23 (CC8/8/44, 51) 1607 Apr 23
                                        (ibid.)

LEFNORES, Ayrshire MRf NS5420
Cumnock par
Houston, James, MA   1622 Feb 11 (343, 92)

LEGGATIS BRIG, Fife MRf NT1087 (Dunfermline)
Dunfermline par
Hislop, John   1606 Nov 3 (*Dunfermline Recs.*, 24)

LEIGHTONHILL, Angus MRf NO6381
Brechin par
Moncreiff, Alexander, MA   1620 Nov 23 (354, 220v)

LEITH, SOUTH (par), Midlothian
Grammar School (Trinity House)
no grammar school   1598 Oct 30 (CH2/121/2)
Provand, Thomas, MA,   *boys separated from girls* 1602 Jul 25 (*South Leith*
    min of Leswalt 1614   *Recs.*, 5) 1608 May 16 (154, 366v)
no schoolmaster   1610 Apr 3 (*South Leith Recs.*, 9)
Hogg, Thomas, MA (AbK)   1612 Apr 2 (205, 26) 1616 Aug 8 (*South Leith*
                               Recs., 15)
Spens, William, MA   1622 Oct 10 (RS25/7, 60) 1626 Aug 23
                               (CC8/10/9)
Shaw, John, MA (Gl)   *temporary* 1629 Oct 8 (*South Leith Recs.*, 16–17)
Sanderson, Bernard, MA   1629 Oct 8 (*South Leith Recs.*, 17) *occurs* 1634
                               Nov 13 (489, 398)

Doctors
Cranston, John, MA (SA),   1612 Apr 20 (265, 82)
    later min of Leith
Reid, Alexander, MA, d   1613 Mar 20 (CC8/8/48, 147)
Abernethie, William, MA   1618 Aug 29 (289, 421)
Hedderwick, Robert, MA   1621 Oct 9 (351, 340)
Adinston, David, MA (Ed)   1629 (*South Leith Recs.*, 17)

Music School
Cumming, David, p,   1583 Apr 19 (*RSS*, viii, 1264) Aug 24 (ibid.,
    preceptor and master of   1469)
    the college kirk of
    Restalrig
Cumming, William   1596 Jun 9 (54, 91v)
Makeson, Eleazer   *'professor' of music* 1604 Jun 18 (RS15/2, 250)
Thomson, Martin   1617 Feb 3 (260, 484v)

Vernacular Schools
Hay, James, r, *'teichar'*   1598 Jun 27 (*South Leith Recs.*, 2) *to take all*
                            the girls 1602 Jul 25 (ibid., 5) 1604 Dec 21
                            (RS24/5, 82)
Blacklaw, Daniel, *'teichar'*   1598 Jun 27 (*South Leith Recs.*, 2) *slack in*

	attending on the youth 'committed to him by the congregation' Oct 3 (CH2/121/2, unfoliated)
Anderson, William	1626 Jan 26 (RS25/11, 81)
Campbell, Archibald, d	1628 Oct 25 (428, 284v)

Dame School

Morton, Elspeth	1598 Apr 27 *order to close by Whitsun* (*South Leith Recs.*, 2)

LEITH, NORTH (par), Midlothian
(also known as North Kirk or Brigend of Leith)
North Leith parish was founded in 1599 on a section of Canongate parish in the chapel of St Ninian reconstructed. The school was at the 'brigend'. On 18 Aug 1614 schools other than the reader's were prohibited because part of his stipend was for schoolmastering (CH2/621/1, page [sic] 684).

Grammar School

Wardrope, Moses, cl, r	1606 Jun 18 (127, 9) 1633 Dec 22 (CH2/621/1, unfoliated)

Doctor

Wood, George, d *'on the north side of the brig'*	1595 Jul 24 (49, 570)

Dame Schools

Pinkerton, Katherine *and* Hunter, Jean	*order to close* 1614 Aug 18 (CH2/621/1, page 684)
Kilbowie, Janet *and* Gourlay, Margaret, *mother and daughter, and another*	1633 Dec 22 (CH2/621/1, unfoliated) 1639 Nov 22 (ibid.)

LEITH, WATER OF, *see* Edinburgh, Dean Village

LENZIE (par), Dunbartonshire
Orr, John	1625 Sep 8 (387, 253)

LESLIE (par), Fife
Rollok, Robert, n, r	1623 May 30 (RS31/4, 344)
McClellan, Thomas	1631 May 18 (514, 105)

LESMAHAGOW (par), Lanarkshire
(also known as Abbeygreen)
Arneil, John	1598 May 30 (363, 197)

Dalrymple, John, MA   1621 Sep 27 (325, 310v)
Hamilton, John, MA   1623 May 1 (465, 281) Jul 23 (387, 282)
Matthew, William, MA   1626 Jun 20 (RS40/2A, 270)
Young, Matthew, MA   1626 Nov 13 (392, 19) 1628 Jul 18 (411, 83)
Crawford, John, MA   1631 Jan 5 (RS40/2A, 123) 1632 Nov 5
                            (RS40/2A, 147v)
Watson, Archibald, MA   1633 Dec 11 (483, 24)
Doctor
Young, Thomas, d   1627 Dec 28 (541, 353)

LESSUDEN (par), Roxburghshire
(also known as St Boswell's)
Riddell, John *or* George   1628 Mar 31 (RS56/4, 233) Aug 12 (RS56/4,
                            257)

LETHAM, Fife MRf NO3014
Monimail par
Greig, Walter, MA   1617 Dec 23 (RS31/1) 1619 Apr 28
                            (CC20/4/7, 96)
Cobb, John   1624 Jun 10 (CC20/4/8, 59) 1626 Nov 3
                            (CC20/4/8, 252v)
Busbie, Alexander   1608 Jan 30 (147, 200v)
Baxter, Henry   1622 Feb 16 (RS31/3, 382)

LEUCHARS (par), Fife
Allan, Andrew, MA, r   1593/4 Jan 10 (*RKSSA*, 704n.)
Reid, James, MA (SAS   1606 Mar 22 (282, 185) Aug 28 (125, 252)
  1575)
endowment for school   c.1630 (J. Lee, *Lectures on the History of the
                            Church of Scotland*, ii, Edinburgh 1860, 429)

LEVEN, Fife MRf NO3801
Scoonie par
Sym, David, n   1602 Sep 18 (95, 202v)
Lundie, Robert   1622 Dec 7 (351, 369v)
Black, Robert, MA   1627 Oct 9 (RS31/7, 72v) 1634 Jun 3 (477,
                            140)

LIBBERTON (par), Lanarkshire
(united to Quothquan 1664)
Brown, James   1631 Apr 28 (473, 359)

LIBERTON (par), Midlothian
schoolmaster, unnamed   1598 Jul 25 (CH2/121/2, unfoliated)
Greig (Gray), William   1622 Aug 22 (CC8/8/51, 295)

LICKPRIVICK, Lanarkshire MRf NS6152
East Kilbride par
Nisbet, David   1619 May 19 (CC9/14/7, 64)

LIFF (par), Angus
(united to Logie-Dundee 1613)
Fithie (Futhe), James   1616 Feb 21 (304, 308) 1626 May 30 (486, 96)
Corstorphine, Martin, MA   1631 Feb 15 (516, 397)

LINDEAN, *see* Galashiels

LINLITHGOW (par), West Lothian
Winzet, Ninian, sir   *expelled* 1561 July n.d. (GD215/1877)
schoolmaster, unnamed   1564 Mar 30 (GD215/1877)
Powrie, William, MA   1571 (GD215/1877, 96)
Coill, Alexander, MA, n   1575 May 10 (*RSS*, vii, 182) 1577/8 Jan 10
     (GD215/1877, 79)
Maxwell, Thomas, MA   1587 Oct 31 (39, 148)
Nairn, Robert, MA   1592 Oct 31 (GD76/184)
Monypenny, Patrick, MA,   1592/3 Jan 8 (GD76/185) 1608 May 17
  later min of Haining   (GD215/1877)
student   1606 Jun 25 (156, 40v)
Thomson, Robert, MA   1611 Jul 3 (G.R. Kinloch (ed.), *Ecclesiastical
     Records: Selections from the Minutes of the Synod
     of Fife*, Abbotsford Club 1837, 23)
Haly (Hely), Robert, MA   1616 May 22 (271, 46)
Wiseman, James, MA   1617 Jun 30 (CSP Dom, 92, p. 78; Nicholls,
     Progresses, iii, 326) 1633 Aug 16 (GD215/1877)
     1635 May 8 (ibid.)
Rhynd, Alexander, MA   1618 Jul 8 (280, 30v) 1632 Mar 20 (459, 366v)
Doctors
Donaldson, John, s   1581 May 31 (*Scot. Antiq.*, xi, 131)
Dewar, Patrick, MA, d   1620 Sep 30 (RS25/4, 28) Nov 7 (RS25/4,
     30v)
Haly (Hely), William, MA, d 1623 Feb 14 (GD215/1877)
Russell, James, d   1627 Jan 25 (403, 200v) 1629 May 24 (442,
     83v)
doctor   1629 Feb 14 (GD215/1877)
Keith, Robert, d, r   1633 Sep 6 (GD215/1877)

Music School
Park, Michael   1618 Dec 9 (CC8/8/50, 189v)

LINTON (par), Roxburghshire
Telfer, William   1624 Mar 19 (361, 192v) 1632 Feb 23
                                       (RS1/35, 65)

LINTON BRIGS, East Lothian MRf NT5977 (East Linton)
Prestonkirk par
Burnside, John, r   1604 Jan 26 (180, 378v)

LITTLE DALTON (par), Dumfriesshire
students   1613 Oct 5 (223, 180v)

LITTLE GOURDIE, Perthshire MRf NO1342
chapel of Holy Spirit, Clunie par
Bisset, George *'institutor*   1593 May 25 (*RMS*, vi, 142)
  puerorum'

LITTLEHOPE, Selkirkshire MRf NT2321 (Rodono)
(also known as Rodono Chapel)not in 71 census
Ettrick par
Greig, William   1619 Apr 5 (RS1/3, 88v)

LIVINGSTON (par), West Lothian
Johnston, John   1627 Jun 15 (NP1/74, 312v) 1633 Dec 12
                                       (474, 253)

LOCHHEAD, Argyllshire MRf NR7120
(later called Campbeltown)
Kilchiaran par
Spang, John   1622 May 28 (RS1/11, 43v)

LOCHWINNOCH (par), Renfrewshire
(also known as Semple)
Sellar, Thomas   1619 Nov 20 (412, 2v) 1621 Feb 20 (413, 15v)
Orr, John   1622 Nov 29 (363, 362v) Dec 26 (CC9/14/11,
                                       226)
Carswell, James   1627 May 17 (441, 115)
Adam, James   1632 Oct 14 (CC9/7/25, 559)

LOGIE (par), Fife
(also known as Logie-Murdoch)
Duncan, James   1618 Mar 21 (CC20/4/6, 415)

student   1618 Aug 24 (275, 335)
Burn, James, MA   1630 Dec 14 (RS1/29, 357)

LOGIE (par), Stirlingshire
(also known as Logie-Atheron)
Grammar school *'of old'*   *before* 1627 May 22 (*Reports*, 202)
English school   1627 May 22 (*Reports*, 202)
Speir, Robert, MA   1621 Aug 31 (332, 276v)

LOGIE-COLDSTONE (par), Aberdeenshire
Scroggie, Robert, MA   1630 Apr 30 (RS5/7, 61) Aug 30 (RS5/7,
                                 148)

LOGIE-DUNDEE, *see* Liff

LOGIE-DURNO, *see* Chapel of Garioch

LOGIE-MONTROSE (par), Angus
Gray, William, MA, min   c.1563 (*The Autobiography and Diary of Mr
                                 James Melville*, ed. R. Pitcairn, Wodrow Society
                                 1842, 16)

LOGIERAIT (par), Perthshire
Bairdie, Andrew   1633 May 13 (RS50/6, 297)

LONGCASTLE (par), Wigtownshire
Vaus (Waus), William, r   1581 Apr 22 (CH4/1/1, ii, 57) 1581/2 Feb 15
                                 (CS7/55, 183)

LONGFORGAN (par), Perthshire
Gill, John   1617 Oct 9 (RS49/1, 42) 1643 Nov 7 (582,
                                 212)

LONGFORMACUS (par), Berwickshire
Household School
Martin, William   1613 Jul 26 (CC8/8/48, 8v)

LONGLEY (par), Aberdeenshire (previously in Banffshire)
(also called Inverugie, now St Fergus)
Swan, Alexander, r   1613 Sep 16 (CH2/89/1(2), 151v)
school   1614 Aug 20 (CH2/89/1(2), 166)
schoolmaster, r, unnamed   1615 Aug 31 (CH2/89/1(2), 186)
promise of schoolmaster   1616 Sep 19 (CH2/89/1(2), 201)

school	1617 Oct 2 (CH2/89/1(2), 214) 1619 Sep 9 (ibid., 237v) 1620 Sep 21 (ibid., 255)

LONGNEWTON (par), Roxburghshire

Mather, James	1598 Oct 23 (95, 131)
Bruce, Archibald	1615 Jul 9 (261, 136v)
Ker, Robert	1618 Mar 7 (307, 162v)
Abercrombie, Robert	1620 May 11 (307, 160)
Rodger, Edmund	1621 Sep 14 (338, 147v)

LONGNIDDRY, East Lothian MRf NT4476
Tranent par, transferred to Gladsmuir 1650

Norvell, William	1589 May 15 (30, 469v)
Adinston, William	1603 Jul 7 (97, 141)

LONGSIDE (par), Aberdeenshire
(formerly called Wester Ugie, disjoined from Peter Ugie 1620)

no schoolmaster	1624 n.d. (I.J. Simpson, *Education in Aberdeenshire before 1872*, London 1947, 104)
schoolmaster, unnamed	1625 n.d. (Simpson, *Education in Aberdeenshire*, 104)
Arbuthnott, Alexander, MA, r	1625 Jun 5 (CH2/699/1) 1630 Dec 31 (ibid.)
Robertson, John, MA, r	1626 Oct 30 (CH2/699/1)
Martin, Alexander, MA, r	1631 Jan 10 (CH2/699/1)

LONMAY (par), Aberdeenshire

school	1609 Aug 8 (CH2/89/1, 125)
no school	1610 Sep 13 (CH2/89/1, 134)
Rires, Thomas, min	1613 Jul 29 (CH2/89/1(2), 150)
no school	1614 Jul 7 (CH2/89/1(2), 163v) 1617 Aug 21 (ibid., 212v)
school	1619 Aug 12 (CH2/89/1(2), 236)

LOUDOUN (par), Ayrshire

Melville, William, MA	1624 Sep 30 (373, 264) 1629 Nov 13 (CH2/171/2)

LUDQUHARN, Aberdeenshire MRf NJ4345
Longside par

Martin, Robert, MA	1623 Jun 27 (352, 52v)

LUFFNESS, East Lothian MRf NT4780
Aberlady par
Pringle, William   1626 Feb 7 (463, 148v)

LUNDEIFF (par), Perthshire MRf NO2644
(also known as Kinloch)
Murray, Robert, MA   1618 Aug 17 (RS49/2, 143v) 1620 May 31
                                      (RS49/3, 223v)
Paton, John   1625 Oct 16 (RS50/1, 415) Dec 2 (RS50/2,
                                      14v)

LUTHRIE, Fife MRf NO3319
Creich par
Meldrum, John, MA   1623 Jul 8 (429, 264v)

LYNE (par), Peebleshire
(incorporating Megget 1621)
agreement to sustain a   1600 Jun 26 (CH2/295/1, 64, Report of the
   schoolmaster   Visitation of Lyne)

MADDERTY (par), Perthshire
Donaldson, Thomas   1600 Aug 20 (109, 215)
Ballingall, William   1632 Feb 28 (448, 221)

MAINS-STRATHMARTINE (par), Angus
(location of school uncertain, parishes united 1792)
Petrie, John   *before* 1604 Jan 12 (162, 280v) 1625 Dec 24
                                      (CC20/4/8, 330v)

MAKERSTOUN (par), Roxburghshire
McDougall *or* McDowall,   1608 Apr 10 (173, 417) 1621 Dec 21 (408, 340v)
   Robert

MARKINCH (par), Fife
Melville, Thomas   1603 Apr 21 (227, 77v)
Henryson *or* Henderson,   1607 Sep 24 (146, 123v) 1608 Dec 11
   John, MA   (RS30/11, 342v)
Davidson, Robert   1615 May 7 (258, 116v) 1619 Sep 28 (337,
                                      264)
Duddingston, George, MA, 1620 Aug 5 (431, 174) 1633 Oct 17 (466, 397)
   freeman, b, r

MARYKIRK (par), Kincardineshire
(also known as Aberlethnott)
Irving, James, MA   1618 Jan 16 (289, 418) 1620 Jun 10 (313, 217)
Irving, John, MA   1626 May 18 (388, 163v) Jul 6 (RS7/2, 265)
Barclay, John, MA   1630 Jul 9 (446, 377) 1631 May 6 (RS1/31, 84v)

MARYTON (par), Angus
Ferrour, Richard   1609 Apr 9 (166, 368)
Herring, James, MA   1625 Jul 28 (RS1/17, 338v)

MARYWELL, Aberdeenshire MRf NJ5603
Lumphanan par
Gibbon, George   1612 Jul 11 (201, 337v)

MAUCHLINE (par), Ayrshire
Steven, William, MA   1616 Aug 17 (RS12/2, 498) 1626 Jun 15 (510, 183)
Peebles, Thomas, MA   1627 Feb 16 (RS12/4, 10) 1636 Jan 18 (*Clan Campbell*, v, 206)

MAXTON (par), Roxburghshire
schoolmaster, unnamed   1611 Apr 16 (CH2/327/1, 76)

MAXWELLHEUGH, Roxburghshire MRf NT7333
Kelso par
Mulligan (Mulecin), Robert   1628 Jun 18 (RS56/4, 381)

MAYBOLE (par), Ayrshire
Mure, Robert, MA, cf.   1602 May 11 (Pitcairn, *Trials*, iii, 163)
  Ayr
Power, Gilbert, MA   1605 Nov 15 (RS11/3, 232) 1606 Apr 23 (117, 417)
Porterfield, John, MA   1608 Aug 5 (RS11/4, 212v) Sep 5 (*RPC*, 1st ser., viii, 671)
Ramsay, Patrick, MA   1611 Feb 9 (196, 68)
Burn, John, MA (SA 1610),   1612 May 13 (NP1/67, 14) *'olim'* 1618 Jul 24
  min of Kirkoswald 1616   (RS1/2, 99)
Burn, David, MA   1616 Mar 10 (309, 222) 1618 Jul 24 (RS1/2, 99)
Drysdale, John, MA   1622 Jul 1 (400, 70) Nov 21 (362, 202v)
McKaill, Hugh, MA   1624 Jul 19 (RS12/3, 161)
Henryson, Edward, MA   1627 Jun 6 (CC9/7/21, 369v)

Abercrombie, David, MA   1628 Jan 21 (CC9/7/22, 134v) 1629 Mar 21
  (Gl 1626)   (RS12/4, 386v)
Hume (Home), John, MA, r1631 Nov 11 (GD25/9, Box 44, Bundle 5)
                         1637 May 10 (B18/1/1, 233)

MEARNS (par), Renfrewshire
Skene, David, n   1597 Nov 2 (105, 421)
Moir, Adam   1605 Dec 12 (CC9/14/6, 87)
Hutcheson, Robert, MA   1621 Mar 7 (CC9/14/8, 91v)
Cassells, Robert   1630 Mar 28 (CC9/14/13, 25v) 1631 Oct 15
                         (495, 406)

MEGGET, *see* Lyne

MEIGLE (par), Perthshire
Duncan, Thomas   1601 Jun 2 (85, 105)
Petrie, William, MA   1611 Jan n.d. (205, 130)
Ramsay, David, MA   1618 Apr 13 (373, 72v) Jun 21 (272, 13)
Moncreiff, Alexander   1626 Sep 8 (409, 99v) 1627 May 12 (451, 73)

MEIKLE HARESHAW, Lanarkshire MRf NS8155 (Shotts)
Shotts par
Young, James   1633 Jul 25 (RS40/4A, 134v)

MELLERSTAINS, Berwickshire MRf NT6439
Earlston par
Downs, James   1605 Aug 20 (RS55/1, 37v)

MELROSE (par), Roxburghshire
Coke, William   1608 Apr 20 (*Melrose Recs.*, i, p. 62) Jun 1
                         (ibid., 69)
Cumin, Robert   1611 Jun 16 (190, 285)
Tunno, Robert   1612 Mar 23 (211, 153)
Brown, Robert, MA   1612 Nov 27 (329, 184) 1623 Oct 26 (359,
                         52v)
Mudie, John, MA   1613 Jul 4 (223, 354v) Dec 15 (229, 130)
no schoolmaster, but   1613 Aug 12 (CH2/327/1, 141)
  Alexander Wishart; *'keips*
  the schole'
Mudie, William, MA   1615 Apr n.d. (249, 395)
Mitchell, James   1616 Jul 3 (262, 147v)
student   1624 Jan 12 (RS56/3, 266)
Lawrie, Thomas, MA   1624 Aug 17 (380, 245) Sep 3 (RS56/3, 332v)

| students | 1624 Oct 12 (RS56/3, 339) 1628 Jan 4 (430, 96) |

Doctor

| Crummy, James, *'doctour of the abbacie of Melros'* | 1581 n.d. (29, 12v) |

MENMUIR (par), Angus

| Finlayson, George | 1619 Apr 20 (CC3/9/4) Jun 20 (CC3/9/6) |
| Brokas, Patrick, d, r | 1628 Apr 2 (CH2/264/1, unfoliated) 1637 May 19 (ibid.) |

MENSTRIE, Clackmannanshire MRf NS8496

Logie par (Alva par 1891)

| schoolmaster, unnamed | 1590 Jul n.d. (H. Hutchison, 'Church Control of Education in Clackmannanshire, 1560–1700', *RSCHS*, xviii, 1973, 65) |

MERTOUN (par), Berwickshire

| Shaw, James, MA | 1608 Feb 7 (143, 367v) Sep 30 (*RPC*, 1st ser., viii, 674) |

METHLICK (par), Aberdeenshire

| Henry, John | 1614 Apr 6 (CH2/146/2, 109) |
| Lindsay, Robert, MA | 1617 Sep 6 (CH2/146/2, 131) |

METHVEN (par), Perthshire

students	1604 Aug 27 (RS48/3, 247v) 1605 Jan 15 (181, 214) 1607 Feb 3 (142, 286) 1610 Dec – 1611 May (181, 214)
Berwick, John, MA, r	1617 Dec 4 (RS49/1, 190) 1619 Jun 11 (RS49/2, 325)
Robertson, William, MA	1619 Dec 17 (397, 305) 1620 Sep 5 (354, 305v)
Philp, John, MA	1621 Nov 17 (326, 21v)
Govan, John, MA	1628 Jun 8 (436, 172v) 1632 May 24 (454, 353)
student	1632 Mar 20 (458, 268)

MIDCALDER (par), Midlothian

| Brown, John, MA | 1583 Oct 30 (NP1/30, 106) 1602 Jul 18 (NP1/53, 225v) |
| Johnston, John | 1591 Apr 1 (46, 162v) 1594 Aug 9 (NP1/53, 57v) |

Watson, Thomas	1610 Jan 12 (231, 37)
Hamilton, William	1611 Jun 7 (H.B. McCall, *History of the Parish of Mid-Calder*, Edinburgh 1894, 34) 1612 Mar 17 (202, 387)
Paterson, Oliver	1612 Nov 2 (McCall, *Parish of Mid-Calder*, 34)
Allan, William	1614 Jan 16 (McCall, *Parish of Mid-Calder*, 35) 1616 Sep 1 (ibid.)

MIGVIE, Aberdeenshire MRf NJ4306
Logie-Coldstone par
Thomson, James	1618 Mar 16 (SC1/60/4, 15)

MILLBURN OR FUTHIES MYLE, Fife MRf NT1087 (Dunfermline)
Dunfermline par
Norvell, William	c.1599 (JC26/4/2)

MILLHEUGH, Lanarkshire MRf NS7551
Dalserf par
Hamilton, Blaise	1612 Jun 12 (312, 63v)

MILNATHORT, Kinross-shire MRf NO1204
Orwell par
Morris, John	1625 Oct 20 (516, 376)

MINNIGAFF (par), Kirkcudbrightshire
Little, George	1620 Apr 5 (344, 310) 1622 Jun 14 (*RPC*, 1st ser., xiii, 1)
Elphinstone, Andrew	1623 Apr 14 (RS60/1, 88)
Gray, Andrew	1625 Dec 11 (390, 273) 1626 Jan 17 (383, 197)

MINTO (par), Selkirkshire
Davidson, John	1616 Oct 9 (CH2/198/1, unfoliated)
Lermonth, James	1624 Jun 20 (431, 89v) 1625 Jun 3 (RS1/17, 345v)

MITCHELSTON Mrf (Dysart)
Dysart par
Schoolmaster	1590 (J.M. Beale, *A History of the Burgh and Parochial Schools of Fife*, Edinburgh 1983, 21)

MOFFAT (par), Dumfriesshire
Cockburn, William	1610 Mar 29 (214, 224)
Pollok, James, MA	1612 Nov 21 (494, 208) 1615 May 5 (264, 247)

Wilson, John, MA	1617 Jun 28 (265, 262) 1618 Feb 10 (RS22/1, 54v)
French, Robert, MA	1619 Nov 15 (301, 241v) 1621 Jan 26 (408, 257v)
Waugh, David, MA	1622 Jun 5 (330, 226v) 1623 Nov 29 (356, 286)
Wallace, William, MA	1626 Jun 2 (402, 368v)
Dunlop, George, MA (Ed 1627), r	1628 Jul 14 (RS1/24, 330) 1633 Jul 25 (507, 334)

MONEYDIE (par), Perthshire
Lang, William	1615 Sep 7 (239, 465)

MONIFIETH (par), Angus
no schoolmaster	1599 Oct 30 (GRO OPR 310/1, 98)
Young, Thomas *or* Samuel, MA	1599 Nov 15 (GRO OPR 310/1, 98)
order for schoolmaster	1600 Mar 8 (GRO OPR 310/1, 99v)
schoolmaster, unnamed	1603 Jun 5 (GRO OPR 310/1, 110v)
Morgan, David, MA	1606 Nov 12 (127, 396v)
Haly (Hely), Robert, MA	1610 Jul 30 (176, 147)
Clayhills, Archibald, MA	1619 May 31 (360, 35v)
Morris, David	1632 Oct 2 (CC3/3/5, 111v)

MONIKIE (par), Angus
Dull (Daw, ?Dick), Alexander, MA, cl	1614 Sep 20 (CC3/9/5) *before* 1617 Aug 10 (PRO 311/1, unfoliated)
Durham, Patrick, MA	1617 Aug 10 (PRO 311/1, unfoliated)

MONIMAIL (par), Fife
Busbie, Alexander	1603 Mar 3 (128, 139) 1618 Jan 7 (162, 165v)
Meldrum, David, MA	1610 Feb 9 (175, 64v)
Cobb, John, r	1625 Jul 6 (421, 38v) *reader* 1642 Sep 2 (541, 365)

MONKLAND (par), Lanarkshire
Clydesdale, George, MA	1602 Feb 25 (92, 188)
Hamilton, Claud, MA	1605 Dec 10 (138, 208v)
Hamilton, Allan, MA	1606 Jun 9 (122, 45v)
Brock, Archibald, MA	1610 Mar 4 (187, 473v)
Soutar *or* Sunter, David	1613 Apr 4 (246, 22) 1628 Mar 12 (434, 121v)

MONKTON (par), Ayrshire
(united with Prestwick 1567)

Wight, James	1616 Jun 9 (CH2/809/1, 7)
Sheringlaw (Shillinglaw), John	1616 Nov 17 (CH2/809/1, 8v)
students	1618 Dec 13 (CH2/809/1, 20)
schoolmaster, unnamed	1620 Dec 17 (CH2/809/1, 32v)

Doctors

Burn, John, d	1614 Mar 5 (367, 482)
Urie, John, d	1614 Dec 3 (CC9/7/10, 250)
doctor	1620 May 28 (CH2/809/1, 27v)

MONTROSE (par), Angus
Grammar School

Lindsay, David, MA, later min, bishop of Brechin 1619	*before* 1597 n.d. (A. Maxwell, *The History of Old Dundee*, Edinburgh 1884, 324)
Anderson, Thomas, MA	1566–1585 (*Fasti*, v, 409)
Mylne, Andrew	c.1569 (*The Autobiography and Diary of Mr James Melville*, ed. R. Pitcairn, Wodrow Society 1842, 21)
Hogg, Thomas, MA	1600 Nov n.d. (81, 111v) 1611 Jan 13 (464, 198)
Leighton (Lichton), James, MA (SA 1608), min of Inchbrayock 1615, min of Dun 1622	1616 n.d. (*Fasti*, v, 379)
Petrie, Alexander, MA	1618 Aug 19 (283, 5) 1632 May 24 (457, 6)
Fullarton, William, MA	1632 Jun 23 (483, 217) 1642 Sep 26 (541, 362)

Doctor

Wilson, Adam	1596 Nov 24 (61, 127)

Music School

Keith, James	1620 Sep 25 (CC3/9/6)
Wallace, William	1623 Jun 27 (CC3/9/7) 1626 Aug 17 (B51/1/4, 120v)
Croal, John, r	1629 Mar 8 (*Fasti*, viii, 506)
Irving, Robert	1629 May 9 (435, 1v)

Dame School

Gray, Marjorie	c.1569 (*Autobiography of Mr James Melville*, 21)

MONYABROCH, *see* Kilsyth

MONZIE (par), Perthshire

Daes, Thomas	1633 Aug 20 (J. Hunter, *The Diocese and Presbytery of Dunkeld 1660–1689*, ii, London 1917, 99n.)

MONYMUSK (par), Aberdeenshire

provision for school	c.1584 (J. Robertson (ed.), *Collections for a History of the Shires of Aberdeen and Banff*, Spalding Club 1843, 184–5)
Redford, John, MA	1619 Apr 22 (292, 365v)

MOREBATTLE (par), Roxburghshire

Douglas, James, MA	1628 Nov 14 (RS56/4, 272)
Elliot, Henry, MA	1632 May 16 (33, 242) 1633 Jan 13 (498, 337)

MORTLACH (par), Banffshire

students	1610 Mar 11 (195, 49)
Duff, Alexander, MA	1611 Nov 6 (201, 275v)
Strachan, John, MA	1619 Jun 4 (295, 413) Nov 6 (RS16/1, 170)
Anderson, Gilbert, MA	1622 Jul 4 (334, 93v)
Clark, Alexander, MA	1625 August n.d. (395, 417v) 1630 Jun 25 (435, 411v)

MUIRHEAD, Lanarkshire MRf NS6869

Cadder par	
Semple, John	1622 Aug 4 (338, 386v)

MURROES (par), Angus

no school	1613 Sep 5 (G.R. Kinloch (ed.), *Ecclesiastical Records: Selections from the Minutes of the Synod of Fife*, Abbotsford Club 1837, 69)
Auchinleck, William	1626 Apr 5 (392, 346)

MUSSELBURGH (par), Midlothian

(later in Inveresk par)

Nisbet, George, MA	1579/80 Jan 2 (B52/1/16, 260) 1624 Sep 20 (414, 326v)
Wright, John	1617 Dec 11 (278, 281)
Fiddes, Alexander	1620 Oct 6 (309, 114v) 1631 Sep 4 (CC8/10/9)
March, James, cf. Fisherrow	1625 Dec 14 (RS25/11, 52)
Fairlie, Robert, MA	1629 Aug 9 (RS25/15, 92v) 1632 Oct 16 (483, 462)
Douglas, Archibald, MA	1633 Jun 4 (516, 166) 1637 Oct 16 (527, 135)

Doctors

Provand, Thomas, MA, d	1602 Feb 18 (RS24/1, 274) Oct 23 (88, 87v)
Lowrie, James, d	1602 Oct 23 (88, 87v)
Greig, John, MA, d	1612 Nov 31 (243, 130)

Music School

Blackhall, Andrew	1589 Oct 16 (*IR*, iii, p. 21) died 1609 Jan 31 (*Fasti*, i, 324)
Blackhall, Andrew, younger, son of above	c.1609, *alienated royal endowment* (*Reports*, 76)
school	1627 (*Reports*, 76)

MUTHILL (par), Perthshire

Wood, John	1583 May 21 (*Stirling Presbytery Records*, ed. J. Kirk, SHS 1981, 118)
Balnevis, John	1607 Dec 15 (RS48/6, 268) 1620 Nov 4 (313, 217)
Ayson, Duncan	1626 Jul 18 (RS50/2, 264)
Abernethie, John	1617 Oct 9 (314, 112)

NEILSTON (par), Renfrewshire

Pollok, John	1613 Jul 8 (310, 119v)
Hutcheson, Robert, MA	1617 Jan 18 (282, 246) 1618 Feb 23 (311, 139v)
Logan, Thomas, r	1620 Jan 31 (309, 199) Aug 19 (302, 273v) *still reader* 1639 Dec 5 (551, 156)
Law, John, r	1629 Jun 20 (CC9/7/24, 229) 1632 Dec 17 (528, 242)

NETHER BRACO, Lanarkshire MRf NS8366

Shotts par	
student	1630 Feb 23 (CC9/7/24, 280)

NETHER CRAMOND, *see* Cramond

NETHER HOWDEN, Berwickshire MRf NT5053

Channelkirk par	
Stirling, John	1626 May 23 (406, 270)

NETHER KEIR, Dumfriesshire MRf NX8593 (Keir Mill)

Keir par	
student	1631 Mar 6 (442, 295v)

NETHERTON, Lanarkshire MRf NS7854
Cambusnethan par
Somerville, Claud   1619 Jan 1 (CC9/14/13, 3)

NEVAY (par), Angus
(later united with Eassie)
Boyd, William   1617 Feb 1 (CC20/4/6, 222) 1623 Nov 29
                                              (453, 79)

NEW ABBEY (par), Kirkcudbrightshire
Whyte, David   1626 Mar 14 (382, 107) 1628 Mar 27 (*RPC*,
                                              2nd ser., ii, 579) *reader* 1630 Oct 27 (RS22/3,
                                              119)

NEWBATTLE (par), Midlothian
Sandilands, James   1604 Jul 23 (108, 360)
Drimpis (Dalrymple?),   1605 Nov 15 (122, 4)
   James
Houston, John   1617 Feb 11 (CC8/8/50, 46)
school, Latin, Music and   1626 n.d. (A. Edgar, *Old Church Life in*
Scots   *Scotland*, Second Series, Paisley 1886, 119n.)
                                              1630 May 9 (RS25/16, 100)
Trent, William, MA   1626 Oct 15 (J. Lee, *Lectures on the History of*
                                              the Church of Scotland, ii, Edinburgh 1860, 431)
                                              1627 Jun 24 (413, 311)
Doctor
Wilson, John, d   1617 Nov 30 (Lee, *Lectures*, 431)

NEWBIE, Dumfriesshire MRf NY1865
Annan par
Rorieson, Edward   1614 Jan 9 (221, 253)

NEWBURGH, Aberdeenshire MRf NJ9925
Foveran par
unlicensed school   1605 Aug 26 (CH2/146/1, 132v)
Keith, Robert, *and his son*   *order to close school* 1605 Oct 2 (CH2/146/1,
                                              134v) *permission to teach* 1609 Feb 8
                                              (CH2/146/2, 37)
Innes, Alexander, MA   1617 Feb 12 (356, 43v) Oct 9 (CH2/146/2,
                                              133)

NEWBURGH (par), Fife
(parish disjoined from Abdie 1632)

Grammar School

Drummond, Daniel, MA   1597 Nov 12 (NP1/53A, ii, 60)

Young, John, MA, r   1599 Nov 8 (CC20/4/3, 356v) 1604 Apr 4 (119, 202)

Fairfull, David, MA   1605 Nov 15 (RS30/7, 60) 1618 Apr 17 (NP1/67B, 55)

Reid, Thomas, MA   1608 Jun 9 (219, 327v)

Leslie, James, MA (SAL 1608), min   1611 Sep 2 (*Fasti*, v, 171) 1622 Oct 1 (ibid.)

Barron, James   1630 May 18 (RS31/8, 361)

NEWBURN (par), Fife

schoolmaster, unnamed   c.1630 (J.M. Beale, *A History of the Burgh and Parochial Schools of Fife*, Edinburgh 1983, 54)

NEW DEER, *see* Auchreddy

NEWLANDS (par), Peeblesshire

Young, William   1619 Feb 13 (348, 123v)

NEW LESLIE, Aberdeenshire MRf NJ5825

Leslie par

Strachan, Alexander, MA   1628 Aug 12 (416, 408v)

NEWMILNS, Ayrshire MRf NS5337

part Galston par, part Loudoun par

Dalrymple, Andrew, MA (Gl 1597), n   1600 Feb 2 (GD220/6/2006/8) 1603 Mar 1 (ibid.)

Russell, William, MA   1614 Dec 13 (242, 238)

Aird, John   1617 Oct 11 (*Clan Campbell*, v, 34)

Crooks, William, MA (Gl)   1622 Dec n.d. (*Clan Campbell*, v, 188)

Anderson, James, MA   1630 Dec 16 (RS12/5, 8) 1636 Nov 24 (510, 364)

Doctor

Brown, John, d   1607 May 30 (141, 378) 1620 Nov 13 (315, 336)

NEWTON (par), Midlothian

Jaffrey, Andrew, MA   1632 Aug 14 (RS25/19, 322v)

NEWTON OF CONDIE, Perthshire MRf NO0717

Forgandenny par

Merser, Robert, MA   1619 Oct 21 (RS1/4, 242)

NEWTON ON AYR, Ayrshire MRf NS3523
Monkton par (par on its own 1779)
Baxter, Edward   1622 Nov 14 (333, 56) 1624 Jan 7 (435, 310)

NEWTYLE (par), Angus
Scott, David   1608 Oct 14 (190, 310v)
Murray, Robert, MA   1614 Dec 5 (280, 288) 1616 Jan 30 (270, 391)
Bannatyne, William, MA   1617 Jun 1 (266, 355v) Nov 26 (323, 19)
Sanders, William, MA   1621 May 17 (318, 299) 1622 Jun 19 (470, 443)
Guthrie, Henry, MA   1628 Apr 1 (528, 338) 1631 Dec 20 (465, 311v)

NIDDRIE, Midlothian MRf NT2376 (Granton)
(possibly Niddrie Mill near Granton)
Cramond par
Dungalson, John   1612 Feb 22 (203, 172)

NORTH BERWICK (par), East Lothian
Gibson, John   1580/1 Feb 20 (B56/1/4, 422v)
Nisbet, William   1587 Jul 20 (CS1/3(2), 349v)
Galbraith, William   1603 May 16 (133, 227v) 1605 Jun 25
                                   (B56/1/5, 1)
Morton, George, *'at Bervek'* 1627 Jun 7 (CC8/10/8)
schoolmaster, unnamed   1628, 1633 n.d. (*Common Good*, 47)

NORTHMAVINE (par), Shetland
Thomson, John   1621 Feb 20 (405, 363v)

OAKWOOD, Selkirkshire MRf NT4225
Presumably Selkirk par
Sinclair, Thomas   1608 Dec 6 (155, 90)

OATHLAW (par), Angus
Clayhills, Archibald, MA   1630 Nov 15 (495, 362)

OCHILTREE (par), Ayrshire
Allison, John   1605 May 16 (124, 48v)
Ferguson, John, MA   1615 Jan 16 (252, 145)
Miller, Andrew, MA   1618 Feb 14 (313, 142)
Baird, John, MA   1628 Mar 6 (RS12/4, 237) 1631 Mar 29
                                   (RS12/5, 290v)
Calderwood, John   1629 Sep 25 (435, 403v)

OLD CAMBUS (par), Berwickshire
Crawford, Adam   1620 Jul 20 (RS1/6, 217v)

OLDHAMSTOCKS (par), East Lothian

Park, John	1597 Jun 3 (RS24/2, 5) 1602 Mar 22 (RS24/2, 10v)
Lightbody, George, MA	1611 Feb 14 (194, 343)
school *'aftymes'*	*before* 1627 Apr 22 (*Reports*, 101)

OLD LISTON, West Lothian MRf NT1172
Kirkliston par

Cunningham, John	1609 Aug 19 (220, 318)

ORDENS, Banffshire MRf NJ6161
Boyndie par

Imlach, Robert	1633 May 21 (488, 267)

ORDIQUHILL (par), Banffshire

Darg, Walter, MA (AbK 1623), min of Deskford 1627	1624 Dec 29 (*Fasti*, vi, 284)

ORMISTON (par), East Lothian

Pentland, Robert	1616 Nov 29 (CC8/8/50, 136)
Mylne, George	1625 May 29 (CC8/8/53, 117)

ORPHIR (par), Orkney

Skethewie, Robert	1633 Feb 26 (RS43/4, 374) Mar 31 (ibid., 372v)

OVER CRAMOND, *see* Cramond Regis

OXNAM (par), Roxburghshire

Hislop, Thomas	1628 Jul 17 (RS56/4, 255)
mortification for school	1631 Nov 24 (516, 363–4)

PAISLEY (par), Renfrewshire

Robeson, Thomas, sir	c.1571 (J. Durkan, 'Paisley Abbey in the Sixteenth Century', *IR*, xxvii, 120)
student	1574 Jul 29 (CH4/1/1, i, 117v)
Royal foundation	1576/7 Jan 3 (*RMS*, iv, 2627)
Lochhead, Thomas, *'dene'*	1576 Nov 10 (NP1/201, 3v)
refoundation of grammar school	1577 n.d. (J. Durkan, 'Paisley Abbey and Glasgow Archives', *IR*, xiv, 48)
Maxwell, Thomas, MA	1583 Nov 1 (CC9/14/1, unfoliated) 1585 Apr 28 (ibid.)

Young *or* Younger,   1586 Dec 2 (CC9/14/1, unfoliated) 1587
  Thomas, MA   Sep 29 (ibid.)
Gilchrist, John, MA (Gl   1598/9 Feb 20 (RH6/3607) *removed by*
  1590), b, r, vic of   *minister* 1600 Nov 7 (*RPC*, vi, 171)
  Rutherglen
Henderson, Robert, MA   c.1586 (R. Brown, *The History of the Paisley*
                                    Grammar School, Paisley 1875, 38) 1604 Feb 10
                                    (*Paisley Burgh Chrs.*, 260)
Bell, Thomas, MA, min   1604 Feb 10 (*Paisley Burgh Chrs.*, 259) 1609 Jul
                                    22 (NP1/48, 34)
Park, Robert, MA, b, r, s   1606 n.d. (Brown, *Paisley Grammar School*, 40)
                                    1625 Feb 12 (427, 220v)
Semple, Robert   1613 Nov 20 (218, 50) 1614 Jan 12 (251, 232)
Hutcheson, William, MA   1626 Apr 20 (Brown, *Paisley Grammar School*,
  (Gl 1614), cl, r   45) 1637 Nov 30 (529, 56)

Music School
schoolmaster, unnamed   1618 Oct 5 (Brown, *Paisley Grammar School*,
                                    43)
McKellar, Archibald   1618 Nov 26 (342, 292v)
school apparently given up   1623 May n.d. (Brown, *Paisley Grammar School*,
                                    44)

Sewing School
school   1618 Oct 5 (Brown, *Paisley Grammar School*,
                                    41)

PANBRIDE (par), Angus
Mudie, John, MA   1612 Jan 29 (199, 4)
Whittet, Thomas, MA   1613 Feb 17 (221, 105)

PATH OF CONDIE, Perthshire MRf NO0711
Presumably Dunning par (later in Forteviot par)
Henry, James   1625 Oct 5 (RS50/1, 441)

PAXTON, Berwickshire MRf NT9352
Hutton par
Home, William   1619 May 10 (290, 390)
Horne, John, MA   1619 Jul 24 (RS18/1, 91v)
Murray, William   1621 Jan 12 (RS1/7, 160v)
Shaw, John   1629 May 27 (416, 345v) Jun 2 (463, 239v)

PEASTON, East Lothian MRf NT4265
Ormiston par

Rannald, Gilbert	1622 Jul 1 (CC8/8/54, 83)

PEEBLES (par), Peeblesshire

schoolmaster, unnamed	1562 Oct 24 (*Peebles Recs.*, 287); 1563/4 Mar 9 (ibid., 293); 1565 Apr 7 (ibid., 299)
Craw, James	1568 Oct 13 (*Peebles Recs.*, 307) *discharged* Oct 31 (ibid.)
Crichton, David, n	*discharged* 1569/70 Jan 30 (*Peebles Recs.*, 309) *discharged again* 1571 Beltane (ibid., 326) *'scoilmaister for the tyme'* 1571/2 Mar 12 (*Peebles Recs.*, 336)
Cranston, Andrew, MA	1570/1 Mar 14 (*Peebles Recs.*, 326) *resigned* 1571/2 Feb 6 (ibid., 333) *occurs again* 1572 May 19 (ibid., 339)
order for schoolmaster	1572/3 Feb 7 (*Peebles Recs.*, 353)
Tweedie, John	1585 Nov 16 (CS7/55, 328)
McCall, Gavin, MA (Ed 1596), min 1600, min of Traquair 1603	1596 Dec 23 (CH2/295/1, 4) 1600 Oct 15 (CH2/295/1, 72) *reponed* 1625 Aug 21 (CH2/295/1, 1877)
Young, John, MA	1606 Apr 1 (133, 166) 1612 Jan 2 (206, 166)
Dickson, William, MA	1614 May 31 (227, 12) 1629 Jun 1 (*Peebles Recs.*, 368)
Watson, Andrew, MA	1623 Apr 8 (341, 449) 1629 Jul 28 (423, 209)
students	1629 Aug 24 (SC42/28/1) 1630 Sep 17 (528, 385)
Martin, William, MA	1632 Mar 2 (539, 455) 1633 Dec 19 (512, 111)

Doctors

order for doctor	1565 Apr 7 (*Peebles Recs.*, 299)
doctor, unnamed	1602 Sep 9 (CH2/295/1, 99) 1608 n.d. (*Common Good*, 47)
Foster or Forester, Henry, d	1609 Nov 8 (RD11/Box 73, Warrants)
Brotherstone, William, d	1614 Nov 22 (SC42/28/1)
Crawford, Thomas, d	1614 Dec 14 (262, 59) 1620 Jun 1 (314, 357)
Dyet, William, d	1621 Apr 22 (*Peebles Recs.*, 361)
Bryden, John, MA	1621 Apr 22 (*Peebles Recs.*, 361)
Dunlop, John, d	1627 Apr 30 (*Peebles Recs.*, 367) 1630 Jul 30 (447, 104v)
Dickson, Alexander, d	1631 Feb 1 (SC42/28,2)
doctor, unnamed	1628–1634 n.d. (*Common Good*, 48)

PEEL, Lanarkshire MRf NS6454 (Peelpark)
East Kilbride par
Speir, John, MA   1626 Dec 1 (CC10/11/5, 2v)

PENCAITLAND (par), East Lothian
Kello, John, MA   1589 Aug 1 (33, 84v)
Boigbie, John   1613 Jan 3 (248, 382v) 1618 Jul 24 (372, 190v)
school   1627 May 7 (*Reports*, 128)
Wallace, William   1631 Jun 18 (Rs25/17, 322) 1633 Jun 13 (511,
                                 272)

PENNICK, Nairn MRf NH9356
Auldearn par
Smyth, David   1619 Oct 30 (313, 13) Dec 5 (302, 148v)

PENTLAND (par), Midlothian
Craig, William   1585 May 18 (NP183, 2)

PERTH (par), Perthshire
Grammar School
Simpson, Andrew, MA,   *until* 1562 (E. Smart, *History of Perth Academy*,
  min of Dunning 1562   Perth 1932, 8–11)
Rhynd, William, MA, min   1562 Dec 24 (CS7/39, 294) *died* 1610 Feb 20
  of Kinnoull   (*The Chronicle of Perth*, ed. J. Maidment,
                                 Maitland Club 1831, 12)
Johnston, Patrick, MA, *see*   1604 Apr 26 (RS48/3, 76) *died* c.1623 Nov 24
  below   (Smart, *Perth Academy*, 17)
Durward, John, MA,   1623 Nov 24 (Smart, *Perth Academy*, 17) *died*
  previously doctor, *see*   c.1631 Oct n.d. (ibid., p. 22)
  below
Johnston, Patrick, MA, *see*   1631 Oct n.d., *during Durward's sickness* (Smart,
  above   22)
Rhynd, Patrick, MA, min   *temporary* 1631 Oct n.d. (Smart, *Perth Academy*,
  of Dron, *see also*   23)
  Adventure School
Row, John, MA   1632 Jun n.d. (*Chronicle of Perth*, 33) 1636 Aug
                                 30 (546, 338)

Doctors
Riddoch, Duncan, d   1588 n.d. (Smart, *Perth Academy*, 12)
Abercrombie, John, d   1575 Mar 15 (CC8/8/22, 315v)
Duncan, Denis   1619 Jul 10 (344, 185)
Durward, John, MA, s, d,   1621 Jun 7 (CC3/9/6)
  see above

Robertson, William, MA	1623 Jan 5 (357, 371) (PC6/14) 1631 Sep 15 (Smart, *Perth Academy*, 20)
Sanders, James, MA	1626 Jul 12 (RS50/2, 236v)
doctors	1627 Mar 28 (CH2/299/1, 165)

Music School

Swinton, John, sir	1559 Oct 13 (*The Perth Guildry*, ed. M.L. Stavert, SRS 1993, no. 459) 1572 Aug 2 (GD79/6/91)
Swinton, John, younger, son of sir John Swinton	1575/6 Mar 3 (CS7/55, 85) 1587 Apr 11(J.P. Lawson, *The Book of Perth*, Edinburgh 1847, 167)
Henderson, Samuel	1589 Jul 3 (Stavert, no. 753)
students	1593/4 Jan 7 ('Extracts from the kirk session register of Perth', *Spottiswoode Misc.*, ii, 270)
Wemyss, John, MA	*died before* 1597 Oct 29 (*Chronicle of Perth*, 71) 1604 Jan 4 (103, 216)
Young, James, MA	1604 Oct 21 (*Kirk Session Records*, 72)
Garvie, Thomas	1616 Mar 9 (CC20/4/6, 95v) 1617 Mar 14 (*Kirk Session Records*, 76)
Adamson, Henry, MA, r	1617 Mar 14 (*Kirk Session Records*, 76) 1623 Jul 3 (ibid., 90)

Adventure School

Rhynd, Patrick, MA, min of Dron, *see also* Grammar School	1599 Oct 11 (PS1/56, 37v) 1616 n.d. (Smart, *Perth Academy*, 15)
schools to be closed	1601 n.d. (Smart, *Perth Academy*, 14)
Lamb, William, n	1616 n.d., 1617 n.d. (Smart, *Perth Academy*, 15)
Stark, George, previously assistant to Rhynd	1620 n.d. (Smart, *Perth Academy*, 16)
school	1623 n.d. (Smart, *Perth Academy*, 20)

Dame Schools

schools	1606 n.d. (Smart, *Perth Academy*, 14)

PETERHEAD (par), Aberdeenshire
(formerly called Peter Ugie, disjoined from Wester Ugie 1620)

Grammar School

Alexander, John, r	1597 n.d. (*Fasti*, vi, 187)
Coupland, Patrick, MA	1602 May 20 (RS4/2, 15)

Geddes, Charles, MA	1605 Jul 25 (CH2/89/1(1), 57) 1606 May 1 (ibid., 74)
schoolmaster, unnamed	1609 May 10 (CH2/89/1(1), 121)
Martin, Andrew, MA	1610 Oct 2 (CH2/89/1(1), 135) 1613 Sep 30 (CH2/89/1(2), 152)
Arbuthnott, John	1616 Feb 16 (284, 58v)
no school	1617 Jul 10 (CH2/89/1(2), 210)
school	1620 Oct 5 (CH2/89/1(2), 255v)
Findlater, John, MA	1631 May 31 (445, 426v) 1633 Apr 12 (469, 40)

Music School

Burnett, William	1629 May 13 (SC1/60/8, 49)

PETER UGIE, *see* Peterhead

PETTINAIN (par), Lanarkshire

Hay, Hugh	1622 Sep 2 (CC14/5/2)

PITFOUR, Perthshire MRf NO1920
St Madoes par

Lawson, Andrew	1596 Aug 5 (CC8/8/30, 154v)

PITTENSORN (Pynst), Perthshire MRf NO0840 (Caputh)
Presumably Caputh par

McPhail, George	1622 Apr 15 (341, 110v)

PITTENWEEM (par), Fife
(disjoined from Anstruther Wester 1588)

Harlaw, Nathaniel	1588 Dec 23 (41, 250)
Morris, Robert, MA	1591/2 Feb 18 (RH6/3150)
Irving, John	1591/2 Feb 18 (RH6/3150) 1594 Sep 20 (53, 206)
Welland, James, MA	1599 Jun 2 (80, 207v) Jul 6 (*RPC*, 1st ser., vi, 614)
Black, Thomas, MA	1602 Jan 8 (101, 46) 1607 Dec 16 (143, 15)
Tassie (Caschie), Thomas, MA	1611 Oct 21 (193, 466) 1613 Mar 22 (209, 341)
Rule (Roull), James, MA	1616 May 24 (312, 275v) 1623 Jun 12 (387, 269)
Mearns, David, MA	1625 Jul 8 (421, 453v) 1627 Jun 17 (CC20/4/8, 301)

Seton, James   1630 Mar 31 (RS31/8, 316) 1634 Apr 16 (488, 349)

PITTLESHEUGH, Berwickshire MRf NT7543
Eccles par
Paterson, Thomas   1606 May 28 (149, 240v)

PITTODRIE, Aberdeenshire MRf NJ6923
Chapel of Garioch par
Thom, Gilbert, MA (AbM) 1633 Apr 19 (*RPC*, 2nd ser., v, 550)

POLWARTH (par), Berwickshire
Davidson, John, MA   1585/6 Jan 31 (24, 29v)

PORTRACK, Dumfriesshire MRf NY9382
Holywood par
Paton, John, d   1625 Nov 3 (RS1/18, 230)

POWRIE, Angus MRf NO4234
Murroes par
Petrie, John   1609 Mar 31 (157, 353)

PREMNAY (par), Aberdeenshire
Chessor, William, MA   1620 Mar 4 (306, 292)

PRESTON (par), Berwickshirenot in 71 census
McDowall, Robert   1620 Mar 1 (SC60/56/1, 72v)

PRESTONKIRK (par), East Lothian
(also known as East Linton)
Greig, John   1606 Aug 30 (134, 171v) Jul 6 (219, 231v)
Wilson, Archibald   1611 Jan 20 (208, 169v)
Wilson, James   1620 Jun 25 (329, 91v)
Hamilton, William   1624 Dec 31 (379, 439v) 1628 Jun 12 (447, 333v)

PRESTONPANS (par), East Lothian
(formerly called Preston or Salt Preston)
Rae (Raa), John, MA, n   1570 Dec 21 (NP1/30, 2)
Dickson, George, n   1589 Jun 11 (D. Withrington, 'Schools in the Presbytery of Haddington in the Seventeenth Century', *East Lothian Trans.*, ix, 1963, 91) 1593 Oct n.d. (48, 289) 1603 Jun 2 (139, 19v)

Adamson, George   1605 Apr 4 (RS24/5, 249)

Hume (Home),   1606 Jul 8 (J. Miller, *The Lamp of Lothian*,
   Alexander, MA   Haddington 1844, 445n.) 1611 Oct 25 (*RPC*,
                         1st ser., 272)

Spens, William, MA   1608 Jan 9 (RD4/119) 1635 Jun n.d.
                         (RD4/119)

Dalzell, John, MA   1614 Mar 16 (Withrington, 'Schools in the
                         Presbytery of Haddington', 94) 1617 Jul 7
                         (301, 20)

schoolmaster, unnamed 1620 Apr 9 (*Hist. MSS. Comm., Report on the
                         Manuscripts of the Earl of Eglinton*, London
                         1885)

Lindsay, James, MA   1620 Jul 4 (321, 187v) 1631 Mar 30 (RS25/17,
                         187v)

Doctors

Brown, John, s   1608 Feb 20 (154, 28)

Cuilhill, John, d   1612 Sep 5 (205, 62)

Rutherford, Andrew   1626 Sep 20, Sep 26 (RS25/11, 292v)

PRESTWICK, *see* Monkton

PRIMSIDE MILL, Roxburghshire MRf NT8126
part Morebattle par, part Yetholm par

Ker, John   1611 Jul 26 (333, 314v)

Tait, James   1617 Jul 10 (RS56/1, 49)

Telfer, William   1620 May 19 (366, 298v)

QUOTHQUAN (par), Lanarkshire
(united to Libberton 1664)

Dalzell, Roland   1608 Jul 25 (166, 130)

Adamson, William   1609 May 10 (166, 477)

Brown, James   1630 Mar 27 (RS40/3B, 91v)

Livingstone, James   1633 Nov 5 (RS40/4A, 159) Dec 6 (483, 318)

RAIT, *see* Kilspindie

RAPLOCH, Lanarkshire MRf NS7651 (Larkhall)
Dalserf par

Mackyne, John   1623 Jan 18 (374, 61v)

Cunningham, Robert, MA 1627 Feb 17 (416, 194v)

RATHEN (par), Aberdeenshire
no school   1610 Aug 30 (CH2/89/1(1), 133v)

order for schoolmaster	1614 May 5 (CH2/89/1(2), 159)
school	1617 Aug 7 (CH2/89/1(2), 211v)
Ogston, George, r	1617 Nov 27 (302, 450)
student	1620 Jul 8 (SC1/60/41, 11v) Dec 18 (325, 371)

RATHO (par), Midlothian

no schoolmaster	1598 Aug 29 (CH2/121/2, unfoliated)
Sym, David	1599 Aug 14 (CH2/121/2, unfoliated)
Winram, John, MA	1605 Nov 17 (139, 431)
Knox, Robert	1621 May 8 (320, 113v)
Peacock, John, MA	1631 Jun 25 (RS25/18, 17v)

RATHVEN (par), Banffshire

Geddes, Charles	1600 Aug 21 (*RPC*, 1st ser., vi, 662)
student	1621 Apr 29 (SC2/56/1)
schoolmaster, unnamed	1623 n.d. (W. Barclay, *The Schools and Schoolmasters of Banffshire*, Banff 1925, 98)
Cheyne, John, MA	1628 Nov 8 (RS5/6, 263v)
Moir, John	1631 n.d. (Barclay, *Schools and Schoolmasters*, 98)
Fraser, Walter	1632 n.d. (Barclay, *Schools and Schoolmasters*, 98)

RATTRAY (par), Perthshire

Tough (Teuche), Hugh	1592 Mar 29 (GD6/106, no. 106) 1606 Dec 26 (RS48/5, 337)
Jack, William, MA	1615 Feb 25 (RS1/17, 159) 1625 Aug 5 (388, 62)
Crichton, Robert, MA	1626 Nov 21 (RS50/2, 335) 1631 Nov 25 (RS50/6, 9v)

RAYNE (par), Aberdeenshire

Leith, Henry, MA	1602 May 9 (*RPC*, 1st ser., vi, 729)
Fotheringham, William, MA	1609 Jul 12 (238, 386v)
Glass, William, MA	1631 Jul 23 (506, 97)

REAY (par), Caithness

Campbell, Lachlan	1624 Oct 10 (RS37/3, 59v)

REDPATH, Berwickshire MRf NT5835
Earlston par

Burnett, James	1622 Mar 19 (RS18/2, 10v)

RENFREW (par), Renfrewshire

Brown, John, n, r	1593 Jun 24 (J.A. Dunn, *History of Renfrew*, Paisley 1972, 88) 1600 Feb 4 (CC10/5/2)
McIldowny, Robert, MA	1605 Jul 25 (113, 346v) 1618 Oct 23 (CC10/11/3, 68)
Cameron, Archibald, MA	1610 Jun 3 (CC10/11/4, 25v) Jul 10 (330, 358v)
Lothian, John, MA	1614 Apr 19 (CC10/5/3)
Mudie, John, MA	1616 Dec 9 (292, 348)
Mure *or* Muirhead, Matthew, MA	1618 Jan 15 (277, 217) 1623 May 16 (345, 389v)
schoolmaster, unnamed	1633, 1634 n.d. (*Common Good*, 48)

RESCOBIE (par), Angus

Dickson, David	1603 May n.d. (94, 319v) 1609 Jan 23 (265, 444v)
Ritchie, Thomas, r	1613 May 31 (280, 171) 1618 May 16 (314, 308)
Finlayson, George	1621 Nov 12 (343, 40v)

RESTALRIG, Midlothian MRf NT2874
South Leith par

Cumming, David, preceptor and master of the college kirk of Restalrig	1585 Nov 7 (CS7/55, 327) 1587 Apr 25 (GD20/7/191)
Dunlop, Robert	1607 Nov 27 (*South Leith Recs.*, 5) 1614 Jul 3 (229, 208v)

RHYNIE (par), Aberdeenshire

Youngson, Archibald, MA	1626 Dec 4 (400, 185v)
Ross, John, MA	1628 Dec 2 (465, 368v) 1629 Dec 29 (RS28/3, 248v)
Chalmer, George, MA	1633 Feb 16 (550, 306)

ROBERTON, Ayrshire MRf NS3936
Kilmaurs par

Broom, John	1616 Aug 24 (CC9/7/12, 152)

ROBERTON (par), Lanarkshire

Wilson, John	1621 Mar 14 (318, 423)

RODONO CHAPEL, *see* Littlehope

ROMANNO BRIDGE, *see* Brig of Lyne

RORA, Aberdeenshire MRf NK0650
Longside par
Davidson, William   1613 Oct 10 (227, 122)

ROSS, CHANONRY OF (par), Ross and Cromarty
Grammar School
schoolmaster, unnamed   1574 Jun 3 (CH4/1/1, i, 107v)
Leslie, Robert, MA   1578 Aug 7 (*RMS*, v, 738)
schoolmaster, unnamed   1580 Aug 23 (*RMS*, v, 4)
Crambie, Andrew   1586 Apr 10 (GD297/186/14) 1587 Jul 2
                                          (RS5/55, 224v)
student   1590 Jul 15 (PS61, 10v)
McGillechallum, John, MA   1597 Jun 18 (71, 335) 1600 Feb 9 (RS36/2,
                                          177)
Young, Thomas, MA   1606 Jun 10 (125, 252) 1607 Nov 21 (RS36/2,
                                          309v)
Troup, James, MA   1613 Jan 5 (219, 497) 1616 Jul 18 (GD156, Box
                                          36)
McKenzie, William, MA   1619 Aug 14 (RS37/1, 162) 1620 Jun 6
                                          (RS37/1, 227v)
student   1623 May 26 (532, 399)
Harvie, Francis   1624 Jul 12 (RS1/15, 368v)
Clark, Farquhar, MA   1628 Aug 24 (RS37/4, 110v) 1630 Mar 16
                                          (431, 465v)
Crambie, Thomas, MA   1632 Jan 4 (452, 59) Jun 4 (459, 296)

ROSSIE (par), *Presumably* Perthshire
Anderson, Adam, MA   1604 Mar 1 (200, 41) 1607 Sep 26 (137, 305)
Doctor
Bonar, John, d   1571/2 Jan 24 (12, 45)

ROTHESAY (par), Bute
school and schoolmaster   1619 n.d. (*Common Good*, 48)
Connell, Robert, MA   1619 Nov 3 (292, 335)
Laing, John, MA (Gl)   1623 May 17 (*Lamont Papers*, 140) 1623 Sep 5
                                          (380, 158)
school and schoolmaster   1628 n.d. (*Common Good*, 48)
McGilchrist, Robert, MA   1628 Sep 4 (463, 269)

Music School
Ramsay, William   1631 Sep 29 (NP/171, 21)

ROTHIEMAY (par), Banffshire
Steven, Andrew, MA   1611 May 12 (198, 117)
Abernethie, William, MA   1613 Jul 23 (232, 247v) Nov 20 (344, 180)
Mylne *or* Mill, William, MA 1615 Jun 20 (412, 117v) *before* 1617 n.d.
  (AbM 1610), min of Glass (*Fasti*, vi, 311)
  and Dalbeath 1618
Watson, John, MA (AbK   1619–27 n.d. (*Fasti*, vi, 291)
  1619), min of Rothiemay
  1629

ROWCHESTER, Berwickshire MRf NT7343 (Rowchester Ho)
Greenlaw par
Hewat, Alexander, MA   1619 May 3 (SC60/56/1, 66)

ROXBURGH (par), Roxburghshire
Mure, John   1620 Nov 13 (349, 444) 1621 Jan 12 (443, 188)
McDougall, Robert, cl   1631 May 25 (457, 146)

RUMBLETONLAW, Berwickshire MRf NT6745
Gordon par
Maxwell, William, MA   1622 Oct 31 (*RPC*, 1st ser., xiii, 72) 1624 Aug
                            24 (368, 15v)

RUTHERGLEN (par), Lanarkshire
Grammar School
doctor   1590 (G. Gray, *The Burgh School of Rutherglen*,
                            Rutherglen 1891, 24)
Burn, John   1601 Apr 13 (B64/1/1, 66)
Cook (Cruikis), George   1611 Mar 2 (CC9/14/3, unfoliated) Dec 28
                            (B64/1/1, 330v)
Cumming, Thomas   1617 Apr 9 (349, 12)
Graham, James, MA   1619 Oct 29 (Gray, *Burgh School*, 40) 1620 Mar
                            1 (RU2/1/1, 8v)
Wilson, Gilbert, MA   1624 May 3 (412, 132) 1635 May 25 (506,
                            308)

Reading School
Semple, Robert   1629 Mar 17 (RU2/1/1, 116)

RUTHVEN (par), Angus
Dewar, George, MA   1617 Jun 25 (321, 4)

ST ANDREWS (par), Fife
Colleges
Visitation of 1579 *'we find not Grammer-scuillis neidful nor convenient to be in the Collegeis'* (*Evidence, Oral and Documentary … for Visiting the Universities of Scotland, iii, The University of St Andrews*, London 1837, 190)

St Salvator's
Cranston, William, MA, regent	*Because of plague, teaches grammar to a reduced class with the earl of Cassillis and others* 1588 (*Evidence*, iii, 194)
Martin, David, MA, *rhetoric*	1588 (*Evidence*, iii,194)

St Leonard's
Boyd, Robert, MA, reg	*before* 1563 Nov 9 (SL115, 153) 1565 Nov 5 (ibid., 171)
grammar school	1572 Oct 15 (CH4/1/1, 110v)
Wilkie, Daniel, *grammar*	1588 Apr 17 (*Evidence*, iii, 195)
March, William, *rhetoric*	1588 Apr 17 (*Evidence*, iii, 195)

St Mary's (also known as New College)
grammar school	1552 (*Evidence*, iii, 361–4)
Hamilton, James, MA, r	1569/70 Feb n.d. (St Andrews University Archives, *Acta Rectorium*, ii, 76)
Robertson, John, MA, p	1573/4 Feb n.d. (*Acta Rectorium*, ii, 84)

Holy Trinity Grammar School
Dowie, James, MA (SAS 1544), c	1566 n.d. (W.E.K. Rankin, *The Parish Church of the Holy Trinity, St Andrews*, Edinburgh 1955, 98)
Carmichael, James, MA (SAL 1564), min of Haddington 1570	1570 Apr 5 (*RKSSA*, 334) Jul n.d. (ibid., 335n.)
students	1574/5 Feb 24 (J. Dennistoun and A. Macdonald (eds.), 'Extracts from the buik of the general kirk of Edinburgh', *Maitland Misc.*, i (1), 114–15)
Auchinleck, Patrick, MA	1575 Dec 15 (*RPC*, ii, 478)
Ker, John, MA, min of Haddington 1585, min of Aberlady 1587	1578/9 Mar 13 (B30/13/1, 99v)
Danskin, Henry, MA (SA 1593), p	1605 Sep 28 (RS30/7, 83) 1632 May 24 (477, 112)

Stevenson, Arthur   1612 May 14 (223, 178v)
schoolmaster, unnamed   1626, 1627, 1632, 1633 n.d. (*Common Good*, 49)
Doctors
Donaldson, George, MA, d   1596 Sep 9 (63, 456v)
Mudie, Robert, d, *see also*   1604 Jun 25 (133, 224v) 1606 Aug 5 (125, 353)
    Poor School
Heggie, William, MA, d   1616 n.d. (285, 96v) 1619 Mar 23 (356, 329)
Fairfull, Allan, d   1616 n.d. (285, 96v)
Douglas, John, d   1621 Nov 11 (B65/19/1) 1623 Whitsun (ibid.)

English School
Lawson, John   1591 May 28 (NP3/1, 224)

Music School ('Sang Scole in the Abbey')
Kemp, Andrew   1565 (K. Elliott, 'Scottish Music of the Early
                                 Reformed Church', *Transactions of the Scottish
                                 Ecclesiological Society*, xv (2), 1961, 20)
Rule (Roull), John   1599 Oct 31 (*RKSSA*, 908) 1605 Jun 19
                                 (CC8/8/41, 89)
Murray, George   1621 Mar *damaged* (St Andrews University
                                 Archives, St Andrews Burgh Miscellaneous
                                 Papers, Box 110) 1629 Jan 28 (RS31/7, 421v)
schoolmaster, unnamed   1632, 1633 n.d. (*Common Good*, 49)
Doctor
Smyth, Alexander, d   1560 May 4 (*RKSSA*, 40)

Poor School (also known as the Hospital)
Yule, Robert, MA   1593 Apr 18 (*RKSSA*, 748)
Mudie, Robert, *see also*   1596/7 Mar 2 (*RKSSA*, 824) 1597 Jun 20
Grammar School   (CC20/4/3, 153v) *left by* 1599 Apr 4 (*RKSSA*,
                                 885)
Sourdye, John, '*mercheand*'   1598/9 Feb 21 (*RKSSA*, 880–1) 1599 Oct 31
                                 (ibid., 907)
Adventure School
Liston, Thomas,   *died* 1583 Aug n.d. (CC8/8/12, 282–3)
'*scolemaster and
bukebinder*'

ST BOSWELL'S, *see* Lessuden

ST FERGUS, *see* Longley

ST FORT, Fife MRf NO4125
Forgan par

Mudie (Mowidie), Robert, MA	1624 Jun 2 (366, 188v)

ST JOHN'S CLACHAN, *see* Dalry

ST MADOES (par), Perthshire

Playfair, Andrew, MA (SA 1600), d	1594 Apr 21 (GRO OPR 392/1) 1594/5 Mar 17 (*Fasti*, iv, 194)
Brown, James	1608 Nov n.d. (CC6/5/5, 231v)

ST MARGARET'S HOPE, Orkney MRf ND4493
South Ronaldsay par

Sutherland, John	1623 Oct 29 (RS43/2, 138)

ST MARTINS (par), Perthshire

Boyd, William	1608 Jun 24 (191, 236) Jul 12 (157, 196)
Donaldson, Thomas	1613 Jun 15 (219, 118v)
Young, Alexander, MA	1629 Mar 27 (RS50/4(1), 68v) Dec 5 (RS1/27, 191v)

ST MONANS (par), Fife
(united to Abercrombie 1646)

Dickson, John	1607 Sep 12 (RS30/10, 132)

ST NINIANS (par), Stirlingshire

Murdoch, John	1614 Mar 4 (230, 349v)

ST QUIVOX (par), Ayrshire
(later in Ayr par)

Semple, Robert	1620 Nov 25 (RS12/2, 71v) 1621 Feb 15 (*RPC*, 1st ser., xii, 463)

SALINE (par), Fife

Christie, Thomas, MA	1617 Nov 21 (416, 174)

SALTOUN (par), East Lothian

Stevenson, James	1589 Jun 11 (D. Withrington, 'Schools in the Presbytery of Haddington in the Seventeenth Century', *East Lothian Trans.*, ix, 1963, 91)
Livingstone, William, MA	1623 May 27 (382, 204)

SALT PRESTON, *see* Prestonpans

SAMIESTON, Roxburghshire MRf NT7221
Presumably Oxnam par
Davidson, John   1613 Aug 11 (233, 318v) 1619 Feb 17 (RS56/1,
                               168v)

SANDAY (par), Orkney
Nicolson, David   1625 Mar 12 (RS43/3, 39v)

SANDWICK (par), Orkney
Whyte, Andrew, r   1619 Jun 22 (RS43/1, 70) 1631 Dec 13
                               (RS43/4, 260)

SANQUHAR (par), Dumfriesshire
Weld (Weill), Simon, MA   1606 May 8 (117, 422) 1609 Jun 8 (169, 181v)
Richardson, John   1609 Nov 17 (385, 39v) 1610 Jul 9 (196, 208)
Martin, William   1612 Nov 11 (226, 218v)
Walker, John   1621 May 19 (423, 152)
Chisholm, Archibald   1628 May 1 (RS40/3B, 138) 1640 Dec 14
                               (540, 386)
West (Was, Wast),   1630 Jan 30 (464, 84v) 1631 Jun 1 (RS1/31, 29)
  James, MA
Doctor
Lawrie or Lowrie, Simon, d 1598 Aug 4 (75, 120) Dec 28 (CC8/8/33)

SAUGHTON HALL, *see* Edinburgh

SCALES, Dumfriesshire MRf NY3065
Redkirk par
Gilmour, John   1612 May 4 (255, 50v)

SCALLOWAY, Shetland MRf HU4039
Tingwall par
Humphrey, William, MA,   1612 Aug 22 (232, 256–7)
  min of Bressay, Burra
  and Quarff 1581

SCONE (par), Perthshire
McLaren, Donald   1603 Apr 4 (RS48/2, 396)
Young, Alexander, MA   1610 Oct 10 (NP1/53A(4), unfoliated) 1611
                               Jun 4 (408, 152)
Murray, Robert, MA   1617 Jun 6 (RS49/2, 30v) Nov 27 (298, 207)

Lamb, William, n	1626 Dec 12 (RS31/6, 236) 1627 Jan 12 (RS31/6, 224)

SCOONIE (par), Fife

school	*by* 1626 (J.M. Beale, *A History of the Burgh and Parochial Schools of Fife*, Edinburgh 1983, 63)

SELKIRK (par), Selkirkshire

Guild, John, r	1563 (*Thirds of Benefices*, 284)
Scott, John	1571 Oct 26 (B68/7/1, 94v)
Todd, Alexander	1588 Mar 8 (*Melrose Recs.*, iii, 366)
Henryson, Samuel	1601 Sep 30 (83, 375)
Wood, George	1603 Sep 11 (108, 156v) 1605 Apr 20 (116, 212v)
schoolmaster, unnamed	1606 n.d. (*Common Good*, 49)
Grahamslaw, Andrew	1608 Apr 13 (227, 116v) 1609 Sep 2 (172, 85v)
Paterson, John	*before* 1613 Jun 13 (CH2/327/1, 108)
Shaw, James or Thomas, MA	1614 Mar 3 (224, 223) 1615 Aug 5 (243, 207v)
order for schoolmaster	1617 Jun 3 (CH2/327/1, 139)
Watson, William, MA, r	1617 Aug 1 (CH2/327/1, 140) 1624 Nov 5 (366, 34v)
Wilkie, Thomas, MA	1626 Jun 12, 19 (385, 8v) 1629 Jul 2 (Selkirk Town Archives, Receipt for payment, information provided by W. Elliot)
students	1630 May 20 (433, 67v) 1631 Aug 25 (495, 443)

Doctors

Rutherford, James, d	1563 n.d. (B68/7/1, 321)
Douglas, Andrew, d	1603 Jan 9 (252, 200) 1612 Oct 1 (214, 193v)
Anderson, John, d	1614 Aug 11 (327, 379v)

SEMPLE, *see* Lochwinnoch

SETON (par), East Lothian
(later in Tranent par)

Dunlop, Robert	1609 Nov 16 (168, 41v)
Ferguson, Robert	1633 Mar 30 (480, 272)

SHETHIN, Aberdeenshire MRf NJ8832
Tarves par

order for school and schoolmaster	1617 Aug 6 (CH2/146/2, 131)

Cheyne, John, MA   1622 Nov 25 (385, 185v) 1623 Mar 26
                          (RS5/4, 146v)

SHETTLESTON, Lanarkshire MRf NS6463
Barony par
Greive, John   1631 Oct 25 (CC9/7/25)

SHIELDS, Lanarkshire MRf NS6151
East Kilbride par
Nisbet, David   1625 Dec 2 (410, 429v)

SHIELFIELD, Berwickshire MRf NT5247 (Lauder)
Lauder par
Duncan, John   1601 Nov 10 (CC8/8/41, 70v)

SHIRREL, Lanarkshire MRf NS7361
Bothwell par
Gray, Archibald   1624 May 14 (CC9/14/11, 221v)

SHOTTS (par), Lanarkshire
Semple, Robert   1629 May 29 (CC9/14/14, unfoliated)
Young, James   1630 Nov 12 (447, 180v)

SKIRLING (par), Peebleshire
Smyth, John   1629 Apr 2 (428, 93v)
Forest, Laurence   1632 May 26 (458, 100)

SLAINS (par), Aberdeenshire
Robertson, Andrew, r   1608 Sep 2 (CH2/146/2, 27v)
Clark, George, r   1627 Jul 25 (CH2/146/2, 214v)

SLAMANNAN (par), Stirlingshire
Graham, George   1632 Jun 15 (457, 200)

SMAILHOLM (par), Roxburghshire
Brown, John   1609 May 29 (223, 265v)
Deip (Deipo), John   1621 Apr 18 (310, 124v) 1622 Mar 24 (438,
                          449v)

SMALLBURN, Stirlingshire MRf NS8880 (Falkirk)
Falkirk par (later in Grangemouth par)
Maxwell, John   1596 Jul 22 (54, 177)

SNADE, Dumfriesshire MRf NX8485
Dunscore par
Thomson, Robert   1629 Jul 16 (GD28/1346)

SOUTHANNAN, Ayrshire MRf NS2053
West Kilbride par
Speir, John   1622 Nov 20 (RH11/45/5)

SOUTHDEAN (par), Roxburghshire
Turnbull, Thomas   1620 May 31 (CH2/198/1, unfoliated) Aug 2
                               (ibid.)
Weir, George   1622 May 8 (CH2/198/2, 4v)

SOUTH RONALDSAY (par), Orkney
schoolmaster, r, unnamed   1615 (*Rentals of Orkney*, ed. A. Peterkin,
                               Edinburgh 1820, 87)
Pape, John, cl, r   1624 Feb 13 (RS43/2, 158v) 1633 Aug 5
                               (RS43/4, 414v)
Strang, Andrew, r   1633 Nov 1 (F. Shaw, *Northern and Western
                               Islands of Scotland*, Edinburgh 1980, 144)

SOUTHSIDE, Midlothian MRf NT3663
Newbattle par
Wright, David   1619 Apr 16 (294, 199)

SPEDLINS, Dumfriesshire MRf NY0986
Lochmaben par
Whitehead, William, d   1622 Dec 11 (RS1/12, 86)

SPOTT (par), East Lothian
Simpson, Andrew   c.1560 (J. Miller, *The Lamp of Lothian*,
                               Haddington 1844, 445n.)

SPROUSTON (par), Roxburghshire
Kidd, James   1624 Dec 22 (397, 314v)
Nicolson, Andrew   1617 Jul 25 (411, 257)

STENTON (par), East Lothian
Graham, Daniel   1626 May 17 (544, 11)
Dudgeon, James   1620 May 24 (323, 77) 1621 Aug 23 (334, 24)

STEWARTON (par), Ayrshire
Blair, John   1611 May 23 (192, 175v)

Miller, John, d	1614 Nov 13 (324, 357v)
Montgomerie, Robert, MA (Gl 1613 *or* 1619)	1620 May 4 (RS12/1, 480) Nov 19 (CC9/14/8, 104v)
Walker, John	1623 Sep 7 (352, 33)
Park, Sebastian, MA	1625 Jun 21 (B37/1/1, 244)
Cunningham, Robert, MA	1626 Nov 18 (412, 378)
Walker, William, MA	1630 Apr 17 (CC9/7/23, 360)

STICHILL (par), Roxburghshire

Bairnsfather, Adam	1610 May 4 (191, 115v)

STIRLING, Stirlingshire
Grammar School

Yule, Alexander, MA (*prob* SAS), r at St Ninian's	1574 n.d. ('Register of ministers and readers in the Kirk of Scotland', *Wodrow Misc.*, i, 366) 1610 May 25 (208, 54v)
Buchanan, Thomas, MA	1575 Dec 15 (*RPC*, ii, 478)
Wallace, William, MA	1615 Apr 22 (297, 212v) 1616 Jul 13 (CC21/13/3)
schoolmaster, unnamed	1617, 1618 n.d. (*Common Good*, 49)
Edmeston (Edmondson), James, MA, later min of St Ninian's	1620 May 17 (CC17/5/2, 120–1) *before* 1634 May 29 (474, 230)
Will, David, MA (Ed 1619), p	1629 Mar 27 (RS50/4(1), 68v) 1633 Jul 13 (513, 66)
Johnson, Daniel	1632 Dec 17 (480, 259)

Doctors

two doctors	*appointed* 1602 Aug 20 (B66/20/1)
Ramsay, Patrick	1604 Apr 22 (CC21/13/1)
Edmeston, James, MA	1612 Nov 16 (*Stirling Recs.*, 132) 1622 Aug 28 (ibid., 156)
Thomson, John	1612 Nov 23 (ibid., 132)
Brady, James	*before* 1614 Nov 29 (ibid., 136)
Connell, Robert, MA (Gl 1615), d	1616 Sep 16 (257, 378v)
Burn, John, d	1616 Sep 16 (257, 378v) *before* 1617 Oct 28 (273, 29v)
doctor	1618 n.d. (*Common Good*, 49)
Row, John, MA, pr	1618 May 27 (*Stirling Recs.*, 150)
Murray, David, pr	1620 Dec 9 (ibid., 155)
Forsyth, James, MA, d	1626 Mar 12 (429, 241v)
Rae, Alexander 'englische doctor'	1626 Oct 31 (400, 103)

doctors   1628 n.d. (*Common Good*, 49)
Henryson, Thomas, MA, d   1629 Mar 27 (RS50/4(1), 68v)

Music School
Row, John, MA, pr   1619 Sep 22 (*Maitland Misc.*, i (2), 458)
Murray, David, pr   1620 Dec 19 (ibid., 478)
Row, William, MA (Ed   1620 n.d. (*Fasti*, iv, 209)
  1616), min of Forgandenny
  1624, cf. Airth

Chapel Royal
Castlelaw, James, sir, c, p   1565/6 Jan 3 (*RSS*, v, 2528) 1574 Apr 11
                             (J.R. Oliver, *Upper Teviotdale and the Scotts of
                             Buccleuch*, Hawick 1887, 451)
Hudson, Thomas   1586 Jun 5 (*APS*, iii, 489) 1593 Oct 10
                             (Register of the Privy Seal, vol. 68, fo. 21,
                             transcription in *Thomas Hudson's History of
                             Judith*, ed. J. Craigie, STS 1941, 142)

Vernacular School
Duncanson, James   1603 Nov 18 (*Stirling Recs.*, 107)
Murdoch, Nicholl   1603 Nov 18 (ibid.)
Wallace, James   1631 n.d. (*Maitland Misc.*, i (2), 478)

Dame School
Duncanson, James   *from* 1603 *forbidden to teach boys* (*Stirling Recs.*,
                             107) 1612 Nov 9 (ibid., 132)
Murdoch, Nicholl   *from* 1603 *forbidden to teach boys* (ibid.)

STOBO (par), Peebleshire
Peacock, *name not given*   1604 Jun 21 (C.B. Gunn, *The Church and
                             Parish of Dawyck*, Peebles 1931, 16)
Elder, John   1612 Jun 17 (225, 144v)
Moncreiff, Alexander   1623 May 9 (350, 223)
Waugh (Waich),   1625 Apr 10 (386, 143)
  William, MA
Lowes, William   1629 May 18 (458, 18) 1638 Jun 22 (545, 152)

STOBWOOD, Lanarkshire MRf NS9846 (Carnwath)
Carnwath par
Anderson, Thomas   1620 Jul 29 (RS40/2A, 5)

STONEFOLD, Berwickshire MRf NT7442
Eccles par
Haistie, John, MA   1626 Jul 3 (391, 148) 1630 Apr 27 (RS1/28, 272v)

STONEHAVEN, Kincardineshire MRf NO8786
Dunnottar par
Lepar, Alexander   1613 Jun 4 (227, 239v)

STONEHOUSE (par), Lanarkshire
Macmath, Matthew   1606 Jan 29 (120, 15v)
Young, James, n   1614 Jun 30 (235, 146) Jul 13 (301, 133)
Walker, John, n   1625 Dec 14 (430, 84v) 1627 Apr 19 (432, 183)
Archibald, Hugh   1629 Jan 9 (435, 293)
Aird, John   1629 Oct 29 (432, 151v)
Fairie, James   1630 Apr 27 (503, 527)

STONEYKIRK (par), Wigtownshire
Reid, William   1619 Nov 12 (302, 37v)

STOW (par), Midlothian
Hadden, Andrew   1619 Jun 12 (309, 41v) 1627 Feb 27 (418, 335v)
Johnston, John   1628 Apr 5 (CH2/338/1, 12v) 1629 Apr 5 (ibid.)
schoolmaster, r, unnamed   1629 Jul 12 (CH2/338/1, 21)

STRACATHRO (par), Angus
Brockhouse, Thomas   1616 Jul 4 (254, 199)

STRAGEATH (par), Perthshire
(later known as Blackford)
Brown, John   1583 May 21 (*Stirling Presbytery Records*, ed. J. Kirk, *SHS* 1981, 118–19) Nov 27 (CS1/3(2), 207)

STRAITON (par), Ayrshire
Scrimgeour, John, d   1613 Jan 10 (320, 248v)

STRALOCH, Aberdeenshire MRf NJ8621
New Machar par
Tullidaff, William   1621 Jul 16 (*RPC*, 1st ser., xii, 551)

STRANRAER (par), Wigtownshire
(disjoined from Inch and Leswalt c.1622)

Paterson, James	1610 Jul 29 (187, 336v) 1614 Jul 15 (RH2/8/38, 97v)
Hutcheson, William	1615 Mar 2 (243, 268v)
Haistie, George	1623 Mar 8 (344, 153v) 1636 Jan 26 (502, 60)
Dick, John, MA	1624 Jan 9 (361, 52)
Hutcheson, William	1615 Mar 2 (243, 268v)
Crooks, William, MA (Gl)	1629 Dec 19 (RS60/2, 76v)
Doctor	
Gray, Andrew, d	1622 Feb 12 (325, 320v)

STRATHARDLE (par), Perthshire
(also known as Kirkmichael)

Bairdie, Andrew	1627 Feb 6 (519, 347) 1632 Jan 14 (RS50/5, 439v)
Mollison, Thomas, MA	1633 Jul 3 (RS50/6, 364v)

STRATHAVEN (par), Lanarkshire
(later in Avondale par)

Gilchrist, William	1624 Feb 2 (380, 66v) 1630 Jun 18 (442, 162v)
Aird, John	1626 Jun 13 (408, 214)
Lindsay, William, MA	1626 Oct 11 (RS40/2B, 353v) 1627 Jan 6 (472, 163)

STRATHBOGIE (precise location unspecified)

Jameson, Robert, MA	1608 Dec 25 (215, 259v)

STRATHBROCK (par), West Lothian
(also known as Uphall)

school inadequate	1608 (A. Bain, *The Education Act of 1696 in West Lothian*, Dept of Educational Studies 1974, 135)
McDougall, William	1609 Feb 7 (166, 264v) 1610 Mar 21 (CC8/8/47, 55)
order for maintenance of school and master	1611 Jul 1 (G.R. Kinloch (ed.), *Ecclesiastical Records: Selections from the Minutes of the Synod of Fife*, Abbotsford Club 1837, 22)
Anderson, Robert	1626 Aug 19 (395, 132v) 1627 Dec 6 (421, 126v)

STRATHDON, *see* Innerochtie

STRATHFILLAN, *see* Killin

STRATHMIGLO (par), Fife
Berwick, John, MA   1612 Nov 30 (226, 237v) 1613 Jul 24 (PC6/11,
                          unfoliated)
Graham, James, MA   1629 Jun 23 (RS31/8, 74)

STROMNESS (par), Orkney
Ogilvie, William   1630 [*blank*] (441, 230)
Jack, James, n   1598 n.d. (CS7/195, 357) 1602 Jun 24 (ibid.)

STRONSAY (par), Orkney
Duncan, William   1630 Jul 9 (RS43/4, 103)

STROWAN (par), Perthshire
Horner, John, MA   1600 n.d. (88, 291)

STRUIE, Perthshire MRf NO0811
Forteviot par (detached)
Welsh, John   1598 Sep 30 (78, 141v)

SWINWOOD, Berwickshire MRf NT8962
Coldingham par
  Clarkson, George;   1602 Jan 17 (87, 283)

SYMINGTON (par), Lanarkshire
Tennent, Joseph   1625 Oct 6 (401, 187v) 1627 Jun 19 (412, 227)

TAIN (par), Ross and Cromarty
Grammar School
Moffat, William, MA   1602 Jan 1 (127, 347v) 1605 Jan 15 (110, 297)
Forrester, James, MA   1607 Jun 9 (RS36/2, 260v) Aug 30 (RS36/2,
                          288)
Hossack, Alexander, MA   1610 Feb 10 (*Munro Writs*, no. 150)
Knox, John, MA   1617 Jun 27 (274, 249)
Munro, David, MA   1618 Dec 20 (320, 84) 1619 Oct 22 (299, 4)
schoolmaster, unnamed   1620, 1622 n.d. (*Common Good*, 50)
students   1621 Sep 2 (313, 389) 1621 Nov 26 (337, 59)
                          1622 Aug 8 (343, 351)
Ross, Thomas, MA (SA),   1622 Nov 12 (RS37/4, 243) 1629 Mar 4
  r, also at Music School (RS37/4, 277v)
student   1628 Jun 29 (RS37/4, 92)

Ross, Thomas, MA   1628 n.d. (*Common Good*, 50) 1629 Mar 4
                               (RS37/4, 277)
McCulloch, James, MA   1629 May 16 (RS37/4, 167) 1632 Mar 10 (451,
                               160v)

Music School
Ross, Thomas, MA (SA),   1622 Nov 12 (RS37/4, 243) 1629 Mar 4
  r, also at Grammar School (RS37/4, 277v)
Tullidaff, John, MA, r   1626 May 30 (RS37/3, 271) 1628 May 28
                               (ibid., 85)

TANNADICE (par), Angus
Guthrie, Patrick   1610 Feb 10 (CC3/9/3) Mar 6 (181, 527v)
Rae (Rea), Joseph, MA   1613 Jan 27 (CC3/9/4)
Carr, Archibald, MA   1620 Aug 3 (310, 155)
Crichton, James   1624 Dec 7 (386, 286)

TARBAT (par), Ross and Cromarty
Tullidaff, John, MA   1633 Dec 3 (GD199/7)

TARBOLTON (par), Ayrshire
Stewart, Henry, MA   1602 Jul 29 (RS11/2, 18v)
Primrose, Henry   1619 Sep 3 (289, 392v)
Adam, John   1622 Jan 14 (RS12/2, 289v)
Anderson, James, MA   1627 Feb 19 (RS/21, 64v) Nov 17 (411, 30)
Archibald, Hugh, MA   1630 Oct 6 (450, 403v) Dec 31 (440, 22v)

TARVES (par), Aberdeenshire
Roche, William, MA   1601 Sep 1 (84, 240) 1603 May 9 (110, 482v)
Scroggie, William, MA   1602 Feb 2 (90, 158v)
Lowrie, John   1619 Nov 25 (316, 255) 1620 Jun 6 (322, 50v)
schoolmaster, unnamed   *dismissed* 1621 (I.J. Simpson, *Education in
                               Aberdeenshire before 1872*, London 1947, 11)
order for school and   1621 Jun 14 (CH2/146/2, 170)
  schoolmaster, cl, r
no school or schoolmaster   1622 Apr 24 (CH2/146/2, 170)
'first schoolmaster'   1623 Jul 23 (W.R. Foster, *The Church before the
                               Covenants*, Edinburgh 1975, 196)
Thomson, Robert, MA   1624 Apr 24 (374, 515) 1628 Apr 6 (407,
                               388v)
Gardyne, Thomas, MA, min 1624 Aug 5 (CH2/146/2, 188v)
order for maintenance   1627 May 29 (CH2/146/2, 213)
  of schoolmaster, r

TAYPORT, *see* Ferryport-on-Craig

TEALING (par), Angus
Miller, William, cl   1609 May 22 (GRO OPR 322/1)
Tough (Teuch), Hugh   1620 Jun 19 (333, 245v) 1622 Jun 1 (336, 21v)
Henryson, John   1625 Jun 24 (406, 222v)

TEMPLE (par), Midlothian
Crichton, Patrick   1620 Jul 10 (330, 48v) 1624 Dec 21 (424, 161)

THIRLESTANE, Berwickshire MRf NT5647
Lauder par
Taylor, Gilbert   1616 Jan 20 (257, 370v)

THORN, Lanarkshire MRf NS7360
Bothwell par
Poigis, John *'in muire*   1604 Jul 20 (118, 246v)
magane', i.e. Muirmadkin

THORNTONLOCH, East Lothian MRf NT7574
Innerwick par
Gray, James   1618 Jan 19 (296, 95v)

THURSO (par), Caithness
Cumming, Alexander, MA   1621 Feb 15 (362, 181v)
Nisbet, Alexander   1625 May 28 (RS37/3, 100v) Jun 4 (385, 37)
Allardyce, David, MA, p, r   1628 Jun 2 (478, 121) 1633 Feb 11 (463, 108)

TIBBERMORE (par), Perthshire
Balnevis, Alexander, min,   *for three years, before* 1611 Apr 18 (*Fasti*, iv, 254)
    r at Perth
Anderson, Adam, MA   1623 Jul 5 (349, 289)

TILLICOULTRY (par), Clackmannanshire
school   1627 May 21 (*Reports*, 27)
Rhynd, Alexander, MA   1604 Nov 9 (RS58/3, 289v)
Livingstone, William   1627 Mar 2 (RS58/4, 23v)

TINWALD (par), Dumfriesshire
Paton, John   1627 Nov 19 (539, 369)
Johnston, Daniel   1611 Dec 29 (PC6/11, unfoliated)

TORPHICHEN (par), West Lothian

Mawer, Robert	1623 May n.d. (338, 209v) 1627 Mar 1 (408, 307)
Greig, William, r	1630 Aug 12 (A. Bain, *The Education Act of 1696 in West Lothian*, Dept of Educational Studies 1974, 125) Nov 27 (RS25/17, 181)

TORRYBURN (par), Fife

Norvell, William	*for six months* c.1599 (JC26/4/2)
Rae, Alexander	1620 May 1 (333, 183) 1621 Jul 17 (9445, 291v)
Murieson *or* Morrison, William	1622 Jun 10 (329, 189v) 1623 Jun 20 (370, 438)

TOUGH (par), Aberdeenshire

Scroggie, Robert, MA	1621 Apr 11 (370, 168v)
Schene, James	1627 May 10 (RS5/5, 524v)

TOWIE, *see* Kinbathoch

TRANENT (par), East Lothian

Burnside, John, r	1594 n.d. (D. Withrington, 'Schools in the Presbytery of Haddington in the Seventeenth Century', *East Lothian Trans.*, ix, 1963, 92)
McGhee (Makghe), Andrew	1596 n.d. (Withrington, 'Schools in the Presbytery of Haddington', 93)
Crichton, George	1596 Nov 15 (61, 158) 1599 Sep 27 (75, 152v)
Lithgow, Gilbert	1603 Oct 20 (123, 364v) 1605 Feb 21 (346, 274v)
Dickson, George	1608 Jun 11 (161, 169v)
Hastings, John	1613 Jan 4 (237, 359) 1632 Sep 12 (RS25/20, 31v)
no school *'Excep ane voluntar quha is Reider at the kirk'*	1627 May 6 (*Reports*, 135)

TRAQUAIR (par), Peebleshire
(formerly Kirkbride)

Tennent, Joseph, MA (Ed 1595), min	1598 n.d. (*Fasti*, i, 292)
Wilson, William	1616 Mar 27 (256, 357)
Watson, Archibald, MA	1617 Dec 9 (RS1/1, 205v)

TRINITY GASK, *see* Kinkell

TULLIALLAN (par), Perthshire (later in Fife)
Ramsay, Patrick, d   1604 Apr 22 (CC21/13/1)

TULLIBARDINE, Perthshire MRf NN9214
Strageith par
McCreich, James   1598/9 Mar 1 (73, 344) 1606 Sep 15 (129,
                         299v)

TULLIBODY (par), Clackmannanshire
(united to Alloa 1600)
school   1618 Oct 4 (H. Hutchison, 'Church Control
                         of Education in Clackmannanshire, 1560–
                         1700', *RSCHS*, xviii, 1973, 74)
schoolmaster, r, unnamed 1625 (Hutchison, 'Education in
                         Clackmannanshire', 74)

TULLYMURDOCH, Perthshire MRf NO1952
Alyth par
Paton, John, MA   1603 Nov 4 (451, 101)

TURRIFF (par), Aberdeenshire
Ogston (Austin),   1586 Jul 11 (24, 364) *said to have taught for 40*
  Thomas, MA (AbK)   *years, including regent's post at King's College*
                         (Dempster, *Historia*, i, 55)
Hay, James, MA   1601 Oct 4 (SC1/60/1, 22)
student   1603 Jun 18 (RS4/2, 155v)
Ogston, Andrew, later   c.1586 *taught the 'elements' only* (Dempster,
  min of Canisbay   *Historia*, ii, 514 *bis*)
Ogston, William, MA   1608 Sep 25 (*RPC*, 1st ser., viii, 674) 1620
                         Mar 22 (309, 119)
Gordon (Gorne),   1624 May 15 (360, 442v)
  Thomas, MA
Cheyne, John, MA   1625 Jun 4 (490, 7)
students   1627 Oct 4 (418, 169)
Hempseed, Walter, MA   1627 Aug 21 (409, 72v) 1635 Jun 26 (516, 164)

TUSHIELAW, Selkirkshire MRf NT2917
Ettrick par
Grahamslaw, Walter   1629 Dec 19 (446, 157v)

TYNINGHAME (par), East Lothian

Shorthouse, Robert	1595 Nov 30 (77, 391v) 1605 Jul 30 (NP1/55, 79)
Hay, William	1600 Mar 11 (CC8/17/4) Nov 5 (97, 230)
Wilson, Archibald *or* Edmond	1604 Feb 8 (99, 251v) 1607 Dec 30 (219, 19v)
Aitchison, James	1608 Mar 17 (*Melrose Recs.*, iii, 475)
Adinston, William	1613 May 5 (223, 322v)
schoolmaster, unnamed	1615 Jun 11 (A.I. Ritchie, *The Churches of St Baldred*, Edinburgh 1881, 139)
Wilson, Archibald	1615 Nov 12 (Ritchie, *Churches of St Baldred*, 140)
McQueen, James, MA	1617 Dec 1 (Ritchie, *Churches of St Baldred*, 167) 1619 Oct 17 (ibid., 183)
Davidson, George, p, r	1620 Jul 2 (Ritchie, *Churches of St Baldred*, 186) 1622 Dec 15 (ibid., 202)
Hay, William	*'desyrit to be schoolmaister'* 1623 Nov 30 (Ritchie, *Churches of St Baldred*, 203)
Mills, Henry, MA, r	1626 Feb 12 (Ritchie, *Churches of St Baldred*, 211)
Ferguson, John	1626 Feb 12 (Ritchie, *Churches of St Baldred*, 211) 1632 Mar 2 (497, 286)

TYRIE (par), Aberdeenshire

schoolmaster, unnamed	1614 Jun 2 (CH2/89/1(2), 161)
provision for schoolmaster, r	1615 Jun 2 (CH2/89/1(2), 181v)
no school	1616 Oct 2 (CH2/89/1(2), 195v) 1617 Jun 5 (ibid., 208)
Fullie, Alexander	1618 Oct 5 (RS5/1, 288)

UDDINGTON, Lanarkshire MRf NS8633

Douglas par

Boyd, John	1606 Mar 28 (CC8/8/43, 71v)

UDNY (par), Aberdeenshire

English school

schoolmaster, r, unnamed	1614–1620 (I.J. Simpson, *Education in Aberdeenshire before 1872*, London 1947, 11)

UPHALL, *see* Strathbrock

UPSETLINGTON, *see* Ladykirk

URQUHART (par), Moray

Guthrie, Henry, MA	1613 Sep 10 (222, 296)
Turing, John, MA	1615 Nov 8 (252, 227v)
Duff, John, MA	1627 Apr 13 (RS28/3, 108v)
Tarras, Robert, MA (AbK 1629), later min of St Andrews par, Moray	1631–1640 n.d. (*Fasti*, vi, 399)

URY, Kincardineshire MRf NO8587
Fetteresso par

schoolmaster, unnamed	1618 Jun 17 (D.G. Barron, *The Court Book of the Barony of Urie 1604–1747*, SHS 1892, 28)

WEEM (par), Perthshire

Menzies, John	1587 May 17 (CS1/3(2), 334)

WEST BARNS, East Lothian MRf NT6578
Dunbar par

Hepburn, Thomas	1607 May 11 (139, 105v)

WESTER UGIE, *see* Longside

WEST FENTON, East Lothian MRf NT4981
Dirleton par

Wilson, James	1602 Jul 28 (RS24/2, 145v)

WEST GRANGE, Fife MRf NS9889
Culross par (previously in Perthshire)

Thomson, William	1607 May 29 (RS48/5, 545v)

WEST KILBRIDE (par), Ayrshire

Lowrie, John	1603 Feb 19 (CC9/7/3, 134v) 1626 Apr 14 (B37/1/1, 256v)
Ross, Hugo, MA	1615 May 27 (B37/1/1, 111v)
Taylor, James, MA	1629 Nov 26 (RS12/4, 516v)

WEST LINTON (par), Peebleshire

Nairn, David, MA, min	1602 Sep 8 (CH2/295/1, 99v)
Bell, John	1622 Jul 11 (356, 416)
Dyet, William	1625 Aug 13 (RS1/18, 9)
Chisholm, Archibald	1630 Aug 1 (468, 288)
Alexander, Robert	1632 Jul 10 (RS25/19, 225) 1640 Apr 4 (532, 365)

WEST NISBET, Roxburghshire MRf NT6725
Crailing par
Penston, William, MA   1624 Mar 18 (SC60/56/2, 174v)

WEST RESTON, Berwickshire MRf NT9061 (East Reston)
Presumably Coldingham par
Ruthven, Alexander, MA   1610 Jul 3 (191, 256)
Sym, David, n   1612 Nov 19 (285, 223v)
Horne (*or* Home), John,   1612 Apr 2 (205, 33) Jun 12 (29, 124)
  MA
Sinclair, Thomas   1616 Jul 22 (259, 19) 1619 Mar 17 (259, 195v)
Litster (*or* Little), Henry   1618 May 19 (SC60/56/2, 47) 1619 Jan 16
                             (SC60/56/1, 234)
Hume, Alexander   1619 Dec 22 (357, 112) 1620 Mar 6 (300,
                             375v)
McDougall (McDowall),   1621 Apr 9 (406, 76) Dec 8 (345, 265v)
  Robert

WHISTLEBERRY, Kincardineshire MRf NO8575
Kinneff par
Ramsay, Andrew, MA   1607 Jan 31 (132, 92v)

WHITEKIRK (par), East Lothian
Aird, John, s   1605 Jan 24 (124, 227)

WHITHORN (par), Wigtownshire
Inglis, John   1616 Mar 25 (274, 123) 1619 May 6 (294, 420)
McNeillie, John   1628 Aug 3 (RS60/2, 20v)
Doctor
McNab, Robert, d, n   1608 Sep 12 (152, 102v)

WHITSOME (par), Berwickshire
Davidson, George   1617 Sep 12 (272, 90v) 1624 Aug 18 (415, 46)
Trotter, Andrew   1628 Jul 10 (418, 133) 1654 Feb 2 (608, 365)

WHITTINGHAME (par), East Lothian
Wood, John   1620 Feb 9 (452, 61)

WHITTON, Roxburghshire MRf NT7622
Morebattle par
Couper, William, MA   1620 Jun 16 (324, 201)

WICK (par), Caithness

Annand, James, MA	1617 Mar 22 (530, 565) 1634 Feb 14 (RS37/5, 139)

WIGTOWN (par), Wigtownshire

Adamson, James	1582/3 Mar 6 (CH4/1/1, ii, 187) 1583 May 27 (CS7/55, 245)
Paterson, James	1602 Oct 21 (*RPC*, vi, 762)
Boyd, William, MA	1607 Jul 1 (157, 48) 1614 Jun 7 (301, 276)
Tran, Hugh, MA	1621 Sep 1 (375, 56) 1622 Oct 2 (362, 68v)
Ramsay, David, MA	1628 Jun 24 (440, 408v)
Hutcheson, Hugh, MA	1631 Jul 2 (451, 187)

WINTON, East Lothian MRf NT4271
Pencaitland par

Wilson, James	1627 Aug 22 (425, 73v)

WISTON (par), Lanarkshire

Johnston, Thomas	1629 Feb 2 (450, 393v) 1640 May 13 (532, 412)

WOODHOUSE, Dumfriesshire (unidentified)

Mitchell, James	1609 Apr 15 (165, 305v)

YAIR, Selkirkshire MRf NT4532
Selkirk par (later in Caddonfoot par)

Duncan, Thomas	1612 Jun 3 (216, 37)

YESTER, *see* Bothans

YETHOLM (par), Roxburghshire

Plumber, William	1624 Apr 10 (373, 60)

ABERCHIRDER (Abchirdoch) (par), Banffshire
(later known as Marnoch)
students   1638 Jan 11 (523, 253)

AILLAVURE (unidentified)
Dunlop, George, MA   1651 May 6 (572, 85)

AIRNTULLY, Perthshire MRf NO0935
Kinclaven par
Taylor, Alexander   1650 Mar 2 (566, 140)

ALLOWAY (par), Ayrshire
Nicoll, Thomas   1654 Aug 5 (608, 123)

ANCRUM (par), Roxburghshire MRf NT6224
(also known as Nether Ancrum)
Rutherford, Andrew   1643 Mar 31 (547, 150)

ANWOTH (par), Kirkcudbrightshire
Walker, Robert   *before* 1665 (*Kirkcudbright Sheriff Court Deeds, 1623–1675*, ed. M.B. Johnston and C.M. Armet, Edinburgh 1939, no. 1814)

ARDCHATTAN (par), Argyll
original arrangements for school made 1649 (*Clan Campbell*, i, 81)

ARRAN, Bute (precise location unspecified)
Kilbride or Kilmorie par
Andrew, Matthew   1652 Feb 7 (582, 129)

AUCHINLECK (par), Ayrshire
Campbell, Hugh   1638 Jul 26 (516, 388)

BALMERINO (par), Fife
Sibbald, James, MA   1642 Oct 1 (550, 118)

BARNWELL (par), Ayrshire
Dunbar, John   1648 Dec 26 (593, 158)

BEANSTON, East Lothian MRf NT5476
Prestonkirk par
Wilson, James   1637 Jul 13 (552, 277)

BOLTON (par), East Lothian
Brown, William   1638 Apr 18 (518, 172)

BONHARD, West Lothian MRf NT0179 (Bonhard House)
Carriden par
Hay, Robert, MA   1639 May 25 (528, 40)

BRAIDENHILL, Lanarkshire MRf NS7467
New Monkland par
Ross, Robert   1652 Apr 9 (577, 189)

CAIRNBYRE (unidentified)
Tullidaff, William, MA   1647 Apr 15 (562, 461)

CALDOW, Kirkcudbrightshire MRf NX7278
Balmaclellan par
Thom, James   1648 Feb 1 (577, 106)

CAMLARGO (unidentified)
Marshall, John   1654 Apr 1 (599, 144)

CAMPSIE (par), Stirlingshire
Watt, Henry, MA   1636 Dec 8 (605, 417)

CERES (par), Fife
Craig, James, MA   1636 Dec 7 (504, 378)

CLAYHILLS (unidentified)
Daes, Thomas, n   1637 Sep 14 (569, 211)

CLEGHORN, Lanarkshire MRf NS9045
Lanark par
Paterson, John, MA   1646 May n.d. (613, 265)

COCKBURN, *presumably* Berwickshire, Duns par MRf NT7658 *or*
COCKBURN, Midlothian, Currie par MRf NT1465
Miller, Leonard   1637 Aug 10 (524, 99)

COLLIESTON, Dumfriesshire MRf NX8182
Dunlop, George, MA   1653 Aug 12 (600, 280)

COLVEND (par), Kirkcudbrightshire
Murray, James   1652 Jan 22 (565, 263)

CORTACHY (par), Angus MRf NO3959 (Cortachy Castle)
Watson, William, MA   1634 Nov 6 (504, 24)

COUSLAND, Midlothian MRf NT3768
Cranston par
Halliday, Thomas   1636 May 16 (511, 185)

CREETOWN (Ferryton), Kirkcudbrightshire MRf NX4758
Kirkmabreck par
Cloudslay, William   1634 Nov 13 (540, 100)

CROY (par), Inverness-shire
Smith, George   1642 n.d. (J. Munro and R.W. Munro, *Croy
                                 and Dalcross*, Nairn 1967, 10)

CULSALMOND (par), Aberdeenshire
Watson, William, MA   1653 Apr 22 (619, 253)

DALMELLINGTON (par), Ayrshire
Weir, David   1648 Mar 18 (619, 278)

DALSWINTON, Dumfriesshire MRf NX9385
Kirkmahoe par
Corbett, James   1655 n.d. (CC5/16/1, 40)

DALZIEL (par), Lanarkshire
Leckie, John, pr   1654 May 28 (J. Lee, *Lectures on the History of
                                 the Church of Scotland*, ii, Edinburgh 1860, 440)

DESKFORD (par), Banffshire
Gardiner, William   1655 n.d. (W. Cramond, *The Church and
                                 Churchyard of Deskford*, Banff 1885, 9)

DOLLAR (par), Clackmannanshire
Cormack, John   1637 Feb 15 (512, 31)

DRUM (unidentified)
Rutherford, David, MA   1653 Sep 1 (615, 39)

DRUMBLADE (par), Aberdeenshire
Leslie, Alexander   1652 Dec 15 (599, 144)

DUNDONALD (par), Ayrshire
school   1635 Jan 1 (Dundonald Kirk Session Minute
                            of 1634, quoted in J.H. Gillespie, *Dundonald,*
                            the Parish and its Setting, Glasgow 1939,
                            499–500)

DUNDRENNAN (par), Kirkcudbrightshire
(later known as Rerrick)
Black, John   1658 Jan 29 (CC5/16/1, 17)

DUNTULM, Skye MRf NG4174
Kilmuir par
Mackenzie, William   1660 n.d. (F. Shaw, *Northern and Western Islands*
                            of Scotland, Edinburgh 1980, 145)

EASTWOOD (par), part Lanarkshire, part Renfrewshire
Jenkin, David   1640 Nov 5 (551, 424)

EDINKILLIE (par), Moray
Kinnoch, Alexander   1643 May 31 (551, 352)

FEARN (par), Ross and Cromarty *or* **FERN** (par), Angus
Douglas, James   1653 Jul 18 (621, 144)

FINTRY (par), Stirlingshire
Reid, John   1635 n.d. (CH2/438/1, 14v)

FOULIS, Ross and Cromarty MRf NH5864 (Foulis Castle),
Kiltearn par
Finnie (Phinny), George   1660 Aug 29 (*Munro Writs*, no. 221)

GAIN, Lanarkshire MRf NS7370
New Monkland parnot in 71 census
Shanks, John   1652 Jun 16 (572, 360)

GATESIDE, Ayrshire MRf NS3653
Beith par
students   1638 Oct 15 (579, 204)

GREENOCK (par), Renfrewshire
Crooks, John, MA   1637 Jul 21 (514, 431)

HILL OF MURDOSTOUN, Lanarkshire MRf NS8257
(cf. Murdistoun)
Shotts par
Gray, Gilbert   1652 Nov 23 (590, 92)

HUMBIE (par), East Lothian
Lowrie, Thomas, MA   1655 Mar 6 (615, 215)

HUTTON (par), Berwickshire
Blacklaw, William   1634 Aug 7 (502, 280)

KELBURN, Ayrshire   MRf NS2156
Largs par
Telfer, John   1639 Jan 9 (RH11/19/6)

KELTON (par), Kirkcudbrightshire
Milligan, John   1652 Mar 16 (*Kirkcudbright Sheriff Court Deeds,
                              1623–1675*, ed. M.B. Johnston and C.M.
                              Armet, Edinburgh 1939, no. 7)

KILBARCHAN (par), Renfrewshire
Tennent, Joseph   1640 Nov 11 (611, 99)

KILMORACK (par), Inverness-shire
Ross, Hugh   1650 Feb n.d. (W. Mackay (ed.), *Records of the
                              Presbyteries of Inverness and Dingwall 1643–1688*,
                              SHS 1896, xlvii)

KINCARDINE (par), Ross and Cromarty
Reid, William   *before* 1649 Oct 23 (W. Mackay (ed.), *Records
                              of the Presbyteries of Inverness and Dingwall
                              1643–1688*, SHS 1896, 164)

KINGARTH (par), Bute
order for school   1649 Mar 15 (J. Lee, *Lectures on the History of
                              the Church of Scotland*, ii, Edinburgh 1860, 437)

KINGUSSIE (par), Inverness-shire
Clark, Alexander, MA   1636 May 22 (540, 34)

KINNEDDAR (par), Moray
Keith, Gilbert   1655 Apr 3 (618, 95)

KIPPS, Lanarkshire
Monklands par
Baird, Robert   1635 Apr 14 (504, 574)

KIRKGUNZEON (par), Kirkcudbrightshire
Walker, Robert   *before* 1665 (*Kirkcudbright Sheriff Court Deeds, 1623–1675*, ed. M.B. Johnston and C.M. Armet, Edinburgh 1939, no. 246)

KIRKLISTON (par), West Lothian
Thomson, George   1641 Jul 16 (561, 226)

KIRKPATRICK-IRONGRAY (par), Kirkcudbrightshire
McCrone, John   1641 Jul 16 (528, 469)

KOWEHILL (unidentified)
Ramsay, David   1647 Aug 7 (589, 95)

LAG, Dumfriesshire MRf NX8878
Dunscore par
Rule, Robert   1635 Sep 18 (*Lag Chrs.*, no. 231)

LANGBRIGTOUN (unidentified)
Black, William, MA   1640 Mar 21 (525, 342)

LILLIESLEAF (Lilislie) (par), Roxburghshire
Nicoll, Patrick   1634 Feb 1 (551, 213)

LOANHEAD, Midlothian MRf NT2765
Lasswade par

Dame School
Brown, Alison   1646 n.d. (R. Sutherland, *Loanhead, the Development of a Scottish Burgh*, Edinburgh 1974, 85; L. Aitchison, *Lasswade Parish and Loanhead in the Olden Time*, Edinburgh 1892, 26)

LOCHMABEN (par), Dumfriesshire
Dunbar, William   1636 Jan 2 (567, 370)

LOGIE (*poss* Logie-Dundee) (par), Angus
(united to Liff 1613)
Norrie, John   1645 May 10 (598, 309)

LOGIE (Logie-Wester), *see* Urquhart

LORNE (precise location unspecified)
student   1634 Feb 11 (531, 326)

MANOR (par), Peebleshire
schoolmaster, unnamed   1653 Nov 24 (C.B. Gunn, *Ministry of the Presbytery of Peebles, AD 1296–1910*, Peebles 1910, 111)
Ross, Robert   1656 Jan 3 (618, 188)

MARNOCH, *see* Aberchirder

MARTINABBOT (unidentified), *presumably* Annandale
Machanath (*poss* McKinnell),   1649 Apr 3 (565, 55)
    Robert

MARYCULTER (par), Kincardineshire
Telfer, William, MA   1653 Feb 8 (611, 271)

MAULDSLIE, Lanarkshire
Carluke par
Wilson, Thomas, MA   1643 Apr 18 (547, 241)

MAYNES (unidentified), Kirkcudbrightshire *or* Dumfriesshire
Ritchie, James   1644 Jan 29 (568, 94)

MOCHRUM (par), Wigtownshire
Gillies, William, MA   1641 Feb 8 (546, 148)

MORRISTON, Berwickshire MRf NT6040 (West Morriston)
Presumably Legerwood par
Scott, William   1650 Mar 12 (589, 44)

MOULIN (par), Perthshire
Stewart, Walter   1638 Nov 3 (540, 44)

MUNCHES, Kirkcudbrightshire MRf NX8358
Buittle par
Murray, James   1652 Mar 16 (*Kirkcudbright Sheriff Court Deeds,
                                   1623–1675*, ed. M.B. Johnston and C.M.
                                   Armet, Edinburgh 1939, no. 7)

MURDOSTOUN, Lanarkshire MRf NS8155 (Murdostoun Castle)
(cf. Hill of Murdostoun)
Shotts par
Young, James   1636 Jan 6 (496, 324)

MURROES (Morres) (par), Angus
Marshall, Mungo   1652 Jul 13 (582, 12)

NETHER ANCRUM, *see* Ancrum

NIGG (par), Kincardineshire *or* **NIGG** (par), Ross and Cromarty
Rose, Andrew, MA   1645 Jul 13 (609, 263)

PARVA (unidentified), Aberdeenshire
Mylne (Mill), Patrick   1655 Jan 6 (621, 167)

PENICUIK (par), Midlothian
Lawrie, John   1648 Dec 6 (600, 23)

PENPONT (par), Dumfriesshire
Moir, John, MA, r   1643 Apr 28 (555, 137)

PITKERRO, Angus MRf NO4533 (Pitkerro Ho)
Monifeith par
Granger, George, MA   1634 Jan 21 (RS1/38, 337v)

PLACE OF PARK, Lanarkshire MRf NS6459 (Cambuslang)
Cambuslang par
Row, William, MA   1642 Dec 6 (544, 140)

REDCASTLE, Ross and Cromarty MRf NH5849
Killearnan par
Dunn, William   1645 Nov 16 (*Inventory of Chisholm Writs
                                   1456–1810*, SRS 1992, no. 191)

RERRICK, *see* Dundrennan

ROSLIN, West Lothian MRf NT2763
Lasswade par
Adinston, William   1634 Feb 18 (486, 158)

SALTCOATS, Ayrshire MRf NS2442
part Ardrossan, part Stevenston par
Telfer, John   1646 Jun 27 (SC6/80/1, 180v)

SIMPRIM, Berwickshire MRf NT8445
Swinton par
Courlie or Tourlie,   1638 May 21 (520, 191)
William

SOUTH QUEENSFERRY, West Lothian MRf NT1378
Dalmeny par
Cock, James, d   1636 Jul 7 (504, 513)

STRATHNAVER, Sutherland MRf NC7147
Farr par
Boyd, Hugh, MA   1648 Jul 7 (583, 390)

TOWARD, Argyll MRf NS1168
Presumably Dunoon and Kilmun par
Finlay, Thomas, MA   1643 Mar 4 (*Lamont Papers*, 189)

TYNRON (par), Dumfriesshire
Watson, William, MA   1641 Aug 28 (536, 411)

URQUHART (par), Ross and Cromarty
(united to Logie Wester 15th century)
Reid, William   1649 Oct 23 (*Records of the Presbyteries of
                Inverness and Dingwall 1643–1688*, ed. W.
                Mackay, SHS 1896, 164)

URR (par), Kirkcudbrightshire
Maxwell, Thomas   1643 Apr 3 (587, 281)

UYEASOUND, Shetland MRf HP5901
Unst par
Abernethie, John   1641 Jul 3 (538, 118)

WAMPHRAY (par), Dumfriesshire
Wolly (Wally), Andrew   1650 May 7 (596, 102)

YARROW (par), Selkirkshire
Welsh, William   1652 Oct 13 (567, 390)

BIBLIOGRAPHY

Manuscript Sources

Aberdeen City Archives
Aberdeen Council Register

Archivio Vaticano, Rome
Registra Supplicationum
Vat. Lat. 1744
Urbinates Latini, MS 13

Ayr District Archives (Now in Burns Monument Centre, Kilmarnock)
CH2/751/1(2)   Ayr Kirk Session, 1604–1621
CH2/751/2   Ayr Kirk Session, 1621–1646

Bibliothèque Nationale, Paris
MS Lat 14947
MS 580s

Carnegie Library, Ayr (now in Ayrshire Archive Centre)
B6/7/1   Ayr Burgh Register of Deeds, 1614–1637
B6/11/1 (1&2)   Ayr Burgh Court and Council Records, 1580–1589
B6/11/2   Ayr Burgh Court and Council Records, 1580–1596
B6/11/3   Ayr Burgh Court and Council Records, 1586–1606
B6/11/4   Ayr Burgh Court and Council Records, 1607–1632
B6/12/3   Ayr Burgh Court Books, 1549–1560, 1608–1612
B6/18/1   Ayr Burgh Council Minutes, 1598–1611

Edinburgh City Archives
Charters of the Commendators of Holyrood, Transcripts
Moses Bundle 204

Edinburgh, Columba House Archives
Book of Grisy

Edinburgh University Library
Dc.4.32   Rental of Assumptions, 1561–1566

General Register Office for Scotland, Edinburgh
OPR 294/3   Kettins, 1618–1648
OPR 310/1   Monifieth, 1560–1620
OPR 311/1   Monikie, 1613–1637
OPR 322/1   Tealing, 1599–1699
OPR 392/1   St Madoes, 1591–1819
OPR 481   Gargunnock, 1615–1819
OPR 622   Barony, Lanark, 1654–1749

Glasgow City Archives
CH2/550/1   Glasgow Kirk Session (St Mungo's), 1583–1593
CH2/1277/1   Govan Kirk Session, 1651–1662

Glasgow, Mitchell Library (papers formerly in Strathclyde Regional Archives)
B10/10/1   Glasgow Burgh Register of Deeds, Sasines Old Series Bonds,
               1625–1632
B10/18/1   Register of Services of Heirs, 1625–1676
RU2/1/1   Court and Council Book of Rutherglen, 1619–1635
Glasgow High Kirk Parish Registers, i., Baptisms 1609–1625, Transcripts

Glasgow University Archives
GUA 26620   Rentals and Accounts
GUA 39520   Report of East Kilbride parish
NRAS2808/78   Angus McKechnie Documents relating to Inverness

Glasgow University Library
MS Murray 623
MS General, 326, 643
MS General, 1483/1   Boyd Deeds

National Archives of Scotland, Edinburgh
B9/1/1   Burntisland Burgh Register, Protocol Book of Mr Andrew
               Wilson, 1581–1598
B16/1/3   Dumbarton Burgh Regisers, Protocol Book of William Houston
               (1561–1587)
B16/1/4   Dumbarton Burgh Registers, Protocol Book of William Watson
               (1580–1605)
B18/1/1   Dunbar Burgh Registers, Protocol Book of George Purves
               (1610–1647)
B30/13/1   Haddington Burgh Council Book, 1554–1580
B30/21/52   Haddington Burgh Discharges (40) of schoolmasters' fees,
               1564–1651
B30/21/53   Letters under the Signet, 8 May 1572
B30/21/54   Letters of Gift under the Privy Seal, 20 August 1576
B37/1/1   Irvine Burgh Records, Protocol Book of William Caldwell,
               1611–1632

B37/1/2	Irvine Burgh Records, Protocol Book of Robert Brown, 1620–1640
B37/11/1	Irvine Burgh Court Book, 1621–1660
B37/12/1	Irvine Burgh Council Records, 1593–1606
B38/1/1	Protocol Book of John Wilson, 1550–1572
B51/1/4	Montrose Burgh Records, Protocol Book of James Guthrie (1613–1630)
B52/1/16	Musselburgh Burgh Records, Protocol Book of Robert Bennett, 1560–1585
B56/1/4	Protocol Book of Robert Lauder, 1573–1583
B56/1/5	Protocol Book of William Galbraith, 1605–1661
B64/1/1	Rutherglen Burgh Records, Protocol Book of Robert Lindsay
B68/7/1	Selkirk Burgh Court Book, 1557–1575
CC3/3	Brechin Commissary Court, Registers of Testaments
CC3/9	Brechin Commissary Court, Registers of Deeds
CC5/16/1	Dumfries Commissary Court, Minute Book of Deeds and Protests, 1650–1716
CC6/5	Dunblane Commissary Court, Registers of Testaments
CC6/12	Dunblane Commissary Court, Registers of Deeds
CC8/2/12	Register of Decreets and Acts of Edinburgh Commissary Court, 1582–1584
CC8/8	Edinburgh Commissary Court, Registers of Testaments
CC8/10/5	Edinburgh Commissary Court, Warrants of Testaments, 1607–1610
CC8/10/8	Edinburgh Commissary Court, Warrants of Testaments, 1625–1628 (Will of James Fortoun)
CC8/10/9	Edinburgh Commissary Court, Warrants of Testaments, 1629–1633
CC8/10/52	Edinburgh Commissary Court, Warrants of Testaments, 1796–1797
CC8/17	Edinburgh Commissary Court, Registers of Deeds
CC9/7	Glasgow Commissary Court, Registers of Testaments
CC9/14	Glasgow Commissary Court, Registers of Deeds
CC9/16/1	Warrants of Deeds, 1617–1649
CC10/5	Hamilton and Campsie Commissary Court, Registers of Testaments
CC10/11	Hamilton and Campsie Commissary Court, Registers of Deeds
CC10/13/1	Hamilton and Campsie Commissary Court, Warrants of Deeds and Protests, 1614–1662
CC14/5/2	Lanark Commissary Court, Register of Testaments, 1620–1627
CC17/5/2	Orkney and Shetland Commissary Court, Register of Deeds 1622–1632
CC20/4	St Andrews Commissary Court, Registers of Testaments
CC20/11/3	St Andrews Commissary Court, Register of Deeds, 1618–1624
CC21/13	Stirling Commissary Court, Registers of Deeds

CH2/30/1	Belhelvie Kirk Session, 1633–1650
CH2/32/1	Belhelvie Kirk Session, 1623–1641
CH2/89/1	Deer Presbytery, 1602–1621
CH2/121/2	Edinburgh Presbytery, 1593–1601
CH2/141/1	Edinburgh, Trinity College Kirk Session, 1626–1638
CH2/146/1	Ellon Presbytery, 1597–1607
CH2/146/2	Ellon Presbytery, 1607–1628
CH2/147/1	Ellon Kirk Session, 1602–1641
CH2/171/1	Glasgow Presbytery, 1592–1605
CH2/171/35	Glasgow Presbytery, 1608–1615 (Transcript)
CH2/173/1	Barony Kirk, Glasgow, 1637–1698
CH2/185/1	Haddington Presbytery, 1587–1596
CH2/198/1	Jedburgh Presbytery, 1606–1621
CH2/198/2	Jedburgh Presbytery, 1622–1644
CH2/264/1	Menmuir Kirk Session, 1622–1701
CH2/271/1	Moray Synod, 1623–1644
CH2/292/2	Ormiston Parish Records (Accounts), 1660–1681
CH2/292/9	Ormiston Parish Records (Accounts), 1660–1689
CH2/295/1	Peebles Presbytery, 1596–1624
CH2/299/1	Perth Presbytery, 1618–1647
CH2/327/1	Selkirk Presbytery, 1609–1619
CH2/338/1	Stow Kirk Session, 1626–1643
CH2/377/1	Yester Kirk Session, 1613–1643
CH2/424/1	Dalkeith Presbytery, 1582–1630
CH2/438/1	Fintry Kirk Session, 1632–1659
CH2/562/1	Kirkoswald Kirk Session, 1617–1660
CH2/621/1	North Leith Kirk Session, 1605–1642
CH2/621/69	North Leith Kirk Session, 1571–1572
CH2/699/1	Longside Kirk Session, 1620–1633
CH2/809/1	Monkton Kirk Session, 1615–1654
CH2/1173/1	Kelso Kirk Session, 1622–1647
CH2/1335/2	Galston Kirk Session, 1626–1630
CH4/1/1	Register of Presentations to Benefices, 1567–1578
CH4/1/4	Register of Presentations to Benefices, 1607–1617
CS1/3(1)	Books of Sederunt of Lords of Council and Session, 1575–1583
CS1/3(2)	Books of Sederunt of Lords of Council and Session, 1583–1587
CS5/34	Acts of Lords of Council and Session, 1523–1524
CS5/36	Acts of Lords of Council and Session, 1525–1526
CS5/43	Acts of Lords of Council and Session, 1531–1532
CS6/6	Acts of Lords of Council and Session, 1534–1535
CS7	Registers of Acts and Decreets, 1542–1659
CS15/278	Extracted and Unextracted Processes, First Series, 1527–1698
DI1	General Register of Hornings
DI21/34	Aberdeen Particular Register of Hornings, 1633–1634
DI30/1	Banff Hornings, 1521–1524

DI75/3	Lanark Middle and Upper Wards Register of Inhibitions, 1620–1626
DI75/4	Lanark Middle and Upper Wards Register of Inhibitions, 1628–1647
DI117/2	Glasgow Regality Hornings, 1665
DI121/1	Kilwinning Regality Hornings, 1620–1664
E48	Exchequer Records, Index to Books of Assumption
GD1/382/3	Sandilands of Eastbarns Writs
GD1/413	Wallace-James Notebooks
GD1/509	Notes on Currie, Midlothian
GD6/106	Biel Muniments
GD20/7/191	Crawford Priory Muniments Additional
GD25/9	Ailsa Papers
GD28/1346	Supplementary Calendar of Yester Writs
GD39/172	Glencairn Writs
GD48/727	Rossie Priory Papers
GD76/184	Henderson Collections
GD76/185	Henderson Collections
GD79	Perth, King James VI Hospital Papers
GD90/2/59	Yule Collection
GD112/5/10	Protocol Book of Gavin Hamilton
GD124/17/625	Erskine of Mar
GD125/Box 5	Rose of Kilravock Muniments
GD150/2212	Morton Papers
GD156/Box 36	Irving of Kynnok, 1594–1616, Bundle
GD199/7	Ross of Pitcalnie Writs
GD215/1877	Linlithgow, Beveridge Papers
GD220/6/ 2006/8	Montrose Writs
GD248	Seafield Muniments
GD297/186/14	J. and F. Anderson Collection
GD350/1	Borthwick of Borthwick, Crookston Writs
JC2/6	Justiciary Court Records, Books of Adjournal, 1619–1631
NP1	Protocol Books:
NP1/14	John Robeson
NP1/25	William Cumming, 1564–1573
NP1/30	Alexander Lawson, 1570–1590
NP1/36	Thomas Auchinlek, 1576–1615
NP1/48	John Vaus junior, 1586–1610
NP1/51	John Small, 1587–1603 and John Shaw, 1599–1603
NP1/52	James Fraser, 1588–1593
NP1/53	Alexander Lawson, 1590–1602
NP1/53a	Stephen Paterson, 1590–1612

NP1/54	Thomas Merschell, 1590–1601
NP1/55	Robert Schortus, 1590–1619
NP1/57	Robert Frenche, 1596–1608
NP1/58	James Harlaw, 1596–1616
NP1/61	James Primrose, 1598–1624
NP1/65	William Forsyth, 1603–1634
NP1/66	Hugh Garven, 1605
NP1/67	Gilbert Garven, 1605–1613
NP1/67b	John Philp, 1608–1628
NP1/68	Archibald Millar
NP1/69a	John Lytiljohne, 1615–1629
NP1/71	Thomas Wichtane, 1619–1637
NP1/74	Robert Ker, 1622–1631
NP1/75b	David Heart, 1624–1631
NP1/76	John Nicolson, 1624–1649
NP1/96	Robert Ray, 1652–1658
NP1/171	John McGilchrist, 1627–1656
NP1/183	George Abernethy, 1585–1595
NP1/188	James Kingorne, 1609–1625
NP1/189	David Kingorne, 1614–1630
NP1/196	Robert Lawson, 1534–1541
NP1/197	? Constantine Stewart, 1510–1543
NP1/198	? John McQuhin, 1538–1546
NP1/199	Unnamed notary, Paisley, 1552–1558
NP1/200	John Kessane, 1552–1567
NP1/201	John Vaus senior, 1575–1588
NP2/1	Register of Admission of Notaries, 1563–1567
NP2/2	Register of Admission of Notaries, 1570–1579
NP3/1	Warrants for Admission of Notaries, 1579–1581
NP3/3	Warrants for Admission of Notaries, 1621–1622
NP3/75	Warrants for Admission of Notaries, no. 75
NRAS3094/330	Dunbar of Westfield Papers, Extract Contract, 1629
NRAS3094/338	Dunbar of Westfield Papers, Bond, 1631
NRAS1100	Roxburgh Muniments
PC6/11	Privy Council Registers, Acts of Caution, 1611–1615
PC6/14	Privy Council Registers, Acts of Caution, 1628–1638
PS1/57/146	Privy Seal, 1588
PS1/59	Privy Seal, 1589
PS1/60	Privy Seal, 1589–1591
PS1/61	Privy Seal, 1590–1591
RD1	General Register of Deeds, 1st Series
RD11	Warrants

RH2/8/38	Transcript of the Protocol Book of James Glover, 1588–1618
RH6	Calendar of Charters
RH7	Box of additional miscellaneous writs, Commissariot of Edinburgh
RH11/19/6	Cunningham Baillie Court, Register of Deeds, 1633–1651
RH11/45/5	Regality of Kilwinning, Register of Deeds, 1620–1651
RS1	General Register of Sasines
RS4	Aberdeen Secretary's Register of Sasines
RS5	Aberdeen Particular Register of Sasines
RS6	Kincardine Secretary's Register of Sasines
RS7	Kincardine Particular Register of Sasines
RS11	Ayr Secretary's Register of Sasines
RS12	Ayr Particular Register of Sasines
RS12/2	Ayr Particular Register of Sasines, 1620–1624
RS12/3	Ayr Particular Register of Sasines, 1624–1627
RS12/4	Ayr Particular Register of Sasines, 1627–1630
RS15	Banff Secretary's Register of Sasines
RS16	Banff Particular Register of Sasines
RS18	Berwick Particular Register of Sasines
RS22	Dumfries Particular Register of Sasines
RS22/2	Dumfries Particular Register of Sasines, 1624–1629
RS24	Edinburgh Secretary's Register of Sasines
RS25	Edinburgh Particular Register of Sasines
RS28	Elgin Particular Register of Sasines
RS30	Fife Secretary's Register of Sasines
RS31	Fife and Kinross Register of Sasines
RS33	Forfar Particular Register of Sasines
RS36	Inverness Secretary's Register of Sasines
RS37	Inverness Particular Register of Sasines
RS40/2a	Lanark Particular Register of Sasines, 1620–1627
RS40/2b	Lanark Particular Register of Sasines, 1622–1627
RS40/3a	Lanark Particular Register of Sasines, 1627–1631
RS40/3b	Lanark Particular Register of Sasines, 1627–1638
RS42	Peebles Sheriff Court, Register of Deeds
RS43	Orkney Particular Register of Sasines
RS48	Perth Secretary's Register of Sasines
RS49	Perth Particular Register of Sasines, 1st Series
RS50	Perth Particular Register of Sasines, 2nd Series
RS55	Roxburgh Secretary's Register of Sasines
RS56	Roxburgh Particular Register of Sasines
RS58	Stirling Particular Register of Sasines
RS60	Wigtown Particular Register of Sasines
SC1/60	Aberdeen Sheriff Court, Register of Deeds
SC2/56/1	Banff Sheriff Court, Register of Deeds
SC6/80/1	Ayr Sheriff Court, Register of Deeds

SC42/28   Peebles Sheriff Court, Register of Deeds
SC47/56/1   Forfar Sheriff Court, Register of Deeds
SC60/56   Duns Sheriff Court, Register of Deeds

National Library of Scotland, Edinburgh
Adv MS 29.4.2   Hutton Correspondence 1785–1823
Adv MS 34.7.2   Elgin Cartulary
Adv MS 34.7.3   James Gray Manuscripts
MS 17998   *Virtutes grammaticae*
MS 9447   Duncan Burnett's Music Book (c.1615)

St Andrews University Library Special Collections
B13/10/1   Cupar Burgh Court and Council Book, 1549–1554
B13/10/2   Cupar Burgh Court and Council Book, 1626–1639
B65/19/1   St Andrews Treasurer's Accounts, 1611–1626
UYSL115   Liber Compotorum Divi Leonardi
UYUY350   Acta Rectorum
St Andrews Burgh Miscellaneous papers, Box 110

Stirling Council Archives
B66/20/1   Stirling Council Records, 1597–1619
CH2/438/1   Fintry Kirk Session, 1632, 1640–1659
CH2/722/2   Stirling Presbytery, 1589–1595
CH2/722/3   Stirling Presbytery, 1595–1604
CH2/722/4   Stirling Presbytery, 1606–1614
CH2/723/1   Dunblane Presbytery, 1616–1628
CH2/942/5   Alloa and Tullibody Kirk Session, 1609–1652

Printed Primary Sources

The 1635 Scottish Psalter, ed. R.R. Terry (London, 1936)
'Aberdeen Burgess Register 1631–1700', ed. A.M. Munro, *New Spalding Misc.*, ii (1908)
Abernethy, John, *A Christian and Heavenlie Treatise* (London, 1630)
The Accounts of the Chamberlains of the City of Bath, 1568–1602, ed. F.D. Wardle
    (Somerset Record Society, 1923)
Accounts of the Collectors of the Thirds of Benefices, ed. G. Donaldson (Edinburgh, 1949)
Accounts of the Lord High Treasurer of Scotland, ed. T. Dickson et al. (Edinburgh, 1877–
    1970)
Acta Dominorum Auditorum: Acts of the Lords Auditors of Causes and Complaints (Edin-
    burgh, 1839)
Acta Facultatis Artium Universitatis Sanctiandree, ed. A.I. Dunlop (Edinburgh, 1964)
Acts of the Parliaments of Scotland, ed. T. Thomson and C. Innes (Edinburgh, 1814–75)
Adamson, John (ed.), *Eisodia musarum Edinensium in Caroli Regis, Musarum Tutani,
    ingressu in Scotiam* (Edinburgh, 1633)
Adamson, John, *The Muses Welcome* (Edinburgh, 1618)

Adtimchiol an chreidimh, ed. R.L. Thomson (SGTS, 1962)

Agnew, R.V. (ed.), *Correspondence of Sir Patrick Waus of Barnbarroch* (Ayr-Galloway Coll., 1887)

Allenson, S. (ed.), 'The Inverness Fragments: music from a pre-Reformation parish church and school', *Music and Letters*, lxx (1989), 1–45

Amours, F.J. (ed.), *Scottish Alliterative Poems* (STS, 1897)

Anderson, A.O. (ed.), *Early Sources of Scottish History* (Edinburgh, 1922)

Anderson, A.U. (ed.), *Scottish Annals from English Chroniclers* (London, 1908)

Anderson, J. (ed.), *Calendar of the Laing Charters 854–1837* (Edinburgh, 1899)

Anderson, J.M. (ed.), *Early Records of the University of St Andrews: The Graduation Roll 1413–1579 and the Matriculation Roll 1473–1579* (Edinburgh, 1926)

Anderson, J.R. (ed.), *The Burgesses and Guild Brethren of Glasgow* (Edinburgh, 1925)

Atkinson, S., *The discoverie and hystorie of the gold mynes in Scotland* (Bannatyne Club, 1825)

The Bannatyne Miscellany (Bannatyne Club, 1827–55)

Beveridge, E. (ed.), *The Burgh Records of Dunfermline* (Edinburgh, 1917)

Bibliographia Aberdonensis, ed. J.F.K. Johnstone et al. (Third Spalding Club, 1929)

Black Book of Taymouth, ed. C. Innes (Edinburgh, 1855)

Blair, R., *The Life of Robert Blair* (Wodrow Society, 1848)

Blak, David, *An Exposition uppon the thirtie two Psalme* (Edinburgh, 1600)

Bliss, W.H. (ed.), *Calendar of Entries in the Papal Registers: Petitions* (London, 1896)

Bonar, H. (ed.), *Catechisms of the Scottish Reformation* (London, 1866)

The Book of Deer, ed. J. Stuart (Aberdeen, 1869)

Book of Records of the Ancient Privileges of the Canongate, ed. M. Wood (Edinburgh, 1955)

The Book of the Universall Kirk of Scotland: Acts and Proceedings of the General Assemblies of the Kirk of Scotland, ed. T. Thomson (Edinburgh, 1839–1845)

Breve compendium de concordentiis grammaticalibus (Edinburgh, 1580)

Brown, D., *The introduction to the true understanding of the whole arts of expedition in teaching to write in 6 hours* (London/Edinburgh, 1638)

Brown, D., *The New Invention, intituled Calligraphia: or the arte of faire writing* (St Andrews, 1622)

Brown, D., *A speedy new way of teaching write* (Oxford, c.1640)

Brown, P.H. (ed.), *Vernacular Writings of George Buchanan* (STS, 1892)

Buchanan, George, *Tragedies*, ed. and tr. P. Sharrat and P.G. Walsh (Edinburgh, 1983)

The Buik of the Kirk of the Canagait, 1564–1567, ed. A.B. Calderwood (Edinburgh, 1961)

Burel, J., 'Description of the Queen's Entry', in *Watson's Choice Collection*, ed. H.H. Wood (STS, 1977)

Burel, J., *Pamphilus speakand of lufe* (Edinburgh, c.1590)

Burne, Nicol, *A Disputation* (Paris, 1581)

Calderwood, D., *The History of the Kirk of Scotland*, ed. T. Thomson and D. Laing (Wodrow Society, 1842–49)

The Calendar of Fearn, ed. R.J. Adam (Edinburgh, 1991)

Calendar of Patent Rolls Elizabeth I, iii (1563–1566) (London, 1960)

Calendar of State Papers, Foreign, Elizabeth, ed. J. Stevenson et al. (London, 1863–1950)

Calendar of State Papers relating to Scotland and Mary, Queen of Scots, 1547–1603, ed. J. Bain et al. (Edinburgh, 1898–1969)

Cameron, J.K. (ed.), *Letters of John Johnston c.1565–1611 and Robert Howie c.1565–1645* (Edinburgh, 1963)

Campbell, H. (ed.), *Argyll Sasines* (Edinburgh, 1933)

Cartularium Ecclesiae Sancti Nicholai Aberdonensis, ed. J. Cooper (Aberdeen, 1888–1892)

Casaubon, I., *Epistolae* (Rotterdam, 1709)

Cassander, G., *Tabulae breves et expeditae in praeceptiones rhetoricae* (Antwerp, 1544)

Catena in Exodum (Paris, 1550)

Chambers, W. (ed.), *Charters and Documents relating to the Burgh of Peebles* (Edinburgh, 1872)

Charters of the Hospital of Soltre, of Trinity College, Edinburgh, and other Collegiate Churches in Midlothian, ed. D. Laing (Bannatyne Club, 1861)

Chartulary of the Abbey of Lindores, ed. J. Dowden (SHS, 1903)

The Chronicle of Perth, ed. J. Maidment (Maitland Club, 1831)

Clariodus: a Metrical Romance, ed. D. Irving (Maitland Club, 1830)

Colkelbie Sow and the Talis of the Fyve Bestis, ed. G. Kratzman (New York, 1982)

Commentary on the Rule of St Augustine by Robertus Richardinus, ed. C.G. Coulton (SHS, 1935)

The Complaynt of Scotland, ed. J.A. Stewart (STS, 1979)

Cooper, W.S. (ed.), *Charters of the Royal Burgh of Ayr* (Edinburgh, 1883)

Copiale Prioratus Sanctiandree, ed. J.H. Baxter (Oxford, 1930)

Corpus Christianorum Continuatio Mediaevalis, ed. L. Holtz (Turnhout, 1979)

Correspondence of Robert Bowes (Surtees Society, 1842)

The Court Book of the Barony of Urie, 1604–1707, ed. D.G. Barron (SHS, 1892)

Craig, John, *A shorte summe of the whole catechisme* (Edinburgh, 1581)

Craigie, J. & Law, A. (eds.), *King James, Minor Prose Works* (STS, 1944)

Cramond, W. (ed.), *The Annals of Banff* (Aberdeen, 1891–93)

Cramond, W. (ed.), *Extracts from the Records of the Kirk Session of Elgin* (Elgin, 1897)

Cramond, W. (ed.), *The Records of Elgin* (New Spalding Club, 1908)

Cranstoun, J. (ed.), *Satirical Poems of the Time of the Reformation* (STS, 1891–1893)

de Vio, Thomas, *Evangelia cum commentariis* (Paris, 1543)

Dennistoun, J. & Macdonald, A. (eds.), 'Extracts from the buik of the general kirk of Edinburgh', *Maitland Miscellany*, i (1833)

'The Diarey of Robert Birrel [sic], burgess of Edinburgh, 1532–1605', in J.G. Dalgleish (ed.), *Fragments of the Scotish [sic] History* (Edinburgh, 1798)

Dumbarton Common Good Accounts, 1614–1660, ed. F. Roberts & I.M. MacPhail (Dumbarton, 1972)

Duncan, A., *Appendix Etymologiae, ad copiam exemplorum, una cum indice interprete* (Edinburgh, 1595)

Duncan, A., *Latinae grammaticae pars prior* (Edinburgh, 1595)

Duncan, A., *Studiorum Puerilium Clavis, miro quodam compendio ac facilitate, Latinae linguae ac Poeticae Rudimenta complectens* (Edinburgh, 1597)

The Earl of Stirling's Register of Royal Letters relative to the Affairs of Scotland and Nova Scotia 1615 to 1635, ed. C. Rogers (Grampian Club, 1885)

Easson, D.E. (ed.), *Charters of the Abbey of Coupar Angus* (SHS, 1947)

Edinburgh Records: The Burgh Accounts, ed. R. Adam (Edinburgh, 1899)

Elliott, K. (ed.), *Early Scottish Keyboard Music* (London, 1967)

Elliott, K. (ed.), *Fourteen Psalm Settings of the Early Reformed Church* (London, 1960)

Evidence, Oral and Documentary taken by the Commissioners for Visiting the Universities of Scotland, iii, The University of St Andrews (London, 1837)

The Exchequer Rolls of Scotland, 1557–1567, ed. G.P McNeill (Edinburgh, 1898)

'Extracts from the Accounts of the Common Good of Various Burghs in Scotland, relative to Payments for Schools and Schoolmasters, between the years 1557 and 1634', *Maitland Miscellany*, ii (1840)

The First Book of Discipline, ed. J.K. Cameron (Edinburgh, 1960)

Forbes-Leith, W. (ed.), *Narratives of Scottish Catholics* (London 1889)

Foster, C.W. (ed.), *Lincoln Episcopal Records. Thomas Cooper, Bishop of Lincoln 1571–1584* (Lincoln, 1912)

Foxe, John, *Acts and Monuments* (London, 1858)

Fragmenta Scoto-monastica, ed. W.B.D.D. Turnbull (Edinburgh, 1842)

Gideon Guthrie: a monograph written 1712 to 1730, ed. C.E.G. Wright (Edinburgh, 1900)

Gillon, S.A. et al. (eds.), *Select Justiciary Cases, 1624–50* (Stair Society, 1953)

Grant, F.J. (ed.), *The Commissariot Record of Edinburgh: Register of Testaments* (SRS, 1897–1898)

Grant, F.J. (ed.), *The Commissariot Record of Lanark: Register of Testaments 1595–1800* (SRS, 1903)

Grant, F.J. (ed.), *The Commissariot Record of St Andrews: Register of Testaments, 1549–1800* (SRS, 1902)

Harvey, C.C.H. & Macleod, J. (eds.), *Calendar of Writs preserved at Yester House* (Edinburgh, 1930)

Hepburn, A., *Grammaticae Artis Rudimenta breviter et dilucide explicate* (Antwerp, 1568)

Hill, A., *The Defence of the Article: Christ descended into Hell* (London, 1592)

Historical Manuscripts Commission, Report on the Manuscripts of Colonel David Milne-Home (London, 1902)

Historical Manuscripts Commission, Report on the Manuscripts of the Earl of Eglinton (London, 1885)

Historical Manuscripts Commission, Report on the Manuscripts of the Earl of Mar and Kellie (London, 1930)

'Holyrood Ordinale', *Book of the Old Edinburgh Club*, vii (1916)

Hume, A., *A rejoynder to Doctor Hil concerning the descente of Christ into hell* (Edinburgh, 1594)

Hume, A., *A diduction of the true and Catholik meaning of our Saviour his wordes, This is my bodie* (Edinburgh, 1602)

Hume, A., *Grammatica nova* (Edinburgh, 1612)

Hume, A., *Of the Orthographie and Congruitie of the Britan Tongue*, ed. H.B. Wheatley (Early English Text Society, original series, no. 5, 1863)

In hoc volumine haec continentur Aristotelis … (Paris, 1524)

Innes, C. (ed.), *Fasti Aberdonenses: Selections from the Records of the University and King's College of Aberdeen* (Spalding Club, 1854)

Innes, C. (ed.), *Munimenta Alme Universitatis Glasguensis* (Maitland Club, 1854)

Innes, C. (ed.), *The Thanes of Cawdor* (Spalding Club, 1859)

Inquisitionum ad Capellam Regis Retor natarum … Abbreviato, ed. T. Thomson (Edinburgh, 1811–1816)

'Inventories of Buikis in the Colleges of Sanctandrois, 1588–1690', *Maitland Miscellany*, i (1833)

Inventory of Chisholm Writs, 1456–1810, ed. J. Munro (SRS, 1992)

The James Carmichael Collection of Proverbs in Scots, ed. M.L. Anderson (Edinburgh, 1957)

James, H. (ed.), *Facsimiles of National Manuscripts of Scotland* (Edinburgh, 1872)

Johnson, John, *An Comfortable Exhortation* (Paris?, 1535)

Kinloch, G.R. (ed.), *Ecclesiastical Records: Selections from the Minutes of the Synod of Fife* (Abbotsford Club, 1837)

Kirk, J. (ed.), *The Books of Assumption of the Thirds of Benefices* (Oxford, 1995)

Kirk, J. (ed.), *Records of the Synod of Lothian and Tweeddale, 1589–1596, 1640–1645* (Stair Society, 1977)

Kirk, R.E.G. & E.F. (eds.), *Returns of Aliens in the City and Suburbs of London* (Publications of the Huguenot Society, 1907)

The Kirkcaldy Burgh Records, ed. L. Macbean (Kirkcaldy, 1908)

Kirkcudbright Sheriff Court Deeds, 1623–1675, ed. M.B. Johnston & C.M. Armet (Edinburgh, 1939)

Kirkcudbright Town Council Records, 1606–1658, ed. John, Marquis of Bute & C.M. Armet (Edinburgh, 1958)

Laing, D. (ed.), *Early Metrical Tales, including the history of Sir Egeir, Sir Gryme and Sir Gray-Steill* (Edinburgh, 1826)

Laing, D. (ed.), rev. W. Carew Hazlitt, *Early Popular Poetry of Scotland and the Northern Border* (London, 1895)

Laing, D. (ed.), *Miscellany of the Wodrow Society* (1844)

Laing, D. (ed.), *Registrum domus de Soltre necnon ecclesie collegiate S. Trinitatis prope Edinburgh etc.* (Edinburgh, 1861)

Lamont, N. (ed.), *An Inventory of Lamont Papers* (SRS, 1914)

A last will and testament of Mr Andrew Duncan, Minister of Crail, ed. Peterson, W. (Montreal, 1919)

Law, T.G. (ed.), *Catholic Tractates* (SHS, 1901)

Lawson, A. (ed.), *The Poems of Alexander Hume* (STS, 1902)

Leach, A.F. (ed.), *Educational Charters and Documents, 1598–1909* (Cambridge, 1911)

The Ledger of Andrew Halyburton, ed. C. Innes (Edinburgh, 1827)

Lee, J. (ed.), *Tracts by David Fergusson, Minister of Dunfermline, MDLXIII–MDLXXII* (Bannatyne Club, 1860)

Libellus de administratione beati Cuthberti virtutibus, by Reginald of Durham (Surtees Society, 1835)

Liber Cartarum Sancte Crucis (Bannatyne Club, 1840)

Liber Collegii Nostre Domine, ed. J. Robertson (Maitland Club, 1846)

Liber Protocollorum M Cuthherti Simonis. Rental Book of the Diocese of Glasgow, 1509–1570, ed. J. Bain & C. Rogers (Grampian Club, 1875)

Liber Sancte Marie de Calchou, 1113–1567, ed. C. Innes (Bannatyne Club, 1846)

Liber Sancte Marie de Dryburgh, ed. W. Fraser (Bannatyne Club, 1847)

Liber Sancte Marie de Lundoris, ed. W.T.D.D. Turnbull (Abbotsford Club, 1841)

Liber Sancte Thome de Aberbrothoc, 1178–1329, ed. C. Innes (Bannatyne Club, 1848–1856)

Lightbody, G., *Quaestiones Grammaticae* (Edinburgh, 1628)

Lindsay, E.R. & Dunlop, A.I. (eds.), *Calendar of Scottish Supplications to Rome* (2 vols., Edinburgh, 1934, 1956)

Lindsay of Pitscottie, R., *The Historie and Cronicles of Scotland*, ed. A.J.G. Mackay (STS, 1899–1901)

Lippe, R. (ed.), *Selections from Wodrow's Biographical Collections: Divines of the North-East of Scotland* (New Spalding Club, 1890)

Littlejohn, D. (ed.), *Records of the Sheriff Court of Aberdeenshire* (New Spalding Club, 1904–1907)

Livingston, N. (ed.), *The Scottish Metrical Psalter* (Glasgow, 1864)

MacCarthy, B. (ed.), *Annals of Ulster* (Dublin, 1893)

McInnes, C.T. (ed.), *Calendar of Writs of Munro of Foulis* (Edinburgh, 1940)

Mackay, W. (ed.), *Chronicles of the Frasers: The Wardlaw Manuscript* (SHS, 1905)

Mackay, W. (ed.), *Records of the Presbyteries of Inverness and Dingwall, 1643–1688* (SHS, 1896)

Mackay, W. & Boyd, H.C. (eds.), *Records of Inverness* (New Spalding Club, 1911–1924)

Macphail, J. (ed.), *Highland Papers* (SHS, 1916)

Maidment, J. (ed.), *Analecta Scotica* (Edinburgh, 1834)

Mair, T. (ed.), *Records of the Parish of Ellon* (Aberdeen, 1846)

Maitland Folio Manuscript, ed. W.A. Craigie (STS, 1919)

Maitland Quarto Manuscript, ed. W.A. Craigie (STS, 1920)

Major, J., *A History of Greater Britain*, ed. A. Constable (SHS, 1892)

Marwick, J.D. (ed.), *Charters and Documents relating to the City of Glasgow* (Edinburgh, 1894–1906)

Marwick, J.D. (ed.), *Extracts from the Records of the Burgh of Glasgow, 1573–1642* (SBRS, 1876–1916)

Marwick, J.D. (ed.), *Extracts from the Records of the Convention of Royal Burghs of Scotland* (Edinburgh, 1880)

Maynard, J.D. (ed.), 'An Anonymous Scottish Treatise on Music from the Sixteenth Century, British Museum Additional Manuscript 4911, Edition and Commentary' (Indiana University Ph.D. thesis, 1961)

The Melvill Book of Roundels, ed. G. Bantock & H.O. Anderson (Roxburghe Club, 1916)

Melville, James, *The Autobiography and Diary of Mr James Melville*, ed. R. Pitcairn (Edinburgh, 1842)

Melville, James, *Fruitfull and Comfortable Exhortatioun anent Death* (1597)

Memorabilia of the City of Glasgow (Glasgow, 1835)

Metcalfe, W.M. (ed.), *Charters and Documents relating to the Burgh of Paisley* (Paisley, 1902)

Minutes of the Synod of Argyll 1639–1651, ed. D.C. McTavish (SHS, 1943)

'Miscellaneous Charters and Contracts', *Spalding Misc.*, v (1852)

Mooney, J. (ed.), *Charters and Other Records of the City and Royal Burgh of Kirkwall* (Aberdeen, 1952)

Morgan, A. (ed.) with historical introductions by R.K. Hannay, *University of Edin-*

burgh: Charters, Statutes and Acts of the Town Council and the Senatus 1583–1858 (Edinburgh, 1937)

Moysie, D. (ed.), *Memoirs of the Affairs of Scotland* (Maitland Club, 1830)

Muir, W. (ed.), *Notices from the Local Records of Dysart* (Maitland Club, 1853)

Muniments of the Royal Burgh of Irvine (Ayr-Galloway Coll., 1878–1899)

Murray, A.L. (ed.), *The Lag Charters, 1400–1720* (SRS, 1958)

Musa Latina Aberdonensis, ed. W.K. Leask & W.D. Geddes (3 vols., New Spalding Club, 1892–1910)

Nichols, J., *The Progresses and Public Processions of Queen Elizabeth* (London, 1788–1821)

The Original Chronicle of Andrew of Wyntoun, ed. F.J. Amours (STS, 1903–1914)

Page, W. (ed.), *Letters of denization and acts of naturalization for aliens in England* (Huguenot Society Publications, 8, 1893)

A Pairt of the Life of Lady Margaret Cuninghame, Daughter of the Earl of Glencairn, ed. C.K. Sharpe (Edinburgh, 1827)

Papers from the Collection of Sir William Fraser, ed. J.N.R. MacPhail (SHS, 1924)

Parish Registers of Dunfermline, 1561–1700, ed. H. Paton (SRS, 1911)

Parkinson, D.J. (ed.), *Alexander Montgomerie: Poems* (2 vols., STS, 2000)

Paton, H. (ed.), *The Clan Campbell* (Edinburgh, 1913–1922)

Paton, H.M. (ed.), *Accounts of the Master of Works* (Edinburgh, 1957)

Patrick, D. (ed.), *Statutes of the Scottish Church* (SHS, 1907)

Patrologia Latina, ed. J.P. Migne (Paris, 1893)

Pellegrini, E. et al. (eds.), *Les manuscrits classiques latins de la bibliothèque Vaticane* (Paris, 1991)

The Perth Guildry Book, 1452–1601, ed. M.L. Stavert (SRS, 1993)

Peterkin, A. (ed.), *Rentals of the Ancient Earldom and Bishoprick of Orkney* (Edinburgh, 1820)

Petit, F. (ed.), *Ad Viros Religiosos: Quatorze Sermones d'Adam Scot* (Antwerp, 1934)

Picot, G. (ed.), *Documents relatifs aux Etats Generaux sous Philippe le Bel* (Paris, 1901)

Pitcairn, R. (ed.), *Ancient Criminal Trials* (3 vols., Edinburgh, 1833)

Pont, R., *Against Sacrilege* (Edinburgh, 1599)

The Presbytrie Booke of Kirkcaldie, ed. W. Stevenson (Kirkcaldy, 1890)

Protocol Book of Gavin Ros, ed. J. Henderson & F.J. Grant (SRS, 1908)

Protocol Book of James Young, ed. G. Donaldson & H.M. Paton (SRS, 1952)

Protocol Book of Sir Robert Rollock, ed. W. Angus (SRS, 1931)

Protocol Books of Dominus Thomas Johnsoun, 1528–1578, ed. J. Beveridge & J. Russell (SRS, 1920)

Protocol Books of James Foulis and Nicol Thounis, ed. J. Beveridge & J. Russell (SRS, 1927)

Pryde, G.S. (ed.), *Ayr Burgh Accounts 1534–1624* (Edinburgh, 1937)

Register of Apprentices of the City of Edinburgh, 1583–1666, ed. F.J. Grant (Edinburgh, 1906)

'Register of Burgesses of Guild and Trade of the Burgh of Aberdeen', ed. A.M. Munro, *New Spalding Misc.*, i (1890)

Register of Marriages of the City of Edinburgh, 1595–1700, ed. H. Paton (Edinburgh, 1905)

Register of the Minister, Elders and Deacons of the Christian Congregation of St Andrews, ed. D.H. Fleming (SHS, 1898–1890)

Register of Ministers, Exhorters and Readers and of their Stipends, ed. A. Macdonald (Maitland Club, 1830)

'Register of Ministers and Readers in the year 1574', ed. D. Laing, *Wodrow Misc.*, i (Edinburgh, 1844)

The Register of the Privy Council of Scotland, ed. J.H. Burton et al. (Edinburgh, 1877–1908)

Registrum Cartarum Ecclesie Sancti Egidii de Edinburgh, ed. D. Laing (Edinburgh, 1859)

Registrum de Cambuskenneth (Grampian Club, 1872)

Registrum de Dunfermelyn, ed. C. Innes (Bannatyne Club, 1842)

Registrum de Panmure, ed. J. Stuart (Edinburgh, 1874)

Registrum Domus de Soltre, ed. D. Laing (Bannatyne Club, 1861)

Registrum Episcopatus Aberdonensis, ed. C. Innes (2 vols., Spalding and Maitland Clubs, 1845)

Registrum Episcopatus Brechinensis, ed. C. Innes (2 vols., Bannatyne Club, 1856)

Registrum Episcopatus Glasguensis, ed. C. Innes (2 vols., Bannatyne and Maitland Clubs, 1843)

Registrum Episcopatus Moraviensis (Bannatyne Club, 1837)

Registrum Magni Sigilli Regum Scotorum, ed. J.M. Thomson et al. (Edinburgh, 1882–1914)

Registrum Monasterii de Passelet, ed. C. Innes (Maitland Club, 1832)

Registrum Prioratus Sancti Andree (Bannatyne Club, 1841)

Registrum Sancte Marie de Neubotle, ed. C. Innes (Bannatyne Club, 1849)

Registrum Secreti Sigilli Regum Scotorum, ed. M. Livingstone et al. (Edinburgh 1908–1982)

Reid-Baxter, J. (ed.), *Elizabeth Melville, Lady Culross: Poems and Letters* (forthcoming)

Rental Book of the Cistercian Abbey of Cupar [sic] *Angus*, ed. C. Rogers (Grampian Club, 1879–1880)

Rentale Dunkeldense, ed. R.K. Hannay (SHS, 1915)

Renwick, R. (ed.), *Abstracts of Protocols of the Town Clerks of Glasgow* (Glasgow, 1894–1900)

Renwick, R. (ed.), *Extracts from the Records of the Royal Burgh of Lanark* (Glasgow, 1893)

Renwick, R. (ed.), *Extracts from the Records of the Burgh of Peebles* (SBRS, 1910)

Renwick, R. (ed.), *Extracts from the Records of the Royal Burgh of Stirling* (Glasgow, 1887–1889)

Reports on the State of Certain Parishes in Scotland (Maitland Club, 1835)

Robertson, D. (ed.), *South Leith Records* (Edinburgh, 1911)

Robertson, J. (ed.), *Illustrations of the Topography and Antiquities of the Shires of Aberdeen and Banff* (Spalding Club, 1862)

Romanes, C.S. (ed.), *Selections from the Records of the Regality of Melrose* (SHS, 1914–1917)

Rotuli Scotiae in Turri Londinensi et in Domo Capitulari Westmonasteriensi Asservati, ed. D. Macpherson et al. (London, 1814–1819)

Row, J., *The History of the Kirk of Scotland*, ed. D. Laing (Wodrow Society, 1842)

St Andrews Formulare, ed. G. Donaldson & C. Macrae (Stair Society, 1942)

'A Schoolboy's Letter, 1610', ed. J.S. Ritchie, *SHR*, xxxvii (1958), 35–37

Scomajolo, C. (ed.), *Codices Urbinates Latini* (Rome, 1902)

The Second Book of Discipline, ed. J. Kirk (Edinburgh, 1980)

Series B: Reprinted Glossaries, ed. W.W. Skeate (London, 1874), 65–7

Shearer, A. (ed.), *Extracts from Burgh Records of Dunfermline* (Edinburgh, 1951)

Shire, H.M., 'Court Song in Scotland after 1603: Aberdeenshire', parts i and ii, *Edin. Bibl. Soc. Trans.*, iii (1957), 161–8, and part iii, ibid. (1960), 3–12

Shire, H.M. & Giles, P.M., 'Scottish Song-book, 1611', *Saltire Review*, i (2) (1954), 46–52

Smith, J., *The Hammermen of Edinburgh* (Edinburgh, 1907)

State Papers of Henry VIII, ed. J.S. Brewer et al. (London, 1862–1932)

The Statutes of the Faculty of Arts and the Faculty of Theology at the Period of the Reformation, ed. R.K. Hannay (St Andrews, 1910)

Stevenson, G. (ed.), *Poems of Alexander Montgomerie (Supplementary volume)* (STS, 1910)

Stirling Presbytery Records, ed. J. Kirk (SHS, 1981)

Struther, William [sic], *Christian Observations and Resolutions: Centurie II* (Edinburgh, 1629)

Stuart, J. (ed.), 'Extracts from the Accounts of the Burgh of Aberdeen', *Spalding Misc.*, v (1852)

Stuart, J. (ed.), *Extracts from the Council Register of the Burgh of Aberdeen* (Spalding Club (1844–1848)

Stuart, J. (ed.), *Records of the Monastery of Kinloss* (Edinburgh, 1872)

Stuart, J. (ed.), *Selections from the Records of the Kirk Session, Presbytery and Synod of Aberdeen* (Spalding Club, 1846)

Suetonius, C.T., *Duodecim Cesares* (Lyons, 1548)

Sutton, D.F. (ed.), *Hector Boethius, Scotorum Historia (1575 version)* (http://www.philological.bham.ac.uk/boece/)

Taylor, L.B. (ed.), *Aberdeen Council Letters* (Oxford, 1942)

Thomae Dempsteri Historia Ecclesiastica Gentis Scotorum: sive De Scriptoribus Scotis, ed. D. Irving (Bannatyne Club, 1829)

Thomas Hudson's History of Judith, ed. J. Craigie (STS, 1941)

Thomson, W. (ed.), *Deeds Instituting Bursaries, Scholarships and Other Foundations in the College and University of Glasgow* (Maitland Club, 1856)

Twemlow, J.A. (ed.), *Catalogue of Entries in the Papal Registers relating to Great Britain and Ireland* (London, 1933)

Vattasso, M. & de Cavalieri, P.F. (eds.), *Codices Vaticani Latini* (Rome, 1902)

Vaus, J., *Rudimenta* (Paris, 1531)

Visitation of the Diocese of Dunblane, 1586–1589, ed. J. Kirk (SRS, 1982)

Wedderburn, D., *Institutiones grammaticae. Editio Secunda* (Aberdeen, 1633)

Wedderburn, D., *A Short Introduction to Grammar* (Aberdeen, 1632)

Williamson, R., *Elementa linguae latinae, e grammaticorum imprimis Donati, Despauterii, etc., cornucopiae grammaticali excepta* (Edinburgh, 1625)

Williamson, R., *Grammatica Latina ad artium methodum, et unius anni stadium, e grammaticorum cornucopiae, praecipue Ioh. Despauterii et Linacri commode concinnata. Jam tertio limata, 1632* (Edinburgh, 1632)

Williamson, R., *Paedagogia moralis tertia R Williamsoni Cuprensis cura aucta et limata in gratiam juventutis Christianae* (Edinburgh, 1635)

Winzet, N., *Certain Tractates*, ed. J.K. Hewison (STS, 1888)

Wodrow's Biographical Collections upon the Lives of the Reformers, ed. W.J. Duncan (2 vols., Maitland Club, 1834–1845)

Wodrow, R., *Select Biographies*, ed. W.K. Tweedie (Wodrow Society, 1845–47)

Wood, M. (ed.), *Extracts from the Records of the Burgh of Edinburgh* (Edinburgh, 1927)

Yule, A., *Poemata sacra* (Edinburgh, 1614)

Secondary Works

Abercromby, C.D., *Family of Abercromby* (Aberdeen, 1927)

Aitchison, L., *Lasswade Parish and Loanhead in the Olden Time* (Edinburgh, 1892)

Anderson, H.M., 'The Grammar School of the Canongate', *Book of the Old Edinburgh Club*, xx (1935)

Anderson, J., *Oliphants of Scotland* (Edinburgh, 1879)

Anderson, P.J. (ed.), *Fasti Academiae Mariscallanae Aberdonensis* (New Spalding Club, 1889, 1898)

Anderson, P.J. (ed.), *Officers and Graduates of the University and King's College Aberdeen* (New Spalding Club, 1893)

Anderson, W.J., 'Narratives of the Scottish Reformation, 1: Report of Father Robert Abercrombie, SJ, in the year 1580', *IR*, vii

Antolín, G., *Catálogo de los códices latinos de la Real Biblioteca del Escorial* (Madrid, 1910)

Ashmall, H.A., *The High School of Glasgow* (Glasgow, 1976)

Bain, A., *The Education Act of 1696 in West Lothian* (Dept of Educational Studies, 1974)

Bain, A., *Education in Stirlingshire* (London, 1965)

Bain, A., *Patterns of Error* (Edinburgh, 1989)

Baird, W., *Annals of Duddingston and Portobello* (Edinburgh, 1898)

Bald, M.A., 'The anglicisation of Scottish printing', *SHR*, xxiii (1926), 107–15

Bannerman, J., 'Literacy in the Highlands', in I.B. Cowan & D. Shaw (eds.), *The Renaissance and Reformation in Scotland* (Edinburgh, 1983)

Bannerman, J., 'The Scots language and kin-based society', in D.S. Thomson (ed.), *Scots in Harmony: Proceedings of the Second National Conference on the Languages of Scotland* (Glasgow, 1990)

Barclay, W., *The Schools and Schoolmasters of Banffshire* (Banff, 1925)

Barrow, G.W.S., *Scotland and its Neighbours in the Middle Ages* (London, 1992)

Baswell, C., *Virgil in Medieval England* (Cambridge, 1995)

Beale, J.M., *A History of the Burgh and Parochial Schools of Fife* (Edinburgh, 1983)

Beattie, W. & Durkan, J., 'An early publication of Latin poems of George Buchanan in Scotland from the press of Lepreuik', *Bibliotheck*, xi (1983), 77–80

Becker, M.V., *Civility and Society in Western Europe 1300–1600* (Bloomington, Indiana, 1988)

Bell, G., 'Notes on some music set to Buchanan's paraphrase of the psalms', in *George Buchanan, Glasgow Quatercentenary Studies* (Glasgow, 1906)

Bentinck, C.D., *Dornoch Cathedral and Parish* (Inverness, 1926)

Black, G.F., *The Surnames of Scotland* (New York, 1962)

Blume, F., *Protestant Church Music: a History* (London, 1975)

Boorde, Andrew, *First Book of the Introduction of Knowledge* (Early English Text Society, 1870)

Broadie, A., *The Shadow of Scotus: Philosophy and Faith in pre-Reformation Scotland* (Edinburgh, 1995)

Brown, J. et al., 'Further observations on W1', *Journal of the Plainsong & Mediaeval Music Society*, iv (1981), 53–80

Brown, K., 'Aristocratic finance and the origins of the Scottish Revolution', *English Historical Review*, civ (1989), 46–87

Brown, K., 'Noble indebtedness in Scotland between the Reformation and the Revolution', *Historical Research*, lxii (1989), 260–75.

Brown, R. *The History of the Paisley Grammar School* (Paisley, 1875)

Bryce, W.M., *The Scottish Grey Friars* (Edinburgh, 1909)

Bushnell, G.H., *From Papyrus to Print* (London, 1949)

Cairns, J.W., 'Academic Feud, Bloodfeud and William Welwood: Legal Education in St. Andrews, 1560–1611', *Edinburgh Law Review*, 2:1–2 (1998), 158–79, 255–87

Cameron, A.C., *History of Fettercairn* (Paisley, 1899)

Cameron, A.I., 'The Canongate crafts: an agreement of 1610', *Book of the Old Edinburgh Club*, xiv (1925)

Cameron, J.K., 'Andrew Melville in St Andrews', in D.W.D. Shaw (ed.), *In Divers Manners: a St Mary's Miscellany* (St Andrews, 1990)

Cant, R.G., *The University of St Andrews: a Short History* (St Andrews, 1982)

Chatillon, J., *Le mouvement canoniale au moyen âge* (Paris/Turnhout, 1992)

Clair, C., 'Christopher Plantin's trade connexions with England and Scotland', *Library*, 5th series, xiv (1959), 28–45

Cleland, J., *The History of the High School of Glasgow* (Glasgow, 1878)

Connolly, M.F., *Fifiana* (Glasgow, 1869)

Couper, W.J., 'The Levitical family of Simson, 1: the founding of the house, 1529(?); 2: The family of Adam Simson, 1594–1771; 3: Alexander, 1570(?)–1638, and his descendants', *RSCHS*, iv (1932), 119–37, 208–66; '4: Families that failed', *RSCHS*, v (1935), 117–39

Courtenay, W.J., *Schools and Scholars in Fourteenth Century England* (Princeton, 1987)

Cowan, I.B. & Easson, D.E., *Medieval Religious Houses, Scotland* (New York, 1976)

Cramond, W., *The Church and Churchyard of Deskford* (Banff, 1885)

Cramond, W., *The Church and Churchyard of Fordyce* (Banff, 1886)

Cramond, W., *The Church of Grange* (Keith, 1898)

Cramond, W., *Municipal Life in Elgin in the Sixteenth Century* (Elgin, 1899)

Craufurd, T., *History of the University of Edinburgh* (Edinburgh, 1808)

Craven, J.B., *History of the Church in Orkney, 1558–1662* (Kirkwall, 1897)

Crawford, A.W.C.L., *Lives of the Lindsays* (London, 1849)

Dart, T., 'New sources of virginal music', *Music and Letters*, xxxv (1954), 93–106

Davidson, J., *Inverurie and the Earldom of Garioch* (Edinburgh, 1878)

de Burgo, T., *Hibernia Dominicana* (Cologne, 1762)

De la Mare, A.C., 'Humanistic hands in England', in A.C. De la Mare & B.C. Barker-Benfield (eds.), *Manuscripts at Oxford: an Exhibition in Memory of R.W. Hunt* (Oxford, 1980)

Delorme, F.M., 'Olivier Maillard et le Tiers-Ordre regulier en Ecosse', *Archivum Franciscanum Historicum*, viii (1915), 353–8

Dennistoun, J., *Memories of the Dukes of Urbino* (London, 1851)

Dibden, J.C., *Annals of the Edinburgh Stage* (Edinburgh, 1888)

Dickinson, W.C., 'The advocates' protest against the institution of a Chair of Law in the University of Edinburgh', *SHR*, xxiii (1926), 205–212

Dickson, R. & Edmond, J.P., *Annals of Scottish Printing* (Cambridge, 1890)

Dilworth, M., 'Two necrologies', *Innes Review*, ix (1958), 173–203

Dobson, E.S., *English Pronunciation, 1500–1700* (Oxford, 1968)

Dondaine, A., 'Documents pour servir à l'histoire de la Province de France: l'appel au Concile (1303)', *Archivum Fratrum Praedicatorum*, xxii (1952), 381–439

Douglas, R. *Annals of the Royal Burgh of Forres* (Elgin, 1934)

Dunlop, A.I., *The Life and Times of James Kennedy, Bishop of St Andrews* (Edinburgh, 1950)

Dunn, J.A., *History of Renfrew* (Paisley, 1972)

Durkan J., *Bibliography of George Buchanan* (Glasgow, 1994)

Durkan, J., 'Chaplains in Scotland in the late Middle Ages', *RSCHS*, xx (1978)

Durkan, J., 'The cultural background in sixteenth century Scotland', in D. McRoberts (ed.), *Essays on the Scottish Reformation, 1513–1625* (Glasgow, 1962)

Durkan, J., 'David Lauxius', *Edinburgh Bibliographical Society Transactions*, iii (1952), 78–80

Durkan, J., 'Education in the century of the Reformation', in D. McRoberts (ed.), *Essays on the Scottish Reformation, 1513–1625* (Glasgow, 1962)

Durkan, J., 'Foundation of the collegiate church of Seton', *IR*, xiii (1962), 71–6

Durkan, J., 'Further additions to Durkan & Ross: some newly discovered Scottish pre-Reformation provenances', *Bibliotheck*, x (1981)

Durkan, J., 'Giovanni Ferrerio and religious humanism in sixteenth century Scotland', in J. Kirk (ed.), *Humanism and Reform: the Church in Europe, England and Scotland, 1400–1643* (Oxford, 1991)

Durkan, J., 'Giovanni Ferrerio, Gesner and French affairs', *Bibliothèque d'Humanisme et Renaissance*, xiii, 349–60

Durkan, J. 'Grisy burses at Scots College, Paris', *IR*, xxii (1971), 50–2

Durkan, J., 'Heresy in Scotland: the second phase, 1546–1558', *RSCHS*, xxiv (1992), 320–65

Durkan, J., 'Hospital scholars in the Middle Ages', *IR*, vii (1956), 125–7

Durkan, J., 'The laying of fresh foundations', in J. MacQueen (ed.), *Humanism in Renaissance Scotland* (Edinburgh, 1990)

Durkan, J., 'Medieval Hamilton: Ecclesiastical', *IR*, xxviii (1977), 51–3

Durkan, J., 'Paisley Abbey and Glasgow archives', *IR*, xiv (1963), 46–53

Durkan, J., 'Paisley Abbey in the sixteenth century', *IR*, xxvii (1976), 110–26

Durkan, J., 'Richard Guthrie: books left at Arbroath Abbey in 1473', *Bibliotheck*, iii (1962)

Durkan, J., 'The royal lectureships under Mary of Lorraine', *SHR*, lxii (1983), 73–8

Durkan, J., 'St Andrews in the John Law Chronicle', *IR*, xxv (1974), 49–62

Durkan, J., 'Scottish reformers: the less than golden legend', *IR*, xlv (1994), 1–28

Durkan, J., 'William Murdoch and the early Jesuit mission to Scotland', *IR*, xxxv (1995), 3–11

Durkan, J. & Kirk, J., *The University of Glasgow 1451–1577* (Glasgow, 1977)

Durkan, J. & Ross, A., *Early Scottish Libraries* (Glasgow, 1961)

Durkan, J. & Russell, J., 'Further additions to Durkan and Ross, *Early Scottish Libraries*, in the National Library of Scotland', *Bibliotheck*, xii (1984–5)

Durkan, J. & Watt, W.S., 'Adam Mure's *Laudes Gulielmi Elphinstonii*', in *Humanistica Lovaniensia*, xxviii (1979), 199–233

Edgar, A., *Old Church Life in Scotland* (Paisley, 1886)

Eeles, F.C., *King's College Chapel, Aberdeen* (Edinburgh, 1951)

Elliott, K., *The Paisley Abbey Fragments* (Glasgow, 1996)

Elliott, K., 'Scottish music of the early reformed church', *Transactions of the Scottish Ecclesiological Society*, xv (2) (1961), 18–31

Elliott, K., '*Some helpes for young schollers*: a new source of early Scottish psalmody', in A.A. Macdonald, M. Lynch & I. Cowan (eds.), *The Renaissance in Scotland* (Leiden, 1994)

Elliott, K. & Shire, H.M. (eds.), *Music of Scotland 1500–1700* (3rd edn, London, 1975)

Emerson, R.L., 'Calvinism and the Scottish Enlightenment', in Joachim Schwend et al. (eds.), *Literatur im Kontext: Literature in Context, Festschrift für H.W. Drescher* (Frankfurt/Bern/New York/Paris, 1992)

Esposito, M., 'Les hérésies de Thomas Scotus d'après le Collirium Fidei', *Revue d'Histoire Ecclésiastique*, xxxiii (1937), 56–69

Everist, M., 'From Paris to St. Andrews: the origins of *Wᴵ*', *Journal of the Plainsong & Mediaeval Music Society*, xliii (1990), 1–42

Ferguson, F.S., 'Relations between London and Edinburgh printers and stationers', *Library*, viii (1927), 145–98

Ferguson, J., *Ecclesia Antiqua* (Edinburgh, 1905)

Finlayson, C.P., 'An unpublished commentary by George Buchanan on Virgil', *Transactions of the Edinburgh Bibliographical Society*, ii (1948–1955), 271–88

Flynn, J., 'The education of choristers in England during the sixteenth century', in J. Morehen (ed.), *English Choral Practice 1400–1650* (Cambridge, 1995)

Ford, P. & Green, R.P.H. (eds.), *George Buchanan: Poet and Dramatist* (Swansea, 2009)

Foster, W.R., *The Church before the Covenants* (Edinburgh, 1975)

Fraser, W., *Chiefs of Grant* (Edinburgh, 1883)

Fraser, W., *Elphinstone Family Book* (Edinburgh, 1897)

Fraser, W., *Frasers of Philorth* (Edinburgh, 1879)

Fraser, W., *The Lennox* (Edinburgh, 1874)

Fraser, W., *Memoirs of the Maxwells of Pollok* (Edinburgh, 1863)

Fraser, W., *Scotts of Buccleuch* (Edinburgh, 1878)

Fraser, W., *The Stirlings of Keir* (Edinburgh, 1858)

Fraser, W., *Sutherland Book* (Edinburgh, 1892)

Frost, M., *English and Scottish Psalm and Hymn Tunes, c.1543–1677* (London, 1953)

Garden, G., 'The Life of John Forbes of Corse', *Opera Omnia* (Amsterdam, 1703)

Gibson, A.J.S. & T.C. Smout, *Prices, Food and Wages in Scotland, 1550–1780* (Cambridge, 1995)

Gillespie, J.H., *Dundonald, the Parish and its Setting* (Glasgow, 1939)

Godsman, J., *A History of the Burgh and Parish of Ellon* (Aberdeen, 1958)

Grant, J., *History of the Burgh and Parish Schools of Scotland* (London, 1876)

Gray, G., *The Burgh School of Rutherglen* (Rutherglen, 1891)

Gray, W.F. & Jamieson, J.H., *A Short History of Haddington* (Stevenage, n.d.)

Gunn, C.B., *The Church and Parish of Dawyck* (Peebles, 1931)

Gunn, C.B., *Ministry of the Presbytery of Peebles, AD 1296–1910* (Peebles, 1910)

Gwynn, A., *The Irish Church in the Eleventh and Twelfth Centuries* (Dublin, 1992)

Haws, C., *Scottish Parish Clergy at the Reformation* (SRS, 1972)

Hay, G., *History of Arbroath* (Arbroath, 1876)

Heijnsbergen, T. van, 'The Scottish Chapel Royal as cultural intermediary between town and Court', in J.W. Drijvers & A.A. Macdonald (eds.), *Centres of Learning* (Leiden, 1995)

Henderson, E., *Annals of Dunfermline* (Glasgow, 1879)

Henderson, J.H. (ed.), *History of the Society of Advocates in Aberdeen* (New Spalding Club, 1912)

Herbert, M., *Iona, Kells and Derry* (Oxford, 1988)

Herkless, J. & Hannay, R.K., *The College of St Leonard* (Edinburgh, 1905)

Hill, W.H., *History of the Hospital and School Founded in Glasgow, 1639–41, by George and Thomas Hutcheson of Lambhill* (Glasgow, 1881)

Hist. MSS Comm., 11th Report (London, 1888)

Holmes, S., 'The meaning of history: a dedicatory letter from Giovanni Ferrerio to Abbot Robert Reid in his Historia abbatum de Kynloss', *Reformation and Renaissance Review*, 10.1 (2008), 89–115

Holtz, L., *Donat et la tradition de l'enseignement grammatical* (Paris, 1981)

Hume, D., of Godscroft, *De Familia Humia Wedderburnensi* (Abbotsford Club, 1839)

Hume, D., *History of the House and Race of Douglas and Angus* (Edinburgh, 1743)

Hutchison, H., 'Church Control of Education in Clackmannanshire, 1560–1700', *RSCHS*, xviii (1973)

Hutchinson, H.P., 'The St Andrews Psalter' (University of Edinburgh Ph.D. thesis, 1957)

Huyshe, W., *Devorgilla, Lady of Galloway and her Abbey of the Sweet Heart* (Edinburgh, 1913)

Illich, I., *In the Vineyard of the Text* (Chicago, 1993)

Jessop, J.C., *Education in Angus* (London, 1931)

Kastner, L.E. (ed.), *The Poetical Works of William Drummond of Hawthornden* (2 vols., STS, 1913)

Ker, N.R. & Piper, A.J. (eds.), *Medieval Manuscripts in British Libraries* (Oxford, 1992)

Kirk, J., *Patterns of Reform* (Edinburgh, 1989)

Laing, A., *Lindores Abbey and its Burgh of Newburgh* (Edinburgh, 1876)

Laing, D., *A Catalogue of the Graduates in the Faculties of Arts, Divinity, and Law, of the University of Edinburgh* (Edinburgh, 1858)

Laing, D., 'Notes relating to Mrs Esther Langlois (Inglis), the celebrated calligraphist', *Proceedings of the Society of Antiquaries of Scotland*, vi (1865), 284–309

Lapidge, M., 'The Welsh-Latin poetry of Sulien's family', *Studia Celtica*, viii–ix (1973–74), 68–106

Lawson, J.P., *The Book of Perth* (Edinburgh, 1847)

Lee, J., *Lectures on the History of the Church of Scotland* (Edinburgh, 1860)

Lees, J., *The Abbey of Paisley* (Paisley, 1878)

Leslie, J.B. & Swanzy, H.B. (eds.), *Biographical Succession Lists of the Clergy of the Diocese of Down* (Enniskillen, 1930)

Lorimer, P., *Precursors of Knox, or, Memoirs of Patrick Hamilton* (Edinburgh, 1957)

Love, J., *The Schools and Schoolmasters of Falkirk* (Falkirk, 1898)

Lythe, S.G.E., *The Economy of Scotland in its European Setting 1550–1625* (Edinburgh/London, 1960)

McCall, H.B., *History of the Parish of Mid-Calder* (Edinburgh, 1894)

McCraw, W., *More about Monimail* (Cupar, n.d.)

McCrie, T., *Life of Andrew Melville* (2nd edn, 2 vols., Edinburgh, 1824)

MacDonald, A.A., 'The Renaissance household as centre of learning', in J.W. Drijvers & A.A. Macdonald (eds.), *Centres of Learning* (Leiden, 1995)

McFarlane, I.D., *Buchanan* (London, 1981)

Macgill, W., *Old Ross-shire and Scotland* (Inverness, 1909)

McGrath, F., *Education in Ancient and Medieval Ireland* (Dublin, 1979)

McGregor, M.D.W., 'Political History of the McGregors before 1571' (University of Edinburgh Ph.D. thesis, 1989)

Mackenzie, G., *Lives and Characters of the Most Ancient Writers of the Scottish Nation* (Edinburgh, 1708–1722)

McKerlie, P.H., *History of the Lands and their Owners in Galloway* (Edinburgh, 1870)

Mackintosh, M., 'Education in Lanarkshire up to the Act of 1872' (University of Glasgow Ph.D. thesis, 1968)

McLean, D.G., *History of Fordyce Academy* (Banff, 1936)

McNeill, W.A., 'Scottish entries in the *Acta Rectoria Universitatis Parisiensis*', SHR, xliii (1964)

McQuaid, J., 'Scottish Musicians of the Reformation' (University of Edinburgh Ph.D. thesis, 1949)

MacQueen, J., *Humanism in Renaissance Scotland* (Edinburgh, 1990)

McRoberts, D. (ed.), *Essays on the Scottish Reformation, 1513–1625* (Glasgow, 1962)

McRoberts, D., 'The glorious house of Andrew', *IR*, xxv (1974), 127–9

Mathew, D., *Scotland under Charles I* (London, 1955)

Maxwell, A., *The History of Old Dundee, narrated out of the Council Register* (Edinburgh, 1884)

Maxwell, A., *Old Dundee: prior to the Reformation* (Edinburgh, 1891)

Mill, A.J., *Mediaeval Plays in Scotland* (Edinburgh, 1927)

Miller, J., *History of Dunbar* (Dunbar, 1830)

Miller, J., *The Lamp of Lothian* (Haddington, 1844)

Milne, R., *Blackfriars of Perth* (Edinburgh, 1893)

Motherwell, W., *Memorabilia of the City of Glasgow* (Glasgow, 1835)

Munro, G., '"Sang Schwylls" and "Music Schools": Music Education in Scotland 1560–1650', in R.E. Murray (ed.), *Music Education in the Middle Ages and Renaissance* (Indiana, 2010)

Munro, J. & Munro, R.W., *Croy and Dalcross* (Nairn, 1967)

Murray, A.L., 'The revenues of the bishopric of Moray in 1538', *IR*, xix (1968), 40–56

Murray A.L., 'The Parish Clerk and Song School of Inverness', *Innes Review*, 58 (2007)

Notes and Queries of the Society of West Highland and Island Historical Research, nos. 7, 8, 18

O'Day, R., *Education and Society 1500–1800: the Social Foundations of Education* (London, 1982)

Oehler, J., *Der akademische Austausch zwischen Köln und England-Schottland zur Seit der ersten Kölner Universität* (Cologne, 1989)

Oliver, J.R., *Upper Teviotdale and the Scotts of Buccleuch* (Hawick, 1887)

Orme, N., *English Schools in the Middle Ages* (London, 1973)

Ormond, G.W.T., *The Arniston Memoirs: Three Centuries of a Scottish House, 1571–1838* (Edinburgh, 1887)

Padley, G.A., *Grammatical Theory in Western Europe, 1500–1700* (Cambridge, 1976)

Paterson, J., *History of the County of Ayr* (Paisley, 1852)

Paterson, J., *History of the Regality of Musselburgh* (Musselburgh, 1957)

Patrick, J.M., *Four Centuries of Scottish Psalmody* (London, 1949)

Porter, J., 'The historical importance of Jean Servin's settings of Buchanan's psalm paraphrases', in P. Ford and R.P.H. Green (eds.), *George Buchanan: Poet and Dramatist* (Swansea, 2009)

Proceedings of the Orkney Antiquarian Society, iv (1925)

Quitslund, B., *The Reformation in Rhyme: Sternhold, Hopkins and the English Metrical Psalter, 1547–1603* (Aldershot, 2008)

Raine, J., *History and Antiquities of North Durham* (London, 1852)

Rankin, W.E.K., *The Parish Church of the Holy Trinity, St Andrews* (Edinburgh, 1955)

Reid-Baxter, J., 'Elizabeth Melville, Lady Culross: 3500 new lines of verse', in S. Dunnigan et al. (eds.), *Women and the Feminine in Medieval and Early Modern Scottish Writing* (Basingstoke, 2004)

Reid-Baxter, J., 'Metrical psalmody and the Bannatyne Manuscript: Robert Pont's Psalm 83', *Renaissance and Reformation*, 30.4 (2006/7), 41–62

Reid-Baxter, J., 'Montgomerie's Solsequium and *The Mindes Melodie*', in J.D. McLure & J.H. Williams (eds.), *Fresche Fontanis: Proceedings of the 13th Triennial Conference on Mediaeval and Renaissance Scottish Language and Literature* (Cambridge, 2013)

Reid-Baxter, J., 'Poetry, passion and politics in the circle of James VI', in A.A. Macdonald and S. Mapstone (eds.), *A Palace in the Wilds* (Groningen, 1998)

Reid-Baxter, J., 'Presbytery, politics and poetry: Maister Robert Bruce, John Burel and Elizabeth Melville, Lady Culross', *RSCHS*, xxxiv (2004), 6–27

Reid-Baxter, J., 'The songs of Lady Culross', in G. Munro et al. (eds.), *Notis Musycall* (Glasgow, 2005)

Reid-Baxter, J., 'Thomas Wode, Christopher Goodman and the curious death of Scottish music', *Scotlands* (Edinburgh University Press), 4.2 (1997), 1–20

Ritchie, A.I., *The Churches of St Baldred* (Edinburgh, 1881)

Ritchie, J.B., *Forres: its Schools and Schoolmasters* (Forres, 1926)

Robb, J., *History and Guide to Haddington* (Haddington, 1891)

Roberts, F., *The Grammar School of Dumbarton* (Dumbarton, 1948)

Robertson, J. (ed.), *Collections for a History of the Shires of Aberdeen and Banff* (Spalding Club, 1843)

Robertson, J., 'On scholastic offices in the Scottish Church', *Spalding Miscellany*, v

Roesner, Edward, 'The origins of W1', *Journal of the Plainsong & Mediaeval Music Society*, xxix (1976), 337–80

Rogers, C., *History of the Chapel Royal of Scotland* (Edinburgh, 1882)

Ross, A., 'Notes on the religious orders', in D. McRoberts (ed.), *Essays on the Scottish Reformation, 1513–1625* (Glasgow, 1962)

Ross, J., *Musick Fyne* (Edinburgh, 1993)

Ruddiman, J., *A catalogue of a rare and valuable collection of books ... to be sold by auction. ... 1st February 1758* (Edinburgh, 1758)

Russell, J.A., *History of Education in the Stewartry of Kirkcudbright* (Newton Stewart, 1950)

Sadie, S. (ed.), *New Grove Dictionary of Music and Musicians* (London, 1980)

Samaran, C. et al. (eds.), *Catalogue des manuscrits en écriture latine portant des indications de date* (Paris, 1962)

Sanderson, M., 'Catholic recusancy in Scotland in the sixteenth century', *IR*, xxi (1970), 87–107

Scott, H., *Fasti Ecclesiae Scoticanae* (Edinburgh, 1915–1981)

Scott-Elliot, A.H. & Yeo, Elspeth, 'Calligraphic manuscripts of Esther Inglis (1571–1624): a catalogue', *Papers of the Bibliographical Society of America*, lxxxiv (1990), 11–86

Seton, G., *History of the Family of Seton* (Edinburgh, 1896)

'Seventeenth century landlords asserted their new powers', *Shetland Times*, 21 March 1986

Shaw, F., *Northern and Western Islands of Scotland* (Edinburgh, 1980)

Shaw, L., *History of the Province of Moray* (1775)

Sheehy, M., *When the Normans Came to Ireland* (Dublin, 1975)

Shirley, G.W., 'Fragmentary notices of the burgh school of Dumfries', *Dumfriesshire Trans.*, xxi (1939)

Simpson, G.G., *Scottish Handwriting 1150–1650* (Edinburgh, 1973)

Simpson, I.J., *Education in Aberdeenshire before 1872* (London, 1947)

Simpson, W.D., 'The Augustinian priory and parish church, Monymusk', *Proceedings of the Society of Antiquaries of Scotland*, lix (1924), 34–71

Smart, E., *History of Perth Academy* (Perth, 1932)

Smith, G.G. (ed.), *The Poems of Robert Henryson* (STS, 1906)

Smout, T.C., *Scotland and Europe* (Edinburgh, 1986)

Somerville, A.R., 'The sundials of John Bonar, schoolmaster of Ayr', *Antiquarian Horology*, xvi (1986), 233–42

Southern, R.W., *Scholastic Humanism and the Unification of Europe* (Oxford, 1995)

Spottiswoode, J., *The History of the Church of Scotland*, ed. M. Napier and M. Russell (Spottiswoode Society, 1847–51)

Starnes, D.T., *Renaissance Dictionaries* (Austin, Texas/ Edinburgh, 1954)

Stein, G., *The English Dictionary before Cawdrey* (Tübingen, 1995)

Stephen, W., *The Story of Inverkeithing and Rosyth* (Edinburgh, 1938)

Steven, W., *History of the High School of Edinburgh* (Edinburgh, 1908)

Stevenson, D., *King's College, Aberdeen, 1560–1641: from Protestant Reformation to Covenanting Revolution* (Aberdeen, 1995)

Stevenson, D., *Scotland's Last Royal Wedding* (Edinburgh, 1997)

Stevenson, W., *The Kirk and Parish of Auchtertool* (Kirkcaldy, 1908)

Stewart, C.P., *Memoirs of the Stewarts of Forthergill* (Edinburgh, 1879)

Strawhorn, J., *The History of Irvine* (Edinburgh, 1985)

Sutherland, R., *Loanhead, the Development of a Scottish Burgh* (Edinburgh, 1974)

Tachau, K., *Vision and Certitude in the Age of Ockham* (Leiden, 1988)

Tachau, K. & Courtenay, W., 'Ockham, Ockhamists and the English-German nation at Paris, 1339–1341', *History of Universities*, ii (1982), 53–96

Terry, C.S., 'The Music School of Old Machar', *Miscellany of the Third Spalding Club*, ii (Aberdeen, 1940)

Theiner, A., *Vetera Monumenta Historiam Hibernorum et Scotorum Illustrantia* (Rome, 1864)

Thomas, T., *Dictionarium Linguae Latinae et Anglicanae* (Menston, 1972)

Thomson, D.S., 'Gaelic learned orders and literati in medieval Scotland', *Scottish Studies*, xii (1968), 57–78

Thomson, D.S. (ed.), *Scots in Harmony: Proceedings of the Second National Conference on the Languages of Scotland* (Glasgow, 1990)

Thomson, J., *The History of Dundee* (Dundee, 1874)

Upton, C., 'The teaching of poetry in sixteenth century Scotland', in R.J. Lyall and F. Riddy (eds.), *Proceedings of the Third International Conference on Scottish Language and Literature, Medieval and Renaissance* (Stirling/Glasgow, 1981)

Voet, L., *The Plantin Press, 1555–1589* (Amsterdam, 1980–1983)

Watson, C.B.B. (ed.), *Roll of Edinburgh Burgesses and Guild-brethren* (SRS, 1929)

Watson, T., *Kirkintilloch: Town and Parish* (Glasgow, 1894)

Watt, D.E.R., *Biographical Dictionary of Scottish Graduates* (Oxford, 1977)

Watt, D.E.R., 'Education in the Highlands in the Middle Ages', in Maclean, L. (ed.), *The Middle Ages in the Highlands* (Inverness Field Club, 1981)

Watt, D.E.R. & Murray, A.L. (eds.), *Fasti Ecclesiae Scoticanae Medii Aevi ad Annum 1638* (SRS, 2003)

Webster, J.M., *Dunfermline Abbey* (Dunfermline, 1948)

White, Raymond, 'Music of the Scottish Reformation 1560–1650' (University of St Andrews Ph.D. thesis, 1972)

Wilson, J., *Hawick and its Old Memories* (Edinburgh, 1858)

Wilson, J.A., *A History of Cambuslang* (Glasgow, 1929)

Withrington, D., 'Education in the 17th century Highlands', in L. MacLean (ed.), *The Seventeenth Century in the Highlands* (Inverness, 1986)

Withrington, D., 'Schools in the presbytery of Haddington in the seventeenth century', *East Lothian Trans.*, ix (1963)

Wood, A., *Athenae Oxonienses* (London, 1813–1815)

INDEX OF SCHOOLMASTERS' NAMES

The following index does not attempt to distinguish between individuals of the same name, except where Dr Durkan's research itself did so. This occurs primarily where schoolmasters with MAs were distinguished from those without, or occasionally where father and son of the same name are distinguished. This almost certainly means that in some places different individuals may be listed in the same entry, but in the absence of certainty it was felt to be preferable to include all references in a single entry, so that in such cases readers may identify all references to that name and form their own judgement.

GENERAL INDEX

This index excludes the schoolmasters named in the Lists, but includes other persons discussed in the main text of the book (e.g. writers, clergy), as well as places and subjects. For schoolmasters, readers should refer to the Index of Schoolmasters' Names, above. Places with schools or schoolmasters which are included in the Lists but not discussed in the main text are excluded, since their entries can be readily identified in the alphabetical Lists.